Fundamentals of Crime Mapping

Bryan Hill
Crime Analyst
Glendale Police Department
Glendale, AZ
Retired Officer, Phoenix Police Department
Member, Arizona Association of Crime Analysts
Member, International Association of Crime Analysts

Rebecca Paynich, PhD
Director, Master of Arts in Criminal Justice
Professor of Criminal Justice
Curry College
Member, Academy of Criminal Justice Sciences
Member, American Society of Criminology
Member, International Association of Crime Analysts

JONES & BARTLETT
LEARNING

World Headquarters
Jones & Bartlett Learning
5 Wall Street
Burlington, MA 01803
978-443-5000
info@jblearning.com
www.jblearning.com

Jones & Bartlett Learning books and products are available through most bookstores and online booksellers. To contact Jones & Bartlett Learning directly, call 800-832-0034, fax 978-443-8000, or visit our website, www.jblearning.com.

Production Credits
Executive Publisher: Kevin Sullivan
Editorial Assistant: Audrey Schwinn
Production Manager: Tracey McCrea
Production Assistant: Leia Poritz
Marketing Manager: Lindsay White
Online Products Manager: Dawn Mahon Priest
Manufacturing and Inventory Control Supervisor: Amy Bacus

Composition: Cenveo® Publisher Services
Cover Design: Michael O'Donnell
Rights & Photo Research Assistant: Ashley Dos Santos
Cover Image: © Rebecca Paynich
Printing and Binding: Edwards Brothers Malloy
Cover Printing: Edwards Brothers Malloy

To order this product, use ISBN: 978-1-284-02806-5

Library of Congress Cataloging-in-Publication Data
Paynich, Rebecca.
  Fundamentals of crime mapping / Bryan Hill, Rebecca Paynich.—Second edition.
    pages cm
  Includes bibliographical references and index.
  ISBN 978-1-4496-4865-7 (pbk.)—ISBN 1-4496-4865-7 (pbk.)
1. Crime analysis. 2. Geographic information systems. 3. Digital mapping. I. Hill, Bryan. II. Title.
  HV7936.C88P39 2014
  363.250285—dc23
                              2012046658
6048

Printed in the United States of America
23 22 21 20 19   11 10 9 8 7 6 5 4 3

Contents

Foreword

Learning the fundamentals of crime mapping is important for any person wishing to be a crime analyst, criminologist, or any position that supports law enforcement in efforts to mitigate criminal activity. Virtually every crime incident has a geographic location and can be mapped. This allows us to easily compare, in a geographic sense, crime incidents to other real-world activities, locational attributes, and persons. The study of crime and place is vital to making sense of relationships between crime and the world around it. Crime mapping has proven over the past 2 decades to be fundamental to the analysis, presentation, and sharing of information and insight about criminal activities.

Since the authors paint their presentation of crime mapping as a set of real-world processes, it is less philosophical and more based upon logical workflows leading to actionable results. While many crime analysts unfortunately spend much of their work days processing data to get into statistical tables and maps that a particular command staff requires, there is much more to crime mapping that allows for the careful analysis and development of useful products based upon the needs of the problem. This book allows the reader to see what these are and how this is done.

In recent years, new technology has taken great strides toward allowing for the automation of much of the crime mapping process, from extracting source data, to geocoding, the creation of hotspots, and the delivery of these data to the end users. However, any automation is useless without a grounded knowledge of the intricacies of the source data, local geography, an agency's goals and objectives, appropriate use of analyses for the problem at hand, and the capabilities and special needs of the end users of any crime mapping products. These are some of the fundamentals necessary for success that cannot be replaced by technology, but only enhanced by new software and processes.

Crime mapping has become a hot topic as of late with the more recent thinking in law enforcement organization and analyses such as intelligence-led policing and predictive policing. Neither of these approaches can exist without crime mapping playing a vital role in establishing the necessary intelligence and sources of analytics needed for decision making. The essentials of understanding crime and place, crime analysis, and how to present these data as actionable products are fundamental to support the law enforcement needs of the day.

Looking outside of the world of law enforcement, the same skills that can be acquired from this book can be applied to mapping other data. In particular, there is a rapidly growing trend of requiring location-based information in all Business Intelligence (BI) products. In fact, some of the analytics found in BI are now creeping into crime analysis in the form of predictive analytics, a driving force behind the development of predictive policing strategies. As within the realm of crime analysis, the mapping, spatial analysis, and appropriate presentation of data, as well as development of useful products for decision makers, is still a fundamental need.

Fundamentals of Crime Mapping, Second Edition helps to equip any practitioner of crime mapping and its related fields with the tools and understanding necessary to meet the challenges of the day. New to this second edition is a chapter on basics of cartography by Dr. Jim LeBeau, a chapter on police methodologies and how that impacts crime mapping, as well as new and shorter exercises using ArcGIS 10. In addition, there is a revised appendix tutorial on Microsoft® Excel 2010 and, of course, the authors have shined and polished everything. New and revised instructor materials, including additional exercises available on jblearning. com, enhance the course and students' learning experience. So, this text is and will continue to grow with the needs of the discipline and its practitioners.

Bruce Silva
Director, R&D
The Omega Group, Inc.
San Diego, CA

Preface

The second edition of *Fundamentals of Crime Mapping* offers both full-time college students and practitioners alike who are currently working in the field of law enforcement a great way to learn ArcGIS software, and along the way get an introduction to criminological theory. We know that beginning students and analysts who want to gain introductory skills and knowledge about crime mapping, practical uses of the software, and some of the basics about the theory of crime have come to the right place. Our experience with instruction of various topics related to GIS, crime mapping, and crime theory has helped us recognize that some students need a precursor in criminological theory; some students need a discussion of crime statistics; some students need a discussion of statistical analyses that are commonly used in crime analysis; some students simply need a review of the existing research; and all students need exercises that utilize a range of law enforcement data that they could complete to hone those GIS skills. Acquiring skills in crime analysis and crime mapping that are relevant and purposeful is of paramount importance.

Section I contains an introduction to crime mapping and several chapters on the theoretical approaches to the study of crime and place, as well as a brief explanation of policing theories and methodologies. The discussions in these chapters are meant to be concise but comprehensive, and provide students with enough information to understand the importance of theory in creating crime maps and performing crime analyses. Section II focuses more narrowly on the existing research in the field and the types of law enforcement data that are most commonly used in crime analysis and mapping. This section ends with a discussion of people and places involved in current crime trends. Section III discusses common types of statistical analyses that are employed in crime mapping, as well as distance and hotspot analyses. Section IV provides a chapter that gives useful suggestions about tailoring map presentations based on the needs of particular audiences, a new chapter on the basics of cartography, and a final, brief chapter on future issues in crime mapping.

Mapping is a tool, and it is a powerful one when used appropriately and correctly. This book will teach you how to use that tool with skill and knowledge so that your maps will connect you and others to the geography and the crime stories they depict. With knowledge and understanding, you have the opportunity to find answers to your questions about crime; and more importantly, answers to the questions your supervisors, citizens, and public figures ask of you. We hope you enjoy the chapters and exercises and that we have helped turn law enforcement data into relevant information, and with your diligence in practice with the software, knowledge you can use over and over again.

Exercise Appendices and the Accompanying Data Files

This book includes two appendices that each contain a variety of exercises. It is recommended that faculty use these exercises as assignments to enhance their students' understanding of the practical applications of crime mapping, and also to assist readers in developing the necessary computer skills to execute such applications.

Appendix I outlines how a crime analyst might use Microsoft Excel. Appendix II addresses the use of ArcGIS and takes readers through a variety of situations that crime analysts are often faced with as part of their work. The data files necessary to complete these exercises as well as additional exercises covering more advanced topics can be found on the book's companion website at go.jblearning.com/CrimeMapping2eCW.

To access the companion website, redeem the access code in the front of your book or purchase an access code at www.jblearning.com. Log into the website and select the Crime Mapping Data Files. Download the zipped file and save it to your computer. Please be aware that the data on this disc will require approximately 3 GB of hard drive space. It could take up to ten minutes or more for the data to transfer to your computer.

Once you have downloaded the C:\CIA folder to your computer, you can begin to use the files within it to complete the exercises. The C:\CIA folder has four subfolders:

- The "Data" folder contains the GIS data used for every exercise.
- The "Exercises" folder has the actual .MXD files and other files specific to each exercise.
- The Photos_Graphics folder is a variety of miscellaneous graphic items for use within the exercises.
- The "Resources" folder includes some models and samples that are provided as practical examples of tasks that professionals who map crime perform every day, and some of which will also be used in the exercises.

Use of ArcGIS and CrimeStat with This Book

Fundamentals of Crime Mapping, Second Edition contains a number of practice exercises that utilize the software programs Microsoft® Office, ArcGIS, and CrimeStat. While the Publisher makes every effort to direct users of this book to resources that will allow the user to download the most up-to-date versions of these programs, the Publisher is not responsible for providing the software directly. Any issues regarding technical support or assistance regarding usage of Microsoft® Office, ArcGIS, or CrimeStat should be made directly to the software provider.

Acknowledgments

Bryan Hill—I would like to acknowledge my co-author, Becki Paynich and her family for making this possible, and for taking me into their family as a friend for life. I always thank my beautiful wife, Barbara, for having patience while waiting for me to write a book someday. She is my inspiration in life for everything. I would also like to thank my son Joshua for helping me learn patience, and my son Lucas for teaching me humility. To our granddaughter Jayden and our new granddaughter set to arrive in May 2013, don't run so fast, life catches up to you eventually.

I would also like to thank my many colleagues in the field who have contributed greatly to my knowledge, and especially those analysts who belong to the Arizona Association of Crime Analysts (AACA) who educate me on a daily basis. I owe special thanks to Dr. James LeBeau for being the satellite crime analysis department for the City of Glendale, Dr. Ned Levine for being patient with my many questions, George Rengert, John Eck, Jerry Ratcliffe, Spencer Chainey, Richard and Becky Block, and Paul and Patricia Brantingham, as well as hundreds of other outstanding academicians in this field who have furthered my ability to put theory into practice. Leaders in the crime analysis software business such as Dale Harris, Bruce Silva, and Lew Nelson have also been great teachers and inspirations. I would especially like to thank the past and present board members of the International Association of Crime Analysts (IACA) for being awesome leaders and teachers. As Albert Schweitzer once said, "I don't know what your destiny will be, but one thing I know: the only ones among you who will be really happy are those who have sought and found how to serve." Everyone mentioned above and many others I've known have sought to serve and have done so elegantly; bringing us all along as educators, friends, and leaders in to the world of crime mapping; and staying there to hold our hands while we struggled. I am sure they are smiling now, or should be because I am certain it is due to their great teaching.

Rebecca Paynich—I would like to acknowledge co-author Bryan Hill for signing on to help with the first project and for taking the lead on this edition. Without his expertise and dedication, this book would have never come into fruition. You rock Bryan! Also, to my family for all of the help and support they gave me throughout the process. To Jason, for all of his editing and words of encouragement, and for taking the kids out of the house so I could get my work done; to Spencer, Dylan, and Jack for being patient; to Bonnie, Dan, Mom, and Dad for always being there; to the reviewers for their helpful suggestions; to my professors at WSU, my students, and to all of my colleagues in the field from whom I continue to learn on a daily basis. Without them, none of this would be possible.

Foundations and Theoretical Perspectives

SECTION

I

Introduction to Crime Mapping

▶ LEARNING OBJECTIVES

This text is written for individuals who are interested in the study and practice of crime mapping. Whether you are a practitioner or a college student, we hope you will find this text useful in your endeavor to learn more about crime mapping. This text, however, is not meant to provide you with an in-depth analysis of theory or an extensive discussion of methods in crime mapping. Rather, it is meant to convey the academic and practical skills the beginning student and analyst need to create crime maps that will be useful and accurate. For students who desire more than a cursory approach, there is a plethora of existing literature, both practical and academic, that is more appropriate for advanced studies. We have listed some of these sources in the Recommended Reading section at the end of each chapter. The exercises included with this text will be challenging and will provide you with skills needed to use ESRI's ArcGIS 10 software to complete a variety of analysis projects. Many other topics could be covered in a text such as this, but we have chosen to include only those that are most appropriate for the students we teach—foundational skills for the beginning crime mapping student and crime analyst. We hope this text will inspire your interest in geographic information systems (GIS) and provide a strong foundation for your future crime mapping success.

As a person interested in the field of crime mapping and analysis, you should understand that it is not a simple field of study. The technology is expanding rapidly, and you will need to work vigilantly to stay current in the field.

This chapter introduces the notion of crime as a "criminal event," which stresses the importance of understanding how both victims and offenders interact with their environments. This allows us to examine crime from multiple angles and further our understanding of how human behavior and the environment play pivotal roles in the occurrence of crime. This chapter also contains a brief history of crime mapping and introduces the student to the basics of using mapping tools in the analysis of crime. After studying this chapter, you should be able to:

- Define and explain the *criminal event* and understand the basic theoretical explanations offered for the relationship between crime and place.
- Define and explain the concepts of crime mapping and analysis.
- Identify key research that is rooted in crime mapping and analysis.
- Identify and explain basic map information, data, and various types of maps used by crime analysts.
- List key software and resources used by crime mappers and analysts.
- List the resources available to crime mappers and analysts.

> ▶ **Key Terms**

Administrative Crime Analysis	Criminal Investigative Analysis	Police Operational Analysis
Cartography	Criminology	Projection
CompStat	Geocoding	Scale
CPTED	Geographic Profiling	Strategic Crime Analysis
Crime Analysis	Hypotheses	Tactical Crime Analysis
Criminal Intelligence Analysis	Macro	
	Micro	

■ Introduction

This chapter begins with a discussion of crime as a criminal event. This view differs from other approaches to the study of crime in that it not only seeks to understand the motivations and behaviors of offenders or victims, but also seeks to explain how offenders and victims interact with each other and their environment. Thus, we are studying crime from multiple dimensions (the dimensions of the offenders, victims, and environment) rather than simply trying to understand it from one point of view (for example, trying to understand the motivation of the offender without factoring in victim or environmental characteristics). Viewing crime as a criminal event (Sacco & Kennedy, 2002) allows us to understand crime in a spatial context in that the environment provides varying opportunities for crime by providing cues to both offenders and victims that impact their decision making. Thus, properties of the immediate space in and around criminal events are contributing factors to victimization and cannot be excluded from the study of crime.

Also included in this chapter is a brief discussion of the history of crime mapping. Understanding the history of this field (or any field, for that matter) is important to the discussion of present and future issues in crime mapping. An introduction to basic map terminology and a brief examination of the different types of maps that crime analysts produce are also included in this chapter. A discussion and listing of resources, including mapping and analysis software options, are also provided.

■ Theoretical Explanations of Crime and Place

Crime has been a part of life for as long as people have gathered into social groups. A great deal of time and effort has been invested in trying to understand crime, most notably examining why some people engage in criminal behavior and others do not. As a result, there is a plethora of theories under the larger heading **criminology** (the study of crime and criminal behavior) that attempt to answer these questions. However, thus far, we have no generally accepted theory that explains the existence of crime in a society. For example, *consensus* perspectives of criminology approach crime as a normal and healthy part of any society. *Conflict* perspectives, on the other hand, argue that crime is the result of group conflict and unequal distributions of power. There is no single theory that accounts for all crime in a society. Some are more comprehensive than others, but we do not have a unified or general theory of crime (at least not one that everyone agrees with!).

Criminological theories also differ in their level of application. **Macro**-level theories make assumptions about societal-level variables, including the structure of government and the economy and how these variables impact crime rates within a society (which could be a city, state, country, or even the world). **Micro**-level theories make assumptions about individual characteristics (such as IQ, mental state, temperament, biological characteristics, and personal finances) and how they influence a person's decision to commit a crime. Sometimes, what holds true at the macro level does not work at the micro level and vice versa.

Unfortunately, many theories of crime focus solely on the individual or group that commits a crime and ignore other contributors to crime, including the environment. Recently, theorists have begun to broaden their approach from simple explanations of the criminal and his or her act to include other variables, such as victims' behaviors (Clarke & Felson, 1993; Cohen & Felson, 1979) and the physical environment (Brantingham & Brantingham, 1981, 1993). Thus, theorists began to examine crime as an "event" that was not simply a product of an interaction between persons but an interaction among victims, offenders, and their environments. When researchers began to examine the contributions of time and space on various criminal events, crime mapping became an important tool in crime analysis. In addition, with the introduction of widespread geographic information systems (GIS) data collection efforts and improved technology, the importance of crime mapping has grown exponentially over recent years to the development of theory and to the development of policy aimed at understanding and preventing crime.

Shaw and McKay (1942) put forth their social disorganization theory, which suggests, in part, that the economic composition of a community contributes to crime by affecting neighborhood order. Building upon the earlier works of Park (1915) and Burgess (1925), they observed that higher juvenile delinquency rates tended to cluster in certain neighborhoods within urban areas. Through their research, they determined that various factors about these neighborhoods contributed to higher levels of crime. The neighborhoods suffered from the effects of poverty and residential instability, which impacted both the physical appearance and the social structure of the neighborhood itself. In these socially disorganized neighborhoods, poverty, high population density, and high population mobility created an atmosphere where higher numbers of suitable targets and motivated offenders coexisted with little or no guardianship. Thus, the clustering of motivated offenders and a lack of guardianship in certain areas of a city, often in socially disorganized neighborhoods, produces higher rates of crime. Shaw and McKay made an important discovery that helped guide the development of more recent theoretical approaches; they found that socially disorganized neighborhoods suffered from higher rates of crime regardless of who lived there. That is, whether the neighborhood was inhabited by Italians, Russians, Cape Verdeans, or Cubans, for example, the crime rate remained high. Thus, this discovery suggests that the area, not the people, is criminogenic.

Three primary theoretical perspectives have built upon Shaw and McKay's discovery and have made enormous contributions to the study and understanding of crime in a spatial context: Routine Activities Theory, Rational Choice Theory, and Crime Pattern Theory, all of which are housed within a larger theoretical framework called Environmental Criminology. Each theory provides assumptions about empirical observations of the environment, victims, and/or offenders, allowing predictions to be made about the criminal event. In turn, this provides insight into possible solutions to combat crime, which incorporate environmental factors such as crime prevention through environmental design (CPTED) and other situational crime prevention strategies (Crowe, 2000; Rosenbaum, Lurigio, & Davis, 1998). For example, simply improving lighting or limiting access to a parking lot may reduce thefts from automobiles in that lot, or installing emergency phones and well lit walkways may reduce personal crimes on a college campus.

Environmental Criminology suggests that we analyze a variety of characteristics about the physical landscape, such as land use, access, and visibility, to determine likely areas that are conducive to crime. Brantingham, Dyreson, and Brantingham (1976), in their "cone of resolution," examined why there existed regional differences in crime rates. In their subsequent work, *Environmental Criminology,* they suggested that to have a better understanding of crime, theorists must examine four key elements to crime, including the law, offenders, targets, and place (Brantingham & Brantingham, 1981). In 1993, they proposed the groundwork for crime pattern theory, which combines Environmental Criminology with rational choice and routine activities perspectives in understanding crime (Brantingham & Brantingham, 1993).

Routine Activities Theory (Cohen & Felson, 1979) offers that when three core elements coexist in time and space, crime is more likely to occur: These include a motivated offender, a suitable target, and the absence of a capable guardian. When all three elements come together in time and space, the opportunity for crime is greater than when one or two of these elements are missing. Essentially, Routine Activities Theory suggests that at the micro level, individuals are more likely to be victimized in some situations than others. For example, a person walking alone in a park at night listening to an expensive iPod is more likely to be robbed than a couple in the same park walking their large dog, not listening to expensive iPods.

At the macro level, this theory suggests that patterns in victimization have changed, in part, due to patterns in the routine activities of society in general. For example, in the last 3 or 4 decades, the number of women who work outside of the home has dramatically increased. According to the Bureau of Labor Statistics (2011), 40.8% of civilian, noninstitutional women aged 16 years and older were employed in 1970. In 2009, this percentage increased to 59%. This jump left an increased number of homes during the daytime hours unguarded, which may have contributed to an increase in daytime residential burglaries. Women's civilian employment is projected to increase by 9% from 2008 to 2018, suggesting that this trend (and perhaps its impact on crime) will continue. In addition, this theory explains that crime rates will vary spatially due to increased opportunities caused by higher numbers of suitable targets and motivated offenders and lower levels of guardianship. Neighborhoods that are characterized by physical and social disorder have more opportunities for crime because they tend to hold more motivated offenders and have a greater lack of guardianship.

Crime as a Criminal Event

The criminal event, under Routine Activities Theory, requires that a suitable target, a motivated offender, and the absence of a capable defender or guardian come together at the same time and place. That place might be private, such as at a home (burglary or domestic violence, for example); a more public place than the home, such as work or school (workplace assaults or embezzlement); or in very public spaces, such as public roads, paths, parks, or entertainment spots (robbery, assault, and riots, for example). The specifics of who is assaulted, what is stolen, or who commits the crime may change from place to place, but whenever the three elements of the criminal event converge in time and space, the likelihood of crime is increased. By the same token, if one or more of the elements is missing from the equation, a crime is less likely to occur. Clarke and Eck (2005) expanded Routine Activities Theory and developed the problem analysis triangle (or crime triangle) to include the "controllers," who are *handlers*, *managers*, and *guardians* (see **Figure 1-1**).

In this model, guardians are those persons who keep a watchful eye on people and property, including people themselves and police or private security personnel. Handlers are people who know and interact with motivated offenders. They include agents of informal social control, such as family members, friends, or teachers, and agents of formal social control, such as

Figure 1-1 Problem Analysis Triangle

Source: Adapted from Clarke, R. V., & Eck, J. (2005). *Crime analysis for problem solvers in 60 small steps.* U.S. Department of Justice, Community Oriented Policing Services.

probation or parole officers. Last, managers are those persons who have some level of responsibility for the behaviors of persons within a specific location. For example, homeowners are responsible for controlling behavior in their homes, teachers are responsible for maintaining order in their classrooms, and bar managers are responsible for controlling behavior in their bars. Homeowners, teachers, and bar managers, in this sense, are managers.

In studying and mapping the criminal event, it is possible to study not just the individuals involved, but also to map crime and the spatial and temporal variables needed to understand how the specific event occurred, how the elements came together, what actually transpired, and how the event was concluded. When it is understood how a specific event occurred, it becomes possible to examine similar events in an attempt to identify similarities, patterns, and ways to keep that type of event from occurring again.

McGloin, Sullivan, and Kennedy (2012) in their edited volume, *When Crime Appears: The Role of Emergence,* argue that the "messy" nature of understanding crime must be from an emergence perspective such that:

> … criminologists need to consider the individual, the situation, the interaction of the individual and the situation, the role of learning and its impact on future behavior, and the range of alternative methodologies necessary to gain perspective on the complex dynamics involved in explaining crime (p. xi).

In the emergence perspective, McGloin and colleagues (2012) argue that crime analysis should not only examine areas where crime is prevalent, but also areas where crime is likely to emerge in the future. In addition, crime emergence is not tied to any single theoretical approach nor does it adhere to strict linear statistical patterns. Thus, theories to explain crime and methodologies to analyze crime must be developed to capture the role of emergence.

It is also essential to realize that mapping criminal events is only the first step in the crime-fighting process. The criminal event and the circumstances surrounding it must be analyzed to find meaning in the data. Facts do not speak for themselves! They must be critically analyzed. **Hypotheses** (statements derived from theory that can be tested to either support or disprove a theory or its assumptions) must be generated about individual criminal events and criminal events that take place in combination with other, similar events. Could the perpetrator be the same in a series of crimes? Is the method of committing the crime similar? Are times and locations connected in some way? Examining criminal events to identify relationships is the role of a crime analyst, and data collection, analysis, and mapping are the analyst's methods of fighting and preventing crime.

■ Crime Analysis

There are three broad categories of analysis that fall under law enforcement analysis: crime analysis, criminal intelligence analysis, and investigative analysis (Bruce, 2004; Gottlieb, Arenberg, & Singh, 1994). There is a wide array of definitions for crime analysis in the existing literature. **Crime analysis**, as Boba defines it, "is the systematic study of crime and disorder problems as well as other police-related issues—including sociodemographic, spatial, and temporal factors—to assist the police in criminal apprehension, crime and disorder reduction, crime prevention, and evaluation" (Boba, 2005, p. 6). The International Association of Crime Analysts (IACA; 2005) defines crime analysis as:

> ...a type of law enforcement analysis that is focused on the study of criminal incidents; the identification and analysis of patterns, trends, and problems; and the dissemination of information that helps a police agency develop tactics and strategies to solve patterns, trends, and problems.

Essentially, crime analysis draws on a variety of different types of data, including crime data, to gain a better understanding of criminal activity and the root causes of criminal activity, and to develop more effective means of combating crime and preventing victimization.

The field of crime analysis appeared to gain both significant attention and momentum in the late 1990s after the successes in New York City with the computerized statistics program (otherwise known as **CompStat**) and the large reductions in crime associated with this intelligence and analysis philosophy. The various policing methods and philosophies associated with CompStat (including the now in vogue intelligence-led policing and evidence-based practice are discussed later in this text).

In general, analysts look at crime and other law enforcement data using formal analytical and statistical techniques and research methods that have been developed in the social sciences. They study arrests, crime reports, offender and victim characteristics, and crime scene evidence. They also examine other types of data collected, such as calls for service, traffic citations and accidents, census data, weather and traffic patterns, and data from other criminal justice agencies, including probation and parole reports. By analyzing numerous sources of information, the crime analyst can provide useful information to assist decision makers in a police department to fight and prevent crime.

Crime analysis includes tactical and strategic analysis (focused on criminal activity) and administrative analysis (focused on police activity). **Tactical crime analysis** examines recent criminal events and potential criminal activity by analyzing how, when, and where the events occur to establish patterns and series, identify leads or suspects, and to clear cases (Boba, 2005). Tactical analysis focuses on specific information about each crime, such as method of entry, point of entry, suspects' actions, victims' characteristics, type of weapon used, and the date, time, and location of the crime. It also considers information developed in the field from patrol officers, such as suspicious activity, calls for service, criminal trespass warnings, field interrogation cards, and personal identifying marks (such as scars and tattoos) (Boba, 2005). Usually, crimes examined under tactical crime analysis are those in which the victim and offender are unknown to one another. The focus of tactical analysis is the daily examination of data to identify trends and patterns concerning recent criminal activity. When a crime pattern, suspect, or investigative lead is identified, the information is compiled and disseminated to patrol officers and detectives. Crime mapping is used in tactical analysis to reveal clusters of criminal activity and to identify spatial relationships between crime and various geographic variables (Boba, 2005). Tactical analysis is used to develop a prediction of an offender's future behavior so surveillance units can be deployed to where an offender is predicted to strike again. Another type of tactical analysis entails predicting where an offender may live based on the locations of his or her crimes in the series.

Strategic crime analysis involves the study of crime and other law enforcement issues to identify long-standing patterns of crime and other problems and to assess police responses to these problems (Boba, 2005). Typically, this analysis involves collecting a great deal of information about criminal events. In addition, "helping agencies to identify root causes of crime problems and develop creative problem-solving strategies to reduce crime" is a key goal in strategic crime analysis (IACA, 2005). Strategic analysis is the backbone of most police agency crime analysis efforts, as this is where the analyst identifies problems and begins to work toward prevention strategies.

Administrative crime analysis involves the presentation of key findings of crime research and analysis to audiences within law enforcement, local government, and citizenry based on legal, political, and practical concerns. Bruce (2004, p. 22) provides several examples of administrative crime analysis, including:

- A report on demographic changes in the jurisdiction
- Miscellaneous crime statistics to support grant applications
- Preparation of Uniform Crime Reports (UCRs) or National Incident-Based Reporting System (NIBRS) reports

Another example of administrative crime analysis is the establishment of a department website to inform the general public about public safety issues. **Police operational analysis** is another type of analysis that is also conducted. Its focus is on the operations of police agencies, including staffing and resource deployment. Operations analysis seeks to identify how to better organize the internal operations of a police department to minimize inefficiency and maximize effectiveness (Bruce, 2004).

Crime analysis is different from **criminal intelligence analysis** in that criminal intelligence analysis typically looks at organized criminal activity and seeks to link people, events, and property. Much of the information that is analyzed is obtained by law enforcement efforts, including surveillance, informants, and undercover operations (Boba, 2005). Information that is analyzed is not necessarily criminal information and can include telephone taps, travel information, financial and tax records, and family and business relationships of the person(s) being investigated (Boba, 2005).

Crime analysis is also separate from **criminal investigative analysis** in that with criminal investigative analysis, the focus is on serial criminals (Boba, 2005). Victim characteristics and elements of crime scenes are studied to discover patterns that link related crimes together. Sometimes, in **geographic profiling**, a profile of the offender based on the nature of the crime and the facts of the case is developed. Often these types of serial crimes cross jurisdictional lines, and many different law enforcement agencies may become involved in high-profile cases. (See Rossmo [2000] for a more in-depth discussion of geographic profiling; a discussion on geographic profiling and journey to crime analysis is also provided elsewhere in the text).

Analysis has been utilized for many years on an informal basis, but with newer technology, especially since the 1990s, its prominence and utility in law enforcement applications has grown. After the events surrounding 9/11, the need and demand for good analysis has exploded. Good analysis and presentation are essential. This text is dedicated to providing you with the tools necessary to complete useful and accurate analysis that, when properly presented, can make a difference in fighting crime.

Jack Dangermond (2007), the president and cofounder of Esri (the company that created the ArcGIS software that is used to complete the exercises contained elsewhere in this text), suggests that:

> To gain a greater understanding of our world we need a framework that I call the "geographic approach." The geographic approach uses geographic science supported by geographic information system (GIS) technology as a framework for understanding our world and applying geographic knowledge to solve problems and guide human behavior.

The ability to utilize such an approach has not always been an option for law enforcement. However, with the arrival of GIS and inexpensive desktop computers and printers with speed and large memory/storage capacity, even the smallest agency can use analysis and crime mapping in its daily battle against crime and disorder.

■ A Short History of Crime Mapping

This chapter contains only a brief discussion of the history of crime mapping. For a deeper understanding of its history, there are several sources you may want to look at, including Weisburd & McEwen (1988), Harries (1999), Boba (2001), and Chamard (2006). In addition, for a good general resource for crime analysis, see Osborne and Wernicke (2003).

Mapping itself has a long history, but crime mapping, the subject of our study, has been traced to the early 1800s when social scientists began creating maps to illustrate their crime theories and research. Social scientists Adolphe Quetelet and A. M. Guerry are credited as being two of the first people to use spatial analysis to research crime. Using crime and other social data from France, they determined that crime was not evenly distributed across space and that it also clustered geographically with other observable social-level variables, such as socioeconomic status and population density.

In the early 1900s, the New York Police Department and other large departments began to utilize single-symbol point maps (pin maps) to illustrate crime locations. In the 1920s and 1930s, sociologists at the University of Chicago used graduated area maps of crime and delinquency to show the relationships between crime and social variables, such as poverty. These maps were drawn by hand and were very labor intensive.

It was not until the 1960s and 1970s that crime maps were created with the use of computers. These early computers were large, mainframe computers that were affordable only to the largest agencies. They were very expensive to operate, and producing maps was still very labor intensive. In addition, the maps that were produced were of poor quality and unsuitable for many law enforcement purposes.

Desktop computers that were capable of mapping (still with limited quality) became available in the 1980s, but they had slow processing speeds, limited memory, and poor printer quality. In the 1990s, desktop computers with GIS capabilities and the ability to be integrated with law enforcement record management systems and other data made mapping possible for many law enforcement agencies. The additional contributions of government funding, expanded training, a more tech-savvy workforce, and higher quality computers and printers further enhanced this ability. Studies that examined the use of crime mapping in law enforcement agencies suggest that the utilization of crime mapping software, the program(s) being used, and how crime mapping is applied within an agency vary significantly (Chamard, 2006; Mamalian et al., 1999; Paynich, Cooke, & Mathews, 2007). In general, large departments with an expansive data collection effort that serve a diverse and geographically dispersed population and that provide adequate funding and personnel to accommodate training and equipment expenses have been the most successful in adopting mapping as a strategy and have maintained their involvement through networking, conferences, and the Internet. Mid-sized and smaller agencies have been slower to adopt a crime mapping policy, primarily due to a small service population, a low crime rate, and a lack of resources and personnel. However, with examples of successful implementation, decreasing equipment costs, rising workforce capabilities, and increased training and funding available in the post-9/11 era, crime analysis and mapping will continue to grow and improve law enforcement agencies' analytic capabilities.

■ Mapping Basics

A map is a two-dimensional or flat-scale model of the Earth's surface or a portion thereof (Rubenstein, 2003). Maps portray a portion of the real world in a form we can use to find our way or find answers to questions we may have about an area we are interested in. They may be rough sketches of the way to "Aunt Trudy's house" or a precise computer map of a community that details every important landmark. The science of mapmaking is called **cartography** and is centuries old.

Map Information

For our purposes, we will focus on geographic information systems (GIS)—high-performance computer software that allows users to process geographically related data. This data (topography, political boundaries, population density, calls for service, crimes, etc.) is stored as information in virtual layers (one layer for each variable) to be displayed on the computer in the form of a multilayer, virtual map. A single layer may be displayed, or several layers can be combined to show relationships among the layers (types of information or what is called geoprocessing). In crime mapping, the layers sit atop one another, resulting in an overall picture of crime and its spatial context. This is much like an anatomy textbook that contains different transparency sheets with drawings of the skeletal, muscular, cardiovascular, central nervous, and digestive systems. You may choose to look at the systems individually or layer them atop one another to see how they overlay and get a better picture of the entire human anatomy. In crime mapping, you may have a map with layers representing police boundaries, streets, key landmarks, and various crimes. Using GIS, you can select various layers to use in your analysis. The use of GIS to analyze environmental and social phenomena, such as crime, is what crime analysis and mapping is all about.

The Earth is very nearly a sphere, and while it may be accurately portrayed as a globe, that is not practical for most uses. Problems arise when you try to draw a sphere on a flat surface because the image is distorted. The method used to transfer locations on the Earth's surface to a flat map is called **projection**. Mapmakers have devised numerous ways of producing flat maps, but none are without flaw. There are cylindrical and conical projections, but each has distortions. The distortion produced is more severe when you attempt to map the entire world and less so as the mapped area becomes smaller. For most law enforcement purposes, the geographic area of interest is small enough that projection does not cause serious problems and can be ignored (Harries, 1999). Projection systems are discussed in more detail in the exercises elsewhere in this text, but for our purposes here, you should know that there are many different projection systems to choose from, and it is important to know what system your data is projected with. Nevertheless, you should be aware of the problem and work with local experts to address this issue and, if necessary, create solutions for your purposes. The problem becomes more important as the **scale** of the map increases (from municipal to regional level, for example) and when importing and exporting data between applications. This is especially important in **geocoding** events onto a map. In the geocoding process, street addresses are positioned onto a map using latitude and longitude coordinates. "*Projections* determine how the latitude and longitude grid of the earth is represented on paper. *Coordinate systems* provide the x-y reference system to describe locations in two-dimensional space" (Harries, 1999, p. 14). Different states use different projections, and it is important for the analyst to understand which projections are used by the map layers he or she is working with. This becomes especially important when using data from multiple sources because without knowing the projection of each data layer, it may be difficult to get them all to line up on the map surface as expected.

Types of Maps Used by Crime Analysts

There are many different types of maps that might be constructed depending on what information the analyst wants to present and what audience will receive the information. He or she might map a simple, single event (such as that depicted by traditional pin maps) or show the distribution of crime across a particular area (a choropleth map or shaded grid map, such as a police beat or district or a census block), multiple hotspots located across a jurisdiction that are related to multiple criminal events (which typically include liquor stores, pawn shops, high schools, drug houses, shopping malls, etc.), or a series of connected criminal events (such as crimes committed by a child molester or serial murderer). An analyst might also utilize the statistical capabilities provided in GIS software and other programs, which expand the programs' capabilities to attempt to predict an offender's next target (such was the case in the Washington sniper case) or areas where offenders might live, work, play, or retreat to after performing a criminal event. Caplan and Kennedy (2011) have also developed a method to produce risk terrain maps that analysts can use in efforts to identify variables, or risk factors, most associated with a particular crime or crimes and to predict emerging hotspots.

Map Data

Many different maps can be created. However, most crime maps include a limited number of map components. The five major components of a GIS include hardware, software, data, personnel, and methods. Real-world data are represented by four feature types in a GIS:

- *Point features*: A discrete location usually depicted by a symbol or label. It is like a pin placed on a paper wall map. Different symbols are used to depict the location of crimes, motor vehicle crashes, traffic signs, buildings, police stations, cell towers, etc.
- *Line features*: A geographic feature that can be represented by a line or set of lines, such as railways, streets, rivers, powerlines, bus routes, etc.
- *Polygon features*: A multisided figure represented by a closed set of lines, such as city boundaries, census tracts or blocks, patrol beats, neighborhood boundaries, and gang turf. Polygon features may be as large as countries or as small as a single place (like a park or cemetery) or even a single building (such as a school). Points, lines, and polygons are typically called "vector" types in that they have finite limits, locations, or beginning and ending points, and do not cover the entire surface of the map.
- *Image features*: A vertical photo (usually taken from an airplane or satellite) that is digitized and placed within the geographic information system coordinates that are associated with it. These and hotspot maps are often called "raster" images in that they are actually small pixels of data which cover the entire map surface and each pixel has some value as in the colors and locations of an aerial image.

Each type of feature has "attributes" or a table of data that describes it. The ability to view, query, relate, and manipulate the data behind these features is the real power of a GIS. Simply clicking on a point, line, polygon, or image can produce the data associated with that particular feature. For example, you can very easily identify a specific point on the map and be instantly given detailed information (as long as it is contained in the attribute table). In crime data, this information may include victim and offender characteristics, motives for the crime, and temporal (date and time of incident) and spatial (address and name of location) details.

■ Mapping Software and Resources

In today's world of crime analysis, the beginner analyst is fortunate to have a plethora of crime mapping tools, software, and resources at his or her disposal from a variety of sources. This section provides a brief overview of some of the most known and commonly used programs and resources. It is by no means a complete listing of the wonderful resources available to analysts. The field is rapidly changing and growing and these changes bring new software and resources on an almost daily basis.

Software

The wide use of crime mapping and analysis has greatly increased due to the development and availability of relatively inexpensive computers, printers, and analysis software that are adequate to the task. Today there are many mapping and GIS programs available on the market, and more are being developed each year. For the purposes of this introduction, we will look at five of the more common programs. Three are professional, commercial systems, and two are programs that were developed for special use under government funding and are available free online. The first two programs, currently the leaders in GIS systems used by law enforcement in the United States, are MapInfo (www.mapinfo.com) and ArcGIS (www.esri .com). ArcGIS is the most commonly cited program used by police departments that utilize crime mapping applications in the United States (Paynich et al., 2007). GeoDa is a standalone spatial analysis program developed by Dr. Luc Anselin, then at the University of Illinois, for use as an introduction to spatial analysis. CrimeStat is a standalone spatial statistics program for the analysis of incident locations. It was developed under research grants from the National Institute of Justice (NIJ) by Dr. Ned Levine & Associates, who is the sole distributor of CrimeStat and makes it available for free to law enforcement and criminal justice analysts and researchers (Levine, 2003). You will use CrimeStat in several of the exercises contained elsewhere in this text. CrimeStat must be used in conjunction with a mapping program, such as ArcView or MapInfo, to project the analysis onto a map. Without it, the analyses are simply numerical outputs to be interpreted by analysts. Another commercially available tool for crime mapping and analysis is CrimeView (put out by the Omega Group). CrimeView is an extension for ArcGIS that allows the user to perform specific analyses as needed or to create automated analyses, including hotspot maps, threshold alerts, and cyclical reporting. There are many tools available for analysts for a variety of procedures—some are developed by other crime analysts or academics in criminal justice; some are borrowed from other fields entirely such as earthquake prediction, animal science, or anthropology; and some analysts who are proficient in programming syntax can make their own.

Mapping Resources

There are also a variety of online and other resources for beginning analysts to use in their quest for information about crime analysis and mapping. Many of these sites have links to free software, with accompanying workbooks and tutorials, and publications written about topics pertinent to the analysis of crime and related social problems. New sources are always being developed and older sites might be abandoned. For example, the Mapping and Analysis for Public Safety (MAPS) program at the NIJ (www.nij.gov/nij/topics/technology/maps/welcome.htm), along with the Community Oriented Policing Services (COPS) office (www .cops.usdoj.gov/), and the Center for Problem-Oriented Policing (www.popcenter.org/about/?p=sara) are all good places to start to learn more about how crime mapping fits in with law enforcement's mission to prevent crime. In addition, students may want to join an email group list, such as the LeAnalyst listserv (http://sites.google.com/site/joinleanalyst/), to learn and share information about crime mapping and analysis with other people interested in the topic. The email content of this group ranges from discussions about the best software to buy, how to use various applications, where to find data, and recommendations of various publications and general crime analysis questions. Other online sources worth looking at are listed at the end of the chapter.

■ Conclusion

This chapter introduced you to the world of crime mapping and analysis. A discussion of the basics of crime mapping, along with a brief history of how crime mapping has evolved, was provided. Various types of data, analyses, and maps were described, and outside sources were recommended. This chapter by no means covers all of what you should learn to be a trusted crime mapper, but it will get you started. There are many other discussions concerning the effect different police methodologies and philosophies have had on crime mapping and crime analysis in general. Many of these discussions are found elsewhere in this text. Programs such as the Problem-Oriented Policing (POP) program, Community Oriented Policing Services (COPS), Data-Driven Approaches to Crime and Traffic Safety (DDACTS), intelligence-led policing, and predictive policing or predictive analytics have all had an impact in one form or another to increase (and often guide) the use of crime mapping technologies in the day-to-day crime suppression efforts of many law enforcement agencies.

■ Chapter Glossary

Administrative crime analysis   Administrative crime analysis involves the presentation of key findings of crime research and analysis to audiences within law enforcement, local government, and citizenry based on legal, political, and practical concerns.

Cartography   The science of mapmaking.

CompStat   The term generally associated with the New York model of policing which includes accountability, crime mapping and analysis, and problem-solving processes by the police department to reduce crime; often utilized by other police departments in a variety of forms to help focus efforts in targeted areas in an organized, strategic manner.

CPTED   The acronym for crime prevention through environmental design. Refers to strategies to reduce crime that incorporate making changes to the physical environment to limit the opportunity for crime to occur.

Crime analysis   Several good definitions exist for crime analysis, but essentially, crime analysis is the study and analysis of crime and crime-related factors in efforts to inform and develop strategies to reduce crime and the fear of crime.

Criminal intelligence analysis   Criminal intelligence analysis typically looks at organized criminal activity and seeks to link people, events, and property.

Criminal investigative analysis   With criminal investigative analysis, the focus is on serial criminals. Victim characteristics and elements of crime scenes are studied to discover patterns that link related crimes together.

Criminology   The study of crime and criminal behavior.

Geocoding   In geocoding, street addresses and other geographic reference points are positioned onto a map using latitude and longitude coordinates for computer mapping and analysis.

Geographic profiling   In geographic profiling, a profile of the offender, based on the nature of the crime and the facts of the case, is developed.

Hypotheses   Statements derived from theory that can be tested to either support or disprove a theory or its assumptions.

Macro   Macro-level theories of crime focus on societal-level variables, including the structure of government and the economy and how these variables impact crime rates within a society. Macro-level theories could focus on city-, state-, country-, or global-level influences.

Micro   Micro-level theories of crime focus on individual characteristics, including (but not limited to) IQ, mental state, temperament, biological characteristics, and personal finances, and how they influence a person's decision to commit a crime.

Police operational analysis   Police operational analysis focuses on the operations of police agencies, including staffing and resource deployment.

Projection   The method used to transfer locations on the Earth's surface to a flat map.

Scale   The scale of a map indicates how miniature the representation is; the larger the scale, the smaller the area shown on a map.

Strategic crime analysis   Strategic crime analysis involves the study of crime and other law enforcement issues to identify long-standing patterns of crime and other problems and to assess police responses to these problems.

Tactical crime analysis   Tactical crime analysis examines recent criminal events and potential criminal activity by analyzing how, when, and where the events occur to establish patterns and series, identify leads or suspects, and to clear cases.

■ Questions for Review

1. What is the difference between micro- and macro-level theories of crime?
2. What is the problem analysis triangle?
3. What is crime analysis?
4. How does crime analysis differ from criminal intelligence analysis? From criminal investigative analysis?
5. Briefly define and provide an example for each of the following: strategic crime analysis, tactical crime analysis, and administrative crime analysis.
6. What are projections and coordinate systems?
7. What are the four types of map data? Provide an example of each.
8. Describe raster and vector data. Provide examples of each.

■ Online Resources

A list of online resources is as follows. Please note that this is far from a complete list.

Arizona Association of Crime Analysts: www.aacaonline.org
Center for Problem-Oriented Policing: www.popcenter.org/about/?p=sara
ESRI Mapping Center: http://mappingcenter.esri.com
International Association of Crime Analysts: www.iaca.net

International Association of Law Enforcement Intelligence Analysts: www.ialeia.org

International Association of Law Enforcement Planners: http://www.ialep.org/

Mapping and Analysis for Public Safety (MAPS): www.nij.gov/topics/technology/maps/welcome.htm

Massachusetts Association of Crime Analysts: www.macrimeanalysts.org

Office of Community Oriented Policing Services: http://cops.usdoj.gov

The Omega Group: www.crimemapping.com and www.theomegagroup.com

Police Foundation: www.policefoundation.org

Rutgers Center on Public Security: www.rutgerscps.org/rtm/

■ Recommended Reading

Boba, R. (2012). *Crime analysis and crime mapping* (3rd ed.). Thousand Oaks, CA: Sage.

Chainey, S. & Ratcliffe, J. (2005). *GIS and crime mapping.* Southern Gate, Chichester: West Sussex, Wiley.

Dana, P. H. (1999) at the Department of Geography, University of Texas at Austin gives a good discussion of map projections: www.colorado.edu/geography/gcraft/notes/mapproj/mapproj_f.html.

Johnson, M. R. (2000). Applying theory to crime mapping. *Crime Mapping News, 2*(4), 5–7.

Kelly, J. (1999). MapInfo helps take a byte out of crime. *Crime Mapping News, 1*(4), 5–7.

Levine, N. (2000). CrimeStat: A spatial statistics program for the analysis of crime incident locations. *Crime Mapping News, 2*(1), 8–9.

Levine, N. (2005). CrimeStat III. *Crime Mapping News, 7*(2), 8–10.

Nelson, L. (1999). Crime mapping and ESRI. *Crime Mapping News, 1*(4), 1–4, 8.

Osborne, D. A., & Wernicke, S. C. (2003). *Introduction to crime analysis: Basic resources for criminal justice practice.* New York: The Haworth Press.

Paulsen, D., & Robinson, M. (2008). *Crime mapping and the spatial aspects of crime* (2nd ed.). Boston: Allyn & Bacon.

Swartz, C. at the Center for Applied Studies of the Environment, City University of New York, maintains a rather extensive list of references related to crime mapping and analysis. To view this list, visit: www.geo.hunter.cuny.edu/capse/projects/nij/crime_bib1.html.

■ References

Boba, R. (2001). *Introductory guide to crime analysis and mapping.* Washington, DC: U.S. Department of Justice, Community Oriented Policing Services.

Boba, R. (2005). *Crime analysis and crime mapping.* Thousand Oaks, CA: Sage.

Brantingham, P., & Brantingham, P. (1981). *Environmental criminology.* Beverly Hills, CA: Sage.

Brantingham, P., & Brantingham, P. (1993). Environment, routine, and situation: Toward a pattern theory of crime. In R. Clarke & M. Felson (Eds.), *Routine activity and rational choice: Advances in criminological theory* (Vol. 5). New Brunswick, NJ: Transaction Publishers.

Brantingham, P. J., Dyreson, D. A., & Brantingham, P. L. (1976). Crime seen through a cone of resolution. *American Behavioral Scientist, 20*(2), 261–273.

Bruce, C. (2004). Fundamentals of crime analysis. In C. W. Bruce, S. R. Hick, & J. P. Cooper (Eds.), *Exploring crime analysis: Reading on essential skills.* Overland Park, KS: IACA Press.

Bureau of Labor Statistics. (2011). BLS spotlight on statistics: Women at work. Retrieved from www .bls.gov/spotlight/2011/women/pdf/women_bls_spotlight.pdf.

Burgess, E. (1925). The growth of a city. In R. Park, E. Burgess, & D. McKenzie (Eds.), *The City.* Chicago: University of Chicago Press.

Caplan, J. M., & Kennedy, L. W. (2011). *Risk terrain modeling manual: Theoretical framework and technical steps of spatial risk assessment.* Rutgers Center on Public Safety. Retrieved from www .rutgerscps.org/rtm/.

Chamard, S. (2006). The history of crime mapping and its use by American police departments. *Alaska Justice Forum, 23*(3), 1, 4–8. Retrieved from http://justice.uaa.alaska.edu/forum/23/3fall2006/a_ crimemapping.html.

Clarke, R., & Felson, M. (Eds.). (1993). *Routine activity and rational choice. Advances in criminological theory* (Vol. 5). New Brunswick, NJ: Transaction Publishers.

Clarke, R. V., & Eck, J. (2005). *Crime analysis for problem solvers in 60 small steps.* U.S. Department of Justice, Community Oriented Policing Services. Retrieved from www.popcenter.org /learning/60steps.

Cohen, L. E., & Felson, M. (1979). Social change and crime rate trends: A routine activities approach. *American Sociological Review, 44,* 588–608.

Crowe, T. D. (2000). *Crime prevention through environmental design: Applications of architectural design and space management concepts* (2nd ed.). Boston: Butterworth-Heinemann.

Dangermond, J. (2007). Taking the "geographic approach." *Arcwatch.* Retrieved from www.esri.com /news/arcwatch/0907/feature.html.

Gottlieb, S., Arenberg, S., & Singh, R. (1994). *Crime analysis: From first report to final arrest.* Montclair, CA: Alpha Publishing.

Harries, K. (1999). *Crime mapping: Principle and practice.* Washington, DC: U.S. Department of Justice. Retrieved from www.ncjrs.gov/html/nij/mapping/pdf.html.

International Association of Crime Analysts (IACA). (2005). Frequently asked questions. Retrieved from http://iaca.net/faq_training.asp.

Levine, N. (2003). CrimeStat II. *Crime Mapping News, 5*(2), 2–4.

Mamalian, C. A., LaVigne, N. G., & Staff of the Crime Mapping Research Center. (1999). The use of computerized crime mapping by law enforcement: Survey results. *NIJ Research Preview.* Retrieved from www.ncjrs.gov?pdffiles1/fs000237.pdf.

McGloin, J. M., Sullivan, C. J., & Kennedy, L. W. (2012). *When crime appears: The role of emergence.* New York: Routledge.

Osborne, D., & Wernicke, S. (2003). *Introduction to crime analysis: Basic resources for criminal justice practice.* New York: The Haworth Press.

Park, R. (1915). The city: Suggestions for the investigation of human behavior in the urban environment. *American Journal of Sociology, 20,* 577–612.

Paynich, R., Cooke, P., & Mathews, C. (2007). Developing standards and curriculum for GIS in law enforcement. Presented at 9th NIJ Crime Mapping Conference, Pittsburgh, PA. Retrieved from www.nij.gov/nij/events/maps/pittsburgh2007/panels.htm.

Rosenbaum, D. P., Lurigio, A. J., & Davis, R. C. (1998). *The prevention of crime: Social and situational strategies*. Belmont, CA: West/Wadsworth.

Rossmo, D. K. (2000). *Geographic profiling*. Boca Raton, FL: CRC Press.

Rubenstein, J. M. (2003). *An introduction to human geography* (7th ed.). Upper Saddle River, NJ: Pearson Education.

Sacco, V. F., & Kennedy, L. W. (2002). *The criminal event: Perspectives in space and time* (2nd ed.). Belmont, CA: Wadsworth/Thomson Learning.

Shaw, C. R., & McKay, H. D. (1942). *Juvenile delinquency and urban areas* (5th ed.). Chicago: University of Chicago Press.

Weisburd, D., & McEwen, T. (1988). Crime mapping: Crime prevention. In R. V. Clarke (Ed.), *Crime prevention studies*. Monsey, NY: Willow Tree Press.

Social Disorganization and Social Efficacy

CHAPTER

2

▶ LEARNING OBJECTIVES

Crime mapping is not a new practice of crime analysts. The literature is rich with theoretical justifications of ecological influences upon crime. This chapter discusses several early theoretical approaches beginning with the Chicago School and ending with a discussion of Wilson and Kelling's more recent Broken Windows approach to crime prevention. After studying this chapter, you should be able to:

- Understand a brief history of criminology and how theories focused on social-level variables developed and fit within the larger discipline of criminology.

- Exhibit a solid understanding of the Chicago School and its contribution to the study of crime and crime mapping.

- Explain Burgess and Park's concentric zone theory.

- Explain how Shaw and McKay's social disorganization theory expanded upon the concentric zone theory by adding social-level variables to explain how people interact with their environment.

- Discuss the key elements to social efficacy.

- Identify the key elements to Broken Windows and critically analyze this approach through the lens of social and physical elements found in the theories discussed in this chapter.

▶ **Key Terms**

Broken Windows Theory
Cartographic School
  of Criminology
Chicago School
  of Criminology
Classical School
  of Criminology

Collective Efficacy
Crime Fuse
Determinism
Differential Association
  Theory
Ecological Fallacy
Gentrification

Heterogeneous
Positivist School
  of Criminology
Social Disorganization
  Theory
Utilitarianism

■ Introduction

At this point, you may be wondering why a text on crime mapping has several chapters dedicated to criminological theory. Theory is very important to the creation of crime maps. Theories provide useful suggestions about the types of variables and sources of data that should be included in maps of crime. Some examples might include measures of socioeconomic status and other social variables, population density, and land use types. As emphasized throughout this text, it is crucial that crime maps and analyses convey the whole picture, and theory is instrumental in helping us paint a comprehensive picture of the criminal event.

Maps created without providing the accompanying environmental and social context are limited in their usefulness. Block (1998) emphasizes this point:

> The successful analysis of spatial patterns of crime requires that mapping technology be guided by theory that can link place to crime, can unravel the spatial characteristics of different types of crime, and can provide explanations and suggest prevention strategies for the high vulnerability of some neighborhoods or demographic groups (p. 37).

Eck (1998) furthers this notion by suggesting that "everything displayed on a map should be of theoretical importance" (p. 381). In addition, "the choice of the features that describe the relevant context depends on the theory being examined. To interpret the dots we need a theory so we can display the relevant context and leave out the irrelevant context" (p. 383).

So let us begin with a *very* brief history of criminology. Theories of crime causation have come a long way since Cesare Beccaria published his classic essay "On Crimes and Punishments" (1764) and Jeremy Bentham put forth his *Introduction to the Principles of Morals and Legislation* (1789). Prior to Beccaria and Bentham, crime was primarily viewed as a product of evil and demonic possession or inferior bloodlines. Punishments for committing crimes during the Middle Ages were barbaric and cruel and included various types of torture and execution. By the mid-18th century, however, the prevailing philosophy, rooted in **utilitarianism**, maintained that human behavior is, by and large, the result of reason and logic. Beccaria believed that people act of their own free will, and thus criminals make a conscious decision to commit crime. He advocated for humane forms of punishment and for punishment that "fit the crime." Bentham, also believing in free will and rational thought, argued that punishment itself is harmful and that if it is to outweigh the harm it produces, it must achieve four main objectives:

- The primary goal of punishment is the prevention of crime.
- When punishment does not prevent crime, it must persuade the offender to choose to commit a less serious offense.
- Punishment must persuade future offenders to use the least amount of force in committing a crime.
- Punishment must prevent crime at a cost-effective rate.

Beccaria, Bentham, and others believed that crime was a product of rational thought; their collective works are termed the **Classical School of Criminology**, with the major premise that punishment should be swift, certain, and severe. If this goal was achieved and punishment was publicly exhibited to the general population, rational criminals, weighing the costs and benefits of their actions, would choose to commit either a lesser crime or no crime at all. Thus, under the classical view, criminals were not inherently evil but were people with poor decision-making skills and weak morals. The classical perspective heavily influenced the development of the criminal justice system in the United States and is still evident today. Modern initiatives designed to control crime, including mandatory and enhanced sentencing policies and three strikes laws (popular in the 1990s), are based on the rational offender model. There are many ways in which the classical school of criminology and more recent enhancements of rational choice theory inform crime analysis and crime mapping. For example, being able to assign different values to levels of risk or effort in committing a crime based on environmental variables allows us to create more precise prediction models, such as used in the probability grid method.

The **Positivist School of Criminology** gained prominence during the late 19th century and spurred new methods for studying crime. The scientific method heavily influenced the way positivist philosophers and researchers approached the study of human behavior and their immediate environment. Positivism holds two primary elements. First, human behavior is influenced by biology, psychology, and to some extent the larger environment (social positivists). Second, criminologists can learn about human behavior and solve social problems by embracing the scientific method. Theorists from the positivist perspective by and large have a deterministic view of the world (**determinism**), arguing that human behavior is largely predetermined by psychological, biological, and environmental factors. A major assumption of positivist criminologists was that a criminal could be "cured" of some known or unknown biological and/or psychological defect. Crime control strategies stemming from this school of thought included sterilization (crime is genetic and thus can be propagated), lobotomies (to eliminate the "infected" part of the brain that causes criminal behavior), and various drug and chemical treatments to "fix" criminals. The Positivist School still retains influence today with modern research continuing to focus on biological and psychological factors and their relationship to criminal behavior. Contemporary positivists, however, would support less invasive methods than their earlier counterparts, including genetic counseling, drug therapies, and community-based programs that could help offenders overcome psychological, biological, and environmental risks of crime. The most influential remnant from the Positivist School is the application of the scientific method to the study of crime (which is key to crime analysis).

Both the early classicalists and the positivists were primarily focused on the individual and to some extent ignored many of the environmental factors that impact human behavior. Another group of criminologists, sociological criminologists, emerged in the late 18th through mid-19th centuries. These criminologists began to pave the way for modern theorists and analysts who study crime in a social context. Quetelet and Guerry are credited as being two of the first persons to use spatial analysis in their research and are thought to be the founders of the **Cartographic School of Criminology** (Levin & Lindesmith, 1971). Guerry, using several data sources, determined that crime in France was unevenly distributed across people and places. For example, property crimes were more prevalent in the northern regions of France (and occurred more often in the winter) while crimes against people were more prevalent in the southern regions (and occurred more frequently during the summer). Guerry also concluded that age, education, poverty, and population density were important in understanding the distribution of crime.

Quetelet also looked at how crime was distributed across France (Quetelet, 1842/1973). Using social and spatial variables in his analysis, he determined that crime was more heavily concentrated in the summer, in the southern regions, and among **heterogeneous** populations that, as a group, were both uneducated and poor.

What Quetelet and Guerry discovered is that crime and other social problems are distributed unevenly across space and time—the fundamental justification for crime mapping. This is nothing new, even to the beginning criminal justice student and crime analyst. If crime were randomly distributed, there would be little need for crime mapping. So why is theory so important to crime mapping and analysis? The answer to this question is that criminological theory is instrumental in identifying the individual, social, and ecological factors that allow us to better predict where and when crime will occur. Theory can also help identify which variables we should target in our crime control strategies that will be most beneficial in yielding the greatest reduction in crime. That said, the following sections examine the key theoretical arguments from major sociological and ecological theories of crime causation. In addition to helping us understand theories of crime causation, an examination of theory also helps us identify important variables and data sources to use in crime analysis and crime mapping. We begin with the Chicago School of Criminology.

■ The Chicago School of Criminology

Scholars from the **Chicago School of Criminology** began the arduous task of developing hypotheses and constructing theoretical models about how crime was related to, and caused by, various social and environmental factors. The Chicago School of Criminology, so named because the prominent theorists of this school were scholars at the University of Chicago, comprises the work of several prominent sociologists, including Robert Park and Ernest Burgess. Park (1915) was primarily interested in the myriad social problems that existed in cities. He observed that cities were made up of individual divisions that were based on race and ethnicity, socioeconomic status and occupation, and the physical characteristics of structural components of the city, such as whether an area was used for business or residential purposes. Using concepts from the discipline of plant ecology, Park argued that cities grew from the inside out through a process of invasion, dominance, and succession. Burgess (1925), continuing Park's plant analogy, also studied the growth of cities. He argued that cities grow outward from the center in concentric circles starting with the inner loop (the business district in the center of a city), then the zone in transition (the zone characterized by high rates of crime and other social problems), and then several zones that contain the homes of people who commute varying distances into the city to work (modern-day suburbs). He further argued that people who live in the loop immediately surrounding the business district (zone in transition) would experience the highest levels of social disorganization, including the uppermost crime and victimization rates of the city. Modern critics of the concentric zone theory make the important point that this model does not explain all cities. Many cities in the West, for example, did not grow in concentric circles. In addition, modern cities that once fit this model have changed through the processes of **gentrification**. Areas in the zone in transition once characterized by high rates of delinquency and disorder are now desirable high-rent areas that are affordable only by the wealthy. However, what can be taken from the concentric zone model that is still applicable today is that crime and disorder are not randomly distributed throughout a city and that the areas most plagued by these problems will also have high levels of poverty.

Two other Chicago scholars, Clifford Shaw and Henry McKay (1942), furthered Park's and Burgess's works by studying juvenile delinquency and social structure variables within the zone in transition. Using the term **Social Disorganization Theory**, Shaw and McKay sought to study the processes responsible for creating higher rates of juvenile delinquency in this area. They determined that three primary dynamics exist in socially disorganized neighborhoods; these include high rates of residential turnover, a heterogeneous population, and high levels of poverty. Essentially, they argued that the constant turnover of people moving in and out of the neighborhood combined with self-segregation of ethnicities inhibited the neighborhood cohesion necessary to solve common problems associated with high levels of poverty. That said, poverty is not the *cause* of crime, but it is correlated with other factors, such as high residential mobility and heterogeneity that affect crime rates. When these factors are concentrated in a localized area, the likelihood of a high crime rate noticeably increases. Shaw and McKay also observed that this is true for *all* populations that live in socially disorganized neighborhoods. Thus, crime was not the product of a certain racial group of people but of any group living in high poverty areas with high diversity and turnover.

Edwin Sutherland (1947) expanded upon Shaw and McKay's work by suggesting that high crime areas were not socially disorganized, just organized differently from other areas, and thus the cultural values surrounding crime were different. That said, many juveniles who lived in these disorganized neighborhoods learned values and techniques *favorable* to committing crime via their peer associations. Termed **Differential Association Theory**, Sutherland focused on the social learning processes that aided in the cultural transmission of criminal values and argued that some neighborhoods are not "disorganized" but rather organized around different values. He argued that criminal behavior is learned amongst close-knit groups and that both the techniques needed to commit crime and the values favorable to committing crime are learned. Differential association theory is not meant to replace, but to supplement Social Disorganization Theory, and modern theorists are still testing both theoretical approaches today. In addition, modern theories of crime attempt to integrate the characteristics of physical space and social relationships to explain why crime occurs more frequently in some areas than others.

■ Social Efficacy

More recent research examining social disorganization has determined that crime is not necessarily the problem but rather a symptom of inadequate social networks (or lack of collective efficacy) that exist in these neighborhoods (Reisig & Cancino, 2004; Sampson, Morenoff, & Earls, 1999; Sampson & Raudenbush, 2001; Taylor, 2001). The lack of **collective efficacy** in a neighborhood (inhibited by neighborhood turnover, heterogeneity, and poverty) is a more difficult and complex problem for law enforcement to address. Programs designed to weed crime out of an area by police sweeps and neighborhood clean-up programs ultimately fail in the long run if they do not address the notion of collective, or social, efficacy. Sampson and Groves (1989) contend that the lack of supervision, lack of community involvement, and reduced friendship and other social networks are the primary cause of crime and disorder in a neighborhood. That is, residents in socially disorganized neighborhoods do not know or trust one another, and thus the supervision of the neighborhood people and property is limited. In addition, when residents are aware of a problem, they are less likely to get involved in any collaborative efforts to develop a solution. Taylor (2001) studied neighborhoods he observed as having conditions of collective efficacy. These neighborhoods are characterized as having residents who hold common values about what is right and wrong, strong ties based on physical proximity, informal social control, and high levels of community participation in neighborhood programs. These neighborhoods typically have little to no crime problems. Neighborhoods without collective efficacy are more susceptible to crime and disorder and typically exhibit a host of social and physical incivilities signaling to motivated offenders that this is a good place to set up shop. For example, **Figure 2–1** shows an abandoned house in Providence, Rhode Island.

Abandoned houses such as this can signal to potential offenders that the owners are either unable or unwilling to care for the property. Abandoned houses also emit signals about the lack of social efficacy that is common in poverty-stricken areas, as well as areas where neighbors mind their own business and areas where people can act as they wish with little community disapproval. In addition, abandoned buildings serve as free housing for the homeless and act as places of business for drug activity, prostitution, gang activity, and the like. Wilson and Paulsen (2008), in an issue of *Geography and Public Safety,* discuss the foreclosing crisis in recent years and its impact on neighborhoods. Observing that foreclosures are not randomly dispersed but are clustered in recently revitalized, middle-class neighborhoods, Wilson and Paulsen suggest that:

> Although neighborhood decline is normally a long, slow process occurring over a generation, the foreclosure crisis is expediting this decline, bringing with it the traditional outcomes of theft, drugs, vandalism, vagrancy, prostitution, and arson . . . . As neighborhoods fall further into disrepair, these crimes are only the immediate impact. Long-term trends could undo the significant progress that many metropolitan areas have made in the last few decades in both neighborhood quality of life and economic progress (p. 1).

Other physical indicators within neighborhoods beyond abandoned buildings may also signal a neighborhood's struggle with crime. In **Figure 2–2**, target hardening measures, such

Figure 2–1 Abandoned Property

Figure 2–2 Target Hardening

as barred windows, signal to potential customers (and potential witnesses) that this is not a safe store to shop at, decreasing the store owner's potential profits. Potential customers may not just perceive this store to be a frequent target of crime but the neighborhood at large to be unsafe, thereby affecting other business or social activities within the immediate area.

■ Broken Windows Theory: Can It Be That Simple?

An understanding of the relationship between community variables, such as social and physical disorder, and crime is not new to law enforcement. Within the last several decades, strategies based on the philosophy of community-oriented policing and problem-oriented policing have become very popular. Many of these strategies are geared toward social and physical incivilities within neighborhoods. The popularity of these strategies is often attributed to Wilson and Kelling's "Broken Windows" piece, which was published in 1982. However, most practitioners can tell you that community-oriented policing strategies were being implemented long before this work was even conceptualized, especially in rural law enforcement agencies where budgets are smaller, manpower is sparse, and officers or deputies are highly integrated into the community. The **Broken Windows Theory** (or Broken Windows Approach) is based on an experiment conducted by Stanford psychologist Philip Zimbardo in 1969. In this now classic experiment, Zimbardo placed two unoccupied vehicles in two different neighborhoods: Palo Alto, California and Bronx, New York. Within just 10 minutes of its placement, the car in Bronx was vandalized, and within 24 hours, nothing of value remained inside the car. After it was stripped of its value, passersby continued to vandalize the car by ripping its upholstery and smashing its windows. The car in Palo Alto, however, was left alone for almost a week. It was only after Zimbardo smashed it with a sledgehammer that people began to vandalize the car. Within a few short hours, the car was completely destroyed.

What Zimbardo's experiment tells us is that when the "no one cares" cue is sent out, crime can occur in any neighborhood. Wilson and Kelling (1982) contend that the only reason the car in Bronx was vandalized so soon is because the social and physical structure of the neighborhood emitted the message to potential offenders that no one cared. In Palo Alto, it was the smashing of the car by the researcher that signaled no one cared about the car. This suggests that if the car in Palo Alto had been left intact by the researcher, it may have sat for a much longer period of time before it was vandalized. Community-oriented and problem-oriented police strategies seek to address neighborhood problems that are thought to be root causes of crime. For example, proponents of community policing maintain that a law enforcement concentration on "minor disorders" will, in turn, "lead to a reduction in serious crime" (Mastrofski, 1988, p. 48). That is (in broken windows lingo), minor disorders, when not addressed, often lead to more serious disorders and ultimately to community decay. Supporters of community policing claim that its application can help break this destructive cycle through the coproduction of order and greater community involvement.

However, can crime prevention be as simple as cleaning up the signs of neighborhood decay? The answer is complicated. An illustration of some of the complicated relationships between geographic and social variables can be found in popular culture and movies.

For example, in the popular movie *Boyz n the Hood* (Nicolaides & Singleton, 1991), Furious (played by Laurence Fishburne) takes his son Tre (Cuba Gooding, Jr.) and Tre's friend, Ricky (Morris Chestnut), for a drive in inner city Los Angeles. He stops at a residential neighborhood that could easily be described as a socially disorganized, or a "broken windows" neighborhood (visible signs of both social and physical incivilities). Loud rap music plays in the background, and the audience can also hear a woman yelling. As Tre and Ricky exit the car, they look around nervously, and Ricky expresses to Furious his level of anxiety about stopping in this neighborhood. Furious directs the boys toward a billboard sign that says "Cash for your home." He explains to them the message that the sign displays—that of gentrification. He explains the process as one where "they" bring the property value of a certain area down, get all of the current residents out of the neighborhood, then raise the property value and sell it at a profit. At this point in the scene, a small crowd of people from the neighborhood gather around Furious and the boys and begin a dialog. An old man from the crowd exclaims that it is not people from *outside* the neighborhood bringing down the property value, but it is those *within* the neighborhood who do so by selling drugs and "shooting each other."

Furious then asks why there are so many gun shops in this community. Furious contends that the reason that gun shops and liquor stores are so prevalent in this community is because "they want us to kill ourselves," making a very noticeable distinction between "us" and "them," which can be interpreted in several ways—an important interpretation for this discussion being the "haves" versus the "have nots."

In this movie, Laurence Fishburne's character touches upon several important ideas relevant to our discussion in this text. First, communities are set within a larger environment that must be understood when analyzing crime. Macro-level forces, such as economics, play a part in crime trends over time and must be factored into analyses that examine general crime trends. Ignoring macro-level influences in analyses presents an incomplete picture. Second, individual decisions and behaviors (for example, selling your home to move to a better neighborhood or putting bars on your windows to protect your property) may be beneficial for the individuals for the immediate future, but are detrimental to the neighborhood at large in the long term. Third, structural components of neighborhoods (density of liquor stores and gun shops, for example) are important in understanding the neighborhood's social problems and how they impact the physical space. It is important to remember that relationships between geographic and social variables are complicated and in many ways reciprocal in nature. Fourth, incorporating the notion of a **crime fuse** (a theoretical concept that argues a society *allows* problems such as crime to exist in certain areas and not others), such as Furious alluded to in the "us" versus "them" statement, may help explain the source of some of the frustration in a neighborhood that can manifest itself as crime (Barr & Pease, 1990). Last, cultural components of violence (often escalated in heterogeneous neighborhoods) are not quickly or easily fixed by the criminal justice system. They require more complicated approaches that demand community participation in both the development and implementation of crime-reduction strategies. Skogan (2008) argues that "we cannot arrest our way out of crime problems" and that effective problem solving for neighborhoods suffering from crime and social disorder problems "calls for examining patterns of incidents to reveal their causes and to help plan how to deal with them proactively" (p. 198; such is the task in crime analysis and mapping). Furthermore, solutions will most certainly require the involvement of organizations inside and outside the criminal justice system and will depend upon community support and participation for their success.

The Chicago School did much to further our understanding of the relationship between crime and space, but it is not without criticism. First is the **ecological fallacy**, which, in simple terms, means it is inaccurate to make assumptions about individuals based on aggregate-level data. That is, there are plenty of people who happen to have characteristics that put them at a higher risk to become criminals, including living in socially disorganized neighborhoods. However, they do not always turn to a life of crime. They live under the same conditions with the same environmental cues and the same opportunities to commit crime, yet they do not. Thus, while it is important to include macro-level forces in analyses, it is not always appropriate.

A second problem with the Chicago School is that its approaches do not explain all crime types and are often tested using street crimes within urban areas. This, of course, is a problem with many criminological theories. A third problem has to do with misidentifying the causal order of the relationship between variables. For example, research on **Social Disorganization Theory** suggests that crime and social disorder have a reciprocal relationship (Markowitz, Bellair, Liska, & Liu, 2001), thus crime control efforts must focus on *both* issues to be successful. Simply cleaning up a neighborhood and not promoting activities to build social or collective efficacy will only yield temporary results in crime reduction, giving the "Band-Aid on a bullet hole" analogy a whole new meaning.

A fourth problem with research on social disorganization is multicollinearity. Essentially, when variables in an equation exhibit multicollinearity, it means that the concepts they are measuring overlap. For example, think about the social-level variables we discussed throughout this chapter, such as income and education. We know that both of these variables are associated strongly with crime. However, income and education, in what they represent, overlap at least partially. That is, to some extent, education level can be explained by income, and income is a function of education level. Another example might be overcrowding and substandard housing. Overcrowded neighborhoods tend to contain a lot of substandard housing. Thus, these variables are not completely separated from one another. Multicollinearity is highly problematic in some of the analyses that are routinely run in crime analysis and theory testing. Analyses containing multicollinearity issues can produce inaccurate and misleading findings.

Finally, research on social disorganization suffers from imprecise measurements. The concept of social disorganization itself cannot be measured precisely, and researchers are forced to employ proxy variables that measure *indicators* of social disorganization, such as residential mobility. Gau and Pratt (2008) found that citizen perceptions of disorder and crime were highly correlated, suggesting that treating these concepts as separate constructs is inappropriate. Research on social efficacy and its measurement of friendship networks and neighborhood supervision is more promising in its operationalization of social disorganization; however, these can be difficult concepts to measure. This is an important notion to keep in mind for various types of crime analyses.

■ Conclusion

Regardless of these criticisms, understanding criminological theory is crucial to crime analysis and crime mapping. However, it is important to be aware of limitations of theory, just as it is important to be aware of the limitations of your data and analysis techniques. Eck (1998) sums this up best:

> If the police do not know much about the area then they cannot form a testable hypothesis. This is the case in most situations when the police look for fast-breaking crime patterns so they can focus enforcement activity on a troubled area . . . police, like researchers, should pay as much attention to criminological theories as they do to the data they examine (dots) and the methods they apply (maps) (pp. 402–403).

The theories discussed in this chapter supplement other theories discussed throughout this text. In some cases, they simply address crime at a different level, and in other cases integrate several theoretical approaches into a larger and more comprehensive paradigm of understanding crime.

■ Chapter Glossary

Broken Windows Theory   Broken Windows Theory was introduced by James Q. Wilson and George L. Kelling in the early 1980s. Essentially, it argues that if police focus on social disorder and minor crimes in neighborhoods that contribute to social disorder (for example, public drinking and street prostitution), then they are likely to make an impact in reducing or preventing more serious crimes.

Cartographic School of Criminology   Under this school, early 19th-century researchers in Europe used demographic information to explain the spatial distribution of crime. Variables measuring population density and socioeconomic status, among others, were used to explain uneven distributions of crime.

Chicago School of Criminology   Theories and research on crime classified in this school were developed by urban sociologists (primarily in Chicago) who were interested in the relationship between environmental conditions and crime. They studied social and physical variables to understand the distribution of crime in cities.

Classical School of Criminology   Theories of crime in this school rested on the notion of "free will." Classical theorists maintained that criminals were by and large rational and chose to commit crimes for personal gain. Thus, crime was best prevented by implementing criminal sanctions that were high enough to deter potential offenders from committing crimes.

Collective Efficacy   Sometimes referred to as "social efficacy," this term refers to the level of social control (supervision of neighborhood children, maintaining public order, etc.) wielded by communities. Collective efficacy is high in cohesive communities with mutual trust and is low in communities that are not cohesive and that do not have mutual trust.

Crime Fuse   A theoretical concept that argues a society *allows* problems such as crime to exist in certain areas and not others.

Determinism   The philosophy of determinism argues that human behavior is largely pre-determined by psychological, biological, and environmental factors. In essence, people are victims of their own circumstances.

Differential Association Theory   According to Sutherland (1947), criminal behavior is related to the extent offenders were exposed to antisocial attitudes and values. Sutherland outlined nine principles explaining how criminal behavior is learned through association.

Ecological Fallacy   The problem that occurs when making assumptions about individuals based on aggregate-level data.

Gentrification   In the process of gentrification, existing buildings in a neighborhood, typically in urban areas, are replaced or upgraded. As a result, property in these areas becomes more desirable and results in a shift in population demographics of both residents and business owners. Usually, during gentrification, persons classified as having lower socioeconomic status move out of the neighborhood, and persons with higher levels of wealth move into the neighborhood.

Heterogeneous   Used to denote variation; in the context for which it is used in this text, it refers to populations that have high levels of diversity, primarily in culture and ethnicity.

Positivist School of Criminology   The positivists used scientific methods to examine human behavior. Positivists maintained that crime was a result of biological, psychological, and social factors.

Social Disorganization Theory   Under this theoretical approach, crime is more prevalent in neighborhoods that exhibit social and physical incivilities. In these neighborhoods, levels of social control is low due to a breakdown in institutions such as the family and school.

Utilitarianism   Attributed to Jeremy Bentham, utilitarianism refers to "benefit maximization." Essentially, decisions are made (rationally) in favor of less pain and the greatest good for the greatest number of people. Thus, people are motivated to avoid pain or to pursue pleasure.

■ **Questions for Review**

1. Why is it important to consider theories of crime when creating maps of crime?

2. According to early Chicago School theorists, how is the structure of a city related to the spatial distribution of crime?

3. How has *gentrification* changed crime distributions in urban areas?

4. When examining crime in socially disorganized neighborhoods, why must the analyst include both social and physical variables in his or her analysis to get a more complete picture of crime?

5. What is *social* or *collective efficacy*, and how is it related to the prevalence of crime in a neighborhood?

6. What are some of the problems in researching and/or applying theoretical principles of Chicago School theories of crime?

■ Online Resources

Center for Spatially Integrated Social Science, Clifford R. Shaw and Henry D. McKay: The Social Disorganization Theory: www.csiss.org/classics/content/66

Criminology: www.criminology.com/

History of the Chicago School of Criminology: http://sociology.uchicago.edu /department/history.shtml

National Institute of Justice and Community Oriented Policing Services, Geography and Public Safety Bulletins: www.nij.gov/topics/technology/maps/bulletin.htm

National Criminal Justice Reference Service (NCJRS) Publication on Social Disorganization and Rural Communities: www.ncjrs.gov/html/ojjdp/193591/page1.html

Social Disorganization and Social Efficacy: www.homeoffice.gov.uk

■ Recommended Reading

Akers, R. L. (2000). *Criminological theories: Introduction, evaluation, and application.* Los Angeles: Roxbury.

Cullen, F. T., & Agnew, R. (Eds.). (1999). *Criminological theory, past to present: Essential readings.* Los Angeles: Roxbury.

Cullen, F. T., Wright, J. P., & Blevins, K. R. (Eds.). (2006). *Taking stock: The status of criminological theory.* New Brunswick, NJ: Transaction Publishers.

Kelling, G. L., & Coles, C. M. (1996). *Fixing broken windows: Restoring order and reducing crime in our communities.* New York: Martin Kessler Books.

Sampson, R. J., & Wilson, W. J. (1995). Toward a theory of race, crime, and urban inequality. In J. Hagan & R. D. Peterson (Eds.), *Crime and inequality.* Stanford, CA: Stanford University Press.

Taylor, R. B. (2001). *Breaking away from broken windows: Baltimore neighborhoods and the nationwide fight against crime, grime, fear, and decline.* Boulder, CO: Westview Press.

■ References

Barr, R., & Pease, K. (1990). Crime placement, displacement, and deflection. In M. Tonry & N. Morris (Eds.), *Crime and justice* (Vol. 12). Chicago: University of Chicago Press.

Block, C. R. (1998). The geoarchive: An information foundation for community policing. In D. Weisburd & T. McEwen (Eds.), *Crime mapping and crime prevention: Crime prevention studies* (Vol. 8, pp. 27–81). Monsey, NY: Criminal Justice Press.

Burgess, E. (1925). The growth of a city. In R. Park, E. Burgess, & D. McKenzie (Eds.), *The city.* Chicago: University of Chicago Press.

Eck, J. E. (1998). What do those dots mean? Mapping theories with data. In D. Weisburd & T. McEwen (Eds.), *Crime mapping and crime prevention: Crime prevention studies* (Vol. 8, pp. 379–406). Monsey, NY: Criminal Justice Press.

Gau, J., & Pratt, T. (2008). Broken windows or window dressing? Citizens' inability to tell the difference between disorder and crime. *Criminology & Public Policy, 7*(2), 163–194.

Levin, Y., & Lindesmith, A. (1971). English ecology and criminology of the past century. *Journal of Criminology and Criminal Law, 27,* 801–816.

Markowitz, F., Bellair, P., Liska, A., & Liu, J. (2001). Extending social disorganization theory: Modeling the relationships between cohesion, disorder, and fear. *Criminology, 39*(2), 293–320.

Mastrofski, S. D. (1988). Community policing as reform: A cautionary tale. In J. R. Greene & S. D. Mastrofski (Eds.), *Community policing: Rhetoric or reality?* (pp. 47–68). New York: Praeger Publishers.

Nicolaides, S. (Producer), & Singleton, J. (Director). (1991). *Boyz n the Hood* [Motion picture]. United States: Columbia Pictures.

Park, R. (1915). The city: Suggestions for the investigation of human behavior in the urban environment. *American Journal of Sociology, 20*, 577–612.

Quetelet, M. A. (1973). A treatise on man. In *Comparative statistics in the nineteenth century* (pp. 25–75). Germany: Gregg International. (Reprinted from *A treatise on man*, by M. A. Quetelet, 1842, Edinburgh, Scotland: William and Robert Chambers.)

Reisig, M., & Cancino, J. M. (2004). Incivilities in nonmetropolitan communities: The effects of structural constraints, social conditions, and crime. *Journal of Criminal Justice, 32*, 15–29.

Sampson, R. J., & Groves, W. B. (1989). Community structure and crime: Testing social disorganization theory. *American Journal of Sociology, 94*, 774–802.

Sampson, R. J., Morenoff, J., & Earls, F. (1999). Beyond social capital: Spatial dynamics of collective efficacy for children. *American Sociological Review, 64*, 633–660.

Sampson, R. J., & Raudenbush, S. W. (2001). *Disorder in urban neighborhoods: Does it lead to crime?* Washington, DC: National Institute of Justice.

Shaw, C. R., & McKay, H. D. (1942). *Juvenile delinquency and urban areas* (5th ed.). Chicago: University of Chicago Press.

Skogan, W. G. (2008). Broken windows: Why—and how—we should take them seriously. *Criminology & Public Policy, 7*(2), 195–201.

Sutherland, E. (1947). *Principles of criminology* (4th ed.). Philadelphia: J. B. Lippincott.

Taylor, R. B. (2001). The ecology of crime, fear, and delinquency: Social disorganization versus social efficacy. In R. Paternoster & R. Bachman (Eds.), *Explaining crime and criminals*. Los Angeles: Roxbury.

Wilson, J. Q., & Kelling, G. (1982, March). Broken windows: The police and neighborhood safety. *Atlantic Monthly*, 29–38.

Wilson, R., & Paulsen, D. (2008). Foreclosures and crime: A geographical perspective. *Geography and Public Safety, 1*(3), 1–2.

Environmental Criminology

▶ LEARNING OBJECTIVES

This chapter continues the discussion on theories of crime causation but narrows the scope to theories and approaches that use both individual behaviors and physical characteristics of space to explain crime. The physical characteristics of an environment communicate social clues to the people who live, work, and play there. These clues provide potential offenders and victims with information about how they should behave to ensure their safety, pleasure, and the successful fruition of their interests. For offenders, these clues help identify the method by which they might commit a crime successfully and avoid getting caught. For potential victims, these clues provide information about how to avoid being victimized. This chapter reviews several theoretical approaches that are used in developing environmental design aspects to prevent crime. These aspects include lighting, landscaping, natural surveillance and crime-prevention boundaries, and building design, to name a few. After studying this chapter, you should be able to:

- Identify and explain core elements to crime prevention through environmental design (CPTED) approaches.
- Explain the basic tenets to rational choice perspectives.
- Explain the Crime Pattern Theory.
- Explain and discuss the Routine Activities Theory and its utility in understanding and analyzing crime.
- Discuss lifestyle exposure approaches and understand their utility in understanding repeat offenses and repeat victimization.
- List and describe the types of *crime displacement*, and discuss the relevant research that examines the existence (or lack) of crime displacement.
- Explain the concept of *diffusion of benefits* and its utility in understanding crime patterns.

▶ **Key Terms**

Activity Space	Diffusion of Benefits	Victim Precipitation
Awareness Space	Event Dependency	Victim Provocation
CPTED	Hedonism	Virtual Repeats
Crime Displacement	Risk Heterogeneity	
Defensible Space	Victim Facilitation	

■ Introduction

Several theoretical frameworks identify the social and physical incivilities that are important in understanding community-level crime rates. These theories emphasize the flaws in the physical environment and the gaps in social networks that are common to high-crime areas. These theories also identify characteristics of individuals who are typically found (residing or working) in socially disorganized neighborhoods. This chapter narrows our focus to the individual characteristics and the physical properties of space related to crime and victimization through the creation of increased opportunities for motivated offenders to commit crime. Every person has routines and rhythms of their daily lives that become part of who they are and what they do. Have you ever been so absorbed by a project at work that on some Saturday or Sunday your significant other has asked you to run an errand, and you found yourself on the way to work or even pulling into the place where you work when you had intended to go to the store? That drive back and forth to work has become an important part of your social makeup—so much so that you can often automate that journey. On your way to your activities and employment, you might look around and see a new construction site and ask yourself, "I wonder what they are building there?" People who are prone to crime and hunting for targets do the same thing—only their question might be, "I wonder if that compressor is locked up or if I could steal it later tonight?"

Using environmental design to control human behavior is not only popular in developing crime-prevention efforts; it is also used in the private sector to increase profit margins. Casinos, for example, are strategically designed to keep people gambling for as long as possible. Big casinos incorporate several design aspects to keep customers happy, comfortable, and, most importantly, gambling. For example, carpets exhibit bright, elaborate, and fun designs, while pumped-in oxygen, mirrors, and bright lights create a stimulating environment that makes it difficult to be bored or sleepy. Alcoholic drinks are also served 24 hours a day, often free of charge, to gambling patrons by casino staff members who are typically dressed in "barely there" outfits. Event halls and auditoriums are located adjacent to gambling areas, requiring patrons to walk through those areas upon arrival and departure. Even arrival to and departure from the Las Vegas airport requires people to walk past slot machines!

One does not have to look farther than a local supermarket to grasp the concept of environmental design and how it impacts human behavior. In another example outside of criminal justice, to pick up a gallon of milk at a grocery store, customers must walk to the far corner of the store, usually past impulse and convenience food items, to reach the dairy section. Knowing that people are likely to pick up milk on their way home from work (and are probably hungry and tired), the store places various snack foods and ready-to-eat items on the path to commonly needed items (such as milk) in an effort to increase sales.

Thus, the notion of physical design to control behavior, particularly criminal behavior, also is not new. Attention in both the academic and practical realm shifted to the physical environment and how it could be modified to control human behavior when crime increased exponentially in the late 1960s and early 1970s. Jane Jacobs (1961) was one of the first researchers to propose a relationship between crime and the urban city environment. In her book, *The Death and Life of Great American Cities*, she made several observations about crime and the physical environment. She was also one of the first to suggest that the physical environment could be manipulated by improving the natural surveillance (the ability of the persons living in an area to be aware of what is going on in their portion of the neighborhood) of an area to reduce crime. Other researchers during this time period, including Elizabeth Wood (1961) and Schlomo Angel (1968), focused their research on the effects the physical environment could have on human behavior and how environments could be manipulated to achieve social objectives.

The point to environmental design is to guide, manipulate, and/or encourage people to behave in a desirable manner in a given situation. In neighborhood crime control strategies, this can mean a variety of things. First, the environment needs to be created in a way that encourages informal social control efforts by the people who work and reside in a neighborhood. An example of informal social control is the existence of a block watch group in a neighborhood. All of the neighbors actively participate in reporting, interceding, or watching their portion of the neighborhood for criminal or socially unacceptable behavior. They cannot literally arrest someone, in most cases, but they can give the impression to unauthorized persons in the neighborhood that everything they are doing is being watched and will be reported to the police. Second, the physical properties of a space should allow for maximum visibility so that residents can observe what is happening in their surroundings. Third, environmental clues emanating from the neighborhood should send the message to outsiders and potential offenders that committing crimes in this place would be risky and unprofitable. A very important point here is that the *interaction* of physical design and informal social control is what creates an environment that is resistant to crime. If the environment cannot control human behavior in the way in which it was intended, then the design aspects examined in this chapter will likely have few affects on crime.

■ The CPTED Approach

Let us first examine crime prevention through environmental design (**CPTED**) approaches. CPTED suggests that the design of physical space is important in understanding criminal behavior. C. Ray Jeffrey (1971) and his contemporary Oscar Newman (1972) are credited with providing the foundations that outline how physical space should be designed to maximize its crime-prevention potential.

Newman's Defensible Space

Through the Safe Streets Act of 1968, grant funding was made available to research new crime-prevention efforts. The focus of Newman's research on crime-prevention strategies in public housing projects emphasized how architectural design could play a role in reducing crime. Newman's **defensible space** model argues that physical space can be structured in a way that fosters and reinforces a social structure that defends itself. Newman, focusing his work primarily on housing projects, suggested that by improving natural surveillance and encouraging tenants to assume responsibility for the public areas within the housing project, boundaries might reduce crime due to an increase in the risk of observation. Newman identified four key elements of defensible space: territoriality, natural surveillance, image, and milieu.

Territoriality refers to the ability of legitimate users of an area or physical space to frequently use and to protect the space from nonlegitimate users. For example, an outdoor courtyard nestled within several apartment buildings might have walkways and benches for people to use at their leisure. However, if legitimate users (residents of the apartment buildings) do not use the space, others, perhaps nonlegitimate users, may use the space in ways that are harmful. *Natural surveillance* involves designing physical space in a way that allows legitimate users to observe the behaviors of friends and strangers. In theory, this allows residents to augment and bolster law enforcement by being the eyes and ears of police and by taking action against criminal and/or other socially undesirable activities. Action could include calling the police or even intervening when appropriate. *Image* has to do with fostering a neighborhood environment that creates the appearance that the neighborhood is well cared for and is not isolated from the communities that surround it or the people who inhabit the area. Environmental design of this type might include landscape lighting, clean grounds and garbage receptacles, working fountains, and manicured lawns and bushes. A great example of this is the many fantastic squares of historic Savannah, Georgia. There, the squares serve as tourist attractions, historic landmarks, resting and conversational spots, and speed constraints. When one thinks of Savannah, the beauty and romance of its squares surely create the imagery. In contrast, socially disorganized neighborhoods serve as good examples of what the concept of the image is *not*. Last, *milieu* (the French word for "environment") involves placing an area within a larger community or physical space that contains territoriality, natural surveillance, and image, creating a defensible space that remains free of criminal activity. If a neighborhood with defensible space borders neighborhoods *without* defensible space, milieu is not achieved. One might think of this as the total social landscape of a neighborhood or a group of neighborhoods that border each other. In other words, if you drive through your own neighborhood and adjacent neighborhoods today, what would you find there? Would all of the homes be clean, well cared for, and project the image of the entire neighborhood, or would there be some homes with uncut grass, shabby paint, or trash in the front yard?

Newman's work focused on a comparison of public housing projects in New York City. In his study, he examined several variables, including access points, the ability of residents to observe, the size of the project, and the building structure itself. He concluded that defensible space could be accomplished in public housing projects by installing doors and windows in places that allow for increased observation of surrounding areas by the residents. In addition, he argued that installing better lighting and creating common areas that residents could both use and control would also bolster crime prevention, because residents would be better able to see the behaviors of legitimate and nonlegitimate persons and could thus take action when necessary. Newman identified four types of zones:

- *Public spaces*: These are areas that are open to the general public and serve a variety of uses, such as a public street.

- *Semipublic spaces*: These are areas, such as an apartment lobby, that are limited in their use but are still open to everyone. They are used most often by residents and their friends or families.
- *Semiprivate spaces*: These include areas that are more restricted in use, such as an apartment hallway or stairwell, which are open to nonresidents but are most often used by residents and their friends or families.
- *Private spaces*: Most notably the apartments themselves, these are areas that are not open to the public and are restricted to the use of residents and their friends or families.

In comparing two adjacent housing projects (one with and one without defensible space characteristics), Newman found that the project without defensible space had both higher maintenance costs and higher crime. He extended his research to include analyses of more than 100 housing projects in New York City and reported that there was enough substantial evidence to conclude that physical design aspects have important consequences regarding crime and disorder. Newman was also opposed to high-rise projects and argued that public housing should include as much private space as possible. Newman theorized that this would move people to maintain more guardianship over the spaces in and around their residences.

Subsequent tests of defensible space in other cities mirrored Newman's results. An examination of residential burglary in Boston identified several physical site characteristics that were important in predicting which homes were more likely to be victimized (Reppetto, 1974). Wilson (1978), in his analysis, found that areas of London that lacked defensible space characteristics suffered more incidents of vandalism.

Newman added much to the study of crime and its relationship to the physical environment, but his work is not without criticism. He has been criticized for ignoring the social elements of tenants in housing projects and of those residents in surrounding areas. That is, the physical design elements, while important, may offer far less value in predicting crime rates than social-level variables. Taylor, Shumaker, and Gottfredson (1985) found that the relationship between crime and physical design features was spurious and that neighborhood social status was much more predictive of crime. Merry (1981) also touched on the fact that while environments could certainly be redesigned to better suit defensible space, residents must want to assume a role in the guardianship of the space. Furthermore, her results suggest that physical design strategies may not be entirely effective in spaces with heterogeneous (culturally, racially, or ethnically diverse) populations.

CPTED: Theory and Research

In *Crime Prevention Through Environmental Design*, Jeffery (1971) examined design aspects that contribute to crime prevention and how they could be applied in nonresidential areas, such as schools, to control human behavior. By incorporating elements of behavioral learning theory, Jeffery argued that the removal of reinforcements for crime from schools would reduce incidents of crime. While Jeffery's original model has been revised, the basic concept of crime prevention through environmental design (CPTED) is that by changing the environment (stimulus) we can change the behavior of the offender (response). Crowe (2000) outlines the assessment of CPTED with what he calls the "Three-D approach." Essentially, the Three-D approach is based on the notion that human space is designed to fulfill three functions (Crowe, 2000, p. 39):

- All human space has some designated purpose.
- All human space has social, cultural, legal, or physical definitions that prescribe the desired and accepted behaviors.
- All human space is designed to support and control the desired behaviors.

Space, then, can be evaluated based on *designation*, *definition*, and *design*. **Table 3–1** utilizes the Three-D approach to assess a well known theme park as a useful example. However, the Three-D approach could be used to assess a building or physical space relative to crime prevention. Essentially, space that is designated with a specific goal in mind, that is well defined, and that is designed appropriately for the purposes it was intended is least likely to experience crime or other socially undesirable behaviors. From the perspective of a theme park, spaces that are designed to provide hours of family fun with well maintained areas for visiting, playing, eating, and shopping encourage people to engage in the structured fun that is provided. Furthermore, signs, landscaping, lighting, and other physical design features tell park visitors which activities are appropriate and which are inappropriate.

Kushmuk and Whittemore (1981) argue that there is an indirect relationship between crime and the physical design of the environment and that these changes operate through four intermediate goals: improved access control, surveillance, activity support, and motivation reinforcement. Their model is similar to Newman's defensible space. Good access control exists when we have the ability to regulate who enters and exits an area or building. Surveillance is the ability for the legitimate users of a space to observe their surroundings. Activity support and motivation reinforcement have to do with creating a community atmosphere where people feel vested in their neighborhood and watch out for one another. Kaplan, O'Kane, Lavrakas, and Hoover (1978) propose that opportunity, target, risk, effort, and payoff (OTREP) explain variations in crime across people and places. This model assumes that offenders are rational and that if physical design changes limit opportunities by increasing the risk and effort and reducing the payoff, then crime will decrease. Thus, physical design elements that increase the offender's risk of getting caught or increase the effort required to commit the crime will, in theory, reduce the likelihood of crime.

In their review of the literature, Rosenbaum, Lurigio, and Davis (1998) divided CPTED strategies into the categories of target hardening measures, access control strategies, surveillance enhancement efforts, and community-building measures. Target hardening measures appear to be fairly successful in increasing the effort and risk for potential offenders. Measures including deadbolt locks, solid-case doors, window restrictions, steering column locks on cars, and alarms have all produced some measurable decrease in specific crimes. Access control measures can also be successful but may be difficult to implement. Research suggests that buildings and areas with multiple access points (and limited surveillance) have more crime. The most common type of surveillance enhancement is to

TABLE 3-1 The Three-D Approach: Anywhere Theme Park, USA

Designation

What is the designated purpose of this space?	Family entertainment for people of all ages. This space also caters to people with disabilities.
What was it originally intended to be used for?	Family entertainment, same as above.
How well does the space support its intended use?	Very well. Park designed with a high degree of safety and security for the patrons. Park structures are properly gated, metal is coated with rust-resistant, thick paint, and structures are designed with few hard or sharp edges. Grounds are kept in neat and safe order, trash is properly contained, and parking lots are well lit and well attended by live personnel and CCTV. Fences and gates are locked and signed as needed, pathways are relatively free of tripping hazards, and restroom facilities are well marked and placed in numerous locations. Ride lines are housed under roofs and are relatively out of the weather. Exit routes are well marked, and emergency staff is on duty all open hours.
Is there conflict?	No. Nothing in the park suggests the area is to be intended for anything other than family entertainment. There is no structure, pathway, or area designed for anything unrelated to family entertainment or the administration of the park.

Definition

How is the space defined?	Spaces are defined with clear pathways and borders, signs, lighting, music, and themes. Also, a wide array of colors is used to mark specialized areas, such as first aid and restaurant areas.
Is it clear who owns it?	Yes. Theme park insignia and corporate logos are everywhere. Ownership is a sense of pride.
Where are its borders?	The park has fencing and heavy signage around its perimeter. Individual areas within the park use landscaping, walkways, and physical obstacles, such as a waterway or animal enclosures and fencing, to define borders. In some areas the space is designated by music and the design of buildings. Generally an omnipresent theme designates each area, such as that of the food court, small children's area, gaming area, and general ride area.
Are there social or cultural definitions that affect how that space is used?	Yes. The culture of this park is about innocent family fun. Themes of friendship, fun, and happiness abound. Characters are typically on display and act as ambassadors of kindness, fun, and imagination. Nowhere will one find a theme related to negativity or harmfulness. Even those characters who may be thought of as harmful in the real world (such as pirates) are friendly, full of spirit and adventure, and neglect to harm a soul. While stereotypes of sexism may be observed, traditional gender roles are often combined, resulting in male heroes who take care of infants or female warriors who also take care of their families. Elements of racism are stricken in exchange for themes of multiculturalism and diversity.

(*continued*)

TABLE 3-1 The Three-D Approach: Anywhere Theme Park, USA *(Continued)*

Are the legal or administrative rules clearly set out and reinforced in policy?	Rules are clearly printed on park handouts, such as maps and signs. There is ample staff present to enforce the rules, and all seem keenly aware of various restrictions and park guidelines. Visitors are searched upon entering the park to prevent various items from entering the park, identification is required to purchase tickets, and close monitoring is conducted via CCTV.
Are there signs?	Yes. For every occasion, at every turn.
Is there conflict or confusion between the designated purpose and definition?	No. Each area is specifically designed for its purpose. This not only creates a richer guest environment but facilitates the movement of people through the area, increasing its overall productivity. The numbers of people who use these areas are too great to allow confusion. This would create a bottleneck in the flow of foot traffic and general dissatisfaction among the guests.
Design	
How well does the physical design support the intended function?	Very well. The color, design, and landscaping set the mood of family fun. Colors and characters are age appropriate, music is thematic, and structure sizes are appropriate to the user. There are no structures that do not contribute to the theme of the area or the park. Walkways are wide and well lit, clean, and level. Exits are clearly marked, doorways are well marked and wide, and walkways are indirect, leading to a sense of exploration and bigness.
How well does the physical design support the definition of the desired or accepted behaviors?	Very well. There are signs everywhere indicating directions, rules, and suggestions for park visitors to follow. Rides, games, and sitting areas are clearly separated or integrated, depending on the design of the area. Facilities and distractions are properly restricted where movement and traffic flow is necessary.
Does the physical design conflict with or impede the productive use of space or the proper functioning of the intended human activity?	No. All facilities and structures contribute to the purposeful movement of traffic. Again, restrictions are kept to a minimum so as not to create a greater problem in traffic management.
Is there confusion or conflict in the manner in which the physical design is intended to control behavior?	No. All facilities are designed to control and direct large amounts of traffic. Confusion would hinder the operation and productivity of the park.

increase lighting. However, the jury is still out on whether or not simply improving lighting is effective in reducing crime. Research in this area has found conflicting results. (See Farrington & Welsh, 2002 for a summary of the literature.) One reason for these conflicting results may be how improved lighting is operationalized. Another issue is the choice of crime measurement. Pease (1999) suggests that lighting may reduce crime if it increases outdoor activities, which then increases surveillance abilities. In addition, lighting increases visibility and thus increases the risk to the potential offender.

The use of closed-circuit television (CCTV) for surveillance has grown in popularity in recent years, especially in England. In an evaluation of 13 CCTV ventures, Gill and Spriggs (2005) found mixed results on its ability to thwart crime. In some cases, areas with CCTV sustained more crime than control areas, and in other cases CCTV-equipped areas sustained less crime than the control areas. An interesting report by Black (2003) in *Business Week* suggests that British residents are fed up with the use of CCTV cameras (used primarily for catching speeders) and that they have destroyed many of these surveillance cameras:

> Farmers in Somerset have been charged with using speed cams and closed-circuit TV cameras (CCTV) for target practice. In Cambridgeshire, vandals set one afire. Earlier this month, one creative hooligan knocked down a speed cam by attaching a rope from the back of his car to the camera's pole and driving away (para 2).

Furthermore, "Ten years later, it is clear that CCTV has done little to clean up the streets. Study after study shows that CCTV simply displaces crime to areas where no cameras are present rather than preventing it" (Black, 2003). This suggests that while some areas utilizing CCTV have found success, other communities adopting this strategy have found limited or no success; in the Cambridgeshire example, their use has upset the residents in the process.

Lastly, well intentioned efforts designed to build community cohesion have found varying levels of success and failure. This may be in part due to the operationalization of key variables. For example, what exactly *is* a "community"? In addition, a primary assumption of CPTED approaches is that changing the physical environment will change the social environment. What happens if courtyards are constructed, benches are placed, and lighting improves, but the legitimate users of an area still do not use the spaces? Or worse, the non-legitimate users come in and monopolize and destroy them!

■ The Environment, Opportunity, and Decision Making

Felson and Clarke (1998) outline 10 principles of opportunity—the cornerstone for all criminal behavior. Essentially, opportunities are important in understanding crime, and these opportunities are usually highly specific, concentrated in time in space, and dependent on everyday movements. In addition, opportunities for crime differ with social and technological changes, and some opportunities are more tempting than others. Furthermore, crime opportunities can be reduced, producing significant impacts on crime with little to no displacement. The theoretical approaches framing these 10 principles of opportunity include the Rational Choice, Routine Activities, and Crime Pattern Theories.

Rational Choice Theory

The roots of rational choice perspectives can be traced back to the Classical School of Criminology. Recall that the major premise of the Classical School of Criminology is that offenders choose to commit crime based on their perceptions of risk and reward. Thus, offender behavior is guided by **hedonism,** the principle of pleasure versus pain. Essentially, criminals make decisions based on what is best for them at the time—seeking pleasure and avoiding pain. Sounds simple, right?

More recent rational choice perspectives argue that offender decisions are based on the perceived effort and rewards in comparison to the consequences of committing crime, including the likelihood and severity of punishment (Cornish & Clarke, 1986, 2003). Modern rational choice theorists identify multiple factors in offender decision making, including time constraints, cognitive ability, and available information. These theorists argue that decision making must be examined from a crime-specific focus. In addition, theorists contend that criminality and crime are fundamentally distinct concepts and must be separated under analysis. For example, Cao (2004) states that:

> Crime is an event; criminality is a personal trait. Criminals do not commit crime all the time; noncriminals may on occasion violate the law. Criminal involvement refers to the processes through which individuals choose to become initially involved in particular forms of crime, to continue, and to desist. The decision processes at these three stages are influenced by different sets of factors and need to be separately modeled. Some high-risk people lacking opportunity may never commit crime; given enough provocation and/or opportunity, a low-risk, law-abiding person may commit crime. The offender is seen as choosing to commit an offence under particular conditions and circumstances. The decision making is not always fully rational, or even properly considered; instead the perspective emphasizes notions of the limited rationality. The offenders thus are variable in their motives, which may range from desires for money and sex to excitement and thrill seeking. Offenders' ability to analyze situations and to structure their choice, to switch between substitutable offenses may also vary, as may their specific skills to carry out a crime (p. 33).

Borrowing from the field of public administration, we can apply Simon's (1976) notions of "bounded rationality" and "satisficing" to the study of criminality. Bounded rationality assumes that people approach decision making with imperfect and incomplete information and that because it is impossible to make completely rational decisions with this information and we are constrained by time and other obstacles, we stop searching for solutions when we come across one that is good enough; in other words, we are not satisfied with perfect decisions but are satisfied with imperfect ones we think will work.

Apply this to known crime trends. For example, we know that most crime is intraclass (poor people offend against poor people, rich people offend against rich people, etc.). Working on a rational offender model, a poor offender committing robbery against a poor victim does not seem to make much sense. Wouldn't a rational offender want to rob someone with more money? The short answer is yes, and given the opportunity to do so, he probably would. However, it may be riskier or take more effort to find someone with more money. The robber may have to travel farther to find a wealthier victim, which further increases the effort required. In addition, if the offender has to travel to an area he is not familiar with, his perceived risk of getting caught also increases. In the end, the meager payout from robbing a poor person, in an area the robber is somewhat close to and familiar with, might in fact be a better deal. It is even possible that an offender's drug addiction may cause him to feel a sense of urgency, and thus close targets with little reward (that can be hit more frequently) could be part of his decision-making process to have enough money to buy the drugs he needs. Thus, recent rational choice perspectives offer a better framework for understanding imperfect decisions in an imperfect and dynamic environment.

In crime mapping and analysis, offender decision making is an important variable and must be understood for analysts to make useful predictions about future criminal offending. For example, using geographic information systems (GIS) to analyze a series of robberies in and around Phoenix, Arizona, Catalano, Hill, and Long (2001) included some important assumptions about offender decision making in their model. First, they separated earlier and later crimes in this series based upon the assumption that decisions about where to commit crimes changes as the level of professionalism increases (thus, decision making is dynamic). Second, they only included those potential targets within 3 miles of a freeway (the average plus one standard deviation distance of the past targets' locations from freeway access), assuming that future decisions about the attractiveness of a target would be similar to past targets. Furthermore, an average daily net (the total score of a robbery divided by the number of days between it and the next robbery) was utilized to make predictions about when the next robbery would occur. Thus, Catalano et al.'s model attempted to make predictions about criminal decision making as to *where* and *when* the robbers might strike again, and included within their model was the notion that decisions later in a crime series are influenced by decisions offenders make early in a series.

As you can see, an understanding of criminal decision making is important to the analysis and mapping of crime. The next section takes the notion of rational decision making to the next level by including a discussion of which factors are most important to understanding crimes of opportunity. Specifically, the highest likelihood for crime exists in certain situations where the perceived risk and effort to commit crime are low and the perceived payout is high.

Routine Activities Theory

In Routine Activities Theory, offenders and victims both play a role in the criminal event. In everyday life, people travel back and forth to work, school, play, and home. It is during these normal movements and activities that potential offenders and victims come in contact with one another. Thus, through the normal course of business, people may increase or decrease their risk of victimization based on their patterns. For example, a person who works in an office building Monday through Friday and returns home after work probably has a fairly low chance of becoming a victim of robbery or assault, depending on the pathways he travels to and from work. However, when that same person attends a crowded or rowdy bar or takes part in a volatile situation (for example, a sports victory celebration that is out of control), the risk of being assaulted or robbed increases. In two recent instances, a pattern of excessive substance use (suitable target, motivated offender) combined with the lack of a capable guardian resulted in the deaths of two young, college-aged women in Aruba (the Natalee Holloway case) and New York City (the Imette St. Guillen case). In addition, patterns of movement and activity have changed dramatically since the 1980s. For example, many households today require two incomes. Having both guardians removed from the home every day (and removed from neighbors' homes as well) significantly reduces the offender's risk of getting caught during a daytime burglary. The routine activities perspective argues that crime is most likely to occur when three criteria are present: a suitable target, a motivated offender, and the absence of capable guardians (Cohen & Felson, 1979).

Operating on the premise that most crime results from an exploited opportunity, this perspective holds that offenders, rather than engaging in extensive planning, choose to commit crime simply upon meeting an opportunity to do so, and some opportunities are more tempting than others. For example, to examine the suitability of targets for crime, Felson and Clarke (1998) put forth the VIVA risk quotient; VIVA stands for value, inertia, visibility, and access. Essentially, visible targets that are deemed valuable by offenders and are portable and easy to get at are at highest risk. Another useful acronym, CRAVED (concealable, removable, available, valuable, enjoyable, and disposable), is expanded to include the elements of concealability and disposability (Clarke, 1999). That is, offenders must also be able to hide the item(s) during the commission of a crime and quickly dispose of the stolen items in the black market.

Roman (2005) operationalized several concepts from Routine Activities Theory to examine the spatial and temporal influences on violent crime. In his study of youth crime in Prince George's County, Maryland, he developed a model of opportunity that incorporated variable clusters measuring (1) place-associated risk, (2) the potential level of guardianship (from Routine Activities Theory), (3) informal social control measures of guardianship (from Social Disorganization Theory), (4) the potential for motivated offenders, and (5) the influence of violent crimes from bordering neighborhoods. Temporal influences were measured by the time of day, day of the week, and the time of year. (All of these were grouped based on the school session, for example, commuting times to and from school, evenings, curfew period, and weekends.) The analysis also included a spatial lag of violent crimes (computed by using a weighted average of crime rates in neighboring locations). Roman's findings indicate strong support for Routine Activities Theory and argue for the inclusion of temporal influences in understanding violent crime:

> Individuals are vulnerable to violence during times when the flow of youth is highly concentrated. At certain times of the day there will be places with high concentrations of youth and limited adult supervision. Youth hangouts, schools and busy retail establishments all influence levels of violence, but their impact on violence is mediated by the time of day (Roman, 2005, p. 306).

Thus, routine activities approaches hold some interesting opportunities for crime mapping and analysis and can help guide strategies for crime control and resource deployment. The inclusion of contextual variables that measure various aspects of routine activities can improve the prediction power of crime maps and analyses, increasing their usefulness.

Crime Pattern Theory

Crime Pattern Theory intersects Rational Choice Theory, Routine Activities Theory, and environmental factors to provide a comprehensive explanation of crime (Brantingham & Brantingham, 1981, 1984, 1993). In crime pattern theory, individuals have both activity spaces and awareness spaces. A person's **awareness space** is comprised of those areas with which he is familiar. Rossmo Laverty, and Moore (2005) state that this is "similar to the concept of a comfort zone" (p. 106). An individual's awareness space is typically (but not always) derived from the individual's activity space. An **activity space** is comprised of various *nodes* of activity or locations that represent where people live, work, and play. The routes people take to travel back and forth from nodes are called *paths*. These paths are important in calculating journey-to-crime distances. The importance of these paths to Crime Pattern Theory is that potential offenders tend to search for opportunities to commit crimes along the nodes and paths of their own activity and awareness spaces. In addition to nodes and paths, *edges* are those areas on the periphery (physical and perceptual) of an activity space. These edge areas are premier locations for criminal offending. This is because the level of diversity encountered here (in people from both sides of the edge and their activities) limits the surveillance capabilities of potential guardians. **Figure 3–1** illustrates a simplified model of how a person's activity space may look.

Of course, depending on how far one travels and how many different nodes and paths an individual has, activity spaces can be vast and complex. Private investigators, for example, are likely to have very large and very complex activity spaces because their job requires them to drive to multiple locations on any given day. Awareness space also consists of places that individuals have visited or are aware of, such as landmarks and relatives' homes. We also have to consider that some people are very transient and may frequently move throughout their lives, and thus their awareness and activity spaces change over time.

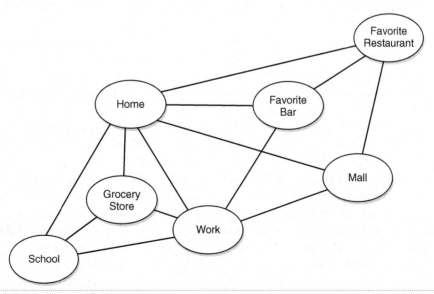

Figure 3–1 Activity Nodes and Paths

Crime Pattern Theory provides a framework for understanding both offender and victim behavior patterns. Individuals, including offenders, create cognitive maps of areas they are familiar with while traveling from one node of activity to another. Offenders use these maps to help them choose targets of crime. What we see here can often be that offenders search directly around them for opportunities to commit crime that are within their own awareness space, or they may also travel to specific locations (bus stations, ATM locations, shopping malls), often called "crime attractors," and wait for a victim. Through the processes of *recognition*, *prediction*, *evaluation*, and *action* (Smith & Patterson, 1980), cognitive maps are created, targets are chosen, and crime is committed.

Whichever type of hunting one offender or another does may also relate to the obligatory time and discretionary time that they have available. Offenders who work will most likely be obligated during their work hours and not be able to commit crime; however, when they get off work, they can commit crime during this discretionary time. In any case, if the analyst can determine what type of thought processes the offender may be using, he or she can be better at predicting a new hit or determining where the offender may reside.

■ Lifestyle Exposure Approaches

Lifestyle exposure approaches to the study of victimization suggest that understanding offender behavior and decision making is only one component to crime and that victim behavior is also important, sometimes *more* important, to understanding a criminal event. The notion of *shared responsibility* (while this term is not meant to place blame upon victims) implies that both victims and offenders contribute to a criminal event, sometimes in minor and sometimes in major ways. For example, a victim who leaves his car unlocked with the keys in the ignition (which was a common practice in colder climates during the winter season prior to the mass production of remote car starters) shares some responsibility in the theft of his automobile. A victim of robbery walking alone in a crime-ridden neighborhood at night shares some responsibility in his victimization. This is not to say that either of these victims *deserved* to be victimized. What we mean is that the decisions and behaviors of victims can create, in part, more attractive opportunities for motivated offenders. Recognizing this and taking active measures to reduce risks of victimization is the first step in preventing crime.

Karmen (2004) categorizes differential risks of victimization into several dimensions. First, the degree of *attractiveness* refers to the levels of risk and potential rewards for an offender. Victims who are likely to be carrying large amounts of cash (restaurant employees, for example) may be more attractive to potential robbers than poor college professors carrying bags full of books. However, a college professor with her arms full may be an easier target for sexual assault. Second, *proximity* refers to the geographic and social closeness of an offender to a potential victim. Targets that are easiest to reach geographically and socially are at highest risk. The *deviant place* factor (such as hotspots of crime), for example, allows greater access to victims for a variety of reasons (a large number of potential targets, lack of social efficacy, poor physical design characteristics). *Vulnerability*, a third dimension, has to do with how capable a potential victim or target is to resist being attacked. The college professor previously described would be more at risk as her arms were occupied by heavy bags of books (which could also be used as weapons of self defense in an attack). Karmen also places victim behavior on a continuum as it relates to shared responsibility in the victimization. **Victim facilitation** refers to victims whose behavior was negligent in making themselves a more attractive or vulnerable target. **Victim precipitation** or **provocation** refers to situations where victims contributed *significantly* to the criminal event. A burglar getting assaulted by an awakened homeowner would be an example of precipitation. In the case of provocation, the crime would not have occurred if it was not for the victim's behavior. An example would be a person who provoked a fight in a bar but ended up being injured by the person with whom he started a fight—thus, he would be a victim even though he caused the fight from which he received an injury.

Along these lines, lifestyle approaches suggest that the reason that victimization risks are higher for some and not others is because of the movements and activities associated with various factors. For example, younger persons in general (under 25 years of age) are far more likely to be victims of violent crimes than are persons older than 25 years of age. In addition, single persons are more likely to be victims of certain crimes (such as robbery) than married persons. These increased risks are not simply due to age or being married, but they are due to the changes in movement and activities that being older and being married bring. Young and single persons are more likely to be out and about in places or events (parties, concerts, sporting events) that may put them in a higher risk bracket for being victimized than older and married persons.

A person's profession may also affect his or her risk of certain types of victimization. Police officers, for example, held the highest rate of workplace violence compared to all other occupations studied during the years 1993 to 1999, accounting for 11% of all workplace violence (Denhardt, 2001). Between 2000 and 2009, the percentage of officers who were injured by assaults on the job remained fairly steady (between 26% and 28.2%; Federal Bureau of Investigation, 2010). Recent statistics suggest that workplace violence against police officers has been escalating steadily. Sgueglia and Dignam (2011) reported that the number of officers killed in the line of duty in 2011 jumped to 173, a nearly 14% increase from 2010. In that same year, the Los Angeles Police Department reported that assaults against their officers had increased almost 27% from the prior year (Romero, 2011). Denhardt observed that during his study period, those working in mental health occupations were second to police officers in their rates of workplace victimizations. College professors were victimized the least. Persons employed in the transportation (bus and taxi drivers, for example) or retail sales fields were more likely to be victims of robbery. Those employed in the transportation field held the highest rates of being victimized with a weapon. Persons working in retails sales had slightly higher risks of workplace violence overall than persons in transportation, teaching, and medical fields.

In addition to legitimate activities and movements, nonlegitimate activities can also place some persons at higher risks of victimization. For example, it's not hard to imagine why prostitutes, drug addicts, and gang members have very high rates of victimization compared to the rest of the population.

Repeat victimization (similar to repeat offending) can be explained in several ways. First, **risk heterogeneity** suggests that the characteristics of targets, or places that made them attractive to offenders in their first victimization, were also attractive to other offenders in subsequent victimizations (Gill & Pease, 1998). For example, an openly gay man practicing homosexual behavior in an atmosphere inhospitable to homosexuals may become a target for victimization of a hate crime. Continuing this behavior on subsequent occasions in the same atmosphere may make this person a target for future victimizations by the same types of offenders. **Event dependency** explains that offenders choose to revictimize a person or place based on their successful past experiences. Places where offenders successfully committed crimes are attractive places for repeat performances. For example, it is not uncommon for a liquor store to be robbed several times by the same offender. Consider also the repeated victimization of individual citizens and shop owners by organized criminal enterprises offering protection from other thugs and troublemakers. Last, **virtual repeats** are when similar targets are chosen based on their similarities to past targets (Pease, 1998). For example, grocery or convenience stores with similar layouts may be hit in a robbery series.

Lifestyle approaches and explanations of repeat victimization help us understand why some people and places are victimized at greater frequency than others. They also provide valuable cues to crime analysts and mappers about which people and places are at highest risk of being victimized, allowing law enforcement officials to implement proactive measures aimed at reducing and preventing crime. Sometimes, however, in discouraging offenders from committing crimes against specific persons and places, we may encourage them to perpetrate their crimes elsewhere.

■ Displacement and Diffusion

Some research suggests that many crime-intervention efforts do not reduce crime, but simply displace it (Barnes, 1995; Clarke, 1998; Clarke & Weisburd, 1994; Reppetto, 1976). There are two general kinds of **crime displacement**: benign and malign (Barr & Pease, 1990). *Benign* displacement is viewed as a success in that while criminals have not been prevented from committing crime altogether, they have at least been displaced to committing crimes that are less harmful or serious in nature. *Malign* displacement, on the other hand, is when criminals begin to commit crimes that are more serious and/or harmful due to the continued successful thwarting of their previous efforts. When evaluating the success of a crime-control strategy, crime analysts must make maps and perform analyses to check for displacement, examining changes in different types of crime and changes in neighborhoods beyond the area targeted by the intervention(s) to ensure that crime was truly reduced and not simply displaced.

Types of Displacement

Reppetto (1976) identified five types of displacement. Spatial or *territorial* displacement occurs when crime is moved from one place to the next. This is often thought to be the most common type of displacement. However, research is mixed concerning the amount of territorial displacement that occurs. Santiago (1998) found that efforts to reduce auto thefts in Newark, New Jersey displaced the crime to adjacent areas. Canter (1998) also observed displacement of residential burglaries occurring in Baltimore. Chainey (2000) found that the use of CCTV was effective in reducing both street robbery and auto theft, but that some displacement of the auto thefts occurred in surrounding areas. Displacement of street robbery, however, did not occur. Last, Ratcliffe (2002), in his analysis of crime data in Canberra, Australia, determined that "Operation Anchorage" (antiburglary strategy involving surveillance, selective targeting, use of intelligence analysis, and traffic enforcement) showed success, with no significant signs of displacement occurring.

Temporal displacement occurs when crime is moved from one time to another but stays within the same area. This could mean that an offender or offenders move from operating on a weekend day to a weekday or from early morning to late afternoon. This is important to understand, especially in a series analysis where patterns of offending may change to mitigate risks of getting caught.

Target displacement occurs when criminals choose another target due to target hardening and other strategies to reduce crime. Target hardening measures, such as house alarms or dogs, may displace a burglar to a different house in the same neighborhood without such protection measures. *Tactical* displacement is when criminals develop new methods to commit the same crime. For example, automobiles are much more difficult to steal today than they were 15 or 20 years ago. It is theorized that the rise in carjackings that occurred in the 1990s was due to the increased difficulty of stealing unattended vehicles that were armed with sophisticated alarm systems and other devices. While carjacking is technically a fairly new crime, the offender's goal of stealing an automobile remains the same. The methods, however, have changed.

In carjacking, the offender takes (or attempts to take) a motor vehicle by force or the threat of force. This is a perfect example of malign displacement, where crime-prevention efforts (target hardening of automobiles) created a change in tactics (and also in this example, a change of crime) that is more harmful and serious in nature than the original crime of auto theft.

Functional displacement occurs when the offender has difficulty committing one crime due to target hardening strategies and is forced to commit a different crime. The previous example of carjacking also works as an example of functional displacement because carjacking is a separate crime from auto theft. Another example would be a burglar switching to armed robbery due to the increased target hardening efforts, such as the installation of alarms by property owners.

The final type of displacement, offered by Barr and Pease (1990), is *perpetrator* displacement. Perpetrator displacement is most common in drug manufacturing and distribution crimes. For example, law enforcement efforts may cause a drug dealer to desist from further drug dealing (perhaps he was arrested and is in jail). However, in the drug market, these efforts create a vacant position for another drug dealer to step in and take his place. Thus, we have traded one drug dealer for another.

Diffusion of Benefits

Now that we have made you skeptical about whether or not crime prevention is ever truly achieved because of possible crime displacement effects, let us discuss another possible effect of crime-prevention efforts (a much more positive one), the **diffusion of benefits**. The diffusion of benefits is defined as:

> The spread of the beneficial influence of an intervention beyond the places which are directly targeted, the individuals who are the subject of control, the crimes which are the focus of intervention or the time periods in which an intervention is bought (Clarke & Weisburd, 1994, p. 169).

Clark and Weisburd argue that two possible sources for diffusion exist: deterrence and discouragement. For example, imagine that your local police department has announced through the media that it will be targeting shoplifters at various local stores throughout the summer months. Potential offenders may be deterred from shoplifting at stores that are not identified in the announcement for fear that they are too close in location to the stores that will receive the enhanced enforcement. Likewise, it is possible that offenders will wait until late fall to return to the stores to shoplift, fearing that increased enforcement may persist until sometime in September. This buffer of space or time provides the benefit of crime-prevention efforts without actually engaging in them. Offenders are discouraged from shoplifting at the stores during these times because their perceived risk has been increased by the enhanced enforcement. What are often seen in typical police departments are enforcement activity areas, or what could be referred to as selective enforcement areas. These are small geographic sections of town that have been designated for extra patrols, increased offender apprehension, or other crime-prevention programs. Depending on the effectiveness of the increased enforcement in this small geographic area, we may see beneficial diffusion results not only within the small area but surrounding it as well.

■ Applied Crime Theory

Rengert (1995) notes that:

> Law enforcement personnel have been conducting spatial analysis since the beginning of modern policing. Much of this analysis has been carried out in the brains of seasoned detectives. These days, however, more and . . . more of this analysis is conducted on desktop computers. Rather than have seasoned officers pass down techniques to their colleagues by word of mouth and example, . . . we now house this knowledge in the memory of a computer. This change is important not only because it supplements the experience of an experienced police officer, but also . . . because the knowledge and techniques accumulated over the years do not retire with a veteran detective. They are there for others to build on (p. xiii).

Clearly we have come a long way since 1995 in being able to collect both knowledge and intelligence in systems that allow us to retrieve a variety of data about people, incidents, and places involved in criminal activity. These data are then used to test theories, or use theories, to develop strategies that help reduce crime, dissuade offenders, or capture offenders involved in crime. A perfect example of this can be found in a computerized crime analysis and mapping system developed in the late 1990s in Los Angeles (Moore, 1995).

Along with the recognition that officer experience needs to be computerized and saved for crime analysis, we also have to use the data in a manner consistent with theory and our goals and objectives.

So now that we are collecting all this data, what has actually been done with it? There are many studies in journals and books concerning the use of some aspect of one of these theories of criminology. For example, in *Journeys to Crime: GIS Analysis of Offender and Victim Journeys in Sheffield, England* (Costello & Leipnik, 2003), the authors came to the conclusion that most offender trips are relatively short and that more than 40% of burglary journeys were less than 1 mile. They also learned that offenders were opportunistic in nature and did not typically travel with the intent to offend. Furthermore, Costello and Leipnik discovered that in high-crime areas, victims were often victimized closer to home than in noncrime areas. The victims who lived in low-crime residential neighborhoods often were victimized in the city center, which was farther from their homes. This type of analysis helps to provide the basic knowledge of where an offender might live in relation to a crime series and greatly limit the search distance and number of records we may initially comb through to find a potential suspect from our databases.

An interesting look at a day in the life of a criminal can be found in Chainey and Ratcliffe's (2005) work, in which they follow a criminal from the time he wakes through his travels to a friend's house, describing the various opportunities for crime, and the defenses through CPTED that were put up in his path as well as the decision-making processes he goes through as his trip progresses.

Chainey and Ratcliffe (2005) suggest, "Having a variety of base layer data is beneficial to the Compstat process, but equally important is the way in which the crime data itself is viewed" (p. 263). In addition, the data needed for the CompStat process focus on the immediate need and identification of problems and situations where police response would provide the most beneficial reductions in crime. Furthermore, problem solving in relation to these issues will impact one or more of the sides of the crime triangle. We might want to create an analysis of the known burglars in an area (offenders) and notify the neighbors (target) living within 1 mile of those burglars, that they are at highest risk of a burglary and work with them to target-harden their homes. Using the same analysis results, we could also use a search radius of 1 mile around a series of burglaries to identify potential suspects (offenders) from a pool of people who might be on probation, known to have committed, or have precursor crimes associated with burglary, to help supply possible suspect lists for detectives. It is not sufficient to have knowledge of the theories of crime, or know how to be a police officer (guardian), or have experience doing crime mapping with accurate data by themselves; it is the combination of good data, analyzed with respect to the theories and research in mind, by a well-informed crime analyst that can direct the skills of a police officer to places where crime can be prevented, or suspects apprehended, that works.

In *The Hammer Gang*, Overall and Day (2008) describe a robbery series in Durban, South Africa where they applied GIS and multilayer geoprocessing to reduce the area where the offender might strike next from 11 potential targets to 2. This suggests that knowledge of offender behavior, derived from crime theory, can assist in maximizing and strategizing law enforcement resources.

In another example of applied crime theory, we enter the "sci-fi" world with research by attempting to simulate a human environment and then control the "agents" that are within the simulation. (If you have ever played the game SimCity, then you have the general idea.) Basically, you set up agents within the simulation that have characteristics of the society you are trying to simulate. These characters can have race, sex, income, and tendency for crime programmed in, and then you let the offenders loose to test various routine activities and other crime theories as they autonomously wander through their environment. Groff (2008) indicates that "although the use of simulation modeling is still very much in its infancy within the environmental criminology research community, the potential implications for informing both policy and practice are numerous" (p. 140).

These are just a few of the examples of where crime theory is put into practice every day to try to impact crime, or actually gain a handle on it. Applying all of this is vital for the crime analyst, researcher, or student learning this field of study, and necessary to form a basic understanding of the theory and its application through active research, or applying the theories to active cases and data within or in conjunction with a law enforcement agency. It is imperative that we continue to use applied research that informs the analyst of what tactics and responses would yield the best results for crime prevention strategies. We want to make sure that we use high quality data and analysis grounded in theory, as well as utilize good policing tactics and methodologies to combat crime. Neglecting these things will make the crime analyst a "paper pusher" and potentially have limited resources looking in the wrong places.

■ Conclusion

Crime and victimization are not evenly distributed across people or places. Several approaches to the study of victimology suggest that understanding the targets, or victims of crime, that make them more attractive to offenders can provide valuable information to the examination and study of crime. Knowing which places or people are most likely to become victims of crime allows us to make better predictions about where and when crime is most likely to occur and better informs the mapmaking and crime analysis process—a critical part of preventing and reducing crime. We also see how important data is to this process. If we do not have quality data or data that can stand in for and adeptly represent another variable, a proxy if you will, we can only guess if our analyses are useful and based on theory.

■ Chapter Glossary

Activity space   In Crime Pattern Theory, activity space denotes the areas that offenders and victims are most familiar with on a daily basis. It contains nodes (home, work, school) and pathways (how people travel to and from their nodes on a daily basis), which define the borders (edges) of the space where people live, work, and play.

Awareness space   In Crime Pattern Theory, awareness space includes any area that an offender is familiar with; it is typically a broader area than activity space.

CPTED   Acronym for crime prevention through environmental design. Attributed to Jeffrey (1971), this approach examines the environment as a stimulus that potential offenders and victims respond to. Essentially, CPTED argues that we can reduce crime opportunities by changing the physical environment.

Crime displacement   When offenders change their offending patterns in response to crime control strategies, crime displacement occurs. There are six types of crime displacement: territorial, functional, tactical, temporal, perpetrator, and target.

Defensible space   Newman (1972) argued that areas with defensible space are less likely to suffer from high crime rates. Areas with defensible space could be characterized as having high levels of territoriality, natural surveillance, image, and milieu.

Diffusion of benefits   The benefits of a crime control strategy extend beyond the borders where the strategy is employed.

Event dependency   Situations where the same offender (usually) commits the same offense against the same target or victims.

Hedonism   The principle that people act to pursue pleasure and avoid pain.

Risk heterogeneity   Something about the victim or target is attractive to different offenders and is thus more likely to be victimized multiple times.

Victim facilitation   When victims, whether carelessly or unknowingly, make it easier for an offender to commit a crime against them.

Victim precipitation   When victims who are hurt significantly in a crime in some way, usually violence related, contributed to the outbreak of the violence.

Victim provocation   When victims who are actually responsible for their own victimization.

Virtual repeats   When similar targets or locations are being victimized, usually by the same offender(s); for example, a robbery series of a chain of convenience stores.

■ Questions for Review

1. How is environmental design used to reduce or prevent crime? What crime-prevention strategies utilize environmental design elements?

2. What are the four key elements to Newman's *defensible space*? Explain each briefly.

3. How do public, semipublic, and semiprivate spaces differ? Give an example of each.

4. Explain how designation, definition, and design are used to assess space in crime-prevention efforts.

5. What factors are included in offender decision-making models by modern-day rational choice theorists?

6. According to Routine Activities Theory, crime is most likely to occur when three criteria exist. Briefly explain these three criteria and provide an example of a scenario in which crime is most likely to occur.

7. How do VIVA and CRAVED explain offender decision making and opportunity? Based on these models, which items are most likely going to be stolen from a motor vehicle? Which items would be least likely to be stolen from a motor vehicle?

8. Explain the concepts *nodes*, *pathways*, and *edges* in Crime Pattern Theory. How does Crime Pattern Theory explain both offender and victim behavior? Draw a map of your own activity space.

9. According to Karmen, what are the differential risks of victimization?

10. In what ways do victims contribute to their own victimization?

11. Explain *risk heterogeneity*, *event dependency*, and *virtual repeats*. Provide an example of each.

12. What is the difference between malign and benign displacement?

13. Explain *diffusion of benefits*.

■ Online Resources

CPTED Vancouver–Environmental Criminology: www.designcentreforcpted.org/Pages/EnvCrim.html

Crime Prevention Through Environmental Design Training Conferences: www.cptedtraining.net

Design Center For CPTED: www.designcentreforcpted.org/Pages/CrimeAn.html

Environmental Criminology Research Inc.: www.ecricanada.com

New South Wales Government CPTED: www.police.nsw.gov.au/community_issues/crime_prevention/safer_by_design

UC MASC Project—Mathematical and Simulation Modeling of Crime: http://paleo.sscnet.ucla.edu/

■ Recommended Reading

Dempkin, J. (Ed.). (2004). *Security planning and design: A guide for architects and building design professionals*. Hoboken, NJ: Wiley.

Fleissner, D., & Heinzelmann, F. (1996). *Crime prevention through environmental design and community policing*. National Institute of Justice. Retrieved from www.ncjrs.gov/pdffiles/crimepre.pdf.

■ References

Angel, S. (1968). *Discouraging crime through city planning*. Berkeley, CA: Institute of Urban and Regional Development, University of California.

Barnes, G. C. (1995). Defining and optimizing displacement. In J. E. Eck & D. Weisburd (Eds.), *Crime and place* (pp. 95–113). Monsey, NY: Criminal Justice Press.

Barr, R., & Pease, K. (1990). Crime placement, displacement, and deflection. In M. Tonry & N. Morris (Eds.), *Crime and justice* (Vol. 12). Chicago: University of Chicago Press.

Black, J. (2003, October 17). Smile, you're being watched. *Business Week*. Retrieved from www.msnbc .msn.com/id/3225985/.

Brantingham, P. J., & Brantingham, P. L. (Eds.) (1981). *Environmental criminology*. Beverly Hills, CA: Sage.

Brantingham, P. J., & Brantingham, P. L. (1984). *Patterns in crime*. New York: Macmillan.

Brantingham, P. L., & Brantigham, P. J. (1993). Environment, routine and situation: Toward a pattern theory of crime. In R. V. Clarke & M. Felson (Eds.), *Routine activity and rational choice* (pp. 259–294). New Brunswick, NJ: Transaction.

Canter, P. (1998). Baltimore County's autodialer system. In N. Lavigne & J. Wartell (Eds.), *Crime mapping case studies: Successes in the field* (Vol. 1, pp. 81–91). Washington, DC: Police Executive Research Forum.

Catalano, P., Hill, B., & Long, B. (2001). Geographical analysis and serial crime investigation: A case study of armed robbery in Phoenix, Arizona. *Security Journal, 14*(3), 27–41.

Cao, L. (2004). *Major criminological theories: Concepts and measurements*. Belmont, CA: Wadsworth.

Chainey, S., & Ratcliffe, J. (2005). *GIS and crime mapping*. West Sussex, UK: Wiley.

Chainey, S. (2000). Optimizing closed-circuit television use. In N. Lavigne & J. Wartell (Eds.), *Crime mapping case studies: Successes in the field* (Vol. 2, pp. 91–100). Washington, DC: Police Executive Research Forum.

Clarke, R. V. (1998). The theory and practice of situational crime prevention. Retrieved from www .e-doca.eu/docs/Situational_crime_prevention.pdf.

Clarke, R. V. (1999). *Hot products: Understanding, anticipating and reducing the demand for stolen goods*. London: Home Office Police and Reducing Crime Unit.

Clarke, R. V., & Weisburd, D. (1994). Diffusion of crime control benefits: Observations on the reverse of displacement. In R. V. Clarke (Ed.), *Crime prevention studies* (Vol. 2, pp. 165–183). Monsey, NY: Criminal Justice Press.

Cohen, L. A., & Felson, M. (1979). Social change and crime rate trends: A routine activities approach. *American Sociological Review, 44*, 588–608.

Cornish, D. B., & Clarke, R. V. (Eds.). (1986). *The reasoning criminal: Rational choice perspectives on offending*. New York: Springer-Verlag.

Cornish, D. B., & Clarke, R. V. (2003). Opportunities, precipitators, and criminal decisions: A reply to Wortley's critique of situational crime prevention. In M. J. Smith & D. B. Cornish (Eds.), *Theory for practice in situational crime prevention* (pp. 41–96). Monsey, NY: Criminal Justice Press.

Costello, A., & Leipnik, M. (2003). Journeys to crime: GIS analysis of offender and victim journeys in Sheffield, England. In M. Leipnik & D. Albert (Eds.), *GIS in law enforcement: Implementation issues and case studies* (pp. 228–231). London: Taylor & Francis.

Crowe, T. D. (2000). *Crime prevention through environmental design: Applications of architectural design and space management concepts* (2nd ed.). Boston: Butterworth-Heinemann.

Denhardt, D. (2001). *Violence in the workplace, 1993–1999* [Special report]. Washington, DC: U.S. Department of Justice, Office of Justice Programs, Bureau of Justice Statistics.

Farrington, D. P., & Welsh, B. C. (2002). *Effects of improved street lighting on crime: A systematic review*. London: Home Office.

Federal Bureau of Investigation. (2010). Law enforcement officers killed and assaulted, 2009. Retrieved from www2.fbi.gov/ucr/killed/2009/data/table_70.html.

Felson, M., & Clarke, R. V. (1998). *Opportunity makes the thief: Practical theory for crime prevention.* London: Home Office Police and Reducing Crime Unit.

Gill, M., & Pease, K. (1998). Repeat robbers: Are they different? In M. Gill (Ed.), *Crime at work: Increasing the risk of offenders.* Leicester, UK: Perpetuity Press.

Gill, M., & Spriggs, A. (2005). *Assessing the impact of CCTV.* London: Home Office.

Groff, E. (2008). Simulating crime to inform theory and practice. In S. Chainey & L. Thompson (Eds.), *Crime mapping case studies: Practice and research* (pp. 133–142). West Sussex, UK: John Wiley & Sons.

Jacobs, J. (1961). *The death and life of great American cities.* New York: Random House.

Jeffery, C. R. (1971). *Crime prevention through environmental design.* Beverly Hills, CA: Sage.

Kaplan, H., O'Kane, K., Lavrakas, P. J., & Hoover, S. (1978). *CPTED final report on commercial demonstration in Portland, Oregon* [Mimeo]. Arlington, VA: Westinghouse Electric.

Karmen, A. (2004). *Crime victims: An introduction to victimology* (5th ed.). Belmont, CA: Wadsworth.

Kushmuk, J., & Whittemore, S. (1981). *A reevaluation of crime prevention through environmental design in Portland, Oregon.* Arlington, VA: Westinghouse Electric.

Merry, S. E. (1981). *Urban danger: Life in a neighborhood of strangers.* Springfield, IL: Mombiosse.

Moore, M. (1995). Keeping it simple. In B. Block, M. Dandoub, & S. Fregly (Eds.), *Crime analysis through computer mapping* (pp. xiii–xiv). Washington, DC: Police Executive Research Forum.

Newman, O. (1972). *Defensible space: People and design in the violent city.* New York: Macmillan.

Overall, C., & Day, G. (2008). The hammer gang: An exercise in the spatial analysis of an armed robbery series using the probability grid method. In S. Chainey & L. Thompson (Eds.), *Crime mapping case studies: Practice and research* (pp. 55–62). West Sussex, UK: John Wiley & Sons.

Pease, K. (1998). *Repeat victimization: Taking stock.* London: Home Office.

Pease, K. (1999). A review of street lighting evaluations: Crime reduction effects. In K. Painter & N. Tiley (Eds.), *Surveillance of public space: CCTV, street lighting and crime prevention.* Monsey, NY: Criminal Justice Press.

Ratcliffe, J. (2002). Burglary reduction and the myth of displacement. *Australian Institute of Criminology: Trends and Issues in Criminal Justice.* Retrieved from www.popcenter.org/Responses/video_surveillance/PDFs/Ratcliffe_2002.pdf.

Rengert, G. (1995). More than just a pretty map: How can spatial analysis support police decisions. In B. Block, M. Dandoub, & S. Fregly (Eds.), *Crime analysis through computer mapping* (pp. xiii–xiv). Washington, DC: Police Executive Research Forum.

Reppetto, T. (1974). *Residential crime.* Cambridge, MA: Ballinger.

Reppetto, T. (1976). Crime prevention and displacement phenomenon. *Crime and Delinquency, 22,* 166–177.

Roman, C. G. (2005). Routine activities of youth and neighborhood violence: Spatial modeling of place, time, and crime. In F. Wang (Ed.), *Geographic information systems and crime analysis* (pp. 293–310). Hershey, PA: IDEA Group Publishing.

Romero, D. (2011). Assaults on L.A. cops up nearly 20 percent in 2011, even as crime went down. *LA Weekly.* Retrieved from http://blogs.laweekly.com/informer/2011/12/lapd_officer_assault_up_crime_down.php.

Rosenbaum, D. P., Lurigio, A. J., & Davis, R. C. (1998). *The prevention of crime: Social and situational strategies.* Belmont, CA: West/Wadsworth.

Rossmo, D. K., Laverty, I., & Moore, B. (2005). Geographic profiling for serial crime investigation. In F. Wang (Ed.), *Geographic information systems and crime analysis* (pp. 102–117). Hershey, PA: IDEA Group Publishing.

Santiago, J. J. (1998). The problem of auto theft in Newark. In N. Lavigne & J. Wartell (Eds.), *Crime mapping case studies: Successes in the field* (Vol. 1, pp. 53–59). Washington, DC: Police Executive Research Forum.

Sguegli, K., & Dignam, C. (2011). Number of police officers killed in line of duty spikes in 2011. *CNN*. Retrieved from http://articles.cnn.com/2011-12-12/us/us_law-enforcement-deaths-2011_1_death-toll-police-officer-craig-floyd?_s=PM:US.

Simon, H. (1976). *Administrative behavior: A study of decision making processes in administrative organization* (3rd ed.). New York: Free Press.

Smith, C. J., & Patterson, G. E. (1980). Cognitive mapping and the subjective geography of crime. In D. E. Georges-Abeyie & K. D. Harries (Eds.), *Crime: A spatial perspective*. New York: Columbia University Press.

Taylor, R. B., Shumaker, S. A., & Gottfredson, S. D. (1985). Neighborhood links between physical features and local sentiments: Deterioration, fear of crime, and confidence. *Journal of Architectural and Planning Research, 2,* 261–275.

Wilson, S. (1978). Vandalism and defensible space on London housing estates. In R. V. Clarke (Ed.), *Tackling vandalism* (pp. 14–26). London: Her Majesty's Stationery Office.

Wood, E. (1961). *Housing design: A social theory*. New York: Citizens' Housing and Planning Counsel of New York.

Geography and Individual Decision Making: Victims and Offenders

By Lorie Velarde

▶ LEARNING OBJECTIVES

This chapter continues the discussion about how offenders interact with the environment to make decisions. Crime patterns are influenced by both the offender's knowledge of the environment as well as the spatial and temporal availability of targets. Essentially, offenders operate within the boundaries of their awareness space and are influenced by target availability, among other factors, when selecting locations to commit crimes. This chapter also reviews findings from studies about journey to crime, and the distances offenders travel when committing crimes. Journey-to-crime research has identified patterns in the distances offenders travel, and we can use this information to create a journey-to-crime estimate of where the offender's anchor point could be. Just as offenders use clues about the environment to select targets, law enforcement uses knowledge about the criminal hunting process to find them. This chapter introduces the concept of geographic profiling—a police investigative methodology that uses the locations in a connected crime series to locate the responsible offender. This chapter concludes with two geographic profiling case examples. After studying this chapter, you should be able to:

- Define and explain awareness space.
- Define and explain target backcloth.
- Define journey to crime.
- Understand the findings of several journey-to-crime studies.
- Define and explain geographic profiling and how it is used in a police investigation.
- List and describe the types of hunting methods used by offenders.
- Describe several different investigative strategies used with geographic profiling.

▶ **Key Terms**

Buffer Zone	Geographic Profiling	Mental Maps
Crime Series	Hunting Methods	Search Base
Distance Decay	Investigative Strategies	Target Backcloth
Expected Crime Pattern	Journey to Crime	

■ Introduction

This chapter builds on the discussion of the theoretical frameworks for crime site selection based in environmental criminology—including Rational Choice Theory, Routine Activities Theory, and Crime Pattern Theory—by focusing on other concepts related to crime site selection, such as activity and awareness space, mental maps, and target backcloth. Crime Pattern Theory explains how offender interaction with the environment produces patterns of criminal activity. Studies examining the distance an offender travels from his home to a crime location are also discussed in the journey-to-crime section.

Researchers and law enforcement practitioners alike have been interested in the influence of the environment on where, when, and how crimes occur. By reviewing research conducted in the area of environmental criminology, the police have been able to use empirical findings about offenders' interaction with their environment to help apprehend criminals. One promising methodology in this area is geographic profiling. The principles of geographic profiling technique and two profiling case examples are discussed later in this chapter. But before we can discuss geographic profiling, we must discuss a little more theory.

■ Mental Maps and Awareness Space

Everyone has daily activities that he or she participates in. Such activities include going to and from work, school, shopping, or recreation areas. Over time, making repetitive journeys to various locations gives us knowledge of the routes and characteristics of these places. We form cognitive images of the places we frequent, the routes to these places, and the areas we pass through. These cognitive images are known as **mental maps** (Brantingham & Brantingham, 1984).

Mental maps are the interpretation of the environment by the individual and are the result of perception, coding, and interpretation of information. Mental maps not only reflect the spatial features of the environment, but also the attitudes, experiences, and feelings of the individual about his or her environment. While mental maps vary from person to person because they are influenced by individual experiences, they also have much in common (Brantingham & Brantingham, 1984).

As people pass through a city, they begin to become familiar with areas. However, people do not know the entire city, either physically or temporally. There are areas that individuals know well and areas they have little or no knowledge of. The well known areas, those places visited frequently, and the routes that connect these areas comprise our *activity space* (Jakle, Brunn, & Roseman, 1976). If you wish to test this, sit down and draw a map of your world as you see it. Draw the major arterial roads and streets you travel on frequently. Also draw the places you go to shop, eat, work, attend school, meet friends, run errands, and other locations you may visit during a 2-week time period. When you are done creating your map, show it to someone who does not know where you live. It is likely that he or she will be able to roughly determine where you live based on where you spend most of your time (see **Figure 4–1**).

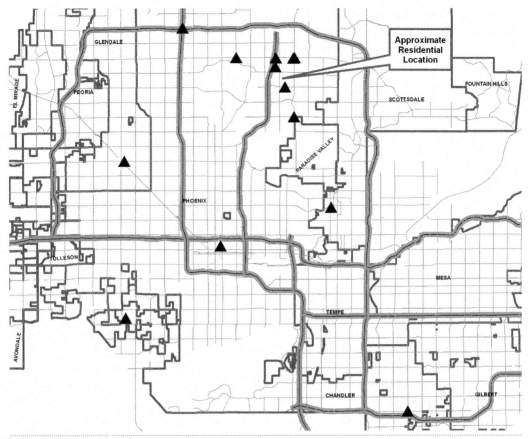

Figure 4–1 Sample Activity Space Map

Criminals, just like noncriminals, have locations they visit frequently. An offender's activity space is comprised of his or her habitual geography, which includes locations he or she visits for both criminal and noncriminal reasons (Brantingham & Brantingham, 1981).

There are also locations that, while we do not regularly frequent them, we still know about them. Along with those places we visit as part of our day-to-day activities, these locations form our *awareness space*.

Awareness space is comprised of those locations for which we have some minimum level of knowledge. It is even possible to have awareness of places we have never visited (Clark, 1990). For example, an offender who regularly steals scrap metal may learn of a new target-rich location for this type of crime from a fellow thief. While the offender has not been to the new location, he is now aware that it exists and may eventually visit it to examine its potential crime opportunities.

When an offender decides to commit a crime, he searches through his awareness space for a location that provides an opportunity for crime. For some offenders, the search will be minimal, perhaps even opportunistic. For others, the search will be extensive before a suitable target is encountered (Brantingham & Brantingham, 1981).

An example of an opportunistic offense might be a juvenile who burglarizes an unlocked home while he was on his way home from school. On the other hand, an example of offenders who show more planning might be a group of adults who commit robberies of banks, or specifically, only of Wells Fargo banks that have limited security. Presumably, the robbers would spend more time searching and planning before committing their crime than an opportunistic offender.

Both types of searches at the aggregate level produce an **expected crime pattern**, areas in the city where crime is likely to occur. Some of these locations, through the overlap of multiple offenders, become hotspots of criminal activity. Target availability also affects the expected crime pattern (Brantingham & Brantingham, 1993). In the previous robbery example, if Wells Fargo banks in the city were few and far between, the target availability would affect the pattern of crimes in a series of these events.

■ Target Backcloth

The daily activities of an offender define the location and time that he or she is likely to commit a crime. The routine activities of potential victims also shape crime patterns. For example, it is from this distribution of victims or targets that offenders must choose. The distribution of targets in the environment is called **target backcloth** (Brantingham & Brantingham, 1993).

The understanding of target availability is important to the understanding of crime site selection because it is from this availability that the offender must make his criminal choices. Targets are typically assessed by criminals on the basis of suitability and risk. *Suitability* refers to the gain or profit of the target as seen by the offender. *Risk* refers to the probability of apprehension of the offender. Both criteria can differ significantly depending on the target selected (Felson & Clarke, 1998).

Target availability is comprised of both temporal and spatial opportunity structures. Because opportunity is different at different times of the day, criminal targets must be examined both geographically and temporally. Depending on the criminal offender's target preference, the availability of that target might vary significantly from neighborhood to neighborhood. Targets might also vary by time of day, day of week, and season of year (Rossmo, 2004).

Because the location of potential victims plays a key role in the determination of where a criminal event will occur, nonuniform or rare target opportunities can distort the spatial pattern of crimes. For example, some target opportunities require more searching by the offender to find them or may result in crime sites determined strictly based on the limited availability of that specific target. The locations of crimes against street prostitutes, for example, are mainly a function of the locations of red-light districts (Rossmo, 2000).

A uniform target backcloth provides the offender with many opportunities; the locations of his or her crimes are mainly a function of what he or she knows. A nonuniform target back-cloth provides fewer opportunities; offenders are forced to the locations of the opportunities because their choices are limited and less can be determined about the spatial choices the offender has made because his choices have been a function of target availability (Rossmo, 2000).

Activity space, awareness space, and target backcloth all influence crime patterns. Law enforcement can use knowledge about how offenders interact with the environment to pri-oritize areas to search for them. This is discussed later in the chapter under geographic profiling.

■ Journey to Crime

Empirical research has examined the distances that offenders travel when committing crimes. The distances differ based on a variety of factors, including the type of crime, whether an area is urban or rural, and whether or not an area has a well developed public transportation system. A **journey-to-crime** trip is the journey an offender travels when he or she commits a crime, assuming the starting point of that journey is his or her home or another *anchor point*. While offenders may begin their actual journey to a crime from anywhere, researchers generally measure journey to crime as the distance between an offender's home and the location of his or her crime, regardless of the distance actually traveled on the day of the criminal event. This starting point then is the anchor point. Some crimes, such as domestic homicide, have a journey-to-crime distance of zero since the offender does not make a trip.

Many studies have been conducted on journey to crime. Some studies have analyzed crime trips based on the offense committed, while other studies have analyzed trips by factors such as demographics of the offender or day of week of the offense (Canter & Gregory, 1994).

Oftentimes, a journey-to-crime study will report its findings using measures such as the mean, median, or mode for the group studied. While these describe the studied group in general, they may not apply to any one individual within the group. It is important to remem-ber that crime trips will always vary by individual; some offenders make short journeys, while others make longer ones.

An example of a typical journey-to-crime study from the City of Glendale, Arizona is shown in **Table 4–1**. Note that for the crime of burglary, offenders travel an average of 2.34 miles from home to commit a crime. Based on the table, it is apparent that the mean distances traveled by offenders vary somewhat by crime type, and the mean trips for robbery, theft, and auto theft are longer than trips for other crimes in the city.

By studying many journeys, researchers have found that the majority of crimes occur close to home. What "close" means is somewhat subjective, but the studies reviewed by Brantingham and Brantingham (1981) found that the majority of crimes occurred within 2 miles of the offender's residence. Research has also found that crimes against persons, such as homicide, assault, and rape, occur closer to home than property crimes, such as larceny and burglary (Brantingham & Brantingham, 1981).

TABLE 4-1 Average Distance to Crime in Glendale, Arizona

Crime Type	Number of Crimes	Mean Crime Trip (Miles)	Standard Deviation (Miles)	68% of Crime Trips Within (Miles)	Furthest Distance
Aggravated assault	8526	1.18	2.86	4.04	6.91
Arson	62	1.32	2.68	4.00	6.67
Auto theft	1058	2.88	3.55	6.43	9.97
Burglary	1356	2.34	3.73	6.07	9.79
Curfew/loitering	164	1.59	1.85	3.44	5.28
Drug offenses	3970	2.27	3.39	5.66	9.06
Murder	70	2.38	4.42	6.80	11.23
Other miscellaneous	18,237	2.42	3.90	6.32	10.22
Other sex offenses	404	1.61	2.66	4.27	6.92
Rape	85	1.35	2.79	4.14	6.94
Robbery	567	3.23	4.21	7.44	11.65
Runaway	5958	0.19	1.29	1.48	2.77
Theft	5139	3.18	4.28	7.46	11.75

Note: The date range was January 1, 2004 through July 24, 2004.

Source: Bryan Hill, Glendale, Arizona Police Department.

Research has also found that crime trips show **distance decay** from the offender's residence. Distance decay refers to the decreasing probability of an offender traveling far from home to commit a crime. Generally speaking, the probability decays or drops off as distance from the offender's residence increases (Brantingham & Brantingham, 1984).

Most criminals, however, have a **buffer zone**. The buffer zone is an area around the offender's residence within which he commits fewer crimes. The buffer zone often exists for two main reasons: a perceived lack of anonymity and reduced number of targets. That is, while offenders often prefer to commit crimes in areas they are familiar with, they do not want to be in areas where they would be recognized (Rossmo, 2000). A burglar, for example, would prefer to steal from a stranger's home a few blocks away than risk being recognized while stealing from his next-door neighbor's home—even if he is more familiar with how to gain access into his neighbor's house. The stranger's house a few blocks away is still in an area familiar to the burglar, but the distance from his own home increases his anonymity and therefore lowers his risk of apprehension.

The number of potential targets increases with distance from a fixed point, such as the offender's residence. For example, if targets were randomly distributed throughout the environment, there would be twice as many targets available 1 mile away from the offender's residence than there would be one-half mile away. For this reason, offenders may not commit as many crimes close to home as they do a short distance away (Rossmo, 2000).

It is important to note that offenders do commit crimes within their buffer zone; however, there may be areas outside their buffer zone where they commit more crimes. The buffer zone represents an area of reduced activity, not an area of *no* criminal activity (Rossmo, 2000).

Geographic Profiling

Geographic profiling is a police investigation strategy that uses the locations in a connected crime series to narrow the search for likely suspects. A smaller search area can result in the apprehension of an offender faster and more efficiently, resulting in fewer victims and a savings in expended resources. In larger investigations, this cost savings can be quite large. Geographic profiling has now been used with success in many different types of criminal investigation (Rossmo, 1995).

Geographic profiling is based on three theories: Rational Choice Theory, Routine Activities Theory, and Crime Pattern Theory. These theoretical approaches, while examining crime differently, share the perspective that crime setting and opportunity are very important determinants as to why crime occurs at one particular location and not at another (Rossmo, 2000).

Geographic profiling is a decision-making tool that can help law enforcement solve cases of serial crime, but it does not solve crimes by itself. It is only through a confession, eyewitness testimony, and/or physical evidence that a crime can be solved and successfully prosecuted. The purpose of geographic profiling is to manage large amounts (sometime overwhelming amounts) of information and help focus limited resources on the most likely area of offender residence (Rossmo, 2000).

Geographic profiling is essentially a method that allows us to infer spatial characteristics of an offender from his crime patterns. For example, the offender's activity space is determined from the locations of the crime sites. Investigators, using this information, determine the target backcloth for the crimes, paths the offender is likely to be using, and other factors that may influence the crime pattern, such as offender hunting method (discussed later in this chapter), offender type, and land use in the area. From this information, sense can be made of the pattern from both subjective and objective perspectives (Rossmo, 1995).

Geographic profiling is typically applied to a **crime series**, a set of crimes believed to have been committed by the same offender. These crimes can be linked by physical evidence, offender description, or modus operandi. Essentially, characteristics about crimes in a series are similar in many ways, thus an inference can be made that they were committed by the same person(s). Identifying a crime series allows the crimes to be analyzed as a pattern rather than as isolated events. As each crime location gives an indicator of the offender's awareness space, more crime locations provide more information about the offender (Rossmo, 2006).

Hunting Methods

Criminals, especially predatory criminals, employ various **hunting methods** when selecting their victims. An offender's hunting method affects the spatial distribution of his crime sites, and any effort to predict the offender's residence must consider hunting style. There are criminals who set out specifically to find a victim, while others happen upon a victim while involved in other noncriminal activities (Rossmo, 2000). The various search and attack methods are discussed in the following paragraphs.

Offenders, when committing a crime, must first find a suitable target. Finding this target involves a search. Four types of search methods exist: *hunter, poacher, troller,* and *trapper*.

A *hunter* (also called "marauder" in the literature) is an offender who sets out from his home specifically to find a victim. A *poacher* (also called "commuter" in the literature) is an offender who also specifically sets out to find a victim, but his search is from a location other than his home, such as work or a recreation site. Poachers also can be offenders who commute to another city to commit their crimes. *Trollers* are offenders who are involved in their everyday activities when they opportunistically encounter a victim. *Trappers* are offenders who set up a situation in which victims come to them. This is usually done through an occupation, want ads, or the taking in of boarders (Rossmo, 2000).

There are three types of attack methods: *raptor*, *stalker*, and *ambusher*. A *raptor* is an offender who attacks the victim upon encounter. Most criminals use this attack method. A *stalker* is an offender who does not attack upon encounter but follows the victim away from the encounter point then attacks. An *ambusher* is an offender who attacks a victim that he has lured to a location he controls (Rossmo, 2000).

Investigative Strategies

An investigative strategy is any method used during the investigation of a crime that helps law enforcement identify the responsible offender. A variety of **investigative strategies** can be used after a geographic profile has been prepared.

Investigative strategies that can be used with geographic profiling include prioritizing records from the various computerized police files, such as arrest files, crime report files, and jail booking files. These files often include the offender's address, physical description, and modus operandi. Other databases may also be used in conjunction with a profile, such as parole, probation, and sex offender records. A profile used with this information could help in the search for the offender by prioritizing persons based on their geography (Rossmo, 2000).

A geographic profile can also be used to prioritize areas for directed police patrols or area canvasses. This strategy can be especially effective if the offender is operating during a narrow time period. Area canvassing might also include providing specific information to local area residents and neighborhood watch groups. The police may also want to use the profile to direct community mailings and/or conduct a media campaign (Rossmo, Laverty, & Moore, 2005).

Geographic profiles can be useful in homicide and missing person cases. In a missing person case where the victim is suspected to be dead, a profile can help determine the likely location of the body. Geographic profiles also have utility in suspected homicide cases where the body is missing because they prioritize areas to be searched based on information about the probable suspect. Location information about the suspect is analyzed to determine where the body might be. Likewise, a profile can help direct the search for a criminal fugitive by determining probable hiding places based on new crimes, sightings, telephone calls, and areas that are familiar to the fugitive (Rossmo, Laverty, & Moore, 2005).

Computerized Geographic Profiling

Geographic profilers can make use of advances in technology to determine the most probable location of an offender's residence. Computerized geographic profiling systems assign scores to areas based on offender movement, hunting behavior, and journey-to-crime distances. The scores are used to create a probability surface (jeopardy surface) that is displayed over a map of the crimes. The profile map (geoprofile) is then used to prioritize locations in the search for the offender. There are three main computerized geographic profiling systems, which are discussed in the following paragraphs.

The Rigel geographic profiling system, developed by Environmental Criminology Research Inc. (ECRI) of Vancouver, British Columbia, Canada, uses the Criminal Geographic Targeting algorithm invented by Dr. Kim Rossmo in 1991 to produce a probability map. Rigel integrates with various mapping programs to display the geoprofile over city streets (Rossmo, 1995, 2000). Rigel is available for purchase by law enforcement agencies that have personnel trained in its use. Training in the use of Rigel is currently offered at several universities and police departments internationally as part of the Geographic Profiling Analysis training program, discussed later (ECRI, 2008).

The Dragnet geographic profiling system, created by Dr. David Canter of the University of Liverpool, England, uses a negative exponential mathematical function to produce a probability map. Dragnet does not integrate with mapping programs or geographic information system (GIS). Dragnet is available for purchase from the University of Liverpool's Centre for Investigative Psychology. Users are not required to obtain training before downloading and using the system, but training in the use of the system may be obtained by contacting Dr. Canter directly (Canter, 2008).

The CrimeStat 3.3 spatial statistics program's journey-to-crime routine, created by Ned Levine & Associates of Houston, Texas, allows the use of any of five different mathematical functions to produce a geographic profile. Users also have the option of calibrating and using a model based on known offender behavior. Bryan Hill, coauthor of this text, has found that a journey-to-crime model calculated from local offenders to be the best routine in the profiling of unidentified offenders (B. Hill, personal communication, July 8, 2011). The profile produced by CrimeStat 3.3 can be exported as several different types of GIS data, including ArcMap Shapefiles, ArcMap Grids, and ASCII files. This program is free to download via the Internet thanks to a series of National Institute of Justice (NIJ) grants, which funded the original development of this program and continues to fund program updates. In May 2005, version 3 of this program was released (Levine, 2007). Several of the crime mapping exercises in this text utilize CrimeStat 3.3.

All of the current computerized geographic profiling systems work by applying a mathematical function over the area of the crimes to predict a likely search base for the offender within the area bounded by the crimes. Because most crimes are committed by hunters or offenders who have specifically set out from their residence to find a victim, the profile usually outlines the offender's home area (Rossmo, 2000). However, not all crimes are committed by hunters (see the previous discussion of criminal search methods). Researchers have questioned whether the current systems have applicability in other types of cases, specifically cases for which the offender does not live within the area bounded by the crimes (van der Kemp, 2005).

Law enforcement practitioners in the field of geographic profiling have found that the area a geographic profile prioritizes is the offender's **search base**. A search base is the location from which the offender consistently begins his search for new targets. For most offenders, their search base begins at their home, and this is the location that a geographic profile prioritizes. For other offenders, such as poachers, their search base is somewhere else. This could be a freeway exit ramp, street intersection in a target-rich neighborhood, or supply location (Velarde, 2008).

Geographic profiling may be used to locate the offender's search base, a location of investigative value. By tailoring investigative strategies to the offender type, a geographic profile can be used to locate the offender, even if he does not live in the area (Velarde, 2008). One successfully geoprofiled case in which the search base for the offender was not his home is detailed later in the chapter.

Training in Geographic Profiling

While some of the computerized geographic profiling systems do not require any training before their use, training in geographic profiling methodology is essential, according to Rossmo and Filer (2005), professional geographic profilers who authored "Analysis versus Guesswork: The Case for Professional Geographic Profiling." They warn that crime locations are just one part of the information used in the preparation of a geographic profile. The other information comes from factors such as offender type, site type, demographics, land use, location of arterial routes, hunting method, target backcloth, temporal patterns, and displacement. To ignore this information could reduce the accuracy of a profile, in some cases quite significantly. Rossmo and Filer (2005) stress the use of analysis based on training, experience, and research in the field rather than guesswork.

For CrimeStat users, NIJ has created a user workbook which is designed specifically for crime analysts and explains several of the different functions within the CrimeStat program. (This workbook is available as a free download at www.icpsr.umich.edu/CrimeStat/workbook .html.) The comprehensive workbook allows users to teach themselves the basics of program operation and also provides information on many of the routines contained within the program. Training in the use of CrimeStat is available from NIJ to a limited number of law enforcement students. However, the current 3-day CrimeStat training program provided by NIJ does not include training in the use of the journey-to-crime module, which is the routine used by CrimeStat to create a geographic profile (Mapping and Analysis for Public Safety, 2008). Other training is being offered online by the International Association of Crime Analysts (IACA) to their members at different times. (You can locate those courses via their website at www.iaca.net/training.asp.)

Formal training in geographic profiling is available through the Geographic Profiling Analysis (GPA) training program. This training program was originated to bring the methodology to local law enforcement agencies that are concerned with property crime (Weiss & Davis, 2004). The training, while open to anyone, is mainly taught to police detectives and analysts and involves classroom courses, work in a computer lab, and field evaluation/ mentorship. The GPA curriculum consists of two 1-week courses. The first week provides an overview of environmental criminological theories, the geography of crime, crime linkage, and the geographic profiling methodology. The second week is taught in a computer lab and provides instruction in the use of the Rigel geographic profiling system, developing a geo-graphic profile map, casework exercises, and report preparation (Velarde, 2004). As of 2011, approximately 600 people, representing 274 police agencies from 14 countries, had been trained in geographic profiling analysis (S. Church, personal communication, September 6, 2011).

■ Geographic Profiling Case Example One

The Chair Burglary case is a good example of how law enforcement can use geographic profiling to help find the offender who is responsible for a crime series.

For several years, the City of Irvine, California, experienced a high number of residen-tial burglaries, and it was suspected that a serial offender was active in the city. In years past, investigators and patrol officers from the Irvine Police Department had initiated surveillances, searched police databases of arrestees, and perused pawn shops, but they were unable to locate the offender or recover any of the stolen property, and the crimes continued. In early 2005, investigators decided to try another approach to the problem that involved searching for new evidence, crime forecasting, and geographic profiling (Rossmo & Velarde, 2008).

Upon reviewing the crimes, analysts decided they needed to identify which burglaries, if any, were linked. A preliminary analysis of all residential burglaries was conducted to deter-mine if a crime series existed. This analysis produced a list of 42 burglaries believed to be linked by modus operandi and target characteristics (see **Figure 4–2**). The linked burglaries

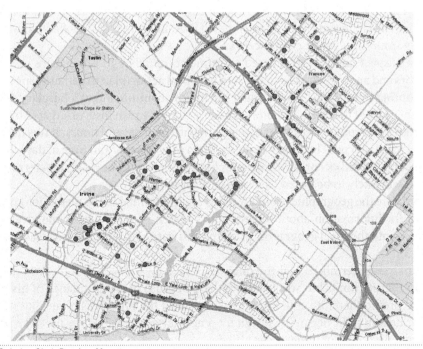

Figure 4–2 Irvine Chair Burglary Map

Source: Created with Microsoft MapPoint software.

were then used to determine offender patterns, such as a target preference, temporal and spatial consistencies, and specific modus operandi.

The analysis concluded that the offender had a consistent pattern of behavior. The targeted residences were in upscale but older neighborhoods. He preferred corner lot homes, particularly those with a greenbelt or park to the rear. Entry to the targeted house was always made at the back through an open window or door, a pried door, or a smashed window. Many of the windows on the homes were metal framed with only one pane of glass (many newer home windows are dual paned and/or framed in vinyl). This assisted the offender in the event that he had to break a window to gain entry. The offender consistently burglarized one neighborhood for about 6 months before moving to another neighborhood.

The offender often placed a lawn chair belonging to the home owner against the rear fence of the backyard. Based on footprints seen on the chair, it was believed the offender used the chair to make his escape over the fence after completing a burglary. The property stolen from the crimes was mostly cash and jewelry, items easily carried by the offender in pockets or a small bag. No fingerprints were recovered at any of the crime scenes. It became apparent to investigators that the offender was a professional burglar (Rossmo & Velarde, 2008).

Crime scene investigators from the Irvine Police Department had begun DNA swabbing at many residential burglaries (DNA swabbing involves running a cotton swab over surfaces that the offender may have touched). These swabs were retained for DNA analysis. In reviewing the evidence collected for the chair burglary series, it was found that DNA swabs were collected at 21 of the 42 crime scenes. In June 2005, these swabs were sent to the crime lab for analysis. The lab found that common male DNA, likely that of the offender, was present on samples from three of the crime scenes.

Now a suspect could be compared to crime scene DNA to see if there was a match. Investigators and analysts worked to develop a tactical action plan to gather suspects. Rather than attempting to find the Chair Burglar during the commission of a burglary, a very difficult task because of the offender's short exposure time, the plan instead targeted the burglar's search for new targets, a process that can take the offender several hours. It was decided that a temporal forecast would be used to predict when (day of week and time of day) the offender's next search would occur, and a geographic profile would be used to determine where that search was likely to be based (Rossmo & Velarde, 2008).

To complete the geographic profile, a crime analyst trained in the methodology analyzed the crimes for information about the offender's search process. The crime locations were then entered into the Rigel geographic profiling software, and a profile map was created (see **Figure 4–3**).

The analysis determined that the offender was likely a poacher, someone who did not live within the city limits but was traveling there because of an abundance of his preferred target. The profile therefore could not be used to find the offender's home, but it could be used to locate him as he began his search for a new target. Investigators used the profile for the strategic placement of undercover officers.

In September 2005, undercover officers began to gather suspect information from the peak area of the geographic profile during the times and dates predicted by the temporal

Figure 4–3 Geographic Profile of Irvine Chair Burglary

Source: Created with Microscoft MapPoint software.

forecast. This information consisted primarily of the license plate numbers from vehicles seen driving in the area. The license plate numbers were researched for driver information through the California Department of Motor Vehicles (Rossmo & Velarde, 2008).

Investigators planned to continue this process for 5 weeks, but as luck would have it, the offender's vehicle, a rental car, was in the group of license plates gathered the very first night of surveillance. A DNA sample from the suspect was submitted to the lab and was a positive match for that found at the crime scenes. Raymond Lopez, a 47-year-old exconvict from Los Angeles County, was arrested for the crimes. He later pled guilty and is now serving a 13-year state prison sentence (Rossmo & Velarde, 2008).

The Irvine Police Department received several awards for their work in solving this case, including the prestigious International Association of Chiefs of Police (IACP)/ChoicePoint Award for Excellence in Criminal Investigations (Rossmo & Velarde, 2008).

■ Geographic Profiling Case Example Two

While some offenders do not live in the area of their crimes, many do. The following is an example of how geographic profiling was used to literally lead investigators to a serial offender's front door.

The city of Glendale, California had several robberies attributed to the "Bad Hat Bandit," so dubbed by investigators because of the unusual brown Western style hat he wore during the robberies. There were three robberies linked to the same offender, and after the last robbery, the offender was observed leaving the crime scene in a red Ford truck (B. Hill, personal communication, July 8, 2011).

Based on information about the crimes, Glendale Police Department's investigating detective believed the offender lived locally and was familiar with the area where he was offending. Glendale's crime analyst, experienced in the use of GIS and knowledgeable in the analysis of serial crimes, believed that a geographic profile could be helpful in this particular case. After analyzing the crimes, the crime analyst created a journey-to-crime geographic profile for the series using data from the robberies and calibrating information from a dataset of known robbery offenders and their travel distances. This information was entered into CrimeStat's journey-to-crime module. The peak area of the geographic profile identified a small area of town that contained a few houses and one large trailer park (B. Hill, personal communication, July 8, 2011). A police database search of all known offenders and probationers was conducted, and the geographic profile was used to prioritize these persons by their home address. Approximately 50 known offenders were identified as living within the peak profile area; these persons were then prioritized based on how closely they matched the robbery offender's physical description including height, weight, and hair color. After prioritization, Glendale's crime analyst then browsed through recent booking and department of motor vehicle photos for each of the top 20 prioritized subjects to determine if their photo was a match for a bank surveillance photo of the robber. Five of the subjects from the list resembled surveillance photos of the robber, and all lived in the same trailer park identified within the peak part of the profile.

Glendale's investigating detective, Det. Mark Lankford, went to each matching person's mobile home at the trailer park, but he was unable to make contact with any of the subjects. The detective also did not see a red truck at any of the mobile homes. As the detective was leaving, he stopped at the trailer park office and showed the surveillance photos to the park manager. The trailer park manager immediately identified the images as that of a completely different subject who also lived in the trailer park, and the manager said, "You will know his trailer by the red truck outside," or words to that effect.

The detective went to that subject's home, knocked on the door, and the offender answered, wearing the same brown cowboy hat worn during the robberies. He simply said, "I was wondering how long it would be before you caught me," or words to that effect. The subject admitted to committing the robberies and was booked into jail.

The geographic profile in this case led detectives to the area of the offender's residence. Information gained about the offender from the crime scene, an analyst's knowledge and use of the CrimeStat program and geographic profiling, and detective legwork resulted in a violent serial offender being apprehended sooner rather than later.

While this report is only anecdotal, one of the authors of this book (Hill) has done research with approximately 50 different crime series for the City of Glendale. Twenty percent of the crime series data analyzed through a journey-to-crime function of CrimeStat 3.3 successfully identified the anchor point of the offender's home within a peak profile area.

In 40% of the cases, the offender's home was just outside the peak profile area of the journey-to-crime analyses. In the other 40% of the cases, the offender's reported home address was nowhere near the peak profile area. This indicates that in 20%–60% of the crime series that police departments investigate, they could help identify the offender, prioritize areas to canvass, or use the information to help surveillance units intercept an offender returning to the peak profile area after a current crime.

■ Conclusion

Offenders use their knowledge of an area, in the form of mental maps and awareness space, to find criminal opportunities or targets. Targets may not be evenly distributed through the environment; target availability varies by neighborhood. Crime patterns are driven by offender awareness space and the spatial availability of targets.

The commission of a crime often involves a crime trip for the offender. This crime trip, or journey to crime, typically starts at the offender's residence. Crime trips often show distance decay from the offender's residence; more trips occur to locations close to home, and fewer trips occur to locations far from home. Offenders typically have a buffer zone around their residence within which they are less likely to offend.

Geographic profiling is a law enforcement technique that helps find offenders based on the geography of their crimes. Based on Rational Choice, Routine Activities, and Crime Pattern Theories, geographic profiling uses knowledge about how criminals interact with their environment. The methodology takes into account offender awareness and activity space as well as information about target availability and criminal hunting methods. There are several different computerized geographic profiling systems available, and formal training in geographic profiling is important for profile accuracy. When properly applied in appropriate cases, geographic profiling can have significant investigative utility.

■ Chapter Glossary

Buffer zone   An area around an offender's anchor point(s) where he or she is less likely to commit a crime due to risk of being identified.

Crime series   A crime series is a set of crimes believed to have been committed by the same offender or offenders.

Distance decay   Distance decay refers to the decreasing probability of an offender traveling far from home to commit a crime.

Expected crime pattern   Expected patterns of crime at the aggregate level indicate areas in the city where crime is likely to occur.

Geographic profiling   Geographic profiling is a police investigation strategy that uses the locations in a connected crime series to narrow the search for likely suspects.

Hunting methods   Hunting methods include the various search and attack methods an offender uses to commit crime. There are four types of search methods: *hunter*, *poacher*, *troller*, and *trapper*.

Investigative strategies   An investigative strategy is any method used during the investigation of a crime that helps law enforcement identify the responsible offender.

Journey to crime   A journey-to-crime trip is the journey an offender travels when he or she commits a crime. Typically, journey to crime is measured from an offender's home to the location of the crime. However, the offender could also be traveling from another anchor point, such as his workplace.

Mental maps   Mental maps are cognitive images of the places we frequent, the routes to these places, and the areas we pass through.

Search base   A search base is the location from which the offender consistently begins his or her search for new targets.

Target backcloth   The distribution of targets in the environment.

■ Questions for Review

1. What are mental maps, and how are they related to offender decision making?

2. Explain the notion of *target backcloth* and how it explains when and where an offender may choose to commit a crime.

3. What is a *journey to crime*? What do we know about distances traveled by offenders?

4. How do the terms *distance decay* and *buffer zone* work together to explain the likelihood of an offender to commit crime within his neighborhood?

5. What computer programs are in existence to aid in geographic profiling?

6. What is a crime series? What factors can be used to link crimes in a series?

7. What are the four types of hunting methods offenders may use to commit a crime? Which method is most often used? Why?

8. What is an investigative strategy? Provide an example.

■ Online Resources

CrimeStat Chapter on Journey to Crime Estimation: www.icpsr.umich.edu/CRIMESTAT /files/CrimeStatChapter.10.pdf

Environmental Criminology Research, Inc.: www.ecricanada.com/

Forensic Psychology Page on Geographic Profiling: www.all-about-forensic-psychology .com/geographic-profiling.html

Geographic profiling Wikipedia page: http://en.wikipedia.org/wiki/Geographic_profiling

A Journey-to-Crime Meta-Analysis Paper: http://citation.allacademic.com/meta/p_mla_ apa_research_citation/0/3/2/3/4/p32344_index.html

The Juvenile Journey to Crime Paper: http://citation.allacademic.com/meta/p_mla_apa_ research_citation/0/3/3/7/2/p33729_index.html

Mapping Crime: Principle and Practice—Chapter 6, Geographic Profiling: www.ncjrs .gov/html/nij/mapping/ch6_1.html

National Institute of Justice article on Predicting a Criminal's Journey to Crime: www
.ojp.usdoj.gov/nij/journals/253/predicting.html

National Institute of Justice page on geographic profiling: www.ojp.usdoj.gov/nij/maps
/gp.htm

Ned Levine paper on modeling the journey to crime using the Crime Travel Demand
Model: www.ucl.ac.uk/scs/events/mapping-conf/conf-2010/downloads-2010/class3e
-levine.pdf

Problem-Oriented Policing page on Journey to Crime: www.popcenter.org/learning
/60steps/index.cfm?stepNum=16

Texas State University–San Marcos page on Geographic profiling: www.txstate.edu/gii
/geographic-profiling/overview.html

■ Recommended Reading

Levine, N. (2007). *Chapter 10 of the Manual for CrimeStat: A spatial statistics program for the analysis of crime incident locations (v. 3.3)*. Washington, DC: National Institute of Justice.
Rossmo, D. K. (2000). *Geographic profiling*. Boca Raton, FL: CRC Press.

■ References

Brantingham, P. L., & Brantingham, P. J. (1981). Notes on the geometry on crime. In P. J. Brantingham & P. L. Brantingham (Eds.), *Environmental criminology* (pp. 27–54). Beverly Hills, CA: Sage.
Brantingham, P. J., & Brantingham, P. L. (1984). *Patterns in crime*. New York: Macmillan.
Brantingham, P. L., & Brantingham, P. J. (1993). Environment, routine and situation: Toward a pattern theory of crime. In R. V. Clarke & M. Felson (Eds.), *Routine activity and rational choice* (pp. 259–294). New Brunswick, NJ: Transaction.
Canter, D. V. (2008). *Offender profiling training*. Retrieved from www.ia-ip.org/training/geographical -offender-profiling-2.html.
Canter, D. V., & Gregory, A. (1994). Identifying the residential location of rapists. *Journal of the Forensic Science Society, 34*, 169–175.
Clark, A. N. (1990). *The New Penguin dictionary of geography*. London: Penguin Books.
Environmental Criminology Research Inc. (ECRI). (2008). *Geographic profiling analyst training calendar*. Retrieved from www.ecricanada.com/geopro/ref_training.html.
Felson, M., & Clarke, R. V. (1998). *Opportunity makes the thief* (Crime Detection and Prevention Series, Paper 98. Police Research Group). London: Policing and Reducing Crime Unit, Home Office.
Jakle, J. A., Brunn, S., & Roseman, C. C. (1976). *Human spatial behavior: A social geography*. Prospect Heights, IL: Waveland Press.
Levine, N. (2007). *CrimeStat: A spatial statistics program for the analysis of crime incident locations (v. 3.3)*. Washington, DC: National Institute of Justice.
Mapping and Analysis for Public Safety. (2008). *CrimeStatIII for crime analysts*. Retrieved from www .nij.gov/topics/technology/maps/crimestat.htm.
Rossmo, D. K. (1995). Place, space, and police investigations: Hunting serial violent criminals. In J. E. Eck & D. A. Weisburd (Eds.), *Crime and place: Crime prevention studies* (Vol. 4, pp. 217–235). Monsey, NY: Criminal Justice Press.

Rossmo, D. K. (2000). *Geographic profiling.* Boca Raton, FL: CRC Press.

Rossmo, D. K. (2004). Geographic profiling. In Q. C. Thurman & J. Zhao (Eds.), *Contemporary policing: Controversies, challenges, and solutions* (pp. 274–284). Los Angeles: Roxbury.

Rossmo, D. K. (2006). Geographic profiling in cold case investigations. In R. Walton (Ed.), *Cold case homicide: Practical investigative techniques* (pp. 537–560). Boca Raton, FL: CRC Press.

Rossmo, D. K., & Filer, S. (2005). Analysis versus guesswork: The case for professional geographic profiling. *Blue Line Magazine, 17*(7), 24–25.

Rossmo, D. K., Laverty, I., & Moore, B. (2005). Geographic profiling for serial crime investigation. In F. Wang (Ed.), *Geographic information systems and crime analysis* (pp. 102–117). Hershey, PA: Idea Group.

Rossmo, D. K., & Velarde, L. (2008). Geographic profiling analysis: Principles, methods, and applications. In S. Chainey & S. Tompson (Eds.), *Crime mapping case studies: Practice and research* (pp. 35–43). Chichester, UK: John Wiley & Sons.

van der Kemp, J. J. (2005, September). *When to use, when not to use, that's the question.* Paper presented at the Crime Mapping Research Conference, Savannah, GA.

Velarde, L. (2004, April). *Applying geographic profiling to property crimes: The geographic profiling analyst program.* Paper presented at the Crime Mapping Research Conference, Boston.

Velarde, L. (2008, July). *Operational geographic profiling of poachers.* Paper presented at the National Institute of Justice Conference, Washington, DC.

Weiss, J., & Davis, M. (2004, December). Geographic profiling finds serial criminals. *Law and Order, 32*, 34–38.

Policing Models, CompStat, and Evidence-Based Practice

▶ LEARNING OBJECTIVES

This chapter highlights the different types of policing methodologies and philosophies that use analysis based on theory and crime mapping to guide them. The influences these different policing methodologies and philosophies have had on the role of crime analysis and crime mapping are enormous. There has been a gradual change within the field of law enforcement since the early 1990s to move away from reactive methods (responding to crime as it happens, often in an ad hoc basis) to proactively addressing crime problems by utilizing crime mapping and analysis to help inform and develop police strategies that "treat" problems long term. This chapter discusses the differences between various models of policing and how the CompStat process has influenced the use of crime mapping and analysis to further accountability and problem solving within law enforcement agencies. After studying this chapter, you should be able to:

- Identify and understand the SARA model.
- Summarize the differences between the major models and philosophies of modern policing.
- Identify and understand community-based or community-oriented policing.
- Describe how community policing and problem-oriented policing are similar and different.
- Identify the key elements of intelligence-led policing.
- Identify the key elements of predictive policing.
- Identify the seven guiding principles of data-driven approaches to crime and traffic safety (DDACTS).
- Explain what CompStat is and how it is used.

▶ **Key Terms**

CECAD
Community-Based or
   Community-Oriented
   Policing

CompStat
DDACTS
Intelligence Cycle

Predictive Analytics
   (or Predictive Policing)
Problem-Oriented Policing
SARA

■ Introduction

Depending on which text you select, the history of policing, complete with reform efforts and "new" models of policing, includes several different waves. Kelling and Moore (1988), for example, discuss the political era, the reform era, and the community policing era. In addition, some use the term *model* while others use the terms *philosophy*, *theory*, or even *strategy* to discuss the same thing. For example, Bayley (1999) examines "the development of modern police" through the lens of the development of the public police, specialized police, and professionalized police. Our intent here is neither to fully cover the history of policing, nor is it to add to the debate about whether something is a model or a philosophy; rather, our goal here is to provide you with enough background to allow for a deeper understanding of how police practice has evolved throughout history and how we got to the evidence-based model we are currently in today (regardless of what you might want to call it).

Although the roots of policing certainly start before this time period, for our purposes, let's start with what one many call "traditional policing." Traditional policing is generally thought to be rooted in the reform era. The reform era (typically includes the time period 1930–1980, although some texts identify roots of the reform era as early as the 1890s) gained prominence with the Wickersham Commission's report highlighting the political corruption and incompetence widely found throughout law enforcement during the "spoils era." August Vollmer and O. W. Wilson are strongly associated with the reform movement (often called "The Progressive Movement") and called for police to enhance their accountability to the public, to ensure equality in their policing by not targeting (or favoring) select groups, and to separate as much as possible the politics from administration in law enforcement (Conser, Paynich, & Gingerich; 2013; Stevens, 2009).

Throughout this era, the police took on the role of professional crime fighter and in this role, combined with technological advances (the radio, telephone, and automobile), police became physically and socially isolated from the communities they served. This isolation, combined with escalating crime and very public and bloody conflicts between the police and the public at civil rights and anti-Vietnam demonstrations, created a crevasse of distrust between the public and the police. The public lacked both the trust and the confidence in the police to do their jobs (both effectively and fairly), which spurred the need for police to step outside of the role as "experts" in crime fighting and invite the communities they served to participate in the coproduction of law enforcement.

The term *community policing* (also frequently called **community-based or community-oriented policing**) appeared somewhere between the late 1960s through early 1980s when there was concern about rising crime rates and the national civil rights movement was in full force. In addition to a shift in policing philosophy, the community policing movement came with federal funds to implement a variety of programs that were geared toward strengthening the relationships between police departments and the communities they served and more proactively addressing and solving crime problems. This impacted police in every aspect—including recruitment and hiring practices, training, and methods of policing on a daily basis. This of course led to demands that more money be put into research and policy development. Citizens were also demanding more police interaction in their neighborhoods, improved relations with police, tolerance for diversity, and controls on unethical police practices such as discrimination. The federal government allocated funds for research that included two key projects relevant to our discussion:

1. Kansas City Preventative Patrol Study (carried out between 1972 and 1973)
2. Rand Corporation Criminal Investigation Study (using data spanning from 1970–1973)

First, the Kansas City Patrol Experiment examined the impact of traditional routine preventative patrol using an experimental design where some areas of the city received an excessive amount of patrol, some areas received the same amount of patrol, and some areas received no patrol (although police officers did respond to calls for service emanating from these areas). Although much discussion and debate about this experiment has led to many important findings, the biggest impact of this research was to discredit the long-held belief that routine patrol was an effective method of preventing crime.

The findings do not prove per se that a highly visible police presence has no impact on crime in selected circumstances. What they do suggest, however, is that routine preventive patrol in marked police cars has little value in preventing crime or making citizens feel safe. The overall implication is that resources ordinarily allocated to preventive patrol could safely be devoted to other, perhaps more productive, crime-control strategies. More specifically, the results indicate that police deployment strategies could be based on targeted crime prevention and service goals rather than on routine preventive patrol (Kelling, Pate, Dieckman, & Brown, 1974).

The Rand Corporation Criminal Investigations Study (Greenwood & Petersilia, 1975, pp. v–vii) examined police practices in investigating and solving crimes. The major findings of this study include:

- Differences in investigative training, staffing, workload, and procedures appear to have no appreciable effect on crime, arrest, or clearance rates.
- Substantially more than half of all serious reported crimes receive no more than superficial attention from investigators.
- For cases that are solved (i.e., a suspect is identified), an investigator spends more time in post-clearance processing than he does in identifying the perpetrator.
- The single most important determinant of whether or not a case will be solved is the information the victim supplies to the immediately responding patrol officer. If information that uniquely identifies the perpetrator is not presented at the time the crime is reported, the perpetrator, by and large, will not be subsequently identified.

These studies showed that police were limited in their ability to impact crime levels and this resulted, at least in part, in more interest in how citizens could work with police to solve local crime problems. In addition, it spurred a plethora of research on community-oriented methods such as foot patrols and neighborhood watch groups and other community-centric issues in law enforcement.

Community-based policing broadened the police role from just responding to calls for service to being proactive in problem solving and working with the community through partnerships to identify local needs and issues that could be addressed together. Core elements to the community-based policing model included:

- Community partnerships
- Problem solving
- Organizational transformations

These core elements are crucial to understanding the evidence-based era that we are currently in as well as how crime analysis and mapping are utilized to develop, implement, and evaluate problem-solving efforts of the police (and the community).

Community Partnerships

Community partnerships include multidisciplinary collaborations with community organizations, other city departments and government agencies, nonprofit agencies, businesses, and the media. These partnerships are often established to target specific problems within neighborhoods. This might include the police identifying a "crack house" in the neighborhood in response to tips from the neighborhood block watch group. The police might then discover (by working with various city organizations and businesses) that the house is actually a foreclosure and work with the listed bank to board it up and secure it. If the problem worsens, police may get the city housing authority to work through the paperwork to get the house demolished. The point is to work collaboratively with people and organizations outside of law enforcement to creatively solve crime-related problems.

Problem Solving

There are four basic steps to problem solving under the community-based policing methodology. This process is often called the **SARA** model. The SARA model was developed by the Community Policing Consortium, International Association of Chiefs of Police (IACP), National Organization of Black Law Enforcement Executives (NOBLE), National Sheriffs' Association (NSA), Police Executive Research Forum (PERF), and the Police Foundation. SARA stands for:

- *Scanning*: Identifying crime problems
- *Analysis*: Identifying causes of crime problems
- *Response*: Developing and implementing strategies to address crime problems
- *Assessment*: Evaluating the effectiveness of the response(s) (Strategies deemed effective are continued. Less effective strategies are retooled or discontinued.)

This is, in reality, the scientific method at work within the crime analysis and law enforcement agency. In crime analysis, a similar acronym used is **CECAD** (collection, evaluation, collation, analysis, dissemination; see **Figure 5–1**). CECAD comprises five of the seven steps in the intelligence cycle (Federal Bureau of Investigation, 2012). Essentially, the **intelligence cycle** outlines the key steps in identifying, collecting, evaluating, and disseminating information that can be used to combat crime. If you look at this with an analyst's eye you can see that in collecting and collating information, information is very similar to the scanning step in the SARA model. Basically, analysts here are observing and collecting information they will use in identifying and defining a problem. Analysis of course is present in both acronyms.

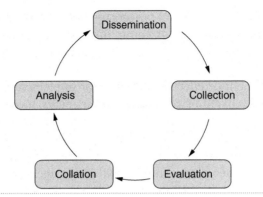

Figure 5–1 Intelligence Cycle

Source: Ratcliffe, J. (2002). Intelligence-led policing and the problems of turning rhetoric into practice. *Policing and Society* 2(1), 53–66. NSW Police Service, 1999, The Intelligence-Based Policing Development Program, p. 39. Reprinted by permission of the publisher (Taylor & Francis Ltd, www.tandf.co.uk/journal). Courtesy of Professor Jerry Ratcliffe.

During this stage, causes of a problem are identified and the combined resources held by law enforcement and other entities are examined in developing a suitable response. Then, we implement our plan during the response phase. Once we have employed our targeted plan for solving the crime issue at hand, we then assess or evaluate the success of that project and what we did.

An emphasis on problem solving under community-oriented policing is crucial to both crime reduction and community satisfaction. To work collaboratively with people and organizations outside of law enforcement to effectively (as well as efficiently and equitably) solve problems, police departments must be transformed to accomplish this. And as you will see throughout the remainder of this chapter, organizational change can be a challenge, but is necessary for successful problem solving and thus crime reduction.

The last phase of the intelligence cycle is dissemination. It is important to the field of crime analysis that we get our work out there. There are a variety of venues in which to do this: presenting results at regional or national conferences, such as the International Association of Crime Analysts (IACA) or the National Institute of Justice MAPS conferences, is a common forum for disseminating research. In addition, you may submit a research paper for publication in a variety of academic journals. There are multiple avenues of dissemination. The point is to get your results out there so that other analysts and departments can benefit from your work and perhaps try out similar strategies to address their own crime problems.

Organizational Transformations

There may be many organizational transformations that need to occur within a police department before the organization can effectively work with the community to solve problems. Depending on which agency you examine, community policing might be implemented in a variety of ways. For some, simply hiring or identifying a community policing officer charged with communicating with the community is defined as community policing. For others, creating a specialized unit with a team of officers to work with residents and business own-ers is considered community policing. Or, community policing as a philosophy or operating model may be engrained deeply at every level of the department, informing much of daily operations and strategic planning.

While the most efficient or effective structure for implementing community policing may be up for debate and is likely different across departments, there are several basic organ-izational changes that will likely need to occur. These can include organizational shifts in assignments to better cover the issues identified during the SARA or the CECAD process. Leadership within the organization must also be designated so that planning and policies are developed to enhance the communication within the agency and the transparency to handle issues without bureaucracy. Units may need to be despecialized and geographically distributed in the areas that require more manpower and resources. Data and information must be accurate and accessible to line-level officers who are now the problem solvers on the street within the agency. And because problem solving is a critical component of com-munity policing, recruitment and hiring of officers with the skills and abilities to competently deal with the public and address problems is paramount. In addition, training and evaluation techniques must be updated to reflect current practice.

■ Problem-Oriented Policing

Problem-oriented policing and community-based policing are very similar and are sometimes thought to be the same. Most literature places problem-oriented policing as a component of community policing because problem solving is a key component of community-oriented policing. Generally attributed to Herman Goldstein (1979, 1990), the main premise of problem-oriented policing is that police should focus their efforts more on problems than incidents. Some argue that problem-oriented policing is not a "new" venture:

> The view that problem-oriented policing represents a revolution is not enthusiastically accepted by everyone. There are officers who convincingly argue (sometimes in aggrieved tones) that "problem-oriented" is simply a new label for old police wine in a more fashionable bottle (Toch & Grant, 2005, p. 13).

There are, however, some subtle differences, as shown in **Table 5–1**. Again, our goal is not to join the debate about subtle definitional or operational differences across various models or strategies of policing, but to give you a sense of different ways of approaching problem solving and to emphasize that collecting and using data to inform how a strategy is developed, implemented, and evaluated are vital to the success of any police effort.

Cordner and Scarborough (2007) describe problem-oriented policing best:

> Simply put, problem-oriented policing (POP) posits that police should focus more attention on *problems,* as opposed to *incidents.* Problems may be recognizable as collections of incidents related in some way . . . or as underlying conditions that give rise to incidents, crimes, disorder, and other substantive community issues that people expect police to handle. By focusing more on problems than on incidents, police can address causes rather than mere symptoms and, consequently, have a greater impact (pp. 397–398).

TABLE 5-1 Problem-Oriented and Community-Oriented Policing

Principle	Problem-Oriented Policing	Community-Oriented Policing
Primary emphasis	Substantive social problems within police mandate	Engaging the community in the policing process
When police and community collaborate	Determined on a problem-by-problem basis	Always or nearly always
Emphasis on problem analysis	Highest priority given to thorough analysis	Encouraged, but less important than community collaboration
Preference for responses	Strong preference that alternatives to criminal law enforcement be explored	Preference for collaborative responses with community
Role for police in organizing and mobilizing community	Advocated only if warranted within the context of the specific problem being addressed	Emphasizes strong role for police
Importance of geographic decentralization of police and continuity of officer assignment to community	Preferred, but not essential	Essential
Degree to which police share decision-making authority with community	Strongly encourages input from community while preserving ultimate decision-making authority to police	Emphasizes sharing decision-making authority with community
Emphasis on officer skills	Emphasizes intellectual and analytical skills	Emphasizes interpersonal skills
View of the role or mandate of police	Encourages broad, but not unlimited role for police, stresses limited capacities of police, and guards against creating unrealistic expectations of police	Encourages expansive role for police to achieve ambitious social objectives

Source: Scott, M. (2000). Problem-oriented policing: Reflections on the first 20 years. Washington, DC: U.S. Department of Justice, Office of Community Oriented Policing Services.

The key here is that problem-oriented policing is much more focused on problem-solving efforts within the department using outside resources where needed, and not as much on creating permanent community partnerships (as in community-oriented policing). Problem-oriented policing is driven by the problem and can be either initiated or implemented top down or bottom up based on the needs and nature of the problem itself.

Problem-oriented policing, then, is a focused, proactive approach designed to attack the root causes of crime rather than just crime itself. Hill (2003) argues that police departments are very good at the SAR stages but fail in the A (assessment) stage. In addition, analysis is always difficult for police officers and police supervisors. Focusing on the "problem" rather than the just the frequently reported incidents can be a hard nut to crack without good crime analysis. Clarke (2004), in his review of several hundred applications that were submitted for the Herman Goldstein Award for excellence in Problem-Oriented Policing, found that:

> ...a majority of police agencies did not fully use a POP approach. For example, "officers frequently fail to specify the problems they are addressing. They make this mistake in one of two ways: either they undertake a project that is too small to fit the definition of problem-oriented policing," or they select an issue that is too big of a problem for POP to tackle (p. 18).

Clarke (2004, p. 20) offers some of the more common limitations of problem-oriented policing ventures including:

- Police report reductions in calls for service or arrests without relating the results to specific actions taken.
- Police consider assessment only as an afterthought, rather than building it into the original outline for the entire project.
- Police fail to present any control data.
- On the rare occasion that control data are presented, police fail to ensure that the control is adequate.
- Police fail to study displacement.

Utilizing geographic information systems (GIS) can improve officers' ability to correctly identify and define the problem(s) at hand and assess the effectiveness of their responses. Comprehensive and conscientious mapping and analysis can help agencies be more effective in their problem-solving efforts and avoid some of the pitfalls identified earlier. Sidebottom, Tilley, and Eck (2012) suggest that borrowing from the medical realm and adapting from the surgical safety and other checklists to create a problem-oriented policing checklist may aid in addressing the most common failures in problem-oriented policing ventures. **Table 5–2** presents Sidebottom et al.'s proposed checklist for addressing problems during the implementation of problem-oriented policing.

■ Intelligence-Led Policing

Intelligence-led policing was developed in the United Kingdom and there the tenets of its use were experimented with long before it became popular in the United States. With the terrorist attacks on the United States on September 11, 2001, the need for better data-gathering and information sharing was imperative, and the necessity for developing "intelligence" from the disparate databases came to be a major priority. Intelligence-led policing is often misunderstood and many agencies profess to be using this methodology in their day-to-day activities. However, what they are actually doing is using an intelligence analyst to apply information and knowledge to substantiate evidence, timelines, and other factors to successfully prosecute a case against an individual or a group of individuals (Ratcliffe, 2008). Ratcliffe points out that the term is often thought to define itself so formal definitions are few and

TABLE 5-2 Intelligence-Led Policing Model: Questions to Ask Yourself

Scanning

1. Have relevant data been examined to establish the extent of the alleged problem?
2. Have relevant data been examined to establish the seriousness of the alleged problem?
3. Does the problem meet the CHEERS (Community, Harmful, Expectation, Events, Recurring, and Similarity) criteria? (Center for Problem-Oriented Policing, 2013)

Analysis

4. Has the problem been analyzed prior to the development of a response?
5. Has the analysis focused on potential pinch-points for situational measures, using all three sides of the problem-analysis triangle?
6. Has the analysis assessed crime distribution: whether the identified problem concentrates among a small group of relevant units (people, places, facilities)?
7. Have relevant experts on the problem been consulted during analysis?

Response

8. Does the response follow from the analysis?
9. Have related preventative responses been critiqued with respect to their application to the identified problem and context?
10. Have the most important aspects of the problem and its harm been addressed in the response?
11. Does the proposed response activate one or more mechanisms (risk-increase, effort-increase, reward-decrease, provocation-decrease, rule-reminder) relevant to the behavior of those whose actions comprise the problem?

Assessment

12. Is the assessment focused on the intended outcome of the response: to reduce, remove, or ameliorate the effects of the problem?
13. Has the assessment attempted to measure offender adaptation, including displacement and diffusion of benefits?
14. Has the assessment documented whether the response was implemented as planned? Have any in-project modifications been recorded?
15. Does the evaluation design explicitly address potential threats to internal validity?
16. Have findings from the evaluation been disseminated to improve future evidence-based problem solving?

far between. Citing NCIS (2000), Ratcliffe (2003, p. 2) identifies four key components to intelligence-led policing:

- Targeting offenders (especially the targeting of active criminals through overt and covert means)
- The management of crime and disorder hotspots
- The investigation of linked series of crimes and incidents
- The application of preventative measures, including working with local partnerships to reduce crime and disorder

As you can see, the importance of community partnerships, the use of data and information to inform police efforts, and the emphasis on problem solving are evident in intelligence-led policing. The general keys to successful implementation of intelligence-led policing are enthusiastic leadership that promotes the concept throughout the department, a strategy for proactive policing, an integrated intelligence structure so that the analysts have the right data and are the hub of the activities, performance measures to determine the effectiveness of the process, and effective partnerships with other local agencies and groups (Ratcliffe, 2008).

A simple demonstration of intelligence-led policing might be when an analyst determines there is a hotspot of burglary activity through analysis of crime *data* within a neighborhood. The analyst provides the *information* to the property detectives and patrol officers, and further information comes back indicating that a known burglar has recently been released from a juvenile facility and that he is now living with his grandmother at a residence in the affected neighborhood. The detectives develop a plan to address the issue and respond to the problem identified, which includes surveillance or other activities to track the suspected burglar. They also identify several businesses and homes in the area that could use crime prevention through environmental design (CPTED) reviews and include that in their plan of response to this problem. We now have actionable knowledge or "intelligence" related to this issue. Intelligence-led policing takes all of the data a police department has, analysts then churn it into information, and then, through interactive dialogs and strong command structure, information is transformed into an organized response strategy based on additional information and knowledge from the field, investigators, or other units who may provide valuable input concerning the problem. This collation of efforts becomes actionable intelligence that can then be evaluated. A strong emphasis on identification of and enforcement of persons responsible for crime through the intelligence process is one key element. In intelligence-led policing, the information guides the response(s).

■ Data-Driven Approaches to Crime and Traffic Safety (DDACTS)

DDACTS is a fairly new policing philosophy that makes the assumption that persons in the United States are very mobile (using vehicles to get them back and forth to their destinations). Criminals also travel through the same venue and are often passing through intersections within cities on their way to commit crimes (recall Crime Pattern Theory). "Drawing on the deterrent value of highly visible traffic enforcement and the knowledge that crimes often involve motor vehicles, the goal of DDACTS is to reduce crime, crashes, and traffic violations across the country" (National Institute of Justice, 2010).

A program developed by the National Highway Traffic Safety Administration (NHTSA) with support by several other federal agencies, DDACTS is a model of policing that allows law enforcement to consider the crime and traffic issues that are most important to reduce the most amount of *social harm* to the public. The model focuses on collaboration with law enforcement, community members, and organizations to reinforce the crucial role that partnerships play in reducing social harm. Its goal is to make officers more "highly visible" in hotspots and reduce crime and traffic issues. There are seven guiding principles of the DDACTS model of policing:

- Partnerships and stakeholder participation
- Data collection
- Data analysis
- Strategic operations planning
- Information sharing and outreach
- Monitoring, evaluation, and adjustments
- Outcomes

By now, you should be recognizing that many of the common ingredients in DDACTS are found in other policing strategies discussed in this chapter: partnerships, data collection and analysis, strategic planning based on intelligence, and evaluation.

DDACTS is geared toward finding areas that are high in crime and traffic issues and then applying multiple resources to that problem area, including those of partnerships and other stakeholders. A strategic plan is put into place that includes information and outreach goals or outcomes, and how the response will be monitored and evaluated. A strong emphasis on dedicated analysts and analytical processes to determine which areas should receive the focus of the plan is a large part of the DDACTS model. This model of policing is structured top down, as the police management and analysis of the plan directs the activities of the department and the line-level officers.

■ Predictive Analytics or Predictive Policing

Predictive analytics is a new term that is being seen on the forefront of policing methodologies and philosophies. There is much argument about what this really means with respect to law enforcement; however, the business community has been using predictive analytics for a long time to develop marketing trends by watching what we buy, and redirecting their inventory based on predictions about what we may want to buy in the future given any set of conditions. For example, Pearsall (2010) writes that Walmart, through predictive analytics, has discovered that the three most purchased items after the forecast of a major weather event are duct tape, bottled water, and strawberry pop tarts. Predictive analytics is the process of using data mining, statistical techniques, and possibly game theory to predict where crime will be so that the police can be there to prevent it. Pearsall (2010) says that "Predictive policing, in essence, is taking data from disparate sources, analyzing them, and then using the results to anticipate, prevent, and respond more effectively to future crime" (para 5). **Predictive policing** borrows components from successful models and strategies of policing, including community-oriented policing, problem-oriented policing, intelligence-led policing, and evidence-based policing (Pearsall, 2010).

Due to the demand for more sophisticated types of analyses by predictive policing, regression analysis and other more technologically enhanced endeavors to predict future crimes have recently been developed and utilized across many law enforcement agencies in the United States. Shown in **Figure 5–2**, Risk Terrain Modeling (RTM), developed by

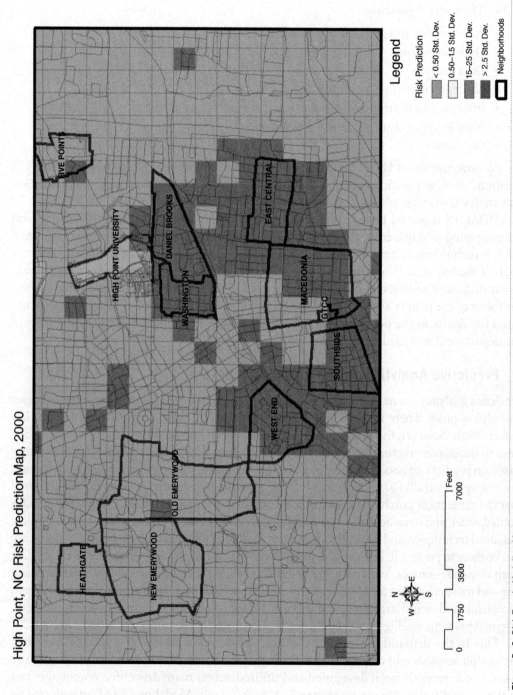

Figure 5–2 Risk Terrain Modeling Map

Dr. Leslie Kennedy and Dr. Joel Caplan at Rutgers University, seeks to combine those factors most predictive of future crime in ways that will identify future and emerging areas of concern.

This GIS modeling technique could be considered predictive policing in that it uses multiple GIS layers of factors correlated with past crime to determine a geographic area where there is a higher risk for new crimes. This can be used to determine which areas in an entire city are at higher risk for burglaries, for instance, based on the number of households by census block, vacant homes, locations where burglaries have already occurred, and perhaps a spatial trend between two recent time periods to show where burglaries have been increasing between the two time periods. These are all collected together and manipulated in GIS software to develop one surface where risk can be separated into low and high categories. The key is to find noncrime risk factors that correlate well to the presence of crime to build a model that will predict crime without the need for knowing where past crime occurred (as is done with traditional hotspot mapping). Resources can then be directed at those areas, information can be gathered about persons living in these areas that could be the source of the problems, and a plan can be developed to then address those problems with the resources available. Alternatively, we can use RTM in an intelligence-led policing model and ask the question, "If I did not have sufficient police resources to fix this problem, what could I do here with the community and other resources to fix this problem?" The risk terrain process is becoming more popular in many agencies.

Another predictive analytics technique we see is tactical predictions such as the probability grid method. This method uses multiple statistical and others GIS layers that the analyst feels may help understand the directionality, frequency, and target selection of the criminal and predict where the offender may strike again. Very similar to the risk terrain model approach, this model of tactical prediction can also be developed as a raster risk terrain, but is inherently a vector process. The idea is that we combine the area where the offender has hit in the past, the hotspots of similar targets, and perhaps other attributes such as closeness to a freeway, path, or direction they have taken in the current series of events. There may be other factors specific to the crime series we are predicting that we want to use such as entertainment venues and percentage of census blocks with persons 65 years or older. The final result is a combination of all of these factors into one map, as shown in **Figure 5–3**.

There are also many more sophisticated predictive analytics like the game SimCity—along with data mining and game theory applied that are currently being researched in police departments across the nation. The most energetic work is being done at Simon Fraser University by Drs. Paul and Patricia Brantingham. They call their work with artificial intelligence "computational criminology" or CCI. This process models everyday life and there are what they call agents in the system that interact. Each agent can be assigned specific traits (Brantingham, 2011). Some can have tendencies to crime and others may not. Some may be police officers and other judges, bailiffs, or whatever else we might find in society today (www.sfu.ca/icurs/research-areas.html).

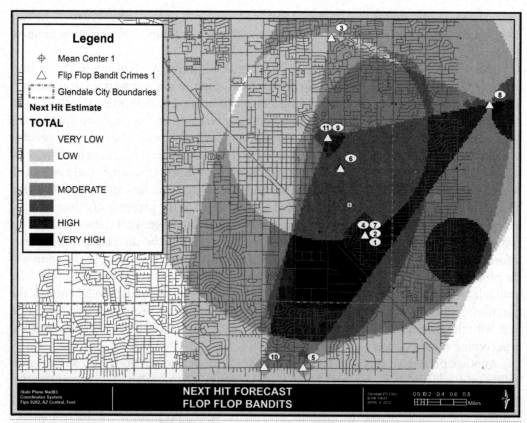

Figure 5–3 Probability Grid Method (PGM) Map

Predictive policing then is focused on top-down supervision and direction to problems identified by the crime/intelligence analysts based on sophisticated computer models, statistical techniques, or processes that direct police to problem areas to prevent future crime.

■ CompStat

CompStat, or computerized statistics, became popular after its huge successes in reducing crime when used by the New York City Police Department in the late 1990s. This is a process and a philosophy of sorts that stresses accountability and the joint participation of most units within the police department in regular meetings to discuss crime problems. These are formal problem-solving sessions where a strong command person will direct the meetings, ask questions, and work through problems with the other units in attendance to direct the proper resources to those problems. There are many variations across the United States and variation in the degree of accountability required of the attendees to these meetings.

These meetings typically involve a crime analyst generating a multitude of reports, making sure that the mapping software and data are working prior to a meeting, and that the data or problem area being discussed is available for live broadcast during the meeting. Staff usually goes over the hotspot areas and the crimes that have occurred within the last 28 days, week, month, or other period that is applicable to the analysis done for the meeting. The attendees may have to answer questions about what they are doing about a particular problem, or be asked for resources to assist another unit in working on a problem. Oftentimes, these meetings will also serve to provide a recap of crime and calls for service counts for the current year, or measure goal achievement for the police department. CompStat can actually be used as a tool with any of the other police methodologies mentioned in this chapter. For the DDACTS model, accountability and measurement of what an agency is doing in a DDACTS area could be discussed and evaluated in a CompStat meeting, for instance.

■ Conclusion

As you can see, the philosophies of policing can be varied and have shifted in society over time. They may also differ in many ways from one methodology to another. There are still some common threads between each of these different philosophies. Good analysis is a major component of each and every one of them. From the sophisticated analysis methods in predictive policing to the simpler officer as the problem solver under community-based policing, *analysis always has a key role*. Whether you are an analyst working in an office or an officer in the field, you both need to know the key theories related to crime and how they can play a part in your analysis effort for the problems you are identifying. In addition, maps and geographic analysis have played a huge part in many law enforcement agencies to assist with comprehensive analysis of areas, whether in identifying problem areas or making predictions of future crime. Each of these methods of policing has its weaknesses and strengths, but all of them are dependent on support throughout the ranks of the police department, good analysis, accountability, and planned responses to problems. Each method also strongly emphasizes the need to evaluate what happened when the law enforcement agency put its plan into place, but also to evaluate what the agency did while implementing the plan. We always need to measure not only whether or not crime went up or down in the target area, but also whether or not we completed all of our tactical responses in that area as planned. Without knowing if we did all of our plans properly, any reduction in crime cannot be adequately ascribed to the methods and tactics we employed. **Figure 5-4** is a great visual for understanding how many of the models, strategies, and philosophies discussed in this chapter work in concert to address problems. Through community- and problem-oriented policing, the careful and thoughtful development of collaborative responses to crimes, and the careful implementation and assessment of those responses is what good policing is all about. And a crime analyst plays a pivotal and critical role from beginning to end.

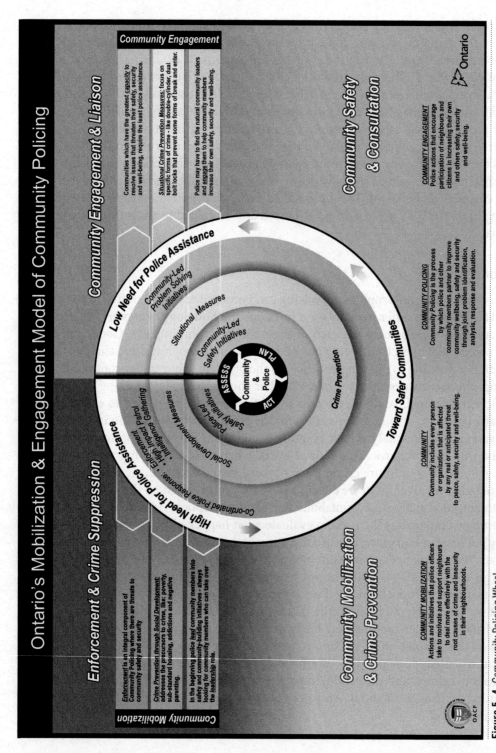

Figure 5–4 Community Policing Wheel

Source: Courtesy of Ontario Association of Chiefs of Police.

■ Chapter Glossary

CECAD   Collection, evaluation, collation, analysis, dissemination—steps in the intelligence cycle.

Community-based or **community-oriented policing**   A philosophy of policing that includes a stronger collaboration between law enforcement to both identify and address community crime problems.

CompStat   Short for computerized statistics. A process and a philosophy of sorts that stresses accountability and the joint participation of most units within the police department in regular meetings to discuss crime problems.

DDACTS   Data Driven Approaches to Crime and Traffic Safety, which is a concept derived around seven guiding principles, including partnerships and stakeholder participation; data collection; data analysis; strategic operations planning; information sharing and outreach; monitoring, evaluations and adjustments; and assessing outcomes.

Intelligence cycle   The process of turning unrefined data into usable intelligence that informs policy and practice.

Predictive analytics (or **predictive policing**)   These are analyses that may utilize risk analysis methods and tools found in the business world and apply them to police work as well as other empirical research and standardized methods to predict future events, forecast elements within an investigation or investigative strategy, or predictive tools and data that can be used based within valid theory to allow police to be at the right place, at the right time, to prevent crime.

Problem-oriented policing   A focused, proactive approach designed to attack the root causes of crime rather than just crime itself.

SARA   Four step process for addressing crime problems. The four steps include scanning, analysis, response, and assessment.

■ Questions for Review

1. What are several similarities of each of the policing philosophies covered in this chapter?
2. Explain what DDACTS is. How does it differ from SARA model policing? How are they similar?
3. What is CompStat and how can it be applied to any of the policing philosophies?
4. Which philosophies are driven by a management-down approach and which are driven from the bottom up (officer initiates)?
5. What is predictive analytics? Provide an example of how that would be used in law enforcement, and for what purpose.
6. Which of the philosophies discussed in this chapter stress traffic issues as important in determining police responses? Why is this philosophy important to both traffic and crime?
7. What does POP stand for?

8. Give an example of the way that intelligence-led policing might be employed in a law enforcement agency.

■ Online Resources

Center for Problem-Oriented Policing (POP): www.popcenter.org/

Community Oriented Policing (COPS) Office: www.cops.usdoj.gov/default.asp?item=36

CompStat on Wikipedia: http://en.wikipedia.org/wiki/CompStat

Data-Driven Approaches to Crime and Traffic Safety: www.ddacts.com

Department of Justice Blog on Predictive Policing: http://blogs.usdoj.gov/blog/archives /385

Dr. Jerry Ratcliffe's website: http://jratcliffe.net/research/ilp.htm

Harvard Kennedy School, Program in Criminal Justice Policy and Management: www .hks.harvard.edu/programs/criminaljustice/research-publications/executive-sessions /past-executive-sessions/old-executive-session-perspectives-on-policing-1985-1991

Police Chief's Magazine, Article on Intelligence-Led Policing: www.policechiefmagazine .org/magazine/index.cfm?fuseaction=display_arch&article_id=1942&issue_ id=112009

Police Foundation, CompStat in practice: An in-depth analysis of three cities: www .policefoundation.org/content/compstat-practice-depth-analysis-three-cities

Risk Terrain Mapping, Rutgers University: www.rutgerscps.org/rtm/

Smart Policing Initiative: www.smartpolicinginitiative.com/

U.S. Department of Justice, Intelligent-Led Policing: www.ncjrs.gov/pdffiles1/bja/210681 .pdf

■ Recommended Reading

Braga, A. (2008). *Problem-oriented policing and crime prevention* (2nd ed.). Monsey, NY: Criminal Justice Press.

Ratcliffe, J. H. (2002). Intelligence-led policing and the problems of turning rhetoric into practice. *Policing and Society, 12*(1), 53–66.

Ratcliffe, J. H. (2008). *Intelligence-led policing.* Cullompton, UK: Willan Publishing

Weisburd, D., & Braga, A. A. (Eds.). (2007). *Police Innovation: Contrasting perspectives.* Cambridge, UK: Cambridge University Press.

■ References

Bayley, D. (1999). The development of modern police. In L. Gaines & G. Cordner's (Eds.), *Police perspectives: An anthology.* Cary, NC: Roxbury Publishing Company.

Brantingham, P. L. (2011, September 12–14). *Computational criminology, EISIC* (p. 3). Athens, Greece: European Intelligence and Security Informatics Conference.

Center for Problem-Oriented Policing. (2013). Analysis for problem solvers in 60 small steps: Use the CHEERS test when defining problems. Retrieved from www.popcenter.org/learning/60steps/index.cfm?stepNum=14.

Clarke, R. V. (2004). Defining police strategies: Problem-solving, problem-oriented policing, and community-oriented policing. In Q. Thurman & J. Zhao (Eds.), *Contemporary policing: Controversies, challenges, and solutions.* Cary, NC: Roxbury Publishing Company.

Conser, J., Paynich, R., & Gingerich, T. (2013). *Law enforcement in the United States* (3rd ed.). Burlington, MA: Jones & Bartlett Learning.

Cordner, G. W., & Scarborough, K. E. (2007). *Police administration.* Newark, NJ: Lexis Nexis.

Federal Bureau of Investigation (FBI). (2012). Directorate of intelligence: Intelligence cycle. Retrieved from www.fbi.gov/about-us/intelligence/intelligence-cycle.

Goldstein, H. (1979). Improving policing: A problem-oriented approach. *Crime & Delinquency, 25,* 236–258.

Goldstein, H. (1990). *Problem-oriented policing.* New York: McGraw-Hill.

Greenwood, P. W., & Petersilia, J. (1975). *The criminal investigation process: Volume I: Summary and policy implications.* Santa Monica, CA: The Rand Corporation. Retrieved from www.rand.org/content/dam/rand/pubs/reports/2007/R1776.pdf.

Hill, B. (2003). Operationalizing GIS to investigate serial robbery offenders in Phoenix, AZ. In M. Leipnik, & D. Albert, *GIS in law enforcement* (pp. 146–158). London, England: Taylor and Francis.

Kelling, G. L., Pate, T., Dieckman, D., & Brown, C. (1974). *The Kansas City preventive patrol experiment: A summary report.* Washington, DC: The Police Foundation. Retrieved from www.policefoundation.org/content/kansas-city-preventive-patrol-experiment.

Kelling, G. L., & Moore, M. H. (1988). Evolving Strategy of Policing. *Perspectives in Policing, 4.* Washington, DC: U.S. Department of Justice. Retrieved from www.ncjrs.gov/pdffiles1/nij/114213.pdf.

National Institute of Justice. (2010). About data-driven approaches to crime and traffic safety. Retrieved from www.nij.gov/topics/law-enforcement/operations/traffic-safety/ddacts.htm.

Pearsall, B. (2010). Predictive policing: The future of law enforcement? Retrieved from www.nij.gov/journals/266/predictive.htm.

Ratcliffe, J. H. (2003). Intelligence-led policing. *Australian Institute of Criminology: Trends and Issues in Crime and Criminal Justice, 248,* 1–6.

Ratcliffe, J. H. (2008). *Intelligence-led policing.* Cullompton, UK: Willan Publishing.

Sidebottom, A., Tilley, N., & Eck, J. (2012). Towards checklists to reduce common sources of problem-solving failure. *Policing (Oxford): A Journal of Policy and Practice, 6*(2), 194–209.

Stevens, D. J. (2009). *An introduction to American policing.* Sudbury, MA: Jones & Bartlett Learning.

Toch, H., & Grant, J. D. (2005). *Police as problem solvers: How frontline workers can promote organizational and community change* (2nd ed.). Washington, DC: American Psychological Association.

Research and Crime Data

Research and Applications in Crime Mapping

▶ LEARNING OBJECTIVES

This chapter highlights the relevant research on crime mapping and its applications in the field. This chapter is meant to provide the student with a cursory examination of the existing literature on how characteristics of place and space impact crime and how geographic information systems (GIS) can assist criminal justice agencies in developing strategies that reduce crime, prevent victimization, and assist in the investigation and prosecution of offenders. After studying this chapter, you should be able to:

- Identify and discuss research in the field of crime mapping.
- Summarize and explain key research findings about crime at various places.
- Be able to identify different applications of GIS in criminal justice.

▶ **Key Terms**

Boston Miracle	Hotspots	Socially Disorganized
Drug Crime	Proactive Patrol	Neighborhoods

■ Introduction

To understand the theoretical justifications behind crime mapping and analysis, a basic foundation of knowledge is required, including key theoretical perspectives of why crime is unevenly distributed across people and places. These theories cover the individual, social, and environmental factors thought to be associated with offending and victimization. Various policing methodologies, the CompStat process—which contributed greatly to the use of GIS, and additional scientific analytical techniques can be used to identify problem areas and assess whether or not an intervention employed has any impact on preventing or reducing crime. After all, if crime analysis and mapping are not helping the police do their jobs, then why do research and analysis if it cannot be applied in an operational environment? This chapter provides a cursory review of the empirical research found in numerous publications geared toward practitioners and academics. This literature discusses not only the use of GIS to examine spatial relationships of crime, but also the GIS applications utilized by various criminal justice agencies. In these studies, the use of crime mapping is built on the knowledge gained from statistics and data, as well as examining theory. Thus, students should understand that maps are not created out of thin air but are carefully constructed using the rules and assumptions provided by both statistics and theory.

■ Research

This chapter is organized into research and applications sections, examining the literature based on the nonmutually exclusive categories of research and application. This chapter is meant to provide students with an introduction to the empirical literature in GIS and law enforcement. In GIS (as with other criminal justice research), the line between research and application is fuzzy at best. Many research studies are based on practical applications, and many applications are subsequently evaluated and then published in peer-reviewed journals. Thus, almost any given study could legitimately be discussed in a number of subsections within this chapter. However, the research examined in this first section focuses primarily on spatial relationships of crime. While the findings have practical utility, the primary research objective is to gain a better understanding of crime in a specific place or area—not necessarily to develop strategies to address it. The following discussions examine the research and analyze some places typically thought to be associated with different types of crime problems. The first section considers some of the research on public housing. Perceived higher rates of crime have consistently existed in poorer areas—including public housing. However, as best practice evolves from empirical research, we need to look at what the research tells us.

Public Housing

The common perception about public housing projects is that they are violent and dangerous places. However, only a few studies have empirically linked disorder and crime to public housing projects. Recall Newman's (1972) principles of defensible space: Newman argued that there were key design flaws found in some public housing projects which facilitated victimization by reducing the visibility and the use of areas by legitimate users. More recently, Suresh and Vito (2007) examined hotspots of aggravated assaults in Louisville, Kentucky between 1989 and 1999. They found that a consistent clustering of assaults occurred around many of the public housing projects. Analysis revealed that several variables were important in understanding these hotspots. While income remained the most important variable, other variables of importance included the proportion of the population younger than 18 years of age, the proportion of the male population that was unemployed, and the percentage of vacant housing. In addition, a distinct change in one of the historic hotspots of assaults in 1997 and 1998 (near the Park DuValle neighborhood) led the authors to investigate further. They discovered that:

> Park DuValle was one of the major historic hotspots until 1996. The disappearance of the hot spot at Park DuValle, in the years 1997 and 1998, suggested some type of intervention. Revitalization of two of the vulnerable low-income public housing projects; the removal of the adjacent dilapidated, unattended private apartments; and the relocation of the former residents of those two low-income public housing projects were the main reasons for this shift (Suresh & Vito, 2007).

Other research suggests that certain crimes are more prevalent in public housing projects than they are in other places. For example, Holzman, Hyatt, and Kudrick (2005) examined public housing areas in three different cities. They found that while "clearly the image of public housing developments as violent, dangerous places finds support in this study" (p. 322), the risk of victimization for different crimes varied. For example, aggravated assaults and robberies were higher in public housing areas, while burglaries, larcenies, and thefts tended to be lower in public housing areas in comparison to surrounding areas.

Holzman, Hyatt, and Dempster (2001) examined the victimization rates of aggravated assault of public housing residents in two cities. They found that black females who lived in public housing in both cities were at higher risk of being victims of aggravated assault than black or white women who did not live in public housing. In addition, the rate of victimization for black female residents of public housing varied due to "different agricultural design and geographic dispersion of the respective cities' public housing developments" (p. 662). In addition, the authors argue that one of the developments "offered less privacy and accessibility, thus discouraging would-be assailants" (p. 662).

Roncek's (2000) study on robbery in the Bronx found that after demographic, socioeconomic, and other variables were controlled for, the existence of public housing projects had no effect on robberies. Thus, the characteristics of *people* may be more important than characteristics of *places* for some types of crimes. This is a very important finding given the recent move toward transforming the physical and social design of public housing through initiatives such as HOPE VI (which began initially in 1992). Oakley and Burchfield (2009) found that the public housing residents in Chicago who were displaced into the private housing market through a system of vouchers were spatially limited in where they could reside: "Findings indicate that voucher housing tends to be clustered in poor African-American neighborhoods where the majority of relocated public-housing residents settle" (p. 589). If, in fact, crime is more strongly correlated with people rather than place, we should not expect reductions in crime with HOPE VI or other similar programs. Another recent study in Louisville, Kentucky suggests that crime is still prevalent regardless of the type of public housing that is being studied. In a review of 19 years of homicide data, Suresh and Vito (2009) found that "low-income public housing and section 8 housing properties provide an environment where homicides are likely to occur" and that "this pattern remained in effect even when the nature of public housing changed" (p. 411).

Fagan and Davies (2000) suggest that very little research exists on crime in public housing and that most is based on neighborhoods or areas where public housing projects are likely to exist: "The official eligibility criteria and social selection processes in public housing also contribute to a concentration of individuals with social deficits and below-average human capital" (p. 123). The authors point to three primary issues within the research on public housing, including:

- There are spatial and temporal differences in crime rates across public housing sites.
- Crime rates are not stagnant but are dynamic and have cycles.
- Various problems exist in calculating population denominators.

One reason Fagan and Davies suggest that people perceive crime to be so prevalent in public housing projects is that these areas have high "spatial and social concentrations of poor people" (p. 124). Suresh and Vito (2009), for example, found that the median-income level of residents was an important predictor for homicide clusters. In addition, there is a general lack of informal social control in the **socially disorganized neighborhoods** where public housing areas are typically located (recall collective efficacy and social disorganization theories). Furthermore, the physical structure of some public housing projects limits the "guardianship" within the area. Thus, Fagan and Davies suggest that crime could be both migrating into public housing and out of public housing, producing a two-way diffusion effect. Their study examined interpersonal violence in 82 public housing projects and the immediate surrounding areas in Bronx County, New York. Using data from the census, the New York City Housing Authority, and official crime reports for the study areas, they found "significant diversity in both social characteristics and the violent crime rates across public housing projects" (p. 127). They found that, in general, crime is greater within a 100-yard perimeter surrounding a housing project than it is within the boundaries of the project itself. Violent crime, while still high, begins to decrease within 100 to 200 yards of the project. Using a two-stage least-squares regression to identify the direction that crime travels, Fagan and Davies concluded that assaults appear to both come from public housing and travel to surrounding neighborhoods and travel into public housing from surrounding neighborhoods. Limitations of the regression analysis included the omission of potentially important variables, including residential mobility, social interaction between neighbors, processes of informal social control, and income inequality. In addition, random selection of public housing sites was not accomplished in this study, limiting the ability of these authors to generalize their findings.

Businesses

Certain business types are also perceived to experience greater levels of crime and disorder than others. Some of the greater risk can be explained by the increased availability of suitable targets. Construction sites, for example, have long been a source of expensive equipment that is often unattended at night and other times. Using mapping and other analyses to guide the development and implementation of law enforcement responses is vital to our effectiveness. Wernicke (2000) employed GIS in a multipronged strategy aimed at reducing incidents of theft at construction sites in Overland Park, Kansas. The first layer of the strategy was to alert the public that the police department would be cracking down on construction site burglary. The second layer was to work closely with builders and contractors to help them identify ways to better secure the sites. The third layer was to identify known offenders in the area who specialized in this type of burglary. Last, through the use of checkpoints and with detectives working weekend hours, the Overland Park Police Department noted a 26% reduction in stolen equipment.

Another business that can attract crime is cheap motels. In Chula Vista, California, an analysis of calls for service (CFS) data indicated a high concentration of calls for service from several of the motels on the west side of the city (Eisenberg & Schmerler, 2004). In 2003,

2091 calls for service were documented in Chula Vista motels, resulting in 129 arrests. The analysis indicated that five motels accounted for a disproportionate number of CFS. The typical reasons for disturbance CFS included: guests would not leave and/or pay; guests/ visitors were having loud parties; guests/visitors were arguing or fighting; and finally, people were loitering and would not leave the property. A temporal analysis revealed that CFS were highest at about noon and again at about 11:00 P.M. Using theory to guide the analysis, it was determined that several factors were related to the high number of CFS from motels. These included lower room prices (attracting a lower class clientele), local residents renting the rooms (indicating that persons had nowhere else to go or wanted a temporary place to party), a higher than normal percentage of guests on probation or parole compared to the population, and a long length of stay. A basic environmental assessment found that many motel rooms did not have chain locks, deadbolts, or peepholes, and very few signs were posted to display the rules of the motel. Several strategies were implemented, including strict screening of both guests and visitors, increased access control, employing security guards, clearly conveying the rules to guests, and posting signs around the motel property that displayed the rules. In addition, employee training, code enforcement, and limits on the length of stay were implemented in efforts to reduce the number of CFS from the motels (Eisenburg & Schmerler, 2004).

Both of these examples reinforce that we need to use theory and data to adequately analyze what the parameters of the problem are, to thoughtfully develop and implement a targeted response, and to assess how effective our response was at combating the problem at hand. The problems at both businesses were clearly different in many aspects—and thus required very different approaches. However, both strategies were successful in their own way.

Schools

Schools are also thought to be related to crime in several ways. For middle and high schools, the immediate areas around the school may experience higher rates of property crime as the school allows for more young persons to congregate within the same space and time, and because the peak age for crime appears to be between the ages of 16 and 18 years; having more of this age group in one spot will naturally increase the likelihood for crime. For colleges, the availability of electronic devices combined with lax target-hardening measures is an attractor for those seeking to grab an easy haul. The interaction of space and time are important in understanding how schools influence local crime trends.

Reno (1998) utilized GIS to examine residential burglaries in Shreveport, Louisiana. The analysis identified that daytime burglaries were more prevalent than nighttime burglaries and that a concentration of daytime burglaries was located near a high school. Based on this analysis, officers were deployed to target areas located near the school and performed investigative stops. They also coordinated their efforts with the high school, focusing on the problem of truancy. The strategy was successful in reducing the burglaries by 67% and virtually eliminating the truancy problem.

Hendersen and Lowell (2000) focused on campus crime at Temple University. Using GIS to map self-reports of assaults (instead of relying on official reports), the researchers identified four clusters. In these four areas, they added security kiosks, improved lighting, increased **proactive patrols**, and provided escort services. Subsequent self-reports suggested a dramatic decrease in assaults (from 57 to 16).

Roncek (2000) analyzed the proximity of robberies to schools. His research at the block level in the Bronx concluded that proximity to schools accounted for a very small percentage of crime and that the type of crime associated with schools varies across different schools. In addition, ordinary least-squares regression analysis (explaining 36.4% of the variation in robbery) identified other variables, including the block population and the presence of a subway stop, as important in understanding the number of robberies. Furthermore, "higher concentrations of the three largest minority groups—African Americans, Asians, and Hispanics—are associated with more robberies, as is lower socioeconomic status" (p. 160). A subsequent negative-binomial regression found that:

- 29.5% more robberies occurred in blocks adjacent to public senior high schools.
- 30.8% more robberies occurred in blocks adjacent to public junior high schools.
- 11.4% more robberies occurred in blocks adjacent to public elementary schools.
- 21.3% more robberies occurred in blocks adjacent to private grammar schools.

The relationship between schools and crimes is complicated, and while it appears that the proximity to some types of schools in some areas is important in understanding some crimes, other variables, such as demographic and socioeconomic factors, may have more influence over the crime rates within these neighborhoods. Although some of these statistics sound like they may be conflicting or confusing, the real benefit comes with the knowledge that research is being done related to crime and place. Many of these studies can be duplicated by analysts within their own jurisdictions. Analysts can thereby add to the research and eventual publications that deal with these crime issues to benefit everyone involved in crime prevention and control.

Transit Stops

The relationship between mass transportation and crime is studied in a variety of contexts. Mass transportation systems allow offenders to travel quickly and efficiently away from their anchor points. For juveniles especially, mass transportation may be integral to their offending patterns. In addition, the commerce that is situated conveniently at many well established transit stops can make for a great place for offenders to commit crime with little suspicion.

Block and Block (2000) examined street robbery in proximity to rapid transit stations in the Bronx and Chicago. They argue that characteristics of transit stops make them ideal places for motivated offenders:

> Transit stops provide cover for potential offenders. There are transitional breaks in transportation, where standing around is not suspicious activity. By definition, transit stops are easy to enter and exit. Potential targets usually live some distance from the transit stop, are not always familiar with the surrounding area, and are unlikely to have previously met potential offenders (p. 138).

Block and Block's (2000) data included both attempted and completed street robberies in Chicago in 1993 and 1994 and New York City police data on street robberies that occurred between October 1995 and October 1996. Hotspot analyses indicated that 10 of the 13 hotspots in the Bronx either contained a transit station or were adjacent to one. Every transit station in the Chicago analysis was found in a hotspot (11 total hotspots, 10 hotspots that contain transit stations). The authors, citing Angel's theoretical model about different types of land use and crime, suggest there is a "critical intensity zone" (p. 146) of land use where there are enough targets to attract offenders while potential witnesses are insufficient in numbers to deter the offenders. Utilizing an intensity analysis of these hotspots, Block and Block determined that 39% of street robberies that occurred in Chicago's Northeast Side in 1993 and 1994 were within 1000 feet of a transit station, with a critical intensity zone located between one and two blocks away from the station. A second peak occurred approximately five blocks away on a commercial strip that parallels the transit line. In the Bronx, approximately 50% of street robberies occurred within 737 feet of a transit station, with the critical intensity zone located within 400 to 500 feet of a station. "In both cities, the number of robberies peaks where the density of targets is still high but civilian and police surveillance are declining" (p. 148). Furthermore, to understand overall crime patterns, it is important to understand the characteristics of areas in which transit stops are located. For example:

> The backcloth, the stations and shops and services that serve their transit riders, may attract predatory offenders. The blocks surrounding the EL stations in Chicago are sometimes a convenient market location for both drug buyers and sellers. These areas also have cash transaction businesses frequently patronized by transit travelers . . . a small strip mall near the Howard station contains a liquor store, a laundromat, a video shop, a pawn shop, and an adult book store (p. 149).

Hotspots

The literature on hotspots is as prevalent and as varied as the definitions of hotspots. Generally, **hotspots** are viewed as small geographic areas that experience higher than average levels of crime for a consistent period of time. Taylor (1998) suggests that three primary forces are leading hotspot research: frustration, tools, and theory. Identifying hotspots is not as simple as counting the dots that appear on the map: "Such complexities suggest that it may not be easy for police to define crime hot spots precisely and allocate patrol resources accordingly. This raises general questions about the clarity of the concept of hot spots" (Taylor, 1998, p. 3). In addition, many analysis programs produce hotspots in the form of circles and ellipses, but real hotspots do not conform to exact geometric shapes.

In his review of the relevant literature, Taylor (1998) suggests that hotspot-based strategies, in general, have produced minimal impacts on crime and that these impacts are typically only achieved for the short term. Basing his suggestion on the literature, he also advised that "we know more about reducing disorder than about reducing crime" (p. 9).

When an analyst or researcher looks at hotspots, we have to assume that this is where crime "has" happened. Although we have a fairly secure history that locations where crime has already occurred are likely to be repeated spots for crime, we have to look at additional factors when working with hotspots. These can be type of crime, consideration of any crime series or trends, and temporal aspects. Some hotspots may be transitory or move around quite a bit, while others may remain no matter what police resources we put there.

An example might be a large department store where security arrests numerous people every day for shoplifting. Another difference we may see is in crime prevention through environmental design (CPTED) policies at various convenience stores. We may find that QT stores have a better policy of having two clerks on duty, locking the beer coolers after 1:00 A.M., and overall better lighting and placement of commonly stolen items; whereas Circle K stores may place their beer right out front, not lock their coolers or put away the beer after hours, and may only have one clerk on duty during late shifts. All of these issues could be and should be considered when looking at hotspots identified in and around these locations.

In addition to hotspots identified by empirical data, other research on hotspots suggests that the identification of hotspots based on one's experience with an area (such as law enforcement) is not necessarily an easy task. For example, Ratcliffe and McCullough (1998) asked police officers in South Nottingham, England, to pick out hotspot areas of crime. When these areas were compared with actual hotspots of crime (identified through analysis), the researchers found that police perceptions about hotspots did not match actual hotspot locations. In another interesting study, Paulsen (2003) compared "media" hotspots with actual hotspots. Paulsen utilized GIS to create maps of homicides covered by the local media in Houston, Texas. Upon comparison with actual homicide hotspots, he found that the actual homicide hotspots tended to be closer to the center of the city than hotspots identified by media coverage.

Martin, Barnes, and Britt (1998) examined arson hotspots in Detroit, Michigan. Using GIS to map arsons, they developed a multipronged approach to reduce arson hotspots. The strategies included forming a citywide task force, identifying community resources, and mapping current arson hotspots and abandoned buildings that might become future targets. In addition, letters were sent to residents to alert them about the arson hotspots and explain the strategies that were being developed to address and reduce those threats. This strategy resulted in fewer fires and the elimination of several hotspots. Unfortunately, a number of hotspots still remained after implementing several of the new strategies. These "stubborn" hotspots were situated in areas of high crime and a large number of abandoned buildings, a low level of community organization, and high levels of poverty. These factors suggest that additional strategies may need to be developed to address them in the neighborhoods with remaining arson hotspots.

Lockwood (2007) made several interesting observations when he examined the relationship between violent crime and land use in Savannah, Georgia. First, assaults were related to the type of land use within an area, specifically with retail/commercial/office, renter, and public/institutional land uses. Second, both homicide and assault were strongly and positively correlated with social disadvantage. In addition, commercial areas with high robbery rates tended to be adjacent to residential block groups with high rates of both homicide and assault.

In examining the distribution of homicides in three cities, Adams (2001) found that although the physical environment was important in understanding homicide hotspots, the more important variable was economic deprivation. The author suggests that more research to examine the impact of rejuvenation projects aimed at both physical and social issues is necessary.

Drug Hotspots

GIS is also useful in researching **drug crime** and the spatial dispersion of drug activity. Romig and Feidler (2008) utilized GIS to better understand methamphetamine (meth) activity in the state of North Dakota. They created map layers displaying meth-related arrests, meth lab seizures, and various demographic characteristics. Using completed maps, they identified uneven distributions in abuse, arrests, and distributions of meth across North Dakota.

> When examining the spatial pattern of methamphetamine-related arrests, our research discovered that they are more likely to take place in counties that are urban, closer to containing a larger city, highly populated, higher per capita income, have a larger proportion of vacant houses, a higher percentage of the population in their late twenties, and a growing population (p. 217).

For clandestine lab seizures, the trends are very different. Lab seizures were higher in "counties that are more rural, further away from larger cities, and have smaller populations" (Romig & Feidler, 2008, p. 217). In their research, they discovered an anomalous county, Williams County, that suffered from both a high seizure rate *and* a high arrest rate. The authors also note that the distribution of rehabilitation programs throughout the state is limited and currently cannot support the numbers of addicted persons who need treatment.

Another example of the drug and crime relationship relative to space comes from High Point, North Carolina. Kennedy (2009) describes what is now known as the High Point Drug Market Initiative (DMI) as a focused deterrence approach where known dealers within a neighborhood are targeted as a means of convincing them to stop dealing drugs. For each targeted dealer, the federal, state, and local law enforcement work together to implement videotaped, undercover buys. After this occurs, the High Point Police Department schedules a community meeting that all targeted offenders are asked to attend. In addition to the offenders, various representatives of the community and the criminal justice system participate in this meeting—including family members of the offenders. At this meeting, offenders are informed of the "banked" cases and are told they are being given a second chance—if they choose to stop dealing drugs. Kennedy reported evidence that this initiative was highly successful in reducing the violence and other crimes thought to be associated with the drug market. A more recent analysis suggests that the success may not have been as dramatic as earlier reported, but still reported modest success in reducing violent crime (Corsaro, Hunt, Hipple, & McGarrell, 2012).

■ Applications

Again, the line between research and application is by no means clear. This section examines some of the research conducted on applications of GIS in various capacities and is organized by the criminal justice function that it serves. While reading the following subsections, it is important to keep in mind that the utilization of GIS varies from department to department. In some agencies, GIS is used extensively for multiple purposes. In other departments, GIS is employed sparingly for only a few types of analyses. Focused, targeted efforts informed by empirical data and sound theory hold the most promise in long-term problem solving. A 2002 publication by the Arizona Criminal Justice Commission indicates that only 14.5%

of law enforcement agencies in Arizona used any type of crime mapping at all. A notation in the executive summary of this publication indicates:

> The average length of time that agencies report having had crime mapping capabilities is approximately 4.5 years. This is actually longer than was found nationally (3.3 years) and would strongly indicate that the potential of mapping in criminal justice systems is in its infancy (p. 5).

Ratcliffe (2004) proposes an interesting "hotspot matrix" that looks promising as an approach to planning both long-term and short-term policing strategies. Using an example for a housing estate, the matrix is composed of spatial patterns (dispersed, clustered, and hotpoint) and temporal patterns (diffused, focused, and acute); matrix cells provide possible police strategies, such as uniform vehicle patrol, foot patrols, surveillance units, and closed circuit television (CCTV) monitoring, among many suggestions.

Investigation and Prosecution

There are endless applications of crime analysis and mapping for investigation purposes. The Lincoln Police Department (LPD) in Nebraska, for example, used GIS to successfully stop a series of automobile breakins. In addition, with the use of GIS, the LPD investigated and solved a sexual assault case of a young boy by linking previous incidents of indecent exposure in the area near the crime (Casady, 2003). In another case, detectives in Knoxville, Tennessee, used maps of known sex offenders who lived in the area of a rape incident to conduct a photo lineup for the victim. The perpetrator was quickly identified, apprehended, and subsequently confessed (Hubbs, 1998).

In Spokane, Washington, GIS was used in the investigation of two high-profile cases: the Brad Jackson case and the Robert Yates case (Leipnik et al., 2003). Brad Jackson was a suspect in the suspicious disappearance of his 9-year-old daughter, Valerie, on October 18, 1999. In the Jackson case, the Spokane Police Department used global positioning system (GPS) tracking and GIS mapping capabilities to follow Jackson's whereabouts for a period of 18 days. The information about his travels and length of stay at various locations was collected and analyzed and led to the discovery of a temporary gravesite and a permanent gravesite where his daughter's body was found.

In the Yates case, police used GIS analysis of body dump sites and of supermarkets in efforts to prioritize areas of Spokane where a serial murderer resided. In the murders, several of the victims' heads were covered with plastic bags. The bags had store markings that could be traced to individual franchise stores. The stores where these plastic bags came from were mapped using GIS capabilities, and an area of probable activity was created. This helped investigators narrow their search by giving them a high probability area to start investigating. Although GIS was not instrumental in solving the case (blood evidence in a white Corvette once owned by Yates was the zinger), Leipnik and colleagues (2003) argue that:

> Although GIS and geographic profiling did not solve this case, in retrospect it could have narrowed down the focus of interest to a five square mile area out of 1800 square miles within the greater Spokane metropolitan area. The suspect's home residence turned out to have been located within this five square mile "high probability" area; in fact he lived less than a mile from the mean locations (centroids) of both the body dump and the grocery store clusters (p. 179).

An interesting twist to the Yates case is that a GPS unit containing 72 waypoints was recovered from Yates's home. That information is still being analyzed to help determine whether or not those waypoints represent dump sites for yet unidentified victims (Leipnik et al., 2003). Yates pleaded guilty to killing 13 of his victims in Spokane County and later received the death penalty for killing two women in Pierce County. Despite the closure of those cases and the fact that Yates will die behind prison walls,

> …detectives throughout the state of Washington have been investigating Yates' GPS waypoints since January 2001. Authorities in Alabama and Germany have also contacted Spokane County, inquiring about Yates' travels. (Though no GPS information is available for those locations, Yates is suspected of three murders in Germany and one in Alabama—both places where he was stationed while in the Army.) (Spatial Industries Business Association, 2012).

In a series of indecent exposure cases, GIS analysis identified information about spatial and temporal clustering of incidents that was disseminated to the public and informed the development of surveillance operations. The subject was ultimately arrested (Woodby & Johnson, 2000). Investigators in Seattle, Washington, used crime mapping to identify and make predictions about a robbery series. Based on the findings of the analysis, crime bulletins were created and distributed to the public via television and newspaper. The suspects were apprehended based on a tip provided by a confidential informant. Additional analysis was performed to review suspect activity and help discover additional crimes perpetrated by the suspects in which weapons were stolen and used in several robberies (Robbin, 2000).

In Edmonton, Alberta, Canada, Warden and Shaw (2000) examined clusters of breaking-and-entering crimes. Spatial and temporal analysis identified patterns that were useful to surveillance, which led to the arrest of the individuals responsible for the breakins.

Crime incidents are not the only points that are plotted during investigations. For example, the murder investigation of a young man in St. Petersburg, Florida, was facilitated by mapping the locations of cellular telephone transmitter sites. In this case, a young man's dismembered body was found in Tampa Bay. The victim had been involved in a bungled drug deal and was subsequently tortured and killed. The times and the locations of the suspects' cell phone use was plotted and mapped to corroborate eye witness testimony of the times and locations that the offenders and victim were seen together (Moland, 1998):

> In the end, the weight of the expert testimony provided by the two detectives, the AT&T cell phone technician, and other witnesses was sufficient to convict the two suspects and sentence them to life in prison. This case shows the difficulty of explaining complex, technical but verifiable information in its purest form. The old expression "a picture is worth a thousand words" was proven during this trial (p. 72).

In another similar example, several violent hijackings of persons over the course of a few days occurred in South Africa. Four persons were suspected in these incidents. Of these hijackings, only two victims (a father and son) were left alive. Two couples were shot and killed. Of these, one woman was raped before she was killed. DNA analysis of evidence implicated two suspects in the rape; they were shot and killed in a police shootout. Two suspects remained at large. During the investigation, it was learned that the woman's cell phone was missing, so phone records of calls made and received were acquired. Further investigation revealed that one phone number was called multiple times at about the same time she was last seen alive. The recipient of these calls happened to be one of the suspects who had been shot and killed in the police shootout. Subsequent investigation of cell phone records revealed that suspects were in constant contact between one another on various cellular phones and landlines. These phone records were mapped and used in court to corroborate eye witness testimony of the suspects' whereabouts (Schmitz, Cooper, Davidson, & Roussow, 2000).

Overall and Day (2008) employed a post hoc analysis to determine the prediction ability of a probability grid method (PGM) outlined by Hill (2003) on the Hammer Gang robbery series in the city of Durban, KwaZulu-Natal, South Africa, between October 2003 and January 2004. The analysis proved to be highly successful in that:

> The resultant probability map produced two very high-probability offence locations in close proximity to each other, one being the seventh and last offence in this series . . . . Both of the very high probability target locations were located within the first ring buffer and the calculated radius was in line with the offenders' directional path. Taking into account the number of potential targets, the PGM reduced the potential target locations from eleven to two (Overall & Day, 2008, p. 60).

In another example of the potential prediction ability of crime mapping and analysis, Casady (2008b) discusses the arrest of a bank robber in Lincoln, Nebraska. In this case, GIS was used to prioritize potential sites for deploying stakeouts. In the analysis, spatial, temporal, and other characteristics of bank robberies in a series were analyzed to produce predictions about when and where the next bank would be hit:

> Crime mapping helped determine Erving's *modus operandi*, helped locate his potential victim banks, helped determine the best locations for stakeout and helped identify likely escape routes. The case is illustrative of the nexus of the art and science of policing: the creativity, initiative and intuition of experienced police officers informed by geographical crime analysis and traditional investigative analysis (p. 68).

Proactive Policing

The term *proactive policing* typically means employing strategies to *prevent* crime and to address the root causes of crime rather than just responding to calls for service ("reactive" policing). Depending on the agency, this might mean randomly running license plates throughout an officer's shift or developing multileveled strategies to address social and physical incivilities associated with crime in a neighborhood. Whatever the case, proactive policing assumes that rather than simply responding to crimes that have already occurred, law enforcement can develop and implement tactics that prevent future crimes. The previously mentioned case in Overland Park, Kansas, would be a good example of creating a multifaceted strategy to reduce or prevent crime.

Casady (2008a) describes an automated system implemented by the Lincoln Police Department (Nebraska) in which maps and reports that alert officers to increases in crime and recently issued warrants, display crime trends for such crimes as burglaries, and monitor sex offender registrations are automated, providing officers with up-to-date information that is useful to their daily operations.

Mapping techniques are useful to police and other agencies in preparation of large events. For example, the Lincoln Police Department uses GIS to plan traffic and crowd control details for large events, including the University of Nebraska's Cornhusker football games (Casady, 2003). Crowd control, traffic management, and other related concerns are planned in advance to ensure public safety and minimize public inconvenience before, during, and after the games.

The Lincoln Police Department has also used GIS to develop a number of proactive approaches to crime and other community problems that are related to proximity to the college. First, "using GIS LPD analyzed the number of complaints received from the public concerning wild parties, and found a 27% reduction in complaints from neighborhoods located within one mile of the campus, as compared to the same period in 1997" (Casady, 2003, p. 115). Second, an analysis of burglaries identified trends in residential burglary in which offenders entered open garages. Officers armed with informational fliers went door to door and told homeowners to shut their garage doors (Casady, 2003). A similar strategy was employed in Overland Park, Kansas. An analysis that used GIS identified several neighborhoods that experienced high numbers of "garage shopping" in which residential burglars entered open garages and stole valuable tools, bikes, and other items. Officers targeted these neighborhoods and handed out brochures to residents alerting them of these thefts. This effort resulted in a reduction of these burglary incidents and facilitated approximately 1200 citizen contacts in the process (Wernicke, 1998).

The LPD has also used GIS for other proactive strategies, including reducing the number of police incidents at a specific apartment complex, decreasing the number of thefts of self-service gasoline, supporting community development in weak neighborhoods, and keeping the public informed about crime in their community and the LPD's commitment to reducing crime (Casady, 2003).

The Knoxville Police Department (Tennessee) used GIS to map the area's crimes and calls for service, including shots-fired calls and auto burglary, and overlaid this information on top of parolee addresses. They identified a clustering of several different crimes and disturbance calls near the end of a cul-de-sac where a parolee (who was also a drug dealer) resided. The parolee was arrested after a search of his home, and it was later discovered that many of the drug dealer's friends were responsible for the crimes and disturbance calls that initiated the analysis (Hubbs, 2003). Hubbs argues that police can effectively use mapping capabilities to track known sex offenders. He cites several successful cases from the Knoxville Police Department (KPD), including one where they found an abducted little girl and arrested a serial rapist. The KPD has also used GIS to extensively map and analyze gun violence in Knoxville.

In Hartford, Connecticut, law enforcement believed that drug calls in the Blue Hills neighborhood were severely underreported. The officers who worked in this neighborhood brought this to the attention of the residents, which resulted in a 170% increase in the number of drug calls for service. These calls resulted in the subsequent arrest of 11 people (Rich, 1998).

Citizen satisfaction can also be affected by the use of GIS and crime analysis. For example, Canter (1998) examined the impact of Baltimore County's Autodialer System—a system that utilizes GIS to systematically alert citizens to crime problems occurring in the community and provide suggestions about how they can reduce their chances of being victimized.

The system has been successful from a community-oriented policing perspective in that it provides a direct line of communication from police to citizens about their community. An evaluation of the system indicates that the citizens really like it.

Goldstein (1990) argues that police should pay less attention to "incidents" and more attention to "problems" if they want to have any impact on crime. The identification of crime problems can be achieved through the use of multiple data sources. In addition, solutions to these crime problems should include both legal and nonlegal applications where appropriate.

> Problems are defined either as collections of incidents related in some way (if they occur at the same location, for example) or as underlying conditions that give rise to incidents, crimes, disorder, and other substantive community issues that people expect the police to handle. By focusing more on problems than on incidents, police can address causes rather than mere symptoms and consequently have a greater impact (Cordner & Biebel, 2005, p. 155).

Recall in problem-oriented policing, problems are addressed utilizing the SARA model (scan, analyze, respond, and assess), with the ultimate goal being to eliminate the problem rather than simply continually responding to it (Eck & Spelman, 1987). Analysis is always difficult for police officers and police supervisors. Focusing on the "problem" rather than the just the frequency of reported incidents can be a hard nut to crack without good crime analysis.

For example, the Springfield Police Department and Illinois State Police collaborated to reduce gun-related incidents and gang-related shootings (Bitner, Gardner, & Caldwell, 2000). An analysis indicated that gang violence was emerging in an area where recently relocated gang members from Peoria, Illinois, resided. Utilizing GIS, a summer strike force that targeted gang- and gun-related violence yielded substantial reductions in the rates of violence and forced gang members to relocate to another area. Otto, Maly, and Schismenos (2000) used GIS to identify gang hot zones in Akron, Ohio, by mapping graffiti that marked gang boundaries. Hot zones were those areas where gang boundaries overlapped and were thus more likely to experience intergang-related violence.

Using repeat address mapping (RAM), Gersh and Beardsley (2000) utilized GIS analysis to identify the top 10% of addresses accounting for drug calls for service to guide the development and implementation of a crackdown (Operation Clean) in the Langley Park area of Washington, DC. Mapping and analysis of the area after the crackdown indicated a substantial reduction in the number of hotspots and in the number of calls for service within the remaining hotspots. In the Lincoln Park area of San Diego, gang boundaries and overlapping areas were mapped along with personal crimes, property crimes, and calls for service to identify problem locations concerning gang-related crimes. The civil injunctions were used to prevent gang members from hanging out in specific areas, associating with other known gang members or affiliates, and engaging in various gang behaviors. This strategy netted Lincoln Park a crime rate reduction of 29.3 to 18.1 (per 1000 inhabitants; Polk, Hammond, Yoder, & Burke, 2000).

In the early 1990s, the Boston Gun Project and other strategies were implemented simultaneously to produce substantial reductions in gang and youth violence in the city of Boston.

GIS was utilized to map gangs and gang territory based on the current gang intelligence of police officers, probation officers, and street workers. A strong consensus existed amongst the practitioners about the active gangs, their rivals, and their territories. Using network analysis, key gangs and their conflict network were identified:

> The Boston Gun Project is a problem-solving exercise aimed at preventing youth violence in Boston by: convening an interagency working group; performing original research into Boston's youth violence problem and illicit gun markets; crafting a city-wide, interagency problem-solving strategy; implementing that strategy; and evaluating the strategy's impact (Kennedy, Braga, & Piehl, 1998, p. 228).

Deemed the **Boston Miracle** by many, youth homicides dropped dramatically:

> The '90's were a remarkable decade for Boston. Not only did Boston enjoy a period of nearly unprecedented economic prosperity, but it was also a time of historically low crime rates and unusually good police–community relations. Most dramatically, the number of homicides plummeted over the decade . . . . For the twenty-nine month period ending in January 1998, there were no teenage homicide victims. Thus, the so-called Boston Miracle (Winship, 2002, p. 1).

In Newark, New Jersey, the problem of auto theft was examined in semimonthly CompStat meetings. An analysis indicated that the time of day these auto thefts were occurring was a critical factor. The last known addresses for people who were arrested for receiving stolen property and the vehicle recovery locations were mapped. Strategies employed in the East district, based on the analysis, yielded a decrease from an average of 40 to 30 auto thefts per week (Santiago, 1998).

McGuire (2000) argues that the key to CompStat's success in New York City was the involvement of multiple agencies including the District Attorney, New York State Department of Parole, City Probation Department, and City Corrections Department. Other city agencies, such as Consumer Affairs, Social Services, and Environmental Protection, also attend the CompStat meetings. CompStat is attributed as being responsible for the 41% drop in crime that New York City experienced between 1993 and 1997, which included a 60% reduction in murder and nonnegligent manslaughter. Again, we see that regardless of the strategy label (CompStat, problem-oriented policing, etc.), it is clear that collaborative efforts focusing on a specific problem in a targeted area can yield long-term success. The key is that these strategies are not superficially developed or applied—using the SARA model, agencies that experience the most success fully incorporate crime analysis at every stage. Data is used to inform, implement, and evaluate practice.

Other Miscellaneous Applications of GIS Analysis

Rieckenberg and Grube (1998) examined traffic fatalities in Cook County, Illinois. They collected and mapped information about the type of accident, location of accident, the condition of the driver and roadway conditions at the time of the accident, and the time and day of the accident to inform a concentrated enforcement effort in high-accident areas. Using a zero-tolerance approach, they achieved a 35% reduction in traffic fatalities in the first 6 months.

In Lowell, Massachusetts, mapping was used to pinpoint and chronicle evidence in a homicide trial (Cook, 1998). In Florida, information on the whereabouts of probationers and parolees being tracked through the use of GPS is stored and accessed using a web-based interface system whereby participating agencies can query tracked offenders to determine if they were within 1000 feet and 30 minutes of a crime (Frost, 2005). In addition, the system signals zone violations of offenders leaving their "inclusion" and "exclusion" zones. The system then automates an email to officers, including a hyperlink to the offender's track points.

Freisthier and colleagues (2007) employed mapping techniques to look at the effects of alcohol outlets on child protection services (CPS) referrals, substantiations, and foster care entries in the state of California. Using data at the zip code level, they found a positive relationship between the number of off-premise alcohol outlets and the percentage of black residents with higher rates of maltreatment.

More specifically, the model derived estimates that an average decrease of one off-premise outlet per zip code would reduce total referrals to CPS in the 579 zip codes by 1040 cases, substantiations by 180 cases, and foster care entries by 93 cases. Characteristics of adjacent zip codes also were related to maltreatment rates in local neighborhoods, indicating a spatial dynamic to this relationship (Freisthier et al., 2007, p. 114).

■ Conclusion

As you can see, the possibilities for crime mapping in small, medium, and large departments are endless. The applications range from the facilitation of simple presentations to the development of complicated prediction models. In addition, the enhanced supervision and monitoring of parolees and probationers is also aided by the use of GPS and GIS. Several tools and approaches are utilized pervasively:

> The most common approach is to have a crime analyst use GIS to analyze the spatial and temporal factors associated with a series of crimes or to detect patterns, trends, and exceptions. In most police departments, crime analysts view GIS as in important but non-essential tool . . . . The reason that many departments use GIS selectively is that it is a relatively new technology in policing (Leipnik & Albert, 2003, p. 5).

As the familiarity of GIS technology increases, crime mapping applications in both research and practice will continue to expand.

■ Chapter Glossary

Boston Miracle   An interagency problem-solving strategy operation in the City of Boston to enforce gang and weapon crimes to reduce murder of teenagers.

Drug crime   Those crimes which are directly involved in the use of drugs and related crimes such as money laundering, forgery, fraud, property crimes, and others that support drug sales and production.

Hotspots   Areas identified through crime mapping as having a larger than normal number of crimes within a certain geographic area with crime points that are clustered.

Proactive patrol   Patrolling areas in an attempt to actively prevent crime through strategic and targeted enforcement and patrolling operations.

Socially disorganized neighborhoods   Those neighborhoods that have three characteristics; these include high rates of residential turnover, a heterogeneous population, and high levels of poverty.

■ Questions for Review

1. Based on the literature review, what areas are promising for GIS to assist law enforcement in the investigating and prosecuting of crime? What weaknesses in utilizing GIS in law enforcement still need to be addressed?

2. Why would automated maps and reports be useful to police agencies? What types of reports or maps do you think would be most useful in an automated format? Why?

■ Online Resources

Center for Problem-Oriented Policing (POP): www.popcenter.org/

Crime Solutions: http://crimesolutions.gov/default.aspx

Eck, Chainey, Cameron, Leitner, Wilson, National Institute of Justice, Mapping and Analysis for Public Safety website, "Mapping Crime: Understanding Hotspots": www.ncjrs.gov/pdffiles1/nij/209393.pdf

Great criminal justice-related articles and publications, including crime mapping studies: http://www.nij.gov/topics/technology/maps/welcome.htm

Hotspots Policing—NIJ Research for the Real World Seminar NCJ 234700, October 2009, Recorded Seminar, by Dr. David Weisburd: www.nij.gov/multimedia/welcome.htm#video-weisburd

National Criminal Justice Reference Service: www.ncjrs.gov

Police Executive Research Forum: www.policeforum.org

Smart Policing Initiative: www.smartpolicinginitiative.com/

■ Recommended Reading

Asbell, B. (2003). National Guard Bureau counterdrug GIS programs: Supporting counterdrug law enforcement. In M. R. Leipnik & D. P. Albert (Eds.), *GIS in law enforcement: Implementation issues and case studies* (pp. 211–227). New York: Taylor & Francis.

Chainey, S., & Tompson, L. (Eds.). (2008). *Crime mapping case studies: Practice and research*. Hoboken, NJ: Wiley.

Goldstein, H. (1979). Improving policing: A problem-oriented approach. *Crime and Delinquency, 25*, 236–258.

Paul, B. (2001). *Using crime mapping to measure the negative secondary effects of adult businesses in Fort Wayne, Indiana: A quasi-experimental methodology.* Paper presented to National Institute of Justice, Crime Mapping Research Center, 2001 International Crime Mapping Research Conference, Dallas, TX.

■ References ■

Adams, T. M. (2001). *Historical homicide hot spots: The case of three cities.* Ann Arbor, MI: UMI.

Arizona Criminal Justice Commission. (2002). Crime mapping in Arizona report. Retrieved from http://azmemory.azlibrary.gov/utils/getfile/collection/statepubs/id/3333/filename/3618.pdf.

Bitner, L., Gardner, J., & Caldwell, R. (2000). Analyzing gun violence. In N. Lavigne & J. Wartell (Eds.), *Crime mapping case studies: Successes in the field* (Vol. 2, pp. 13–18). Washington, DC: Police Executive Research Forum.

Block, R., & Block, C. R. (2000). The Bronx and Chicago: Street robbery in the environs of rapid transit stations. In V. Goldsmith, P. G. McGuire, J. H. Mollenkopf, & T. A. Ross (Eds.), *Analyzing crime patterns: Frontiers of practice* (pp. 137–152). Thousand Oaks, CA: Sage.

Canter, P. (1998). Baltimore County's autodialer system. In N. Lavigne & J. Wartell (Eds.), *Crime mapping case studies: Successes in the field* (Vol. 1, pp. 81–91). Washington, DC: Police Executive Research Forum.

Casady, T. (2003). Lincoln Police Department—specific examples of GIS successes. In M. R. Leipnik & D. P. Albert (Eds.), *GIS in law enforcement: Implementation issues and case studies* (pp. 146–158). New York: Taylor & Francis.

Casady, T. (2008a). Automating briefings for police officers. In S. Chainey & L. Tompson (Eds.), *Crime mapping case studies: Practice and research* (pp. 27–32). Hoboken, NJ: Wiley.

Casady, T. (2008b). Rolling the dice: The arrest of Roosevelt Erving in Lincoln, Nebraska. In S. Chainey & L. Tompson (Eds.), *Crime mapping case studies: Practice and research* (pp. 63–68). Hoboken, NJ: Wiley.

Cook, P. (1998). Mapping a murderer's path. In N. Lavigne & J. Wartell (Eds.), *Crime mapping case studies: Successes in the field* (Vol. 1, pp. 123–128). Washington, DC: Police Executive Research Forum.

Cordner, G., & Biebel, E. P. (2005). Problem-oriented policing in practice. *Criminology & Public Policy, 4*(2), 155–180.

Corsaro, N., Hunt, E., Hipple, N. K., & McGarrell, E. F. (2012). Overview of "the impact of drug market pulling levers policing on neighborhood violence: An evaluation of the High Point Drug Market Intervention." *Criminology & Public Policy, 11*(2), 165–199.

Eck, J. E., & Spelman, W. (1987). *Problem solving: Problem oriented policing in Newport News.* Washington, DC: Police Executive Research Forum.

Eisenberg, D., & Schmerler, K. (2004, May 19). The Chula Vista Motel project. Presentation at the Massachusetts Association of Crime Analysts, Hyannis, MA.

Fagan, J., & Davies, G. (2000). Crime in public housing: Two-way diffusion effects in surrounding neighborhoods. In V. Goldsmith, P. G. McGuire, J. H. Mollenkopf, & T. A. Ross (Eds.), *Analyzing crime patterns: Frontiers of practice* (pp. 121–135). Thousand Oaks, CA: Sage.

Freisthier, B., Gruenewald, P. J., Remer, L. G., Lery, B., & Needell, B. (2007). Exploring the spatial dynamics of alcohol outlets and child protective services referrals, substantiations, and foster care entries. *Child Maltreatment, 12*(2), 114–124.

Frost, G. A. (2005). Integrating GIS, GPS, and MIS on the web: EMPACT in Florida. In F. Wang (Ed.), *Geographic information systems and crime analysis* (pp. 183–195). Hershey, PA: IDEA Group.

Gersh, J. S., & Beardsley, K. C. (2000). Evaluating the impact of a drug crackdown. In N. Lavigne & J. Wartell (Eds.), *Crime mapping case studies: Successes in the field* (Vol. 2, pp. 19–27). Washington, DC: Police Executive Research Forum.

Goldstein, H. (1990). *Problem oriented policing.* New York: McGraw-Hill.

Hendersen, K., & Lowell, Lt. R. (2000). Reducing campus crime through high definition mapping. N. Lavigne & J. Wartell (Eds.), *Crime mapping case studies: Successes in the field* (Vol. 2, pp. 3–12). Washington, DC: Police Executive Research Forum.

Hill, B. (2003). Operationalizing GIS to investigate serial robberies in Phoenix, Arizona. In M. R. Leipnik & D. P. Albert (Eds.), *GIS in law enforcement: Implementation issues and case studies* (pp. 146–158). New York: Taylor & Francis.

Holzman, H. R., Hyatt, R. A., & Dempster, J. M. (2001). Patterns of aggravated assault in public housing: Mapping the nexus of offense, place, gender, and race. *Violence Against Women, 7*(6), 662–684.

Holzman, H. R., Hyatt, R. A., & Kudrick, T. R. (2005). Measuring crime in and around public housing using GIS. In F. Wang (Ed.), *Geographic information systems and crime analysis* (pp. 311–329). Hershey, PA: IDEA Group.

Hubbs, R. (1998). The Greenway Rapist case: Matching repeat offenders with crime locations. In N. Lavigne & J. Wartell (Eds.), *Crime mapping case studies: Successes in the field* (Vol. 1, pp. 93–98). Washington, DC: Police Executive Research Forum.

Hubbs, R. (2003). Mapping crime and community problems in Knoxville, Tennessee. In M. R. Leipnik & D. P. Albert (Eds.), *GIS in law enforcement: Implementation issues and case studies* (pp. 127–145). New York: Taylor & Francis.

Kennedy, D. M. (2009). *Deterrence and crime prevention: Reconsidering the prospect of sanction.* New York: Routledge.

Kennedy, D. M., Braga, A. A., & Piehl, A. M. (1998). The unknown universe: Mapping gangs and gang violence in Boston. In D. Weisburd & T. McEwen (Eds.), *Crime mapping and crime prevention: Crime prevention studies* (Vol. 8, pp. 219–262). Monsey, NY: Criminal Justice Press.

Leipnik, M. R., & Albert, D. P. (2003). How law enforcement agencies can make geographic information technologies work for them. In M. R. Leipnik & D. P. Albert (Eds.), *GIS in law enforcement: Implementation issues and case studies* (pp. 3–8). New York: Taylor & Francis.

Leipnik, M., Botelli, J., Von Essen, I., Schmidt, A., Anderson, L., & Cooper, T. (2003). Apprehending murderers in Spokane, Washington using GIS and GPS. In M. R. Leipnik & D. P. Albert (Eds.), *GIS in law enforcement: Implementation issues and case studies* (pp. 167–183). New York: Taylor & Francis.

Lockwood, D. (2007). Mapping crime in Savannah: Social disadvantage, land use, and violent crimes reported to the police. *Social Science Computer Review, 25*(2), 194–209.

Martin, D., Barnes, E., & Britt, D. (1998). The multiple impacts of mapping it out: Police, geographic information systems (GIS) and community mobilization during devil's night in Detroit, Michigan. In N. Lavigne & J. Wartell (Eds.), *Crime mapping case studies: Successes in the field* (Vol. 1, pp. 3–13). Washington, DC: Police Executive Research Forum.

McGuire, P. G. (2000). The New York Police Department COMPSTAT process: Mapping for analysis, evaluation, and accountability. In V. Goldsmith, P. G. McGuire, J. H. Mollenkopf, & T. A. Ross (Eds.), *Analyzing crime patterns: Frontiers of practice* (pp. 11–22). Thousand Oaks, CA: Sage.

Moland, R. S. (1998). Graphical display of murder trial evidence. In N. Lavigne & J. Wartell (Eds.), *Crime mapping case studies: Successes in the field* (Vol. 1, pp. 69–79). Washington, DC: Police Executive Research Forum.

Newman, O. (1972). *Defensible space: people and design in the violent city.* New York: Macmillan.

Oakley, D., & Burchfield, K. (2009). Out of the projects, still in the hood: The spatial constraints on public-housing residents' relocation in Chicago. *Journal of Urban Affairs, 31*(5) 589–614.

Otto, A. C., Maly, K. W., & Schismenos, D. (2000). Cracking down on gangs with GIS. In N. Lavigne & J. Wartell (Eds.), *Crime mapping case studies: Successes in the field* (Vol. 2, pp. 101–107). Washington, DC: Police Executive Research Forum.

Overall, C., & Day, G. (2008). The Hammer Gang: An exercise in the spatial analysis of an armed robbery series using the probability grid method. In S. Chainey & L. Tompson (Eds.), *Crime mapping case studies: Practice and research* (pp. 55–62). Hoboken, NJ: Wiley.

Paulsen, D. J. (2003). Comparing actual hot spots v. media hot spots: Houston, Texas, homicides 1986–94. In M. R. Leipnik & D. P Albert (Eds.), *GIS in law enforcement: Implementation issues and case studies* (pp. 98–102). New York: Taylor & Francis.

Polk, J., Hammond, M. M., Yoder, C. S., & Burke, M. L. (2000). Enforcing civil gang injunctions. In N. Lavigne & J. Wartell (Eds.), *Crime mapping case studies: Successes in the field* (Vol. 2, pp. 123–131). Washington, DC: Police Executive Research Forum.

Ratcliffe, J. H. (2004). The Hotspot Matrix: A framework for the spatio-temporal targeting of crime reduction. *Police Practice and Research, 5*(1), 5–23.

Ratcliffe, J. H., & McCullough, M. J. (1998). The perception of crime hot spots: A spatial study in Nottingham, U. K. In N. Lavigne & J. Wartell (Eds.), *Crime mapping case studies: Successes in the field* (Vol. 1, pp. 45–51). Washington, DC: Police Executive Research Forum.

Reno, S. (1998). Using crime mapping to address residential burglary. In N. Lavigne & J. Wartell (Eds.), *Crime mapping case studies: Successes in the field* (Vol. 1, pp. 15–21). Washington, DC: Police Executive Research Forum.

Rich, T. F. (1998). Crime mapping by community organizations: Initial successes in Hartford's Blue Hills neighborhood. In N. Lavigne & J. Wartell (Eds.), *Crime mapping case studies: Successes in the field* (Vol. 1, pp. 35–41). Washington, DC: Police Executive Research Forum.

Rieckenberg, E. J., & Grube, T. (1998). Reducing traffic accidents using geographic analysis. In N. Lavigne & J. Wartell (Eds.), *Crime mapping case studies: Successes in the field* (Vol. 1, pp. 23–26). Washington, DC: Police Executive Research Forum.

Robbin, C. A. (2000). Apprehending violent robbers through a crime series analysis. In N. Lavigne & J. Wartell (Eds.), *Crime mapping case studies: Successes in the field* (Vol. 2, pp. 73–79). Washington, DC: Police Executive Research Forum.

Romig, K., & Feidler, A. (2008). A therapeutic landscape? Contextualizing methamphetamine in North Dakota. In Y. F. Thomas, D. Richardson, & I. Cheung (Eds.), *Geography and drug addiction*. Berlin: Springer Science and Business Media.

Roncek, D. W. (2000). Schools and crime. In V. Goldsmith, P. G. McGuire, J. H. Mollenkopf, & T. A. Ross (Eds.), *Analyzing crime patterns: Frontiers of practice* (pp. 153–168). Thousand Oaks, CA: Sage.

Santiago, J. J. (1998). The problem of auto theft in Newark. In N. Lavigne & J. Wartell (Eds.), *Crime mapping case studies: Successes in the field* (Vol. 1, pp. 53–59). Washington, DC: Police Executive Research Forum.

Schmitz, P., Cooper, A., Davidson, A., & Roussow, K. (2000). Breaking alibis through cell phone mapping. In N. Lavigne & J. Wartell (Eds.), *Crime mapping case studies: Successes in the field* (Vol. 2, pp. 65–71). Washington, DC: Police Executive Research Forum.

Spatial Industries Business Association (SIBA). (2012). GIS and GPS track and convict serial killer: Investigations continue. Retrieved from www.xyz.au.com/public/general_info/details.cfm?info_id=726&sub_cat=56&category_id=15.

Suresh, G., & Vito, G. F. (2007). The tragedy of public housing: Spatial analysis of hotspots of aggravated assaults in Louisville, KY (1989–1998). *American Journal of Criminal Justice, 32*(1–2), 99–115, 130.

Suresh, G., & Vito, G. F. (2009). Homicide patterns and public housing: The case of Louisville, KY (1989–2007). *Homicide Studies, 13*(4), 411–433.

Taylor, R. B. (1998). Crime and small-scale places: What we know, what we can prevent, and what else we need to know. In National Institute of Justice (Ed.), *Crime and place: Plenary Papers of the 1997 Conference on Criminal Justice Research and Evaluation* (pp. 1–22). Washington, DC: U.S. Department of Justice.

Warden, J., & Shaw, J. (2000). Predicting a residential break-in pattern. In N. Lavigne & J. Wartell (Eds.), *Crime mapping case studies: Successes in the field* (Vol. 2, pp. 81–87). Washington, DC: Police Executive Research Forum.

Wernicke, S. (1998). Close the door on crime: A mapping project. In N. Lavigne & J. Wartell (Eds.), *Crime mapping case studies: Successes in the field* (Vol. 1, pp. 27–33). Washington, DC: Police Executive Research Forum.

Wernicke, S. (2000). Reducing construction site crime. Overland Park, Kansas. In N. Lavigne & J. Wartell (Eds.), *Crime mapping case studies: Successes in the field* (Vol. 2, pp. 29–36). Washington, DC: Police Executive Research Forum.

Winship, C. (2002). *End of a miracle? Crime, faith, and partnership in Boston in the 1990s.* Retrieved from www.wjh.harvard.edu/soc/faculty/winship/End_of_a_Miracle.pdf.

Woodby, K., & Johnson, A. (2000). Identifying a serial indecent exposure suspect. In N. Lavigne & J. Wartell (Eds.), *Crime mapping case studies: Successes in the field* (Vol. 2, pp. 55–63). Washington, DC: Police Executive Research Forum.

Crime Mapping and Analysis Data

▶ LEARNING OBJECTIVES

This chapter is designed to provide the beginning crime analyst and mapping student with an awareness of the different types of data commonly used in crime analysis and mapping. Data for crime analysis is produced in several different forms and can be obtained from many different places. While it is important to understand *how* and *when* to use different data types, it is first important to understand the key sources of data available and their characteristics. In this chapter, key data sources and different types of data are identified and discussed. In addition, readers will learn the importance of clean data, and the strengths and weaknesses of different data sources are examined. After studying this chapter, you should be able to:

- Know what is meant by the term *clean data*.
- Identify and explain different *units of analysis* for incident characteristics, including time and space.
- Know the appropriate uses for both qualitative and quantitative data.
- Understand the difference between *structured* and *unstructured* data.
- Identify and explain the major sources of crime data in the United States and be able to recognize their strengths and weaknesses.
- Understand the *crime funnel* of the criminal justice system and how it affects the crime data that mappers and analysts use.
- Explain different types of *contextual* data used in crime analysis and mapping, and list various resources for finding this data.
- Have a basic understanding of various issues with crime mapping data, including data sharing and ethical and legal issues.
- Have a basic understanding of the various tools that crime mappers and analysts use to create and modify crime maps and the tools used to present their findings to others.

▶ **Key Terms**

Attribute Table	Institutional Review Board	Probability Sample
Contextual Data	National Crime	TIGER
Data Cleaning	Victimization Survey	Uniform Crime Reports
Geocoding	National Incident-Based	
	Reporting System	

■ Introduction

Typical crime analysts work with different types of data and data sources throughout their careers. The audiences these analytical efforts attract could be the public, fellow analysts, police officers, command staff, other law enforcement agencies, and even other governmental entities. In a large number of these analytical efforts, the question at hand will not involve forecasting or predicting but simple production of maps that describe a crime problem. An example might be creating a beat map that shows patrol officers where new beat boundaries have been drawn, or showing the hotspots of armed robbery incidents in the city. The second type of analytical effort involves forecasting or predicting where something is likely to happen again, how many crimes of a specific type we might expect in a given area, and even where an offender could potentially live in relation to a series of crimes committed. When making a forecast or a prediction, the description of the problem is very important—how you define a problem significantly impacts any predictions you might develop about future developments of that problem.

Currently, a large number of excellent data sources are available for crime analysis and mapping, many of which are free of charge. Police departments, social welfare agencies, and even the U.S. Census Bureau are just a few of the data gold mines available to crime analysts. However, crime analysts must use a level of caution in the analysis process with all data, regardless of the source. The old adage "garbage in, garbage out" will serve you well. We must always address the data needs and analysis to be performed based on the audience to whom the analytic product will be directed. For example, we would likely need much less information about several specific incidents within a certain geographic boundary if we were presenting that information to a neighborhood watch group instead of a group of detectives within our own agency. The audience and the data that is available for the analysis requested will generally guide your mapping product to fruition. This works for not only the descriptive types of maps, but also those developed for problem solving and prediction. When we wish to make meaningful assumptions or assertions based on data we have collected, we need to take this concept a bit further and add the scientific process to the collection, collation, dissemination, and evaluation of the data we wish to use. Any analyst can make a map; the key is knowing your data well enough to make a map that turns data into information and information into actionable knowledge for your audience. There has been and will likely continue to be much argument about whether data collected by a police department is a sample or the entire population. From the police officers' perspective, the crime reports and information they write reports about is the true crime problem and represents the picture of crime within their jurisdiction. From the researchers' perspective, they know that not all crime is reported, and even policies within police departments may cause anomalies in the formal reporting of certain crimes (gas drive outs, very minor thefts, etc.). These policies are generally put into place to save time for officers to deal with more serious crimes and save money in the police department's budget. On the other hand, not all crime is actually reported to the police, so from a researcher's perspective, the data collected by a police department should be viewed as the entire population of *reported* crime and thus represented as such—keeping in mind that reported crime does not always represent true population characteristics of all committed crime.

Another important point to make here is that data will be organized and structured in a variety of forms. Qualitative data are often found in narrative, or nonnumeric, form. To use qualitative data, you will have to restructure it in a way that can be analyzed (often called "coding"). Quantitative data can also be found embedded in a narrative but are numeric in nature. Data can also be *structured* or *unstructured*. Structured data are contained within distinct fields (such as in a labeled column in a spreadsheet, or in fields on a form or report) that can be easily queried, manipulated, and analyzed on command. Many records-management systems are structured so that analysts can quickly access information based on queries, such as searching via computer database for all gang-related homicides in which the victim was under 18 years old. In this example, data about gang affiliation, crime, and age are contained in unique fields and the computer program essentially grabs the information based on the commands and presents it to the analyst in whatever form he/she requested. Structured data are nice because they are quick and easy to work with.

Unstructured data are trickier to access but arguably contain incredibly rich information that is very useful to crime analysis. Unstructured data are anything found in a records-management system that are not accessible by a unique field. The narrative in a police report is unstructured data, for example. Think about the potential of unstructured data for a minute. What if you could search everything in an agency's records-management system or a regional database or even the World Wide Web based on a few search terms? For example, at a recent International Association of Crime Analysts conference (IACA; 2011), a representative from uReveal (a data organization and analysis software company) recounted how using simple search terms of "male," "hostile toward police," who "carries a silver gun" yielded several police documents that enabled police to identify a suspect in a crime. uReveal's software took these simple search terms and identified similar search terms (so in addition to "silver gun," the program searched for "chrome pistol" and other similar search terms) and located all files that contained those terms and/or phrases. Of course, the analyst must be skilled and patient during the search process, and this type of software is not free, but it shows how powerful the ability to search unstructured data can be. (For more information on this product and unstructured data analysis, visit www.ureveal.com/.)

Another type of data is social network data. More and more, having an understanding of an offender's (or victim's) social network is becoming crucial to analyzing many different types of crimes. There are many different sources of data for performing social network analysis. First, much information can be gleaned from a department's own database. Simply analyzing how different offenders are connected through co-offending patterns can be useful. Social network analysis can also be helpful in identifying patterns of violence between gangs: Mapping out where gang members and gang affiliates live and where the violence occurs can provide rich detail to the problem of gang violence and may yield valuable information that would not have been discovered otherwise. At the 2011 IACA conference, a panel discussion on Blue Spider Analytics (commercial social network analysis software) outlined how social network analysis revealed two gangs who had been friendly in the past but were now fighting were connected by two females—it turns out that higher ranking males in both gangs were fighting over their girlfriends!

Another source of social network data can be found on various social networking sites such as Facebook, MySpace, and LinkedIn. Although gaining access to this information can be tricky at times (users can adjust privacy settings to keep information safeguarded), these social media sites can be goldmines for all kinds of information related to crime.

When doing meaningful research, it is important to determine if the data were properly collected following the guidelines of the scientific process. This includes the requirement that the data be a scientifically selected **probability sample** (which can be difficult or even impossible in many types of crime analysis). A probability sample is a scientifically selected sample group chosen from a larger population where all cases within that population have an equal chance of being selected to be in the sample group. There are many different sampling techniques that can be applied to the selection of both probability and nonprobability samples, and any good research methodology book will have detailed descriptions of each technique. For our purposes, you need to be able to justify that the cases you include in your analysis include all or are representative of the larger population that you are trying to explain. In crime mapping, this typically means including all cases or units that fit the required characteristics in the analysis. For example, if your analysis or crime map seeks to understand robbery-motivated homicides within city limits for a given time period, *all* known robbery-motivated homicides must be included in the analysis. If any are excluded, the analysis will be limited in its power to explain or predict these crimes. The problem is that the complete information about a particular crime is not always available, and analysts are left to make assumptions that may or may not be correct. For example, there may be a series of homicides that were motivated by robbery, but the evidence left behind fails to show a complete enough picture to rule them as such. In addition, there may be more than one motivation for the offender to commit homicide and robbery, but the data entry person may only list the most apparent one. Thus, the more assumptions an analyst must make in his or her analysis, the more likely there will be errors.

A second issue of concern for crime analysis is **data cleaning**. This process involves eliminating information that is unnecessary to your analysis and making sure there is no bad information. It can also mean taking the coded data and normalizing it so that anyone would understand what the codes mean. For example, a records-management system stores gender values as 0, 1, or 2, where 0 is unknown, 1 is male, and 2 is female. We would want to clean this field so that a layperson would understand what 0, 1, or 2 means when we get the data ready for a mapping production process. With quantitative analysis, most available data comes in a database management format (such as SPSS, Stata, SAS, Crystal Reports, a vendor's database product [records management system (RMS)], or Microsoft Access) or spreadsheet format (such as Excel). Cleaning the data simply involves running frequency reports or manually scanning the data for information that does not appear to be correct. This process, to many analysts, is a daily event. Any field within the dataset's rows could have errors that are created from commission (incorrectly entering the wrong information) or omission (leaving the field blank or null). For example, if you come across someone who is 157 years of age when computing frequencies or scanning the column that holds information of victims' ages, you obviously need to correct or clean up this person's file. It is possible that the person who entered the data (you, in some cases) accidentally hit the "1" key before typing in the person's true age of 57 years. In this case, simply deleting the extra numeral is the solution. The data could also just be incorrect, and if there are too many errors within one record, it may have to be excluded. Another example might be a victim whose cause of death is listed as gunshot to the head, but under the weapon field heading, a knife may be listed. Obviously, this does not make sense. The analyst will need to go back to the original report (if available) and clean up the data-entry mistakes. Depending on where the data come from, this may not be possible, and in this case, the entry may have to be removed from your analysis. An important point to make here is that you must never make assumptions about what the correct information is. In the first example, it may be possible that the 5 or 7 were incorrect, leaving the victim's true age to be 17 or 15 years—a far distance from 57. In the second example, it is possible that the perpetrator also used a knife, and thus simply replacing the knife with a gun would not present the entire picture. Another possible example would come from changes in policies, or even software and hardware, over time within a police agency. For example, when a department's records-management system (RMS) was first created, its creators might have used the race variables of B (black), W (white), S (Spanish), A (Asian), and O (other) as the only allowable entries. Over time and due to racial profiling complaints, the RMS may have undergone changes that shifted these variables to A (African American), C (Caucasian), H (Hispanic), and U (unknown or other). Chances are the data entered for older cases were not modified when the new format was made policy, and if you go back in time to do analysis, you may find the need to modify entries to match current policies and procedures to get good quality data to work with. Analysts need to be intimately familiar with their department's RMS to know what garbage needs to be sifted through in the cleaning process. There is a philosophical debate as to *who* in the department should be keepers of the data. In some departments, the belief is that correcting errors in the RMS is the responsibility of crime analysts. However, most analysts believe (and we agree) that this responsibility should be held by the records department or a similar custodial department, leaving the analyst the time required to perform crime analysis.

In addition to clean data, another topic often discussed with regard to crime mapping is the concept of scale. For example, if your analysis is general in nature and only covers a citywide scale, then chances are your detail and ultimate cleanliness of the data may not be as demanding as if you were analyzing a specific robbery series occurring within a geographic area of your city.

Choosing a unit of analysis or scale that is too small or too large may obscure important relationships. An illustration of this in crime analysis would be a comparison of two well known studies, the first being the infamous Kansas City Preventive Patrol Experiment. Published in 1974 by the Police Foundation (Kelling, Pate, Dieckman, & Brown, 1974), this study evaluated an experiment that was conducted by the Kansas City Police Department (KCPD). In this experiment, KCPD varied their patrol levels in 15 police beats. For approximately 1 year, 5 beats received no routine patrol (although police did respond to calls for service),

5 beats received at least double the amount of patrol they would normally receive, and 5 beats received the normal amount of patrol they had always received. Using multiple sources of data, including victimization surveys, reported crime rates, arrest data, a survey of local businesses, attitudinal surveys, and trained observers who monitored police–citizen interaction, the major findings were that crimes thought to be preventable by routine patrol, such as burglaries, auto thefts, robberies, and vandalism, were not changed. Based on these results, the utility of routine patrol, a key component of policing, was questioned. In addition to its inability to prevent crime, routine patrol was also determined in this study to have no impact on fear of crime or satisfaction with the police. This study's unit of analysis (the police beat) was based on political boundaries that were meaningless to crime control efforts. Recall from earlier discussions that caution must be used when selecting which unit of analysis to employ in analysis. This is very important in crime mapping and analysis. If the boundaries of an area that are being examined do not have spatial meaning to crime or the social context of crime, important relationships can be obscured. This point is supported by the results of another study of police patrol that was conducted almost 2 decades after the Kansas City experiment. In this study, the unit of analysis was a hotspot, a much smaller area than a police beat, whose borders are a function of crime itself and therefore are very meaningful to crime control efforts.

Sherman and Weisburd (1995) conducted their study of preventative patrol in the city of Minneapolis. This 1-year study also examined crime and disorder in 110 hotspots, 55 of which received increased levels of police patrol. Their findings indicated that hotspots that received a higher dosage of routine patrol showed modest reductions in crime and significant reductions in disorder. In this study, the unit of analysis, identified hotspots, intensifies the deterrent effects of preventative patrol.

Scale is also an important consideration when mapping crime. If we are doing analysis at a citywide scale, perhaps only the main streets are important and the residential streets only confuse the viewer. At a neighborhood scale, the main streets might not be as useful as the residential streets and alleyways, for instance, The quality of your geographic information system (GIS) data may also be affected by measures of scale. When the engineering department of your city drew in a lakefront, they may have drawn it at a citywide scale, thus when you zoom in, each cove and eddy within the lake's shorefront does not align with the actual shorefront, but may be straight lines, or only have some of the general tracings of the shoreline. In a burglary series where the offender is hitting lakeshore cabins, but then escaping by boat, having the shoreline drawn accurately to scale might be important not only for describing the problem, but also for making more precise forecasts or predictions.

As you can see, choosing the appropriate unit of analysis or scale is extremely important in analyzing crime. We cannot assume that the Kansas City Preventive Patrol Experiment would have yielded different results had the researchers chosen a smaller unit of analysis, but it is plausible that this could be the case. The following sections of this chapter narrow our discussion to examine specific types of data that are commonly used in crime mapping and analysis and their respective strengths and weaknesses. As you read this chapter, keep in mind the importance of having representative, clean data collected at the appropriate unit of analysis.

■ Measuring Crime

Crime is measured in a variety of ways, utilizing a variety of methodologies, each with its own strengths and weaknesses. Whether using "official" data or self-report measures, crime mappers must be intimately familiar with their data sources and be mindful of the limitations of these sources and how they impact the interpretation of their results. The following sections discuss some of the most common ways in which we currently measure crime, beginning with official crime data.

Provided in the discussions of commonly used data is also an examination of the strengths and weaknesses that impact interpretations of crime analysis performed using these data sources.

Official Crime Data

Official crime data can be classified into a few general categories: incidents, people, places, and things. Incident data typically include reported offenses, calls for service, arrests, traffic citations, and accidents. People data involve persons listed in reports, corrections data, probation information, parole records, and sex offender registry information. Places data include such things as locations (addresses) or boundaries for businesses, schools, beats, and council districts, and information about locations within the city that the analyst might use. Data surrounding things include property taken or recovered in a criminal incident, evidence found at a crime scene, stolen vehicles, weapons, and other items of interest to the analyst.

In addition, you need to consider that when working as a crime analyst within an agency, you are going to have access to essentially everything your agency collects in the four categories just discussed, but as a researcher, you need to build positive relationships with law enforcement agencies first, and then be specific about what data you would like them to provide for your analysis. Most data on calls for service, number and types of arrests, and reported offenses are public record in many states. Most states have legal restrictions on releasing any kind of persons data for privacy reasons. Often, persons data can only be released on people convicted of a crime; if a law enforcement agency arrested someone, information about that person does not fall into the conviction category and therefore privacy issues and legal ramifications exist if the data are released to the general public. There could also be restrictions on releasing the names and other information of homicide, rape, and child abuse victims within some agencies. Establishing a good working relationship and collaborative analysis agreement with a law enforcement agency will often reap great rewards in both data quantity and quality. You may have to pass a background examination and sign a non-secondary disclosure document to obtain privacy-protected data, if needed for your analysis. Although this was not meant to scare you from seeking this type of data, you do need to realize the issues facing law enforcement in many states and their seeming unwillingness to share their data.

Let's look at some of the more commonly available data, beginning with the most well known source of crime data for the general public. The **Uniform Crime Reports** (UCR) are published annually by the Federal Bureau of Investigation (FBI). Participating law enforcement agencies keep track of known offenses and report monthly aggregate totals to the FBI, which then analyzes this information to produce the Crime Index. Thus, the UCR is *summary* data. The UCR collects information on Part I index crimes, which consist of murder and nonnegligent manslaughter, forcible rape, robbery, aggravated assault, burglary, larceny–theft, motor vehicle theft, and arson. In addition, arrest data for Part II crimes (less serious crimes, including simple assaults and driving under the influence) are also collected. A major strength of the UCR is that it has been in operation since 1930 and thus is useful for trend analysis. The UCR is a great resource for analysts who are performing large-scale analyses. However, because the information that is collected represents crime totals for grouped categories and is measured at the agency level, comparisons based on place can only be made at the precinct or larger level (this is important for the analyst to keep in mind if he or she needs a smaller scale).

Other weaknesses of the UCR data for crime analysis include:

- The program is voluntary, and therefore not all agencies participate.
- Included offenses are only those known to police. Crimes not reported or discovered by police are not included in the UCR.
- The definitions for crimes differ from state to state, so what one agency considers to be a burglary based on its local criminal statutes may not be a burglary under UCR definitions. This often causes some confusion and potential weaknesses in the UCR data collection.
- UCR data are based on the primary or most serious offense that occurred during the commission of a crime. For example, if a suspect kidnapped, raped, and then murdered a victim, under UCR hierarchy rules, only the murder would be reported.
- UCR counts some crimes by the number of victims, not the number of incidents (e.g., assaults on officers and homicides).

Another source of publicly available data, the **National Incident-Based Reporting System** (NIBRS), a component of the UCR, provides greater detail in its crime reporting ability. In contrast to the UCR, it provides *incident*-level data. It was developed because the law enforcement community recognized a need for more detailed information about crime. While the UCR collects most of its crime data in the form of category totals, NIBRS breaks down data into specific subcategories. For example, the fraud offenses category contains the crimes of false pretenses/swindle/confidence game, credit card/automatic teller machine (ATM) fraud, impersonation, welfare fraud, and wire fraud. NIBRS collects information at the incident level for 22 different offense categories (Group A offenses) and records incident and arrest data about the incident, including victim and offender characteristics and types and value of property stolen and recovered (see **Table 7–1**). In addition, NIBRS collects arrest data (only) on 11 other offense categories (Group B offenses, see **Table 7–2**). The NIBRS program does not have the hierarchy rule and thus will provide information for *all* crimes a criminal commits within an incident. Furthermore, NIBRS includes updated definitions for crimes such as rape (the UCR does not account for male victims of rape, however, NIBRS does) and differentiates between attempted and completed crimes (the UCR Summary Reporting

TABLE 7-1 NIBRS Group A Offenses

1. Arson	12. Homicide offenses
2. Assault offenses: Aggravated assault, simple assault, intimidation	13. Kidnapping/abduction
3. Bribery	14. Larceny–theft offenses
4. Burglary/breaking and entering	15. Motor vehicle theft
5. Counterfeiting/forgery	16. Pornography/obscene material
6. Destruction/damage/vandalism of property	17. Prostitution offenses
7. Drug/narcotic offenses: Drug/narcotic violations, drug equipment violations	18. Robbery
8. Embezzlement	19. Sex offenses, forcible: Forcible rape, forcible sodomy, sexual assault with an object, forcible fondling
9. Extortion/blackmail	20. Sex offenses, nonforcible: Incest, statutory rape
10. Fraud offenses	21. Stolen property offenses (receiving, etc.)
11. Gambling offenses	22. Weapon law violations

Source: Data from the Federal Bureau of Investigation (FBI). (n.d.). UCR general FAQs. Retrieved from www.fbi.gov/about-us/cjis/ucr/frequently-asked-questions/ucr_faqs.

System does not). Last, NIBRS accounts for victimless crimes (e.g., drug offenses), whereas the Part 1 UCR Summary Reporting System only counts crimes against persons and crimes against property.

Although the NIBRS is a wonderful addition to the UCR and greatly enhances our abilities in crime analysis, it suffers from the same limitations as the UCR. In addition, NIBRS has not been around as long as the UCR, and not every state reports NIBRS data. The FBI reports that as of 2007, approximately 6444 law enforcement agencies reported NIBRS data to the UCR program, and there are 31 state programs certified for NIBRS participation. The Federal Bureau of Investigation (n.d.) states that "the data from those agencies represent 25 percent of the U.S. population and 25 percent of the crime statistics collected by the UCR program."

TABLE 7-2 NIBRS Group B Offenses

1. Bad checks	7. Liquor law violations
2. Curfew/loitering/vagrancy violations	8. Peeping Tom
3. Disorderly conduct	9. Runaway
4. Driving under the influence	10. Trespass of real property
5. Drunkenness	11. All other offenses
6. Family offenses, nonviolent	

Source: Data from the Federal Bureau of Investigation (FBI). (n.d.). UCR general FAQs. Retrieved from www.fbi.gov/about-us/cjis/ucr/frequently-asked-questions/ucr_faqs.

Both the UCR and NIBRS data can be accessed online and free of charge through the National Archive of Criminal Justice Data (NACJD) held by the Inter-University Consortium for Political and Social Research (ICPSR) housed at the University of Michigan. These data files can be easily downloaded to a personal computer, or the user can perform a limited, but useful, number of analyses online using the provided Survey Documentation and Analysis (SDA) program. In addition to the UCR and NIBRS, the NACJD hosts a website dedicated to GIS datasets that are organized into the following categories:

- Geographic data in mapping software files
- FIPS county codes
- Collection-specific county codes
- Census tract codes
- Zip codes
- Block groups
- Police precincts
- Police beats
- Addresses
- *XY* coordinates
- Reference collections to link geographic identifiers

Crime analysts may also access data from local law enforcement agencies. Depending on the agency, this may be a very simple or very complicated process, as discussed earlier. Typically, the analyst is employed by an agency, and thus data access is mostly a nonissue. Students, academic researchers, and outside analysts must usually go through a public records request process from the agency. Depending on how the data are collected and stored within the police department, the data may be furnished in a variety of electronic formats and may even be supplied in hard copy form. In this case, the researcher must enter the data into a database prior to analysis. A crime incidents database typically houses a wealth of information, including a record number; date of reported incident and occurrence (if known); type, method, and location of crime; and disposition. In most cases, characteristics about the victim and offender can also be included. When an arrest is made in the case, an arrest report is completed. This information is entered into an arrests database and contains basic information on the charge, date and often the location of the arrest, arrestee's address, and characteristics of the arrestee.

Calls for service data are generated from citizen- and officer-initiated calls for service. Typically, 911 dispatchers record information from a call, including the date and time of the call (and the time of police arrival), the type of call (what the complaint is), the location of the call (sometimes this is an exact address, sometimes it is a street segment or intersection), and the disposition(s) of a call. Calls for service records are useful to analysts, especially in performing evaluation of department performance measures, such as response times (which are often more important to citizen satisfaction than solving crimes). However, there are limitations that must be understood when using these data. First, when a citizen calls for police assistance, his or her depiction of the situation may be misleading or inaccurate, leading the dispatcher to enter an incorrect call type. However, many computer-aided dispatch (CAD) systems distinguish between an initial call type and a verified or final call type, or the initial call type may be verified by a detective after the call is investigated further. Second, many people may call police regarding the same incident. For example, several people may hear gunshots or someone screaming. Third, the address that the citizen calls from may not always be the address where the incident or crime occurred. A good example is a theft from a vehicle where the victim discovers the theft at his or her place of business, but drives home and calls police to make a report from there. In crime mapping, if each caller to an event receives a point on the map, analysis can count each caller as an incident, potentially producing artificially inflated results. Last, errors in inputting addresses can lead to difficulty in **geocoding** (the process of taking street addresses from a tabular file and matching them to a reference file to produce the points on a map). In addition to data and information values that could need a good cleaning, we also need to make sure that the address is in a format that will ensure that it geocodes properly when brought into a GIS system for mapping. For example, the person who entered the data may have typed the address as 123 Main St. when in fact it is 123 Main *Rd.* This is a threat to validity because unmatched addresses must either be matched manually (which can be time consuming) or removed from the analysis.

Police departments also keep track of traffic and accident information. Accident databases typically house information on the time and date of accidents, road conditions at the time of the accident, and violations of traffic laws, including whether or not alcohol played a role in a crash. Some states also collect information about whether or not one or more parties were using a cell phone at the time of the accident. Traffic databases hold information on traffic citations and vehicle stops. These data have a variety of uses. For example, in more recent years, these data have been used to perform racial profiling research.

A persons database contains information about people involved in a criminal incident. Usually linked to the criminal incident database, files contain information on witnesses, victims, and suspects. Probation and parole departments also maintain records about their parolees and probationers. These records are vital to investigations in crime mapping and can be used to prioritize a list of suspects who live or work near a criminal incident or within a journey to crime or geographic profile peak prediction area.

In addition to parolees and probationers, police departments maintain information on sex offenders who live within their jurisdiction. Known addresses of registered sex offenders can be examined in light of regulations that outline where this type of offender can live and work (most cities, for example, have laws forbidding sex offenders to live or work within 2000 or 2500 feet of a school, park, or daycare facility). Mapping capabilities make this analysis much more efficient. There may be challenges in court to distances that are calculated using mapping software, so analysts should verify the distance accuracy of their software and layers, which is considered spatial cleaning of the data. Additional "boots on the ground" verification will also often be used for court purposes in this case; or in other words, someone goes out to the location with a measuring tape.

Police departments may also maintain records on property and vehicles that have been stolen or recovered or have been used in the commission of a crime. These databases may also be linked to the criminal incident database through a record number. The primary information held by these databases is physical descriptions of the vehicle or property, vehicle identification numbers (VIN) and serial numbers, or other identifying information. Somewhat related to this category are files and information that are collected in reference to the location of evidence collected during an investigation. This could be such things as locations where a murder victim was taken, murdered, and his or her body dumped; where evidence was found; photos of the scene or evidence; or where cell phone towers from which phone calls were received or made from a suspect's phone are located.

All of these datasets are a wealth of information that can be formed into maps that provide actionable knowledge to police administrators, provide opportunities to test current research, do new research with new ideas on predicting, validate police responses, or simply inform the public of crime problems so they can help protect themselves.

Self-Report

The most widely known self-report data used in crime analysis is the **National Crime Victimization Survey** (NCVS). Launched in 1873 and housed by the NACJD, approximately 77,290 households (see the Bureau of Justice Statistics website at http://bjs.ojp.usdoj.gov for complete methodology) are selected in which household members (older than 12 years of age) are asked to report their victimization experiences, if any. The NCVS is especially interesting because it captures crimes that are unreported to police and elicits detailed information about crime victims and their experiences. However, the NCVS is not without its faults, which include:

- There is no way to verify if a respondent is providing truthful and accurate information.
- Information on homicides is not collected. ("Dead men can tell no tales.")
- Crime victims under the age of 12 years are unaccounted for.
- Victimless crime is unaccounted for.

As shown in this section's discussion of official and self-report crime data, analysts must take caution to ensure their data is the correct data, is clean, and is measured at the appropriate scale prior to performing any analyses. Remember, every dataset has its strengths and weaknesses and must be used appropriately if analysts wish to get accurate and usable results from their analyses.

The Crime Funnel

The crime funnel is an important model of crime in the criminal justice system and provides an important lesson for crime analysts. The basic premise is that as criminals progress through the criminal justice process (beginning with a crime being committed and ending with sentencing of the offender), the number of criminals who are processed within the formal criminal justice system becomes progressively smaller (see **Figure 7–1**).

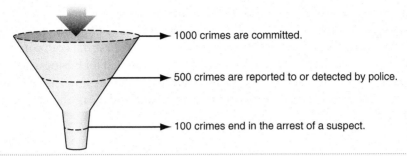

1000 crimes are committed.

500 crimes are reported to or detected by police.

100 crimes end in the arrest of a suspect.

Figure 7–1 Criminal Justice Funnel Model

Based on yearly comparisons of the UCR and NCVS data, it is argued that approximately half of crime is not reported to or detected by police. Of the 50% of crime that is known to police, only about 20% ends in the arrest of a suspect. This means that a suspect is arrested in only about 10% of all crimes committed. The likelihood of arrest is not evenly distributed across all crime types, however. Homicides, for example, generally obtain the attention of law enforcement, and murderers usually leave behind important physical evidence that helps aid in the successful investigation of the crime. On the other hand, business or residential burglary, if detected long after the burglars leave and if there are no witnesses to the crime, rarely ends in an arrest. Homicide, a crime that is most often reported to or detected by police, has a high clearance rate. Burglary, also often reported to police (because one needs a police report to submit to insurance agencies) has a low clearance rate due to the low arrest rate.

What does this mean to crime analysis? It means that the data crime analysts use to explain crime and make predictions about crime is often incomplete. This is a common limitation in crime mapping and analysis. For example, when examining a robbery series, an analyst may not have information on *all* of the robberies committed by an offender because some of them may not have been reported or another nearby agency had one or more currently unknown related robberies that met the series' modus operandi. Information about these unreported or unknown robberies may be important, even critical, in predicting where the next robbery is likely to take place or where the offender is likely to live or work.

The next section continues this chapter's discussion of data sources available to police. Here, we examine non-crime data that is important in crime analysis. Contextual data— information about the people or places involved in crimes—is just as important in understanding the larger picture of crime as the crime data itself.

■ Contextual Data

Contextual data contain information about people or places that is not crime related. For example, in crime mapping, analysts often include information about population characteristics, such as median income or the percentage of single-female-headed households. In addition, analysts often include places, such as bars or pawn shops, in their maps to provide context to the crimes they are analyzing. Contextual data are typically supplied by other public and private organizations outside of the criminal justice system. Census data are most commonly used in crime analysis. In crime mapping, locations of places such as businesses and areas such as school and voting districts are often used. These data can come from a city sales tax licensing department or commercial software designed for businesses that contains this information. In some cases you can even collect this data from Google Maps, Yahoo! Maps, or other types of Internet applications, manipulate and clean the data in Excel, and then geocode the results.

U.S. Census Bureau

The U.S. Census Bureau is a gold mine for crime analysts and crime mappers who are looking for contextual data. According to the U.S. Census Bureau website (2012), the first U.S. census (after America's independence) was taken in 1790. At this time, people were simply counted by U.S. Marshalls on horseback. In addition to the population census taken every 10 years, the U.S. Census Bureau has grown and expanded to include gathering information on fisheries, manufacturing, poverty, and crime, and today it collects information year round from households and businesses on a variety of important issues. Many of these issues have important implications in crime analysis. The following is a list of some categories of data that the Census Bureau collects, which are often used in crime research and analysis:

- Age
- Race/ethnicity
- Gender
- Marital status
- Education
- Income
- Poverty status
- Employment
- House value
- Own/rent

The Census Bureau website makes it very easy to download files in a variety of formats. In 2010, the bureau made some drastic changes to the American FactFinder website (http://factfinder2.census.gov/) that is now a place where you can do a multitude of queries for your geography and pull out various bits and pieces of census data. Those data are still being uploaded slowly but surely from the 2010 census. In addition, they have an online mapping component that allows users to quickly make basic maps of crime and other social variables that are important in understanding crime. The Topologically Integrated Geographic Encoding and Referencing (**TIGER**) system "is a Census Bureau computer database that contains all census-required map features and attributes for the United States and its possessions, plus the specifications, procedures, computer programs, and related input materials required to build and use it" (U.S. Census Bureau, 2004). Several states have direct links to these files from their own GIS websites, making it even easier for crime analysts to access locally relevant information.

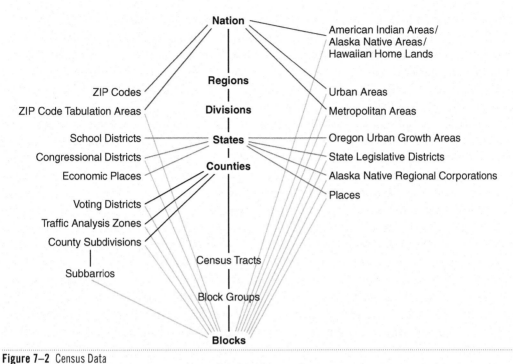

Figure 7–2 Census Data

Source: U.S. Census Bureau. (2002). Census Bureau geographic hierarchy. Retrieved from www.census.gov/geo/www/geodiagram.html.

Census information is organized by different units of analysis, beginning at the block level. **Figure 7–2** is a diagram developed by the Census Bureau to explain all levels of analysis for which data are available.

However, not *all* data are available at *all* levels of analysis. There are several reasons for this, the primary reason being the protection of privacy. Most information comes in the form of a mean or median or a percentage. For example, crime mappers could access the median household income or the percentage of persons who do not hold a high school diploma or equivalent at various levels (block, block group, tract, etc.).

Another noteworthy issue is that the recent changes to the American FactFinder website operated by the Census Bureau has, in an attempt to make obtaining census data much easier, actually made it more difficult in the opinion of some analysts. Chatter amongst various analyst listservs suggests that more work needs to be completed to make the data-collection process more user friendly.

Local Social Agencies

If the analyst does not find the contextual data he or she is looking for in the Census Bureau data, he or she may want to contact local government and/or social agencies. One of the best places to acquire current, local GIS files is at city and/or county planning departments. Some states even have a dedicated GIS agency. Massachusetts, for example, has the Office of Geo-graphic and Environmental Information, which maintains a publicly accessible website with links to state-specific data. It is extremely rare that a crime analyst would have the skills and training necessary to create the base map files necessary for geocoding and analyzing crime. Today, however, these skills are not required for the analyst because these files are almost always easily accessible from other agencies.

In addition to GIS files, other public agencies collect a variety of data that is useful to the crime analyst. Information about establishments with liquor licenses, public assistance and housing, abandoned buildings, and even graffiti cleanup are collected by various agencies and are great resources for crime analysts. However, it is up to the analysts to perform the legwork necessary to access these data files. Sometimes this may mean a simple phone call or email, but at other times, the process may be more lengthy or complicated. Regardless, these data can be very valuable to crime analysts. Furthermore, the analyst should always ask what the quality and accuracy of the data may be and how often they are updated or when they were last updated. A quick search and review of the metadata in ArcGIS might also be a wise endeavor for any dataset you might retrieve from one of these agencies if it is included. Know-ing the data well allows you to make useful assumptions rather than wild guesses.

Universities also store data that analysts can use. Earlier in this chapter we discussed ICPSR, which is housed within the University of Michigan. Many universities hold GIS-related data as part of their responsibility as data repositories. They also employ researchers who, in addition to data sharing, often collaborate with practitioners on a variety of research projects related to crime prevention, and these collaborations have often produced interesting and innovative research. In addition to universities, there are multiple websites (such as www .gislounge.com and www.esri.com/data/free-data) that hold GIS data free for the taking. Of course, caution must be employed when using these free sources of data because (depending on its original source) the data may contain errors that will impede accurate analysis.

■ Tools for Crime Analysts and Mappers

Aside from GIS software, crime mappers must also be proficient in a variety of other com-puter software programs. This text only discusses a few of these; however, as with crime mapping software, there are a variety of options to choose from depending on the applica-tions the analyst wishes to complete. Remember, the programs vary widely in their applica-tions and cost. In this text, we briefly discuss Microsoft programs because they are the most commonly used applications for crime analysts. These programs are relatively inexpensive but have powerful applications for crime analysts.

Microsoft

Microsoft Access is a desktop database program commonly used to store, query, and analyze data. Access is also capable of creating reports by using fairly simple functions. It is a relational database system, which allows an analyst to link related files and organize and analyze the data. It allows for a multidimensional view of tabular data and has tremendous capabilities in law enforcement and in crime analysis. Hicks (2007), for example, used Access and Microsoft Outlook (an email system) to develop a system whereby automated probationer contacts were created and compiled into a relational database. Every 24 hours this system checks police reports for the names and dates of birth of approximately 120,000 probationers. If an exact match is found, an email alert is generated and sent to Hicks and the assigned probation officer, giving a brief summary of what transpired (e.g., suspicious person? arrest?). This information can then be imported into Microsoft Excel for future quantitative analysis, or it can be geocoded onto a map for spatial analysis.

Excel is a spreadsheet application that allows the user to create multiple charts and graphs and to perform quantitative analyses as simple as counting or as complex as multivariate regression. It is the computational engine behind Access. One can also create an **attribute table** in Excel, which can be geocoded as a map layer. An attribute table contains the information that makes up a map's layer. For example, an attribute table of homicides would contain key information in columns (address, crime type, weapon used, victim and offender characteristics, etc.) for individual cases (listed in rows).

Microsoft Word and Microsoft PowerPoint are software programs used primarily for presentation purposes. In Word, one can type a professional-looking report by importing charts, graphs, tables, and even maps. It also has merging applications so that the user can quickly and easily print labels and envelopes for mailing. PowerPoint is often used for oral presentations, allowing the presenter to write text or import pictures, charts, tables, and even audio and video clips to slide presentations. It is also used to create flowcharts and other diagrams used in professional presentations.

Statistical Package for the Social Sciences

Statistical Package for the Social Sciences (SPSS) is commonly used in academia, government, and the private sector to enter, store, organize, and analyze data. Although it is much more expensive than Excel, SPSS is easier to use than Excel due to its point-and-click application. In a few short keystrokes, SPSS can perform complicated computations. While not part of its base software package, users also have the option to purchase a variety of extensions, including a mapping component. When analyzing survey data and doing regression analysis, SPSS can be very useful and speed up your ability to create reports or validate data.

Another very powerful, and free, resource is *R*. R is "a language and environment for statistical computing and graphics" (The R Project for Statistical Computing, n.d.). It was developed in the 1960s in the Bell Systems labs and can be used to perform a variety of mathematical and other functions and works easily with SPSS, SAS, Excel, and other data analysis programs, including OpenOffice. The language is pretty straightforward and allows for high-quality graphics. In addition, a variety of tools, plugins, and documentation are available, including the R commander, which allows for many "point-and-click" functions.

Other Software Tools

There are many different analysis tools to choose from, and it matters little which package is ultimately selected. The decision should be based on how user friendly the software is, what applications the analyst needs it to perform, what training the individual already has, and how much money the analyst/department is prepared to spend. One common tool, Crime Stat III, is a free program, sponsored by the National Institute of Justice (NIJ) and developed by Ned Levine and Associates, that allows the analyst to perform a wide variety of functions including hotspot, distance, journey-to-crime, and other analyses with relative ease. Microsoft Office, SPSS, and many other computer tools allow an analyst to perform many different types of analyses at varying degrees of ease and cost. Regardless of which tools the analyst selects for his or her toolbox, it is important to remember the lessons learned about the limitations of different types of statistical analyses and the weaknesses of different types of data that are discussed throughout this chapter.

It is also important to consider your audience again. If you are an academic creating your report for other academics, more complicated discussion of the specific regression models you used may be appropriate. If you are speaking to a group of police administrators, you may want to generalize the terms you use to a typical layman's vocabulary and by all means, make sure what you are telling them has some operational value to the mission of the police department. Telling a chief that you have proven through multiple-regression bivariate models that calls for service go up during storms likely will get you booted out of his office; however, telling the chief that you have developed a model that will allow officers to enter a beat, and it will tell them where they can go to be the most successful at preventing crime in that beat, might get you applause.

■ Data-Sharing Issues

The last section of this chapter finishes our discussion of data by examining issues of data sharing, including ethical issues and legal issues. There are a number of entities and persons who might request data from crime analysts and mappers. First, other agencies may wish to access data for their own analyses. Cities, for example, are not islands. They have borders that touch other towns or cities. Criminals often pay no attention to these borders and commit crimes in multiple jurisdictions. After all, have you ever seen lines in the street denoting which city you are in or which police beat? Well, the criminals do not see them either. An analysis that is conducted in only one town and ignores the white space of bordering jurisdictions will provide an incomplete picture of crime. Another issue regarding interagency data sharing has to do with the compatibility of computer programs. Many records-management systems were custom built for individual departments and may not interface well with other systems. Many law enforcement regional data–sharing systems are in the process of being developed nationwide, but the cost is substantial and often requires changes within the participating agencies that are difficult to implement. These systems may also provide only query capability for specific items or persons, and not "give me all the calls for service in the surrounding 1200 square miles."

Second, academic researchers are often interested in acquiring data for their own research projects. Traditionally, this relationship between police agencies and academics has been collegial and productive. However, it is important that both parties be clear about what the data will be used for and how issues of confidentiality will be maintained, as mentioned in the "Measuring Crime" section earlier in this chapter. In addition, when academics are doing research with police data, **institutional review boards** (IRBs) should review the research proposal to identify problems in methodology and ethics of the research design.

Third, citizens and community groups may also make periodic requests of crime analysts. In fact, many agencies have crime mapping availability for citizens on their department website. Some departments publish monthly or quarterly maps, while others allow interested citizens to interact with an online mapping component by entering an address or landmark to retrieve crime information. Upon doing so, aggregated crime data are presented in map form for the area surrounding the entered address or landmark. In many states, the addresses and names of persons involved in a criminal event are considered to be public information (except in the case of juveniles or sexual assault victims, where it can be argued that a victim's right to privacy outweighs the public's right to know), and thus maps that depict crime incidents at the address level would not normally pose privacy issues. However, with the widespread use of the Internet and increased mapping abilities, one can argue that the public's access to crime data is greater now than it has ever been. This may pose potential problems depending on who is accessing the crime maps and for what reasons (Wartell & Thomas, 2001).

A fourth issue has to do with the commercial use of crime maps that are made available by law enforcement. Private businesses, such as mortgage brokers, insurance agents, or businesses dealing in private security, may use crime maps in devious and discriminatory ways. Mortgage brokers and insurance agents, for example, could use crime information to refuse loans or insurance (or require overpriced premiums) to persons living in high-risk neighborhoods (a process called *redlining*; Zenou & Boccard, 1999). In addition, the people who live in these neighborhoods may be exploited by businesses that use crime maps to scare people into buying security measures. Remember that all data are relative. A hotspot map like those found on the Oakland Police Department's website (www.infoalamedacounty.org/index.php/Research/Crime-Safety/Crime-Research/Oakland-Crime-Hot-Spot-Maps-for-the-1st-Quarter-of-2011.html) show hotspots of data for Oakland alone. So, they are only relative to the other data and areas within Oakland, but not to the entire county or any neighboring cities. The analyst should keep this in mind as the places that are "hot" or densest are determined by the crimes in that jurisdiction and do not consider the other city counts in the surrounding area, or other data that were not included. It is possible that the hotspots shown on the Oakland map might actually be in other places if we used data from all of Alameda County in our hotspot map.

Last, the misuse of crime data or the analyst's failure to follow statistical rules in analysis (intentionally or unintentionally) may lead to maps that are difficult to interpret or mislead the viewer. For example, a map that displays crime information at the census tract level could be misinterpreted to mean that the *entire* census tract suffers from high rates of crime when it may only be one small section of the tract that has a large crime problem. People who view this information may decide not to conduct business in this tract, including purchasing homes or starting businesses.

■ Conclusion

As you can see, knowing which data sources to use and how to share the completed analysis (whether in report or map form) is a diverse and complex skill. Understanding and clearly articulating the limitations of analyses is critical to limiting the possibility of misinterpretations by your audience. Furthermore, understanding the legal and ethical issues involved with distributing crime maps, data, and analysis is imperative for crime analysts.

The Massachusetts Association of Crime Analysts' website contains an article entitled "The Ten Commandments of Crime Analysis" (Bruce, 1999), which provides a useful framework for summarizing the main points presented in this chapter. Several of these commandments are useful to our current discussion. First, commandment three states, "thou shalt take responsibility for thine own data." Crime analysts must be accountable in using appropriate, clean, timely, and accurate data in their analyses. Second (commandment five): "thou shalt never present statistics (or maps) by themselves." Analysts should always provide qualitative descriptions of the maps and analyses they present, making sure to include any limitations of the analyses. Commandments six and seven, "thou shalt know thy jurisdiction from one end unto the other," and, "thou shalt not stop crime analysis at thy jurisdiction's borders," reinforce the notion that many jurisdictional or municipal boundaries commonly used in mapping files have no real meaning to crime and/or criminals. It is important for analysts to have an understanding of the hotspots in their jurisdiction as well as an understanding of how crime in bordering jurisdictions affects one another. The eighth commandment of crime analysis is, "thou shalt focus equal attention on the six Ws." Thus, the analyst should attempt to answer the who, what, where, when, how, and why of crime series, patterns, and hotspots. Finally, commandment nine asks that analysts "remember thy community, and keep it holy." This includes prioritizing crime analysis activities and providing as much information as you can without violating the privacy of crime victims and others or causing harm to ongoing investigations.

■ Chapter Glossary

Attribute table   An attribute table contains the information that makes up a map's layer. It is contained in a spreadsheet or database application, such as Excel or Access. For example, an attribute table of homicides would contain key information in columns (address, crime type, weapon used, victim and offender characteristics, etc.) for individual cases listed in rows.

Contextual data   Contextual data include information on variables related to crime, but not crime itself. Contextual data often include information about population or spatial characteristics.

Data cleaning   The process of eliminating information unnecessary to your analysis and making sure there is no bad information. It may also mean creating or computing new variables needed for an analysis or recoding existing variables into a format that is more useful or easier to use in the analysis.

Geocoding   Geocoding is the process of taking street addresses from a tabular file and matching them to a reference file to produce the points on a map.

Institutional review board   An internal review system typically found in colleges and universities that is concerned with the potential ethical issues in research proposed by faculty, staff, and students.

National Crime Victimization Survey   A self-report survey of crime in the United States, launched in 1873 and housed by the National Archive of Criminal Justice Data (NACJD). Approximately 77,290 households are selected in which household members (older than 12 years of age) are asked to report their victimization experiences, if any. The NCVS captures those crimes that are unreported to police and elicits detailed information about crime victims and their experiences.

National Incident-Based Reporting System   NIBRS collects information at the incident level for 22 offense categories (Group A offenses) and records incident and arrest data about the incident, including victim and offender characteristics, and types and value of property stolen and recovered. In addition, NIBRS collects arrest data (only) on 11 other offense categories (Group B offenses). NIBRS collects incident-level data and breaks down the data into specific subcategories. Not every state participates in the NIBRS data collection system.

Probability sample   A probability sample is a sample group scientifically selected from a larger population in which all cases within that population have an equal chance of being selected to be in the sample group.

TIGER   The Topologically Integrated Geographic Encoding and Referencing system is a computer database operated by the U.S. Census Bureau that contains all of the census-required map features and attributes for the United States, including the specifications, procedures, computer programs, and related input materials that are necessary to develop and utilize it.

Uniform Crime Reports   Participating law enforcement agencies keep track of known offenses (primarily Part I index crimes) and report monthly totals to the Federal Bureau of Investigation (FBI), which then analyzes this information to produce the Crime Index. The UCR data are published annually by the FBI.

■ **Questions for Review**

1. What are the limitations of using department crime data in crime analysis?
2. What is the difference between structured and unstructured data?
3. Why is the selection of scale or unit of analysis so important in creating crime maps or performing crime analysis?
4. What are the strengths and weaknesses of the UCR?
5. What are the strengths and weakness of the NIBRS?
6. What are the limitations of using calls for service data?

7. What is contextual data, and how is it useful to crime mapping and analysis? Provide an example of contextual data in your discussion.

8. What is geocoding?

9. What are the ethical and legal considerations in sharing data with other agencies or the public?

10. What are the "ten commandments" of crime analysis?

■ **Online Resources**

Blue Spider Analytics: www.bluespiders.net/

Bureau of Justice Statistics: http://bjs.ojp.usdoj.gov/

Crime Stat III: www.icpsr.umich.edu/CrimeStat/

FBI Stats and Services: www.fbi.gov/stats-services/fbi-resources

The R Project for Statistical Computing: www.r-project.org/index.html

U.S. Census Bureau: www.census.gov/

uReveal Software: www.ureveal.com/

■ **Recommended Reading**

Adler, J. (2010). *R in a nutshell: A desktop quick reference.* Sebastopol, CA: O'Reilly Media.

Cornillan, P. A., Josse, J., Guyader, A., Kloareg, M., Husson, F., Matzner-Lober, E., . . . Rouviere, L. (2012). *R for Statistics.* Boca Raton, FL: CRC Press.

Crawley, M. (2007). *The R Book.* New York: Wiley.

Stallo, M. A. (2003). *Using Microsoft Office to improve law enforcement operations: Crime analysis, community policing, and investigations.* Analysis Consulting and Training for Law Enforcement, Inc. Retrieved from www.actnowinc.org/.Stallo, M. A., & Bruce, C. (2008). *Better policing with Microsoft Office.* Charleston, SC: BookSurge.

Teetor, P. (2011). *R Cookbook.* Sebastopol, CA: O'Reilly Media.

■ **References**

Bruce, C. (1999). *The ten commandments of crime analysis.* Retrieved from www.macrimeanalysts .com/articles/tencommandments.pdf.

Federal Bureau of Investigation. (n.d.). *National incident-based reporting system: Frequently asked questions.* Retrieved from www.fbi.gov/about-us/cjis/ucr/frequently-asked-questions/nibrs_ faqs#agencyparticipation.

Hicks, D. (2007). *Spatial analysis of probationer contacts and automated email alerts: NIJ workshop.* Presented at the 9th Crime Mapping Research Conference, March 28–31, 2007, Pittsburgh, PA.

International Association of Crime Analysts. (2011). Joint Training Conference, Hyannis, MA. September 19–23, 2011.

Kelling, G. L., Pate, T., Dieckman, D., & Brown, C. E. (1974). *The Kansas City preventive patrol experiment: A summary report.* Washington, DC: Police Foundation.

The R Project for Statistical Computing. (n.d.). *Introduction to R*. Retrieved from www.r-project.org.

Sherman, L. W., & Weisburd, D. (1995). General deterrent effects of police patrol in crime "hot spots": A randomized, controlled trial. *Justice Quarterly, 12*(4), 625.

U.S. Census Bureau. (2004). *Maps in American FactFinder*. Retrieved from http://factfinder2.census .gov/faces/nav/jsf/pages/index.xhtml.

U.S. Census Bureau. (2012). Census of population and housing *1790 Census*. Retrieved from www .census.gov/prod/www/abs/decennial/1790.html.

Wartell, J., & Thomas, J. T. (2001). *Privacy in the information age: A guide for sharing crime maps and spatial data*. Washington, DC: National Institute of Justice. Retrieved from www.ncjrs.gov/ txtfiles1/nij/188739.txt.

Zenou, Y., & Boccard, N. (1999). Racial discrimination and redlining in cities. *Journal of Urban Economics, 48*, 260–285.

People and Places: Current Crime Trends

▸ LEARNING OBJECTIVES

Students from every major discipline can acknowledge that crime is not randomly or equally distributed across population, time, or space. Crime rates can be affected by such things as geographic considerations and/or changes within an infrastructure, weather conditions and major weather events, economic conditions and political changes, isolated events such as a mass killing or terrorist attacks, the use of the death penalty, and many others. While many of these conditions change with some level of **predictability** (like the change of season), others are spontaneous events that create a wave of change that can be both unanticipated and long lasting (such as hurricane Katrina, 9/11, and the Virginia Tech shootings). This chapter provides a snapshot view of what crime looks like today and how it has changed over the last few decades. We also discuss crime trends and their changes over time. Current trends in criminal offending and victimization, offender and victim characteristics, and how crime trends exist in time and space are emphasized. After studying this chapter, you should be able to:

- Identify who is at the greatest risk of becoming a victim of various crimes based on age, gender, and race.
- Identify who is most likely to commit various crimes based on age, gender, and race.
- Identify different motivations for offending.
- Understand the nature of victim and offender relationships.
- Explain patterns in group crimes.
- Understand the role victims play in their own victimization.
- Understand the role of drugs and alcohol in crime.
- Identify the relationship between geographic size, location, time, and crime.

▸ **Key Terms**

NVAT	Victim Precipitation	Victimization Rates
Part I Index Offenses	Victim–Offender	Violent Victimization
Predictability	Relationships	

■ Introduction

This chapter examines data—including calls for service, arrest data, victimization surveys, and information collected by the U.S. Census Bureau—to identify the trends and patterns found in criminal offending and victimization. This chapter also includes a discussion of any changes in trends or patterns that have occurred within the last few decades. Students should view the information contained in this chapter with a critical eye using what they have learned about the strengths and weaknesses of crime measurement and statistical analysis. The majority of the information discussed in this chapter comes from the Uniform Crime Reports (UCR) and the National Crime Victimization Survey (NCVS). You should keep in mind that depending on what information you are viewing (or looking for), the data may be collected differently, and the most recently available data may not be within the same year. Thus, we have attempted to present you with the most recent information, but by the time this text is published, for at least some of the information, newer information could be available. This is something you may run into as a crime analyst. There are different ways to deal with it—understanding the long-term trends can be very important in this process—but it can make analysis much like doing a treasure hunt and putting a puzzle together at the same time.

The overwhelming majority of calls to police are not crime related. Durose, Schmitt, and Langan (2005) reported for the Bureau of Justice Statistics (BJS) that of the 45.3 million people who had personal contact with police in 2002, only 2.9% were arrested by police. A more recent report suggests that contacts with the police have been decreasing, with an estimated 40 million persons (age 16 and older) having contact with police (Eith & Durose, 2011). The most common reason for police–public contact is traffic stops. The second most frequent contact involves crime-related incidents. Only about 8.3 million of the face-to-face contacts in 2008 involved a crime or related problem. This approximate 30% drop in crime-related contacts was consistent with the NCVS reported reductions in victimizations for 2008. This is an important notion for the analyst to understand because he or she will most likely be called upon to complete analyses for the department that focus on quality of life issues, such as barking dogs or loud parties. In the sections that follow, a description of a current snapshot of crime in the United States is provided, organized by trends across people and places.

■ People

The primary people involved in criminal incidents are, of course, victims and offenders. When these two types of people interact, you have a criminal event. Witnesses, responsible parties, investigative leads, and other persons help us to collect information about how the event happened, where it happened, and who did what to whom. The following sections discuss characteristics of both victims and offenders based on crime data from the UCR and the NCVS. When reading this chapter, keep in mind the strengths and weaknesses of each of these data sources. Also, try to imagine why and how characteristics of people interact with time and space for a more comprehensive picture of crime.

Victims

The UCR is a voluntary reporting system for law enforcement agencies that measures **Part I index offenses**. (Remember, the UCR crime rates are reported as rates per 100,000 people. This is done to make the statistics more meaningful to the reader and is used as a way to make the data comparable across jurisdictions of various sizes.) According to the Federal Bureau of Investigation (FBI), an estimated 1,246,248 crimes of violence (murder, forcible rape, robbery, and aggravated assault) were reported to the UCR in the United States in 2010. This is approximately a 6% reduction from 2009, and a 13.4 % reduction from 2001. (Crime trends often show minor fluctuations over short time periods while reflecting more consistent patterns over longer time periods.) In 2010, reported property crimes (burglary, larceny–theft, motor vehicle theft, and arson) totaled 9,082,887. This is a decrease of 2.7% from 2009 and a decrease of 19.6% from 2001 (see **Figure 8–1**).

In 2010, murder was the least frequent form of violent victimization (approximately 6 murders per 100,000 persons). In 2010, this rate decreased to 4.8 murders per 100,000 inhabitants. While males of all races accounted for approximately 77% of murdered victims between 1976 and 2010, for victims where the race is known (all but 152 cases), 50.4% were black, 47.0% were white, and 2.6% were from other racial backgrounds. Persons aged 18–24 years were at highest risk of being murdered during this same time period.

The NCVS indicates similar crime trends over time. However, it consistently estimates that there is approximately twice the number of crimes committed as are reported to the UCR, supporting the general assertion that this report may be a better indicator of victimizations in the United States (see **Figure 8–2**). A recent BJS report (Truman, 2011) stated that approximately 50% of all violent crime and 40% of property crime victims reported the incident(s) to police—and that this reporting behavior had been consistent for the last decade.

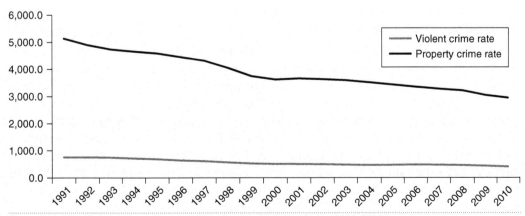

Figure 8–1 UCR: Violent Crime and Property Crime Rates in the United States, 1991–2010

Source: Data from NCVS study.

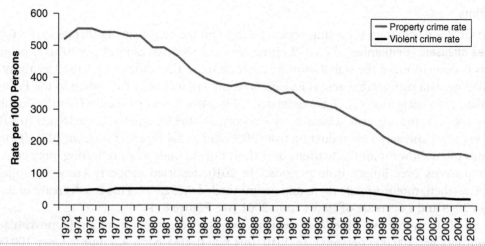

Figure 8–2 NCVS: Violent Crimes and Property Crime Rates in the United States, 1973–2005

Source: Data from NCVS study.

Note that in Figure 8-2, violent crime rates are separated into "series included" and "series excluded" categories. The series included category contains *all* victimizations, regardless of whether or not they were repeat victimizations (such as in a domestic violence relationship). By excluding repeat victimizations, we get a much different picture about victimization (as you can see, repeat victimizations account for a significant portion of events). The NCVS uses three criteria to determine whether an incident is considered a "series" victimization:

1. The incident occurred 6 or more times during the previous 6 months.
2. The incidents are similar to each other in detail.
3. The respondent is unable to recall enough detail about each event to adequately distinguish them from each other.

According to the NCVS (recall that the NCVS reports crime rates per 1000 people, only measures crimes perpetrated against victims age 12 years and older, and excludes victims of murder), 18.7 million crimes were committed against U.S. residents 12 years of age or older in 2010. Of these crimes, an estimated 14.8 million were property crimes, 3.8 million were violent crimes, 1.4 million were serious violent crimes (rapes or sexual assaults, robbery, and aggravated assault), and 138,000 were personal thefts. Of the approximately 3.8 million violent crimes during this period, slightly over 36% were serious violent crimes (Truman, 2011). In 2010, the national violent crime rate was down 34% from what it was in 2001, and for the most part, it has been steadily decreasing since about 1993. This does not mean, however, that every city in America has been enjoying lower crime rates. As will be discussed later in this chapter, while crime has been steadily declining for the nation as a whole, it has been increasing for different demographic groups and in different areas of the country.

According to the NCVS, males were at a slightly higher risk for violent victimization in 2010, at 15.7 per 1000 males age 12 years and older (this higher risk for males is true for all violent crime categories with the exception of sexual assaults). Females were victims of violent crimes at a rate of 14.2 per 1000 females age 12 years and older. This is the first time in history that males and females have had such similar violent victimization rates. When looking just at **victimization rates** for simple assault, there is not a significant or substantive difference in victimization rates across gender (males = 9.7 per 1000 and females = 9.2 per 1000).

In 2010, the NCVS reported that persons between the ages of 18 and 20 years held the dubious honor of being the group with the highest rate of most types of **violent victimization**: 33.9 per 1000 persons within this age group. Persons in the age groups 50 to 64 years and 65 years or older held the lowest risks of violent victimization. This trend remains fairly consistent over time, with the highest risk of being a victim of a violent crime belonging to persons under the age of 24 years. Thus, the risk of violent victimization progressively decreases with age.

This crime trend presents an excellent opportunity for the budding analyst to ponder a few questions about this victimization trend and what influences it. When considering the violent victimization rate previously shown for those over age 50 years, how do you think the following considerations affect that rate, and why does it appear to remain so stable?

- Activities of the victim
- Location of the victim
- Environment of the victim
- Age of the victim
- The number of potential victims in that community or particular location
- The extent of the violence perpetrated upon those victims

Now consider what is known about the victim population. In general, we can say with some certainty that this population (people aged 50 years and older) in general is more likely to perform its daily activities during the day and tends to curtail its movements in the evening hours. We can also say that this population tends to live in one location for longer periods of time and probably has a sense of its community. We can also say that this population, by and large, tends to be physically weaker than the typical offender population and may live alone, as with the case of widows and widowers. How do you think these factors combine to create or thwart victimization? As the baby boomer population bubble enters the retirement years (beginning in 2008), do you think this trend will remain consistent? If one considers the cities where large segments of the population are in these age groups (such as Phoenix, Arizona), how might that affect the mapping process, and what data characteristics might analysts screen when performing their analyses?

When using the online NCVS Data Analysis Tool (**NVAT**), persons younger than age 20 years had the highest risk of victimization of property crimes. Persons between the ages of 50 and 64 years and those 65 years old or older were the least likely to experience property victimization. However, while the elderly were least likely to be victims of property crime, more than 90% of crimes against the elderly between 1993 and 2002 were property crimes. An article reporting on Maricopa County, Arizona quoted the Area Agency on Aging as having more than 50% of their calls in the area of financial exploitation (Tabachnick, 2009). (Is this a matter of better reporting, being easier targets, or more property ownership? Again, these are things to consider when analyzing crime trends.) Teens and young adults experienced the highest rates of victimization for both property and violent crimes. Approximately 40% of crimes against persons aged 12 to 24 years between 1993 and 2002 were property crimes.

When examining the impact of race on victimization, the NCVS data show that "black victims experienced higher rates of violence than whites or persons of other races" (Rand & Catalano, 2007, p. 4). However, in 2010, American Indian and Alaskan Native and households reporting two or more races showed the highest rate of violent victimization (52.6 and 42.2 per 1000 respectively). The overall rate of violent victimization for black individuals was 20.8 per 1000 black persons in 2010. For white individuals for the same year, the overall rate of violent victimization was 13.6 per 1000 whites. Property crime rates for Hispanics (152.1 per 1000 households) were higher than property crime rates for non-Hispanic white or black households (115.5 and 150.5 per 1000 households; BJS NVAT, 2010). Again, however, households with more than one race accounted for the highest risk, 296.1 per 1000 households.

According to NCVS data, in 2010 black women were at a higher risk to be victims of violent crime (with a rate of 25.9 victimizations per 1000 black women) than white women (16.7 victims of a personal crime per 1000 white women; Truman, 2011). Black women were also at almost a three times greater risk for being the victim of a rape or sexual assault. The risk of being a victim of a rape or sexual assault for Hispanic women (1.1 per 1000) was slightly higher than for non-Hispanic women (0.7 per 1000; BJS, 2005).

When examining variations in victimization rates based on socioeconomic status, persons in households with an annual income between $7500 and $14,999 (in 2010) had higher rates for burglary victimization. This is true for both black and white victims. Households with an annual income below $7500 suffered the highest rates of violent victimization.

When examining the impact of marital status on victimization, a few interesting trends emerge. According to NCVS data, persons who never married have the highest rate of victimization for violent crimes (39 per 1000 persons never married). This group is followed in risk by persons who are divorced or separated (32.8 per 1000 divorced or separated persons), then persons who are married (10.8 per 1000 married persons), followed by widowed persons, who are at the lowest risk of being victimized of a personal crime (6.9 per 1000 widowed persons; BJS, 2005). These trends follow common sense in that a large number of persons who have not yet married are young (hence the highest risk), and a large number of persons who are widowed are older (hence the lowest risk). Much of the victimization risk of divorced or separated persons can also be explained by other factors, such as age and socioeconomic status because divorces are expensive and often leave one partner with a worse financial condition than he or she had during the marriage. Divorced or separated females, for example, have slightly higher rates of victimization for crimes of violence overall and are at higher risk to be victimized of completed acts of violence, rape and sexual assault, and simple assault (BJS, 2005).

When looking at the number of persons living within a household, it appears that the more people living under one roof, the higher rate of victimization the household suffers. For example, the rate of household victimization for a property crime in 2010 was 92.0 per 1000 households for households with only one occupant. This rate increases progressively, and households with six or more persons suffer a rate of 218.5 property crimes per 1000 households with six or more occupants (Truman, 2011).

Last, in examining the notion of time, in 2008 approximately 53.6% of violent victimizations (excluding murder) occurred during the daytime (6:00 A.M. to 6:00 P.M.). Forty-three percent of violent crimes occurred between the hours of 6:00 P.M. and midnight. For property crimes, this pattern changes modestly. In 2008, approximately 40.5% of property crimes were committed between the hours of 6:00 A.M. and 6:00 P.M., and 42.9% of the crimes were committed during the nighttime (12.7% between 6:00 P.M. and midnight, and 17.8% between midnight and 6:00 A.M.; for the remaining nighttime crimes, an exact time was not specified; BJS, 2008).

Offenders

Many of the same trends and patterns of victimization also appear in patterns of offending. This is because *most* crime is largely intra-age, intra-race, and intra-class—meaning that offender and victim populations tend to be within the same group. That is, a young, white male is most likely to be victimized by a young, white male. For example, in 2008 according to NCVS data, male victims of single-offender crimes perceived 77.6% of their offenders to be male for overall crimes of violence (Rand & Robinson, 2011). Consistently, white victims of violent crimes perceived their offenders to be white most (67.4% in 2008) of the time and perceived their offenders to be black only some (15.9%) of the time. Black victims of violent crimes perceive the race of their offenders most often to be black (64.7% of the time in 2008) and white only some (15.4%) of the time.

Overall, approximately 58.4% of offenders were perceived by their victims to be white compared with 22.8% who were perceived to be black. However, when examining individual crime categories, victims perceived their offenders to be white a higher percentage of the time for the categories of attempting to take property with injury (attempted robbery) and for both categories of assault (simple and aggravated). For the categories of rape and sexual assault and robbery (completed and attempted without injury), victims perceived the race of their offenders to be black a higher percentage of the time.

The FBI estimated that 13,120,947 arrests for all offenses (excluding traffic violations) were made in 2010. Approximately 1,643,962 of these arrests were for property crimes and 552,077 were for violent crimes. Drug abuse violations accounted for 1,638,846 of total arrests. Approximately 87.4% of the total arrests in 2010 were of persons aged 18 years and older. Almost 90% of the drug abuse violation arrests were adults. Adults accounted for 86.3% of all violent crime arrests and 77.5% of property crime arrests.

Males accounted for a larger percentage of the distribution of arrested persons (74.5% for total crimes, 80.5% of violent crimes) for every crime category measured by the UCR except embezzlement and prostitution, although males and females were very close in larceny–theft offending (56.1/43.9). (Females accounted for 50.5% and 68.7% respectively.) Females also accounted for 10.9% of persons arrested for murder and nonnegligent manslaughter.

For total offenses, whites accounted for 69.4% of arrested persons, and when compared to blacks on various crime types, whites accounted for more of the arrests for all other categories except for robbery and gambling (FBI, 2010).

Motivations for Offending

Depending on the type of crime, offender motivations may not be completely known. Oftentimes they are assumed by clues left at a crime scene or by victim and witness accounts of the crime. Sometimes the offenders themselves offer their motivations for committing crimes. For most property crimes, such as larceny and burglary, and violent crimes, such as robbery, the motivation is usually assumed to revolve around economics. However, motivations become more difficult to ascertain for crimes such as vandalizing property, auto theft, and arson. In some instances of auto theft, for example, the offender may have simply needed to get somewhere; other times, especially with juveniles, the thrill of stealing a car is the motivation. In addition, the motivations for burglary are thought to be much more complex than simple economic gain, and self-report studies have identified several motivations beyond monetary gain, including the excitement of the job, the challenge, and using one's intelligence to beat the police (Wood, Gove, & Cochran, 1994). Research also suggests that criminals typically do not specialize in any one crime type and that a majority of crime is opportunistic, negating the need for high levels of forethought and planning (Farrington, 1992; Gottfredson & Hirschi, 1990). Wood et al. (1994), in their study of incarcerated adults in Oklahoma, found that a variety of motivations existed for the crimes of shoplifting, burglary, robbery, rape, and assault, including:

- Ease of opportunity
- Thrill or excitement
- Money and property rewards
- Difficulty and challenge
- Anger, frustration, and rage
- Power and control
- Sexual relief and/or satisfaction
- Revenge/hatred/payback
- Sudden impulse or whim
- Unintentional/accident
- Offender was on drugs
- Respect and admiration of others
- To buy or steal drugs or alcohol
- Need money for food, rent, or bills
- Peer pressure or group behavior

For shoplifting, offenders in Wood et al.'s (1994) study ranked money and excitement as the most important motivations for their crime. For burglary, monetary motivations were ranked as very important by most offenders, while the ease of opportunity and the thrill or excitement were also very important. This is also true for robbers who indicated that power and control were important motivations behind their crimes. For the crime of rape, offenders ranked the ease of opportunity, the thrill or "high" of performing the act, anger/frustration/rage, power and control, sexual satisfaction, revenge/hatred/payback, and a sudden impulse as very important motivations for their crimes. Last, for assault, offenders noted the motivations of the thrill of excitement and the "high," anger/frustration/rage, power and control, revenge/hatred/payback, a sudden impulse, being on drugs, earning admiration and respect from others, and peer or group pressure as being important. Felson and Boba (2010) suggest that:

> Most criminals take a rather casual approach to crime, still making decisions. The point of crime is to get things without having to work hard and without much dedication; thus, most crime is quick and easy, and most offenders are unskilled. That does not mean they are stupid, merely that they do not usually put forth a lot of effort (p. 50).

Determining the motivations for crimes is often a difficult task because we are left to make assumptions based on the information left at crime scenes and the self-reports of victims, witnesses, and offenders involved in the crimes (which can be suspect). Information about bias, however, is typically more readily available in hate crimes. For example, the FBI reports that in 2010, there were 8208 victims of hate crimes. Of these, 48.2% were targeted because of their race, 18.9% were targeted because of their religion, and 18.6% were targeted because of their sexual orientation. In addition, 13.7% of hate crime victims were targeted because of their ethnicity or national origin, and less than 1% were targeted because of their disability. For hate crimes motivated by racial bias, 70% were targeted because of anti-black sentiment, 17.7% because of anti-white bias. Approximately 67% of religious-based hate crimes were anti-Jewish attacks, and 12.7% were attacks based on anti-Islamic bias. For hate crimes motivated by a bias against sexual orientation, the majority of attacks were credited to anti-male-homosexual bias. When examining ethnicity, 66.6% of attacks were anti-Hispanic. Finally, of the 48 persons targeted because of their disability, half were attacked because of a mental disability, the remaining half because of a physical disability.

Victim–Offender Relationships

Victim-offender relationships are important in understanding heightened risk for certain crimes in specific places. For example, you are much more likely to be victimized by someone you know or are acquainted with. For violent crimes in 2008, approximately 36% of victimizations were committed by persons who were strangers to their victims (another 5% were not sure who their offender was). Most homicide victims knew their murderers in some capacity (BJS, 2005). The number of homicides where the relationship between the victim and offender is unknown has been decreasing since 1999 (BJS, 2005). The percentage of homicides where the offender was unknown in 2009 was 46.8% (Puzzanchera & Kang, 2011). The nature of victim and offender relationships varies by crime type. For example, when examining rape and sexual assault, only about 35% of offenders were strangers to their victims. For robbery, only 39.5% of offenders were known to their victims (BJS, 2008). When examining relationships between victims and offenders, some interesting patterns emerge. For example, the NCVS indicates that for 2008, approximately 62.8% of the offenders who victimize males were strangers (for violent crimes). For female victims of violent crime, however, only 35.8% were strangers. Each year most murder victims are male. In 2009, approximately 65.6% of murder victims were male. Of all murder cases where the relationship between the victim and offender is known, 53% of victims were killed by someone they were acquainted with, and 24.8% were killed by family members (FBI, 2010). In 2010, approximately 56.5% of murder victims knew their offenders. These offenders are overwhelmingly males aged 18 years or older. Approximately 41.8% of murder victims were killed during arguments; another 23.1% were killed during the commission of other felonies.

Only one in 320 households in 2005 experienced intimate partner violence (Klaus, 2007). Nonfatal intimate partner violence has been declining since 1993 (Catalano, 2006b). Young females victimized by males have been the typical picture historically. Within same-sex relationships, rates of intimate partner violence are similar to those of heterosexual relationships—however, their reporting behavior is much lower. Married females reported the lowest rates of nonfatal intimate partner violence, while separated females reported the highest rates. Hispanic and black females have slightly higher rates of experiencing intimate partner violence than white females. Alcohol or drugs were present in approximately 42% of all incidents of nonfatal intimate partner violence.

Domestic violence is a serious problem and targeted interventions focused narrowly on domestic violence have had some success. For the crime analyst, domestic violence incidents pose two issues. First, they account for repeated events within the data (called series in the NCVS data discussed earlier in this chapter). If not excluded for some types of analyses, these repeat events can skew your analyses. Second, the nature of domestic violence assaults is different from other assaults (bar fights, for example). Creating a map, for example, including all assaults is worthless in terms of practical applications. It makes more sense to create two different maps—a map for domestic violence assaults, and a map for nondomestic assaults.

Group and Other Miscellaneous Patterns

The following sections discuss group and other patterns in offending including weapon use and gang-related crime. General patterns of behavior that occur in criminal events within your own geographic region can be specific to that region, or more global in nature. Understanding the who, what, when, where, and how of criminals in your region can aide you in developing better analysis products for your agency. It is important for the analysts to have an understanding of these patterns when performing analyses and creating crime maps as they can help inform the analyses. As with individual characteristics, these patterns are dynamic and are not absolute, but may be useful in understanding criminal incidents in a broader context.

Group Offending Patterns

In 2008, for all crimes of violence, approximately 75.8% of incidents involved only one offender. When comparing crimes committed by strangers with crimes committed by nonstrangers, 62.5% of stranger crimes were committed by only one person, and 89% of nonstranger crimes were committed by only one person. These percentages historically do not vary much. However, when multiple offenders were present, offenders aged 12–20 years accounted for 37.5% of these crimes (based on victims' perceptions of the age of their offenders; BJS, 2008). When examining the perceived race of offenders for crimes committed by more than one person, victims perceived their offenders to be white 33.3% of the time and black 29% of the time.

Weapon Use

For 2008, approximately 73.7% of all violent incidents (excluding murder) were committed without the use of a weapon. In 6.6% of violent incidents, the presence of a firearm was indicated (BJS, 2008). The presence of some sort of weapon (club, knife, firearm, etc.) was indicated in 39.9% of robbery victimizations and 18.1% of assaults, and firearms were used in 23.7% of robberies and only 4.8% of all assaults. Crimes of violence were more likely to be perpetrated without a weapon when the victim and offender knew each other than when the victim and offender were strangers. For intimate partner violence, a weapon of some type was present during the offense less often for incidents with female victims than for male victims.

Gang-Related Crime

It is difficult to separate crimes that are gang related from crimes that, while they are committed by known gang members, are not gang related. Thus, while victims' perceptions about the gang status of their offenders are important, this does not necessarily mean that the crimes themselves were gang related. Data about gang-related violence are also not often collected by the patrol officer and may often be discovered by the detective units upon re-interviewing the victims. For example, say that the victim of an armed street robbery heard the suspect shout, "63rd Ave," while running away from the scene. This could be considered a gang-related robbery in one jurisdiction, but in another it may not. It all depends on how a department defines, collects, and documents gang-related crimes and just because an offender has participates in a gang does not mean that all of his crimes are gang related. In fact, a good number of his crimes are probably individually motivated outside of normal gang activities.

According to NCVS data, between 1998 and 2003 approximately 6% of violent victimizations were perpetrated by persons believed to be gang members (this is down from 9% during the years 1993 to 1996). This estimate is based on the perceptions of the crime victims themselves, so the true figure could be higher or lower. According to the FBI's supplementary homicide reports, the percentage of homicides that were gang related between 1993 and 2003 ranged from just under 5% to a peak of 6.9% (Harrell, 2005).

The nature of gang recruitment, organization, and gang crime has been changing in recent years. According to the FBI (2011), "gangs are responsible for an average of 48 percent of violent crime in most jurisdictions and up to 90 percent in several others. Major cities and suburban areas experience the most gang-related violence" (p. 9). Furthermore:

> Local neighborhood-based gangs and drug crews continue to pose the most significant criminal threat in most communities. Aggressive recruitment of juveniles and immigrants, alliances and conflict between gangs, the release of incarcerated gang members from prison, advancements in technology and communication, and Mexican Drug Trafficking Organization (MDTO) involvement in drug distribution have resulted in gang expansion and violence in a number of jurisdictions.
>
> Gangs are increasingly engaging in non-traditional gang-related crime, such as alien smuggling, human trafficking, and prostitution. Gangs are also engaging in white collar crime such as counterfeiting, identity theft, and mortgage fraud, primarily due to the high profitability and much lower visibility and risk of detection and punishment than drug and weapons trafficking (pp. 9–10).

We are also beginning to see third and fourth generation gang members. They come from a long line of gang members and are raised with the values and culture of the gang. Many of them, however, would be difficult to identify as a gang members by their dress, tattoos, and rap sheet. They forego the ink, get college and professional degrees, and gain employment in many respectable fields—including the military and law enforcement. However, they use their education and status to further the goals of the gang—it is just in a much more covert and organized fashion than that of their parents or grandparents. This makes it much more difficult and complicated for law enforcement to address. (See Nagle, 2008 for a discussion of third generation gangs.)

Reporting Crime

The crimes that are reported to or detected by law enforcement only represent about 50% of total crime. Therefore, a discussion of *why* people decide to report their victimizations (or why they do not) is important.

According to the Bureau of Justice Statistics (BJS), the reporting of crime to the police across crime types or crime victims is neither random nor equal. The BJS estimates that 50% of violent crimes and 40% of property crime were reported to the police during 2010 (Truman, 2011). For violent crime, robbery and aggravated assaults are more likely to be reported to police than rape and sexual assaults. For property crime, motor vehicle thefts are most likely to be reported to police. For personal crimes, victims of purse snatching or pocket picking and victims of rape or sexual assault are least likely to report their victimizations to police. Victims of robbery are most likely to report the crimes to police (especially victims of completed robberies and robberies with injuries).

For property crimes, victims of motor vehicle thefts were most likely to report their victimizations to authorities (91.1% for completed motor vehicle thefts in 2008). Female victims of violence were more likely to report their victimizations than were males. Females were more likely to report victimizations for every violent crime category concerning stranger and nonstranger offenders. There were no substantive or significant differences in reporting across gender for victims of property crimes.

The most often cited reason for not reporting personal crime victimization was that the offender was unsuccessful or that the object was recovered. The second most often cited reason was that the incident was a private or personal matter. For victims of property crimes, 26.7% of those who did not report their victimizations to police cited that the object(s) were recovered or that the offender was unsuccessful (BJS, 2005). This makes sense given that the most cited reason for reporting a property crime is to recover stolen property (23.8% in 2008).

Victim Precipitation

Victim precipitation occurs when a victim does something that increases their risk of victimization. According to NCVS data, 9.8% of violent crime victims reported being the first to use or threaten physical force during the incident. A victim being the first to use or threaten physical violence was more likely in assault crimes as well. Approximately 60.9% of respondents who were victims of a completed violent crime in 2008 reported using self-protective measures of some kind. Self-protective measures by victims were highest for attempted robberies (89.2%) and lowest for completed robberies (46.2%). An estimated 63.1% of rape and sexual assault victims reported taking self-protective measures prior to the offense occurring. Interestingly, there do not appear to be significant differences across race or gender, but white victims were more likely to report taking self-protective measures before being victimized in nearly every violent crime category except rape and sexual assault (although the percentages here are very close). Persons aged 20–34 years and 35–49 were more likely to report using self-protective measures than any other age groups for all crimes of violence. Persons aged 50–64 years were least likely to take self-protective measures.

Resisting or capturing the offender was the most frequently cited self-protective measure for victims of violence in 2008. This held true for every completed violent crime category (rape and sexual assault, robbery, and assault) with the exception of aggravated assault and robberies with injuries. In these instances, the most common protective measure was running away or hiding. Running away and getting help or giving an alarm were cited as the second and third most employed measure of self-protection used for most crime types. Both male and female victims of violence were more likely to cite resisting or capturing the offender than any other self-protective measure. Female victims of violence were most likely to get help or give alarm, scare the offender, or run away and hide than male victims. There were subtle, but few significant differences across race. Both black and white victims reported resisting or capturing the offender to be the most prevalent self-protective measure.

In every crime category, victims who took self-protective measures were far more likely to report their behaviors as helpful to the situation. Approximately 66% of violent crime victims in 2008 reported that their self-protective measures helped them. When victims reported that their self-protective measures hurt the situation, the majority (66.1%) indicated that their behavior made the offender angrier and/or more aggressive. Analysts might consider this when examining crime rates across their jurisdictions. For example, they might consider if the presence of a college community and the attendant housing decreases the rate of crime or causes criminal events to be dispersed to different parts of the community. Could the use of protective measures entice criminals to do harm to other, less defensive populations, such as the elderly as discussed earlier, or are there equal attempted victimizations across the jurisdiction but more successful attempts upon the elderly population? For example, perhaps robbery attempts on one ethnic group are more successful than another. In addition, what if some protective measures appear to be more successful in thwarting certain types of crimes? How might you consider this information when producing a crime map, and how would you present this information to your chief or sheriff? As you can imagine, a crime analyst could elicit several conclusions from the same data, all of which could be based on firm analysis.

Alcohol and Drug Use

In 2008, 24.2% of victims of crimes of violence perceived their offenders to be under the influence of drugs or alcohol during the commission of the crime. For rape and sexual assault, this figure increased to 30%. The category with the lowest percentage of victims who perceived their offenders to be under the influence of drugs or alcohol was robbery (23.3% of victims).

In 2002, approximately "68% of [jail] inmates reported symptoms in the year before their admission to jail that met substance dependence or abuse criteria" (Karberg & James, 2005, p. 1). Approximately 16% of inmates reported that the reason they committed their offense was to get money for drugs, and approximately 50% of all convicted inmates reported being under the influence of drugs or alcohol at the time of the offense. Of these offenders, 71% were dependent upon or abused drugs or alcohol.

A larger percentage of female inmates reported substance dependence (51.8%) than did their male counterparts (44.3%). White inmates reported more substance dependence (55.4%) than did black (40.4%) or Hispanic inmates (35.7%). Female and white inmates were more likely to report using drugs at the time of their offense. Convicted females were more likely to report being under the influence of drugs (34%) than alcohol (22%) at the time of their offense. Males were more likely to report using alcohol at the time of their offense. An astounding 41.6% of inmates convicted of homicide reported using alcohol at the time of the offense. Marijuana and cocaine or crack were most often cited as the inmate's substance of choice. This example again presents another opportunity to discuss mapping considerations. Knowing that a large proportion of violent offenders use drugs, an analyst might consider the trends in drug arrests and the geographic location of those arrests when predicting future violent crimes. For example, can you see how a chief might appreciate knowing that a division in his jurisdiction is about to undergo an increase in the homicide rate due to drug activity? When analysts can appreciate these connections and nuances, they can then assist the administration with resource allocation and the creation of crime prevention measures. Techniques such as risk terrain modeling might assist the analyst in predicting where the highest risk for homicide might be based on considering drug use by geographic area as one of the possible risk factors.

Self-report studies of school-age students also provide information about the drug and alcohol abuse of minors. "In 2005, one quarter of all students in grades 9–12 reported that someone had offered, sold, or given them an illegal drug on school property in the past twelve months" (Dinkes, Cataldi, Kena, Baum, & Snyder, 2006, p. vi). In 2005, approximately 43% of students in grades 9 through 12 reported consuming at least one drink of alcohol during the past 30 days, and 20% of students reported using marijuana during the past 30 days.

■ Places

As this text's main focus is the importance of spatial relationships to crime, this chapter would not be complete without a discussion of "place." Just as crime is unevenly distributed across people, it is also unevenly distributed across place. The following section provides a cursory review of crime distribution based on geography and basic spatial characteristics (primarily looking at the differences between urban and rural areas).

Location

Persons living in urban areas are far more likely to be a victim of a violent crime, while persons living in suburban areas are far less likely than urban residents to be a victim of a violent crime but slightly more likely than rural residents. Between 2004 and 2005 the rate of violent crimes per 1000 persons aged 12 years or older was 29.4 in urban areas, 18.3 in suburban areas, and 18.1 in rural areas (population below 50,000 persons).

Rates vary significantly across urban areas. For example, in 2010, the UCR reported a rate of violent crime for the Detroit–Livonia–Dearborn metropolitan division to be 1111.2 per 100,000 persons. In the Washington, DC–Arlington–Alexandria metropolitan statistical area, the violent crime rate is a much lower at 380 per 100,000. The FBI cautions, however, not to make comparisons based solely on population and lists the following "known" variables that can cause crime to vary from place to place:

- Population density and degree of urbanization
- Variations in composition of the population, particularly youth concentration
- Stability of the population with respect to residents' mobility, commuting patterns, and transient factors
- Modes of transportation and highway system
- Economic conditions, including median income, poverty level, and job availability
- Cultural factors and educational, recreational, and religious characteristics
- Family conditions with respect to divorce and family cohesiveness
- Climate
- Effective strength of law enforcement agencies
- Administrative and investigative emphasis of law enforcement
- Policies of other components of the criminal justice system (i.e., prosecution, judicial, corrections, and probation)
- Citizens' attitudes toward crime
- Crime-reporting practices of the citizenry

In 2005, the western region of the United States held the highest rate of violent victimization at 25.9 violent crimes per 1000 persons. The South had the lowest rate of violent crime with 18.5 violent crimes per 1000 persons. However, remember that NCVS data does not count homicides (because dead people cannot report their own victimization). According to UCR data, in 2010 the violent crime rate (comprised of murder, forcible rape, robbery, and aggravated assault) was highest in the South (452 per 100,000) and lowest in the Northeast (357 per 100,000). When examining property crime rates, the South again holds the highest rate of victimization with 3438.8 property crimes per 1000 households. The lowest property crime rate is attributed to the northeast with approximately 104 property crimes per 100,000 persons.

Type of Location

For crimes of violence (excluding murder) in 2008, approximately 18.4% of victimizations occurred at or in the victim's home. This location is second only to the percentage of violent crimes committed on a street near the victim's home or within a mile of the victim's home (both at 17.9% of violent incidents). When crimes committed by strangers are compared with crimes committed by nonstrangers, it is not surprising that crimes of violence more often occurred at home when perpetrated by a nonstranger. When examining what victims were doing when victimized, for crimes of violence in 2008, the largest categories included victims involved in leisure activities away from home (20.6%) and victims involved in other activities in the home (25.4%). For property crimes, the largest percentage of victims reported sleeping while being victimized (27.5%).

The number of units in a housing structure is also an important variable in understanding victimization rates. It appears that for most property crime, households occupying housing structures with three units hold the highest rate of victimization (178.9 per 1000 households of the same). NCVS data indicates that housing structures with one unit held the lowest risk for most property crime (BJS, 2008).

Schools

In 2008, 13.3% of violent victimizations occurred inside a school building or on school property. During the period of July 1, 2009 through June 30, 2010, 17 youth from the ages of 5 through 18 years were victims of school-associated deaths (one of these was a suicide; Robers, Zhang, Truman, & Snyder, 2011). "In 2010, a greater number of students ages 12–18 experienced total victimizations (theft and violent crime) at school than away from school" (p. iv). Rates of victimization for students ages 12–18 in schools decreased from 42 per 1000 in 2009 to 32 per 1000 in 2010. The trend since 1992 is declining victimization in schools. This is also true for total victimization rates outside of school. Male students were more likely than female students to report being threatened or injured with a weapon on school property in the past year. White and Asian students were less likely to report being threatened or injured with a weapon than black or Hispanic students. School enrollment size was an important variable in understanding the frequency of discipline problems. In addition, students attending urban and suburban schools experienced slightly higher rates of total victimization.

Own or Rent?

People who rent their homes are far more likely to be victims of property crime than people who own their homes. This is likely the case for several reasons. College students, for example, tend to rent much more often than they own homes and are often less committed to self-protection measures than are other populations. They also have more technological gadgets (smart phones, laptops, etc.) that are easy to fence. In 2005, the rates of property crime victimization for renters was 192 per 1000 households. The property crime rate for people who own their home was approximately 136 per 1000 households (Catalano, 2006a).

Residential Mobility

Residential mobility is also important in understanding victimization risks. In 2005, for crimes of violence, people age 12 years and older who reported living in their homes for a period of less than 6 months held the highest rate of victimization at 51.3 per 1000 persons of the same group. This risk declines as the time spent living in a home increases, while people living in their home for 5 or more years held the lowest risk at 14.6 crimes of violence per 1000 people. This trend also holds true for property crimes. People living in their homes for less than 6 months suffer a property victimization rate of 297 per 1000, while people living in their homes for 5 or more years had a significantly reduced rate of property victimization of 137 per 1000 (BJS, 2005). Using the college student example, combining high residential mobility (and thus lack of collective efficacy and no sense of who belongs in an area and who does not), availability of targets (if you have 3 college students renting the same apartment, you potentially have 3 iPods and 3 laptops to steal—3 times the reward for the effort), and less self-protection measures (not locking doors, open windows, etc.), you have a routine activities theory recipe for burglary.

Urban Versus Rural: Is There Really a Difference?

The short answer to this question is yes. In general, people living in urban areas are at greater risk of victimization than people living in suburban and rural areas, with rural inhabitants typically having the lowest risk. However, this pattern is not constant across regions or across crime types. For example, in 2010, the reported rate of violent crime for metropolitan statistical areas (MSAs) was 428.3 per 100,000 persons and the reported rate for cities outside of MSAs was 399.7. However, when you examine property crime, cities outside of MSAs have a rate of 3602.3, slightly higher than the MSA rate of 3046.5 per 100,000 (FBI, 2010).

In examining the risk of property victimization, rural residents have slightly higher risks for household burglary than suburban residents. This is true in all regions except for the West, where rural residents have lower rates of household burglary than their urban and suburban counterparts (BJS, 2005).

■ Conclusion

So now that your head is spinning with crime statistics, you may be wondering: What does any of this matter to a crime analyst? The answer to your question is this: Knowing that some people and some places are more affected by crime than others is the first step when identifying those factors important in understanding when, where, how, and why crime is distributed the way it appears to be. Understanding the factors associated with criminal events allows us to make better predictions about where and when crime is most likely to occur. In addition, the ability to predict crime provides us with an opportunity to prevent crime—the ultimate goal of law enforcement.

Recall the theories that offer various explanations of both individual and environmental causes of crime. While reading this chapter and recalling these discussions of crime theory, you should begin to make the connections between *how* crime is distributed and *why* it is distributed the way it is. In addition, it is important to keep up with local, national, and global crime trends. As you read earlier in this chapter, the nature of gangs, and their crime patterns, are changing drastically. Knowing this helps to inform your maps and analyses by alerting you to key variables that impact law enforcement response strategies.

■ Chapter Glossary

Part I index offenses   Includes the crimes of homicide, rape, robbery, aggravated assault, burglary, larceny–theft, motor vehicle theft, and arson.

NVAT   The NCVS victimization analysis tool is an online data analysis tool for victimization data.

Predictability   The ability to forecast crime trends, patterns, sprees, and series related to crime to inform supervisory staff, validate research, or provide actionable knowledge.

Violent victimization   The term used to describe victims of violent crime such as murder, rape, robbery, and aggravated assault.

Victimization rates   The statistic related to the number of violent crimes experienced by a study area in relation to another factor such as population, total victims, or total violent crimes. Typically presented as a percentage or a decimal equivalent of the value.

Victim–offender relationships   The relationships between the offender and the victim in relation to a criminal environment and the place where victims and suspects interact.

Victim precipitation   Behavior by the victim, such as prostitution in high-crime areas, or walking in a park late at night all alone, which make the victim at higher risk of crime.

■ Questions for Review

1. Based on the crime statistics discussed throughout this chapter, who is *most* likely to be a victim of a violent crime?
2. Who is *least* likely to be victim of a violent crime?
3. How do crime theories explain some of the crime trends that appear in the UCR and NCVS statistics?

■ Online Resources

National Gang Threat Assessments: www.fbi.gov/stats-services/crimestats

Reports and data on crime and victimization in the United States: www.ojp.usdoj.gov/bjs/

School safety statistics: http://nces.ed.gov/programs/crimeindicators/crimeindicators 2011/index.asp

Sourcebook of Criminal Justice Statistics: www.albany.edu/sourcebook/

Uniform Crime Reports (FBI): www.fbi.gov/ucr/ucr.htm

■ References

Bureau of Justice Statistics. (2005). *Criminal victimization in the United States, 2005 statistical tables.* Washington, DC: U.S. Department of Justice, Office of Justice Programs, Bureau of Justice Statistics.

Bureau of Justice Statistics. (2008). *Criminal victimization in the United States, 2005 statistical tables.* Washington, DC: U.S. Department of Justice, Office of Justice Programs, Bureau of Justice Statistics.

Catalano, S. (2006a). *Criminal victimization, 2005.* Washington, DC: U.S. Department of Justice, Office of Justice Programs, Bureau of Justice Statistics.

Catalano, S. (2006b). *Intimate partner violence in the United States.* Washington, DC: U.S. Department of Justice, Office of Justice Programs, Bureau of Justice Statistics.

Dinkes, R., Cataldi, E. F., Kena, G., Baum, K., & Snyder, T. (2006). *Indicators of school crime and safety: 2006* (NCES 2007-003/NCJ 214262). U.S. Departments of Education and Justice Statistics. Washington, DC: U.S. Government Printing Office.

Durose, M. R., Schmitt, E. L., & Langan, P. A. (2005). *Contacts between police and the public: Findings from the 2002 national survey.* Washington, DC: U.S. Department of Justice, Office of Justice Programs, Bureau of Justice Statistics.

Eith, C., & Durose, M. (2011). *Contacts between police and the public, 2008.* Washington, DC: U.S. Department of Justice, Office of Justice Programs, Bureau of Justice Statistics.

Farrington, D. P. (1992). Explaining the beginning, progress, and ending of antisocial behavior from birth to adulthood. In J. McCord (Ed.), *Facts, frameworks, and forecasts: Advances in criminological theory* (Vol. 3, pp. 253–286). New Brunswick, NJ: Transaction.

Federal Bureau of Investigation. (2010). Crime in the United States. Retrieved from www.fbi.gov/about-us/cjis/ucr/crime-in-the-u.s/2010/crime-in-the-u.s.-2010/index-page.

Federal Bureau of Investigation. (2011). National gang threat assessment. Retrieved from www.fbi.gov/stats-services/publications/2011-national-gang-threat-assessment.

Felson, M. & Boba, R. (2010). Crime and Everyday Life (4th ed.). New York: Sage Publications.

Gottfredson, M. R., & Hirschi, T. (1990). *A general theory of crime.* Stanford, CA: Stanford University Press.

Harrell, E. (2005). *Bureau of Justice Statistics crime data brief: Violence by gang members, 1993–2003.* Washington, DC: U.S. Department of Justice, Office of Justice Programs.

Karberg, J. C., & James, D. J. (2005). *Bureau of Justice special report: Substance dependence, abuse, and treatment of jail inmates, 2002.* Retrieved from http://bjs.ojp.usdoj.gov/content/pub/pdf/sdatji02.pdf.

Klaus, P. (2007). *Crime and the nation's households, 2005.* Washington, DC: U.S. Department of Justice, Office of Justice Programs, Bureau of Justice Statistics.

Nagle, L. (2008). Criminal Gangs in Latin America: The next great threat to regional security and stability. *Texas Hispanic Journal of Law and Policy, 14,* 7–27.

Puzzanchera, C., & Kang, W. (2011). Easy access to the FBI's supplementary homicide reports: 1980–2009. Retrieved from www.ojjdp.gov/ojstatbb/ezashr/.

Rand, M., & Catalano, S. (2007). *Criminal victimization, 2006.* Washington, DC: U.S. Department of Justice, Office of Justice Programs, Bureau of Justice Statistics.

Rand, M. & Robinson, J. (2011). Criminal victimization in the United States, 2008—Statistical tables. Retrieved from www.bjs.gov/index.cfm?ty=pbdetail&iid=2218.

Robers, S., Zhang, J., Truman, J., & Snyder, T. (2011). Indicators of school crime and safety, 2011. Bureau of Justice Statistics, National Center for Education Statistics. Retrieved from http://nces.ed.gov/pubsearch/pubsinfo.asp?pubid=2012002.

Tabachnick, C. (2009). Crimes against the elderly. Retrieved from www.thecrimereport.org/archive/crimes-against-the-elderly/.

Truman, J. (2011). *Criminal victimization, 2010.* Washington, DC: National Crime Victimization Survey, U.S. Department of Justice, Office of Justice Programs, Bureau of Justice Statistics.

Wood, P. B., Gove, W. R., & Cochran, J. K. (1994). Motivations for violent crime among incarcerated adults: A consideration of reinforcement processes. *Oklahoma Criminal Justice Research Consortium Journal.* Retrieved from www.doc.state.ok.us/offenders/ocjrc/94/940650G.HTM.

Statistics and Analyses

A Brief Review of Statistics

▶ LEARNING OBJECTIVES

This chapter is designed to provide students with a basic understanding of data and how data are manipulated by crime mappers and analysts. Basic concepts of statistical analysis and their applications in crime mapping are also discussed. After studying this chapter, you should be able to:

- Understand the difference between *qualitative and quantitative* data.
- Define and explain levels of measurement including *nominal*, *ordinal*, *interval*, and *ratio*.
- Understand the difference between *discrete* and *continuous* variables.
- Understand *descriptive* statistics, including typical measures of *central tendency* and *dispersion*.
- Understand *inferential* statistics, including typical tests of *significance* and measures of *association*.
- Understand what a *regression* model is and how it works.
- Understand the limitations of statistics and how their improper application can yield misleading results.
- Define and explain *classification* in crime mapping and be able to identify strengths and weaknesses of each method.

▶ Key Terms

Antecedent Variable	Intervening Variable	Quantitative
Bimodal	Inverse Relationship	Range
Causal Relationship	Linear Relationship	Ratio
Choropleth Map	Mean	Reliability
Coefficient	Mean Center	Skewed
Contingent Variable	Measures of Association	Spatial Autocorrelation
Continuous	Median	Spurious Relationship
Dependent Variable	Mode	Standard Deviation
Dichotomous	Multicollinearity	Standard Deviation Ellipses
Discrete	Mutually Exclusive	Tests of Significance
Exhaustive	Nominal	Unimodal
Frequency Distribution	Normal Curve	Unit of Analysis
Histogram	Operationalize	Validity
Independent Variable	Ordinal	Variables
Interquartile Range	Positive Relationship	Variance
Interval	Qualitative	

■ Introduction

This chapter explains basic statistical terms and concepts that are necessary for the beginning crime analyst to understand when performing statistical analyses and making crime maps. Our intent here is not to overload the student with a comprehensive and detailed discussion of formulas and equations, but to provide enough information for the beginning analyst to understand the strengths and weaknesses of statistical procedures commonly used in crime analysis and crime mapping (in academic and practical settings). This chapter also discusses various characteristics of data. These characteristics are important in understanding how maps and analyses can be interpreted.

■ A Crash Course in Statistics

As with any scientific approach to finding solutions, we need to analyze data. Crime analysis is no exception. With these analyses comes the responsibility to effectively (and ethically) use statistics to derive adequate answers to questions posed by command officers and others whom we can depend on to make decisions. Having a basic understanding of statistics and statistical methods enables us to analyze our data and avoid mistakes or misinterpretations of the data.

Types of Data

Before we can begin examining the how and why of data analysis, we must first examine the different types of data and how each can be manipulated. Essentially, there are two types of research: **qualitative** and **quantitative**. In the simplest terms, qualitative research typically yields narrative-oriented information (such as the categories "hospital" or "park"), while quantitative research generally produces number-oriented information (usually coined "data"). Of course, as with virtually everything in the social sciences, this concept is not as simple as it appears. For example, suppose an analyst or researcher wanted to know why a certain intersection within a city experienced a higher level of drive-by shootings than anywhere else in the city over the last year and why these types of shootings continue to increase. He or she may choose any number of research designs to study the problem, including a qualitative or quantitative approach or a hybrid of the two. One qualitative design might be to conduct interviews of residents and business owners who live and work in the immediate vicinity of the intersection. Narratives gathered from these interviews might suggest that the neighborhood has recently undergone a transition characterized by high levels of instability and diversity. (For example, a participant might state, "Since they changed the bus schedule, this neighborhood has really fallen apart.") Upon further investigation, the researcher might discover that a nearby factory where many of the residents were employed was recently closed, resulting in high rates of unemployment, which in turn may have caused many families to move out of the neighborhood. The subsequent cheap real estate attracted recent immigrants to move into the neighborhood. This resulted in a culture clash amongst old and new residents in an already strained neighborhood. This situation also increased the tension between rivaling gangs (for example, the battle over drug territories), which increased the violent incidents between them, including drive-by shootings.

Using the same hypothetical problem, suppose the same researcher employed a quantitative design to study the violent intersection. First, he would collect official crime statistics for the area immediately surrounding the intersection of interest. In addition, he would gather information from secondary sources about the neighborhood and its residents, including real estate values, employment rates, residential mobility rates, and income and education levels. This data may tell the researcher that there are high unemployment levels, low real estate values, and high transition rates within the neighborhood. Statistical analysis may then determine that these and other factors contributed significantly to the number of drive-by shootings. However, while statistical analysis provides some explanation of the key factors or **variables** (any trait that can change values from case to case; individual variables are what datasets are made of) that impact the amount of violence in a neighborhood, it cannot explain how and why the neighborhood was transformed to begin with and why it is continually declining. This information comes from the qualitative methods discussed earlier, including resident interviews.

As you can see from this hypothetical example, qualitative approaches are excellent in their ability to collect very rich information. This information is usually in the form of narratives or stories that can provide a great deal of insight to the researcher. In crime analysis and mapping, qualitative information is invaluable to understanding maps and statistical outputs. However, qualitative information is impossible to analyze unless it is converted to a numerical output, which can sometimes be difficult. For example, in mapping gang activity and territory, Kennedy, Braga, and Piehl (1998) collected information from police officers, probation officers, and street workers about gang membership, activity, and territory to create maps as part of a multiagency collaborative effort geared toward reducing gun violence among Boston youth. The qualitative information that was gathered was then combined with Boston police department data on gun assaults, weapons offenses, drug offenses, armed robbery, youth homicide, and calls for service for "shots fired" (Kennedy et al., 1998, p. 245) and mapped to illustrate gang rivalries, gang boundaries, and locations of violent incidents. The resulting analysis produced a better understanding of the links between gangs and crime in the city of Boston.

Qualitative and quantitative research designs have their own strengths and weaknesses. Research designs that incorporate elements of both yield the most comprehensive and accurate information and will have a better chance of providing the answers that researchers seek.

Now that the basic differences between qualitative and quantitative research data have been discussed, the next step is to gain an understanding of the levels of measurement. Variables can be measured using four different levels of measurement. Visualizing the levels of measurement as a four-step ladder is helpful (see **Figure 9–1**).

The lowest step represents **nominal**-level data, which is often referred to as qualitative data. Nominal-level data is that which is measured in categories, or categorical data (in this text, categorical data is defined as data measured in word-based categories, such as "yes" or "no"), and cannot be ranked. Race, for example, is a nominal-level variable. Typical categories for race include African American, Caucasian, Hispanic, and Asian. Nominal variables are often collapsed into the smallest number of categories possible so that they may be used

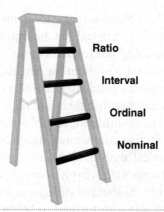

Figure 9–1 Levels of Measurement

in different types of analyses. For example, the variable race on a survey or data collection instrument may be originally separated into the following categories:

- African American
- Native American
- Caucasian
- Hispanic
- Asian
- Other

These six categories can also be collapsed into two categories: Caucasian and non-Caucasian. A variable in this form (**dichotomous**) can be more versatile. Collapsing smaller categories into larger ones makes statistical analysis easier. Categories that hold too few cases are difficult to use in comparisons and thus need to be combined with other categories. An important thing to remember, however, is that collapsing categories into larger ones can hide important relationships between them. For example, the difference between African Americans and Native Americans on a given variable may be significant, but if they are both collapsed into the category of non-Caucasian, any differences between the two groups will be obscured. Similarly, if smaller areas (such as intersections or street segments) are collapsed into larger areas (such as census blocks or block groups), important crime patterns may be hidden. However, a dichotomous or *dummy* variable (one with only two categories as in the earlier race example) is a very powerful form statistically for a nominal variable. Last, categories, whether numeric or alphanumeric, must be **mutually exclusive** (a case should not be able to fit into more than one category) and completely **exhaustive** (every possible answer must be included in the answer set). This makes variables such as race very tricky to measure. It is easy to envision instances where persons could fit into more than one racial category. When categories are not mutually exclusive, this introduces an error to any analysis that is performed using these variables.

Examples of nominal-level variables in crime maps might be city parks or cemeteries. They cannot be ranked as variables themselves, and depending on what data are available about the park or cemetery (the facilities that are located there, different physical attributes), they may be able to be placed into separate categories. However, on the map, they are just shown with different colors that represent the various nominal variables available (often called physical features in mapping terminology). They can be ranked based on other variables—for example, location, size, or criminal activity—but these are separate measures that can be ranked and are attributes "about" the feature or about where the feature is located. We would use a single symbol classification type when trying to map the features on a map, where every item would either have the same symbol, or a categories classification where each feature would be symbolized with a different symbol based on what the feature was (i.e., name or type of feature).

The second step in the ladder represents **ordinal**-level data, which contain categorical or numerical data that can be ranked, but the precise value is not known. The most often used example for categorical ordinal data are variables constructed using the Likert scale. The following survey question, designed as a partial measure of fear of crime, is a useful example:

I feel safe walking in my neighborhood alone at night.
1. Strongly agree   2. Agree   3. Neutral   4. Disagree
5. Strongly disagree   6. Don't know

Note that the answer sets can be ranked in terms of the level of agreement but that there is no meaningful or quantifiable difference between "strongly agree" and "agree." Another point that must be noted regarding any variable is that traits, concepts, and ideas in criminal justice can be difficult to **operationalize**, or measure. Using the previous example of fear, the statement, "I feel safe walking in my neighborhood alone at night" might be interpreted by respondents in several ways. Someone reading this statement may answer "strongly disagree," not because he is fearful of crime, but he is fearful of other things. The road that he lives on may have a lot of traffic, so he might be fearful of getting hit by a car, or his neighborhood may have a chronic problem with loose dogs, and he is fearful of getting attacked by a dog. Neither of these interpretations involves fear of crime, yet if he answers that he strongly disagrees with the statement, he will be counted as a respondent who is fearful of crime. We might commit this data to a mapping project by adding the ordinal-level data to a map by representing the data as a category and each category would have a classification in ArcMap; or, we could create values between "1. Strongly agree" and "5. Strongly disagree" and we could then create a map based on the values or quantities classification based on the values.

When measuring a complex idea such as fear of crime, it is important to construct questions as carefully as possible and to ask multiple questions about the concept to achieve **validity** and **reliability** in the variable's operationalization. (Validity means that a variable accurately reflects the trait or concept it is measuring; reliability means that the measure is representative consistently across people, places, and time.) This is a very important point because available data for crime analysis and crime mapping do not always contain variables that are measured perfectly. When this is the case, maps can describe and illustrate, but analysis is limited in its interpretation or its ability to provide inferences.

A second example of an ordinal measure uses numerical data in ranges:

What is your annual household income?
1. Less than $20,000
2. Between $20,000 and $40,000
3. Between $40,001 and $60,000
4. Between $60,001 and $80,000
5. More than $80,000

Note that while the answer sets have clear numeric ranges and can be ranked in order of income level, the analyst does not know the exact amount of household income attributable to the respondent. Also note that the class intervals are equal (each range within the answer set is $20,000). Numeric ranges for ordinal data must either contain answer sets with equal interval widths or contain ranges that are logically or theoretically based. For example, suppose the analyst needed to create a map at the beat level showing reported burglaries for the past week for a large city. The map will be a **choropleth map** (uses color intensity to show the value of a given variable, often called a shaded grid map), and because this is a very large city with numerous police beats, the analyst cannot use the precise numbers for each beat or the map, while very colorful, will be difficult to read. Therefore, the analyst needs to group the number of burglaries into ordinal ranges. These ranges should be based on equal intervals (1–5, 6–10, . . . 201) or on ranges based on some logic (perhaps in ranges based on natural breaks within the data). An example of natural breaks in both classification within ArcMap and the statistics behind it can be found in an exercise from an educational setting. Let us say we have 10 students in a course on crime mapping and each student was given a test. The following scores were calculated for each of the 10 students:

20
35
55
75
80
81
82
89
90
95

What we would want to look for as a "natural breaks" exercise would be to find the largest differences between the scores depending on how many "classifications" we would want in the map or in our analysis. Assuming we want 4 classifications, we would want to find the largest differences between scores in our distribution. Our first break as a quantities classification using natural breaks classification is going to be between 20 and 35, with a value of 15 separating these scores in our distribution. There are 20 points between 35 and 55, and 20 between 55 and 75. These would be our second two breaks. Between 82 and 89 is a difference of 7, so our last break would be here.

The third step in the level of measurement ladder represents **interval**-level data. With interval-level data, the precise value of a measure is known and thus can also be ranked. For example, suppose the previous survey question regarding income was changed to:

What is your annual household income? _____.

The analyst would know exactly how much money in household income is attributed to the respondent and could rank it from lowest to highest. A mapping example might be to use the total number of burglaries at the beat level for a large city such as Baltimore. An analyst would not want to use the actual total number of burglaries if he or she were creating a map at the beat level of Baltimore because at that **unit of analysis**, the map would be very difficult to read. The analyst can use ArcMap's ability to classify data based on quantities to take the interval-level data and place it in a "classification" based on several different classification and symbology types to create a map that tells a story.

The last step in the ladder represents **ratio**-level data. For most statistical analysis purposes, interval- and ratio-level data are treated the same (all ratio-level data is also interval-level data). The example of income used in the discussion of interval-level variables is also a ratio-level variable. Ratio-level data has a true zero point and continues infinitely to the positive and to the negative. Therefore, some analyses that rely on the assumption of ratio-level data will provide results that do not exist in the real world—for example, predicting that 111.23 crimes will occur within a given area. In real life, this will never happen. Similarly, a prediction of a negative number of crimes cannot exist in the real world (we can reduce crimes by five, but we cannot have a negative number of crimes as a real value for an area).

Using the ladder analogy, the top level (ratio) assumes all the characteristics of lower levels in addition to its own unique characteristics. However, lower levels can only assume characteristics of the levels beneath them. For example, one can take an interval-level variable, such as income, and collapse it into a **frequency distribution** that displays the number of respondents with a range of household incomes (see **Figure 9–2**).

This frequency distribution can also be collapsed further into a distribution that illustrates those above and below a given household income (see **Figure 9–3**).

The reverse, however, is not true. One cannot take information gleaned from an ordinal-level measure and turn it into an interval-level measure. For example, if on a survey, a respondent indicates that he or she commits between 10 and 20 crimes per month, we cannot assume that this person commits 12 crimes per month, only that the number is somewhere between 10 and 20 crimes per month. This is why it is best, when possible, to collect interval- or ratio-level data. This notion will become more and more apparent as you progress in your studies of crime analysis and crime mapping. Depending on the data you have, you are given different possibilities to classify the data using the legend tools in ArcMap. Ordinal data is

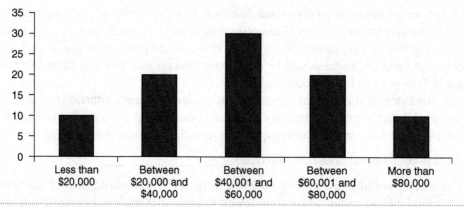

Figure 9–2 Annual Household Income Frequency Distribution, Example 1

limited to single-symbol and category-type legends or classifications, whereas ratio-level data allows you to use all of the classification types available in ArcMap in most cases. Using categories may require the analyst to do some work collapsing the ratio- or interval-level data into categories first by creating a new field containing the new categories, but it can be done fairly easily.

Two more concepts must be addressed before we move into a discussion of statistics: *discrete* and *continuous*. These terms are necessary to the discussion of utility of various spatial analyses (specifically when performing hotspot analyses), so it is important to have a basic understanding of what they mean. **Discrete** variables are variables that cannot be subdivided. The number of persons living in a household is a discrete variable. For example, there cannot be 2.3 persons living in a household. There can be 2, or there can be 3, but not 2.3. Similarly, as discussed earlier, an area cannot have a total of 111.23 crimes. It is either 111 or 112, because crime is a discrete variable. Another example is a variable expressed in rate form.

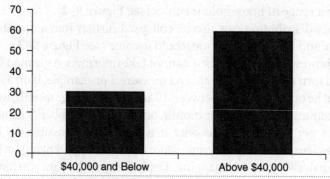

Figure 9–3 Annual Household Income Frequency Distribution, Example 2

In map form, we can see continuous variables in something like a kernel density map where the map appears to be like a weather map and every pixel has a value of some sort. Or the values are laid across the analysis area like a blanket. The opposite would be something like a hotspot map where data are aggregated to census block groups to create a choropleth map. The values within each census block would be considered discrete. The entire census block contains the aggregated value, but different parts of the census block would not have values of their own.

Often, when discrete variables are converted into rates, they will look like continuous variables. For example, 412 burglaries in a city of 300,000, converted to rate form, computes to be 13.73 burglaries per 10,000 persons. **Continuous** variables, on the other hand, *can* be subdivided—theoretically they can be subdivided an infinite number of times. Time is a good example of a continuous variable. Response times could be measured in minutes, seconds, milliseconds, nanoseconds, and so on. Usually, these variables are rounded to the unit that makes the most sense or is the most convenient; for example, there is little sense in comparing response times to the nanosecond (billionth of a second). Response times are usually rounded to the unit of minute or second. Knowing whether a variable is discrete or continuous is important in understanding which statistical analyses can be performed and how they can be interpreted.

Variables can be presented in a variety of ways. For example, as discussed in the next section, variables can be presented using measures of central tendency, such as the most frequent value, the middle value, or the average value in a distribution. Raw values are also often used but are usually standardized in some way to allow for meaningful comparisons. For example, when comparing the number of crimes across cities in eastern Massachusetts, it is necessary to compute a *rate* based on population so that the number of crime incidents for heavily populated cities can be compared to less populated cities in a meaningful way. Rates can be calculated for any number of persons but are typically calculated in crime analysis per 1000 persons, 10,000 persons, or 100,000 persons (usually some power of 10 to eliminate decimal points). The computation is simple: Divide the number of crimes in an area by its population, and multiply this value by whatever number of persons you would like the rate to be based upon. Crime rates as presented in the Uniform Crime Reports (UCR) are per 100,000 persons, whereas victimization rates presented by the National Crime Victimization Survey (NCVS) are per 1000 persons.

We might also use rate maps to see if one area or type of location (single-family residences versus multiresidential properties) might have higher incidences of burglary or auto theft. We sometimes have to be careful when using rate maps in that the grids, census block, jurisdictional boundaries, or other polygon we use to test the rates are as equal in size as possible. If they are too different in size, we might see that an area with only one single-family residence within a business district with 10–25 crimes might have a much higher rate of burglary than a location with 300 homes and 150–300 crimes. We can also create rate maps based on crimes per square mile, also called a *simple density map*.

$$Rate = [(f_1) \div (f_2)] \times (some\ power\ of\ 10\ to\ eliminate\ decimal\ points)$$

Ratios are often used to compare the frequency of values in one category to another. To compute a ratio, simply use the value of category one as the numerator and the value of category two as the denominator, and divide to compute the ratio. For example, if the frequency of property crimes is 300 and the frequency of violent crimes is 10, the resultant ratio is 300 ÷ 10, which equals 30. This is interpreted by stating that for every one violent crime, there are 30 property crimes. Ratio maps can also be created in ArcMap in several ways. The analyst usually needs to aggregate data to a polygon feature class for the variables he or she wants to create ratios for, and then create new fields within the polygon feature classes' attribute table and classify the data based on these calculated fields or ratios. ArcMap also allows you to often create ratios on the fly in the quantities classification type by percentage of total in the field you are classifying, or log of the total, or by another field in the same attribute table; this is called *normalization* in ArcMap.

$$\text{Ratio} = (f_1) \div (f_2)$$

Percentage changes are also useful for comparisons, typically from a given time period to another. The computation for calculating a percentage change is not difficult; simply put, the analyst first takes the value at the later time (f_2) and subtracts the value at the earlier time (f_1) and divides this number by the value at the earlier time (f_1). This computed value is then multiplied by 100 to express the change in the form of a percentage—often expressed as [(new – old) ÷ old] × 100.

$$\text{Percentage change} = [(f_2 - f_1) \div (f_1)] \times 100$$

Descriptive Statistics

Descriptive statistics are used primarily to summarize large amounts of information. The frequency example used earlier (in Figures 9–2 and 9–3) summarized the household incomes of 90 persons by grouping them into ranges. The most common descriptive statistics are measures of central tendency and measures of variation (or dispersion). The most often used measures of central tendency include the *mode, median,* and *mean.*

The **mode** (Mo) is simply the most frequent score that appears in a distribution. Using the earlier example (Figure 9–2), the modal category for household income is "Between $40,001 and $60,000." That is, the highest number of people (30) fall into this category. Another example using age might be as follows: There are 10 members in the fictitious Reservoir Street gang. Bob, Bill, and Jason are 17 years of age; Ted and Tim are 16 years of age; Kevin and Tyler are 14 years of age; and Steve, George, and Ed are 15 years of age. These data ($n = 10$) have a **bimodal** distribution. That is, there are two modes: 17 and 15 (three persons are 17 years of age, and three persons are 15 years of age). Another example of a bimodal distribution is a sample of a robbery series where an offender hits most frequently between 1700 and 1800 hours and also between 0700 and 0800 hours (each the same number of times) in a series of hits.

The mode can be used for variable measures at all levels of measurement, but it is the only measure of central tendency that can be used for nominal and categorical data. That is, the mode requires only frequencies (how many cases are in each category) and thus can be used with variables that are measured categorically or in word-based categories (such as race or gender). For example, in mapping places that sell alcohol in a large city, there may be 100 restaurants that sell alcohol, 80 bars, 15 grocery stores that sell beer and wine, and 10 liquor stores, producing a total of 205 establishments that sell alcohol, with restaurants being the modal category. Other measures of central tendency require at least midpoints (median) or numerical scores (mean) in their computations.

The **median** (Md) is simply the middle score within a distribution. That said, the variable must be represented numerically and thus be able to be ranked from lowest to highest. (We will not go into the mathematics of it in this book, but there are formulas available that use midpoints to compute the median for ordinal data that is numeric. When the data available for crime analysis are measured at the ordinal level, it is necessary to compute an approximate median that can be used for further analysis.) The median cannot be used on nominal or categorical data. In odd-numbered distributions, the median is always the middle score. In even-numbered distributions, there are two middle cases, so the median is defined as the score exactly halfway between the two middle cases. Using the age example again, and ranking the ages from lowest to highest, the median for this distribution is 15.5.

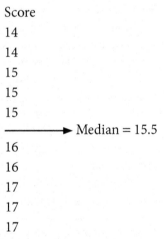

Score
14
14
15
15
15
——————————▶ Median = 15.5
16
16
17
17
17

The **mean** ($\bar{X}$), or average, represents the arithmetic average of a distribution. It is easy to compute. One must simply add up all the scores in the distribution and then divide this sum (Σ) by the number of scores in a distribution. (Using midpoints, there are formulas that will compute an estimated mean for numeric, ordinal-level data, but it is beyond the scope of this text. Most good textbooks on statistics will contain these formulas. Again, if the only data available are measured at the ordinal level, it may be necessary to estimate the mean so that further statistical analysis can be conducted.) Using the age example again, the average is computed to be 15.6. The mean is the most powerful measure of central tendency and thus the most often used. However, because it is computed using every score within a distribution, it is sensitive to extreme values and should not be used for distributions that are highly **skewed**.

Scores	
14	
14	
15	
15	
15	$n = 10$
16	
16	$\bar{X} = \Sigma x_i \div n$
17	
17	$\bar{X} = 156 \div 10 = 15.6$
$\underline{17}$	
$\Sigma = 156$	

An example of a skewed distribution might be best illustrated using the concept of response times for a police department. The computed average response time for a department may be higher than the median response time because extreme scores skew the distribution. The median is a more useful measure of central tendency to use in skewed distributions. This is an important point because most of the data that crime analysts use in their analyses and maps are skewed. This concept will be explained later in this chapter, but, essentially, a distribution is skewed if the majority of cases are in either the low end or high end of the distribution. (However, despite this, many police commanders are accustomed to hearing the average of crime variables and may not readily accept median values without some explanation.) For example, when analyzing calls for service data over 1 year, the majority of addresses will only be represented once within the dataset. That is, the overwhelming number of people who call police within a 1-year period will only call once. However, a select few of the addresses will show multiple calls to the police. This distribution will be skewed, and thus the median and mode number of calls for service should be used instead of the mean to describe the data.

A **mean center** analysis is one of the most common descriptive analyses used in crime mapping. The procedure is similar to computing a mean for a series of scores. The mean center is the approximate center of a series of events (typically crime incidents). It is primarily used to compare the center points of different types of crimes or similar crimes that occurred at different times. As with the mean of a distribution, the mean center is sensitive to outliers. In addition, if a distribution is oddly shaped or has more than one mode (for example, has two clusters within a distribution), the mean center (while in the center of the distribution) is deceiving. One useful bit of information about the mean or median center of a crime distribution on a map is that if the criminal is a marauder, he or she may live very near the mean

TABLE 9-1 When to Use the Mode, Median, and Mean

Measure	When to Use
Mode	• With nominal-level variables. • You want to report the most frequent, or common, score.
Median	• Variables are numeric and measured at the ordinal level or higher. • You have interval- or ratio-level variables with highly skewed distributions. • You want to report the central score.
Mean	• You have variables measured at the interval or ratio level (unless highly skewed). • You want to report the average score.

or median center of the crime series. This location would be a simplistic geographic profile, where canvassing operations or searches of crime databases for offenders who match the description would have the most likelihood of identifying a suspect in a crime series.

A useful hint is to compare the mode, median, and mean of a distribution to get a better understanding of a variable. If the mode, median, and mean are fairly close, the distribution is not skewed, and reporting the mean on its own is appropriate. If the measures are vastly different (indicating a skewed distribution), it might be more appropriate to report just the median. **Table 9-1** provides some helpful reminders of when it is appropriate to use the mode, median, and mean.

The next subject to tackle in this crash course on statistics is measures of dispersion (also called measures of variability). Measures of central tendency report the most common, the middle, and the typical (or average) scores. Measures of dispersion take us further in our understanding by reporting the shape of the distribution. There are several simple and familiar statistics that report dispersion. The most common include the **range** (the distance between the lowest and highest score), **interquartile range** (the distance between the 25th and 75th percentiles), **variance** (the average squared distance of each score in a distribution from the mean of the distribution), and **standard deviation** (the average distance of each score from the mean). Reporting the range provides the audience with an understanding of the lowest and highest point, providing perspective to where an individual score may lie in a distribution. For example, if a neighborhood experienced 15 burglaries in a week, knowing the lowest number of burglaries any neighborhood experienced that week and the highest number of burglaries any neighborhood experienced that week provides more meaning to the number 15 burglaries. Using the interquartile range provides the audience with an even better understanding of where an individual score lies in relation to other scores in a distribution. For example, knowing the interquartile range allows for understanding whether or not a neighborhood is in the top 25 or 50%, or the lower 25 or 50%, for burglaries. There are several other measures of dispersion that are used less often, but for our purposes we will focus our efforts on the most important measure of dispersion to crime analysis and mapping: the standard deviation.

The standard deviation requires that a mean be computed and thus is only appropriate for interval-level variables. (Again, there are formulas that allow you to compute a standard deviation for ordinal-level numeric data, but these computations, found in most good statistics books, are beyond the scope of this text.) The computation for standard deviation is simple enough, and the information it provides is invaluable to crime analysts. As defined, the standard deviation is the square root of the squares of the deviation. It gives us the average distance of each score from the mean, which tells us the shape of the distribution and whether or not a distribution is tight or dispersed (that is, how far away from the mean any given score is likely to be). The problem is that if the mean is subtracted from each score in the distribution, the sum of these values will be zero. This is because the mean represents the balancing point of the distribution. Thus, dividing the sum of these values by the number of scores in the distribution (to find the average deviation from the mean) will also be zero. Therefore, one must square each of the distances (the individual scores minus the mean) and *then* add them up and divide them by n. This will provide the variance (S^2) of the distribution. To compute the standard deviation (S), one simply needs to take the square root of the variance. (When using a random sample instead of the whole population, the formula uses $n - 1$ instead of n to account for error when using smaller samples.) The following is how to compute the variance and standard deviation for the age example we have been using:

Scores (x_i)	$x_i - \bar{X}$	$(x_i - \bar{X})^2$	
14	−1.6	2.56	$S^2 = \Sigma (x_i - \bar{X})^2 \div n - 1$
14	−1.6	2.56	$S^2 = 12.4 \div 9$
15	−0.6	0.36	$S^2 = 1.38$
15	−0.6	0.36	
15	−0.6	0.36	$S = \sqrt{1.38}$
16	0.4	0.16	$S = 1.17$
16	0.4	0.16	
17	1.4	1.96	
17	1.4	1.96	
17	1.4	1.96	
$\Sigma = 156$	$\Sigma = 0$	$\Sigma = 12.4$	
$n = 10$			
$\bar{X} = 15.6$			

The average age of this sample is 15.6 years. The standard deviation of this sample indicates that for the variable age, the standard deviation from the mean is 1.17 years. Later in this chapter, distributions that are based on the bell-shaped, or normal, curve will be discussed. Understanding the meaning of a standard deviation is vital to understanding *normal* distributions.

In crime mapping, the standard deviation is used in several ways to illustrate levels of crime dispersion. For example, an analyst may compute and compare the standard deviation distances for crimes within a large city. The larger the standard deviation distances, the more dispersed the crimes are. **Standard deviation ellipses** (oval and circular shaped) are used to illustrate the size and shape of the distribution. The smaller the ellipse, the closer together crime events are located. A tall and skinny ellipse indicates a distribution that is more tightly clustered from west to east and more dispersed from north to south. ArcMap also allows you to create a quantities legend using a standard deviation classification type with ratio and interval data. We often use this classification type with hotspot maps.

Inferential Statistics

The goal of inferential statistics is to study a sample (again, randomly selected) to learn about a larger population. Often in crime analysis, the populations or areas we are interested in studying are much too large to properly survey. For example, if a researcher wanted to know the thought process of burglars in choosing their intended targets and needed to interview all burglars, he would have a difficult time to say the least. Aside from the time and resources involved in such a study (the U.S. Department of Justice estimates that approximately 298,835 arrests for burglary were made nationwide in 2005), not all burglars get caught and thus are not known (the U.S. Department of Justice estimates that 2,154,126 burglaries were reported in 2005), and it is plausible to assume that not all burglars would agree to be involved in any research study (FBI, 2005). That said, it is important to be able to *infer* that what is known about a sample adequately represents the larger population from which it was drawn. To do this, we must rely on the rules of probability.

Probability theory is the foundation of inferential statistics. Probability is defined as the number of times any given outcome will occur if the event is repeated many times. For example, if a random coin was flipped 100 times, and there was nothing wrong with the coin (for example, it was not two headed or weighted on one side), one would expect to see the coin land on heads about 0.5 or 50% of the time. Of course, rarely will the result be exactly 50 heads and 50 tails, but it is usually close, 48 to 52 for example. What is interesting about random samples is that they usually reflect what is called the normal curve or bell-shaped distribution. This means that if you perform the 100-flip coin toss, most of the results should be very close to what you would find if you performed the coin toss 1000 times, 10,000 times, or more. That is, the results should be close to a 50–50 distribution of heads and tails.

The **normal curve** is a concept that is of great importance to statistics. Not only is it key to understanding inferential statistics, it also is a powerful tool that allows us to form precise statements about empirical distributions and to infer sample statistics to a larger population. The normal curve is a theoretical model that is **unimodal** (it has only one mode) and is flawlessly smooth and symmetrical. It is bell shaped, has tails that continue infinitely in both directions, and the value of its peak is the mode, median, and mean for the distribution. The most important point about the normal curve is that the distances along the horizontal axis, when measured in standard deviations, always contain the same proportion of the total area under the curve. That said, if the mean and standard deviation of a distribution are known, they can be used to describe the distribution more precisely, and analysts gain the ability to determine where any given score lies within a distribution. **Figure 9–4** illustrates the normal curve.

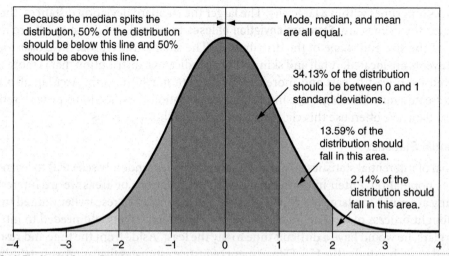

Figure 9–4 The Normal Curve, Example 1

Notice that the mean, median, and mode are all equal. And, because the median is the exact middle of a distribution, the median splits the distribution exactly in half. Also notice that the numbers along the axis represent standard deviations from the mean. Note that the mean is represented by a zero. This is because the mean itself cannot deviate from the mean. Thus, it is 0 standard deviations away from the mean.

The standard deviations along the axis also correspond to a proportionate area under the total curve. Note that the area between 0 and 1 standard deviations encompasses 34.13% of the area under the normal curve. This is also true for the area between 0 and –1 because the normal curve is symmetrical. Essentially, what this means is that if an empirical distribution is normally distributed, we would expect to find 68.26% of the scores to be within one standard deviation above and below the mean. Along the same lines, we would expect 99.72% of the distribution to fall within 3 standard deviations above and below the mean. What this means is that given the assumption of normality, it is highly unlikely that we would find very many scores that are farther away than 3 standard deviations from the mean. **Figure 9–5** illustrates the normal curve for a distribution that has a mean of 100 and a standard deviation of 10.

Note that the range of scores within 3 standard deviations below and above the mean correspond to a range of values between 70 and 130. Thus, 99.72% of the distribution should fall between 70 and 130, with 95.44% of the distribution falling between 80 and 120, and with 68.26% of the scores falling between 90 and 110. We would only expect a score above 130 or below 70 less than 0.28% of the time.

In the world of criminals and their crimes, what this means is that analysts do not have to sample all criminals and all crimes to get a better understanding of criminal behavior. They can randomly sample a proportion of them and be able to *infer* that what they learn about the sample is also true for the entire population. Essentially, if analysts correctly selected

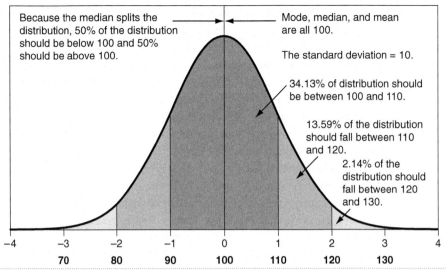

Figure 9–5 The Normal Curve, Example 2

a random sample, 99.72% of the time the sample average on any given variable should be within 3 standard deviations of the true population (the entire population the sample was selected to represent).

Suppose analysts wanted to know the average number of arrests for inmates in a given state. (This would typically be a known parameter of this population, so we could use it to perform a check on our sample to see if it is representative of the population of all inmates in the state.) If the average number of arrests for this population is 5 with a standard deviation of 1, and analysts randomly sampled 1000 inmates, they should find that approximately 683 (68.34%) of the inmates have between 4 and 6 arrests (1 standard deviation from the mean). Approximately 954 (95.44%) should have been arrested between 3 and 7 times (2 standard deviations from the mean). Finally, approximately 997 (99.72%) should have between 2 and 8 arrests (3 standard deviations from the mean). Three or fewer persons should fall into the category of less than 2 arrests or more than 8 arrests. If the parameters of this variable are applied to the entire population of inmates, the distribution should be very similar. That is, less than 1% (0.28%, to be more precise) of the inmates should have less than 2 arrests or more than 8 arrests.

The shape of the normal curve can be tall, short, wide, or narrow, as long as it retains all of the characteristics of the normal curve (unimodal, symmetrical, and smooth). A disperse distribution will be short and wide, while a tight distribution will be tall and narrow.

Recall that this is a theoretical model with infinite tails. Thus, theoretically, it is possible for a score to exist anywhere. However, in the practical world it is highly unlikely, and, in the real world, it may even be impossible. This is a very important point for crime analysts to understand. For example, the average number of arrests for a given population may be 1.67 (which we know is impossible for an individual record) with a standard deviation of

0.85. If this is taken to 3 standard deviations, 99% of the population should fall between 20.88 arrests and 4.22 arrests. Obviously, no one caught up in any state correctional system has less than 1 arrest, and it is also impossible to be arrested a negative number of times. The variable "arrest" is not a continuous variable, and it cannot, in practical terms, carry on past zero on a continuum. In addition, the distribution of arrests across this population is most likely skewed, so applying the normal curve to this particular variable is problematic. It is important for analysts to know how the variables they are using are distributed. Therefore, it is recommended that analysts make frequency tables or create **histogram** charts to help them understand how the data is distributed. A histogram is a specific type of bar chart used to display frequencies of class intervals or scores of a given variable. They use real limits rather than stated limits, so they are most appropriate for continuous, interval-level data. However, because this data rarely exists in crime analysis and mapping, histograms are commonly used for discrete, interval-level variables. **Figure 9–6** is an example of a histogram displaying state violent crime rates.

The totals were grouped into numeric ranges of 100. Notice the modal category is "300" with a frequency of 13 states in this category. Also, notice the shape of the distribution. It looks nothing like a normal or bell-shaped curve. Analysis on this positively skewed variable (the mean is greater than the median in this case) is limited in its interpretation. (This is also true of negatively skewed distributions.)

With criminal justice data, it is often difficult to make the assumption of normality because empirical distributions are often positively or negatively skewed. In their study of offender and victim movement in homicide cases, Groff and McEwen (2005) report that for homicides, both victims and offenders tend to stay close to home, creating a skewed distribution. A distribution can be *positively* skewed (where the mean is greater than the median) or *negatively* skewed (where the mean is lower than the median). When dealing with skewed data, the assumption of normality cannot be made, which limits the interpretability of results produced from analyses that require this assumption. The data can still be described, but assumptions or inferences cannot be made directly from skewed data.

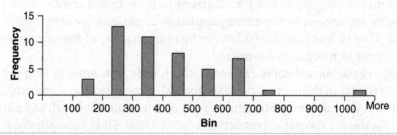

Figure 9–6 Histogram of State Violent Crime Totals

Source: Data from Bureau of Justice Statistics. (2012). Law enforcement, courts, & prisons: Crimes and crime rates. Retrieved from www.census.gov/compendia/statab/cats/law_enforcement_courts_prisons/crimes_and_crime_rates.html.

Many of the models produced by statistical analysis are based on assumptions of a *normal* distribution of a *continuous* variable. Thus, the results that are produced cannot always be strictly interpreted. In spatial analysis, crime (measured in raw counts) is a discrete variable that has a minimum value of zero. Statistical models based on the assumptions of normality and continuity will sometimes produce predictions of negative crime values. These results cannot be directly interpreted to mean that a negative number of crimes will occur in a given area, but that it is highly unlikely for any crime to occur in the given area. The limits of interpretation must be considered when crime maps and analyses are disseminated to others. If not, the results can be confusing and, worse, misleading.

There are far too many statistical tests and analyses that crime analysts have in their toolbox for us to provide a comprehensive discussion of each. As stated earlier in the chapter, it is beyond the scope of this text to provide those detailed discussions. Thus, the definitions and discussions of statistics are very much simplified. Our intention is to provide the beginning student with enough background in statistical operations to be able to understand what different tests in crime mapping do and how they can be interpreted. This is very important. Using the wrong test with the right data and vice versa can yield inaccurate and misleading results. Crime analysts must pay attention to the attributes of their data to avoid running the wrong tests.

The selection of the type of statistical analyses to run depends on some of the concepts and ideas we have already discussed in this chapter. Answers to the following list of questions can help the analyst choose which analyses to perform:

- What variables are available?
- What is the overall n?
- What is the unit of analysis?
- What do I want to know about the variable(s)?
- What is the level of measurement of the variable(s)?
- Are the variables discrete or continuous?
- How many groups will be compared in the analysis?
- Am I interested in just describing the data or finding inferences within it?

Throughout this text, the answers to these questions will be provided in the corresponding discussions for each statistical analysis. However, before discussing statistical tests, we need to examine the nature of relationships between independent and dependent variables.

Relationships Among Variables

The **dependent variable** (Y) is the variable that analysts are trying to explain (in crime mapping, the dependent variable is often some crime measure). **Independent variables** (X) are variables that produce a change in our dependent variable. For example, Catalano, Hill, and Long (2001), in an investigative analysis of a robbery series, created prediction models for where future robberies had the highest probability of occurring and where the offenders were likely to live and work in Phoenix, Arizona. In these models, freeway access and street density (independent variables) were used to predict which grocery stores were most likely to be targeted by the robbery gang (dependent variable).

Relationships can be modeled in many ways. The majority of mathematical formulas that are used in crime analysis require the assumption that X causes Y (**causal relationship**). However, in the real world, X and Y could be related in many ways. A third variable (Z) might even be included as an **intervening variable** ($X \to Z \to Y$), or it could be factored in as an **antecedent variable** ($Z \to X \to Y$) or a **contingent variable** ($X \to Y \to Z$) in the relationship between X and Y. This is important because misspecified models in crime analysis can yield incorrect outcomes, which may result in inappropriate solutions designed to reduce crime problems. Problems of **multicollinearity** (when X, Y, and Z have overlapping measures of the same concept) and **spurious relationships** (when X and Y have no direct relationship but are both affected by Z) can also pose multiple problems for crime analysts. An example of multicollinearity would be median household income and median home value in a neighborhood. The value of a home is in part a function of how much money people make. Thus, these two variables overlap in what the analyst is trying to measure. When multicollinearity exists, special care must be taken in analysis and interpretation. Models that suffer from multicollinearity can produce false significance levels.

An example of a spurious relationship is poverty and crime. Spatial analyses consistently and frequently identify a strong link between areas with high levels of poverty and corresponding high-crime rates. However, it may be the lack of opportunities that produce both. In this case, programs geared toward poverty instead of the lack of opportunities will probably yield minimal, at best, reductions in crime because deficiencies in opportunities produce both crime and poverty.

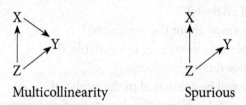

Model specification of the relationship between variables is extremely important to crime analysis. Many common **tests of significance** depend on the assumption of a causal relationship between X and Y. Tests of significance, including *chi-square*, *z-tests* or *t-tests*, and *ANOVA*, should be common in data analysis. Essentially, they work by determining whether or not variable distributions or differences between groups or areas would be expected based on random chance. For example, if crime was distributed by random chance, we would not expect to see clusters or *hotspots* of crime. In crime mapping, tests of significance tell us if the distribution of crime across any given area or the difference between two or more areas is statistically significant. Analysts can also perform tests of significance to look at crime distributions across time. If crime was distributed randomly across seasons, we would not expect significant variations in crime from month to month. Tests of significance tell us how likely the distribution is to occur or how likely differences between groups are to occur by random chance. In crime analysis, if the significance level (often termed the p value) is 0.05 or smaller, analysts determine the results to be statistically significant. A significance level of 0.05 tells us that the probability of getting these results (a variable's distribution or differences between groups or areas) by random chance is expected only 5% of the time. A significance level of 0.01 tells us that we would expect the same results by random chance only 1% of the time.

Tests of significance cannot tell us how strongly related two variables are or in which direction they are related. To determine the strength and direction of a relationship between two variables, **measures of association** must be performed. Some commonly used measures of association in the analysis of criminal justice data (either in academics or in law enforcement) include *lambda, gamma, Kendall's tau statistics, Spearman's rho*, and *Pearson's correlation coefficient*. Each of these tests make certain assumptions about the variables used in their computations, including the level of measurement, so it is important when selecting which measure of association to perform that those important assumptions not be violated. Values for measures of association typically range from 0 to 1 (for tests that cannot determine the direction of a relationship) and 21 to 1 (for tests that can determine the direction of a relationship). Results close to zero indicate a weak relationship, and results closer to 1 indicate a strong relationship. Negative values designate an **inverse relationship** (as X increases, Y decreases; or as X decreases, Y increases), and positive values indicate a **positive relationship** (X and Y both increase or decrease together).

In mapping, there are several spatial correlation analyses. The two primary tests for **spatial autocorrelation** (using aggregate data) are *Moran's I* and *Geary's C*. For the purposes of this chapter, these measures are interpreted similarly to measures of association. In interpreting Moran's I, a value between 0 and 11 indicates positive spatial autocorrelation (or clustering). A value between 21 and 0 indicates negative spatial autocorrelation (random distribution). For Geary's C, values under 1 signify positive spatial autocorrelation, and values over 1 designate negative spatial autocorrelation.

In addition to running tests of significance and measures of association, an analyst may want to run a *regression* model. Regression analysis can be computed by employing one or multiple independent variables to determine their impact on a chosen dependent variable. The most common regression model, *ordinary least-squares (OLS)*, relies on multiple assumptions, including a **linear relationship** between X and Y; continuous, and thus, interval-level or ratio-level variables; and that the **units of analysis** are the same. When using discrete variables or variables that are not measured at the interval or ratio level, direct interpretation of the results is difficult. When using variables that are discrete or measured at the nominal or ordinal level, other types of regression analyses should be employed. In crime mapping, regression models that employ spatial measures must still adhere to model assumptions, or the interpretation of results may be limited.

Regression models allow analysts to include multiple independent variables in the same model to identify how they affect the dependent variable. Depending on the regression

TABLE 9-2 Descriptive Statistics

	Mean	Std. Deviation	N
Assaults per 100,000 population	274.480	136.947	50
% of all births to teen moms	11.852	2.943	50
Median family income	48,957.580	7314.200	50
% of population older than 25 years who have not completed high school	15.922	4.377	50

model, analysts can make precise predictions about the conditions that will increase or decrease their dependent variable (typically crime). Interpreting OLS regression is fairly easy. First, the equation is stated as follows:

$$Y = a + b_1 X_1 + b_2 X_2 + b_3 X_3 \ldots$$

In this equation, Y represents the dependent variable, X_1 and X_2 represent the independent variables, a is the value of Y when both X_1 and X_2 are zero (Y intercept), and b_1 and b_2 are the **coefficients** of X_1 and X_2, respectively. A typical output is contained in Tables 9–2 through 9–5. **Table 9–2** displays the descriptive statistics for the variables included in the model. (Assault rate per 100,000 is the dependent variable; the percentage of births to teen moms, median family income, and the percentage of persons older than 25 years who have not completed high school are the independent variables.) Note that the n is equal to 50 for all variables. This is because the unit of analysis for this dataset is states, and there are 50 states included in this dataset.

Table 9–3 provides the correlations between all the variables. This allows us to check for multicollinearity for variables that could potentially overlap in their measurements. Note

TABLE 9-3 Correlations

		Assaults per 100,000 Population	% of All Births to Teen Moms	Median Family Income	% of Population Older Than 25 Years Who Have Not Completed High School
Pearson's Correlation	Assaults per 100,000 Population	1.000	**0.486	–0.127	**0.431
	% of All Births to Teen Moms	**0.486	1.000	**–0.753	**0.668
	Median Family Income	–0.127	**–0.753	1.000	**–0.513
	% of Population Older Than 25 Years Who Have Not Completed High School	**0.431	**0.668	**–0.513	1.000

** Significant at the 0.01 level

TABLE 9-4 Model Summary

Model	R	R^2	Adjusted R^2	Std. Error of the Estimate
1	0.625	0.391	0.351	110.303

Predictors: (Constant), % of population older than 25 years who have not completed high school, median family income, % of all births to teen moms.

that the Pearson's correlation for the percentage of persons older than 25 years without a high school degree is 20.513 and is significant at the 0.01 level. (Note that ** indicates a significant level at the 0.01 level or better. A separate t-test is conducted on values of association to test for significance.) This tells us that these two variables have a significant and inverse relationship. That is, as the number of persons older than 25 years who have not completed high school increases, the assault rate decreases. It is known that income and education overlap in their measurements, so we must be careful in our interpretations of these results.

Table 9-4 provides the model summary. Analysts are interested in the R^2 and adjusted R^2. Because there may be issues of multicollinearity that might artificially inflate the findings, analysts need to use the adjusted R^2 for their interpretations. The R^2 and adjusted R^2 will range from 0 to 1 and are interpreted as the percentage of variance in the dependent variables that is explained by the independent variables in the model. In our model, we can state that approximately 35% of the assault rate can be explained by the percentage of births to teen moms, median family income, and the percentage of persons older than 25 years who have not completed high school. Not bad, but it also means that other variables not included in our model explain the remaining 65% of variance in the assault rate.

Table 9-5 displays the coefficients for our regression model. The first column "B" underneath the category "unstandardized coefficients" represents the values for "a" (constant) and b_1, b_2, and b_3. Note that the value for "a" or the y intercept is 2762.081. This means that when the percentage of births to teen moms, median family income, and percentage of persons older than 25 years who have not completed high school are all zero, the assault rate should be 2762.081 per 100,000. Obviously, this value does not exist in the real world. An assault rate of

TABLE 9-5 Coefficients

Model		Unstandardized Coefficients B	Std. Error	Standardized Coefficients Beta	t	Sig.
1	(Constant)	−762.081	243.335		−3.132	0.003
	% of All Births to Teen Moms	35.934	9.395	0.772	3.825	0.000
	Median Family Income	1.043E-02	0.003	0.557	3.184	0.003
	% of Population Older Than 25 Years Who Have Not Completed High School	6.273	4.840	0.200	1.296	0.201

Dependent variable: Assaults per 100,000 population.

zero is the absolute low. However, what this should tell you is that without the effects of these three independent variables, the assault rate is very low.

We can also use these coefficient values to make more precise predictions. When substituting our values into the equation, we have the following:

$$\text{Assault Rate } (Y) = -762.081 + 35.934(X_1) + 0.0143(X_2) + 6.273(X_3)$$

If we know the values for our independent variables, we can use them to predict what the assault rate will be. Assume that a state has 5% of all births delivered to teen moms, a median family income of $40,000, and 7% of the population is older than 25 years and has not completed high school. Substituting these numbers, our formula should look like this:

$$\text{Predicted Assault Rate } (Y) = -762.081 + 35.934(5) + 0.0143(40,000) + 6.273(7)$$

$$\text{Predicted Assault Rate } (Y) = -762.081 + 179.67 + 572 + 43.911$$

$$\text{Predicted Assault Rate } (Y) = 33.5$$

Based on the model, if a state has 5% of all births delivered to teen moms, a median family income of $40,000, and 7% of the population is older than 25 and has not completed high school, we would expect about 34 assaults per 100,000 persons. The model is based on probabilities (as all statistics are) and thus it is not perfect. But, depending on how good the model is (determined by a variety of factors, but a high adjusted R^2 usually indicates a strong model), our estimates can be fairly precise.

As you can see, statistical analysis can be quite powerful in crime analysis for describing and making predictions about crime. However, statistical analysis requires analysts to obey rules and follow guidelines. When they do not, their results are inaccurate, misleading, and deceptive. But what, you may ask, does this have to do with making crime maps? The answer is that it has everything to do with crime mapping. Spatial analyses employ the same mathematical computations as nonspatial data analysis and thus rely on the same assumptions and require the analyst to follow the same guidelines and obey the same rules. If not, the crime maps produced can also be inaccurate, misleading, and deceptive. This by no means should keep analysts from making maps and using the various tools and tricks of the trade to identify problem areas when the commander requests their assistance, but it is imperative that they recognize the possible weaknesses in the data, and if they attempt to infer something about that data, that they do so with the utmost sense of responsibility.

■ Classification in Mapping

There are several methods to classify information in crime maps using some of the statistical concepts and ideas discussed in this chapter. Harries (1999) provides a good description of five common classification methods in *Mapping Crime: Principle and Practice*. *Equal interval* classification calculates the range (distance between the lowest and highest scores) and divides the range into equal ranges or intervals. Typically, a map should contain between four and six intervals (or classes) but no more than seven in any case (Harries, 1999).

A choropleth map is shown in **Figure 9–7**. Choropleth maps use shading variations according to their value on a chosen variable; in this case, burglary rates at the town level in the state of Massachusetts are shown.

Maps classified into quantiles place equal numbers of incidents or observations in each category. This method is strongly influenced by the number of categories selected. If five categories are selected (the default in ArcView), areas will be separated into 0–20th percentile,

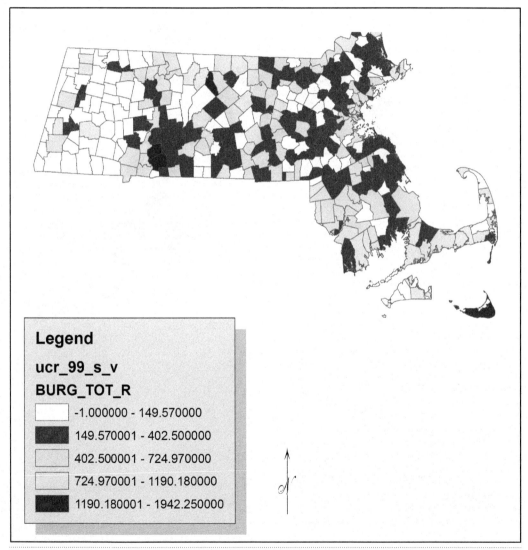

Figure 9–7 1999 Massachusetts Burglary Rate, Equal Interval Classification

Source: Data from the Office of Geographic Information (MassGIS). (2012). Retrieved from www.mass.gov/mgis/crime_statistics.htm.

21st–40th percentile, 41st–60th percentile, 61st–80th percentile, and 81st–100th percentile (see **Figure 9–8**).

Equal area classification divides the distribution based on area rather than incidents or observations. When using the equal area classification, maps with areas that are roughly the same size will look similar to a quantile map. If the areas vary greatly in size, an equal area map will look substantially different from a quantile map.

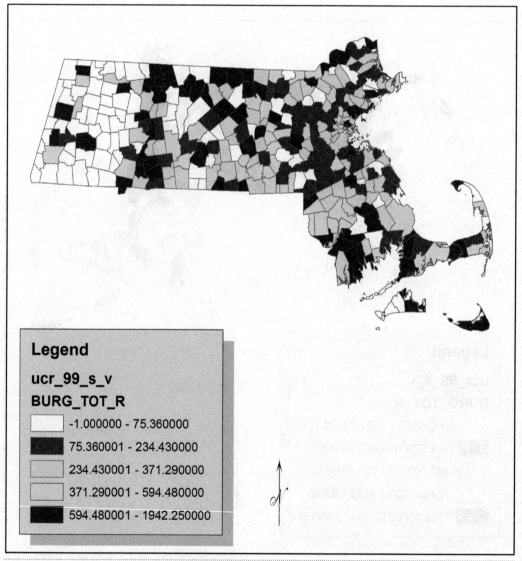

Legend

ucr_99_s_v
BURG_TOT_R

☐	-1.000000 - 75.360000
■	75.360001 - 234.430000
▨	234.430001 - 371.290000
☐	371.290001 - 594.480000
■	594.480001 - 1942.250000

Figure 9–8 1999 Massachusetts Burglary Rate, Quantile Classification

Source: Data from the Office of Geographic Information (MassGIS). (2012). Retrieved from www.mass.gov/mgis/crime_statistics.htm.

Natural breaks classification method uses breaks or gaps in the data distribution to create categories. Typically, a procedure known as Jenks optimization (the default in ArcView) "ensures the internal homogeneity within classes while maintaining the heterogeneity among the classes" (Harries, 1999, p. 51; see **Figure 9–9**).

Standard deviation maps classify data based on the dispersion of data from the mean score. For example, if the average number of homicides for a city at the block group level is

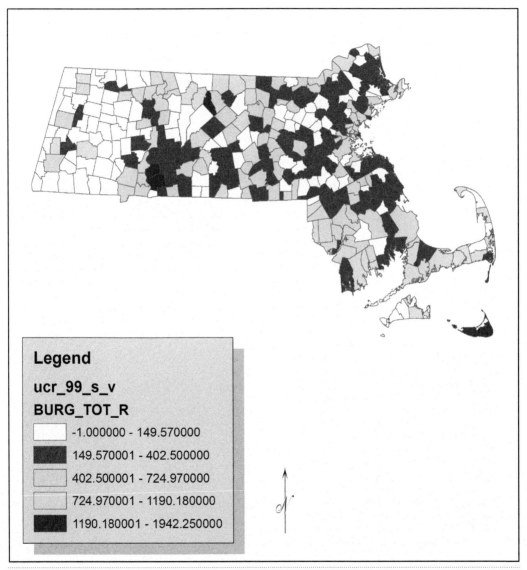

Figure 9–9 1999 Massachusetts Burglary Rate, Natural Breaks Classification

Source: Data from the Office of Geographic Information (MassGIS). (2012). Retrieved from www.mass.gov/mgis/crime_statistics.htm.

three, areas will be categorized by how many standard deviations they fall above or below three homicides (see **Figure 9–10**).

As one can see, each of the four maps, using different classification methods, looks very different and thus paints a different picture to the intended audience. The analyst must balance what classification method is best for the intended audience with rules of statistics. For example, standard deviation classification is a good tool for expressing extreme values. However, using this method assumes the variable is normally distributed. In this case, analysts

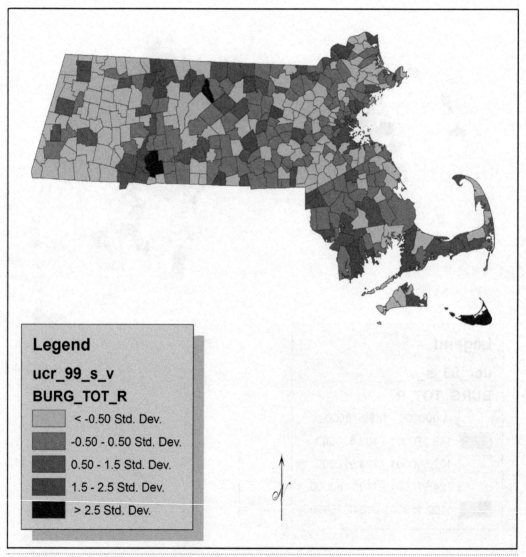

Figure 9–10 1999 Massachusetts Burglary Rate, Standard Deviation Classification

Source: Data from the Office of Geographic Information (MassGIS). (2012). Retrieved from www.mass.gov/mgis/crime_statistics.htm.

cannot assume the burglary rate is normally distributed without looking at the frequency distribution first. This is easy enough to do in most spreadsheet or database programs.

■ Conclusion

This chapter provided a brief discussion of statistics in crime analysis. Elias (1999), drawing on Huff's *How to Lie with Statistics* (1993), identifies six statistical "sins" for the analyst to avoid that form a useful framework for summarizing the main points found in this chapter and integrating other relative points from the study of crime mapping. First, analysts must acknowledge that even in randomly selected samples, statistical analysis, while computed without flaw, can yield inaccurate results. This can happen for a number of reasons. In self-report studies, people may report things that are untrue purposefully or accidentally. In survey research, potential respondents who decide not to participate in the study may be inherently different from persons who do decide to participate on key variables that matter to the study. Even if a sample is randomly drawn, there is still the possibility, although small, that it will not be representative of the larger population. In research that requires interviewing, characteristics of the researcher may influence respondents' answers to questions or their decision to participate in the research.

The second sin analysts engage in is reporting statistics that, while accurate, are deceptive. Reporting the mean, for example, with a skewed data distribution is misleading. Zedlewski (1987) used the arithmetic average in calculations to estimate the cost–benefit ratio for incarceration. He estimated that the typical offender committed 187 crimes per year, producing a "social cost" of $430,000 per offender, per year. DiIulio and Piehl (1991) in a similar study estimated that a typical felon only costs society $28,000 per year. Why are their conclusions so different? They likely used different measures of central tendency to estimate the number of crimes the typical offender commits and the average cost associated with these crimes. Because the distribution of both variables is likely to be skewed (recall that a small proportion of offenders cause a large percentage of the problem), using different measures of central tendency can yield vastly different conclusions.

The third statistical sin analysts commit is not presenting their audience with the whole picture. Focusing on only one month of crime, for example, without placing it in the larger picture of yearly crime can be misleading. Another problem is not including raw numbers along with percentages. Sometimes a large decrease in crime percentage may only amount to one or two crimes in raw numbers.

The fourth sin has to do with interpreting statistical significance. It is common in very large samples to achieve a finding of statistical significance for very small differences between groups or areas simply because there is a large number of cases or observations. It is important for analysts to run both tests of significance *and* measures of associations to determine whether or not their findings have *substantive* significance. For example, one group of offenders might self-report committing an average of 3.1 crimes per month, and the comparison group might report an average of 3.3 crimes per month. If the number of offenders included in the analysis is large enough, tests of significance may identify a statistically

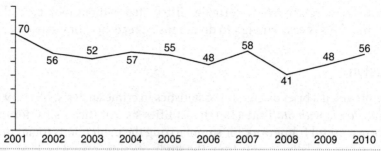

Figure 9–11 Officers Feloniously Killed, 2001–2010, Scale Example 1

Source: Data from the Federal Bureau of Investigation (FBI), Uniform Crime Reports. (2011). Law Enforcement Officers Killed and Assaulted. Retrieved from www.fbi.gov/about-us/cjis/ucr/crime-in-the-u.s/2011/crime-in-the-u.s.-2011/leoka.

significant difference between the groups. However, from a practical standpoint, a difference of 0.2 crimes is insignificant to law enforcement and thus provides no meaningful difference.

The fifth sin relates to our earlier discussion of model specification. Most formulas for determining the nature of relationships assume a causal relationship between the independent and dependent relationship. Further analysis is needed to identify if a third factor, Z, is an intervening, antecedent, or contingent variable that mitigates the relationship between X and Y. In addition, further analyses, such as partial correlations, must be performed to rule out spurious relationships.

The sixth sin an analyst can commit is choosing an improper scale to display his or her results. At one magnitude, the problem (or solution) may look much more impressive than at a different scale. The following figures illustrate the number of officers feloniously killed between 2001 and 2010. **Figures 9–11** and **9–12** use the same official figures but employ different scales.

Note that the changes from year to year look more dramatic in the first example, even though the figures used are the same. **Figure 9–13** shows the same information, except that the 72 officers killed as a result of the 9/11 attacks have been included.

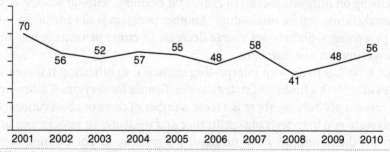

Figure 9–12 Officers Feloniously Killed, 2001–2010, Scale Example 2

Source: Data from the Federal Bureau of Investigation (FBI), Uniform Crime Reports. (2011). Law Enforcement Officers Killed and Assaulted. Retrieved from www.fbi.gov/about-us/cjis/ucr/crime-in-the-u.s/2011/crime-in-the-u.s.-2011/leoka.

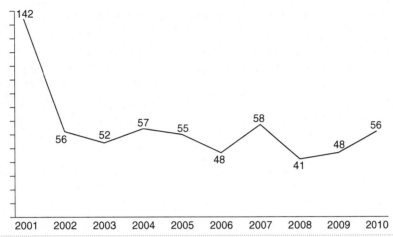

Figure 9–13 Officers Feloniously Killed, 2001–2010, Scale Example 3 [Does not include the 72 officers who lost their lives in the September 11, 2001 attacks]

Source: Data from the Federal Bureau of Investigation (FBI), Uniform Crime Reports. (2011). Law Enforcement Officers Killed and Assaulted. Retrieved from www.fbi.gov/about-us/cjis/ucr/crime-in-the-u.s/2011/crime-in-the-u.s.-2011/leoka.

This example reemphasizes the need to present the whole picture to the intended audience, making them aware of any known reasons for dramatic shifts in variable trends.

A seventh possibly deadly sin would be for an analyst to fail to recognize the audience for whom the analysis is prepared. If an analyst wishes to simply describe crime in terms easy enough to let the audience understand the problems, many of these sins do not apply directly. However, it is incumbent on analysts to learn how to use these inferential statistics tools to better serve their law enforcement audience. Analysts may find that they need to describe their findings and analysis in an executive summary fashion and tell the police command staff what their findings mean in a laymen's terms rather than via statistical jargon. It may make the analysis more useful to them.

In conclusion, it is extremely easy to present inaccurate or misleading statistics (either intentionally or unintentionally), even if the calculations are performed perfectly. It is crucial for crime analysts and mappers to pay attention to the rules and guidelines of statistical analyses that have been addressed in this chapter to produce the most accurate and representative picture of what is occurring. Maps and analyses created by violating the assumptions and rules of various statistical analyses provide misleading information to policy makers and may result in wasted resources.

■ Chapter Glossary

Antecedent variable   In an antecedent relationship, a third variable, Z, is placed before X and Y.

Bimodal   A distribution is bimodal if it contains two modes.

Causal relationship   In a causal relationship, X is assumed to have produced variation in Y.

Choropleth map   Choropleth maps use shade and color to denote different distributions of a variable. Done at the polygon level, they can be at different units of analysis including beats or precincts, census blocks or block groups, or towns.

Coefficient   A coefficient is a value used in a mathematical equation that is a constant multiplicative factor of a certain object, such as in $9X^2$ where 9 is a coefficient of X^2. In simple terms, coefficients are the values and variables we use in statistics calculations.

Contingent variable   In a contingent relationship, a third variable, Z, is placed after X and Y.

Continuous   Continuous variables *do* have values that fall between adjacent values on the same scale.

Dependent variable   The variation in the dependent variable (Y) is thought to be caused by the independent variable(s) (X).

Dichotomous   Variables that are divided into two categories. Often called "dummy" variables, dichotomous variables are typically used in parametric tests that require interval-level variables.

Discrete   Discrete variables do not have values that fall between adjacent values on the same scale.

Exhaustive   When a variable operationalization is exhaustive, there is a category for all values.

Frequency distribution   A frequency distribution is a visualization, in summary form, of how values are spread over categories or scales.

Histogram   In a histogram, the categories of one variable are plotted on one axis, and the responses are plotted on the other axis. Histograms are best used on nominal- and ordinal-level variables but can be used on interval variables with collapsed categories (as in a frequency distribution).

Independent variable   In a causal relationship, the independent variable (X) is assumed to be at least a partial cause of the change in the dependent variable (Y).

Interquartile range   An interquartile range is the distance between the 25th and 75th percentiles.

Interval   Interval-level variables (data) can be ranked, such as ordinal variables, but the distance between each value is known.

Intervening variable   In an intervening relationship, a third variable, Z, is between X and Y.

Inverse relationship   In an inverse relationship, the value of one variable increases as the value of the other variable decreases.

Linear relationship   In a linear relationship, two variables (measured at the interval or ratio level) travel together in a seemingly straight line.

Mean   The average (usually the arithmetic mean) of all scores within a distribution.

Mean center   In mapping, the mean center marks the location of the arithmetic average of all the incident locations on a map. The mean center is the approximate center of a series of events (typically crime incidents).

Measures of association   Statistics that indicate the strength and nature of a relationship between variables.

Median   The middle score in a distribution.

Mode   The most frequent score in a distribution.

Multicollinearity   Multicollinearity exists when variables in a model are highly correlated. This can mean that the variables are measuring the same thing.

Mutually exclusive   When a variable operationalization is mutually exclusive, values can only fit into one category.

Nominal   Nominal-level variables (data) are variables (typically word categories) that cannot be ranked. For example, gender and race are nominal-level variables.

Normal curve   In a normal distribution, the values form a curved shape that is unimodal, symmetrical, and infinite in both directions. In normal distributions, the mode, median, and mean are all the same value.

Operationalize   This term denotes the process of measuring a variable by putting it into categories and assigning numbers to its characteristics.

Ordinal   Ordinal variables (data) can be ranked. In number or word form, the actual value of an ordinal measurement is not known; rather, it is included within a category that ranges in value.

Positive relationship   In a positive relationship, the values of both variables travel in the same direction (either both are increasing at the same time or both are decreasing at the same time).

Qualitative   Qualitative research is usually narrative focused and rich in information. Variables measured at the nominal level are considered to be qualitative data.

Quantitative   Usually number oriented, quantitative research typically utilizes statistical analysis to answer research questions.

Range   The simplest measure of dispersion, the range is the difference between the lowest and highest scores in a distribution.

Ratio   Ratio-level variables (data) are interval-level variables, except that ratio-level variables have a true zero.

Reliability   A variable is reliable if it consistently measures a variable from one study to the next.

Skewed   A distribution is skewed if the mode, mean, and median are not the same value.

Spatial autocorrelation   Spatial autocorrelation tests indicate whether or not distributions of point locations are related to one another.

Spurious relationship   A spurious relationship exists when X and Y are assumed to be related, but a third variable, Z, is actually strongly related to both X and Y. Once controlling for Z, the relationship between X and Y disappears.

Standard deviation   The square root of the variance, the standard deviation represents the average deviation from the mean.

Standard deviation ellipses   Standard deviation ellipses are drawn on a map to represent typically one and two standard deviations from the mean center (the average distance from incident locations to the mean center). It also indicates the direction toward which the dispersion is oriented (north, south, east, west).

Tests of significance   Tests of significance indicate whether or not the distribution of a variable or the relationship between two or more variables is statistically significant.

Unimodal   A distribution is unimodal if it only has one mode.

Unit of analysis   A unit of analysis is the level at which variables are measured. In examining relationships using statistical models, it is important to keep within the same unit of analysis.

Validity   A variable has validity if it measures what it is supposed to measure.

Variables   Called "variable" because they vary in some way, variables are the characteristics of people, space (or even time), or behaviors that analysts study. People-related variables include age, race, gender, victimization, and criminal behavior. Place-related variables include distances from one place to another, or the concentration of bars in an area, for example.

Variance   Variance measures the average of the squared deviations from the mean.

■ Questions for Review

1. Explain *qualitative* and *quantitative* data. Provide an example of each.
2. What is a variable?
3. Explain the four levels of variable measurement. Provide an example of each in your discussion.
4. What is the difference between *discrete* and *continuous* variables?
5. What is a mean center and how is it used in crime mapping?
6. What is a standard deviation ellipse? Why do crime analysts only draw three or fewer standard deviation ellipses?
7. What is spatial autocorrelation? What are two commonly used tests of spatial autocorrelation?
8. Why do crime analysts need to have a solid understanding of statistics to create and explain crime maps?
9. How can data be classified in crime maps? How does an analyst know which classification method to use?
10. What are the statistical sins analysts should avoid?

■ Online Resources

Dr. Tom O'Connor's comprehensive list and guide to modeling relationships: www.drtomoconnor.com/criminology.htm

FedStats: www.fedstats.gov

Kahn's Academy (a great online source for short tutorial clips on statistics and other topical areas): www.khanacademy.org/math/statistics/#math/statistics

Statistics Every Writer Should Know: http://nilesonline.com/stats/

■ Recommended Reading ▬▬▬▬▬▬▬▬▬▬▬▬▬▬▬▬▬▬▬▬▬▬▬▬▬

Walker, J. T., & Maddan, S. (2009). *Statistics in criminology and criminal justice: Analysis and interpretation* (3rd ed.). Sudbury, MA: Jones & Bartlett Learning.

■ References ▬▬▬▬▬▬▬▬▬▬▬▬▬▬▬▬▬▬▬▬▬▬▬▬▬▬▬▬▬▬▬▬▬

Catalano, P., Hill, B., & Long, B. (2001). Geographical analysis and serial crime investigation: A case study of armed robbery in Phoenix, Arizona. *Security Journal, 14*(3), 27–41.

DiIulio, J., Jr., & Piehl, A. M. (1991, Fall). Does prison pay? *Brookings Review,* 28–35.

Elias, G. (1999). *How to collect and analyze data: A manual for sheriffs and jail administrators* (2nd ed.). Lafayette, CO: Voorhis Associates.

Federal Bureau of Investigation (FBI). (2005). Crime in the United States, 2005. Retrieved from www2 .fbi.gov/ucr/05cius/offenses/clearances/index.html.

Groff, E., & McEwen, J. T. (2005). Disaggregating the journey to homicide. In F. Wang (Ed.), *Geographic information systems and crime analysis* (pp. 60–83). Hershey, PA: IDEA Group.

Harries, K. D. (1999). *Mapping crime: Principle and practice*. Washington, DC: National Institute of Justice.

Huff, D. (1993). *How to lie with statistics* (Reprinted). New York, NY: W. W. Norton & Company.

Kennedy, D. M., Braga, A. A., & Piehl, A. M. (1998). The unknown universe: Mapping gangs and gang violence in Boston. In D. Weisburd & T. McEwen (Eds.), *Crime mapping and crime prevention: Crime prevention studies* (Vol. 8; pp. 219–262). Monsey, NY: Criminal Justice Press.

Zedlewski, E. W. (1987). Making confinement decisions. *Research in brief*. Washington, DC: National Institute of Justice.

Distance Analysis

CHAPTER

▶ LEARNING OBJECTIVES

This chapter begins with a discussion of several types of distance analysis. Each type of distance analysis has strengths and weaknesses that must be understood prior to interpretation. After studying this chapter, you should be able to:

- Identify the common types of distance analyses used in crime mapping.
- Explain the appropriate uses of distance analysis.
- Understand the strengths and limitations of distance analysis.

▶ **Key Terms**

Buffer	Euclidean Distance	Manhattan Distance
Distance Analysis	Journey to Crime	Mean Center
Distance Between		Spider Distance
Hits Analysis		

■ Introduction

All analyses that rely on distance measures are distance analyses. Thus, the hotspot analyses that are examined in this chapter could also be viewed as distance analyses in that the determination of a clustering of events requires that individual events are located closer together than we would expect based on random chance. In this case, the distances measured are strictly those between criminal incidents (distances between homicides in a city, for example). This chapter discusses analyses where distance is measured in relation to another point or in efforts to find another point (the mean center of a distribution, an offender's home, predicted next target, or some other point of importance such as a school, bar, or pawn shop). The **distance analyses** to be discussed in this chapter include mean center analysis, journey-to-crime analysis, spider distance analysis, proximity analysis, distance between hits analysis, and distance and time analysis.

There are several different methods of calculating distance. Each has its strengths and limitations in analysis. In crime analysis, the two most common methods of distance calculation are Euclidean and Manhattan. **Euclidean distance** is measured by measuring the distance between two points. Often called the "as the crow flies" measurement, it is the shortest distance between two points on a map. The problem is that there rarely is a road that leads directly from point A to point B on a map (have you ever navigated Boston?), and travelers usually must take a series of twists and turns to reach their destination. Thus, Euclidean calculations of distance are typically smaller than the path actually traveled by an individual. **Manhattan distance** or "street" distance, as it is often called, is calculated by using right angles to get from one point to another. In practical terms, individuals do not always travel in right angles to get to their destination (again, have you ever driven in Boston?). Manhattan calculations are always larger than Euclidean calculations because the shortest distance between two points is a straight line (see **Figure 10–1**).

You may be wondering at this point which is the best calculation method to use. The answer depends on the type of analysis you are performing and the data you are using (including the street layout of the study area). Euclidean distance is much easier to calculate; however, Manhattan more closely approximates the distance traveled by individuals. Rossmo, Laverty, and Moore (2005) observe that:

> Research has shown that Manhattan distance gives the most accurate result in the greatest number of cases, while not being significantly worse than other methods across the entire spectrum of cases—a finding true for both North America and Great Britain . . . As long as these specific exceptional cases can be identified and recognized through training and experience, the most reliable and practical method involves the use of Manhattan distance (p. 111).

The best method of distance calculation is dependent on the type of analysis that is to be performed. Groff and McEwen (2005) found a strong correlation between Euclidean and

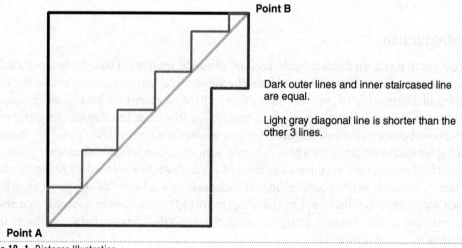

Point B

Dark outer lines and inner staircased line are equal.

Light gray diagonal line is shorter than the other 3 lines.

Point A

Figure 10–1 Distance Illustration

street distances and thus argued that one could use the coefficients of Euclidean measures in a regression model to estimate street distances.

■ Distance Analysis

A variety of distance measures can be used in crime analysis and mapping, and in reality, distance and how features are related to each other on a map are what crime mapping is all about. The very technical term *spatial autocorrelation* has a fairly simple explanation to crime mappers, which is that features that are closest to one another are likely more related to other features near it than to those farther away. If we think about this within our own lives, we might often find more in common with our neighbors, friends, and coworkers nearer to us in geography than persons who live farther away or who have no similar occupation, interests, or residence. The first type of distance analysis we discuss is mean center analysis, which is used for tactical analysis purposes.

Mean Center Analysis

The **mean center** of any distribution is, very simply, the point at which the mean of X (latitude) and the mean of Y (longitude) of events meet on a map. It represents the average or the center of gravity of a spatial distribution (Levine, 2002). The problem with performing a mean center analysis is that it is sensitive to outliers (the mean itself is sensitive to outliers and thus cannot be relied upon in skewed distributions). In addition, the mean center of distributions that are multimodal or oddly shaped (such as in an L-shaped distribution) may be placed at a point where very few crimes actually occur. Thus, the utility of mean center analyses is not in finding a point on the map to throw more resources at or the apex of crime in an area. Rather, it is a reference point to be used in further analyses, such as in the comparison of two different distributions (same crime but different time, or different crime but same time), and as a starting place to begin prioritizing places and persons of interest (such as performing a standard deviation ellipses analysis). There are several different types of mean center analyses that an analyst can perform. CrimeStat performs several different mean center analyses, including the mean center, the harmonic mean, and the geometric mean. Note that when viewing **Figure 10-2** at a smaller scale, the three mean centers appear to be located at the same point. However, in **Figure 10-3**, a larger scale reveals that the three mean center analyses are indeed three separate points.

What does this all mean to the analyst? If we remember that maps are simply representations of the real world and our goal is to be as accurate as possible when doing analyses, then deciding which distance method to use is just part of that well planned analytical process. It also makes a difference in what scale we are looking at. If we had been zoomed out on these points they indeed appear to be about the same place. If we were to target the area that encompasses or is within 500 feet of the points, we might get an area that would be useful to investigators. If we look at recent research we might only want to find the 500-foot radius around the mean center and give that to detectives working the case.

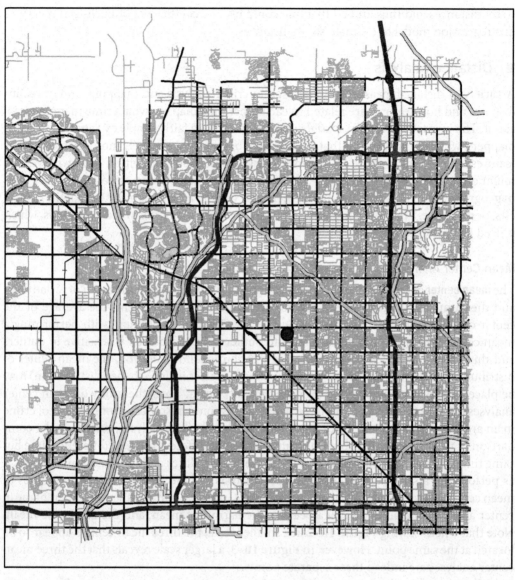

N

Figure 10–2 Mean Center Analysis, Burglaries 2003, Glendale, Arizona, Small Scale

Source: Created with CrimeStat and ArcGIS.

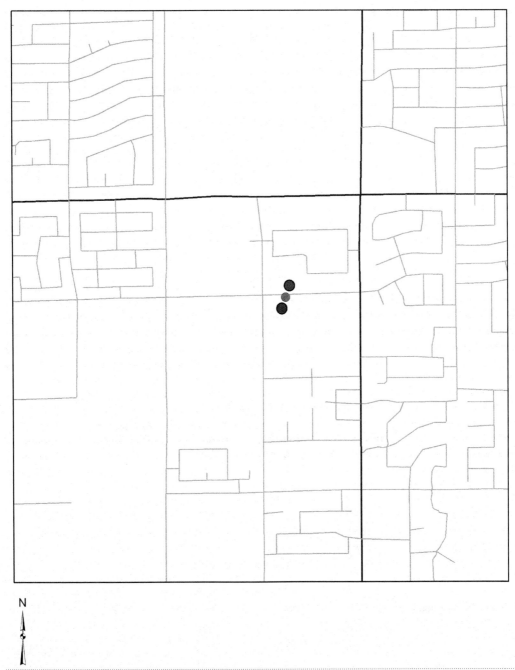

Figure 10–3 Mean Center Analysis, Burglaries 2003, Glendale, Arizona, Large Scale

Source: Created with CrimeStat and ArcGIS.

Journey-to-Crime Analysis

A **journey-to-crime** (JTC) analysis is a type of distance analysis that is used primarily in investigations of crime series thought to be attributed to an individual or group of persons acting together. It is conducted in hopes of prioritizing areas in which the offender or offenders are most likely to live or work. Offenders are fairly routine in their travels for both criminal and noncriminal behavior (see **Table 10–1**).

In addition, offenders generally tend to travel greater distances for property crimes than they do for violent crimes, and the likelihood of offenders to commit any crime dissipates as they get farther away from their home. (However, if offenders commit crime in relation to an anchor point that is not their home—for example, if the anchor point is their place of employment—distance decay measures from home to crime should not be used if more accurate work-to-home distances are available.)

Journey-to-crime research traditionally has examined the route undertaken by offenders between their home and place(s) where the crime was committed. However, this ignores the *victim's* journey to his or her victimization and also ignores other nodes where offenders maybe traveling from (work, school, parole office; Costello & Leipnik, 2003). Groff and McEwen (2005) found "clear differences in travel behavior between victims and offenders" (p. 60) in their study of homicides in Washington, DC. They calculated Euclidean and street distances for offenders and victims and found that for homicides, victims traveled a median of 0.69 street miles (0.54 Euclidean miles). Median distances were chosen due to the skewed nature of the dataset. (Both victims and offenders of homicide tended to stick very close

TABLE 10–1 Average Distance to Crime in Glendale, Arizona

Crime Type	Number of Crimes	Mean Crime Trip (Miles)	Standard Deviation (Miles)	68% of Crime Trips Within (Miles)	Furthest Distance
Aggravated assault	8526	1.18	2.86	4.04	6.91
Arson	62	1.32	2.68	4.00	6.67
Auto theft	1058	2.88	3.55	6.43	9.97
Burglary	1356	2.34	3.73	6.07	9.79
Curfew/loitering	164	1.59	1.85	3.44	5.28
Drug offenses	3970	2.27	3.39	5.66	9.06
Murder	70	2.38	4.42	6.80	11.23
Other miscellaneous	18,237	2.42	3.90	6.32	10.22
Other sex offenses	404	1.61	2.66	4.27	6.92
Rape	85	1.35	2.79	4.14	6.94
Robbery	567	3.23	4.21	7.44	11.65
Runaway	5958	0.19	1.29	1.48	2.77
Theft	5139	3.18	4.28	7.46	11.75

Source: Bryan Hill, Glendale, Arizona Police Department.

to home.) The distance traveled for both victims and offenders varied according to the originating motivation for the homicide. For robbery-motivated homicides, victims were killed about 1 mile from their homes. For retaliatory, drug, and gang-related homicides, victims were killed a median of 0.67 miles from their homes. Male victims traveled farther to their murders than did female victims in every category of homicide (with the exception of domestic violence homicides).

You may be wondering why we are including a discussion of *victims'* travel to crime. The answer is straightforward. Crime, in spatial analysis, must be viewed as a criminal event, and thus the behaviors and travel patterns of victims are equally important to the behaviors and traveling patterns of offenders. Although crime is largely opportunistic, and thus any number of targets may be equally desirable in an offender's eyes (although this not always the case in serial crimes), it is important to understand how victims and offenders interact with their environments to gain a better picture of how a crime unfolds from multiple perspectives. You will also find that law enforcement agencies do not often ask these questions of crime victims, and it may take considerable effort to change the vision of information collection to include collection of travel data and behavior of victims in less serious crimes. JTC analysis can be as simple as choosing the area around the median or mean center of the crime series. The mean center can be calculated by hand, using the spatial statistics toolbox in ArcMap, or by using CrimeStat III. In addition, a more sophisticated model can be run in the journey-to-crime tab in CrimeStat III, which includes the ability to calibrate the model for your own offenders, or by using a variety of mathematical models research has shown can be useful with certain types of crime series (much information can be found in the CrimeStat manual if you have the time to read through the chapter on JTC analysis).

Spider Distance Analysis

Spider distance analysis draws lines from each point in a distribution to its centroid, or mean center. Spider analysis helps to answer several questions in crime analysis. First, in a crime series, is the offender likely to be a poacher or a hunter? Poachers or marauders exhibit fairly predictable patterns in their offending, usually committing crimes short distances around their central base (typically their homes, but not always). Hunters or commuters, on the other hand, are much less predictable in their offending patterns. Spider distance analyses can provide clues to analysts to whether or not a series is expanding outward or shrinking inward. If the mean center does not change very much with each new hit in the crime series, this could mean that you are dealing with a marauder and may be successful in finding his home anchor point, or identifying a potential suspect from records-management databases (RMS) for the small area around the mean center or through a calibrated JTC model in CrimeStat. If the hits seem to bounce back and forth around the mean center, this may be another indicator the analyst has identified as being indicative of a marauder. JTC analysis will be less useful in helping to identify the suspect's home anchor point or in helping to whittle down the list of potential offenders from RMS data when you have a commuter operating.

Buffer Analysis and Queries (Theme Selection)

There are two general types of proximity analysis: **buffer** analysis and queries. A buffer zone analysis is completed by drawing circles around points of reference or polygons (like beats or parks), such as pawn shops or city parks, at distances determined by the analyst. Essentially, the points (locations of pawn shops or parks) serve as centers (or centroids) for the buffers with a radius set at a distance desired by the analyst (this can be done in miles, meters, feet, etc.). For example, an analyst might wish to draw 0.5-mile buffers around all pawn shops in his jurisdiction. He then may wish to add to a map layer of known burglaries within its jurisdiction and visually scan to see those burglaries that occur within a half mile of a pawn shop. At other times the analyst may want to analyze crime around city parks. A specific park may be the local hangout of transients, and the analyst may want to look at the crime around the park to determine if the crime rate in and around that park is higher than other parks in similar neighborhoods. This analysis may assist with planning efforts and enforcement of no camping ordinances and other issues that often surround high transient population areas. In this case, a point is not the center of the buffer, but the limits of the park polygon would act in this manner, and then the buffer would be drawn, following the park outlines outward by 0.5 miles. Buffer zone analysis is a common type of distance analysis and is easily interpreted. **Figure 10–4** provides an example of a buffer analysis.

There are basically three types of queries in ArcMap: (1) attribute queries, (2) spatial queries or location queries, and (3) queries using graphics on the screen. The first type of query, attribute queries, allow the analyst to query any of the data fields in the attribute table that makes the point, line, or polygon a smart piece of data. We could query all the robberies/burglaries that occurred between 4:00 A.M. and 6:00 A.M., or Hispanic male persons who have been listed as suspects in past theft incidents.

An analyst may also want to query incidents that are within a distance of some other type of point data (spatial query), such as schools, liquor establishments, or pawn shops. For example, an analyst may be called upon to produce a map of crimes that are within a given distance of schools. Another example might be to query store robberies that are within a given distance of a freeway entrance. The benefit to using a query over a buffer analysis is that points that are not within the specified distance are removed from the map once we create a layer of just the selected incidents, lessening clutter and improving map clarity. Another related query is one that queries the number of points within a polygon, such as a police precinct or beat. In fact, any concept of space and relationships in space can be queried, such as within a distance of, totally within, intersected by, or adjacent to something else in a map layer in geographic information systems (GIS).

The analyst can even use graphic objects drawn on the map display to query points (graphics query), lines, and polygons in relation to space and distance. In addition, one has the option with queries to create a new theme and save it as its own map layer. However, buffer analysis can be more visually appealing, such as in courtroom illustrations, because

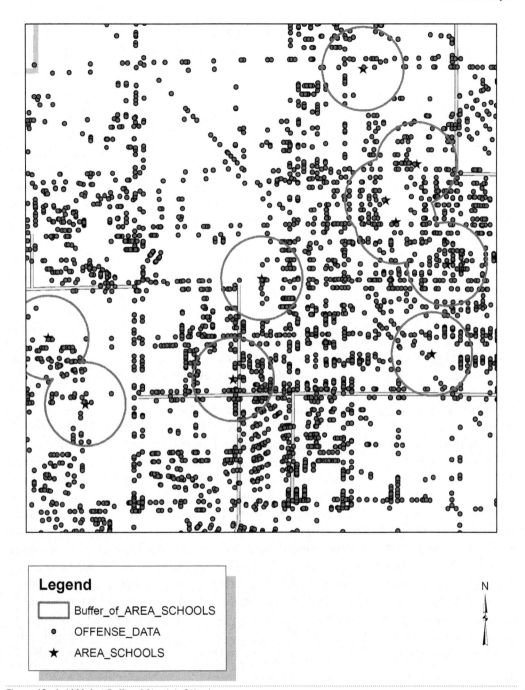

Figure 10–4 1000-foot Buffer of Glendale Schools

Source: Created with ArcGIS.

one can see the physical proximity between the incident and the point of reference. (For example, a map could have one point to represent a school and another to represent the home of a known sex offender.)

Distance Between Hits Analysis

A **distance between hits analysis** is the calculation of the distance between each crime in a crime series (crimes committed by the same offender[s]) to determine the most likely distance the offender may choose from the most current hit. The concept here comes from mean and standard deviation calculations. We place the crimes in a series on the map and measure the distance from the first crime to the second, the second crime to the third, and so on. We then calculate the average and the standard deviation of those distances. Let's say the following were the distances we found between five hits in a crime series:

- First to second: 2.0 miles
- Second to third: 1.5 miles
- Third to fourth: 1.25 miles
- Fourth to fifth: 0.75 miles

By reviewing the distances between crimes in this series, we can determine a few things. First, the average distance this offender traveled was 1.38 miles with a standard deviation of 0.52 miles. This means that 68% of the time the offender traveled from 0.85 to 1.9 miles between hits, and 95% of the time the offender traveled from 0.33 to 2.42 miles between crimes. Second, by looking at the distances the offender traveled between crimes, we can see that a pattern is emerging between each hit in that the distance from one hit to the next decreased over time. Common sense would lead us to the conclusion that the offender will probably travel less than 0.75 miles from the fifth hit in this series to the next crime he will commit in the future. Depending on the circumstances of the crimes, the targets or victims that are chosen, and the modus operandi, we might be able to use this information efficiently to predict where the offender might go in the future.

Another side benefit of this analysis for tactical purposes is that a directional pattern might also be revealed. In **Figures 10–5** and **10–6**, we can see the same crimes where there is no visible pattern and one crime where there is a specific directional pattern to the offender's activities. A common way to use this method is to add the mean plus two standard deviations and then divide this by 3. You would then create a buffer using the multiple-buffer tool, where the number would be 0.81 miles, and each of the 3 buffers would be 0.81 miles from the next. From the authors' experience, the second buffer has the most likelihood for the next hit in the series. Normally, in this series, it seems that it might be the first buffer as discussed earlier based on the pattern of travel this offender has provided.

Distance and Time Analysis

Distance and *time* are also very often related. When an analyst begins looking at the distribution of crimes based on how far away they are from another crime, a specific location, or a

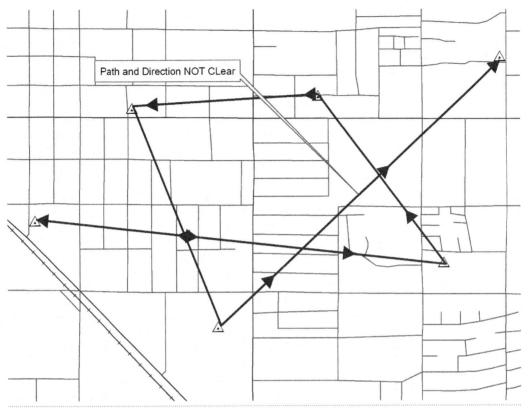

Figure 10–5 Path and Direction Not Clear

Source: Created with ArcGIS.

geographic region, he or she should also consider the tempo of the events. In the simple examples illustrated in Figures 10–5 and 10–6, if we looked at the time element, we might also see a pattern where the longer the offender waits between hits, the farther he or she travels between each crime in the series. This may relate to the amount of money the offender got at each crime site and how much money that offender needs to satisfy a drug habit, for example.

Distance and Social Networks

The last type of "distance" analysis we want to briefly address is the "distance" between people in social networks (distance here can be measured by space and by people). Social network analysis is a powerful tool for analysts. Understanding how offenders and victims are connected within and between social networks can add important intelligence to understanding many different types of crime problems, especially gangs and organized crime groups.

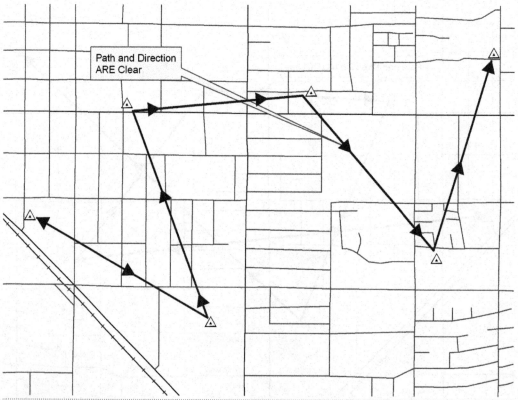

Figure 10–6 Path and Direction Clear

Source: Created with ArcGIS.

■ Conclusion

Distance analyses can be used to examine clusters of seemingly unrelated crimes (as in mean center analysis) or to investigate crimes thought to be committed by a single individual (as in journey-to-crime analysis, spider distance analysis, and distance between hits analysis) or a group of individuals. In addition, distance analyses can be used to provide a wide assortment of information based on the spatial distribution of crime with respect to how near, how far, within what distance, adjacent to what other feature, or simply how distant in space and time crimes have occurred. All of these forms of distance analyses can and should be used in conjunction with other analysis products to help decision makers make effective and productive decisions. These skills are also the ones most needed daily by analysts within the ArcMap software. Being able to successfully query data spatially and by attributes are the bread and butter of crime analysts' jobs. Becoming proficient in these skills is what makes you a good analyst.

■ Chapter Glossary

Buffer   Buffer analysis is completed by drawing circles around points of reference or polygons (like beats or parks), such as pawn shops or city parks, at distances determined by the analyst.

Distance analysis   In this chapter, distance analysis refers to analyses in which distance is measured in relation to another point or in efforts to find another point.

Distance between hits analysis   The calculation of the distance between each crime in a crime series.

Euclidean distance   Euclidean distance is measured by measuring the distance between two points.

Journey to crime   A journey-to-crime trip is the journey an offender travels when he or she commits a crime. Typically, journey to crime is measured from an offender's home to the location of the crime. However, the offender could also be traveling from another anchor point, such as his workplace. Journey-to-crime analyses are used to prioritize search efforts for possible suspects and future hits.

Manhattan distance   Manhattan or "street" distance is calculated by using right angles to get from one point to another.

Mean center   The point at which the mean of X (latitude) and the mean of Y (longitude) of events meet on a map.

Spider distance   Spider distance analysis draws lines from each point in a distribution to its centroid, or mean center.

■ Questions for Review

1. What are the different methods for measuring distance? How does the crime analyst know which method to employ?

2. Explain the different types of distance analyses discussed in this chapter.

■ Online Resources

ArcGIS Spatial Analyst: Distance Analysis: www.esri.com/software/arcgis/extensions/spatialanalyst/key-features/distance

CrimeStat III: www.icpsr.umich.edu/CRIMESTAT/

CrimeStat III User Workbook. This entire workbook is extremely helpful: www.icpsr.umich.edu/CRIMESTAT/workbook/CrimeStat_Workbook.pdf

Spatial Predictive Analysis Crime Extension: www.bairsoftware.com/space/help.html

■ Recommended Reading

Lee, J., & Wong, D. W. S. (2001). *Statistical analysis with ArcView GIS*. Hoboken, NJ: John Wiley & Sons.
O'Sullivan, D., & Unwin, D. (2003). *Geographic information analysis*. Hoboken, NJ: John Wiley & Sons.

Wong, D. W. S., & Lee, J. (2005). *Statistical analysis of geographic information with ArcView GIS and ArcGIS*. Hoboken, NJ: John Wiley & Sons.

■ References

Costello, A., & Leipnik, M. R. (2003). Journeys to crime: GIS analysis of offender and victim journeys in Sheffield, England. In M. R. Leipnik & D. P. Albert (Eds.), *GIS in law enforcement: Implementation issues and case studies* (pp. 229–231). New York: Taylor & Francis.

Groff, E., & McEwen, J. T. (2005). Disaggregating the journey to homicide. In F. Wang (Ed.), *Geographic information systems and crime analysis* (pp. 60–83). Hershey, PA: IDEA Group.

Levine, N. (2002). *CrimeStat: A spatial statistics program for the analysis of crime incident locations* (Vol. 2.0). Ned Levine & Associates, Houston, TX, & the National Institute of Justice, Washington, DC. Retrieved from www.icpsr.umich.edu/NACJD/crimestat.html.

Rossmo, D. K., Laverty, I., & Moore, B. (2005). Geographic profiling for serial crime investigation. In F. Wang (Ed.), *Geographic information systems and crime analysis* (pp. 102–117). Hershey, PA: IDEA Group.

Hotspot Analysis

This chapter explains several types of hotspot analyses and discusses the strengths and weaknesses of each type. The type of hotspot analysis used depends largely upon two factors: the type of data available and the questions about various crime clusters that need to be answered. After studying this chapter, you should be able to:

- Provide a working definition of a "hotspot."
- Explain different types of hotspot analyses.
- Identify the strengths and weaknesses of each hotspot analysis.
- Interpret the results of any hotspot analysis in a manner that is useful for practical applications.
- Explain the difference between a hotdot and a hotspot.
- Define and explain cluster analysis and point pattern analysis, and use spatial deviation ellipses in an analysis.
- Show how you can create a kernel density map and what its uses are.

▶ Key Terms

Choropleth Mapping	Hotspots	Point Pattern Analysis
Grid Cell Mapping	Hot Targets	Standard Deviation
Hotdots	Kernel Density	Analysis
Hot Products	Manual Hotspot Technique	

■ Introduction

The available research provides several definitions for the term **hotspot**, which can be slightly confusing for the beginning student. For example, a hotspot may be loosely defined as "a single address, a cluster of addresses close to one another, a segment of a streetblock, an entire streetblock or two, or an intersection" (Taylor, 1998, p. 3). Conversely, a hotspot may have to adhere to strict requirements, such as being no longer than a standard street block, not being within a half of a block from an intersection, and being at least one block away from another hotspot (Buerger, Cohn, & Petrosino, 1995). Boba (2005) utilizes the definition put forward by Sherman, Gartin, and Buerger (1989) whereby a hotspot is a specific location or small area that experiences large amounts of crime. She distinguishes hotspots from hot-dots, hot products, and hot targets. **Hotdots** represent people who are repeatedly victimized (or addresses that may be frequently victimized), **hot products** are items or property that are repeatedly victimized, and **hot targets** are places that share similarities (fast food stores, convenience stores) that are frequently victimized.

Eck Chainey, Cameron, Letner, and Wilson (2005) suggest that although the definitions of hotspots vary within the literature, the "common understanding is that a hot spot is an area that has a greater than average number of criminal or disorder invents, or an area where people have a higher than average risk of victimization" (p. 2). They suggest that hotspots can be in the form of a hotspot place, hotspot street, hotspot neighborhood, hotspot city, or hotspot region. Selecting the appropriate level of analysis is far more important than adhering to a rigid definition that does not fit the situation.

Another point to make is that hotspots are dynamic; they change over periods of time. They can move, change shape, expand, contract, or disappear and reappear depending on two variables: the types of crimes being analyzed and the duration of time over which those crimes occurred. This chapter reviews some of the common types of analyses used to identify hotspots and clusters of crime. During our examination, we will refer to several concepts and ideas based in statistics. If you find yourself having difficulty understanding some of these analyses, you may need to review the basics of statistics.

Hotspots, hot areas, hot places, or hot street segments are classifications designed to take a large amount of data and identify places where crime is at a higher level than other places and to help identify those areas for problem-solving efforts through enforcement. A hotspot analysis is just the start of any good crime analysis effort and can be used to find single-event hotspots at which to address enforcement or to track progress of a tactical action plan over time. When the analyst has identified a problem area by time of crime and temporal distribution, the work has usually just begun. The analyst will need to drill down into the hotspot and often may need several methods of hotspot analysis to pick up all of the issues causing that particular hotspot. For example, we might look at residential burglary within our city. We want to first look for the hotspots across the entire city, perhaps for the entire year. Our scale at this point is a citywide analysis. This will yield us some results and identify generalized hotspots for residential burglary. Once we have identified several hotspots, we want to choose the ones that have the most number of burglaries and then look at each individual hotspot. We will likely find that apartment complexes make up a large number of our residential burglaries in some of these hotspots. To find out if this is the case, we may want to look at repeat burglary locations or addresses and create a graduated point or "hot place" map (or hotdot). If these hot places are inside our hotspots, we may want to exclude them and retry our hotspot analysis and see if our hotspot remains a hotspot. When this analysis is done, we might even consider changing our unit of measurement from individual crimes to rates such as burglaries per 1000 residents to level out the playing field between the single-family homes and the apartment complexes. Our next step will likely include analysis efforts toward identifying what temporal patterns we may see in our hotspots, what types of specific modus operandi are present, or if the residents are just failing to lock their garage doors. Although a hotspot analysis is a valuable tool with which to analyze crime, as with any tool, it is made for only one job, and you will need other tools and analytical processes in addition to hotspot analysis to make your analysis useful to those decision makers.

■ Types of Hotspot Analyses

There are essentially five broad categories of analyses used to identify and examine clusters of crime (Boba, 2005; Eck et al., 2005; Paulsen & Robinson, 2004). Various software applications (such as the free CrimeStat software) have the ability to perform many of these analyses. CrimeStat even comes with an extensive manual for the beginning analyst to use and learn from. The manual is very technical at times and may take a bit of fortitude to get through, but there is a lot the analyst can learn from this manual if he or she takes the time to give it a try. Christopher Bruce, a past International Association of Crime Analysts (IACA) president, and Susan Smith, a longtime IACA board member, have also written a comprehensive guide to using CrimeStat (see Online Resources at the end of this chapter).

Manual or Eyeball Analysis

The first method for identifying hotspots, the **manual** (or *eyeball*) **hotspot technique**, requires the analyst to produce a simple point or pin map of criminal events. The analyst visually scans the distribution in search of points that are clustered together. This is the modern version of the classic paper-pin map approach. This technique, while simple and seemingly easy to complete, is as limited in its usefulness as it is in its complexity. For example, analysts who are unfamiliar with the areas they are mapping (this is an offense) may incorrectly identify or ignore hotspots. The basic idea here is to look for an abnormally large number of crimes clustered within small areas relative to the overall study area. However, in areas that experience large amounts of crimes, even after filtering for crime type and time, the map may be covered with dots. In addition, addresses that have more than one crime incident will only have one visible dot. This is because in the geocoding process, repeat addresses receive a dot in the same place every time (see **Figure 11-1**). You may also want to change the symbol type to a very simple one and reduce the size to no more than 4 in ArcMap so that the clusters of dots are easier to discern depending on the scale you are looking at. This would not be as important if you are only trying to determine hotspots at the neighborhood scale versus looking at the entire city. (Please note that the maps are not formatted in a way that would be used for presentation. However, for our purposes in this chapter, it is more important that you understand how they differ visually depending on the type of analysis you decide to employ.)

Another technique employs the use of graduated symbols (usually circles) so that addresses with repeat occurrences are represented by larger dots. Addresses with the largest number of incidents will be represented by the largest dots. This can make a cluttered map slightly easier to read, but again the process is imprecise because the size of the circle is

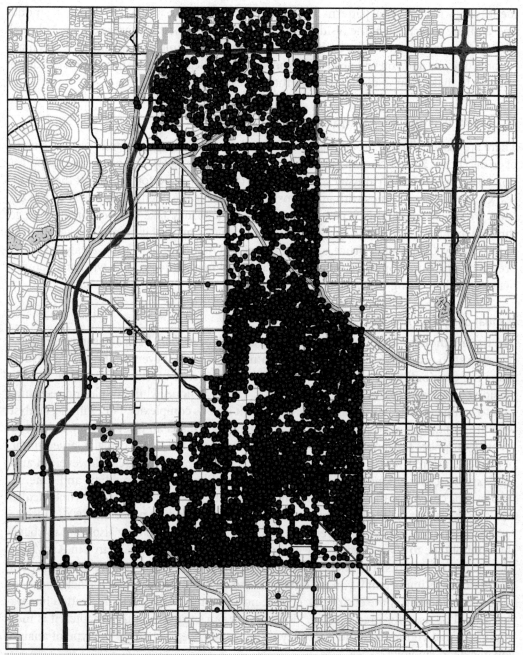

Figure 11–1 Offense Points Map, Glendale, Arizona

Source: Created with ArcGIS.

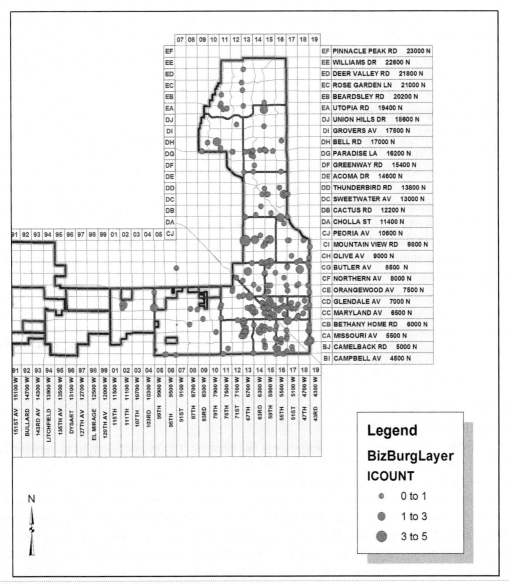

Figure 11–2 Graduated Symbol Map, Glendale, Arizona

Source: Created with ArcGIS.

determined by the analyst's ability to filter the data correctly (see **Figure 11–2**). You can sometimes enhance the ability by limiting the data to only the top 10–25 locations, or by changing the color of the dots as well as the size. The dots with the most activity would be the largest and be colored red for instance. The dots with the fewest incidents would be the smallest and be colored blue for instance.

A second technique, termed repeat address mapping (RAM), allows the analyst to choose the number of incidents an address must be involved in before a dot becomes visible on the map. For example, an analyst can make visible only those addresses representing the highest 10% of repeat incidents. Thus, addresses that do not make the top 10% will not be visible on the map.

Graduated Color Map or Choropleth Map Analysis

A second approach, using *graduated color maps* or **choropleth mapping** (sometimes referred to as shaded grid maps), uses color intensity to shade areas on a map according to the number of criminal events those areas experience. This approach is dependent upon the analyst choosing an appropriate level of analysis (census blocks, block groups, beats, cities, etc.). Caution is advised when choosing the unit of analysis. Selecting a unit of analysis that is too large will result in obscuring smaller hotspots placed in larger areas with limited crime (see **Figure 11–3**). In the map in Figure 11–3, the unit of analysis is a uniform grid layer that is overlaid on top of the city of Glendale, Arizona. However, this process can be done (and may be more useful) with polygons that represent beats or precincts, depending on what the analyst is looking for. In many cases the analyst might start with a map like Figure 11–3 and then zoom in on the hottest spots and create a **kernel density** map for just that area using the spatial analyst extension, or CrimeStat III. This allows the analyst to create a report explaining why the area was chosen initially and then what areas within the grid were actually the source of it being in the top 10% of grids with crime. He or she might then choose to create a RAM map to see if specific addresses are the main reason this area is a hotspot, or if crime is randomly distributed across the hotspot.

Grid Cell Mapping Analysis

The third type of hotspot analysis utilizes **grid cell mapping**. This type of analysis is sometimes called a *density* analysis. There are several individual methods to this approach, and results vary depending upon the assumptions made by the analyst. Essentially, a grid is placed atop a map that contains address-level information for criminal events (similar to Figure 11–3). The grids contain equally sized cells (much like a piece of graph paper), and grids can range in size according to the analyst's needs. However, the typical size is between 50 and 500 ft because this makes for a detailed and visually pleasing map, depending on the scale of the map being developed (Boba, 2005). The analyst determines a *search radius* (also called a bandwidth), which calculates the number of incidents within the radius and divides that number by the size of the search area. In simple density analysis, the score computed for each cell does not represent the number of crimes within that cell; it represents the number of crimes that are near the cell divided by the area around the cell. Thus, the score is not a count of crimes but a ratio of crimes in an area divided by the size of the area (also referred to as a density calculation or a plain distance calculation or distance analysis in the spatial analyst extension). The cells are assigned colors based on their scores. Typically the darkest colors represent cells with the largest scores. The smaller the cells, the greater the resolution

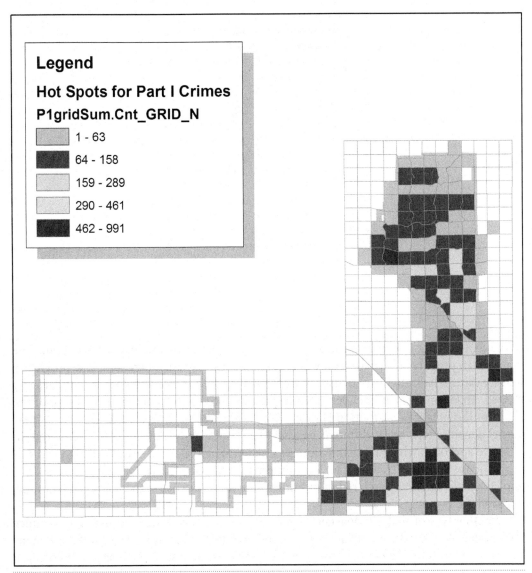

Figure 11–3 Choropleth Hotspot Map, Glendale, Arizona

Source: Created with ArcGIS.

(and the smoother the picture). Map results can vary significantly as the cell size and search radius are adjusted. See **Figure 11–4** for an illustration of a grid cell analysis.

A more precise type of grid cell analysis using kernel density calculations is also common. Kernel density interpolation employs a grid analysis methodology to estimate crime density across an entire study area by assigning greater weight to incidents that occur closer

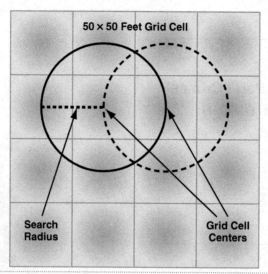

Figure 11–4 Grid Cell Analysis

to the center of the search radius and lesser weight to incidents that occur farther out. The results then provide information on where crime is clustered together, but it also provides a density value relative to the entire study area. In addition, because hotspots are not perfectly shaped circles or ovals, kernel density interpolation projects a more realistic image of the shape of the hotspot distribution (Levine, 2002). **Figures 11–5** and **11–6** represent single kernel density maps set at different bandwidths (search radius). Figure 11–5 employs an adaptive approach where the bandwidth is smaller in crime-dense areas and larger in less crime-dense areas, which allows for a minimum number of points to be found. Figure 11–6 depicts a fixed-interval search radius of 1 mile. Note the difference in the shape of the outputs between the two maps.

Another type of analysis, dual kernel density interpolation, allows the analyst to produce a risk value associated with crime density. This is an important advantage, and these maps can be very useful to law enforcement. For example, in dual kernel density interpolation, analysts can compute victimization risk relative to the population. This allows for a more accurate analysis of areas that are sparsely or densely populated relative to other areas being studied. In addition, this technique can be used to compare crime density for two different crime types and to compare crime densities for two different time periods (Levine, 2002). This is most often used by analysts; a dual kernel density analysis for January 2011 compared to January 2012 would tell us where areas have relatively gone up between the two time periods, or where we have seen relative reduction between two time periods. This can be very helpful at times to see if crime-prevention efforts have served their purpose and prevented crime, or in some cases it can be used to see if crime was dispersed outward from the

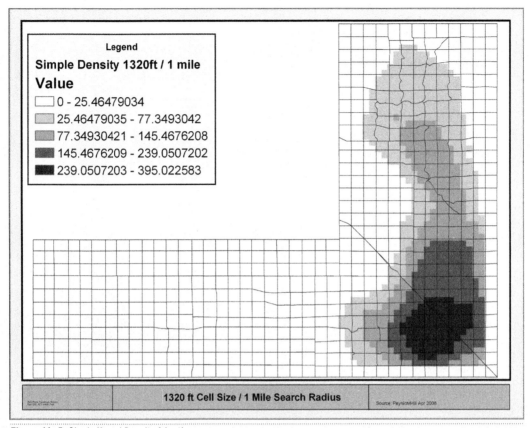

Figure 11–5 Single Kernel Density Adaptive

Source: Created with CrimeStat and ArcGIS.

enforcement area instead of just alleviating it in the target area. This is very easy to do in Spatial Analyst (ArcGIS extension) or CrimeStat III.

Point Pattern Analysis or Cluster Analysis

The fourth type of hotspot analysis, **point pattern analysis** or *cluster analysis*, as it is sometimes called, uses an arbitrary starting point (called a "seed") to calculate whether or not incident points are closer in proximity than we would expect by random chance.

> Typically, an arbitrary starting point ("seed") is established. This seed point could be the center of the map. The program then finds the data point statistically farthest from there and makes the point the second seed, thus dividing the data points into two groups. Then distances from each seed to other points are repeatedly calculated, and clusters based on new seeds are developed so that the sums of within-cluster distances are minimized (Harries, 1999, p. 117).

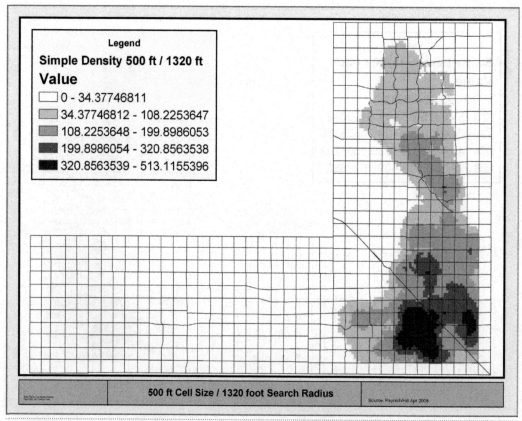

Figure 11-6 Single Kernel Density Fixed 1 Mile
Source: Created with CrimeStat and ArcGIS.

There are several common point pattern analysis techniques. The first, called *fuzzy mode* analysis, works by creating a search radius to use at each point (as performed in a grid analysis) and counting all incidents that occurred at a specific address and in the defined search radius around the location. The key here is to set an appropriate search radius. Using settings of a mile or larger will create false hotspots. Setting the radius too low will ignore true hotspots (Levine, 2002). See **Figure 11-7** for an example of a fuzzy mode map. Note that hotspots are represented by graduated symbols. There are only subtle differences between this method and RAM or repeat location analysis, but there are differences in method. The fuzzy mode looks for nearest neighbors and the RAM method only looks for data at the address chosen.

Again, it is important that the crime analyst intimately knows the study area he or she is working with. The second type of point pattern analysis, *nearest neighbor hierarchical clustering* (Nnh), uses a confidence interval and a set minimum number of incidents in determining hotspots. The confidence interval (similar to the concept of statistical significance)

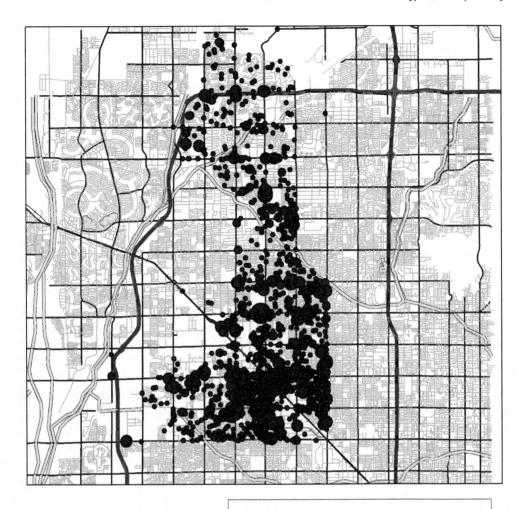

Figure 11–7 Fuzzy Mode, Burglaries 2003, Glendale, Arizona

Source: Created with CrimeStat and ArcGIS.

is set in an effort to more accurately identify clusters that would not be expected to occur by random chance (Levine, 2002). The bigger the confidence interval (usually 0.10 is the largest acceptable confidence interval), the bigger the search area. A confidence interval of 0.10 allows for a 10% margin of error. That is, we are 90% confident that this is a true hotspot in the case of a 0.10 confidence interval. Another component to Nnh is its ability to identify second and third order clusters of crime. Essentially, several hotspots might be clustered in close proximity in a larger area that has high concentrations of crime. Milieu is the placement of defensible space within a larger area that is also characterized as defensible space. This notion also works in reverse. In second and third order groupings, Nnh identifies local hotspots that are placed within larger crime clusters. In other words, smaller hotspots of crime are situated in larger hotspots of crime. Another type of point pattern analysis, *Risk-adjusted Nnh* (Rnnh), allows analysts to control for a third variable (often population) to identify hotspots of crime based on the relative risk of victimization based on the third variable (such as population) rather than just using simple counts and proximity (Levine, 2002).

Spatial autocorrelation analyses assume that criminal events that occur in different locations (yet close in proximity) are related; said in another way, events that occur in time and place closer to one another are more likely to be related than those events that occur farther away or later in time. The computations and interpretations are similar to those of measures of association. The two most commonly employed tests for spatial autocorrelation are Moran's *I* and Geary's *C* (Levine, 2002). Both tests require aggregate data (point data aggregated to some polygon feature, such as a census block). The variable that is being computed must be in a continuous format (such as a crime rate). In Moran's *I*, the value is computed by comparing each area's crime rate to all other areas. The value ranges from −1.0 to +1.0. Positive results indicate that spatial autocorrelation exists: Areas with high-crime rates are clustered together, and areas with low-crime rates are clustered together. A negative value indicates no spatial autocorrelation and thus a random distribution of crime (Levine, 2002). Geary's *C* is a little more precise and is used for small neighborhoods. Because the computations are based on the squared deviations of incidents (similar to computing a variance), the resulting value for Geary's *C* ranges between 0 and +2.0. Results between 0 and 1 indicate that spatial autocorrelation exists (high-crime areas are clustered with high-crime areas, and low-crime areas are clustered with low-crime areas). No spatial autocorrelation exists if the value is greater than 1. Because Geary's *C* is more sensitive in smaller areas, it is possible to get conflicting results when running both a Moran's *I* and a Geary's *C* on the same data. If this occurs, analysts should visually scan the graduated color maps to determine the appropriate interpretation to use (Levine, 2002). In the most recent version of CrimeStat III, the output for many of these methods can either be ellipses or convex hull polygons.

Standard Deviation Analysis

A fifth type of hotspot analysis is called **standard deviation analysis**. The outputs are in the shape of a rectangle or an *ellipse*, depending on the specific type of analysis performed, and they are drawn around criminal incidents that are clustered together and that would not be expected based on random chance. Ellipses are oval shapes that vary in size in accordance with the incident distribution. Ellipses and rectangles can be short or tall, narrow or wide, depending on the north to south distribution of incidents and the east to west distribution of incidents. Of course, visually, these analyses cannot illustrate the true shape of a hotspot, but they are useful in comparing changes across crime types and across time. In addition, some standard deviation analyses, such as *standard deviational ellipse analysis* (SDE), are better suited for skewed data distributions (this is common with crime data; Levine, 2002). See **Figures 11–8** and **11–9** for illustrations of different types of standard deviation analyses.

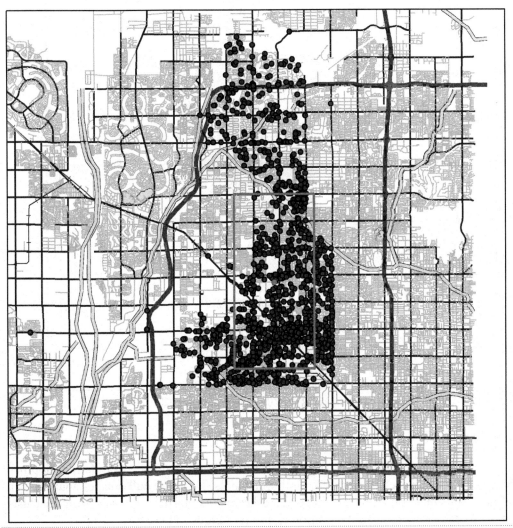

Figure 11–8 Standard Deviation of *X* and *Y* Coordinates, Burglaries 2003, Glendale, Arizona

Source: Created with CrimeStat and ArcGIS.

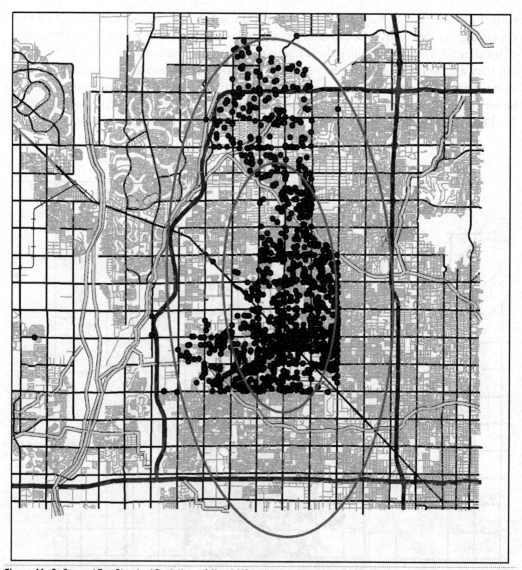

Figure 11–9 One and Two Standard Deviations of *X* and *Y* Coordinates, Burglaries 2003, Glendale, Arizona

Source: Created with CrimeStat and ArcGIS.

A slight variation of these standard deviation ellipses that uses a similar development method is the convex hull representation of hotspots. A convex hull hotspot analysis technique results in an odd polygon shape that follows the outermost points within the cluster of points rather than a spatial deviation ellipse (see **Figure 11–10**).

The concept here is that if you have a group of points that has been determined to be included in the hotspot, the software application (CrimeStat III) will then draw a polygon

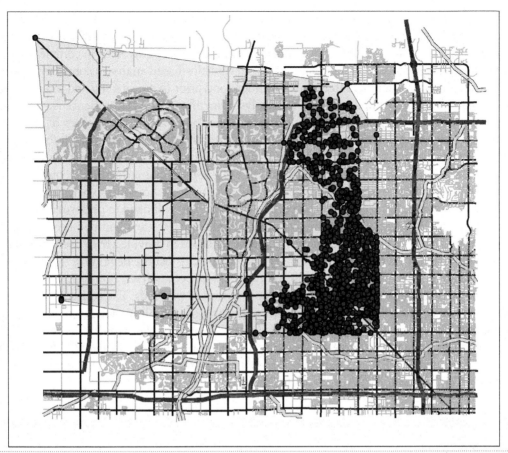

Figure 11–10 Convex Hull, Burglaries 2003, Glendale, Arizona

Source: Created with CrimeStat and ArcGIS.

that joins the outermost points so that all of the other points fall within the convex hull polygon. Because this process differs only in the output of a convex hull rather than a standard deviation ellipse, it is not considered to be a different hotspot analysis technique.

■ Conclusion

Various analyses exist for identifying hotspots. Some of these are very simple (the eyeball method), and some are much more complex (dual kernel density interpolation). Because the choice of which analysis to employ is dependent upon the type of data (Do we have point or aggregate data? Is the distribution skewed?) and the types of questions that need to be answered (Do we need to know the shape of the distribution? Are we comparing changes across crime types or different periods of time? What do the commanders understand the best?), the type of hotspot analysis we choose makes a difference. Of course, the analyst's skill level is important in selecting the appropriate method, but most software applications come with a manual that will school the analyst on the finer details and practical steps involved in completing the analysis. Each type of hotspot analysis (as with all statistics-based analyses) comes with varying strengths and weaknesses that must be understood prior to performing and interpreting the results. It is vitally important that the analyst remembers who the audience is, what the purpose for developing the hotspot is, and remembering to avoid the offenses of analysis. Creating a beautiful hotspot map is a great thing, but if the audience you made it for already knew the areas on the map were "hot" based on their enforcement experience, then what did you accomplish, except for maybe validating their opinions? The analyst should consider that the hotspot analysis chosen may not be the only method that should be experimented with for a given analytical project; in fact, you may find that you will need to perform a hot area, hot place, and hot street segment analysis to really get down to the identified problem, and then perform temporal, modus operandi, and other analyses to provide a truly useful product. A hotspot map is never the end of an analysis; it is typically just the beginning. This chapter provided an overview of the most common types of hotspot analyses; however, students are encouraged to seek alternative sources for more advanced methods. The authors would also suggest that students become familiar with CrimeStat III and all its hotspot methods and processes. The manual can be useful, especially the second chapter, which provides a quick start guide to using the software. There is also a new tutorial that was created by Christopher Bruce and Susan Smith that can quickly help get you up and running with the product (www .icpsr.umich.edu/CrimeStat/workbook.html).

■ Chapter Glossary

Choropleth mapping   The analyst uses color and shading to display areas that experience higher frequencies or rates of crime.

Grid cell mapping   This type of analysis is sometimes called a *density* analysis. Using equally sized cells contained in a grid, the analyst, using a set search radius, (also called a bandwidth), which calculates the number of incidents within the radius and divides that number by the size of the search area to produce a hotspot map.

Hotdots   Represent people who are repeatedly victimized (or addresses that may be frequently victimized).

Hot products   Items or property that are repeatedly victimized.

Hotspots   A specific location or small area that experiences large amounts of crime.

Hot targets   Places that share similarities that are frequently victimized.

Kernel density   This is another term for grid cell mapping where the cells overlap during the calculation and gives the map a smoother appearance between locations on the map.

Manual hotspot technique   The analyst visually scans the distribution in search of points that are clustered together to identify potential hotspots.

Point pattern analysis   Uses an arbitrary starting point (called a "seed") to calculate whether or not incident points are closer in proximity than we would expect by random chance.

Standard deviation analysis   The outputs are in the shape of a rectangle or an *ellipse*, depending on the specific type of analysis performed, and they are drawn around criminal incidents that are clustered together and that would not be expected based on random chance.

■ Questions For Review

1. Explain the different methods an analyst can use to identify hotspots.
2. What are the strengths and weaknesses associated with each method of identifying hotspots?

■ Online Resources

Christopher Bruce's CrimeStat III Manual: www.cbruce.com/CrimeStatIII.pdf

"Crime Hot Spot Analysis and Dynamic Pin Map" paper: http://proceedings.esri.com/library/userconf/proc97/proc97/to600/pap575/p575.htm

Crime Reduction Toolkit: www.crimereduction.homeoffice.gov.uk/toolkits/p031306.htm

ESRI Mapping Center's Hot Spot Analysis of 911 Calls: http://mappingcenter.esri.com/index.cfm?fa=maps.hotSpot911

■ Recommended Reading

Anselin, L., Cohen, J., Cook, D., Gorr, W., & Tita, G. (2000). Spatial analyses of crime. In *Measurement and analysis of crime and justice: Criminal justice 2000* (Vol. 4, pp. 213–262, NCJ 182411). Washington, DC: U.S. Department of Justice, Office of Justice Programs.

Holden, K. (1995). Vector autoregression modeling and forecasting. *Journal of Forecasting, 14*, 159–166.

■ References

Boba, R. (2005). *Crime analysis and crime mapping.* Thousand Oaks, CA: Sage.

Buerger, M. E., Cohn, E. G., & Petrosino, A. J. (1995). Defining the "hot spots" of crime: Operationalizing theoretical concepts for field research. In J. E. Eck & D. Weisburd (Eds.), *Crime and place* (pp. 237–258). Monsey, NY: Criminal Justice Press.

Eck, J. E., Chainey, S., Cameron, J. G., Letner, M., & Wilson, R. E. (2005). *Mapping crime: Understanding hot spots.* Washington, DC: National Institute of Justice.

Harries, K. D. (1999). *Mapping crime: Principles and practice.* Washington, DC: National Institute of Justice.

Levine, N. (2002). *CrimeStat: A spatial statistics program for the analysis of crime incident locations* (Vol. 2.0). Ned Levine & Associates, Houston, TX, & the National Institute of Justice, Washington, DC.

Paulsen, D., & Robinson, M. (2004). *Spatial aspects of crime: Theory and practice.* Boston: Pearson.

Sherman, L. W., Gartin, P. R., & Buerger, M. E. (1989). Hot spots of predatory crime: Routine activities and the criminology of place. *Criminology, 27*, 27–55.

Taylor, R. B. (1998). *Crime and small-scale places: What we know, what we can prevent, and what else we need to know* (pp. 1–22). Crime and Place: Plenary Papers of the 1997 Conference on Criminal Justice Research and Evaluation, U.S. Department of Justice, Washington, DC.

Mapping for an Audience, Cartography, and the Future!

Mapping for Your Audience

12

▶ LEARNING OBJECTIVES

This chapter discusses the importance of creating appropriate maps for your audience. Elements of content, style, and color are addressed. As an analyst, you must also be able to tell stories with your maps that give the command staff interesting information on how they are doing with their battle on crime, accountability factors (are they doing the job right?), or measurements of crime to see if they have been successful. Being able to put the data on the map so that the most important information is the most prominent in your story is also important. Because crime maps must also be accompanied by explanations for those who will be reading and using the maps, it is important to tailor maps and their discussions to the intended audience. After studying this chapter, you should be able to:

- Identify the different uses of crime maps by different criminal justice practitioners.
- Create different maps and write tailored descriptions for the intended audience.
- Learn which key items should be on every map.
- Discover the things you should consider when making maps for an specific audience.

▶ Key Terms

Administrative Crime Maps
Aerial Images
Business Intelligence
Cartographic Methods
Center of Attention
Clustering Algorithms
Geoprocessing
Reference Map
Strategic Crime Maps
Tactical Crime Maps
White Space

■ Introduction

The belief that "one map fits all" is severely flawed. Each audience has a unique set of objectives it is trying to achieve (Harries, 1999). For example, patrol officers need maps that can help them make day-to-day decisions about the people and places where they are assigned. Investigators need maps to help them locate suspects in the crimes they are investigating as well as help them predict where and when perpetrators are likely to strike again. Administrators need maps to help them improve the effectiveness and efficiency of their operations.

Community members want maps to inform them about problem areas in their communities that need attention. Court officers need maps to tell a story to the jury about a criminal event. And finally, corrections officers need maps to help them track and assist offenders who are under their supervision. Given this wide array of goals, one can see how maps and analysis must be tailored for each unique audience. This chapter provides suggestions about how the beginning analyst might create different maps for different audiences. The audiences discussed in this chapter by no means represent a complete list; however, they are the most common audiences a crime analyst must please and thus are included in the discussion. There are powerful geographic information systems (GIS) desktop applications with which you can create maps and analyze data that has some spatial or geographic relationship to something else (on the Earth's surface). We could also say that GIS is any data a police department collects as a normal part of its activities. Most data collected by a police department can be related to, or used with, location data (addresses) that deal with crime, disorder, terrorism, or any other issue assigned to a police department to solve. Data about people can also be important, such as the traffic citation data that led to the identification of Timothy McVeigh after the Oklahoma City bombing incident on April 19, 1995. Police departments routinely collect geographic data on where a crime happens or even where an apartment complex is within their jurisdiction. They track where the "bad guys" live and where they arrested them. They keep track of citation data and the related racial-profiling data that many departments have begun to collect or analyze in the past several years.

All of these datasets can be used with a GIS to enable quick access to data and information and put it in the hands of the decision makers. With this increase in the amount of data available to decision makers, we have to be able to make sense of all of it. In the business community this is often described as **business intelligence** or the process of taking the bits and pieces of *data* we collect everyday, ordering it, and organizing it so that it makes sense and provides *information*, which administrators, detectives, and patrol officers can then use as *knowledge* to prevent crimes, catch criminals, or enhance public safety.

■ GIS in Criminal Justice

There are a variety of GIS mapping products that you will use during a career as a crime or intelligence analyst within a law enforcement agency. The general idea you should be thinking about now is that the audience determines what type of map is produced. After the analysis is done, it is possible that a map may not even be needed for a specific audience and the analysis "behind the scenes" that you got to by identification of the problem based on the data you have in a GIS might be what your audience needs. You will have many different people and purposes within the audiences you will address as a crime analyst. One way to classify the maps most often produced is to place them into a few categories that align themselves with the three basic categories of crime analysis:

- Administrative
- Strategic
- Tactical

Administrative crime maps are often **reference maps** (beat maps, city council districts, etc.). They are generally less specific and often show the entire city boundaries. They generally show yearly or monthly data aggregated to some type of boundary layer and one center of focus or purpose for developing the map. They do not always have to be reference maps and can show hotspots, point data, and other incident efforts; however, the goal is to be more general in nature, and the use of these maps is more appropriate for monthly summary CompStat meetings (a sort of "state of the union" presentation), for example.

Strategic crime maps are often the first step toward problem-solving efforts within a police agency. They generally cover shorter time periods and focus on a specific geographic area within the city boundaries, and the overall objective is to identify problems and suggest possible solutions. These maps will evolve within a crime analyst's tenure at an agency and will probably need to be updated often to track problem areas. These maps can also be hotspot, graduated point, pin, or other types of maps, but again, the general purpose is problem solving rather than administrative depiction of data. We often see crime clusters and patterns in this stage of crime mapping.

Tactical crime maps involve very short time periods. Tactical maps are usually used to predict a new crime in a series or spree or identify where the suspect in a series of offenses might live. With tactical mapping products, you wait for the next offense to happen to create a new map and prediction to help catch the offender. The analyst might also be asked to create a map with high-quality **aerial images** for a search warrant, or known locations of offenders for a warrant roundup to aid planning for these events. This is an exciting phase of crime analysis, but sadly, only a few analysts across the country ever do tactical analysis. This function seems to be increasing, but it does require the analyst to work very closely with the case detectives, and that relationship has to be nurtured over time.

Within these three categories of maps, we find that a large variety of **cartographic methods** and **geoprocessing** efforts may come into play. Each of these different ways to portray data (cartography—the art of creating a map) and show relationships between different types of data (geoprocessing) can be used for any of the three mapping categories already discussed. It is not uncommon to have administrative hotspot maps lead to a strategic version of the hotspot map, and finally have a tactical set of what we could call hotspot maps to track a crime cluster, spree, series, or pattern of crimes that was originally identified at the administrative level.

As a simple matter of what looks good and what doesn't, you should think about a few things:

- Who is your audience? The person or group you are generating a map for will often govern the type of data you place onto the map. The issues involved include privacy, data accessibility for that audience, the point you are trying to make with the map, and the political ramifications.
- What type of output is going to be required? If only black and white maps on a laser printer are going to be printed, why use colors for symbols? You should consider changing the symbol to a black and white symbol for each different item rather than use color in this case.

- What size map will be printed? A large map from an E-size plotter will require having symbols that are often larger than your standard 8.5" × 11" map. They also print much slower, and if an aerial photo or graphic is included, the picture will pixelate a little bit and is more useful when viewed from farther away.
- Printing 22 copies of a map at 36" × 48" is possible but not recommended.
- Does the map have the following elements?
  - Title
  - Scale bar
  - North arrow
  - Legend
  - Disclaimer text
  - Notes or file location information so it can be found again later
  - Map with one **center of attention** or point being made
  - Nonpsychedelic color scheme
  - Good use of **white space**

It is important that the area around the center of attention is free from confusing data and allows the eye to see breaks among different items on the map. Each map you create should have only one purpose or story to tell; avoid trying to tell two or more stories in a single map. Is the map at the right scale, and are you zoomed in on the important story you want to tell with the map? Did you look at the data from several different viewpoints to make sure the type of map you are using is the best? Does your map read left to right and top to bottom as we read everything here in the United States? Using really bright colors for unimportant items makes the map confusing and difficult to look at. Try to keep to pastel colors for the reference parts of a map, and use the bright colors to help illuminate the key point of the map.

Other questions to ask yourself in creating useful maps include: Did you use good analytical technique, knowledge, and good mapping technique when creating the analysis behind the map? Did you verify that the data you used were appropriate for the analysis and that they were as up to date as possible? Before publishing the map, did you let a few coworkers review it and tell you what they think the map is telling them? If they get the wrong point from the map, maybe a revision is needed!

The average supervisor or officer within a police department does not normally make maps. They typically have a very limited knowledge of what can be done with crime data and statistics. Both authors of this text have asked the following questions several times with new groups of students and at various presentations, and the audiences' responses provides a demonstration of this lack of knowledge. First we ask, "How many of you have taken a college-level statistics class?" Most of the group raises their hands. The second question is, "How many of you remember what you learned in that statistics class?" This question results in 75% of the hands going down. The third question, "How many of you use statistics on a weekly basis?" typically results in all hands down unless some crime or intelligence analyst sneaked into the classroom or meeting. The results of the questioning would also be very similar if you asked how many people have seen a map and then asked how many know how to make a map. If you then asked about cartography, or the art and science of making a map, chances are only one or two persons in the police group, if any, would raise their hands.

This is where most of the problems lie with crime mapping in law enforcement: (1) The analyst does not know how to make a map that speaks to the issues, or (2) the audience does not know how to read or interpret a map clearly and thus makes mistakes when trying to use the analysis that came with the map. There are also situations where they ignore the analysis altogether and do their own thing. This can be very frustrating for the analyst, but it is your duty to make your products useful to the audience and learn what that audience needs. Working with them and asking their opinions, or talking to them about what would make their jobs easier, always helps make your products more useful.

Crime mapping deals with administrative, strategic, and tactical map assignments. Within these general categories we know that there are reference maps, point or pin maps, hotspot maps, and maps that are derived from slightly more complicated geoprocessing or multilayer analysis. We need to remember that the ultimate goal of mapping is not to make a pretty map or one that makes you feel good about yourself, but one that helps the officer or supervisor make sound decisions. It isn't a matter of making sure the specific cartographic technique you use is technically sound every time. After all, what good is a map if no one will read it after you've spent all day making it? The dilemma appears for the crime analyst when we begin to learn the right way to make a map based on what cartographers say and what our fellow employees can comprehend. Most analysts can tell you of at least one incident where they made a technically sound and accurate map but the audience within the police department simply looked at it once and asked, "So what does this mean?" We can only guess how many maps we've made that wound up in a trashcan someplace as well. Like any other analysis product, maps are temporary and will not hang around very long. Crime is dynamic, so the maps we create must also be dynamic to keep up with the current crime trends and goals or objectives of the police department. Do not become too attached to the maps you create because they will not last very long in the reality of the world of crime fighting.

Analysts need to make every effort to make sure the analyses they perform are accurate and reliable. They should learn about making cartographically sound maps and include things like north arrows, scale bars, legends, and titles to help the user fully understand the map. At least once in your career, you will probably experience a supervisor who asks you to remove these items from your map because "it just clutters it up!" That probably means that the elements are too large or take up too much of the map area, so reduce them in size and place them in an obscure corner, but don't take them out. If the supervisor still insists on removing them, follow orders, but add training about reading maps to your list of things to do within your police department.

You will find that most officers and supervisors are very comfortable with point or pin maps, and most of the requests you get for maps will be for these types of maps. You should always remember scale and multiple points as keys to understanding and making your audience understand your pin maps. Showing multiple points on a map at a small scale (zoomed out from the Earth's surface) can just show there is a lot of crime. At certain scales, having multiple legend categories or showing every crime as a different symbol or marker can be confusing and often a waste of time. In these cases, consider doing more than one map after you have taken time to understand what your audience really wants. Be comfortable with your spatial data as well as the attributes of the data behind each point. Know what it looks like when you zoom to a citywide level and how it changes as you zoom in to a specific beat or reporting district. Keep in mind that the audience does not understand the data as well as you do, and you need to use the KISS ("keep it simple, stupid") method when making pin maps. In cases where you are doing the same map over and over again, consider "publishing" a map to the Internet or creating an automated map of the same data your audience can see in ArcGIS for Sharepoint. All of these tools take time to set up correctly, but could make your job easier by automating your map and training your audience how to use it.

Remember that there are often multiple points under one single dot on the map. Somehow convey this message to the audience through graphs, charts, maybe an additional graduated point map, or a hotspot map that shows those concentrations at one location. Realize that the underlying geography or landscape of a place can determine why the points are arranged as they are. If you have an area that looks like crime is extremely high and everything else around it has no crime at all, be suspicious. What is probably happening is that the surrounding area includes dirt lots or agriculture areas, and the high crime area is the only residential area or apartment complex within a few miles. The best advice anyone can give you is to know your data and city landscape inside and out; it saves you from making analysis errors and saves your audience from making decisions based on faulty assumptions.

When creating hotspot maps, remember that there are different ways and methods to create them. They are all based on spatial autocorrelation and distance decay theories. This simply means that things that are closer together are more likely to be related than things that are farther apart. If we have a classroom full of students and the instructor calls on a student for the answer to a question, the people in the front row are often the victims, so most people want to sit way back in the room. Many crime theories depend on the fact that this assumption is true. In a very mobile society where traveling 15–25 miles to get to work is not unusual, the same may be true for your suspects and neighborhood hotspots may then be affected based on this knowledge, or at least your response to the problem and the analysis products.

You can create hotspot maps that are based on **clustering algorithms** (such as in Crime-Stat III) where the math determines that the points are not randomly generated but are clustered together in significant groupings that are higher than the entire geographic area being analyzed. Another method uses density analysis (like spatial analyst results) where the software counts the number of points within a certain distance of an artificial grid that is laid over the area being analyzed. Areas where the points are closer together and more numerous (within a set search radius) make the hotspot more dense than other areas in the total geographic area being analyzed. Terminology such as nearest neighbor, kernel density, spatial density, cluster analysis, spatial and temporal analysis of crime (STAC) clusters, fuzzy mode, and several other analysis methods relates to different math calculations that attempt to find areas of abnormally high activity for the kind of crime you may be analyzing at the time. Spatial autocorrelation can be tested for using different programs and will tell you if the data are clustered, random, or dispersed. Here is where it is important to understand the landscape under those points and make some of your own decisions about the usefulness of these products. A hotspot map is usually developed to find the source of significant problems that can be addressed through enforcement activities. It isn't really a research project to find out how well hotspot methods work when compared to one another. It is a great idea to do this research and look at the results of the various methods together. Which areas of your city seem to show up with every method? Chances are these are the hotspots you should be focusing on. The final map for your audience does not have to show all of these. In fact, it would be more useful if you just circled the most crime-ridden area for the user and explained the types of crime that are the biggest problem. It is the job of the analyst to provide the maps and information and also to do an analysis, which generally means to provide a presentation of your findings, not just regurgitate the data.

When you need to make a reference map, make sure you interview the people who will use it and find out under what conditions they will use the map. You can make a beautiful color map for daytime patrols, but the nighttime patrols cannot distinguish three of the four areas of the map because of the colors you chose. This is also true when you send an email or electronic document in full color, but the units in the field only have a black and white laser printer. Do not let these issues scare or frustrate you, just adapt and change and learn from each opportunity.

Geoprocessing deals with the concept of logical steps to create data. Much more thought needs to be given to this process to make sure the analysis product is useful and gives us the right answer. What we are doing is using multiple layers of data to come to a single analytical result. Each step in the process needs to be planned out, and we need to make sure that we don't make incorrect assumptions with each individual step. Those steps could include a specific layer or analysis in the form of point data, line data, polygon data, hotspots, and more. Remember that we do not need to show the audience everything we did, only the final result that gives us the "knowledge" we need to prevent crime, intercept an offender and arrest him, or point our proactive patrol philosophy at the most significant problems.

■ Maps for Specific Audiences

In addition to the tips that have previously been discussed, specific products can be created for various units within a police department, the city government, and citizens.

Patrol Officers

Patrol officers utilize maps for several different purposes. They are primarily a way to convey information about what is currently happening in their assigned areas and how crime and other incidents have increased or decreased from the recent past. Maps for these purposes are often distributed prior to the commencement of their shift and/or are discussed during roll call. The most important factor to consider when making maps for patrol officers is that they include real-time information that they can use. Information that is several days old is not necessarily useful to them (although a historic map is helpful, it does not include the most recent data, which is needed to better inform decision making about what to do about crime and other incidents day to day). Remember, the primary purpose of crime maps at the patrol level is so officers can develop strategies to respond to crime (such as the scanning, analysis, response and assessment [SARA] model) within their assigned areas. Another important factor to consider when making maps for patrol officers is that the mapped area should be specific to the areas the officer patrols. Along these lines, some placement of landmarks and street names helps orient the officers to where they are on the map, but placing too many landmarks and providing too many street names clutters up the map and is unnecessary, because patrol officers are usually intimately acquainted with the areas they patrol. Including a table that details key elements of the crime incidents (crime, date, address, and victim or offender characteristics, for example) allows officers to refer back to important variables without cluttering up the map and provides some context to the dots. Last, using sharply contrasting colors and dark, readable fonts on the map is helpful, especially if the map will be printed in black and white or for officers who may have to refer to the maps in low-light conditions. If it is difficult to see important items on the map, the map is of limited use.

Paulsen (2003) suggests that maps are underutilized by patrol officers. Creating maps that are easy to read and include up-to-date statistics that help patrol officers make decisions about their assigned patrol areas may increase their utilization of crime maps. Well informed crime maps can help officers identify trends and patterns of crime that can be relayed to citizens to reduce their victimization (as in the "garage shopping" case where residents were alerted to the increase in garage thefts and were encouraged to shut and lock their garages when not in use). In addition, maps can produce suggestions about where traffic officers might best place themselves to reduce traffic accidents caused by speeding. Finally, maps can indicate how seemingly unrelated crimes are in fact related to suggest possible areas of surveillance that might be most beneficial.

Figures 12–1 through 12–3 are examples of maps that would be useful to patrol officers. **Figure 12–1** depicts an example of a briefing map that is designed for patrol officers to pull up in their patrol cars. It only includes incidents that officers are able to work on and is designed primarily to help officers know what happened in their area during other shifts and for the week. It is a building map, so the first map completed for Monday shows what happened over the week, the next one completed for Tuesday shows what happened on Monday, and so on. It is broken down by shift, and the callout boxes contain information requested by the officers so that if they need more information, they can pull it up on the department's records-management system.

Figures 12–2 and **12–3** depict traffic maps that use two different ways of displaying traffic accident data. Figure 12–2 uses graduated points, and Figure 12–3 uses a join between point and street segments to get a number of accidents per street segment calculation.

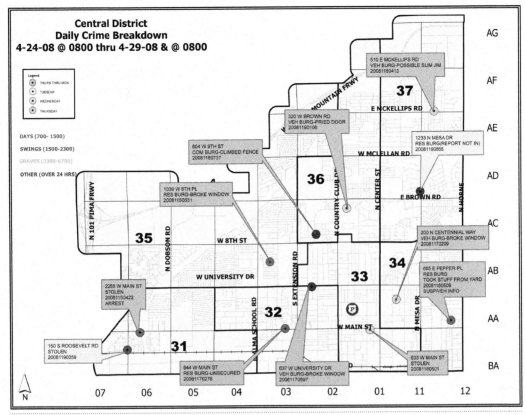

Figure 12–1a Central District Daily Crime Breakdown

Source: Jackie McClanahan, Crime Analyst, Central District Mesa Police Department.

Investigators

There are multiple uses of crime maps for investigators: "A recurring theme is that maps often reveal a whole picture that is greater than the sum of its parts. This happens when many small and seemingly isolated and insignificant pieces of evidence take on critical importance when viewed as part of a pattern" (Harries, 1999, p. 70). For example, there was a case in Knoxville, Tennessee, in which a clustering of seemingly unrelated crimes were related to a drug dealer (who was also a parolee) who lived in a cul-de-sac. Upon arrest of this person, it was discovered that many of the crimes were committed by the drug dealer's clients and friends on their way to and from his house. Maps that can bring together all of the information in a coherent manner to provide a visual of the whole picture are most useful to investigators. Spatial analyses of crime can identify areas most likely for an offender to live, which can reduce the number of persons an investigator needs to investigate. For example, utilizing databases of last known addresses of offenders within a targeted area to perform queries based on the elements of the crimes is an important tool. Maps can then be distributed to investigators

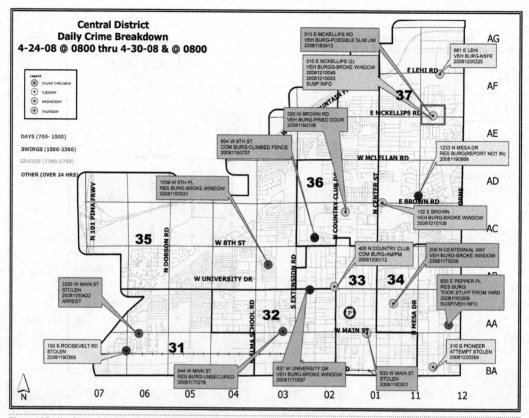

Figure 12–1b Central District Daily Crime Breakdown

Source: Jackie McClanahan, Crime Analyst, Central District Mesa Police Department.

along with a prioritized list of offenders to be questioned. This technique can be successful in apprehending burglars and sex offenders. Maps can also be used to confirm the alibis of suspects and to corroborate eyewitness accounts of crimes, for example by mapping the locations of victims and offenders based on cell phone transmissions.

Again, these maps need to include legible fonts for landmarks, street names, any other text that is important to the map, and contrasting colors that make the map easy to read. Including too much detail clutters a map and does not add to the investigation. Neglecting to add enough information (and the right information) to the map limits its ability to inform an investigation.

Figures 12–4 and **12–5** provide useful examples of maps for investigators. Figure 12–4 depicts a map showing the known associates of a wanted offender. Detectives searched the suspect (Percy), and they thought he was being hidden by his friends or family. Several officers and detectives who were not familiar with any of the characters assisted with the search, so the map was used to show who the parties were and where they lived. The cell

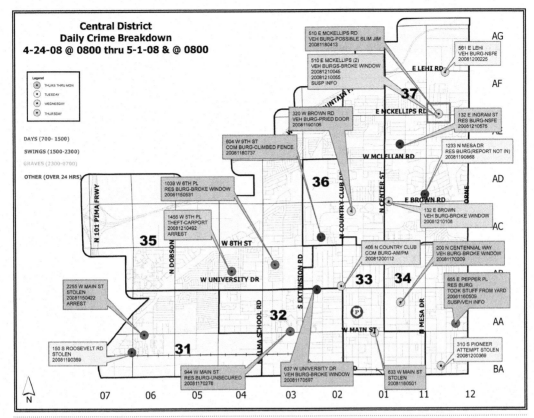

Figure 12–1c Central District Daily Crime Breakdown

Source: Jackie McClanahan, Crime Analyst, Central District Mesa Police Department.

phone tower–hit locations indicated the areas where Percy was located when he made calls from his cell phone.

Figure 12–5 is a map that provides a timeline of a suspect's (Ruiz) activity over a couple of months. Detectives held many briefings to try to identify all of the events and places involved in their search for the suspect. The timeline and map were used to keep all of the events straight during the investigation.

Management

Police managers have a difficult task in that they are responsible for having an effective, yet efficient agency as well as providing equality in the services they provide. The inherent conflicts that arise in achieving these goals are numerous. Managers need maps that present a larger picture of crime and other problems within their jurisdiction. They need maps that can inform them of recent changes in the distribution of crime and that can help them deploy resources based on predictions about crime distributions in the future. For example, one of

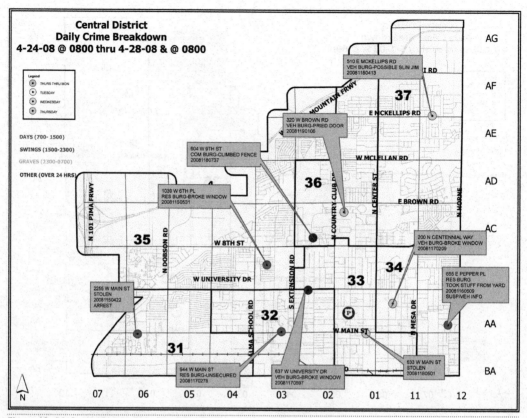

Figure 12–1d Central District Daily Crime Breakdown

Source: Jackie McClanahan, Crime Analyst, Central District Mesa Police Department.

the most common tasks of police managers is resource allocation. As discussed earlier, only a small percentage of calls for service actually involve criminal events.

Maps that depict the demands placed on law enforcement by the community can be helpful in several ways. First, calls for service can be mapped based on the severity of the call. These maps can identify areas of service that need more patrol. In addition, maps can help police managers with redistricting in attempts to equalize the workload for officers. Using techniques such as repeat address mapping (graduated dot maps) can produce maps that clearly show addresses that are responsible for a large percentage of calls for service. Managers can then reach out to these businesses to see if there is any sharing of information that can be had, which may aid in reducing the number of calls for service. Second, hotspot maps can also help managers develop solutions to chronic problems (such as in the case of the Boston miracle) and at the same time minimize the effects of displacement. Third, maps that depict before and after levels of crime can be used to assess the effectiveness of strategies (and to show the community at large the successes) and to inform needed adjustments to

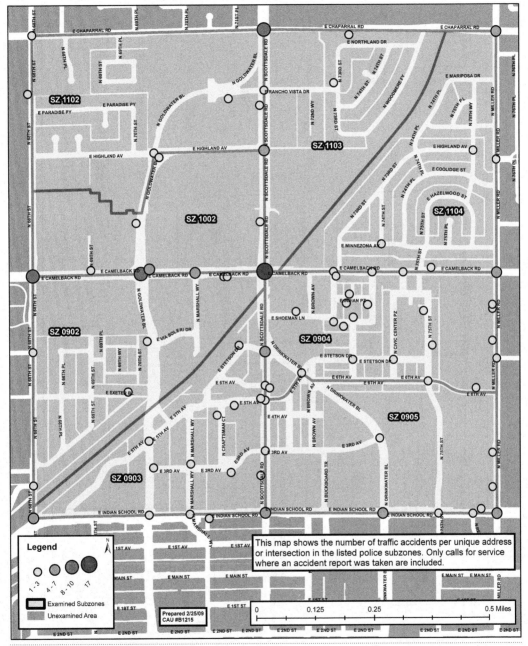

Figure 12–2 Traffic Accidents, Scottsdale, Arizona, Graduated Circles

Source: Scott Peacock, Police Analysis, Scottsdale Police Department.

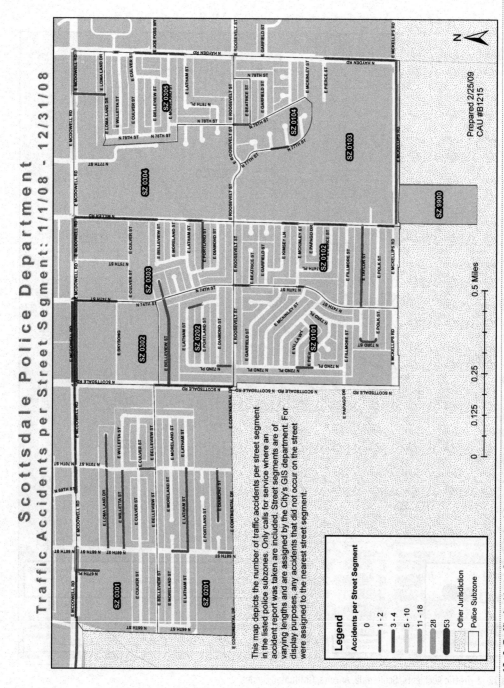

Figure 12–3 Traffic Accidents, Scottsdale, Arizona, Street Segment Colors

Source: Scott Peacock, Police Analysis, Scottsdale Police Department.

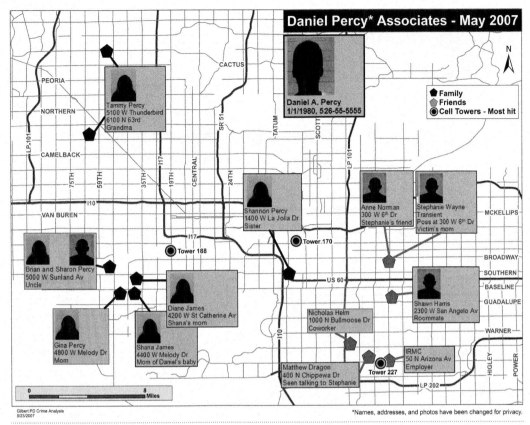

Figure 12–4 Daniel Percy Associates

Source: Judy Fernandez, Crime Analyst, Gilbert Police Department.

crime-prevention efforts. Fourth, maps are also useful as visual representations of need in grant applications for equipment and personnel. Last, in an age of cultural diversity and community policing, it is critical for police managers to have an understanding of the demographics within their jurisdiction. While access to recent data on demographic shifts can be difficult (for example, other than in large cities, the U.S. Census Bureau only collects demographic information every 10 years), it may be useful in understanding how changes in the population may affect crime trends. For example, knowing that some communities have become increasingly more racially and ethnically diverse might help law enforcement understand some of the conflicts that may have occurred and resulted in increased numbers of crimes such as assaults. In addition, a particular neighborhood may have a higher percentage of young persons (perhaps between the ages of 12 and 24 years), which might explain higher than average crime rates within this neighborhood. These maps, if based on solid predictions about demographic and cultural shifts, may be useful in making decisions about future resources, including the hiring of officers who are bilingual.

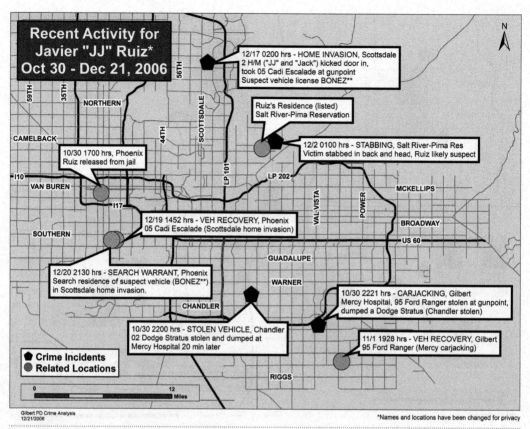

Figure 12-5 J. J. Ruiz Known Activities

Source: Judy Fernandez, Crime Analyst, Gilbert Police Department.

Figures 12-6 and **12-7** are examples of maps that are useful to managers. Figure 12-6 is a choropleth map that was produced at the request of crime-prevention officers when they spoke at neighborhood meetings.

Community

The demographics of neighborhoods can change drastically over a relatively short period of time. This can create conflict amongst the persons who reside in the neighborhood and between residents and police. Under community-oriented policing, law enforcement must work with communities to address crime and other problems that occur in their neighborhoods. One method of sharing information about crime with a community is through interactive mapping programs that are typically available online. Caution should be used in providing information in this format, because it can be used in a deceptive manner by persons who wish to capitalize on a neighborhood's crime problems. The maps (whether created by law enforcement and posted for community viewing or by a system that allows

Scottsdale Police Department
Vehicle Burglaries per Residential Subdivision - Beat 5
1/1/08 - 12/31/08

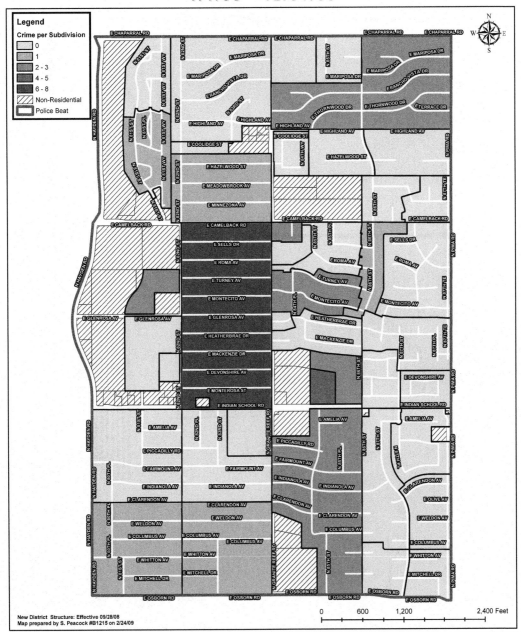

Figure 12–6 Hotspot Map Burglaries/Thefts from Autos

Source: Scott Peacock, Police Analysis, Scottsdale Police Department.

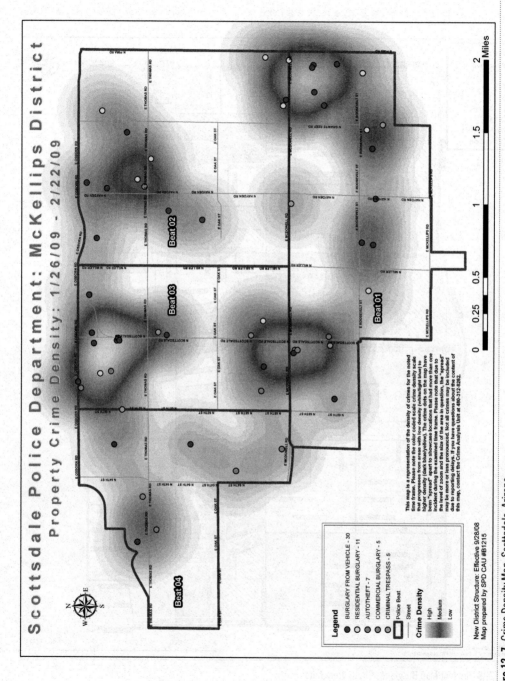

Figure 12-7   Crime Density Map, Scottsdale, Arizona

Source: Scott Peacock, Police Analysis, Scottsdale Police Department.

community members to create their own maps with the use of basic queries) should convey useful information about crime, demographics, and community resources. Access to online mapping capabilities varies from department to department. Some departments allow any user with Internet access to create detailed maps of crime at the address level. Other departments allow open access but only provide aggregate information at the block or larger level. In some cases, departments only allow certain members of community organizations to have access to mapmaking abilities. Last, some departments post static maps that community members can view but cannot change or even query.

Figure 12–8 is an example of a map for communities. It was created and submitted as part of a press conference that the Tucson Police Department/Counter Narcotics Alliance gave regarding the arrests of 39 people who were connected to a meth cell. By showing the areas where the offenders lived, the map demonstrated that meth is not a problem just in disadvantaged neighborhoods or high-crime areas but that meth affects the entire community.

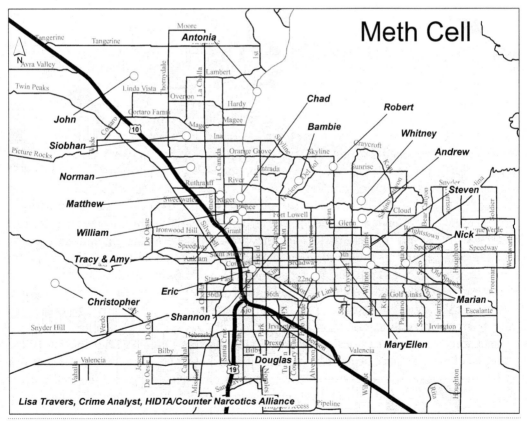

Figure 12–8 Meth Cell Map

Source: Lisa Travers, Crime Analyst, HIDTA/Counter Narcotics Alliance.

Courts

The main function of GIS in the courtroom is presentation. Maps can be created at the building level to reconstruct crime scenes or to illustrate the points where key pieces of evidence were found. Maps can also be useful to show the paths the offenders used to travel from place to place in committing their crime(s). For example, maps of serial offenders' movements can be created to provide the jury with a better picture of how a crime unfolded. In addition, maps can be used to present evidence about an offender's whereabouts in temporal and spatial proximity to a victim (such as mapping locations of offenders and victims based on cell phone call logs). The value here is the visual impact that maps can add, especially in a long and complicated trial. Maps can synthesize a great deal of information and project the complete story in a picture. (Remember, a picture is worth 1000 words.) Many people also naturally believe that maps are always true. This can aid the prosecution of a case if the maps are well prepared. Maps should be simple and easy to follow with bright, engaging colors that project only the information that needs to be projected (anything less minimizes a map's impact, and anything more can confuse jurors or redirect their focus to unimportant elements of the case).

Corrections

The possibilities for GIS applications in corrections are unlimited. Mapping programs can be used to identify problem areas within an institution. For example, assaults within an institution can be mapped to identify areas that need more security, or maps of gang activities within an institution can be created and used to develop strategies to minimize gang problems. In addition, GIS can be used to map the residences (and workplaces) of individuals who are on probation or parole that can be shared with law enforcement to develop strategies that improve the effectiveness of investigation and applications of problem-oriented policing. Furthermore, GIS can be used in conjunction with global positioning systems (GPS) to monitor the movements of parolees and probationers to ensure these individuals are not visiting places (and people) they are barred from by their probation and parole stipulations. Information about offenders' movements can also be compared to current cases to prioritize and investigate suspects in efforts to solve these cases. Also, government and community resources can be mapped to identify areas within large jurisdictions that are lacking in the supports necessary for parolees and probationers to successfully complete their sentences. This is critical to offenders who have limited means of transportation. Last, due to residency restrictions that have been passed in many states for sex offenders, maps can be created to identify areas where these offenders are allowed to live. (Incidentally, these maps can also discover enclaves or clusters of sex offenders living together.) **Figures 12–9** and **12–10** are examples of maps that can be used for correctional purposes. The maps depict offenders on parole for the crimes of robbery and possession of a stolen vehicle and are used by the street crime unit for knock-and-talk applications. These maps are updated monthly and can be made for offenders who are on parole for a variety of crimes.

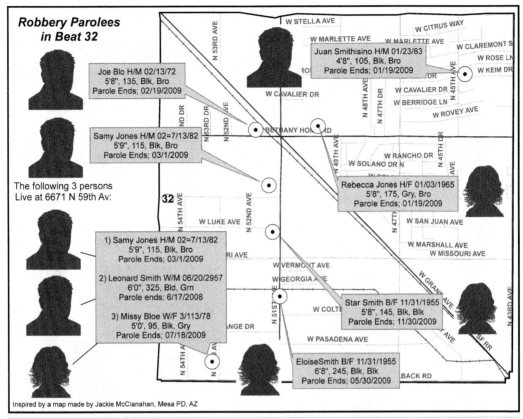

Figure 12–9 Robbery Parolees

Source: Inspired by a map made by Jackie McClanahan, Mesa PD, AZ.

■ Conclusion

As you can see, there is a plethora of GIS applications in the criminal justice system. However, maps must be tailored to the function(s) and audience they serve. The analyst must be willing to spend time to learn what their audience does day to day so that by understanding the needs of their audience, they can better create maps that speak to the issues of that audience and possibly automate a process that can provide more timely data to that audience. Special attention must be paid to scale, color, text, and the data used to create useful and meaningful maps that assist criminal justice in its efforts to manage crime. Maps that are difficult to read due to scale, color, or content are problematic and will be discarded and ignored rather than yielding the intended results.

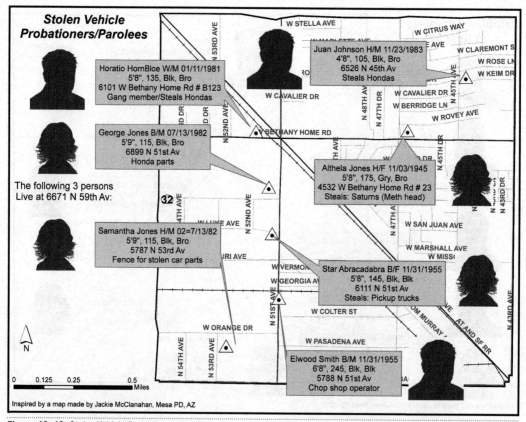

Figure 12–10 Stolen Vehicle Probationers/Parolees

Source: Inspired by a map made by Jackie McClanahan, Mesa PD, AZ.

■ Chapter Glossary

Administrative crime maps   These are maps that are generally citywide, and are often monthly maps with little analysis that just describe a crime problem. These can be maps for the public, websites, and reference maps.

Aerial images   Aerial images are images taken from an airplane or occasionally a helicopter that show the surface conditions on the ground; they are aligned in tiles in a GIS for use by the analyst and others to show the landscape on the ground.

Business intelligence   A type of analysis that takes data from different database systems, combines them into information, and after careful analysis (often automated), becomes actionable intelligence to aid the agency in solving problems.

Cartographic methods   These are methods learned by cartographers to accurately portray a section of the Earth's surface. These can be drawing methods, scale issues, and correct organization of the map contents.

Center of attention   The center of attention on the map is the item(s) that the audience should immediately recognize and the most important item on the map. It is usually a contrasting color to other items, and is the most prominent feature.

Clustering algorithms   Mathematical model that determines if the points are not randomly generated but are clustered together in significant groupings that are higher than the entire geographic area being analyzed.

Geoprocessing   A mapping process that shows relationships between different types of data through contrast and comparison techniques. This is done through a series of sequenced steps in which the analyst takes existing information and uses it to create new information.

Reference map   A map used to provide general direction and "reference" for the area in question, such as a beat map that shows the officers where the boundaries of their beats are.

Strategic crime maps   Maps that generally cover shorter time periods and focus on a specific geographic area within the city boundaries, with the overall objective of identifying problems and suggesting possible solutions.

Tactical crime maps   Maps that involve very short time periods and are usually used to predict a new crime in a series or spree or identify where the suspect in a series of offenses might live. They may also include high-quality aerial images for a search warrant, or known locations of offenders for a warrant roundup to aid in planning for these events.

White space   The space between elements on a map. Having open white space between elements helps to avoid cluttering. White space should normally be regularly sized between elements.

■ Questions for Review

1. Why must an analyst intimately understand the data he or she is working with?
2. What are the three basic categories of maps that are made in crime analysis?
3. What items should be part of any map an analyst makes?
4. What should an analyst keep in mind when making maps for:
   - Patrol officers?
   - Investigators?
   - Managers?
   - Community members?

■ Online Resources

Dr. Jerry Ratcliffe's "Top Ten Crime Mapping Tips": www.jratcliffe.net/papers/Jerry's%20top%20ten%20mapping%20tips.pdf

POP Center, Crime Analysis for Problem Solvers in 60 Small Steps, Make Clear Maps: www.popcenter.org/learning/60steps/index.cfm?stepNum=55

Wikipedia reference on cartography: http://en.wikipedia.org/wiki/Cartography

■ Recommended Reading

Monmonier, M. (1996). *How to lie with maps* (2nd ed.). Chicago: University of Chicago Press.
Brewer, C. (2005). *Designing better maps: A guide for GIS users*. Redlands, CA: ESRI Press.

■ References

Harries, K. D. (1999). *Crime mapping: Principle and practice*. Washington, DC: U.S. Department of Justice Programs.
Paulsen, D. (2003, March). *To map or not to map: Do crime maps have any measurable impact on patrol officers?* Presentation at the Academy of Criminal Justice Sciences, Boston, MA.

Basics of Cartography

By James LeBeau and Katherine E. Wuschke

CHAPTER
13

This chapter covers the basic elements found in a map and some useful cartographic principles and notions to keep in mind when making a crime map with good cartographic design. Without creating useful maps that explain to your users what the map is for and how it can help them do their jobs better, you are just wasting paper. The student is provided with several examples of good maps, and how to take complicated data and display it so that the reader can quickly and easily see the most important parts of the map and the knowledge it should impart. After studying this chapter, you should be able to:

- Identify the key required elements of a good map.
- Discuss the cartographic principles involved in good map making.
- Observe the differences in cartographic design for point, line, and polygon layers.
- Discover proper uses of qualitative and quantitative data.

▶ Key Terms

Cartography	Legend	Ratio
Choropleth Map	Nominal	Scale
Crime Rate	North Arrow	Thematic Map
Interval	Ordinal	Title

■ Introduction

It is a very arduous process mastering the skills of managing, analyzing, and mapping data. However, your blood, sweat, and tears can be all for naught if your map does not effectively communicate with the map reader. If the map reader (your audience) is working very hard trying to understand and interpret your map, then your attempt to communicate knowledge with your map has been a failure (Monmonier, 1993). This chapter discusses some basic elements of **cartography** that can help you create maps that are more effective and efficient in communicating information to any given audience.

Generally, three types of features are found in maps: points, lines, and polygons. In this chapter, we are building on your knowledge about basic statistical techniques and levels of measurement variables (nominal, ordinal, interval, and ratio) and their properties; we are adding to that knowledge by examining how best to represent points, lines, and polygons with symbols representing the different levels of measurement.

■ General Topics

The Basic Elements

Figure 13-1 is a reference map of Canada that reflects some of the basic elements you need to have on your maps. These include a title, a legend or key, a scale, and a north arrow or compass rose.

Title

What is your map about? A short and concise **title** such as "Canada: Provinces, Territories, and Capitals" informs the map viewer that this map is going to be about the political organization

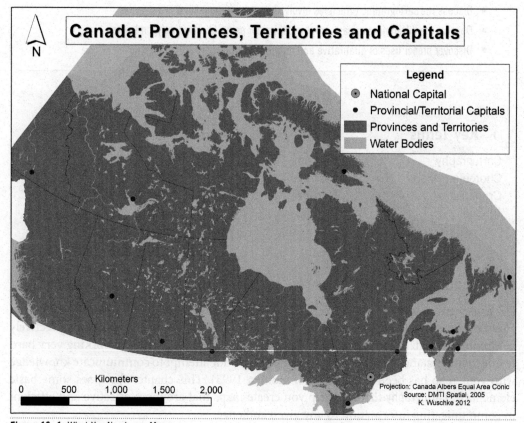

Figure 13-1 What You Need on a Map

of Canada, or where the capital cities are located. The title has the largest font size and is centered between the left and right margins at the upper portion of the map. The title has also been placed into a rectangle that is in a contrasting, lighter color than the rest of the map. Another item that is often in the title is an indicator of the relevant date or time depicted on the map. Since the political organization of Canada has been fairly static, there is less need for an indicator of date or time. However, a map depicting provincial **crime rates** would need to have some indication of the date and time period depicted on the map. In crime mapping, periods of time and dates are vital to understanding what the map is telling us. In addition, including some language about the type of crime is also important. For example, if you are presenting a hotspot map of burglaries in Glendale, Arizona for January–June, 2006, your title should include all of these key points of information. For Figure 13–1, some insufficient titles might be, "Canada," or "Canadian Capital Cities." The current title is the most appropriate because it shows the provincial and territorial boundaries as well as the capital cities.

Legend or Key

The title informs the viewer of what the map is all about, while the **legend**, or key, tells the map viewer how the contents of the title are operationally defined and visualized. More simply, the legend translates what the different symbols, shapes, and shades on the map represent in the real world. The legend in Figure 13–1 is very straightforward, starting with the point symbol for the national capital, a smaller point symbol for the provincial/territorial capitals, and area shadings differentiating between water bodies and the provinces/territories, as well as outlines of each province. In crime mapping, you may choose different symbols or colors to represent different crimes, for example. In addition, the size of those symbols may vary depending on their frequency. For example, a point that represents 10 burglaries would be larger in size than a point that only represents 1 or 2 burglaries. This is of course based on the quantitative or qualitative data we are working with. We often have to depict different political boundaries in crime maps, but they are more often used as reference map layers, and thus are often more muted in either color or hue, or if grey-scale, they may be a lighter shade of gray. It is the analyst's responsibility to not only understand these key elements of a map, but also put them to use together, to provide actionable knowledge to the audience.

Scale

Now that we know the title of Figure 13–1 and how to interpret the symbols with the legend, the next question is: What is the size or geographic extent of the area being presented? This question is answered very quickly by the provision of a **scale** bar *(lower left or southwest corner)*. A scale bar allows one to roughly estimate the distances between and among map features. This scale bar is in kilometers, and usually in professional journals the metric system is the norm. Yet, in the United States, feet and miles are the norm for crime mapping. Sometimes crime mappers will provide both the metric and non-metric scales on their maps. Crime analysts will usually choose whatever the local measurement is for their jurisdiction, or what is commonly known and easy to understand for the audience. The choice depends on your intended audience and the information you are trying to convey. Which scale makes the most sense for the information that is included in your map? If your map zooms onto only a few square blocks, then a scale bar in feet makes more sense than one set to miles. If your map covers a large city in the United States, a scale bar in miles may make the most sense. However, always remember that your goal is to portray information and provide knowledge to the audience, so making the scale bar and all other items on the map easy to understand for that audience is paramount. The analyst should be very familiar with his or her commonly accepted local measurement units, consider what map units their data is in, and determine what would be the best scale to use for every map, again, to inform the reader.

North Arrow or Compass Rose

The **north arrow**, or compass rose, complements the title, legend, and scale information by indicating the orientation of the map. We can see from Figure 13–1 that the top of the map is north. Many people assume that the top of any map is north and that the orientation of small-scale maps depicting large areas is recognizable. Yet, large-scale, small-area maps are the norm for crime mapping so orientation is helpful for the viewer (think about cutting out the middle of a city map and giving it a good spin—how easily would you be able to discern north from south without the larger context—what if you were unfamiliar with the area?). So the closer you zoom into the Earth's surface, the larger the scale is or the range becomes closer to a 1:1 relationship (e.g., 1:2500 scale {0.0004} is larger than 1:250,000 scale {0.000004}).

Internalize these four elements as absolute musts for your maps. These elements, depending on the quality of their design and composition, should greatly enhance your communication. The analyst may be asked by command personnel to remove these items from their maps to clear up the map so they are easier for officers to read. This should never be done because they should always be on the map, but you can place them in inconspicuous places on the map. The analyst must be prepared to teach his or her law enforcement audiences about the significance of these map items, and also show them how to use them. There are, however, other pieces of information that routinely appear on crime maps.

Observe the three additional pieces of information in the lower righthand or southeast corner of Figure 13–1. The first is the graticule *(projection or coordinate system)* of the map (Harries, 1999). This information is helpful for comparing other maps and transforming maps from other projections or coordinate systems. Projections vary across many law enforcement jurisdictions, so analysts must be proficient in not only knowing what their layers are in, but they must also be able to use different sources of data that may be in varied projection types. This information should appear on the map so that other analysts can know what to ask for when they want to share data, and potentially what projection data are in. This enables them to be able to not only share the data, but also make sure their data line up with the other data they may have on the map, which could be in different projections. It is not important to list all of the different projections of the data included, but the projection of the final map is important. The second is a notation of the data source(s). In Figure 13–1 the source is DMTI Spatial, 2005, which indicates the data came from the Canadian company, Desktop Mapping Technologies, Inc. The database is called Spatial, and it was published or released in 2005. Often the source information is placed in the lower left or southwest corner on the map, but given the layout of the different elements in Figure 13–1 the best place for the source was in the lower right corner. Analysts should always list the source of the data they use. Analysts will often also include the current map file location, directory, and file name. This is also useful for being able to find the map project and the data or analysis used to make the map months after it was made. This will enable you to repeat your analysis or update it as needed without recreating the map from scratch.

The third piece of information that appears in the lower right corner is the name or initials of the mapmaker and the year of creation. We can see that K. Wuschke made this map in the year 2012. Often the initials of the mapmaker and year will do. As maps are published and contain a great deal of information and analyses, it is important to be able to identify who created a map so that if we have further questions, we know who to contact. Think about this in terms of publishing an article, or even writing a research paper for school: Don't the authors usually put their name on the finished product? There are some cases where you may not want your full contact information, such as a map made for media and being placed on the news company's website. In other situations where the map is for other law enforcement personnel and contacting you expeditiously with any new information to break a case might be warranted. Along with the file name and location, we can use this information to recreate that map for the chief if he happens to ask for it when the analyst who made it is on vacation.

Summary of Essential Features

We have discussed the essential features of a map and the additional ones that help convey more information. Notice the overall layout of Figure 13–1. There is maximum exposure; in other words, the point of interest is in the main feature of the map, Canada. The map is well balanced with the north arrow and title across the top of the page, which is not significantly obstructing the layout of Canada. The same can be said of the legend. The scale and the text information are in the bottom left and right corners of the map. The placement of these features will vary with the subjects and layouts of the map. There is sufficient white space amongst the various features of the map to avoid cluttering. Some useful references that go into more depth regarding the essential features and map composition appear at the end of this chapter.

■ Mapping Points, Lines, and Polygons, Along with Data Scales

The majority of crime mapping pertains to making **thematic maps**. Thematic maps assess the distributions and relationships between two or more variables or attributes (Dent, 1996, p. 7). Assessing the quantities and distances of drug arrests from school properties is an example of a popular thematic map, given the widespread concern about the effectiveness and efficacy of drug-free school zones.

Constructing thematic maps requires numerous decisions by the mapmaker. Among them is matching the scale of the data with appropriate symbols. Therefore, the points, lines, and polygons the map composer uses can be nominal, ordinal, or interval–ratio scaled. Maps showing these features with different data scales should clarify the relationships between and among different attributes. Crime analysts have a large assortment of methods for developing data that can be thematically portrayed on a map. In addition, analysts must consider how they summarize, aggregate, or collect events when determining the best way to show these "themes" on the map. Analysts cannot collect nominal or ordinal data (character or text) when they want to create a map that needs numerical (ratio or interval) classification. So analysts must consider how the data is to be collected or pulled together for the final product and be mindful of that responsibility when developing data for the map. Most geographic information systems (GIS) software has multiple ways to symbolize or classify data for a map display. Each method of classification comes with some rules, and we must follow those rules of data preparation, collection, and symbolization to make useful maps.

■ Nominal Data

Nominal data use numbers or symbols to classify a phenomenon or concept. In a database or survey, gender may be recorded as: 1 = female and 2 = male. The numbers are labels. You cannot infer that this is a ranking and that females are number 1. Nor can you infer that males rank twice that of females or the latter is half that of the former. The numbers are just labels. Any number that is used to represent nominal factors is just a label. It cannot be used for any mathematical purposes other than classifying or sorting. Think about your social security number. It would make no sense to subtract it from someone else's social security number, because the resulting figure does not have any meaning. Nominal features on a map can be represented with symbols of different colors or characters (Krygier & Wood, 2005, p. 61). These types of maps could include pin maps using two different symbol classes, shaded polygons, or even pie charts that show which dots represent males and females, for instance.

Nominal Points

Figure 13–2 shows the point locations for the arrests of drug dealers in Charlotte–Mecklenburg, North Carolina between 1997 and 2002. The points are differentiated and shaded by race. Thus, the theme is comparing the spatial distribution of arrests by race. This map tells us the following:

- The legend indicates there are many more arrests of black than white suspects.
- The map visually confirms the quantity of arrests.
- Overall, the black arrests appear in a large contiguous area in the center of the map.
- The black arrests spread to the west, southwest, northeast, and east.
- The majority of the white arrests are south of the central cluster of black arrests.
- Some white arrests show a strong linear pattern extending from the center of the map to the southwest for about 10 miles.
- Similar white arrest patterns emanate from the center to the southeast and fork off to the east.
- White arrests predominate outside the contiguous cluster of black arrests in all directions.

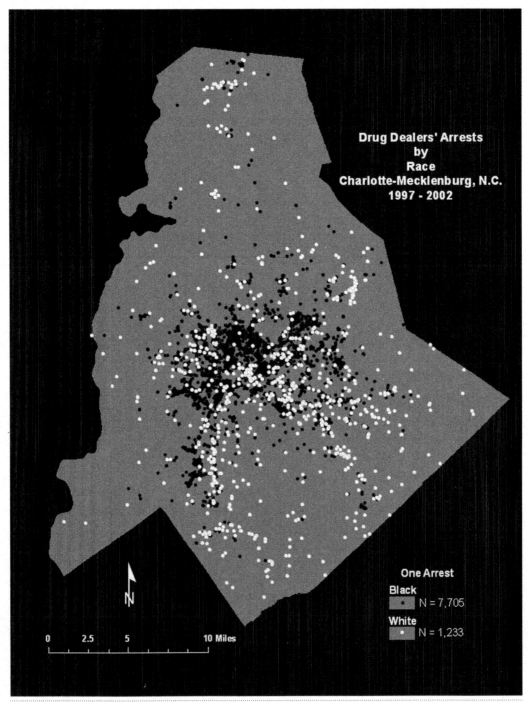

Figure 13-2 Nominal Point Data

Obviously, contributing to the generation of these patterns are varying residential and commercial land uses interacting with diverse populations and a range of socioeconomic statuses across the landscape within the central business district (located in the center of the map). The dark, contrasting gray-scale colors clearly delineate the two variables that are meant to be the main focus of the map. The dark outer area focuses the map even more to the outlines of the Charlotte–Mecklenburg city limits, and the two main variables being shown. The reader should have no problem determining this thanks to the scale bar, title, north arrow, and legend, as well as the overall design of the map, which focuses us on these two most important nominal variables.

Nominal Lines

Figure 13–3 emanates from the same database as Figure 13–2. However, this time travel vectors or lines are drawn between the points of the offenders' residences and arrest locations. The travel vectors are differentiated by the race of the offender. The predominance of the black vectors makes it difficult to ascertain definitive patterns for the white vectors, although almost a half mile due south of the area previously identified as the central business district, one can see two large nodes. These nodes are created because numerous white travel vectors happen to cross at those locations. Thus, future research would have to determine if these nodes are meaningful or if they are simply graphic anomalies. Although these data are much harder to understand for the reader, the title, scale bar, legend, and north arrow help understanding, and the stark contrast between variables and the other elements of the map make this map stand out for the reader.

Nominal Areas/Polygons

Figure 13–4 is an excellent example of how to map **nominal** areal data. This map is more of a reference map than a thematic map. Different hues and texture patterns are employed to distinguish the spatial extent of different policing jurisdictions. Again, the map delineates different areas, including the areas outside the detachment zones, and the title, scale bar, north arrow, and legend play an important part in providing clarity to the reader. This map might look better in color, but the thematic construction of the various pieces is what makes this map stand out. The analyst should keep in mind that the typical human mind can only visually track about seven different things at a time, so by adding more than that you would be causing confusion and difficulty understanding the message of the map. Even with this simple nominal data (detachment names), some thought needs to go into the creation of the map, because we need to determine the detachment name from the legend, and on the map.

■ Ordinal Data

Ordinal data simply imply there is some sort of rank order or hierarchy in the data. Thus, "low, medium, high" is an example of an ordinal scheme. The actual numbers defining each category are usually unknown to the viewer or map user. Moreover, some police agencies and/or the companies they retain to make their maps available to the public will use the ordinal scale as opposed to the interval–ratio scale, leaving the individual map viewer to

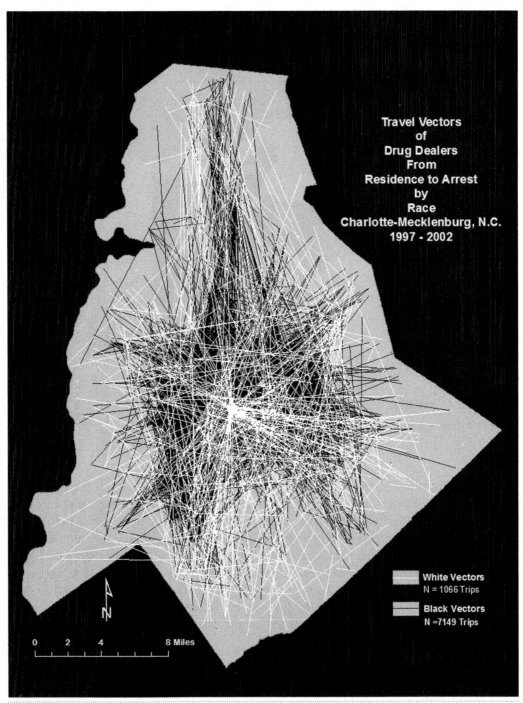

Figure 13–3 Nominal Line Data

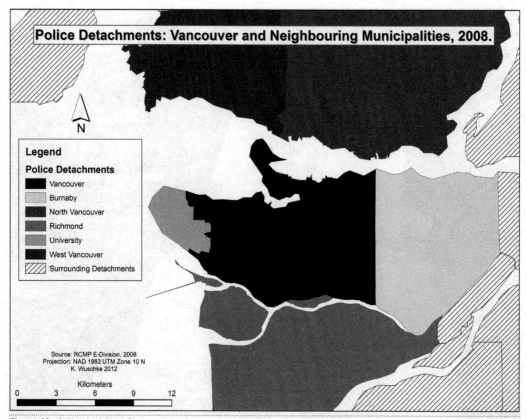

Figure 13–4 Nominal Areal Data

determine what is high, medium, and low. If we have ordinal data, and it is important that rank order is somehow shown on the map, then the analyst must develop a thematic map that depicts this clearly. Polygons showing ordinal data might be depicted with a shaded grid map that shows the high polygons in bright red, with the medium in orange, and the low in faded yellow. We might also see a chart (bar graph or pie chart) within each patrol zone showing the degree of residential burglaries in each zone with a different bar or pie in red, orange, or yellow, for example. Of course, we would probably want to use interval or ratio data for these types of analyses 90% of the time, but in some cases, for privacy issues and other reasons we may only want to compare "scores" for different areas using a rank order rather than a specific number.

Ordinal Points

Figure 13–5 employs different size points or circle symbols to designate the motor vehicle theft rate across major Canadian cities during 2007. There is a stark contrast between the cities in the east and those in the Midwest–Rockies–West region. The east experiences low

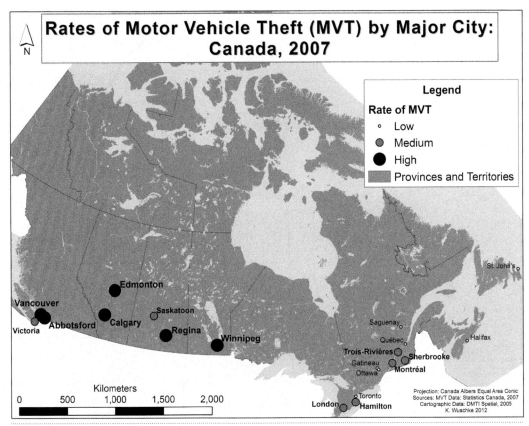

Figure 13-5 Ordinal Point Data

to medium rates of motor vehicle theft, while the Midwest–Rockies–West, with the exceptions of Saskatoon and Victoria, has the highest rates. The difference is that in the east there are many smaller towns and suburban jurisdictions recording motor vehicle thefts, which are not major cities. The provinces heading west, except for British Columbia, have fewer cities and suburbs so a majority of the provincial population resides in a few large cities. Analysts must be intimate with their data. This not only includes the incident data they are analyzing, but also the underlying physical makeup of the various geographies within their jurisdiction. The landscape of their jurisdictions may contribute as much to the display of ordinal or other data (as we see in Figure 13–5) as the events themselves. Being able to know these limitations may not always change the way you make the map; however, disclaimers might be added to the map explaining these issues if they are significant in the analyst's eyes.

Ordinal Lines

Figure 13-6 depicts the visualization of ordinal lines. Line widths and color shadings are combined to represent the hierarchy of street types. These are often called graduated lines,

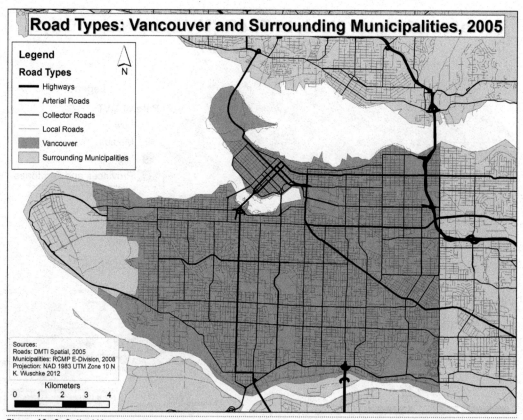

Figure 13–6 Ordinal Lines

or lines that increase in size and/or vary in color depending on the count of incidents along the street or line segment. In this case the different street segments are displayed based on the ordinal structure of the line segment such as highway, arterial, and collector and their relative rank in importance. We could also count the number of traffic crashes along street segments, and calculate a Z score (calculating Z scores standardizes the data and allows for understanding of the relative size and/or position of some event in context of the others), and then rank order the number of crashes based on the Z score, with 4 being the "worst," 3 being second worst, and so on. Each street segment could then be shown in varying thicknesses and/or colors to show the viewer which streets are the worst for traffic crashes. This might be used for solo motor units for traffic enforcement programs, or at least as a start to a tactical action plan for traffic crashes.

Ordinal Areal/Polygon Data

Figure 13–7 is an example of mapping areal/polygon ordinal data. The areal units are census tracts of an anonymous municipality in British Columbia. The crime being mapped

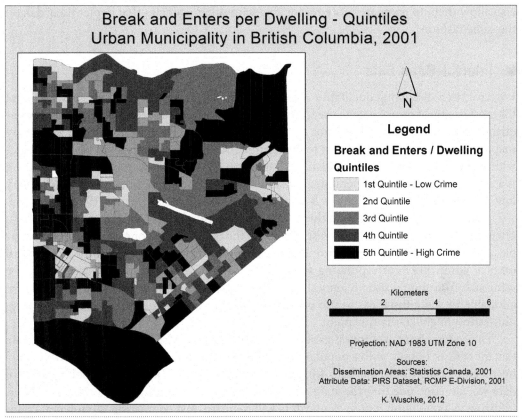

Figure 13-7 Ordinal Areas

is "break and enters per dwelling unit" (burglary rate). This rate is interval–ratio scale data and can be correctly used in a **choropleth map**, but for our purposes here the rate is converted to an ordinal scale.

The rates for the census tracts are rank ordered and placed into quintiles. Using a total of 100%, the quintiles represent 20% increments of data. Therefore, the first quintile represents the lowest values constituting the first 20% of the data while the fifth quintile represents the higher values, constituting a cumulative representation of 81 to 100% of the data (Griffith & Amrhein, 1991, p. 85). The legend indicates the shades for the extremes of low crime and high crime, but the exact numbers or thresholds for these and the intermediate categories are not revealed. For the most part, crime analysts would likely use the counts or rates for internal customers; however, this sort of depiction as ordinal data for the public may be entertained. For internal customers, the actual values can be known and we can share that information with our chain of command. However, with the public and media, they may often misinterpret the data, so providing them with ordinal scale data for the polygon or areal units will prevent them from making improper assumptions. This may also allow them to compare more reasonably with other agencies that depict their data in the same fashion.

■ Interval–Ratio Data

We have been discussing qualitative data to this point, but now embark on a discussion of the most exciting types of data to use for analysis. Interval–ratio scaled data, also known as the quantitative scale reflect a difference in the operationalization of the concept of zero. If we mapped the average January lowest temperature for Canadian cities we will find some cities with averages below zero on the Celsius or Fahrenheit scales. Below zero does not mean there is a complete absence of temperature; it just means for the scale used the temperature is very low. Therefore, the zero is arbitrary. It is just a reference on a scale (Harries, 1999, p. 23).

A general rule of thumb is to think of **interval** as "number of," frequency, or count of a phenomenon. Interval data imply restrictions on the types of maps one can make. For example, analysts should not make choropleth maps using interval data unless the polygon/areal units or some other corresponding standardization unit (population for example) are the same size. You should usually only make choropleth maps with rates. However, it may be allowable in some instances to use other units of measure such as density. The following illustration might clarify this point.

The Federal Bureau of Investigation (FBI) 2010 Uniform Crime Reports (UCR) indicate that the state of Illinois, with a population of 12,830,632 people, recorded 706 murders. During the same time, Louisiana, with 4,533,372 people, recorded 510 murders. Looking at these data we can conclude that the state with the larger population has more murders. Thus, inferring as population increases murders will increase. Just comparing the interval count or frequency data implies this is true. Let's look at these numbers in another way.

Currently, we are comparing the states based on frequencies but the comparison is not exact. We need to standardize the murder rates with another number so the states will be on the same scale. This other number is usually the resident population of each state divided by 100,000 or how many 100,000ths there are in each state. Illinois is 12,830,632/100,000 = 128.3; Louisiana is 4,533,372/100,000 = 45.33. We take this number and divide into the number of murders and we get a murder rate per 100,000 persons. Illinois is 706 murders/ 128.3 = 5.5 murders per 100,000 persons; Louisiana is 510 murders/45.33 = 11.24 murders per 100,000 per persons (FBI, 2010). Thus, the smaller state in terms of population has twice the murder rate of Illinois, which has almost three times the population of Louisiana. Therefore, if we made a choropleth map of murder rates across the states, Louisiana would be in a higher category than Illinois. The lesson learned is that when working with quantitative data, one has to be very aware of when they are working with interval or ratio data, because the type of data one uses implies the type of map that is appropriate (Monmonier, 1993; Harries, 1999; Krygier & Wood, 2005).

In the typical crime analysis world, we might want to find out where the worst areas are in town for theft from a motor vehicle. If we just used the counts of thefts from vehicles, we might find areas that have a high number of thefts from vehicles, but perhaps not the "worst" areas because there are thousands of parking lots in that high-count area. We might want to calculate a rate that represents the number of thefts from vehicles per number of parking spaces in the polygon. This would then show us areas where the theft from vehicle rate was the highest in comparison. We might find that an area in the southern part of town had 100 thefts from vehicles, but it had 100 total parking spaces. In another neighborhood in the north part of town we had the same number of thefts, but only 25 parking spaces. The rate for the northern polygon would then be 4, whereas the rate in the southern polygon would be 1. The northern area had a rate that was 4 times the rate of the southern polygon. If we then looked at the sizes of each polygon and found that the northern polygon was 100 times larger than the southern, then the rate we calculated above may not be quite as valid, again, depending on all of the information analyzed together.

Rates and counts can both be useful for crime analysts as they explore where they can best serve the various audiences within the agency they need to create products for. Knowing when to use nominal, ordinal, interval and ratio data for each analysis product becomes the challenge when trying to provide the most reliable actionable knowledge to prevent or forecast crime or traffic issues.

Interval Point Data

Figure 13–8 is an anomaly in this text about using ArcGIS, because this map is "old school"; it was made with pen and ink, a compass, a Leroy lettering set, and Zip-A-Tone layers of shading, which are cut out of a sheet and placed on a circle. These are some of the tools of traditional cartographers. Whether the analyst has sophisticated electronic mapping software or old school pen and ink, the skill of the analyst to make the map tell the story that needs to be told is what really makes the map speak to the issues.

Three purposes are served by Figure 13–8. The first is to demonstrate the proper mapping of interval count or frequency data through using graduated circles to visualize the number of reported rapes in each census tract for two areas encompassing Northern San Diego, California, during 1971 and 1975. The second visualizes how the types of rapes varied across the landscape. The type of rape or "offender status" is the number of reported rapes committed by the same lone assailant before apprehension. Therefore, there are three categories: Open—the offender is not known or apprehended, but all the evidence indicates the assault was by one person; single—the offender commits one reported rape before apprehension; and series or serial—the offender commits two or more rapes before apprehension (LeBeau, 1985). These categories are nominal data, but the graduated circles are shaded according to the proportion of each type of offender in each tract (pie chart). The third and final purpose of this map is visualizing how the numbers and types of rapes changed between 1971 and 1975. The upper portion of the map represents an area containing the city of Escondido. The area in the lower right by the coast contains La Jolla, and to the south Mission Bay. The community known as Claremont Mesa is to the east. During 1971, both areas accounted for 15 reported rapes, which is the highest number of rapes reported between 1971 through 1974. One year later (1975), the number was 72.

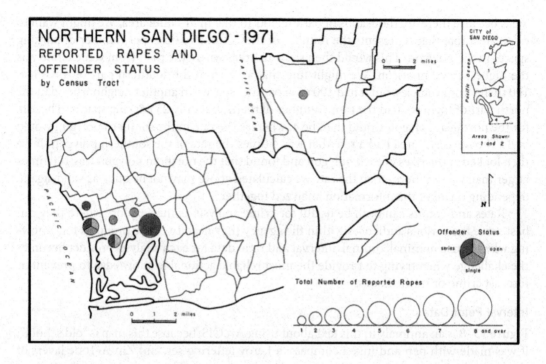

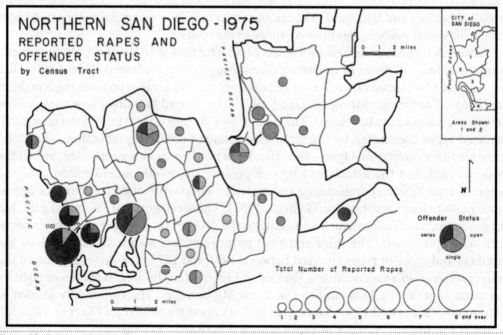

Figure 13-8 Interval Point Data

During 1971, in the La Jolla–Mission Bay area, the majority of the rapes were committed by one serial offender with a few open and single offenders. There are two single assaults in Escondido, but the remaining tracts in both areas are unaffected. Four years later this picture changes dramatically.

The La Jolla–Mission Bay area was the hunting ground for multiple series offenders, but series offenses appeared in Claremont Mesa and in the Escondido area. Moreover, both areas were inundated with open and single assaults. Why the dramatic change? One strong explanatory factor is that in 1975, California implemented a new rape law. This may have led victims who would have otherwise been reluctant to report their rapes to do so (LeBeau, 1988). Thus, changing the geographic patterns of reporting are what can be seen with the map, not necessarily an increase of rapes. This is an example of how the analyst must understand the fabric or landscape of the geography, politics, or policies within the department, because they can dramatically affect interpretation of the data, possibly causing incorrect conclusions if these underlying factors are not understood.

Two other features of these maps need to be noted. First, in the upper right, or northeast, corner one can see a locater index (Monmonier, 1993, p. 29). This feature informs map readers of which portions of the city they are viewing. Second, the two areas are presented at different scales, so there is an appropriate scale bar for each area.

Interval Line Data

Figure 13–9 depicts the "Journey to Burn," with a graduated line map representing the travel vectors between the residences of apprehended arsonists and their targets in Chicago, Illinois, during 1993. This map and supporting tabular data indicate that a majority of arsons where the suspect has been apprehended involve shorter journeys. The average journey is 2.44 miles, but there are 87 incidents where the target is the arsonist's own residence. Moreover, the median and mode travel distances are 0.03 miles. The former indicates that half the journeys are below 0.03 miles. The latter indicates 0.03 miles is the most frequently occurring trip distance, thus implying that the journeys of apprehended arsonists are very short. However, in Figure 13–9 we can see the number of trips, assess the distances, and observe the directional biases of habitual or serial arsonists.

Ratio Areal Data

Figure 13–10 is an example of mapping **ratio** areal or polygon data. The crime being mapped is burglary or breaking and entering. The denominator is not the resident population but the number of dwelling units divided by or per 100 dwelling units by census tract. Break and enters (B&Es) per 100 dwelling units have five categories defined by increments of 3.25 B&Es per 100 dwellings. Supporting the map is a histogram informing the reader of the number of census tracts (count) in each of the five intervals. This shows that only a small number of census tracts are responsible for the largest ratio of B&Es. This kind of mapping has become more frequently seen in problem-solving mapping and analysis products for law enforcement agencies. These types of ratio polygon data allow us to zero in on the most significant problem areas within a jurisdiction and give the responding units better direction. Again, analysts

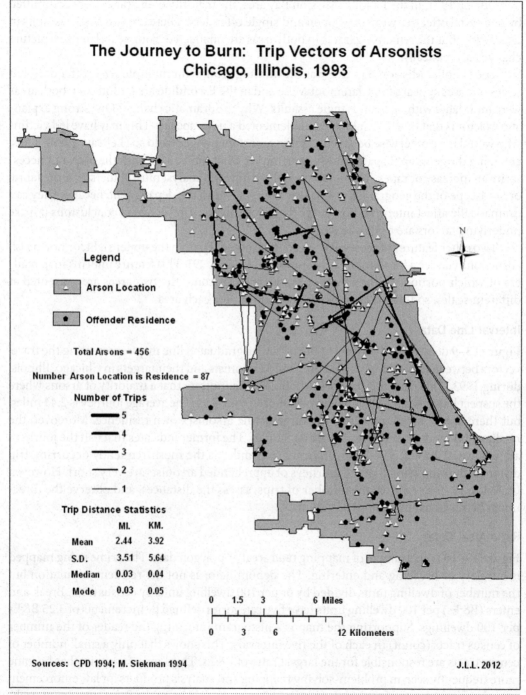

Figure 13-9 Interval Line Data

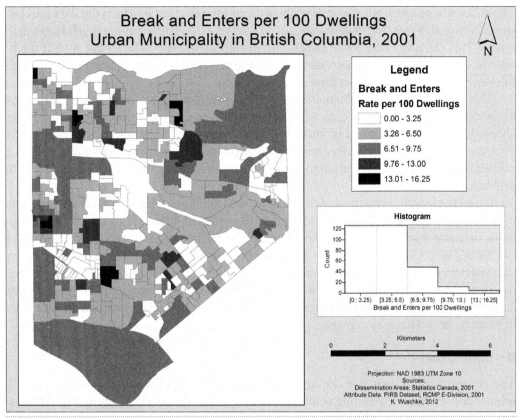

Figure 13–10 Ratio Area Data

must be intimate with their data and not be afraid to get out of their offices from time to time to start collecting data such as number of dwelling units, number of parking spaces, and other counts by various polygon boundaries. At times analysts will find these data have already been collected by their planning or engineering departments, or perhaps by the county association of governments. We can also sometimes work slowly but surely with aerial photos to find counts of parking spaces and other data we can use for calculating rates.

■ Comparing Two Maps and Classifications

The examples of ordinal areal data and ratio areal data maps (Figures 13–7 and 13–10) use the same data about B&Es per 100 dwellings. Yet, if you compare the two maps, it is highly likely that you can have two different impressions of the risk of breaking and entering in the anonymous municipality. Figure 13–7 (using quintiles) creates an image leading one to believe there are many contiguous census tracts with high crime or burglary. Yet, Figure 13–10 projects an image of a few, very small, and dispersed high crime tracts. Both maps are true!

The difference results from the scale of the data and the manner in which the data are classified. Notice also that the polygons are not all the same size, and many are much larger than others. This can also cause some issues with displaying of ratio data, so the analyst might want to edit this layer, or even create a new polygon layer where the polygons are closer to the same size for ratio symbolization or classification.

This dilemma is more problematic with interval–ratio data because there are many ways to classify and categorize these data, which will depict varying images of a problem like crime, although they all will be true. The analyst must also know that although maps are extremely important to sharing knowledge, additional charts, graphs, and reports will probably be needed to give enough information to the audience to make sure they are attacking the right problem.

Given the length limitations of this chapter, this manner of data classification resulting in perceived images of a problem is best left to the works of others. The point is that in thematic or crime mapping there are very few final, deterministic results. The map we make can always be countered by another map using the same data classified in a different way (see Harries, 1999, pp. 51-56; Krygier & Wood, 2005, pp. 214-226; Monmonier, 1996). It is the job of the analyst to make sure that he or she looks at the problem from many viewpoints and presents the data and associated materials that give the best chance of success in support of strategic or tactical action plans.

■ Conclusion

This chapter has just scratched the surface of the basics of cartography. There are three recommended works for expanding your map-making skills. The first is *Mapping It Out: Expository Cartography for the Humanities and Social Sciences* by Mark Monmonier (1993). This work contains all the basics of cartography and more. This is not a crime-mapping book but one discussing and illustrating all the principles of designing, classifying, and constructing maps in general.

The second work is *Making Maps: A Visual Guide to Map Design for GIS* by John Krygier and Denis Wood (2005). This also is not a crime-mapping book, and despite having GIS in its title the book is not customized for any particular brand. This book is for the novice GIS data jockey who has very limited map-making skills. This book, like the previous one, contains all the basics and more.

The third recommendation is *Mapping Crime: Principle and Practice* by Keith D. Harries (1999). Obviously, the title indicates this is a crime-mapping book. This work includes the basics of cartography, design issues in crime mapping, the functions of different types of maps, and many examples of color crime maps depicting different problems from different jurisdictions. Not only is this work very good—it is free! One can download it from the National Criminal Justice Reference Service.

There is a fourth work that I recommended that pertains to the issue of map classifications and varying interpretations by map users. This is another work by Mark Monmonier (1996) titled, *How to Lie with Maps* (2nd ed.). The book starts with an introduction to maps and the basics of cartography. The author then develops his point that maps are actually little white lies, simply because some features on a map are highlighted at the expense of others. Then the author reveals how blunders in map construction have mislead consumers and how maps have been intentionally constructed to advertise, deceive, misinform, seduce, and misdirect. Familiarity with this work should help one become a more informed and more critical map maker and user.

As a crime analyst you will have a large degree of freedom with the data you collect and use. The more you know your data, the landscape of the geography you are responsible for, and the methods and processes involved in classifying data, the better equipped you will be to make maps that speak to the issues within your department. Your task is to provide maps that provide actionable knowledge through a thorough understanding of nominal, ordinal, interval, and ratio data symbolization; statistics; proper thematic design; and cartographic principles. All of this sounds like a huge burden on the analyst's shoulders, doesn't it? The idea is to be the analyst you've been hired to be and not a perfectionist. Your job is to make conclusions and provide research and products that lead your personnel to the right strategic and tactical conclusions that help to reduce or control crime within your jurisdiction by highlighting problem areas with maps. Understanding criminological theory, how to work with data to provide the most reasonable representation of knowledge that leads but does not mislead, and how to be thorough without worrying about perfection when doing analysis is what makes you an "analyst" and not just an employee.

Perhaps many of you will not go on to become crime analysts or mappers of any kind. Nevertheless, you should know, intuitively, there are four features that each crime map should have: a title, a legend, a scale bar, and a north arrow. Each map should also have good thematic design, be visually appealing, tell the story you need it to tell, be mindful of the audience, and be complete in the understanding of the data and the geographic landscape being analyzed. Although we may not wish to be a cartographer tomorrow, we do want to be efficient and thorough.

■ Chapter Glossary

Cartography   This is the art and science of map making and the learned skill of making maps that speak to the issues, correctly portrays the Earth's physical features on a 2D map, and informs the reader.

Choropleth map   A map made by aggregating data to polygons and then shading them in with a range of color indicating the count, density, or rate of the data being analyzed. It is also called a shaded grid map and can represent counts or densities (interval or ratio).

Crime rate   This is a calculation using crime data and typically population to show density or rate of crimes per 100,000 population as in UCR analysis. It could also represent any rate such as burglaries from vehicle per parking spaces throughout a city for instance.

Interval   A statistical term that represents data that is a value from – infinity to + infinity; however, there are finite values associated with it. Examples would be counts of crime within a patrol division, for instance. You cannot have one-half of a crime.

Legend   The key text or graphics on the map that inform the user as to the definition, ranges, and descriptions of the various figures, shapes, colors, and hues the cartographer displays on a map.

Nominal   A statistical term that represents data that can be represented by categories and types of legends, including data such as "City Park," Community Park," and the like.

North arrow   A graphic or text on the map that denotes where north is on the surface of the area with respect to that portion of it that the map displays.

Ordinal   A statistical term that represents data that are nominal but have an order to them. On a map this might be data such as "high" versus "low." Ordinal data cannot be turned into ratio or interval data, but could be collapsed into interval data through aggregation.

Ratio   A statistical term that represents the best kind of data to have that can be any number from − infinity to + infinity and is most often displayed as a quantities classification schema in ArcMap. This is good data to have because you can collapse it into any of the other three categories of data through aggregation. This is most often displayed as a decimal value where there is no absolute value and would be what a kernel density map is often using.

Scale   This is the concept of distance from the Earth's surface on your map as if you were in a spaceship or flying a helicopter over the study area. Related to whether you are at large scale (helicopter) or small scale (spaceship), it also involves the degree of accuracy associated with your data. At small scale a shapefile's features might be very detailed, but at a larger scale the coves and eddies along an oceanfront may be obscured.

Thematic map   The process by which the map maker displays points, lines, polygons, and raster data that represent political or social variables that explain, describe, or inform the reader through proper graphical representation of qualitative and quantitative data.

Title   The key text on a map, usually at the top or a prominent place, which describes the content and primary purpose of the map and may also contain the temporal range of the data depicted on the map.

■ Questions for Review

1. What types of map classifications can you use with interval or ratio data?
2. What are the limitations when using nominal or ordinal data in classifying data?
3. What is the difference between nominal and ordinal data?
4. When are ratio data better to use for making a map layer than ordinal data?
5. Why is scale so important when making maps?

■ Recommended Reading

Harries, K. D. (1999). *Mapping crime: Principle and practice*. Washington, DC: U.S. Department of Justice. Retrieved from www.ncjrs.gov/html/nij/mapping/pdf.html.

Krygier, J. & Wood, D. (2005). *Making maps: A visual guide to map design for GIS*. New York: The Guilford Press.

Monmonier, M. (1993). *Mapping it out: Expository cartography for the humanities and social sciences*. Chicago: University of Chicago Press.

■ References

Dent, B. D. (1996). *Cartography: Thematic map design* (4th ed.). Dubuque, IA: Wm. C. Brown Publishers.

Federal Bureau of Investigation (FBI). (2010). *Crime in the United States*. Retrieved from www.fbi.gov/about-us/cjis/ucr/crime-in-the-u.s/2010/crime-in-the-u.s.-2010/tables/10tbl04.xls.

Griffith, D. A., & Amrhein, C. G. (1991). *Statistical analysis for geographers*. Englewood Cliffs, NJ: Prentice-Hall.

Harries, K. D. (1999). *Mapping crime: Principle and practice*. Washington, DC: U.S. Department of Justice. Retrieved from www.ncjrs.gov/html/nij/mapping/pdf.html.

Krygier, J., & Wood, D. (2005). *Making maps: A visual guide to map design for GIS*. New York: The Guilford Press.

LeBeau, J. L. (1985). Some problems with measuring and describing rape presented by the serial offender. *Justice Quarterly, 2,* 385–398.

LeBeau, J. L. (1988). Statute revision and the reporting of rape. *Sociology and Social Research, 75,* 201–207.

Monmonier, M. (1993). *Mapping it out: Expository cartography for the humanities and social sciences*. Chicago: University of Chicago Press.

Monmonier, M. (1996). *How to lie with maps* (2nd ed.). Chicago: University of Chicago Press.

Future Issues in Crime Mapping

This chapter provides a brief discussion of future issues in crime mapping. These issues include technological opportunities and challenges, the future of crime mapping research and education, implementation issues, and issues related to ethics and privacy. After studying this chapter, you should be able to:

- Identify some future opportunities and challenges facing the field of crime mapping.
- Identify future directions for crime-mapping research, technology, and education.

▶ Key Terms

Epidemiological Research	Hashtag	Tweet
	Modus Operandi	

■ Introduction

This introductory text discusses several issues related to crime analysis and crime mapping: the theoretical underpinnings of the spatial context of crime, data available to crime analysts and the limitations to the use of these data in crime analysis and the creation of crime maps, the relevant research on geographic information systems (GIS) applications in law enforcement, and an introduction to statistics as well as the types of analyses crime analysts perform on a regular basis. This chapter provides a brief examination of the academic, practical, and technological issues that crime analysts will potentially face in the coming years.

■ General Topics

In the world of GIS there are very few sources for data that remain constant over time. As the use of GIS increases in many fields, including crime analysis, there are always new data sources that will be added or modified to provide more knowledge to decision makers. Remember that with GIS, we want to think along the lines of the business intelligence field where data become information and information becomes actionable knowledge. In the future, it may not be enough to know where all the crimes happened; we will need to know (and document) why they happened and what the root causes of crime really are. Obviously, having a better understanding of crime so that we can prevent it (or at least have a good idea where it is emerging so that we can prepare our response) is the larger goal here. There are many sociological theories, psychological theories, and criminological theories of why crime happens, but these are usually very general to crime and society as a whole rather than to individual geographic groups. Often placed into the category of predictive analytics, as crime mapping progresses, we will continue to learn how to use tools from other fields of analytical study and apply them to crime analysis. Some of the lessons learned by biologists who track animals in the wild may have some application with tracking suspects in criminal offenses; we could learn in the future that crime evolves much like a communicable disease and that **epidemiological research** or methods may have some use within the crime analysis field. For example, using analytic software from the field of medical geography, April Zeoli, a researcher in public health, and several of her colleagues from Michigan State University analyzed murder data from Newark, NJ over the span of 26 years. They found that murder spreads in a predictable manner to susceptible groups (in this case, clustering in the inner city and spreading in a southwest direction toward poor and minority communities; Science 2.0, 2012). There are also current predictive policing projects that are using mathematical methods derived from prediction of earthquakes (Dickinson, 2011). Other related fields, such as anthropology, archaeology, biology, psychics, and geology, may provide answers to questions we don't know how to answer with today's GIS crime-fighting tools. In addition, as we explore new methods and new sets of data, we'll be able to add more information behind those points, lines, and polygons. For example, a city may have been drawing sewer and water lines all along in their enterprise GIS, with attributes such as length, material, and build date. As they progress with GIS, they find that they can also do flow analyses but need to add the elevation and material flow values to the pipe segments in the GIS data so that they can do modeling to find out what happens if they add a T branch at a certain juncture. With crime analysis, as we add new elements of information, such as **modus operandi** (MO) data to GIS points of where and when a crime occurred, we can start using the data to find trends, patterns, series, and clusters of crime by type and MO characteristics more easily. Later, we may want to include U.S. Census Bureau data, zoning data, and other elements we do not always use in crime analysis but eventually find might assist in our analysis or trend detection. Using risk terrain modeling (www.rutgerscps.org/rtm/) to review areas that have the highest risk of crime and then digging into why they are highest risk may lead to better risk factor analysis that can further isolate areas that have the highest risk of crime, and thus, make it a better predictive model. This may lead to the desire for additional data from the health department and other agencies concerning welfare programs and teenage pregnancy levels in specific sections with high crime. At some point we may even find out that historical soil contamination from pesticides in certain areas that are now downtown actually may have some causal effect on crime. There is no end to the data we will need when we know how to use the data we already have.

As with any technology implementation, technology itself changes over time, sometimes dramatically. Think about the fact that just a few decades ago a 20-megabyte hard drive for a new computer would be considered huge. Now, the storage capacity of your simple desktop PC has more capability than a whole bank of servers that filled an entire basement of a building not so long ago. Mobile devices (smart phones, tablets, etc.) have now more capability and storage than laptop computers had a few years ago. We will see more and more of our maps being used in patrol cars and other active enforcement activities. This will lead to questions concerning the accuracy of the data for some places that may have been neglected during the data-creation phase or are older than some of the other data. We will find that exact accuracy may become much more important than it is now as courts begin to use GIS analysis to convict persons charged with crimes (e.g., Megan's Law and others, which require suspects to adhere to certain distance requirements from something). Increasing legal issues will probably accompany the use of these new datasets by police as we weigh the rights of the individual with the protection and safety of our society. Presentation devices will change as they already have in the past few years within the court environment. A short time ago, bringing a PC and a movie into the courtroom was somewhat frowned upon, but now, in some modern-day courtrooms, video conferencing and electronic media are status quo.

■ Education and Crime Mapping

The academic future of crime mapping looks very promising. More and more colleges across the country are offering courses that are focused on GIS in law enforcement. In a survey of 26 police agencies across the country, Paynich, Cooke, and Mathews (2007) found that one of the frequent complaints about hiring new crime analysts was that the recruits lacked hands-on experience and/or training. In addition, the new recruits were either very knowledgeable about crime or criminal justice but had very little background in statistics or crime analysis and crime mapping computer applications or vice versa. One respondent stated in the survey, "I'd add in geographic profiling, psychology, and criminology courses. I think that you need to have a working knowledge of criminology and especially . . . how the process flows (from dispatch to the courts). Not that this makes mapping easier, but you can't work in a vacuum." Another respondent observed, "There are plenty of skilled GIS people out there, but very few understand crime data. They often make maps that are misleading and are not really actionable for the guys on the street."

The number of college courses about GIS applications in law enforcement has grown, and the use of crime mapping by law enforcement also continues to grow. The use of crime mapping by law enforcement agencies increased from 14.5% in 2000 to 17.9% in 2003 (Chamard, 2006). In addition, if the use of GIS by smaller agencies is to increase, more widely available training is needed in the academic realm. Smaller departments, for example, are much more likely to discontinue the use of crime mapping. This discontinuance is strongly related to staffing in technical support (Chamard, 2003). In the future, this may lead to new and simpler ways to provide mapping technology to these smaller agencies that do not have staff on hand to develop GIS for their agency. Google Earth and other similar applications seem to be on the forefront of offering such services to smaller agencies without the technical staff to develop dedicated GIS functionality, for example. Private vendors such as the Omega Group offer police departments a line of products that allow officers to simply and easily access crime reports within a few short clicks on a computer or even mobile device. There still needs to be some control over all of these methods of getting maps into the hands of those who need them; without control over the data and the output forms of that data, the usefulness will be limited.

■ Crime-Mapping Research

The future of crime-mapping-related research is also promising. The largest national criminal-justice-related organizations, the Academy of Criminal Justice Sciences (ACJS) and the American Society of Criminology (ASC), both host panels focused specifically on GIS applications in criminal justice at their annual meetings. In addition, the National Institute of Justice (NIJ) has held 11 national research conferences on crime mapping as of October 2011. Other associations, such as the International Association of Crime Analysts (IACA), also hold annual conferences with special panels and presentations on crime-mapping research. There are also many local crime analysis associations that routinely provide training on aspects of GIS with a crime-analysis focus, and several private vendors specialize in various forms of GIS training outside of the academic environment to fulfill training needs.

Many law enforcement agencies also have internship opportunities with the crime analysis and GIS departments that allow a student to become more knowledgeable through on-the-job training. The duties may vary depending on the assignment and can include such things as address verifications, digitizing, reading reports, and doing weekly reports and other analyses to help free up city personnel for other duties. These programs are available in many cities across the country and browsing the Internet and the University's website often reveals them (for example, http://chandlerpd.com/stats/internship/, http://alexandriava.gov/police/info/default.aspx?id=9384, and www.scottsdaleaz.gov/Police/about/adminbureau/Crime_Analysis/CAU_Internship_Info).

In addition to conferences, several publications have emerged in recent years that are dedicated solely to GIS applications in criminal justice. ESRI, for example, publishes *Public Safety Log: GIS for Public Safety*. A fairly recent issue of ESRI's *ArcNews* contained several articles focused on GIS in law enforcement and highlighted how crime mapping and analysis can improve the effectiveness and efficiency of a department. For example, one article discussed how the United States Postal Service (USPS) utilizes GIS to track the purchase and redemption of money orders (a common tool for criminals to launder money because individuals can purchase money orders under $3000 without providing identification). These money orders then can be redeemed anywhere in the United States.

> The department has embraced the use of GIS technology to more effectively detect and in some cases deter crime. GIS maps show where suspicious activities may be occurring and link data on individuals, transactions, and/or offices to reveal potential criminal patterns. Modern mapping and spatial analysis also help USPS managers make sense of extensive transactional databases and millions of bits of data to ensure they are meeting regulatory compliance (ESRI, 2008, p. 33).

Essentially, post offices and individuals with an unusually high number of suspicious money order transactions can be flagged and investigated. The USPS article is a prime example of many other crime-mapping-related pieces that are being published in academic and trade journals. *Geography and Public Safety* (put forth by the NIJ, Mapping and Analysis for Public Safety [MAPS], and the Office of Community-Oriented Policing Services [COPS]) is another recently established news bulletin that is dedicated to crime-mapping-related issues. In this publication, readers can find discussions of theory and practice related to crime mapping as well as helpful tips for crime analysts.

■ Geographic Profiling and Forecasting Crime

In 1999, Harries predicted that geographic profiling and crime forecasting methodologies would continue to evolve and gain more support in the future. The research and literature that has been reviewed throughout this text indicates that Harries' prediction was correct. In geographic profiling, a number of programs, both free and for purchase, are available to help analysts make predictions about offender decision making in efforts to arrest serial offenders. In forecasting crime, analysts are developing models that include related crimes to identify emerging hotspots (for example, examining robbery, assault, and burglary to identify an emerging drug hotspot; Olligschlaeger, 2003).

With this increase in the availability of training and software to perform such analyses, we are also seeing more analysts across the country using such software tools. There is still much disagreement about what works best, when and why it works, and what related skills are needed to make the analysis products useful to the law enforcement officials who are doing the investigations. In many cases and inside many police agencies, these predictions and analyses are still met with skepticism among the investigation personnel, but they are gaining credibility as time goes on and more analysts use these techniques effectively. Using these tools is almost a change in social perception and policies more than just a technological issue.

The IACA has spearheaded several white papers that outline recommendations for GIS requirements for police departments, education suggestions for colleges and universities, and even crime pattern definitions for tactical analysis. Although at the time of this writing only three papers are available through IACA, by the time you read these words, there may be even more. The goal is to provide current and future analysts and the organizations that train and/or employ them with the information they need to ensure the training and tools are of high quality.

■ Technology

Technological advances since about 2000 have provided many opportunities in crime mapping. High-resolution and three-dimensional (3-D) applications have enabled analysts to make maps of buildings, such as apartment buildings or correctional institutions, which illustrate problem areas within these buildings. The use of global positioning systems (GPS) in police cruisers allows for enormous potential in data collection and in producing real time maps for administrators and patrol officers alike. We are already seeing that GPS, photography, and 3-D views can be extended out from the officer's vehicle to handheld devices (such as smart phones) that the officer can carry right to the crime scene. Several departments, utilizing smart phones, provide real-time maps and information to officers on the street to aid them in investigations, pursuits, and other policing activities. A pilot study in Minneapolis is using GPS technology to alert officers and victims when domestic violence offenders are within a given range of their victims. In this study, offenders wear a GPS-equipped anklet and victims carry around a small device that detect when the two are within a predetermined range of one another. At that time, the device alerts both the victim and police dispatch (Powell, 2012). In addition, it is conceivable that in the not too distant future we may see small and accurate GPS devices that can be incorporated on an officer's uniform, or perhaps embedded in the new personal video cameras we are seeing officers carrying now, that can provide up-to-date locational data on an officer whether he is in his car or not.

Many aerial photography companies now do more frequent updates for locations with high growth, so the aerial photos are increasing in detail and accuracy over time as well. There are also some more widely available satellite images that show other elements such as elevation, weather, and many other types of data.

Automated programs, such as the one that Hicks (2007) designed in Minneapolis, allows for maps and analysis to be completed on a routine basis, saving valuable time and resources. Further research and development in geocoding through entity-named extraction is also on the horizon. Many analysts across the country are starting to develop multilevel geocoding processes to increase the accuracy of the points they analyze. An example is to use parcel addresses as the first pass to geocode calls for service data, then use a verified point address file as a second pass, and finally use the street centerline file to geocode the remaining rows of data that did not geocode in the first two passes. With each run through of the data, the addresses that do not match at one level match at the next, so your overall data is more accurate in the long run.

Commercial applications, such as Google Street View, which is a feature of Google Maps and Google Earth, allow the user to see a 360-degree panoramic, street-level view of selected cities at ground level. Launched in May 2007, Google Street view included only five American cities, but it has since expanded and includes many more U.S. cities and locations in France, Italy, Australia, and Japan. Useful in both the practical and academic realms, Google Street View provides enormous detail and power in crime mapping. Many crime analysis product vendors are making use of this functionality to deliver maps in a new way to law enforcement agencies that purchase their products.

Google is also currently developing "Google Goggles," set to be for sale on the private market as early as 2013. Google is currently testing prototypes of the glasses that are installed with GPS, a built-in camera, and the ability to perform email and Internet searches from the surface of the glasses: "The wraparound glasses feature a miniature display that sits above one eye, allowing users to surf the internet, make video calls, listen to music and update the diary without lifting a finger" (Waugh, 2012). The possibilities of these high-tech glasses relative to law enforcement are endless. Already, agencies are exploring the uses of iPhones and other smart devices for relaying and providing real-time information to police about calls for service, locations of known offenders, and more.

Bing Maps (www.bing.com/maps/) has several useful map apps that crime analysts can utilize. Twitter Maps, for example, allows anyone to zoom in on any location in the world and view public tweets that posted within the last 30 days. You can also query **tweets** based on **hashtags**, locations, or keyword. Bing Maps also has a heat map application that allows users to upload data to produce a publishable-quality heat map of anything they desire. The possibilities for these and many other applications for crime analysts are virtually endless and very exciting.

■ Other Issues

When it comes down to it, there are very few limitations to what can happen in the future with GIS. We may find that aerial photos, closed circuit television (CCTV), and 3-D modeling become so advanced that when a call comes out of a robbery, the officer can simply hit a few buttons on his vehicle computer (or handheld device, or computerized glasses), and a map will pop up that shows the quickest way to get to the scene and where all his backup units will come from. With another click of a button (or touch of a screen, or voice command), he will be able to see CCTV images of the robbery scene showing the suspects running behind a building and getting into a white vehicle; the officer will then be able to tag that vehicle electronically while he is responding. CCTV and aerial or satellite images will track the tagged vehicle, and information will be sent directly to all the units that are responding. If the suspects take hostages, a 3-D model of the buildings and access points around the crime scene will pop up to allow SWAT units to position themselves the most advantageously through line-of-site analysis and other tools right from their vehicles on the way to the scene or at the scene itself. Although this may sound somewhat like science fiction or something you might see in a movie, some of these applications of GIS are already available but not yet widely used. We may also see in the near future crime analysis units coming to the scene of major crimes with a vehicle that is equipped with everything analysts have at their desks back at the office. The units will assist and run intelligence and investigative analyses for the on-scene detectives to aid the investigation in real time. This type of crime analysis activity is already happening in Riverside, California.

While crime maps are wonderful tools for crime analysts, and the future holds even more promise for new ways of using this awesome tool, there are still unresolved issues related to ethics and privacy. Modern technology allows for ease in accessing and analyzing large quantities of data. As discussed earlier in this text, if these data (in raw or map form) fall into the wrong hands, they can be used to discriminate against people or areas (such as in the process of redlining). Chicago, for example, currently has its crime data (since 2001) available for the public to download or map online (https://data.cityofchicago.org/). This is an amazing opportunity for academics and crime analysts to be able to analyze big city crime problems over a long time span. It is also, however, an opportunity for others to profit off of the dissemination of information that could potentially negatively impact certain communities. The future will determine whether or not our fears in this regard are warranted. Some municipal departments may also have infrastructure data about streets, public buildings, schools, and other data that could potentially be used by terrorists and thus many ethical and legal discussions have popped up all across the country weighing the need for ease of access to these kind of data with the potential for terrorist attacks.

With the advent of new data-sharing agreements among federal, state, county, and local law enforcement that are either happening now or on the horizon for many states, there will be ownership and need-to-know issues with some of the massive quantity of law enforcement data that are currently or soon will become available. The analyst must be able to be discrete and keep focused on helping the investigation and not hinder the investigation through information overload. GIS enables us to access a lot of data, and sometimes we can manipulate that data enough to give the end users just the right amount of information, because too much information can bury what they really need to know. That is why the analyst must analyze the data and information available and produce maps and other products that provide knowledge that can be acted upon rather than just muddy the playing field.

In addition, crime analysts need to find an appropriate balance between an individual's right to privacy and the public's right to information. Agencies must also continue to address barriers to implementing crime mapping in their agencies, including (but not limited to) money, training, social changes within the department, and staffing.

■ Conclusion

The future holds much promise for crime mapping and analysis. This is an incredibly exciting time to become a crime analyst. However, with the opportunities that come with technological advances comes great responsibility. Using the foundational knowledge contained in this text, it is up to you to ensure your analyses are completed competently, ethically, and with the intent to make an impact in preventing, reducing, or solving crime problems. Following best practices in data collection, storage, and statistical analysis will help you toward that end. In addition, we all need to become more open to new analytical methods and be persistent in applying new technology to solve the age-old problem of crime. Throwing technology at a problem just because it might seem cool may be fun, but without the theory and best practices behind that technological implementation, the cards are against you and it may fail.

■ Chapter Glossary

Epidemiological research   The systematic and scientific study of health problems.

Hashtag   A word in social media messages that is preceded by the hash mark (#) that indicates a topical/keyword that facilitates searching for a particular topic or conversation thread for interested users.

Modus operandi   A method or way of doing something. In crime research, this refers to the methods a criminal employs to commit a criminal act. This can be the clothing they wear, statements they make, the kind of weapon or tool used, or the items they steal.

Tweet   A short message that is posted on the Twitter online message service. It can be used as a noun or a verb.

■ Review Questions

1. What are some future challenges facing the field of crime mapping relative to data collection and dissemination?
2. What other fields of study (including their tools) can we use to study crime?
3. Explore some of the online resources contained in this chapter. Choose your favorite and provide a brief description of this resource and how it might add to the study or practice of crime analysis.

■ Online Resources

Bing Maps: www.bing.com/maps/

Esri Mobile Mapping Information: www.esri.com/software/arcgis/arcgismobile/

Google Earth: www.google.com/earth/index.html

The International Association of Crime Analysts: http://iaca.net/

The Omega Group (mobile mapping information): www.crimemapping.com/mobile/app.aspx

SpotCrime for I-Devices: www.apple.com/webapps/travel/spotcrimeknowyourneighborhood_spotcrime.html

■ Recommended Reading

Boba, R. (2008). A crime mapping technique for assessing vulnerable targets for terrorism in local communities. In S. Chainey & L. Tompson (Eds.), *Crime mapping case studies: Practice and research* (pp. 143–151). Hoboken, NJ: Wiley.

Chainey, S., & Tompson, L. (Eds.). (2008). *Crime mapping case studies: Practice and research.* Hoboken, NJ: Wiley.

Groff, E. (2008). Simulating crime to inform theory and practice. In S. Chainey & L. Tompson (Eds.), *Crime mapping case studies: Practice and research* (pp. 133–142). Hoboken, NJ: Wiley.

Lersch, K., & Hart, T. (2011). *Space, time, and crime* (3rd ed.). Durham, NC: Carolina Academic Press.

Monmonier, M. (1991). *How to lie with maps.* Chicago: University of Chicago Press.

Olligschlaeger, A. M. (1997). Artificial neural networks and crime mapping. In D. Weisburd & T. McEwen (Eds.), *Crime mapping and crime prevention* (pp. 313–347). Monsey, NY: Criminal Justice Press.

Paulsen, D., & Robinson, M. (2004). *Spatial aspects of crime: Theory and practice.* Upper Saddle River, NJ: Pearson.

Ratcliffe, J. (2002). Damned if you don't, damned if you do: Crime mapping and its implications in the real world. *Policing and Society: An International Journal of Research and Policy, 12*(3), 211–225.

Sorensen, S. L. (1997). SMART mapping for law enforcement settings: Integrating GIS and GPS for dynamic, near-real time applications and analysis. In D. Weisburd & T. McEwen (Eds.), *Crime mapping and crime prevention* (pp. 349–378). Monsey, NY: Criminal Justice Press.

■ References

Chamard, S. E. (2003). Innovation-diffusion networks and the adoption and discontinuance of computerized crime mapping by municipal police departments in New Jersey. PhD Dissertation, Rutgers University, New Brunswick, NJ.

Chamard, S. E. (2006). The history of crime mapping and its use by American police departments. *Alaska Justice Forum, 23*(3), 1, 4–8.

Dickinson, B. (2011). Police forecast crimes using earthquake prediction models. Retrieved from www.smartplanet.com/blog/science-scope/police-forecast-crimes-using-earthquake-prediction-models/9840.

ESRI. (2008, Summer). USPS fights crime with GIS: GIS pinpoints potential money laundering. *ArcNews, 30*(2), 1, 33.

Harries, K. D. (1999). *Crime mapping: Principle and practice.* Washington, DC: U.S. Department of Justice Programs.

Hicks, D. (2007). *Spatial analysis of probationer contacts and automated email alerts.* National Institute of Justice Workshop. Washington, DC: U.S. Department of Justice Programs.

Olligschlaeger, A. (2003). Future directions in crime mapping. In M. R. Leipnik & D. P. Albert (Eds.), *GIS in law enforcement: Implementation issues and case studies* (pp. 103–109). New York: Taylor & Francis.

Paynich, R., Cooke, P., & Mathews, C. (2007). *Developing standards and curriculum for GIS in law enforcement.* Presentation at 9th NIJ Crime Mapping Conference, Pittsburgh, PA.

Powell, J. (2012, November 1). Ramsey County project will use GPS on stalkers. *Star Tribune.* Retrieved from www.startribune.com/local/east/176700931.html.

Science 2.0. (2012, November 29). Like infectious disease, homocide spreads throughout a city. Retrieved from www.science20.com/news_articles/infectious_disease_homocide_spreads_throughout_city-97571.

Waugh, R. (2012). "They're a lot further along than people imagine": Google co-founder reveals that hi-tech Project Glass techno-goggles could be on sale next year. Retrieved from www.dailymail.co.uk/sciencetech/article-2152140/Googles-Sergei-Brin-reveals-Project-Glass-techno-goggles-sale-2013.html.

Microsoft Excel: A Generic Primer for Crime Analysis

This appendix is a tutorial for using Microsoft Excel 2010 and earlier (PC version). The majority of these functions will also work in Excel 2007; however, the location of the menus, buttons, and functions may be in a slightly different place on the ribbon menu that is part of Excel 2007. This tutorial covers basic Excel skills that the analyst may need on a daily basis and allows the student to learn more about Excel through practical exercises. *(Note: The majority of these functions will also work on the MAC version of Excel, however they may be found in different places than in the PC versions.)* All of the files referenced in this appendix will be located in the CIA/Exercises/Excel folder in the directory where the data was installed (typically the C:\drive). Your educational institution, employer, or teacher may have installed these files on another drive name, so follow their directions to find the data and the CIA folder.

■ Introduction

Crime analysts often need a variety of software tools to create a final analysis product. One of the most widely used tools for day-to-day analysis by analysts across the United States is the Microsoft Office suite of products. Excel probably tops the analysts' most wanted list in any crime analysis unit in the country and is used in a variety of ways. Analysts can collect intelligence information on persons, do analytical studies of crime phenomena, or simply use it to balance their checkbooks. One obvious use for Excel is to create administrative, strategic, or tactical analytical products and bulletins. Practicing analysts could use Excel for creating the bulletin itself or they could use it to clean and prepare their data, make calculations, and then cut and paste that information into Microsoft Word or other applications.

This tutorial does not intend to suggest what an analyst should use. It is only a how-to manual for Excel that contains some of the lessons and processes we have learned over the past 15 years or so. There are often many other ways of doing the same things as shown in this tutorial, and it is not intended to be a definitive source about Excel.

This tutorial is divided up into sections that cover specific topics and examples in Excel, and the included Excel exercises also follow the section numbers. You may also find the following websites to be useful for Excel hints and tricks:

- www.ce.memphis.edu/1112/excel/xlstart.htm
- http://spreadsheetpage.com/

- www.ozgrid.com/Excel/
- www.xlhelp.com/Excel/help.htm
- www.meadinkent.co.uk/excel.htm
- http://homepage.ntlworld.com/noneley/
- www.addictivetips.com/windows-tips/office-excel-2010-tutorial-pivot-tables/
- http://office.microsoft.com/en-us/excel/
- http://office.microsoft.com/en-us/excel-help/
- http://en.wikipedia.org/wiki/Microsoft_Office_2010

■ Section 1

Introduction to Excel and Some General Information

When you first open Excel, the spreadsheet application should look something like **Figure A1–1**. Your menu bars and items may be slightly different depending on who has used your computer last and how they left Excel, but generally, this should be the way it looks. If you are using Excel for Windows XP or Windows 7, you might see some minor changes or functionality as well. In Windows XP and Excel 2007, you will also see a window to the right that shows some shortcuts for using basic Excel functions and creating new spreadsheets. We typically close this window because it takes up working space, but that is up to you.

We will not spend a great deal of time showing you the Excel interface, as we assume you are already familiar with it to some degree. We will point out a few things so we can find them easily later.

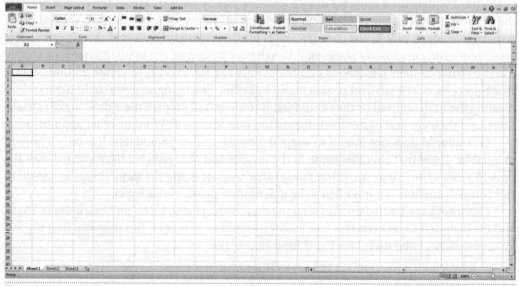

Figure A1–1

Screenshot used with permission from Microsoft.

The **Data** menu provides you with several functions, such as retrieving data from an external source, removing duplicates, and sorting.

The **Home** menu allows you to format text and cells as well as conditional formatting and find functions.

The **File** menu can be used to find one of the most useful add-ins in Excel, the Analysis Toolpak (for Excel 2007, please check the **Help** menu for how to turn on the Analysis Toolpak). This set of tools adds several new statistical functions for the user and enables you to do some slightly more advanced work. To enable the Analysis Toolpak add-in using Excel 2010, follow these steps:

1. Click on the **File** menu.
2. In the **File** menu, select **Options**.
3. In the popup dialog, click **Add-Ins**.
4. Click on the Analysis Toolpak.
   a. There is also an Analysis Toolpak—VBA, if you are going to do programming with these functions.
5. At the bottom where it reads, "Manage," click the GO button.
6. In the new popup window, click the checkbox next to Analysis Toolpak to turn it on.
7. To find the added functions, click on the **Data** menu and then look to the far right for "Data Analysis."
8. Double click Data Analysis to bring up the Toolpak add-in additional functions:
   a. Histograms
   b. Descriptive statistics
   c. Regression, and more…

General Information

Excel uses some odd terms at times to describe differences in various things you may see on the screen. For example, the entire Excel application, whether you are using one or more worksheets, is called a *workbook*. If you close Excel and it asks if you want to save your work, you are saving an Excel workbook. At the bottom of the Excel application window, you will see one or more tabs with wording such as Sheet1, Sheet2, etc. Figure A1–1 has three tabs in the workbook, and they are labeled Sheet1, Sheet2, and Sheet3. You can create several of these individual sheets, and Excel refers to them as worksheets. Think of an Excel file as a book that contains multiple pages called sheets.

Within each sheet, the working surface is separated into cells. Each cell is represented by the gray squares (gridlines) on the worksheet surface. These gridlines can be turned on and off so you do not see them when viewing a worksheet, but typically we want them there to help us organize our projects. These gridlines are really only for the user, and unless you set Excel to print them, they will not show up on the printed page. If you want the gridlines to be print-able, they are called *borders* (rather than "printable gridlines," which might be what you would intuit). The width, line color, and style of the borders can be changed for each cell, or a group of cells, by selecting the cells you want to change and then pressing CTRL+1, or you can change them by selecting **Format**, then Cells from the **Home** menu bar. The background color, text color, and a variety of other things can be changed for each individual cell, or groups of cells, to make the final product more eye-catching and appealing. You can practice this whenever you want to, and any basic Excel course should have introduced you to these items.

Another useful tip is to know what Excel Help screens mean when they indicate that you can make *relative cell references*, or *absolute cell references*, in a worksheet. Absolute cell references just means that we only want to use that one cell in every place a formula can be found using that cell reference. For instance, let's say you want to create a percentage for three different rows of data. The sum of these three rows is the cell we wish to have absolute reference to. So, assume we have data in cell A1, A2, and A3, and the sum of these cells is in cell A4. In cell B2, we want to calculate the percentage of A1/A4. Now we could just type that in and be done, then type in A2/A4 in the next, and so on. However, we want each cell to absolutely reference A4 and as we drag the formula down from B2 we want it to correctly calculate for the other cells. So we absolutely reference A4 as "$A$4" in the formula. The relative cell reference will be A2 and the absolute cell reference will be $A$4 in the following formula—"A2/$A$4." If we now drag this formula down to the other cells, it will reference the cell on the left and change as we drag it down to A2 and A3, but the absolute cell reference will stay the same (see example 1 in CIA\Exercises\Excel folder). As a further explanation, if cell A1 were to contain the value of 31, and we wanted to add it to cell B1, which has a value of 40, we would want to enter a formula in cell C1 that reads something like "=A1+B1". This would give the value of 71 in cell C1. This is called *relative cell referencing*, because you are saying that cell A1 should be added to B1, and they are "relative" to each other for the value you want in cell C1. You will always take whatever is in column B at that level and add it to whatever is in column A at the same level, or in the same row. Now, expand this thought to the data you have entered into cells A1 through B25. You have two columns worth of data (columns A and B), and in column C you want to use the previously described formula, but you want it to change as it moves from row 1 to row 2, to row 3, and so forth. By simply entering the formula as previously shown in cell C1 and then double clicking the bottom right-hand side of that cell (indicated as a black plus sign), you can copy the formula into all of the cells below it down to the end of your data (open CIA\Exercises\Excel\Section1.xlsx to practice this). You can also drag the cell and formulas down by clicking on the bottom right-hand corner of the cell with the formula, holding your left mouse button down, and dragging it to the cells below. In the individual rows in column C, you see that the formula also changed because it was a relative formula. Cell C2 has the formula =A2+B2, cell C3 has the formula =A3+B3, and so on. This is the use of the relative cell reference function in Excel.

On the other hand, if we want an absolute reference to a particular cell, we need to modify our formula a little to make Excel calculate it the way we want it to. Think of the rows of data as the following examples show, where column E contains some text value, column F contains a numerical value, and we want column G to calculate the total percentage of all the different types. We will want to use an *absolute cell reference* in our formula to accomplish this.

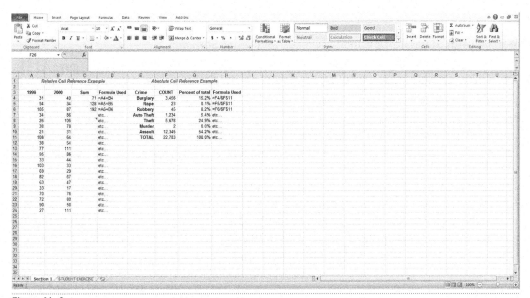

Figure A1–2

Screenshot used with permission from Microsoft.

As you can see from the "formula used" columns in Section1.xlsx, for the two types of referencing (see **Figure A1–2**) the absolute cell reference (column H) uses the "$" sign before the column and row numbers to make it refer to the total crimes cell for each of the calculated percentages. The first operator, which refers to column F, is a relative reference, so the formula changes as it is copied down, but the last operator is an absolute cell reference with the $F$11 type of notation, so it always looks "absolutely" to that cell for the second half of the formula.

Practice finishing the Section 1 sheet in Section1.xlsx, and then recreate the top section of the Student Exercise tab with the data displayed in the bottom section, which is formatted the same. Use relative and absolute references to cells to get all the data from the bottom sheet into the top sheet without actually typing any of the numbers in by hand.

Absolute references should not be confused with R1C1 reference style, which is discussed here. Click on the **File** menu and then go to Options, click on Formulas in the popup menu, and then about halfway down on the right you will see a menu item for R1C1 reference style. If you are an old Lotus user this may look familiar to you. When you have R1C1 checked, instead of seeing columns labeled A, B, C, D, etc., the rows and columns are both labeled with numbers (1, 2, 3, 4, etc.). This means that you need to type in R1C1 instead of A1 when you refer to the same cell (C1R1 instead of A1 or Column 1 Row 1 instead of a single cell reference of A1). This is not particularly useful unless you are a hardcore Lotus or SPSS user who cannot get into the A1 cell reference style.

This concludes the general information about Excel, because you should already have basic abilities with it, so we will approach some harder topics and uses of formulas and functions in Excel for crime analysis.

■ Section 2

Working with Standard Deviation, Average, and Other Statistics

Start this exercise with the file named CIA\Exercises\Excel\Section2.xlsx (see **Figure A1–3**).

You want to be able to give your command staff a prediction of how many crimes will probably be reported for your jurisdiction by the end of 2012. We deliberately left out any crimes that have already been reported in 2012 so that we can use the previous 19 years to predict 2012 levels. Typically, the more data you have, the more likely your prediction will be accurate, and most of the time you will want at least 20 months, days, weeks, or years to predict the next period you are aiming at with any degree of certainty. This will change depending on the variability of your data from year to year and you may use as little as 5 years, or as many as 35 years, if needed. Keep in mind that this prediction is really only reasonably accurate for the predicted next year, week, or month, and the reliability of the prediction decreases as you try to use your data to predict farther into the future. Inferring what may happen based on the past is always a shaky proposition, and with crime data, it is often not as accurate as we may want it to be. Combining a description of what has happened in the past with an inference of what *may* happen helps your analysis to be understood and should at least be considered each time you try this.

As an analyst you should be able to look at the data to get a feel for what your prediction will most likely look like, especially with this example. Based on the data from 1993 through 2011, what would you expect the total number of crimes to be in 2011 by simple observation of the "Crimes" column? (Will it be higher than 2011, lower than 2011, or about the same as 2011?)

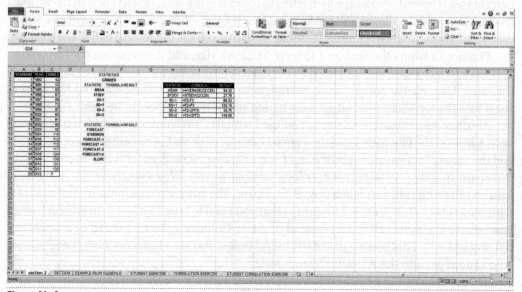

Figure A1–3

Screenshot used with permission from Microsoft.

The data show that crime appears to be steadily increasing from year to year for the most part, and except for 2010, each year has always been higher than the previous year. You should expect that if you use the mean and standard deviation, or the slope and standard error, to predict 2012's count, either method will most likely predict 2012 to be higher than 2011. This is reasonable for this data set, so why do we need Excel? Law enforcement agencies have been using "gut feelings" and "by the seat of their pants" types of analyses very successfully for many years. Most of that past analysis is based on pure common sense. Make sure that when you start applying scientific methods and statistics to crime analysis, you keep common sense!

Let's test this theory by calculating the following statistics for our set of numbers. Enter the formulas as shown in column F of the Section 2 worksheet (see example to the right of column G in Section2.xlsx, sheet name, "section 2") and match your results to those in the example table in column J. If you get any numbers different from those listed in the table, make sure you entered the formulas correctly and make sure that your data matches the data in the sample provided.

Now that we have used Excel's statistical functions to calculate the mean and standard deviations of our yearly data, what does that allow us to say about this data?

We could say that we average at least 94.3 crimes per year in this city. We can also say that 68% (mean plus or minus 1 standard deviation) of the years experienced between 55.5 and 122.1 crimes, or that 95% (mean plus or minus 2 standard deviations) of the years experienced between 38.8 and 149.9 crimes. We cannot really predict what the total will be for 2012 using the mean and standard deviation, and we can only *describe* the crimes per year for the previous years. That is why they call this descriptive statistics!

To predict what 2012 is most likely to experience, we have to use Excel's **Forecast, Slope**, and **Steyx** (standard error) functions. These will allow us to know if the *linear trend* is up or down and give us an estimate of what might be expected in 2012. The statistics we will need to calculate are shown in section 2 in columns I and J again.

Enter the formulas into column F in the Section2.xlsx/section 2 worksheet as shown in the examples in column I. Work with and understand these formulas and make them common in your day-to-day analysis efforts.

This shows that with no standard error calculated, the forecasted number of crimes in 2012 should be 142.9 crimes. If you add in the standard error (or standard differences between numbers from year to year), then within one standard error, the predicted range for 2012 is between 138.3 and 147.4 crimes. Extending this to two standard errors brings the range to between 133.7 and 152.0 crimes. If you look at the slope of the linear trend line (see **Figure A1–4**), it is a positive number, meaning that the trend over the past 19 years has been a positive one, or upward.

The chart of the forecasted information that we will create in the following steps may help you to understand it better. We have found that the linear trend line works about as well as any other trend or forecasting tool with crime data. There are more sophisticated methods, such as polynomial, logarithmic, moving average, and many others, that can be used, and you should take the effort to look at these other methods at some point in your career and

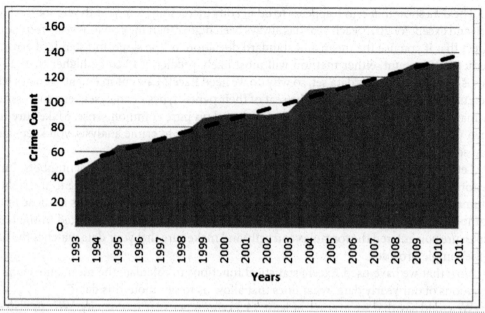

Figure A1–4

empower yourself to be able to use them as the data lends itself to those analysis methods. The only method covered in this tutorial will be the linear trend line.

To create this chart in Excel, follow these steps:

1. Highlight cells B1 through C20 with your mouse.
2. Click on the **Insert** menu and select the **Area** chart type about midway on the menu ribbon.
3. Choose the top left **2d Area** chart type. Your chart should appear on your worksheet.
4. Reposition it as needed.
5. To add a trend line, right click the area and pick **Add Trend Line** from the drop-down menu.
6. Select **Linear** from the **Trend/Regression Type** section, and click **Close** to add the trend line.
7. You can reposition the legend to the top by right clicking it, selecting **Format Legend**, and checking **Top**.
8. You can also apply several preset formats by choosing one from the **Chart Tools-Design** tab at the top of the menu ribbon.

You can clearly see that the statistics we calculated for this data seem to match up to the chart/graph that we created of the data. Combining these visual objects with the analytical data allows the analyst to not only make sound analytical statements, but also allows the

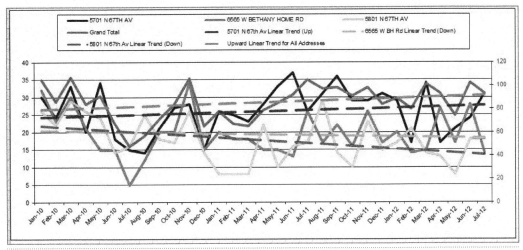

Figure A1–5

command staff users to understand the significance of the statistics you used through a very simple chart or graphic of the data.

The tab in the Excel exercise spreadsheet labeled "Section 2 Example from Glendale" (see Figure A1–3) shows how this type of analysis was used on an actual analysis effort that tracked calls for service (CFS) information for several apartment complexes in Glendale that were hot locations. The chart (see **Figure A1–5**) is a visual representation of the data and should be reviewed so you can decide what conclusions you would make in a written document to describe this data.

Based on this information, provide a short description of the data presented for the addresses shown on the chart, describe how the data has changed over the past months shown, and provide information on what the predicted values will be for the next month, which will be August 2012. Refer back to the various fields in the Excel spreadsheet and the calculated data for reference when needed. An example of the descriptive text for our exercise is as follows:

> For all apartment complexes listed, the trend appears to be slightly upward for all calls for service over the last 31 months. 5701 N 67th Av also shows a slight increase in CFS, however 6565 W Bethany Home Rd and 5801 N 67th Av show a slight downward trend over the past 31 months. The monthly average for all apartment complexes is 85 CFS and the forecasted number of calls to these apartment complexes in August 2012 should be between 77 and 107 within 1 standard error of estimate.

For further exercises using these functions in Excel, go to the sheet labeled "Section 2 Student Exercise" and complete the formulas for the data listed. Create a short memorandum that explains the data, what the trend is with each of the crime types listed, what the forecasted number of crimes should be for August 2012 for each type of crime, and any other information you think would be appropriate for a crime analysis effort requested by your chief for Part 1 Uniform Crime Report (UCR) offenses in your jurisdiction. For a more in-depth review of these processes and some other considerations, review Chapters 15–20 in Gottlieb, Arenberg, & Singh (1994). Another option is to take a basic statistics course at a college near you or read one of the many statistics books available.

The following summary is an example of information you may want to include when you describe this data to your chief.

> Based on the information included in the following tables and charts, it appears that the number of homicides has been steadily increasing over the past 31 months. There have been a total of 278 homicides in the past 31 months, with an average of 9 per month across that entire time range. If this basic trend holds true, there will be between 16 and 30 homicides in August 2012, or greater than a 162% increase in homicides from the July 2010 count of 6. From past statistical reports, the reason for the sharp increase in homicides in recent months may be linked to gang violence erupting in the city's downtown area.

Students should review the information in the CIA\Exercises\Excel\Section2.xlsx Student Exercise worksheet tables, insert the correct formulas and functions in the cells that are blank, summarize the information in a similar fashion for each crime type, and be able to make several generalizations about the data and the status of violent crimes and property crimes in the city as a whole in the past 31 months.

Remember that the time period you choose to analyze may often be as important as the data you are analyzing. If you use a short time period in your analysis, your prediction and forecast may be highly inaccurate. If you use a time range that is too long, you may see a trend that does not exist in more recent months or may be changing rapidly from month to month. This is where common sense comes into play when doing these types of analyses using Excel. You can only describe the data you choose to analyze and forecast for that one next time period with any degree of certainty. Make sure you understand these limitations, and make sure that the persons for whom you create your analysis understand the limitations of a linear trend. You may also want to consider seasonality in your trend analyses (crimes go up or down naturally with the weather, school getting out, etc. every year despite the current trend), and look for potential causes to explain severe upward spikes or low troughs in the data. Often these really high spots and low spots may be due to a comprehensive enforcement project your agency was involved in, a change in policy on how certain crimes are recapped, or some other situation that was not normally present (such as a new computer system installation, a statewide auto theft task force or DEA focus in your city, etc.).

When it is possible to list some of these situations as potential confounding variables on your analysis product, you will usually provide a better product than if you did not look for them and reported the information simply from the charts or graphs. Of course, as with any other analysis, the peaks or valleys may not be explainable, and that may need to be a state-ment in your analysis as well. Do not be afraid to state your opinions in your analysis prod-ucts, but be intimate enough with your data to support those conclusions and wise enough not to argue too much if they are not accepted or considered by personnel for whom the analysis was meant.

An example of the same general functions with seasonality calculated in and the use of data regression from the Analysis Toolpak is provided in the sheet labeled "Seasonality." This can be very useful and moderately accurate from year to year when doing monthly CompStat presentations. We will not go into any great detail here, other than to provide this sample you can replicate back at your own agency.

Now that we know how to describe trends in singular datasets, what happens if we want to know how one item, such as population, affects an increase in crime? This is called a correlation, and we have heard this term used incorrectly many times. The most incorrect use of this term is when someone says that population increases "caused" crime to rise because they are highly correlated. Although this statement may have some truth behind it, a correlation is simply looking at the relationships between two sets of data or numbers and whether or not they are going up or down in the same manner over time, not if one "caused" the other. This incorrect usage should be avoided.

There are three basic types of correlation you may deal with when analyzing crime data:

1. Two variables increase over time together (positive correlation).
2. Two variables decrease over time together (positive correlation).
3. As one variable increases, the other decreases over time (inverse or negative correlation).

Items 1 and 2 are typically called "positive" correlation because they both move in the same direction up or down. Item 3 is typically called a "negative" or "inverse" correlation because as one moves up, the other moves down. You can find positive and negative correlations in just about any two columns or rows of data. The common sense part of this entire calculation comes in what two variables you choose to analyze. For example, if your commander asked you to check on whether the color of the dirt in his sector affected the crime rate, your response should be, "Are you kidding?" On the other hand, if he advised you that he has been doing a 90-day increased enforcement activity for traffic violators in his precinct, and he wants to know if it has affected the number of traffic collisions, you may have a different opinion of his request. In this example, you would want to find a negative correlation; as the number of citations went up, the number of crashes went down.

Open the CIA\Exercises\Excel\Section2.xlsx workbook and the sheet labeled "Correlation Exercise." You will see our old data from the previous exercises along with some population data for each year and the chart shown in **Figure A1–6**. By using your common sense and viewing this chart, you can see that as population increased, the number of crimes also rose.

The degree to which these elements changed over time is not exactly the same, but we can use common sense and conclude that there is a positive correlation between population rate and crimes reported. When we use the **Correl** function or the **Pearson** function in Excel, we find that the correlation coefficient (with either function) between the population rate and the reported crimes is 0.99. For both functions, we specify that array 1 equals the population data column (D2:D20), and array 2 equals the total number of crimes (E2:E20). Because the "r value" or degree of correlation (values of +1 to –1 with a value closer to +1 or –1 indicating a very strong correlation, +1 indicating a strong positive correlation, and –1

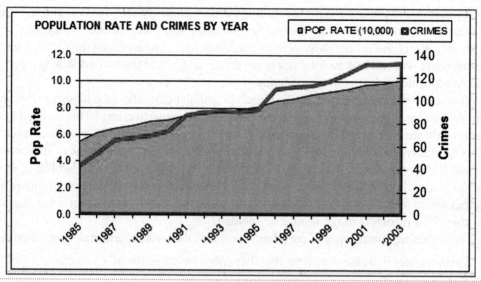

Figure A1–6

indicating a strong negative or inverse correlation) is very close to 1, we can say that there is a *strong positive correlation* between the population rate and the reported crimes. This does not mean that one causes the other, but as population increases, we could expect that crimes will also rise (*pure and simple common sense in action*). The lower the value of the correlation coefficient (or the closer to 0), the less likely that we will see a change in one variable when we see a change in the other. If the value is –0.99, then the relationship would be a strong, negative correlation. What you are looking for is a value that is closest to 1 or –1. A correlation coefficient of 0 would mean that there was no correlation of any sort between your two columns of data. The table labeled "Correlation Values Table" at the bottom of the "Correlation Exercise" sheet in Section2.xlsx explains what we might say about the strength and direction of a correlation, depending on what the value is.

If you use the Correl (this function is only visible when the Analysis Toolpak is on) or Pearson function, you should get the same result for the correlation coefficient or *r* value with most crime datasets. Just knowing whether or not you have a strong or weak correlation and if it is positive or negative is part of the process, but you also need to have an idea of how likely it is that you could arrive at that *r* value by chance or accident. The simplest way to get a handle on this possibility is to either square the *r* value or use the RSQ function, which does the same thing. The RSQ function needs the same data columns as your Correl functions, but you can also just square your *r* value obtained from the Correl or Pearson function by using the following formula in a new cell:

$$= (RValueCell)^2$$

For our example, we had an *r* value of 0.99. If we square it using either RSQ or the preceding formula, we get a value of 0.987. We can then make a statement such as, "When the population goes up, 98.7% of the time the crimes reported will also go up." This doesn't tell us how much it will go up, of course, but that is life in statistics and math.

Using the Section2.xlsx Student Correlation Exercise worksheet, copy the data from Columns A–E and Rows 44–63 into the empty table above and create the correct functions and formulas so that your charts and other data come out correctly. Use the correlation exercise sample sheet as your guide for the correct formulas to enter.

- Is there a correlation between these two sets of data?
- What is the strength of the correlation and the direction of it?
- When the number of traffic citations increases or decreases, what happens to traffic crashes?
- What percentage of the time does this occur?
- Create a summary statement to explain this information to the commander who asked you to check into these statistics.

■ Section 3

Converting Dates and Times

Start this exercise with the file named CIA\Exercises\Excel\Section3.xlsx.

Dates and times can often be among the most difficult pieces of data that you may run into when working with Excel. ESRI's ArcMap products often do strange things to dates and times, and many database products, records-management systems (RMS), and computer-aided dispatch (CAD) software applications store and retrieve date and time data much differently. In this lengthy section, we discuss some of the basic date and time data you may run into and how to utilize the nifty date- and time-handling functions inherent in Excel to make your job as an analyst much easier.

Let's start out by deciding what we want to do with a date or time. Next to the "where" category or location (geography of crime), the "when" (date and time or temporal factors) question seems to pop up most often during an analyst's normal routines. Even in the examples in Section 2, we used year and month as factors in our analysis. If we have a date, we can determine several things about an incident, or we can aggregate or simplify this information. Excel has functions that deal with dates and can calculate all of these different variables when needed. But before we can deal with the data, we first have to tell Excel that the data we are using or have entered is in date and/or time format. If Excel treats the data as a number or text field, then the date and time functions that are built into Excel cannot be used with the data.

Several of the things we may want to know about a date on which an incident occurred may be as follows:

- Date
- Time
- Hour of the day
- Day of the month

- Day of the week
- Month
- Year
- Week

Of course, we may also want to combine several of these factors into some time pre-structured period to make it easier to understand, make the data work better for a chart or table, or explain some aspect of the data being analyzed. We may also want to use the information to describe when something happened or predict when it may happen again based on prior occurrences.

To be able to do all of these things, we first have to provide Excel with data that is in date and/or time format. To enter dates into Excel in a typical crime analysis setting, you should normally enter the information as follows: 08/24/2004 17:34. Notice we used a military or 24-hour time entry, which is pretty commonplace in police departments. If you neglect to enter the time, Excel will normally use 00:00 (midnight) instead of the actual time of the incident, so you should be careful of this when entering data. When you convert data that is only available as a date, such as 08/24/2004, without a time, Excel will store the time as 00:00 for this event. If you need to capture the second that something happened, add the second at the end, for example, 08/24/2004 17:34:42. If you fail to do this, Excel will also make the seconds :00, and any calculations you do could be in error at the seconds level. You also need to make sure that the fields you are entering the data into are formatted as mm/dd/yyyy HH:mm:ss as well or you may not see your seconds or even the time in some cases. For instance, if you entered 08/24/2004 17:34:33 into a field that was only formatted as mm/dd/yyyy, you would only see 08/24/2004 in the field after you hit enter or tab to go to another field. The formatting of the field is almost as important as the way the data are entered. The field retains the values of the time in the aforementioned example, but does not display it.

Using the CIA\Exercises\Excel\Section3.xlsx spreadsheet as a guide, enter the following dates and times starting in cell A5.

- 01/01/1900 12:00:01
- 01/01/1998 12:01:01
- 12/31/2003 13:14:01
- 06/21/1994 06:05:03
- 08/31/2000 00:00:01

As you enter each of these dates and times in the spreadsheet, the day, hour, year, etc. fields should automatically calculate. The week field may show "Number?" or "Value?" instead of a number. This is because the WeekNum function is part the Analysis Toolpak add-in for Excel that has to be turned on before you can use that function. To find out how to enable other Add-ins, open the Help menu and enter "How do I install add-ins?" in the dialog, then follow the directions to install the add-ins.

You will need to refresh the calculations on the screen by clicking in any row under the week column and then pressing enter without changing anything in the field. This will recalculate the WeekNum, and values should now appear in each of the "Week" cells. You should now have a table that looks like **Figure A1–7**.

For each date and time you entered, Excel calculated the year, month, weekday (with 1 representing Sunday), day of month, week of the year, hour, minutes, and seconds. Now click on the cells in each column and see how the formula is entered using the date and time

DATE	YEAR	MONTH	WEEKDAY	DAY OF MONTH	WEEK	HOUR	MINUTES	SECONDS
08/24/2004 17:35:42	2004	8	3	24	35	17	35	42
01/01/1900 12:00:01	1900	1	1	1	1	12	0	1
01/01/1998 12:01:01	1998	1	5	1	1	12	1	1
12/31/2003 13:14:01	2003	12	4	31	53	13	14	1
06/21/1994 06:05:03	1994	6	3	21	26	6	5	3
08/31/2000 00:00:01	2000	8	5	31	36	0	0	1

Figure A1–7

functions of Excel. These have all been entered for you for this part of the exercise. You can refer back to this simple spreadsheet as the lesson progresses for information on how to use each formula.

We often create all of these fields in a set of data we are going to use for analysis even if we do not think we will use them. It helps to remember these functions, and if we decide to do some date and time analyses, we already have everything we need. Some additional fields we often create are concatenations (combinations) of several of these fields. We often create a field called YrMnth, which is the year and month of an incident. This is how the data were analyzed in Section 2. We may also create a field called YrMnthWeek and use it for trend charts by week for some analysis projects. The only trick to these fields is to observe that some months have only one digit in them, and others have two. To make your data sort correctly, you need to make sure all of your data are the same when you combine or concatenate fields. See the table in **Figure A1–8** for an example.

If we use the standard formula for concatenating two fields, the cells under YrMnth before edits would contain a formula that resembles =B12 & C12. It refers to the first cell (B12), the ampersand advises Excel that a new cell or function is coming, and then C12 refers to the second cell to be combined. This formula takes two number fields (right justified), combines them, and converts the data to a text field (left justified), but each cell is not the same length. If you sort them, the list of data will not sort properly. To keep this from happening, change the formula to the following:

=B12 & IF(LEN(C12)=1,"0" & C12,C12)

LEN stands for length, and it finds out whether or not the value in C12 is one or two digits long. If it is one digit, it adds a 0 in front of it, and if not, it accepts the value of C12 and combines it to the year. On the Section3.xlsx sheet, use this same logic to create the YrMnth Week formula so that each of the weeks is also exactly two digits long in the final result.

DATE	YEAR	MONTH	WEEK	YRMNTH BEFORE EDITS	YRMNTH (CORRECTED)	YRMNTHWEEK
08/04/2004 17:35:42	2004	8	32	20048	200408	
01/24/2004 01:01:01	2004	1	4	20041	200401	
12/17/2003 00:02:34	2003	12	51	200312	200312	

Figure A1–8

Remember that you already have the year and month combined correctly in the YrMnth (Corrected) field, so you do not need to concatenate all three fields in this formula. On the exercise spreadsheet you will also see that we added the Excel function INT (integer) to convert the text value of the combined year and month back to a number (right justified). This is sometimes useful when sorting large sets of data because Excel sorts numbers much faster than text. An alternative to using these functions individually is the use of the TEXT function. The data you wish to convert must be a date and time field and you will use the TEXT function to get the parts of the date or time you wish to use. In ArcGIS and other programs, using a date format of yyyymmdd or 20120801 as a number representing August 1, 2012 is oftentimes easier to work with and still sorts in the proper order. You can even add the hours and minutes for a number value such as 20100801192233 which represents August 1, 2012 19:22:33. Some examples include:

- =TEXT(A14, "yyyymm")—provides 200408 from the date and time in A14
- =TEXT(A14, "yyyymmddhhmm")—provides 2004081735 from the date and time in A14
- =TEXT(A14,"HH")—provides the military hour of the time in A14

To convert this to a number, we can use either the VALUE function or the INT function in front of the TEXT function in the aforementioned examples as follows:

- =Value(TEXT(A14, "yyyymm"))—provides 200408 from the date and time in A14, but as a number instead of text. INT(Text(A14,"yyyymm")) would yield the same result.

For more help with the TEXT function, refer to Excel Help or visit the Microsoft website and search for the Excel TEXT, VALUE, and INT functions.

Converting Data into Date Format

There are several ways that temporal information can get into your Excel spreadsheet, and it comes in several different types. The table in rows 20–25 of the Section3.xlsx, sheet Section 3 exercise shows data in several different formats that refer to a date or date and time. The easiest way to tell numeric data apart from textual data (most of the time) is that if the data is left justified it is probably text, and if it is right justified it is normally a number or date. You can change the formatting of every cell in an Excel spreadsheet, however, using the Format → Format Cells function in the menu bar (or press CTRL+1) or by right clicking the cell and then selecting Format Cells from the drop-down box.

These are just a few of the examples that we have seen, and your data may come in a variety of formats and combinations when you are working as a crime analyst. You will need to become intimately familiar with the data your agency collects and know what odd collection methods, programming, or policies make the data come in those various ways to your desktop. An example we like to use is from our days with a police department. When we were creating a crime analysis unit database, we pulled data from our RMS, which was built in house. The date and time were collected in two different fields in the RMS for most incidents, and they were not combined. Going through the data, we noticed that several date fields had "0" instead of a blank or an actual date value. We assumed this was exactly midnight. The fields that did contain dates had text such as 19990101, which represented 01/01/1999. Every time we brought this information from our RMS into Excel, it converted the 19990101 to a number. This seemed to work fine, and we logically concluded that "0" in the date field meant that the date had not been known and was not entered for this incident or was null. Unfortunately we did not conclude the same thing for the time field. The time was also a text item in the crime analysis data tables, but it was entered such that 1 represented 00:01, 23 represented 00:23, 123 represented 01:23, etc. When we brought this data into Excel, it changed the data into a number. For almost a year we did analyses with this data and converted these two separate fields into concatenated date and time fields in Excel through some manipulations of several Excel functions. During a meeting on a totally different subject one day, a programmer mentioned that the value of 0 in our RMS anywhere represented a null value or something that had not been entered. This meant that we had been translating 0 in the time field to be 00:00, or midnight, incorrectly. Luckily, there were not too many incidents where this information had been left out, but it still caused some problems because we had not known enough about our data and how it was collected in our own RMS. In this case, the RMS could not capture midnight as a time because programmers had used 0 instead of 999, 99, or some other common number as a null or missing value. We could only record from 1 minute past midnight to 1 minute before midnight, or 23:59, because, when it was converted, 0 didn't represent 00:00; it represented a null value. Therefore, nothing could happen exactly at midnight in that RMS.

A side note is that if you convert 0 to a date, Excel will show the date as 01/00/1900, because that date is represented by the number 0 in Excel's storage of date and time information (see Excel's Help file for information about how Excel stores date and time data). All other dates are serial numbers counting up from that date or the number 0. For example, 08/24/2012 is 41,145 days from that date, so 08/24/2012 can also be represented by the serial number 41145.

There are several examples of data conversions under the Excel Hints and Tricks tab in Section3.xlsx that may be helpful to you for the remaining lessons in this tutorial and for future use. Feel free to copy, print, or use them as needed.

We cannot tell you how many problems we have solved by simply advising an analyst to combine separate date and time fields into one date/time field and then make the calculations. When you enter a formula into the "Results" column and a number such as 38233 appears in the cell, remember that this is the way Excel stores date/time information. If you want to see this information in a standard date/time format (such as 01/01/2004 15:34) you will need to **format** the cell so that it shows the date and time the way you want to see it (see Formatting Cells in Excel Help).

The general rule for converting data into dates that Excel understands is to do whatever it takes to make Excel think of the information as if you had entered it as in the first part of this lesson: 08/24/2004 17:34. You want to convert the data that was given to you with whatever functions Excel needs so that it interprets the data into that format. For example, let's use the following data and see what we need to do to it to make Excel see the data as a date:

- Cell A21: 01/01/2004; format: text
- Cell B21: 00:01; format: text
- Target cell for formula: C21; format: mm/dd/yyyy HH:mm

This information is almost in the format that Excel likes to see; however, it is contained in two different fields. We need to use the DateValue and TimeValue functions of Excel to look at this text information, see it as a date and time, and then just add them together into a new field. The formula for doing this would be as follows:

=DATEVALUE(A21) + TIMEVALUE(B21)

This would give you the result of 01/01/2004 00:01 in cell C21, where you entered this formula. This kind of date and time manipulation is easy and is what you hope for in life. You may also run into data that look like "01/01/2004 12:34:05," possibly from ArcMap or another application, and appear to be a date already. Usually there is an invisible character somewhere in the date data that Excel translates into a text field, or the application that provided the data advised Excel on the transfer that the data was a text field. Regardless, when you attempt to do calculations between dates, you will get back an error message like #Error or #Value!. This is because Excel is looking at this data as a text field and not a date. You can sometimes simply format the field as "mm/dd/yyyy HH:mm:ss" using the custom formatting function under the Number tab in the Format Cells dialog, and Excel will do your calculations correctly without actually converting the data into a date and time. Formatting simply displays the information in the way you want it, but it does not change the underlying data type in the sheet in most cases. You can also create a new field and use the following function to look at cell C2 and convert the "01/01/2004 13:42:13" data into a date and time field:

=DATEVALUE(left(C2,10)) + TIMEVALUE(RIGHT(C2,8))

If you just used the DateValue function, you would only get the date part of the text data and not the time as well, it would be set to 00:00:00. If you only used the TimeValue function, you would only get the time part of the text with the date of 01/00/1900. Excel will only do what you tell it to do and will not guess what you meant to do. In other cases, either the date or time actually transferred into excel as a date or time. In these instances you would change the formula to drop either the DateValue or TimeValue functions for one or the other set of characters.

Complete the cells in the worksheet under the Section 3 exercise tab for the different date formats. Remember to use the Mid, Left, Right, DateValue, and TimeValue functions in your formulas to arrive at combined date and time fields that reflect the correct dates and times for the data provided. Use the Excel Help dialogs to find out more information about these functions if you need to. The format for using each of these functions can be found in the Help menu; however, a very short description of their use and a few other helpful functions are provided in the "Excel Hints and Tricks" sheet in the Section3.xlsx workbook.

Some other useful text functions taken directly from Excel Help are as follows:

- **Char**: Returns the ANSI character specified by the code number
- **Clean**: Removes all nonprintable characters from text
- **Code**: Returns a numeric code for the first character in a text string
- **Concatenate Concatenate (text1,text2,...)**: Joins several text items into one text item. *(Note: This is an alternative to using A2 & B2 & C2 etc. and basically allows you to skip the & symbol.)*
- **Dollar**: Converts a number to text using currency format
- **Exact**: Checks to see if two text values are identical
- **Fixed**: Formats a number as text with a fixed number of decimals
- **Lower**: Converts text to lowercase
- **Proper**: Capitalizes the first letter in each word of a text value
- **Rept**: Repeats text a given number of times
- **Search**: Allows you to search for a text string and returns a number that represents where that text string was found in the target cell. (The **Find** function is very similar and returns the same information.)
- **Substitute**: Substitutes new text for old text in a text string. (This can be used for much more complicated operations than the **Replace** function.)
- **T**: Converts its arguments to text. (You can sometimes use this to see if a field is actually text or some other type of data. It returns an empty/blank cell if the field does not contain text.)
- **Text**: Formats a number and converts it to text
- **Upper**: Converts text to uppercase
- **Value**: Converts a text argument to a number

In the Section3.xlsx worksheet, there is a tab labeled "Section 3 Example from Glendale." This tab shows a robbery series that occurred in Glendale and shows that the dates and times were in two separate fields and not usable with Excel's date functions as they were. We used a formula that combined several of the functions previously mentioned to calculate the dates and times into one field so that this information could be used for doing day of week, time of day, and next date of hit predictions as shown. In Section 5, we go over how this is done with a tactical crime series bulletin.

A very useful function is the **text** function when you already have the data in date and time format. For instance, if you want the day of the week from a date, and the date and time are in cell A2, you can use the text function to get it in several ways. For the following examples, let's assume the date 03/14/2012 13:14:55 is in cell A2:

- =TEXT(A2,"d") returns 14 or the day of the month
- =TEXT(A2,"ddd") returns Wed or the day of the week
- =TEXT(A2,"dddd") returns Wednesday

Although we do not use this function in this tutorial, you should at least be aware of it for later use in your own analysis efforts.

Using what you have learned from this discussion and from reviewing the spreadsheets and functions provided, click on the Section 3 Student Exercise tab and create a formula for the incomplete columns and rows. These are RptNum, DateTime1 (calculate a date/time field based on any of the date and time columns), Day of Week, Hour of Day, Month, YrMnth, and Days Between Calls columns. Drag your formulas down to fill the remaining cells for every call listed. Make sure they all calculate correctly and there are no problems with your data or formulas for all of the records. Consider that all of the data will need to be sorted by order of occurrence to calculate properly for the "Days Between Calls" column, and make sure you sort the data correctly prior to entering a formula for this field.

After you have completed entering these formulas, see if you can calculate the average number of calls per day of week and hour of day. You might consider placing this information in a graph to make it easier to understand. You should also calculate the average number of days between calls. Consider how this information could be used in your daily crime analysis assignment and what value it could be to your agency. Write a short memo describing the conclusions you came up with concerning these data and your temporal analysis results complete with the charts, tables, and graphs you think most appropriately support your conclusions. After you have completed your analysis, review the Word document titled CIA\Exercises\Excel\Section3.docx as an example of the analysis that was done with this information. The very simple date and time charts were added for this tutorial only.

■ Section 4

In this section, we will briefly discuss data transfers between Excel and GIS software. If you are using Excel 2007, you will need to search for a paper on the ESRI website (www.esri.com) to find out how to work with Excel and Access 2007 data sources. Instead of trying to export to a DBF table from Excel, as we did with previous versions of Excel, you will "save as" a comma delimited text file (CSV) for use in ArcGIS. Excel will read DBF tables for the time being but will not export them. You will need to export data you wish to use in ArcGIS as CSV tables for geocoding and other projects. You can also connect to Excel directly to access any of the sheets in Excel. It is a good idea to name the range of data you wish to import, as this makes it easier to find the proper data in many cases when you link directly to Excel. You also need to make sure that the Excel sheet is closed when you try to link to it, and the field names should be under 10 characters and have no spaces, punctuation, or other odd characters in the field names for the connection to work properly.

Notes on Working with ArcMap and Excel

It is usually very easy to get data from ArcMap to Excel, or from Excel to ArcMap, but there are a few tricks that make this process much simpler. One of the first bits of advice we can give you pertains to an ArcMap shapefile and the format in which it is stored on your hard drive. When you create a shapefile in ArcMap, it actually creates and stores three or more interconnected files that make up a shapefile. The files in the following list are the three files you will find every time that are absolutely necessary for a shapefile to work and cannot be changed or modified independent of one another without corrupting the shapefile and making it totally useless:

- SHP: The shape geometry of a shapefile (polygon, line, point, and related information)
- SHX: The locations and spatial elements of a shapefile (where it is)
- DBF: The data behind the shapefile (the specific rows and columns of data)

In many cases, you will take some time in querying a set of data in ArcMap and create a shapefile of the selected data so that you can use it in Excel or some other application. Many instructional materials teach you that you can use the shapefile's DBF table that ArcMap creates to view and manipulate data in Excel, Access, SPSS, and other products that read DBF files. The problem comes in when they forget to advise you *to avoid editing the DBF table and saving it under the same shapefile name,* same shapefile folder name, and as the same shapefile DBF table where you obtained it. If you write over the shapefile's DBF table with edits you have made in SPSS, Excel, or Access, you will totally corrupt the shapefile, and it will no longer be useful in ArcMap as a shapefile. This can cause regeocoding of a lot of data and some unhappy moments. You can, of course, export data from ArcMap as a DBF table that is not associated with a shapefile, and these are okay to edit as you please in Excel. One of the first lessons in this section is that if you edit data that come from a DBF table that is part of an ArcMap shapefile, *do not* save it under the same name or same directory as the shapefile's DBF source table you took it from. This will save you hundreds of hours of work. We speak from experience here, so learn from our mistakes.

Suppose that you have data in ArcMap and want to do some calculations and create some new fields in Excel so that you do not have to try to use ArcMap's limited database tools. There are a couple of situations that could occur in which it would make more sense to pull your data into Excel to create and calculate some new fields rather than try to do it in ArcMap. The first situation is when you deal with dates or times. ArcMap handles dates much like any other application, but manipulating dates and calculating dates and times can be a bit rough unless you have some programming experience or really like to work slowly. We can do everything we might think of or want to do in Excel, but we can't do it as easily in ArcMap, and sometimes it may just be too much of a headache to try.

The first, most obvious, way to get data from ArcMap into Excel is to simply pull the data into Excel from the ArcMap shapefile's DBF attribute table. Remember that if we edit the shapefile's DBF table in Excel and save it, we will corrupt the shapefile. There are two options to work around this problem. The first is to give every incident in your shapefile an absolutely unique identification (ID) number or record number and then bring only the data you will need from this table into Excel, create and save a new table, add your new fields, and then using that unique record number, **join** it back to your shapefile. This makes the data useable in ArcMap and is a great way to add content to your GIS layers. The second method is to add the X and Y coordinates of your data to the shapefile; bring the DBF file into Excel; create, edit, and add the new fields; then bring these data back into ArcMap as an *event* theme; and display all the information that way in your map. ArcGIS has a tool in the ArcToolbox that will add the *X* and *Y* coordinates to the attribute table. This tool can be found under the Data Management Tools, under Features and Add *XY* Coordinates. We will show you an example of both methods in the next few pages, and you can decide which would work the best for your project.

In example 1, we use a shapefile called CIA\Exercises\Excel\RobSeries1.shp (SHX and DBF). This is a set of data about a robbery series in the City of Glendale, and we have geocoded the addresses and created a shapefile of that information from our RMS. The data are located either in the files from the Companion Website for this book or, if installed by your educational institution, please refer to where your instructor advised you this data can be located, typically located at CIA\Exercises\Excel\RobSeries1.dbf (Shx, Shp). We need to pull the DBF table into Excel from this shapefile to calculate some common tactical analysis fields we will need. This particular table does have *X* and *Y* coordinates in it. The DR_NO field is a unique identifier for each incident in this series. To start using these data in Excel, open Excel and follow these steps:

1. Open Excel and click on **File**.

2. In the drop-down menu, click on **Open**.

3. In the dialog box, navigate to the drive that contains the CIA course data, and find the subdirectory ..CIA\Exercises\Excel\.

4. Change the "Files of Type" box at the bottom right of this dialog box to Dbase Files (*.DBF) to display the RobSeries1.dbf file. (This works for all versions of Excel.)

5. When you have found this file, click on it once, and then click **Open**.

6. The data will now be in your Excel spreadsheet as shown in **Figure A1–9**.

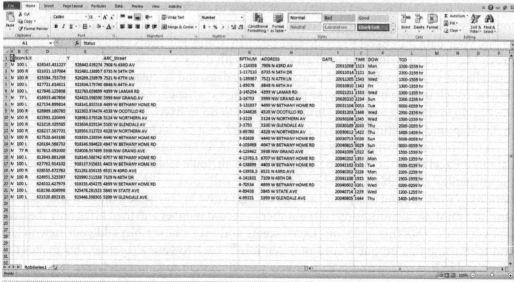

Figure A1–9

Screenshot used with permission from Microsoft.

7. Click on the small box in the upper left-hand side where the rows and columns come together to select all the rows and columns.

8. Now click on **Format → AutoFit Column Width** to resize all of the columns to fit the data. (In Excel 2007, this is under Home → Ribbon → Format.)

9. For the data we need to calculate, we only need the RPTNUM, DATE_, and TIME fields, so delete all of the other columns in this spreadsheet by selecting the entire column and then pressing the Delete key.

10. Now go to the File menu and choose Save As; save this workbook as "MyVersion.xlsx".

11. Create five new fields as follows:

- DateTime
- DBH
- CDBH
- Hour
- DOW

The formulas you will need to enter in these new cells can be found in the workbook CIA\Exercises\Excel\Section4help.xlsx.

If you entered all of these formulas correctly, your Excel table should have the values as shown in CIA\Exercises\Excel\RobSeries1Solution.xlsx in each of the calculated cells.

In your version, the DateTime field may be displaying the serial number for the date and time. This is the default way that Excel stores dates and times. If you want to see this as a date and time, use the Format → Cells (or CTRL+1) dialog and format this to be "mm/dd/yyyy HH:mm." Excel does not need the data to look like this, and it still calculates the days between hits, cumulative days between hits, hour, and day of week correctly, but is easier on the users of the data. Format the DateTime field how you would like to see it in ArcMap. You will see that ArcMap seldom cares how you saved it and will typically make it into a text field when you bring it back in (depending on the version of ArcMap you are using).

Now make sure you **Save** this data again. If using a spreadsheet program that allows you to save the file as a DBF, make sure you *do not* save it as a DBF file under the same name as the shapefile, or that shapefile will no longer be useful to you. Select **Save As** again, and save this Excel spreadsheet as a Comma Separated Values (CSV) file with a new name (RSLU1.csv). This will enable us to use the table in ArcMap and join it to our shapefile. This is the hard part: *Remember where you saved these files so you can find them again!*

After you have saved this spreadsheet as an Excel workbook and an RSLU1.csv table, you can close Excel. You must close Excel or you cannot add the data to ArcMap without some potential issues. Open ArcMap and add the RobSeries1 shapefile. Add the RSLU1.csv table to your project. You need to open the table in ArcMap to make sure that everything is there before proceeding (right click on the table and choose open). If everything is not included, there are a few guidelines you should follow:

1. Open the Excel spreadsheet with your data. Select the entire range of data.

2. Right click, and in the popup menu choose Name a Range (in Excel 2007) or Define Name (in Excel 2010).

3. Call the selected records (all your data) "Database" or another name with no spaces that is not longer than 10 characters.

4. Select **Add** (in 2003/2007) or **OK** (in 2010).

5. Rename all your field names so they are a maximum of 10 characters long.

6. Rename all your fields so there are no spaces or other characters from the Shift + number keys (1–0) in the field names.

   • Underscore can be used in the field name.

7. Save the spreadsheet again.

8. Save As RSLU1. csv again.

9. After replacing the bogus version, close Excel.

10. Bring the file into ArcMap again.

Now the entire table should be complete with the data you calculated. Right click on the RobSeries1 shapefile in the table of contents and choose the Joins and Relates choice. Join the RSLU.csv data to the shapefile's attribute table based on the RPTNUM field. A new shapefile will be created that is a combination of the original shapefile and the new fields concatenated to the right from your CSV file. You can now use it to do some temporal displays of the data, show the ones that occurred on Saturdays or between certain hours in another color, etc.

If you were really observant during all this, you will have noticed that our data had more than 12 characters in the RPTNUM field (yours will not). We have found that it is much easier in the long run to use an DSN/ODBC/OLE DB connection to bring this data from Excel into ArcMap so our field names and data will not be truncated (especially in Excel 2007/2010).

If you have to get these data back into ArcMap, use the following steps:

1. Select all the rows and columns that make up your series of incidents.

2. Insert a name for that data, and save this workbook as an Excel workbook.

3. Close the Excel workbook.

4. Open ArcMap.

5. Create a database connection to the Excel sheet.

6. Select the named range to add.

7. Voilà! The complete data from your Excel spreadsheet is in ArcMap. (See ArcMap Help for creating and adding a new DSN/ODBC/OLE DB database connection for further assistance or refer to class exercises that accompany this text.)

Because the *XY* coordinates were part of the data, you could then add this table to your view as an event theme to get points on the map again, and all the fields you calculated in Excel will come along. It is then a very simple matter to convert the CSV table you added to a shapefile with ArcMap—complete with all of your new Excel fields and calculations.

In summary, our advice to you is:

- When dealing with ArcMap and dates, retreat slowly and use Excel.
- If you really want to bring the data back into ArcMap after you have made several calculations and added data, then name the entire data range (all cells in your worksheet), save it as an XLSX sheet, and use a database connection to bring the data back into ArcMap as an event theme (*XY* coordinates in the table).
- *Do not* edit a DBF file that is part of an ArcMap shapefile, or you will corrupt the file!
- When all else fails, read the Help instructions carefully.

■ Section 5

Tactical Prediction

This section deals with doing date and time predictions in Excel using three different methods, and it mentions another paper and how-to publication we created to do the next date prediction in CrimeStat III. Some of the ideas behind different temporal calculations are also briefly discussed, such as days between hits and dollars per day. These are our own observations and not part of scientific research, although some testing has been done with a multitude of crime series we have analyzed over the past 15 years.

Decimal Time Predictions

Decimal time is simply the process of taking a date and time, converting it to decimals, and then doing basic math calculations on it. This is the method taught by Gottlieb et al. (1994).

We are doing two things here: (1) predicting the next date, and (2) predicting the most likely time for a new hit in a crime series. A third option of predicting the most likely day of the week is also possible from this same data.

For the first part, we are going to use the days between hits (DBH) calculation to figure out the average number of days between hits and the standard deviation. We can use this information to provide a range of dates the offender most likely will strike again *based on his prior behavior*. In Excel, this is a very simple calculation when you have the data in date and time format. We have already seen that getting the data into date and time format is the most complicated part of this process. Open the CIA\Exercises\Excel\Section5.xlsx exercise spreadsheet and view the data in the first tab, S5 Exercise. You will see our old table from the robbery series with all the data calculated and the fields we added correct and ready to go. To predict the next date of hit based on the mean and standard deviation of the DBH data, we first have to calculate the average and standard deviation of that column of data. So, in the cell to the right of the word Average, type in =AVERAGE(E3:E13). You should get an average of around 26 days if you rounded up. Now type in =STDEV(E3:E13) next to the StDev, and you should get a value of 14 (rounded). The values are already calculated for you in cells F15 and F16 as an example. Now calculate the mean minus 1 standard deviation (SD−1), mean plus 1 standard deviation (SD+1), mean minus 2 standard deviations (SD−2), and mean plus 2 standard deviations (SD+2) fields. If you calculated these correctly, you will find that in cells E21 and E22, for the row called 68% range, the prediction is that the suspect will hit between October 25 and November 22. The row called 95% range indicates that the next hit will be between October 11 and December 6. Because October 11 is prior to the last hit in the series, which occurred on October 16, we would change this in any analysis bulletin to between **now** and December 6. If you look at the formulas in E & F 21 & 22, you will see that it is the last date in the series (D13) plus the values in the SD–1, SD+1, etc. fields. These fields were then formatted as dd/mm/yyyy only, as we do not really feel that the date and time together could be accurately forecasted using this singular method.

As with any predictions based on mean and standard deviation, you have to really look at the data to see if it describes this offender's behavior adequately. The closer the standard deviation is to the mean, the more likely your prediction is going to be useful. The bigger the standard deviation, the less likely your prediction is going to be reliable. In this case, the standard deviation is so large that the offender could hit just about any time; the mean is 26 and the standard deviation is 14. We would call this date prediction very "loose," and although we do think the offender will hit in the 95% range timeframe, nailing down which of those 54 or more days he will choose to hit in is much harder. From looking at just the last 5 or 6 hits, we can see that he has not hit any earlier than 21 days between a previous hit. Prior hits were much more widely distributed. Perhaps as this criminal gets better at what he does, he settles down into that 21-day or so pattern that can help you do a better "best guess" for the investigators. By using just the last 6 hits, you would get a much smaller date range for a new hit, and depending on how confident you are of that (based on modus operandi information and reading the reports), you may want to use the shorter time range for your prediction on your bulletin. It is these types of decisions you are being paid for and should be willing to make to help narrow the focus of the investigation to the best chances of nabbing this criminal in the act of committing a new crime. Another factor we may want to look at is if the "tempo" of the hits are increasing or decreasing over time. In other words, is the offender hitting in fewer days from his last crime or in more days as time passes? In this particular case, we do not see a pattern of increased or decreased tempo between hits. Many robberies do see an increasing tempo as the offender seems to hit much more often as the series goes on. This seems to be a confidence factor in many robberies. As the offender starts outdoing robberies, he or she is more timid and commits robberies less frequently, but as the series continues, he or she becomes bolder and more aggressive and the days between robberies shorten.

Now we will work on predicting the time range using decimal time. First we need to convert regular time into decimal time to do average and standard deviation calculations on it. To accomplish this we will need to create two or three new fields to work with. We already have a field called Hour that tells us what the hour of day was for each hit. We need to know the minutes, converted to decimal, and then combine the two into a decimal time number field.

In the Section5.xlsx worksheet, look at the two new fields to the far right: Minutes and DecTime. These fields are already calculated for you.

Click in cell I2 and take a look at the formula entered in cell (=MINUTES(D2)). To convert minutes into decimals, we need to divide by 60, so the formula we want in the Dec-Time field (cell J2) should look something like =G2 +(I2/60) or a decimal equivalent time of 23.41667. Because we have already calculated the mean and standard deviation for the DBH column, we can select all of the cells between Average and SD+2, press CTRL+C to copy them, and then go to cell J15 and press CTRL+V to paste the formulas. Although this has already been done for you here, you may want to practice on your own in a new column to fully understand this formula. We can see that the average for the decimal time is 21.75, and the standard deviation is only 1.06. Therefore, the 68% time range is between 20.68 and 22.81, and the 95% range is between 19.62 and 23.88. That does not make any sense, does it? How can you have a time like 22.81? To avoid confusing friends, loved ones, and cowork-ers, we have to convert these decimal times back into regular times. *For further details on how to do this, please review Chapter 18 in Gottlieb et al. (1994).*

To convert the decimal times you calculated back to regular time, use a formula that looks like the following:

$$=INT(J17)\&":"\&INT((J17-INT(J17))*60)$$

Basically, you take the integer part of the decimal time or hours (20, from 20.68) and then take the decimal remainder or decimal minutes and multiply that by 60 to convert it back to minutes, so 0.68 * 60 = 40.8. Because we do not want the 0.8 part, we then take the integer of 40.8, which is 40, and then separate the 20 and the 40 with a colon, and voilà, instant regular time! The spreadsheet automatically calculates this for you, but you should practice it several times on your own to remember it, understand it, and be able to repeat it later when you need it.

Simple Graph Predictions

Another way to accomplish the same thing in a slightly easier way is to simply graph your data by hour of day, and use the graph to tell you when investigators should do their stakeout activities. Keep in mind that surveillance units typically still work an 8- or 10-hour day, and we need to give them a timespan that gives them the best likelihood of catching the offender in the act. We are probably not going to be able to predict the actual minute the offender strikes with most crime series. You will come to about the same conclusion; however, you will not be accurate down to the minute, of course. Using the Section 5 exercise sheet again, create a new spreadsheet and insert the following new values in a row in cells below the actual robbery data (use the Samples sheet as a guide). Start typing these values in cell A27:

- Time of Day
- HOUR
- COUNT
- Percentage of Total

After adding this cell's values side by side in a row (following the Samples sheet), enter the values of 0 through 23 under the time of day heading and 0000–0059 hrs, 0100–0159 hrs, etc. under the Hour heading. We will use this table to create a chart of the time distribution of this crime series. *(Note: A sample table is located in the sheet named "Samples" in Section 5.xlsx.)*

As a side note, custom lists in Excel can be your friend, although the custom lists dialog is buried deep in the File menu. In order to save the HOUR column as a custom list (0000–0059 hours, etc.), select the entire range of cells you want as a custom list, and then go to File → Options → Advanced. About all the way at the bottom you will see a button labeled, "Custom Lists"; click this button, and you should see the range you have selected in the box at the bottom right of this popup menu. Click the ADD button next to this range and you will see your data appear in the window on the left. Now exit. When you type in 0000–0059 hrs and drag it downward, the entire list will then produce itself down to 2300–2359 hrs and then start over. Cool, huh?

Okay back to work. In the Count field (C2), enter the following formula: =COUNTIF ($G$2:$G$13,A28). $G$2:$G$13 references back to the entire column of data under the heading of HOUR and A28 is the first value of 0 in your new Time of Day column. Now drag this formula down through the other 22 cells. You should see that all of them are 0 except for 2000 to 2359 hours. To calculate the percentage, create a cell with the name TOTAL in it under the 2300–2359 cell, and then calculate cell B52 to be =SUM(C28:C51). You should get a total of 12 incidents in cell B52. Now in cell D28 enter the following formula and copy it down to the other cells: =C28/$C$52. (Remember absolute referencing from Section 1—see the Samples tab if you need help.)

Format (CTRL+1) column D as a percentage with one decimal place, and you should now see the percentage of incidents that occurred during each hour of the day.

Now select cells B27 through C51 and create a graph like the one in the Samples sheet for the time of day. Click on Insert in the menu bar, and then pick the type of chart from the menu Ribbon. Pick the type of chart you feel would display these data the best, an area chart is shown in the Samples tab. A bar, line, or area chart would work. We prefer area charts over bar charts because they seem to be simpler and not as confusing or prone to misconceptions.

By simply viewing the chart you can see that the best time to deploy undercover personnel for stakeout activities is between 2000 and 2359 hours for this crime series. This, of course, falls right into line with the decimal time predictions, and both are likely to be very accurate. In many cases, we have found that if multiple methods predict the same day of week, time of day, or next date of hit, then we can have much greater confidence in the prediction. We are, after all, trying to predict human behavior, so we are never going to be 100% correct or have 100% confidence in a prediction we might do. We should think of these predictions in two manners:

1. The prediction itself—where we try to narrow it as much as possible based on the available information

2. The confidence that we have in that prediction based on the facts of the series we know

You can use a similar approach to predict what day of the week a serial offender will hit next. Count up the number of hits by day of week instead of hour of day as we did with the hour of day calculations. For this offender, based on the chart in the Samples sheet, the prediction would be based on those days with the highest number of hits in prior incidents.

For this robbery series we would make a statement such as, "If the offender continues to behave in the manner that he or she has, the offender will most likely hit between Oct 26 and Nov 22, 2012. The most likely day of week for a new hit in this series is on a Sunday or Monday (50%), and between 19:37 hrs. and 23:52 hrs. I have moderate to high confidence in this prediction." When you use this simple graphing method, you need to pay attention to the sequence of hits to see if the offender's pattern has changed a lot lately. This is also true with other methods for calculating these items. It is the consecutive nature of the days or hours being high in your graph that is actually the signal that a pattern may exist, so what you really want to look for in these charts is days or hours where the largest number of hits occurred next to each other in time.

Split Time or Midpoint and Weighted Averaging Predictions

Weighted averaging is a way to conclude what time an incident may have occurred when you don't have an exact time. For the examples discussed so far, we have had specific times for which crimes happened. This is almost always the case with robberies, sexual assaults, and other violent crimes in which a person was attacked. With property crimes, like burglary or auto theft, victims may see their property when they go to bed and wake up to find it missing.

The normal advice on this topic suggests that any times over 24 hours should not be used in calculations for any series (Gottlieb et al., 1994). This is mainly due to the fact that we don't really have any idea when the crime occurred and thus should probably not use it in our scientific analysis. This is also true with split time or midpoint time calculations, and you would get a major headache trying to find out what time you wanted to use for your best guess split time. When you do not have a single time for all incidents in your series, you can use split time to calculate these date and time differences. It is suggested as a general rule that with time periods longer than 24 hours, you should throw out that incident during your calculations. When doing standard decimal time calculations and graphs, we agree with this statement. When doing weighted averaging, we think you could either throw it out or use it if you are able to justify its use or addition to your analysis. The entire concept of weighted averaging dictates that you could weight this incident correctly and still have it be a valid part of your analysis because you did not really know when it happened, and you can only use an estimate. All you really need to know is when the time range starts and ends and how long is it between them.

First, let's discuss the easier split time calculations and how to do them in Excel. Open the CIA\Exercises\Excel\Section5b.xlsx spreadsheet and take a look at the data. In this spreadsheet you have 25 burglaries that have been committed by the same offender. For most of these incidents there is not an exact minute that the crime occurred, and you have two date fields and two time fields to deal with. We can use Excel to subtract dates and times for us and calculate the midpoint or split time, but we need to convert these all into date/times first. We therefore create two new fields called DateTime1 and DateTime2 and use the functions we previously learned to calculate these two new fields correctly. Format these fields to be mm/dd/yyyy HH:mm style (press CTRL+1). Keep in mind that because your time fields are not all four characters long, you will have to change the formula slightly to accommodate each of the time field lengths to make them come out right. You can also use an "If" statement, but this gets a little more complicated and may not be worth the effort for 25 incidents. Your formula should look something like the following for 3 characters in a time field:

$$=DATEVALUE(MID(B2,5,2)\&"/"\&RIGHT(B2,2)\&"/"\&LEFT(B2,4))$$
$$+TIMEVALUE(LEFT(C2,1)\&":"\&RIGHT(C2,2))$$

We often create a new field called TimeLen to make using the If statement a little easier. We use the formula =LEN(A2) (where A2 is the cell that contains the time in number format) to get the length of the time field first. Then in our datetime formula we use If statements to add 0s or not, depending on the length. This looks something like the following:

$$=DATEVALUE(MID(B2,5,2) \&"/"\& RIGHT(B2,2) \&"/"\& LEFT(B2,4))$$
$$+ IF(LEN(C2)=4, TIMEVALUE(LEFT(C2,2) \&":"\& RIGHT(C2,2))),$$
$$IF(LEN(C2)=1, TIMEVALUE("00:0" \& RIGHT(C2,1))), IF(LEN(C2)=3,$$
$$TIMEVALUE("0" \& LEFT(C2,1) \&":"\& RIGHT(C2,2)),"00:" \& RIGHT(C2,2))))$$

Note that C2 contains the time field, B2 contains the date information in text format, etc.
        You have to embed an If statement inside another If statement, making sure to account for each of the possibilities in your data. Now that we have converted the date and time fields to real datetime data, we can calculate the split time or midpoint between these two dates and times. This formula is quite simple: =DATETIME1 + ((DATETIME2–DATETIME1)/2). Create a new field called Midpoint, and enter this formula, replacing the DateTime1 and DateTime2 above with cell references for your DateTime1 (F2) and DateTime2 (G2) columns (the first row is done for you as an example). You now have a date and time that occurred directly between or halfway between DateTime1 and DateTime2. As you can see, this doesn't tell you when the incident really occurred, but it gives you an estimate. You can then use this estimate like a regular date and time (convert it to decimal time, etc.) and work with it to get your calculation and prediction. Some analysts choose to disregard all times that have a spread greater than a few (24) hours in their final analysis. This is entirely up to you, and it is one of those judgments you make and live by as your experience and knowledge grow in this profession, but it is based on sound practice. One thing you may want to watch out for is if there are any single times or time ranges that are very narrow in your crime series, or those incidents where we have an alarm activation, for instance. Let's say you have five burglaries and three have a timespan of 32 hours, but the other two show exactly when the alarm activated. You would probably use the time the alarms activated instead of trying to calculate a weighted averaging estimate, because doing so makes a lot of sense. Chances are the times the alarms activated are showing when the offenders are active, which is the whole point of doing a prediction. We try to use all the data we can for most analysis products, even if it means using data that is questionable at times, as long as we are sure it does not adversely

affect the analysis. Most of the data we collect as a police department have human error when they are collected, so we try to view the data as a challenge and make use of as much as we can, as long as it makes good sense.

You can visually inspect your data and figure out which incidents will have more than a 24-hour date and time difference. In the workbook Section5b.xlsx, if you have calculated all of the dates and time correctly, you will see that a few of the time ranges are more than 24 hours apart. Now look at cell I2 in the Section 5b exercise sheet. A formula is entered there already, so drag it down to cell I25. The cells in the column labeled Dec Hrs Between simply subtracts DateTime1 from DateTime2. The equivalent decimal number is the difference between the first and second date serial numbers. The integer value (left of the decimal point) represents the total number of days between the two dates. The decimal portion represents the total number of hours, minutes, and seconds. Basically, we have a bunch of information here that we could use, but the key item is that if the integer is 1 or more, then there is a 24-hour or more gap between the two dates and times. With this field you could decide which incidents to ignore when doing your calculations for mean, standard deviation, etc. when you convert the midpoint time to decimal time.

Another way of handling these incidents is to create a weighted averaging table of your incidents and calculate the total for each 24-hour period based on your data. Although it seems a little more complicated the first few times you use this approach, it actually makes quite a bit of sense when you really sit down and look at it. It also is where we got the idea to use the simplified graphing method for determining the next date, most likely time period, and most likely day of the week. We also like to avoid math at times, and being able to look at a chart, see where the offender has been hitting the most frequently in the past, and then advise the investigators of this information sometimes seems simpler. Dr. Jerry Ratcliffe has a slightly different approach to weighted averaging that he has termed *Aoristic analysis* (http://jratcliffe.net/research/aoristic.htm). You can review papers, presentations, publications, and research he has compiled on various subjects at his website (http://jratcliffe.net), which also has his top 10 tips and tricks for effective presentations and other publications that could be of interest to crime analysts.

Weighted averaging uses the idea that if a crime could have occurred, say, between 0800 and 1200 hours, the total possible timespan is 4 hours. Each hour from 0800 to 1200 will get a weighted score for the total possible hours, or one-fourth. As you add up the possible scores per hour for each of the incidents in your series, you get an overall weight assigned to the hour of day of the chance that the crimes occurred during that hour, and thus, a way to predict the next chance for a new crime to occur.

Now take a look at the Weighted Averaging spreadsheet for the burglary series we have been working with in Section5b.xlsx (it will be blank if you have not done the first part of this exercise). You will see that for each incident there is a column of data based on the 24 hour-long periods of a day. We have calculated these based on the dates we calculated in the first steps of this exercise. Each incident is evaluated on how many hours are between the start and end times, so you have to know the start times and end times. If your time period was between 12/31/2012 23:30 hours and 01/01/2011 13:15 hours, we know that there are 15 hours inclusive when the hit could have happened. We score 2300–2359, 0000–0059, all the way to 1300–1359, with a score of 1/15th or 0.067. When we tally up all of the incidents for each of the 24 hour periods, we can see how much weight that hour and incident had on the overall crime series.

In addition, when a crime can be identified as happening at a specific time or within an hour, that hour gets the entire weight of 1. The entire weighting for that incident cannot equal more than 1. We have heard of analysts who complicate the issue and score incidents they think are weakly associated with the series with a value of less than 1, depending on how strongly they think that crime is part of the series. This gets way too complicated for our brains, but it is a thought on how we can rank and weight different crimes in our series depending on how well they reflect the normal behavior of the offender.

When we compare the hour of day chart from the weighted result to the midpoint result, which counted all of the crimes, we cannot see much of a difference for those peak hours we are looking for in the first place (see the graph at the bottom of the Weighted Averaging sheet). Note that the weighted result tossed out 8 of the 24 incidents. We left them all in for the split time calculation, but in theory we should exclude the same 8 incidents from both the weighted and midpoint results.

The peaks are about in the same place, although the 2200–2359 peak is much higher with the midpoint analysis results and may be a bit deceiving. You should expect to see a more level graph with weighted averaging because that is really what you are doing with the data: leveling it off and making each hour the crime could have occurred is less valuable in the overall result, or less weighted. We find that for most analysis efforts, the midpoint is fast, very practical, and works as well as the much longer and more complicated weighted averaging endeavor, even if we leave in the incidents where the timespan is more than 24 hours. Because the graphing helps us understand the hourly distribution of the crime series very well, we also prefer doing the simple graph method for predicting the next time range and day of week range. The midpoint analysis and weighted averaging can both be done rather quickly when you know how to convert and use dates in Excel.

If you wanted to use all of the incidents in the weighted method, you would simply figure out how many possible hours are between the start and end times. Every hour would then get 1/nth of the weight. For example, if there were 48 hours between two times a crime may have occurred. The start time was midnight, and the end time was also midnight 2 days later. Each of the 24-hour periods would be weighted as 2/48 (the same as 1/24) because they have two chances of being the correct time for the actual offense. If the time between the start and end was 26 hours, then every hour would get 1/26, but 2 hours would get 2/26 of weight. This gets confusing, and although you can set this calculation up in Excel, we have never been very successful at creating a spreadsheet that would do this automatically for any crime series. However, we have done this in Access, and it works quite well for most analysis efforts and does not change the outcome very much. (You can download a sample tactical database application created by one of the coauthors here: www.box.net/shared/7mclyk956605aam93ln8.) Dr. Ratcliffe's Aoristic method may also be easier for you to use and it is well worth the time to browse his site and check out this method. The methods shown are not the only ways dates and times can be manipulated in Excel to come to these answers, of course. You may develop your own method and become an expert at manipulating Excel into making your life easier. The idea is that we want to create an analysis that is operationally useful to the investigators, is not confusing to them, and has the best chance of nabbing the offender the next time he tries to commit a crime in this series. When you develop that easier or faster method, share it with other analysts who also want to make their jobs and analysis products better.

CrimeStat's Correlated Walk Prediction

Because this tutorial is getting fairly lengthy, we will not go into great detail about the Correlated Walk Analysis method in CrimeStat III. Please review the CrimeStat III manual for instructions on how to create and use the Correlated Walk Analysis routine. We have found that the next hit date prediction it calculates is very reliable for most crime series and could be useful to you once you learn how to use it.

Take a look at the Correlated Walk Analysis (CWA) Exercise sheet in the Section5b.xlsx workbook. This sheet does the date calculations we use when doing a tactical prediction. If you use the midpoints as the base for your calculations, you will see that for this series, the average number of days between hits is 2.5, and the standard deviation is 2.8. This should tell you that the data are widely variable, and there is no real discernable pattern in hits by date. The last hit was 10 days from the previous one, and this could mean that the offender had been jailed on another offense or you don't have all of the crimes in this series identified. Maybe the offender was sick for a few days or on vacation! Whatever the case, the prediction based on the average and standard deviation has the next hit happening prior to the last one and up to March 7. That is about as good as your next date prediction may get.

Using the three date predictions from CrimeStat III CWA routine, we see that it is predicting a new hit on March 1, 3, or 5. So far in our analysis, the median prediction has always been the most accurate from the CWA routine; therefore, March 5 seems like a good date. We typically then just subtract 2–3 days and add 2–3 days to this prediction to get a range. We find that when the standard method of days between hits predicts a similar time period as the Correlated Walk Analysis routine, then it is a pretty sure bet the suspect will hit during the 7-day span that was calculated with the CWA routine (see columns I through M in the CWA Exercise sheet in Section5b.xlsx). With the CWA process we take the cumulative days between hits count for the last hit in the series and plug that into the CWA routine in CrimeStat III. CrimeStat then determines if there are any temporal patterns and gives us a number that can then be subtracted from the cumulative count and added to the last date a hit was known. This gives us a future date that the CWA routine is predicting a new hit is likely to be on. We can usually provide a more accurate and smaller date range with this method than with the standard methods already discussed.

It is a good idea to try several different types of temporal analyses with your tactical crime series. We find it very validating to know that when the CWA routine, our simple graphing method, and the calculated decimal time all come up with pretty much the same prediction for a lot of crime series, the accuracy and confidence in the prediction goes up. When they do not come out about the same, or the range is very large between them, we have less confidence in the prediction. We also begin to worry that we have done some calculation incorrectly when these results differ greatly, so we make a habit of checking our work for errors. If we find none, then the suspect has no discernable temporal pattern and may be very hard to predict. We may also be missing cases that happened in another jurisdiction nearby or simply missed them in our own review of potential cases from our RMS.

Why Do So Many Calculations?

The comment we made before about several methods all arriving at the same conclusion is the primary reason why you may want to do all of these things on every tactical prediction. If the decimal time calculation, days between hits calculation, Correlated Walk Analysis, and dollars per day calculation all say the same date, time, and day of week are most likely for a new hit in a crime series, then this means that your prediction is very likely to be true, and we have the absolute best chance to apprehend the offender before he can do any more harm. You can thus have high confidence that your prediction is correct or will yield good results if the undercover officers can get out and watch the areas you predicted the suspect will go to next. When they differ a great deal, it can mean that your prediction is based on data that are not reliable enough to make a good prediction, and you can tone down your confidence in the prediction. Picking the days that overlap from the two to four methods you may have tried can narrow a prediction that has a very wide timespan for the prediction. As an analyst, the first thing you have to do is give the **most likely** estimate for a new hit in the series. The second thing you should do is state how confident you are in that prediction. You should also not stop doing analysis if you happen to be wrong now and again. That *is* going to happen, because again, human behavior is very difficult to predict correctly every time.

One of the methods we learned many years ago from Dale Harris, of Corona Solutions, was based on a robbery analysis. He advised that his agency in Colorado had done well with using an average dollars per day calculation for predicting when a robbery offender would hit next. This was based on the thought that if an offender was a drug user and had a $300/day habit, he would need to commit enough robberies to keep him in drugs. If you have a robber who is shown to have a $300 habit based on the dollars per day you've calculated, then if he made $1200 on his last robbery, you have about 4 days before he hits again. This is a very simple thought process and piece of logic, but it often works very well. If you think about your own habits, like drinking milk, for example, you may see this thought process a bit clearer. My family of four used to drink 2 gallons of milk per week when my sons were little, so every week we went shopping for milk at the local grocery store to replenish our supply. One weekend we bought 4 gallons instead of our usual 2 gallons (it was on sale) so we did not go shopping or need milk again for 2 weeks. If you were a robber, and money to feed your drug habit was your motivation, do you think this pattern would be predictable? Of course, we would have to measure the number of gallons of milk the robber received for each of his crimes, but you get the idea.

The formulas for doing all of these calculations are included in the exercise spreadsheet—they are very simple formulas. Review them as needed to understand how this all goes together.

Section 6

Pivot Tables and Administrative, or Strategic, Analysis

A pivot table is a function of Excel that allows you to take rows and columns of data and create summary tables for the fields in your dataset. You can make pivot tables from fields that contain day of week (row) and time of day (column) data and a value field (count of RptNum) to help in describing and analyzing data more quickly.

Pivot Table Web Resources

The websites in the following list have great tutorials on creating pivot tables. You can refer to them to learn how pivot tables can be used and leveraged for crime analysis. Pivot tables and pivot charts are a crime analyst's friend, and the Excel Help file is also useful in learning how to use these powerful summary tools. You can find many other tutorials on pivot tables by searching online for "Excel pivot tables."

- www.exceltip.com/excel_tips/Excel_Pivot_Tables/32.html
- www.mathtools.net/Excel/Pivot_tables/
- www.cpearson.com/excel/pivots.htm
- www.dummies.com/how-to/content/the-essentials-of-excel-2010-pivot-tables-and-pivo.html

Pivot Table Example

The following pivot table example uses some data you have already seen. Open CIA\Exercises\Excel\Section6.xlsx and review the calls for service data. Follow these steps to create a pivot table of this data to determine what radio code type was the highest for this area. *(Note: In Excel 2007, the functions are similar, but these instructions were written for Excel 2010. Please review the pivot table help in your version of Excel for additional directions or visit one of the websites mentioned in the previous section.)*

1. Click on **Insert** in the menu bar and select **Pivot Table** at the far left side of the Ribbon menu.
2. In the Create Pivot Table popup dialog box, click the small spreadsheet-looking icon to the right of the Table/Range box. The Create Pivot Table popup menu will shrink, and then highlight all the cells that contact any data (cells A1 through K1681).
3. Choose "New Worksheet" from the section asking, "Choose where you want the pivot table to be placed." Click the OK button.
4. You should now have a new and empty pivot table to work with in a new worksheet (see Pivot Table Sample tab).
5. Drag the RptNum field from the right side and drop it on the Values part of the pivot table on the left. Drag the Radio_Code field from the right and drop it on the Row Labels part of the pivot table field list.
6. This is your pivot table, and it summarizes the number of calls for service by radio code type.

Click in the **Total** column, and then you can use the **Data** menu's sort buttons to sort these data in descending or ascending order as needed. You can also drag other fields to the pivot table, move the row data to columns, and any number of other things. We modified this pivot table and made the DOW (day of week) field the column heading and the TOD (time of day) field the row heading. The resulting pivot table can be found in the Pivot Table Samples sheet (cells J1 through R29).

Right clicking on the pivot table allows you to refresh the data from your table. If you change anything in your source data sheet, click Refresh to update the data in the pivot table. Then you can use the new fields you inserted between columns. If you added a column to the end, you typically have to click on the pivot table options menu in the ribbon bar. Here you will find a button to change the data source and include those columns you added to the end of the data. Remember that if you insert columns into those already there, you only need to refresh the data because Excel will automatically recognize the new columns.

If, for example, you wanted a list of the details of the incidents that occurred at 2100–2159 hours on Sunday (the spreadsheet shows 19 records), you can double click on the Grand Total cell, for that time period in the pivot table and a whole new worksheet will be created that has a drill-down version of those 19 records and all of the details that are in the original source data, as shown in sample sheet 2100_2159 in the workbook.

This is a super feature for creating subsets of data you may want to use for other analyses, like date and time, trend over time, top addresses, and others based on the analytical product you want to create.

Attempt to create your own pivot table with the data in Section6.xlsx and change it, refresh it, and make several different pivot tables to summarize the data in this table. You can also change the type of data summarized by clicking on the "Values" field and then choosing "Value Field Settings." You can get the following statistics or summaries:

- Sum
- Count
- Average
- Minimum
- Maximum

- Product
- Count Numbers
- STDEV (Entire population)
- STDEVP (STDEV of a sample)

Keep in mind that for sum, average, product, and STDEVs you will need to have your Values field set to a number field in your table.

Another cool use of pivot tables is to use conditional formatting with the results from a pivot table. Highlight all the rows and columns in the DOW and TOD pivot table within the Pivot Table Sample tab and click CTRL+C to copy the entire pivot tables' contents. Now find a blank space on the sheet anywhere to the left of the DOW/TOD pivot table and right click a cell and choose Paste Special Values. You now have a copy of the original pivot table data. Change the Days of week from 1, 2, 3 . . . etc. to Sun, Mon, Tue . . . etc. Additionally, change the Times of day from 0, 1, 2, 3 . . . etc. to 0000–0059 hrs, 0100–0159 hrs . . . etc. Spruce up the column and row headings to make them pretty and add some dark blue background and bold, yellow text to them. Now, add gridlines for each of the cells in the new temporal matrix so that each cell is boxed in. Format the column and rows to fit the cell contents. Now highlight all of the cells under Sun, and right of 0000–0059 hrs to under SAT and right of 2300–2359 hrs. Everything except the total sections and the column and row headings should be selected. Now in the Home menu, choose the Conditional Formatting button. Choose the **Color Scales** option, and the second from the left, top row scale that goes from red to green. You should now have a temporal heat "map" of when these calls are coming in. We can see from the chart that Mon–Tue between 1600–1759 hrs are the peaks for this set of data. We can also create day of week, time of day, or even radar/spoke charts or 3D surface charts with the data (see the conditional formatting example tab for an example of what your chart should look like).

■ Section 7

Now open the spreadsheet called CIA\Exercises\Excel\Practice.xlsx. The file contains a set of 12 different tactical crime series from the City of Glendale, AZ. We have also included four administrative/strategic forecasting projects in this spreadsheet.

The projects can be geocoded, so you can create a map; you can create forecasts, charts, and brief summaries of the data as if you have been assigned them during your work as a crime analyst.

You should create all of the fields you will need to do a date and time analysis and calculate split time where needed. Also complete the next hit date, most likely weekday, and most likely time range for a new hit in the series provided. You can work on these crime series individually or in groups as would be best to assist you in learning how to compute the statistics and information you will need to know in the real world of crime analysis.

- Try to forecast the total number of Part 1 UCR crimes for 2012 in worksheet Admin1.
- Calculate what the total UCR crimes will be in each of the five grids in Admin2 for 2012.
- Calculate the correlations between variables in the strategic worksheets.
- Predict when the offender will hit next in the tactical exercises.

In the CIA\Exercises\Excel folder there are also two helpful excel sheets that were created by Norman J. Harker and Peter Noneley. These are older sheets, so to use them in Excel 2010 you do have to make sure that macros are enabled for the functionality and indexing in these sheets to work. You can try to upgrade them to Excel 2010 versions, but you may run into a few issues with the older code in them. They are both awesome references to the many functions Excel has and how to use them in your analysis. The file names are Excel_Functions_Dictionary.xls and Appendix 01 function list.xls.

■ Recommended reading

Bruce, C., & Stallo, M. (2008). *Better policing with Microsoft Office 2007*. North Charleston, SC: Booksurge.

■ References

Gottlieb, S., Arenberg, S., & Singh, R. (1994). *Crime analysis: From first report to final arrest*. Montclair, CA: Alpha.

Ratcliffe, J. (n.d.). *Research and spatial questions (past and current)*. Retrieved from http://jratcliffe .net/research/index.htm.

Exercises

■ Exercise Introduction

All of the exercises in this text were developed using Microsoft Excel 2010 and ArcGIS 10 with Service Pack 3 installed. Although many of these exercises will work correctly with ArcGIS 9.3 and Excel 2007, you may need to look in a different location for tools, buttons, or functions described in the exercises.

The chapter exercises created for this text were developed by Bryan Hill, a crime analyst for the Glendale Police Department in Glendale, Arizona. Ms. Laura Vittorio from Tucson Police Department, Mrs. Judy Fernandez from Gilbert Police Department, and Mrs. Katherine Foley from Tucson Police Department also reviewed the exercises and provided insight and helpful tips to make the exercises better. The ArcMap 10 exercises in this section are basic, applied exercises for flexing your geographic information systems (GIS) muscles in a practical and operational setting. The exercises will take you through administrative, strategic, and tactical situations that many crime analysts are faced with during their careers. Hopefully, with these exercises, *and lots of practice, and lots of practice* (yes, we said that twice), you will find ways to accomplish GIS crime analysis tasks through some standard geoprocessing tactics. The authors would like to stress that there are many more skills and practiced abilities that the student can learn on their own using the knowledge they get from these exercises. As Bruce Silva explains, "The study of crime and place is vital to making sense of relationships between crime and the world around it. Crime mapping has demonstrated over the past two decades to be fundamental to the analysis, presentation and sharing of information and insight about criminal activities." They will be valuable skills when seeking employment in the crime analysis field, as well as many other fields.

The format of the lessons assumes that you are a beginner or a working analyst or are trying to become one, and you have received or will receive a request for GIS products. The data used in these exercises come from the City of Glendale, Arizona, but they have been sanitized. Any names or addresses found in the data resemble real data, but they have been altered to avoid any relationship to the real world other than the locations. With some intuitive thinking, you should be able to substitute your own data in these exercises where needed. The authors encourage this kind of experimentation with other data that are similar to the exercise data to help you apply the skills you learn here to other data and other situations.

Each exercise demonstrates the skills and job duties you are often asked to do as a crime analyst in the field. Enjoy—be patient! It can take several months to several years to become a proficient GIS analyst of crime. Studying, practicing, and reading about crime mapping will help you attain great skills. You won't get there by osmosis; it takes work. Think of it as trying to learn four new languages all at the same time: (1) geography, (2) GIS and spatial thinking, (3) crime theory and statistics, and (4) the ArcGIS software itself. These are all sciences and arts themselves, and so the world of crime mapping does not come into view quickly; it takes patience and, at times, stubbornness to become proficient.

The texts in the following list contain working copies of ArcGIS that you may find useful for additional practice and reference. The first one contains a 180-day trial version of ArcMap, which is needed to complete these exercises (if your educational institution does not have the software). You may also order an evaluation copy (which usually expires 60 days after it is installed onto your computer) from the ESRI website (www.esri.com/software/arcgis/arcview/eval/evalcd.html). In addition, ESRI offers a 1-year student license for about $100 (you can ask for and obtain a student license for ArcGIS here: www.esri.com/industries/apps/education/offers/promo/index.cfm).

- *GIS Tutorial for Crime Analysis.* ESRI Press, 380 New York Street, Redlands, CA 92373-8100; Copyright 2011, ISBN: 9781589482142.
- *Getting to Know ArcGIS Desktop, Second Edition, Updated for ArcGIS 10.* ESRI Press, 380 New York Street, Redlands, CA 92373-8100; Copyright 2010, ISBN: 9781589482609.
- *GIS Tutorial 1: Basic Workbook, Fourth Edition*, ESRI Press, 380 New York Street, Redlands, CA 92373-8100; Copyright 2010, ISBN: 9781589482593.
- *GIS Tutorial 2: Spatial Analysis Workbook, Second Edition*, ESRI Press, 380 New York Street, Redlands, CA 92373-8100; Copyright 2010, ISBN: 9781589482586.
- *GIS Tutorial 3: Advanced Workbook,* ESRI Press, 380 New York Street, Redlands, CA 92373-8100; Copyright 2010, ISBN: 9781589482074.
- Many more ESRI press books can be found at their website at http://esripress.esri.com/display/index.cfm?CFID=10145828&CFTOKEN=66928842.
- There are several other locations where you can find free tutorials as well, such as Rutgers University's "GIS for Public Safety: An Annotated Guide to ArcGIS Tools and Procedures (for versions 9.3 or 10)": www.rutgerscps.org/gisbook/.

College and university websites are always good places to find tutorials online, and the ESRI software comes with many tutorials that could be of use to you as you work your way through the GIS trade. When working on them on your own, if you get stuck on any of the exercises in this tutorial, you can refer to either of the other ESRI manuals listed here and work out the problems most of the time. These exercises will assume you have some basic knowledge of crime analysis (that can be gained from this text) and a small degree of familiarity with ArcMap (the exercises do contain very basic, introductory instructions to familiarize the student with ArcMap). If you can create a new map from the data you have available to you, you should do very well. These exercises should be simple enough for any new user to develop skills in GIS with practice. They should also be challenging enough for current crime analysts to remain interested. For extra help, various screenshots and other figures have been created. They also include examples of finished maps for comparison to see if you have correctly completed the exercises.

■ The Data Files

Data Needed for This Exercise

- ArcGIS desktop software (evaluation copy is fine, see the previous introduction to the chapter exercises).
- Everything else is included in the files on the companion website.

Task Description

- Download the data files from the companion website and save them on the PC that has ArcGIS installed.
- Run the CIA.exe file. This will create a folder called C:\CIA on your PC and copy all of the data for the class into the appropriate folders.
- Using Windows Explorer, Open the CIA folder on your desktop and browse through the data.
- Install ArcGIS 10x onto your computer. Make sure to also install the most recent patch or service pack for the version of ArcGIS that you own. The patches can be found at the www.esri.com site here: http://resources.arcgis.com/content/patches-and-service-packs. You may have to sign in and create a global ESRI user name and password. At the time of this writing, service pack 3 was the most current service pack, however service pack 4 will be out prior to the publishing of this workbook. If these service packs are not up to date, the software may not perform as desired in these exercises.
- Make sure you have at least 20 gigabytes of available space on your computer. The files downloaded from the website will be about 4 gigabytes.
- To begin using this data, save the entire "CIA" folder from the website to the local C:\ drive of the computer.
- It will take several minutes to copy the files needed for these exercises, so please be patient, and do not use your PC while the copying is being performed. There are approximately 4 gigabytes of data in the CIA folder.
- When the process is completed, you will need to open Windows Explorer to browse the data in the folder on your PC. After the data is completely loaded onto the C:\ drive, right click on the C:\CIA folder, choose properties, and in the dialog menu, make sure that all of the data in the folder is not read only. This is accomplished by unchecking the box next to read only on the General tab and then under the Customize tab, check the box to also apply it to all subfolders.
- The data may be downloaded in read only format, so to make edits to this data you will need to remember this step. (Note: on many college computers, the C:\ drive is restricted and often the entire drive has been made read only by the Information Technology Department at the college or police agency. You may need to contact the Information Technology Department to have the data copied, and then may need to alter the exercises slightly, when trying to edit data. This may not be the case at all colleges and universities, so you will need to check prior to trying to install in a educational setting, or even on law enforcement computers.)
- **You are ready to start working with our data.** All exercise data are located in the CIA\ Exercises folder on the directory where the student or educational institution saved the data from the website. This is typically in the CIA\Exercises directory. Please ask your instructor, or the person who saved the data to find the it. The "CIA" folder is the uppermost level, with the Data, Exercises, Photos_Graphics, and Resources folders directly under the CIA folder. The vast majority of the data for each exercise can be found in the Data

folder and the student (and instructor) are provided with a extensive array of data from file geodatabases, personal geodatabases, and shapefiles. These data include UCR reported crimes, calls for service, boundary data, persons data, and traffic crashes for use in the exercises. It is very important to keep the directory tree the same as provided on the DVD. If any of the sub-directories are moved, not installed, or renamed, the exercises may not work properly, so this is strongly discouraged.

Section 1: Basic Level GIS

■ Exercise 1: Discovering ArcMap Through a Trip Around Glendale, Arizona

Data Needed for This Exercise

- All data are included in the ArcMap document (CIA\Exercises\EX_1\EX_1.mxd).

Lesson Objectives

- The student will learn to open an ArcMap document.
- The student will learn to use the **Standard toolbar** to browse data in ArcMap.
- The student will learn to use the Tools and **Layout toolbars** to browse data in ArcMap.
- The student will discover the basic elements of an ArcMap project.
- The purpose of this exercise is to introduce the student to the ArcMap interface and one way to add data using ArcCatalog. The student will also learn about different types of data that can be used in ArcMap. Additionally students will be introduced to symbol classifications and how to make their maps appear as they wish them to.
- The student will discover where the table of contents (TOC), map display, toolbars, status bar, and other parts of the ArcMap interface are located.
- The student will learn how to add data using ArcCatalog.
- The student will learn the basics of how to change symbology classifications to make a better map.

Task Description

1. To begin this exercise, we will open a saved ArcView/ArcMap project.
2. In Windows, click on the **Start menu ‡ Programs** and find the ESRI or ArcGIS program folder. (*Note*: The authors are using a PC with Windows 7 installed, so if you are using an older version, some windows and views may be slightly different from the graphics in this project.)
3. Double click on the icon for ArcMap 10 to open the program. When ArcMap opens, choose **Existing Maps** and then **Browse for more**.
4. Find the EX_1.mxd file located in CIA\Exercises\Ex_1\EX_1.mxd (see **Figure E1–1**).
5. The file extension for ArcMap documents is .mxd. Like Microsoft Word (.docx) or Microsoft Excel (.xlsx), the .mxd extension stores all of the settings, legend items, location of windows, source locations of data (but not the data itself), and toolbars for the mapping project. It saves these settings when it is closed and will reopen and appear as it was when last saved and exited. This means that whatever queries, joins, and window positions the project was set to when they were closed, will reappear exactly as when they were last closed.

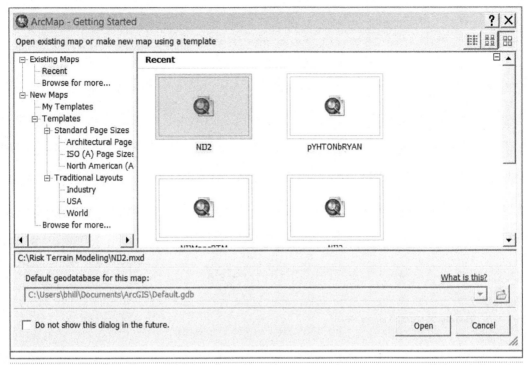

Figure E1–1

The MXD file does not save the actual data for each theme in the TOC within the project, *but it does store the path to that data.* When the EX_1.mxd file opens, you will see an ArcMap document window that has the TOC on the left, map display on the right, status bar at the bottom, and toolbars docked to the top, bottom, center, and possibly floating or in other locations (see **Figure E1–2**).

Do not worry if it does not exactly match or if your toolbars are not located where they are shown in this image. Toolbars can be moved at any time, and their positions are saved when ArcMap closes on your PC. The TOC should look very similar to the TOC in this image because the TOC is saved for each project. You should notice by now that this project is blank and has no data in it.

6. The TOC (left side of screen) displays the themes or layers of data that are linked for this project. It also shows the types of markers, line symbols, and polygon outlines and fills that will be shown in the map display.

7. The map display (right side of screen) is the graphic representation of the data that are listed in the TOC. This can also be called the "drawing canvas," and it basically shows you what is visible and how it would look if you printed this project "map."

8. The Menu bar has commonly seen functions in all Windows types of applications and programs, including File, Edit, View, etc. It also includes such items as adding data and layers, viewing the attribute table of a theme, or adding more toolbars.

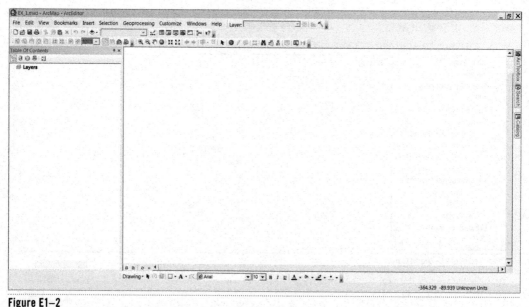

Figure E1–2

9. The Tools toolbar (**Figure E1–3**) contains tools that you can use to browse around the map display and allows you to do such things as zoom in, zoom out, pan, identify an item on the map display, measure distances, and show hyperlinks.

Figure E1–3

10. The Drawing toolbar (**Figure E1–4**, bottom of screen) gives you some tools that allow you to draw rectangles, circles, points, oddly shaped polygons, and add text as graphics to the screen. Think of these tools as the representative of the old standard wall map. They are simply graphics and contain no data or attributes behind the graphic item, unlike a theme or layer in the TOC, which can conceivably store everything there is to know about an incident. Graphics can be useful for quickly portraying graphic information on a map and allowing a lot of freedom in adding individual pieces of annotation (text) to the map display. In an emergency response situation, the Draw toolbar is a lifesaver and allows you to draw a lot of things on the map display without having to create a sophisticated attribute table behind it. Later, when you have more time, you can create the shapefile or data that make the information more permanent.

Figure E1–4

11. The View Choice buttons at the corner of where the map display window meets the TOC window will allow us to move back and forth from the map display view and the layout view of the data (see **Figure E1–5**). It also allows us to pause the drawing of the map when using very large files (far right button), and redraw the map display (second button from the right).

Figure E1–5

12. The Data view (leftmost button) can be thought of as the place where we get our view of the Earth to look like it needs to look to tell the story that we wish to tell. This is the view of the world we see in our map.

13. The Layout view is where we create a printable map that has a legend, scale bar, north arrow, title bar, and other items that make it a good cartographic representation of the world and story we wish to tell. We generally print the map from the Layout view. The Layout view has a different set of standard tools than does the Display view, and you need to get used to recognizing the difference between the two toolbars (compare Figure E1–3 with **Figure E1–6**).

Figure E1–6

14. Both tools control what you see; however, the Data view toolbar (called Tools in the toolbar list) allows the user to browse, select, zoom in, and identify various parts of the geography, or surface of the Earth that are being examined. The Layout toolbar allows you to zoom in and out of the map you will eventually want to print and change the layout template being used. You could think of the Tools toolbar as a device that allows you to interact with the map, or the graphic representation of the Earth's surface, and the Layout toolbar allows you to move around the printable "copy" of the Earth's surface just to enhance the ultimate, printed version.

15. The Selection tab at the top of the TOC (see **Figure E1–7**) allows us to "see" our data in different ways. The leftmost button lets us see our data by the selected sort order. The second to the left allows us to see our data by where the data is stored, or the source of the data. The middle button allows us to see layers we have set to being "visible." The fourth from the left button allows us to see data that have been "selected" and allows us to make settings in our data about whether or not a layer can be selectable. The rightmost button lets us change a few options about the data in the TOC.

Table Of Contents	⊕ ✕

Figure E1–7

16. In addition to these buttons we also have the ability to add or remove the ArcToolboxes and ArcCatalog tabs from the project.

17. If ArcToolbox and ArcCatalog are not visible to the right side of the map display, we can turn them on using other tools in the main menu bar.

18. To turn on ArcToolbox, click on Geoprocessing → ArcToolbox.

19. To turn on ArcCatalog, click on Windows → Catalog.

20. To add the search function to the map display, click on Windows → Search.

21. If you want them to be pinned to a certain part of the screen, grab the function tab by clicking on it and then holding the left mouse button down, and then drag it to one of the blue directional tabs (you must be right on top of one to drop it and have it "stick" to the right side).

22. We can then click each of the AutoHide buttons in each function tab window (top right, looks like a stick pin). This will cause the tabs to autohide and minimize on the right side of the map display as needed.

23. We will now add some data to our project. At the far right of the map display area, there is a tab that reads, "ArcCatalog." Left click this tab. At the top is a row of buttons and functions we can use to work with data. Slowly move your cursor over the buttons until you find the one that has a popup that reads, "Connect to Folder."

24. Left Click this button. Browse to the CIA\Data folder, make sure the data folder is highlighted, and then click OK.

25. Go back to the ArcCatalog tab and you should now see the CIA\Data folder listed under folder connections.

26. Click on the plus sign to the left of this connection to see all of the data available under the data folder.

27. There are several types of data that can be used in the ArcMap software. Some data are GIS data formats we can create with the ArcMap software, and others, although created in a different software product, can be imported. The four primary data types we deal with are:
    a. File Geodatabases: ESRI Proprietary structure
    b. Personal Geodatabases: MS Access Database GeoEnabled Structure
    c. Shapefiles
    d. SDE GeoDatabases: Special Spatial Database Engine (SDE) connection to Oracle, or SQL databases
    We can also have older ArcInfo coverage and of course we can work with .DBF, .CSV, and other tabular data as with any database product. We will not discuss spatial database engine (SDE) databases in this course as they are typically used for large enterprise solutions for GIS, are more expensive, and are more than the average college may need. We will discuss and show the use of file geodatabases, personal geodatabases, and shapefiles.

28. Going back to the ArcCatalog tab and the CIA\Data folder connection, we can see that there are three folders, each with the name of one of the types of data we discussed in step 26. Left click on the plus sign to the left of the **File Geodatabase** folder. You will see that in this folder is a **GIS_layers.GDB** database. The .GDB extension indicates this is a file geodatabase. Double click on the GDB file, and when you do you can see several sections called **Feature Datasets**. We will get to these a little later. At the very bottom are two layers we want to add to our current map. File Geodatabases have a proprietary structure on the Windows directory. They have files that do not make much sense when they are viewed by Windows Explorer alone, but only make sense within the ArcGIS environment. The advantages to a file geodatabase is that several users can more easily work with the same data without running into issues of data locks as we might get with a personal geodatabase. A personal geodatabases could be an MS Access database that contains files that denote the spatial aspects and attributes of the data within the geodatabase. Personal geodatabases are much easier to work with and offer the ability to collect feature datasets

(as with file geodatabases), but also be able to connect to the data within the personal geodatabase through ODBC connections for use in other databases or even spreadsheets. Shapefiles are actually made up of at least 4 different file types:

- *.SHX—Spatial location indexes
- *.SHP—Actual geography of the layer
- *.DBF—Attributes or data behind the GIS layer type
- *.PRJ—The projection of the data

Each of this files are needed to make up the complete shapefile. Without the first three, a shapefile cannot be a shapefile and will not work in the GIS software. Another caution is that when new GIS users start out they often think they can edit the *.DBF table within Excel or some other application and expect it to work in the GIS. However, changing the underlying DBF table in any way will corrupt the shapefile and make it no longer useful within the GIS. It is always a good idea to use the GIS software to make edits to the GIS data no matter what file format it is in. While you might be able to do the edits faster in Excel or Access, doing so may seriously damage your GIS data.

29. Selecting one at a time, drag and drop **Basic_Street_Labels_An** and **Street_Labels** to the TOC.

30. The "An" at the end of the Basic_Street_Labels_An layer indicates that this is a saved annotation (text). For this layer there is really nothing to do unless we wanted to change the font, color, etc. of the text or annotation. The Street_Labels layer is actually a set of polygons that were drawn to surround or "house" the text. We want to change all the boxes around the street names to a very light blue fill and a light grey outline, and the boxes around the grid names (two letter and number text combination) to light yellow with a light grey outline.

31. Double click on Street_Labels. This will bring up the properties of this layer, which allows us to make several changes to the way we see and interact with these data (see **Figure E1–8**).

32. Click on the "Symbology" tab and then click on the colored box to the bottom and right of the word "Symbol." This brings up a dialog box that lets us choose different symbols for the data we have (see **Figure E1–9**).

33. Choose the premade "Jade" symbology and click OK and OK again.

34. Notice that this changed all of the boxes to a light blue color with a black outline. This is because we used the symbology type of single symbol (the default), which means all data in this layer will be displayed with a "single symbol," or our jade coloring scheme.

35. Because we want to change the symbology for those boxes that surround the street names to one fill color and a different fill color for the grid boxes, we need to use the symbology type of "Categories." Double click on the Street_Labels layer again, and when the properties dialog pops up, click on the symbology tab. In the symbology dialog box, in the "Show:" section at the top left, find **Categories** and click it. Choose the Categories type classification of **Unique Values** and then move your cursor to the right where it reads, "Value Field," and click on the small down arrow to see the fields available. Find the field called **LabelType** and choose it by clicking it.

36. Now we need to **Add All Values** (button at bottom of Symbology area). Click **OK**. Well, we can see that we are still not where we wanted to be. We have two different colors for the street boxes and four different colors for the grid name boxes.

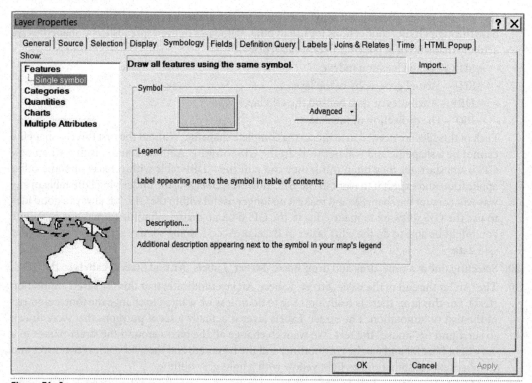

Figure E1–8

37. Double click the Street_Labels layer again and go to the Symbology tab of the Properties dialog one more time. In the Symbology window where you see E grid names, E Street Names, N Grid Names, N Street Names, etc., click on **E Street Names**, hold the **CTRL** key down, and click on **N Street Names** to select them both. Now right click on one of them and choose **Group Values**. Do the same thing with all four "grid"-related classes and make sure you **Group Value** them as well. Now we should only have two classifications or items in the symbology window.

38. Double click on the colored box next to the classification for the combined street boxes you created to bring up our pal, the Symbol Selector, and choose the Jade classification again and click OK. Now double click on the classification type to the left of our combined grid classification type to bring up the Symbol Selector for the grid boxes. Choose the Yellow classification type and click OK.

39. In the Properties/Symbology dialog box, click APPLY or OK at the bottom right of the Properties dialog window. Wow! We are almost done with this stage of the project. We have learned how to add data very easily from ArcCatalog by dragging and dropping it into the map's TOC. We have learned that there are several different kinds of data we can use in ArcMap. We have

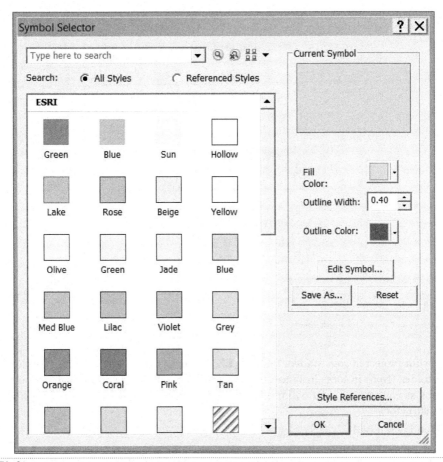

Figure E1–9

also learned that there are different toolbars to use for different features of ArcMap and that a project saves all the window settings from when it was last closed, *but it does not save the data in the project, only the **path** to the data.*

40. Thought I forgot, didn't you? We still do not have a light grey line around our boxes—they are black. Double click on Street_Labels again and go to the symbology tab. Click on our grouped street boxes classification, hold down the CTRL key, and click on the Grid box group classification. When both are selected, right click on either grouped item. This brings up the same popup box we used to group values, but this time we are going to choose **Properties for Selected Symbols**. In the section that reads "Outline Color," we want to click on the same down arrow near the color selection box, make it about a 50% gray, and then click OK and OK. **Figure E1–10** shows how your project should look at this stage.

Figure E1–10

41. **Save** your project in your student folder as EX_1b.mxd, or the folder called "Z_Student" in the CIA folder. (*Note:* In some instances in an educational setting, on educational computers at the school, saving to this folder will not be allowed, so alternative choices should be provided by the instructor).

42. This ends Exercise 1a.

■ Exercise 1b: Continuing our Discovery: ArcMap and Glendale, Arizona

Data Needed for This Exercise

- We will begin with the project you saved in Exercise 1a (EX_1b.mxd). If you do not have this project saved, a copy can be found under CIA\Exercises\EX_1\EX_1b.mxd.

Lesson Objectives

- The student will learn to open an ArcMap document by double clicking the *.Mxd in Windows Explorer.
- The student will learn where the standard toolbar is located.
- The student will learn to add more data.
- The student will learn to Add and Classify other data (points, lines, and polygons).

Task Description

1. Open Windows Explorer.
2. Navigate to your student folder and open the project you named EX_1b.mxd (alternatively, go to CIA\Exercises\EX_1\EX_1b.mxd and open it).

3. We will now continue to build our map so that we have boundaries, streets, some calls for service point data, and some reference features.

4. ArcMap uses three basic types of data: points, lines, and polygons.

5. Point data are represented on the map as dots and are symbolized by any variety of single shapes and colors. They typically represent something that occurred at a specific time and location, like a call for service, or represent a feature (light pole, sewer manhole, police station, etc.). Points can know everything there is to know about an event that happened at that spot, or about the feature. Any number of symbols can be used to represent what the point data are trying to represent in the real world.

6. Line data are usually street centerlines; they can also be boundary lines, streams, water pipes, etc. They are represented on the map as any number of line symbols, which can have different colors, shapes, and can be solid, dashed, or dotted. Lines are usually broken up in segments and have nodes joining the segments. Each segment "knows" what segment is before it and after it, as well as what data is on the left and right. In a street centerline example, the centerline knows which addresses are on the left and right of it, and which segments are before and after it. This is good for network analysis, routing, and *geocoding*. We will discuss geocoding later on in the exercises.

7. Polygon data are shapes that have a fill color and outline color and can represent boundaries such as beats, patrol zones, or jurisdictional political boundaries. They can be filled with solid, gradient, or texture fills; the outline can be changed from thick to thin; and the outline color can also be changed. Polygons "know" what other polygons are adjacent to them, and they can be used to select all points or lines that are within them.

8. Let us begin to shape our view of the world called Glendale, AZ a bit more, shall we?

9. Click on the ArcCatalog button again and find our folder connection to the CIA\Data folder.

10. Click on the file geodatabase folder and open the CIA\Data\File geodatabase\GIS_Layers.gdb geodatabase.

11. Click the plus sign next to the boundaries feature dataset to see the different layers that are in this feature dataset.

12. Find the layer named "City_Boundary_P" and drag it to the table of contents (TOC). Now double click the city boundary layer in the TOC to open the properties and go to the symbology tab.

13. Let's change the classification of this layer to the "hollow" symbol by clicking on the single symbol area where the colored box is located under the word "symbol," as we did in Exercise 1a.

14. In addition, change the outline thickness to 3 and the outline color to a medium blue.

15. Click OK, Apply, and then OK again to make your changes.

16. Notice that with a polygon we do not require a fill color, which means we do not have to have a color filling the entire polygon(s)—they can be completely transparent.

17. We can also get a bit fancier with our outline type and style. Double click on the city boundary layer again to open the properties dialog (alternatively you can right click the layer and then choose properties from the popup menu).

18. Double click on the Symbol box that is currently showing the blue outline and no fill to get into the symbol selector dialog menu.

19. Click on the **Edit Symbol** button.

20. Click on the **Outline** button.

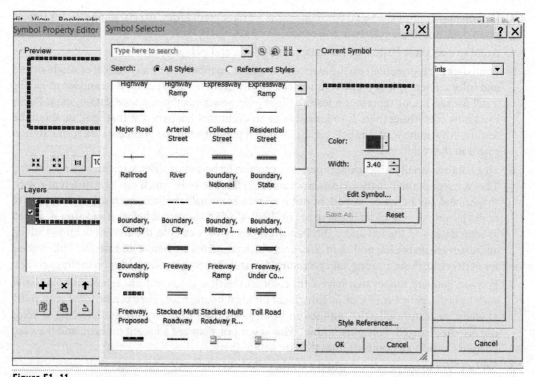

Figure E1–11

21. Choose the Boundary, Township symbol class in the symbol selector window (see **Figure E1–11**).
22. Change the thickness back to 3 if it reverted to 0.40, and also choose a color that is a light or medium brown for the border.
23. Click OK in each of the three dialog boxes to close them, and then Apply and OK on the properties dialog to see your artwork.
24. Find the Grids_P data in the file geodatabase in ArcCatalog and add it to the TOC.
25. Change this layer to be a hollow fill with a medium grey outline, using the skills we have gone through with the three other layers we have added to this project.
26. Double click on each layer one at a time, and when the properties dialog opens, go to the General tab, and rename the layers where it reads, **Layer Name**, as follows:
    a. Basic_Street_Labels_An to *Labels*
    b. Grids_P to *Grids*
    c. City_Boundary_P to *Glendale Boundaries*
    d. Street_Labels to *Reference boxes*
27. Save this project as EX_1c.mxd in your student folder.
28. Your map should now look like **Figure E1-12**.

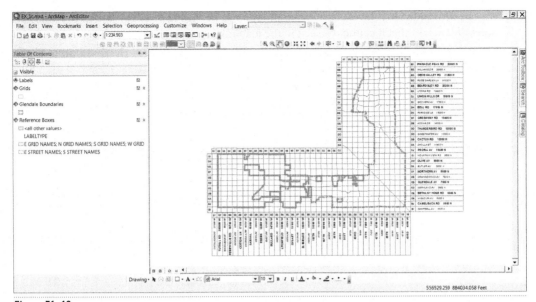

Figure E1–12

29. Another way to add data is to use the **Add Data** button in the Standard toolbar (see **Figure E1–13**).

Figure E1–13

30. The Add Data button is located just below the word "Insert" in the menu bar at the top of the ArcMap project. Click on this button.

31. This opens the Add Data dialog box, which resembles the standard open files or add data dialog you might find with other Windows products.

32. Navigate to the CIA\Data\File Geodatabase\GIS_Layers.gdb and find the feature dataset named "Transportation" and double click it.

33. Click on **Bike_Routes**, then hold the CTRL key down and click on **GLN_Streets_Plus**. In this manner, you can add multiple files in the same feature dataset, or file folder at the same time.

34. Click the **Add** button.

35. Right now we do not want the city streets to be visible, so unselect the bike routes layer by unchecking it. Click on the city streets layer to select only it.

36. At the top of the TOC, just beneath the words "Table of Contents" is a group of icons. Hover your cursor over each and click on "List by Visibility." At the far left of the layer, there is small box that looks yellow and has a black line symbol within the box. As you move your cursor over the symbol, popup text appears which reads, "Click to toggle visibility."

37. Click on this visibility toggle.

38. The city streets layer has been moved down and is now in a separate location within the TOC and it is not visible in the map display area.

39. We can turn individual layers or a group of layers to be visible or nonvisible in this manner. *Nonvisible* means that it cannot be seen in the map display area.

40. Change the Bike_Routes name to Bike Routes and change the symbol classification to Single symbol type of "Boundary, County" classification.

41. Your map should now look like **Figure E1–14**. Save your map document.

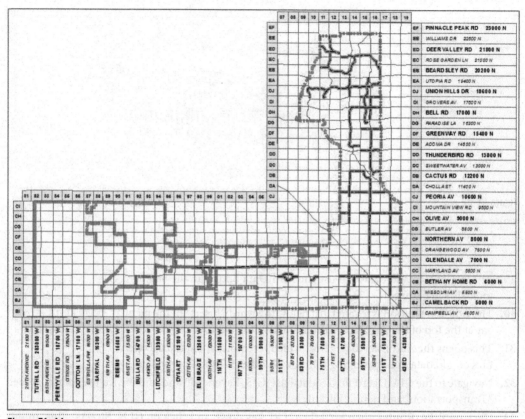

Figure E1–14

42. Another function we find in ArcMap is the ability to select features either on the map, or within the table. The select tool (see **Figure E1–15**) found on the Tools toolbar allows us to select data on the map in several different ways. By clicking the small down arrow at the right of the select button we can choose to:

Figure E1–15

    a. Select by rectangle
    b. Select by polygon
    c. Select by lasso
    d. Select by circle
    e. Select by line

43. To start our selection mania, we usually need to specify which layer we want to be "selectable," so that when we select data we only get a selection in the data we wish, rather than everything on the map.

44. First change the TOC order to "List by Selection" and then, to the far right of each layer except the bike routes, click on the small box by the name of the layer where the popup text reads, "Click to toggle selectable" when you hover your mouse over it. You can also click on the TOC command buttons at the top of the TOC; click the one that reads, "List by selection." You can then right click on the bike routes layer and choose "Make this the only selectable layer."

45. Once you have made the bike routes the only selectable layer, we need to set some options or at least understand the options for selections. In the Menu bar, click on **Selection**, and then **Selection Options**. **Figure E1–16** shows the selection options we can make for our selection processes on the map. The first choice we have is whether or not we want to select items that intersect a polygon, are completely within a polygon, or that the box or graphic is completely within.

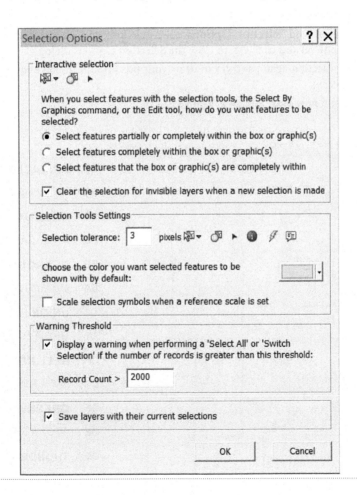

Figure E1–16

46. To experiment a bit, let us set the selection type to select features partially or completely within a box or graphic(s).

47. Close the Selection Options dialog.

48. Use the zoom tool (**Figure E1–17**) found on the Tools toolbar and zoom in to an area around Utopia and N 51st Ave on the map. The easiest way to zoom is to click and hold the left mouse button down at one corner of a box you wish to draw around the area you wish to zoom to. Then, drag the box over the area you wish to zoom to and release the left mouse button.

Figure E1–17

49. Now, click on the select tool (see Figure E1–15), click on the down arrow, and choose select by a rectangle.

50. Try to draw a rectangle that includes all bike routes between W Beardsley Rd and W Grovers Ave, and N 51st Ave to N 59th Ave. Your selection and map should look similar to **Figure E1–18**.

51. The bike routes that are light blue now are the ones selected. However, we have bike routes selected farther west than we wanted.

52. Click on **Selection** and **Selection Options** now, and choose Select features completely within the box or graphic(s) and click OK to close the Selection Options dialog.

53. Now do your selection again, and try to draw your box around the bike routes as close to the one you did before.

54. Your map should now look similar to **Figure E1–19**.

EF	EF	**PINNACLE PEAK RD 2:**
EE	EE	*WILLIAMS DR 22600 N*
ED	ED	**DEER VALLEY RD 218(**
EC	EC	*ROSE GARDEN LN 21000*
EB	EB	**BEARDSLEY RD 20200**
EA	EA	*UTOPIA RD 19400 N*
DJ	DJ	**UNION HILLS DR 1860(**
DI	DI	*GROVERS AV 17800 N*
DH	DH	**BELL RD 17000 N**
DG	DG	*PARADISE LA 16200 N*
DF	DF	**GREENWAY RD 15400**
DE	DE	*ACOMA DR 14600 N*
DD	DD	**THUNDERBIRD RD 138**

Figure E1–18

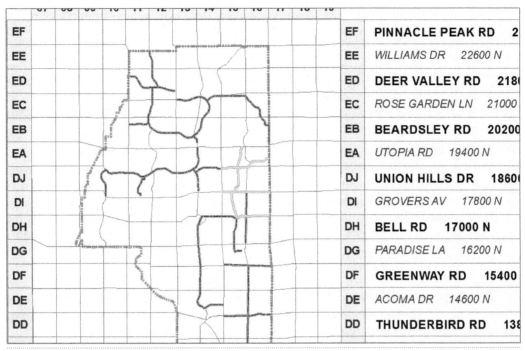

EF		EF	**PINNACLE PEAK RD 2**
EE		EE	*WILLIAMS DR 22600 N*
ED		ED	**DEER VALLEY RD 218(**
EC		EC	*ROSE GARDEN LN 21000*
EB		EB	**BEARDSLEY RD 20200**
EA		EA	*UTOPIA RD 19400 N*
DJ		DJ	**UNION HILLS DR 1860(**
DI		DI	*GROVERS AV 17800 N*
DH		DH	**BELL RD 17000 N**
DG		DG	*PARADISE LA 16200 N*
DF		DF	**GREENWAY RD 15400**
DE		DE	*ACOMA DR 14600 N*
DD		DD	**THUNDERBIRD RD 13&**

Figure E1–19

55. Notice how when you selected the option of select data only within the box or graphic(s) that the bike routes farther west of your box are not selected. This option simply means that only those data elements that are completely within the rectangle, box, or graphic(s) will be selected. In the first option, or selection set, we got more bike routes because that option allows data to be selected whenever any part of the data is within the box or graphic(s).

56. Change the selection options back to the first option and try your selection set again. See how it changes? In most cases we are going to want the first option, but in some cases we may not want points or lines that intersect our selection graphic, and will only want those that are "completely within" what we draw.

57. We can clear this selection by going to **Selection** in the Menu bar and choosing **Clear Selected Features**, then save your map document.

58. Stop, breathe, sigh, expel all those negative vibes and let's go again!

59. Okay, let's try some of the other types of selection graphics with the selection tool.

60. Choose select by polygon after clicking the down arrow next to the select button.

61. On the map, click several spots in a counterclockwise direction and watch as a polygon is created around the bike routes. When you are done making points; double click to make the selection.

62. Now, let's try the Lasso selection option. Click the down arrow on the selection tool, and choose Select by Lasso.

63. Click on the map, and *hold the left mouse button down*. Draw a circle clockwise or counterclockwise around where you clicked, and when you release the mouse button, the data will be selected inside the lasso.

64. Try and see if you can figure out the circle and line options yourself. Notice how the circle option gives you the radius and area of the circle you are drawing at the bottom left side, below the TOC? How can that be of use in your selection projects in the future?

65. Okay, now select some bike routes with any method you choose and leave the selected records visible.

66. Right click on the bike routes layer in the TOC and choose **Open Attribute Table.**

67. The data behind the bike routes, called an attribute table, should open. Depending on how many records you have selected, at the bottom of the attribute table it will read, "*23* out of 104 selected." The 23 will be a different number depending on how many records were selected when you did it. Look in the table and see that the selected records are also light blue in the table. Click on the small grey box to the very far left of the record in the table. Notice first, that all the records that were selected are now unselected and only the one you clicked on is now selected. Second, find the record on the map display that is also light blue.

68. You should have learned that we can select records via the table, and see those selected items on the map, or select items on the map, and see them also selected in the table. This is a powerful tool for crime analysis and provides a small part of the spatial analysis tools we will explore in this text.

69. Clear all selected features (**Selection** in menu bar, and **Clear Selected Features**).

70. Save your project as EX_1c.mxd. Close ArcMap.

■ Exercise 1c: Working with Tables

Data Needed for This Exercise

- We will begin with the project you saved in Exercise 1b (EX_1c.mxd). If you do not have this project saved, a copy can be found under CIA\Exercises\EX_1\EX_1c.mxd.

Lesson Objectives

- The student will load calls for service data.
- The student will learn about records and fields in an attribute table.
- The student will learn how to sort data.
- The student will learn how to add a field.
- The student will discover how to calculate a field and a geographic field.
- The student will learn how to use the find and replace feature.

Task Description

1. Open EX_1c.mxd that you saved in the previous exercise (alternatively you can open CIA\Exercises\Ex_1\Ex_1c.mxd).

2. Once open, click the add data button (alternatively, from the menu bar, you can click on File → Add Data).

3. Navigate to the CIA\Data\File Geodatabase\GIS_Layers.GDB\CFS feature dataset and then double click on the CALLS_FOR_SERVICE data to add it to the map.

Table

CALLS_FOR_SERVICE

OBJECTID *	Shape *	Status	Score	Side	X	Y	Pct_along	ARC_Street	REPORTNOYR	RI
1	Point	M	100	L	614523.03777	922120.49318	6.1	6407 W OCOTILLO RD	1	
2	Point	M	100	L	628418.65571	920777.69484	4.1	4305 W MARYLAND AV	1	
3	Point	M	100	L	615791.47468	920835.04487	6.1	6207 W MARYLAND AV	1	
4	Point	M	100	L	609380.80639	913981.1236	0	7201 W COLTER ST	1	
5	Point	M	100	L	618491.98205	925148.81422	40	5813 W NORTHVIEW AV	1	
6	Point	M	100	L	612691.50921	930565.74593	40.5	8342 N 67TH AV	1	
7	Point	M	100	L	628418.65571	920777.69484	4.1	4305 W MARYLAND AV	1	
8	Point	M	100	L	614971.10592	923453.8924	28.6	6329 W GLENDALE AV	1	
9	Point	M	100	L	623057.46768	913110.30817	14.3	5014 N 51ST AV	1	
10	Point	M	100	L	612617.41826	920603.92367	70.2	6442 N 67TH AV	1	
11	Point	M	100	L	617306.07102	921171.89969	30.6	6530 N 59TH DR	1	
12	Point	M	100	L	617719.88685	916809.7445	38.8	5738 N 59TH AV	1	
13	Point	M	100	R	611427.80051	922258.29456	100	6898 W OCOTILLO RD	1	
14	Point	M	100	R	594288.40751	923308.56575	100	9398 W GLENDALE AV	1	
15	Point	M	100	R	612839.99972	924596.96683	28.6	7129 N 67TH AV	1	
16	Point	M	100	L	613880.0785	921767.66238	63.6	6614 N 65TH AV	1	
17	Point	M	100	L	626241.83247	919322.5867	69.7	4639 W KEIM DR	1	
18	Point	M	100	R	620274.92623	949944.90573	55.1	5554 W THUNDERBIRD RD	1	
19	Point	M	100	R	616639.81247	960133.14389	100	6098 W BELL RD	1	
20	Point	M	81	R	618722.6915	946244.23823	77.6	5776 W CORRINW DR	1	
21	Point	M	100	L	613516.57397	955995.91009	49	6649 W CAROL ANN WAY	1	
22	Point	M	100	L	616767.19619	918190.58744	29.2	6031 W BETHANY HOME RD	1	
23	Point	M	100	L	626988.13911	921413.40938	28.6	4529 W MCLELLAN RD	1	
24	Point	M	100	R	618133.37081	923669.3055	30.6	5848 W GLENDALE AV	1	
25	Point	M	100	L	628472.43329	923420.80178	100	4299 W GLENDALE AV	1	
26	Point	M	100	R	628292.22054	937592.50229	13.1	4326 W ONYX AV	1	
27	Point	M	100	L	627077.39154	939228.54558	86.4	4493 W PEORIA AV	1	
28	Point	M	100	R	620959.81596	948851.95463	69	5444 W EUGIE AV	1	
29	Point	M	100	R	617972.34444	940454.60125	100	5898 W MERCER LN	1	
30	Point	M	100	L	628336.5946	928871.64016	0	8000 N 43RD AV	1	
31	Point	M	100	R	623286.17688	915944.77267	55.1	5555 N 51ST AV	1	
32	Point	M	100	L	609618.3014	921748.98731	23	7129 W KRALL ST	1	

1 (0 out of 328522 Selected)

CALLS_FOR_SERVICE

Figure E1–20

4. Click on the **Click to toggle visibility** icon to the left of the layer so it does not draw on the map display. Who wants an overpopulation of ants anyway?
5. Right click on the CALLS_FOR_SERVICE layer and click, **Open Attribute Table**. (**Figure E1–20** shows the table you should be seeing.)
6. An "Attribute Table" is made up of Records or Rows, and Fields or Columns. Each record in a table represents a different point on our map. Each column has a field name by which we call that particular data element. The field name at the top of the column can be right clicked and sorted, calculated, frozen, or deleted.
7. Using the scroll bars at the bottom of the table, scroll to the right to view all of the fields in the table.
8. Right click on the TOD field at the far right of the table and choose **Properties**.
9. Here you can see you have the ability to view what type of data are contained in the field (field type). We can see that this field is *string* (or text) and is 18 characters in length.
10. Now click on **Highlight field** and click Apply. Observe that it is now highlighted in yellow. This is a good feature if used sparingly to help you see and work with your data by column.
11. Uncheck **Highlight Field** and click **Apply**.
12. Close the Field Properties dialog box.

13. Let's browse some of the other data in the table. Right click on the fields DateTime, Date_Time, and RecvDate. See what type of fields they are and how many characters they each have.

14. We should see the following:
    a. DateTime = Field Type (Date)
    b. Date_Time = Field Type (String)
    c. Recvdate = Field Type (Double)

15. A date field is a field that is just what it sounds like—a field which captures the date of an incident. Dates can be a bit hard to work with in ArcGIS at times. This is often why we want to add a field that is a string version of the date for graphing and such, or a number field (double), which can represent the value of a field in the format of YYYYMMDDHHMM or any variation thereof.

16. Right click on Date_Time's field name and choose Sort Ascending.

17. We are sorting more than 328,000 records so this will take a minute or two.

18. It looks like the dates and times sorted properly in the data set this way, but if we scroll down to about record 25,500 we can see we jump from January 16 to February 1. Right now we do not know if this is because 2004 ended at January 16, or it just did not sort correctly, so continue scrolling down through the records to row number 66,454. Here, we see that February 25, 2004, ends and then March 1, 2001, begins. Obviously, sorting by a string field that looks like a date does not sort the data by date and time order.

19. Now right click the DateTime field and sort by ascending order.

20. If you scroll through the data now, it appears that the date has been sorted appropriately by date of the incident, but there is no time in this field.

21. To solve this little dilemma, we can use advanced sorting to sort by two fields. Right click on RecvTime and notice that it is a string as well? We can then be pretty assured that RecvDate will sort properly because it is a number, and RecvTime will sort properly because it is a string representing a time, but will also sort properly by time because of the leading zeros in it and how strings sort.

22. Right click on RecvDate and choose Advanced Sorting. You will get a dialog box like **Figure E1–21**.

23. Put RecvDate in the first pick box to sort by first, and put RecvTime in the second pick box to sort by it after sorting by RecvDate.

24. Click OK to put the sort process in motion. Again, this may take a few moments due to how many records we are sorting through.

25. Scroll through the data and see that it appears, that the date and then the proper times are in ascending order based on when the incident occurred.

26. After this sorting exercise we can see that the field type, the data in the fields, and

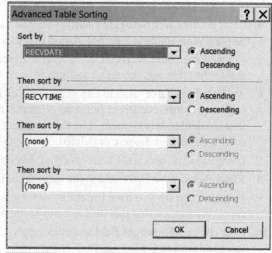

Figure E1–21

how they are formatted can make quite a bit of difference when we sort the data. ArcGIS 10 has made great improvement over the control the analyst has when sorting with the advanced sorting function.

27. In this exercise, so far we have learned that there are rows or records of data in a table and that each record represents an object on the face of the Earth or on the map display. We also learned we have fields or columns of data that are bits of information about each record within the attribute table. Additionally, we discovered that the type of field can be very important in the way data might display and how it sorts.

28. In the previous steps, we did an advanced sort by the RecvDate and RecvTime fields. Now let's add a field to our table so we can concatenate or join together the RecvDate and RecvTime into one number (double) field where we can sort ascending by just that field and get the data in the order we want.

29. Go up to the upper left corner of the table and click on the small icon to the far left of the group of icons.

30. The popup text will read, **Table Options**, as you hover your cursor over it.

31. Click on this icon, and in the drop-down menu click on the sixth item down from the top, **Add Field** (see **Figure E1–22**).

32. Fill out the following in the add field dialog box:
    a. Name = DateTimeFull
    b. Type = Double
    c. Alias = MyDate

33. When you have completed the three fields properly click OK.

34. Scroll to the far right of the table and see that we now have a new field displaying our alias name of **MyDate**.

35. If we right click it and go to properties, we can see that it is a Double number type as we indicated. If you do not have Double number type, or the alias is not showing, right click the new field and click **x Delete Field** and then go back to step 29 and try again.

36. Now we need to calculate our new field by concatenating the RecvDate and RecvTime fields.

37. Click on our Table Properties Icon again and this time choose the third item down, **Clear Selection**, in order to make sure we have no records selected before we begin. *If this is greyed out, then no records are selected.* If we do not make sure there are no records selected, *then only the selected records would calculate.*

38. Right click on the MyDate field and choose **Field Calculator** from the popup dialog.

39. In the Field Calculator window, find the RecvDate field and double click it to bring

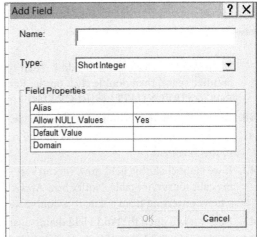

Figure E1–22

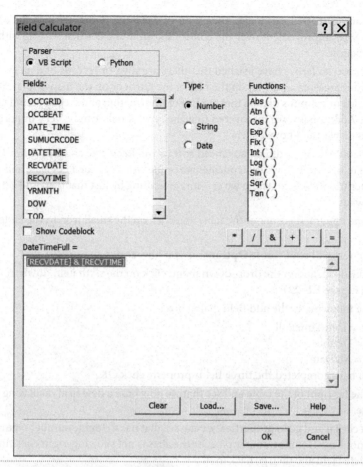

Figure E1–23

it down into the calculator window. Then type a space and then an ampersand (&) symbol and another space, then double click on the RecvTime field to bring it down. Your formula should look like **[RECVDATE] & [RECVTIME]** (see **Figure E1–23**).

40. After entering the formula as indicated, click the OK button to do the calculation.

41. After the calculation is done, you should now see data in the format of YYYYMMDDHHMM in this one field.

42. If we right click this field now, we can sort it in the proper chronological order of the events in the calls for service table. Notice how ArcGIS already knows to format the date as YYYYMMDD when converting from a date to a double number type.

43. Now we will open the Add Field dialog again. Save your map.

44. Click on the **Table Options** icon and click **Add Field**.

45. In the drop-down box in the TYPE section, click on the down arrow to the right of the field to review all of the field types ArcGIS 10 tables will allow.

46. Here are the categories or types of fields ArcGIS 10 allows:
   a. Short integer
   b. Long integer
   c. Float
   d. Double
   e. Text
   f. Date
   g. Blob
   h. Raster
   i. Guid

47. To find out what each field type means, we will use the help feature of ArcGIS. Close the Add Field dialog box, and close the attribute table.

48. In the menu bar click on HELP, and select ArcGIS Desktop Help.

49. Type "Add Field" and hit the **Enter** key.

50. A group of items that match your search criteria comes up. Click on the first one, **Adding Fields**.

51. We can read how to add a field. If we scroll to the bottom of this help screen, we see a hyperlink which reads, **Geodatabase Field Data Types**.

52. Click this hyperlink.

53. Read this very useful help screen from top to bottom. We learn that not only is it important to know the difference between these field types, but also their limitations and how much space they take up in the database, depending on what kind of field it is, what the length of the field is, etc.

54. Only two more items to learn in this exercise! There are many times when you want to find a certain text string in a field and perhaps replace it with another text string. We may want to just find data to see if it is in a specific attribute table or we want to replace bad data and we need to "clean" our data before we can make those beautiful maps we need for our analysis projects.

55. We are going to use the **Find and Replace** function to see if the data we are thinking are in the data are actually in there.

56. If your attribute table is closed, right click on the layer in the TOC and choose Open Attribute Table. Right click on the CALLS_FOR_SERVICE layer and click **Open Attribute Table**.

57. Left click on the field named "RADIONAME" to select that field to search in.

58. Click on the Table Properties icon again; but this time choose Find and Replace at the top.

59. In the Find and Replace dialog, type, "Explosive Device," then click **Find Next** (see **Figure E1–24**).

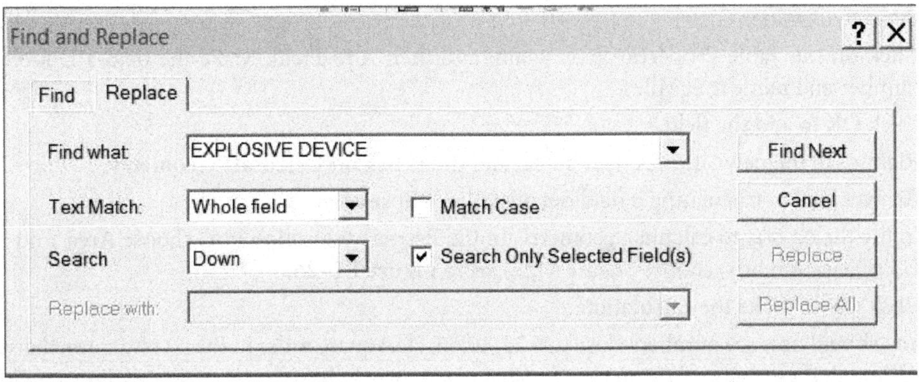

Figure E1–24

60. After a few moments, the search function should have brought you to the first record where EXPLOSIVE DEVICE was found.

61. If you keep hitting Find Next, you will be taken to each successive record in the table. If you continued to click until all records were found, a popup dialog would appear, which indicates you had reached all possible records in the table.

62. So let us assume that we want to change "EXPLOSIVE DEVICE" to "BOMB." We would first need to place the attribute table in edit mode by clicking on Customize in the menu bar.

63. We would then choose Toolbars → Editor.

64. When the editor toolbar is open, we click Editor → Start Editing to start and edit session. Although we will not edit the field values at this time, you should at least know how to do it. Once you started editing, the column headers in the attribute table would turn white, indicating that the table is now editable. Click on the Replace tab in the Find and Replace dialog box. At the top we can type in the field value we wish to search on, and at the bottom of the Replace tab, we can type in the value we wish to replace Explosive Device with, or in this case, "Bomb." Clicking the Replace All button would make those replacements. *(Note: If you wish to practice this skill, please make a copy of the Calls for Service layer and work with it so you can see how this function works.)*

65. The final item to stretch your GIS skills is calculating a geometry field. "Geometry" is the length, area, or *X* and *Y* coordinates of a field. For this exercise we need to add the City_Council_P layer from the CIA\Data\File Geodatabase\GIS_Layers.GDB\Boundaries feature dataset.

66. After adding this layer, right click on it and then click on **Open Attribute Table**.

67. You can see that there is a field at the end called Shape_Area, and a huge number is found for each polygon. This number represents the square feet of each of these city council boundary polygons. We want to add a new field that calculates this in square *miles* instead of square *feet*.

68. *Note*: If the system you are using at a school or another location does not allow you read and write access to the data that would be loaded to the CIA folder, you will need to export the city council polygons to a location where you have edit capability. This is accomplished by right clicking the City_Council_P, and in the popup dialog, choosing **Data → Export Data**. **Figure E1–25** shows what the export dialog looks like. You should save the layer to a location where you can make edits, and make sure to export all features and not just selected features of the City_Council_P polygon layer. Once it has been exported, then you should use this layer instead of the one in the C:\CIA folder.

69. Click on the Table Properties Icon again, and then Add Field. Make the field a Double type number and name it SqMiles.

70. Click OK to add the field.

71. Right click the new SqMiles field name, and then click on **Calculate Geometry**.

72. Answer YES to calculating a field outside of an edit session.

73. In the dialog box to calculate geometry, in the Property selection box, choose Area, and in the Units selection box, choose Square Miles, as in **Figure E1–26**.

74. Click OK to make the calculation.

75. You should now see numbers close to 6.23, 19.66, etc. square miles in the six city council districts. Although there are more than two decimal places, we do have square miles and not square feet in this new field.

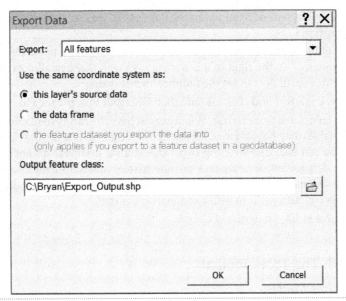

Figure E1–25

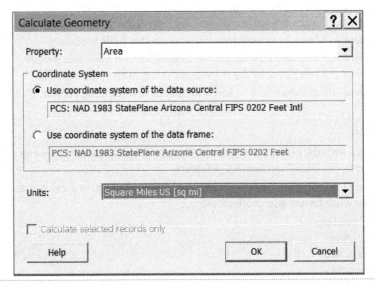

Figure E1–26

76. If we want to see just two decimal places, or none at all, we can right click on the field name, then go to Properties.

77. In the middle of the Properties dialog it reads Number Format and to the right of this is a word that reads "Numeric." To the right of it is a small icon with three small dots in it. Click on this box with the three small dots to get the number format dialog.

78. Change the decimals to 1 and click OK and then OK again to apply the changes.

79. You have now completed this exercise. When analyst have the ability to manipulate the numbers and data in a table, they have a lot of power. It's important to know what data can be cleaned, and how far we can take that cleaning to get the data we need. We do not want to go too far or control the data too much or we may provide false or misleading information, but we often need to improve data quality, make changes to data formats so they are more user friendly, or concatenate several data fields to better summarize our data.

80. Save your project as EX_1d.mxd and close it.

■ Exercise 1d: The Tools Toolbar

Data Needed for This Exercise

- The project you saved as EX_1d.mxd (alternatively you can use EX_1d.mxd located in the CIA\Exercises\EX_1 folder).

Lesson Objectives

- The student will add offense data and persons data to the project.
- The student will learn about grouping data in the table of contents (TOC).
- The student will learn how to use the zoom tools on the Tools toolbar.
- The student will learn how to use the pan tool on the Tools toolbar.
- The student will discover how to use the identify tool on the Tools toolbar.
- The student will learn how to use the measure tool on the Tools toolbar.
- The student will discover how to add bookmarks to a mapping project.

Task Description

1. We will begin with the project you saved as EX_1d.mxd (alternatively, you can open the EX_1d.mxd located in the CIA\Exercises\EX_1 folder).

2. Use the Add Data button to add everything in the Persons feature dataset in the CIA\Data\File Geodatabase\GIS_Layers.gdb geodatabase:
   a. Gang_Members
   b. Person_Data
   c. Persons_Cited
   d. Probationers

3. We can add all four layers from this same feature dataset by clicking on the top one, then holding down the CTRL key and clicking on the other three one at a time.

4. Our first discovery in this exercise is to group layers in the TOC so that they are a little easier to work with.

5. After adding all four layers at one time, they should all be highlighted in the TOC. If not, click on one, hold down the CTRL key, and click on the others until all persons data added are highlighted.

6. Now right click on any one layer that is highlighted. Click on Group from the menu that appears.

7. In the TOC in the topmost area, click on the farthest left icon that has the popup text, "List by drawing order." This will show the persons data listed under an item currently named, "New Group Layer."

8. Right Click New Group layer and choose Properties.

9. In the General tab, change the name to Persons Data and then Click OK.

10. Now the group these files are under is called Persons Data.

11. If you click the small box next to Persons Data now, all of the layers in this group turn off or are no longer visible in the map display. They are still turned on individually (check boxes checked next to their names), however, the group properties now override the individual layer properties. We can also collapse the entire group by clicking the minus sign to the far left of Persons Data and we no longer see all four layers in the TOC until the time comes that we need to see them again.

12. This feature can help unclutter a TOC and help us to organize a bit during complicated mapping and analysis projects.

13. As we move on in showing you the multifunction features of ArcGIS 10, it is important to be as organized as possible. The more data you are working with and the various classifications and uses of the data we apply will get confusing. Even seasoned and skilled analysts may sometimes spend several minutes doing something with the wrong set of data, clear a selection they wanted to keep, or any other number of boo boos we try to avoid. One mistake we may often make is not saving our projects often enough during the course of our map-making sessions. My advice is that you save *every time* you have done something you like and the results ended up like you wanted them to. That way, when you open the project after a crash, you can go right back to work and only lose the past few minutes of work since your last SAVE, instead of hours of work. So save your project often.

14. Save this project.

15. In the CIA\Data\File Geodatabase\GIS_Layers.gdb database, add the following from the OTHER feature dataset:

   a. City_Parks
   b. MultiResident_Areas

16. These are both polygon layers.

17. Toggle visibility of these layers so we cannot see either one in the map display area (uncheck the box to the far left of the layer).

18. You might also want to turn off the city council boundaries and bike routes off by either unchecking the box to the left of the layer, or toggling the visibility.

19. Turn the city parks layer back on and we need to find where Bonsall Park South is located for a project. The chief wants to know how many calls for service (CFS) we received in 2004 around this park for a city council meeting.

20. Open the attribute table of the city parks layer (right click the layer name and choose Open Attribute Table).

21. Click on the Name field to select that field for searching, and then click on the Table Properties Icon we used in the last lesson. Then choose **Find and Replace**.

22. In the find and replace dialog, type in Bonsall South and click **Find Next**. Record number 5 in the attribute table is selected. Click on the small grey box to the left of that record to select it in the table and the map display.

23. After selecting the record, close the attribute table and then right click on the CityParks layer in the TOC, Choose **Selection**, and then **Zoom to Selected Features**.

24. We are now zoomed in to Bonsall Park South. Turn on the calls for service layer so we can see the points near our park.

25. Click on the **Identify** tool in the Tools toolbar (you can refer back to Figure E1–3 for an image of the Tools toolbar). The Identify tool can be found by looking for a blue circle with an "i" in it, or by moving your cursor over the tools in the toolbar until you see "Identify" in the popup text.

26. Click on this tool to activate it.

27. Move your cursor to the map display area and you will find your cursor now looks like an arrow with an "i" in a circle next to it.

28. Click on any one of the dots inside the boundaries of Bonsall South Park.

29. As you click on each point, notice that some are single calls for service, and others are multiple calls at the same address, or same X and Y coordinate (see **Figure E1-27**).

30. If you click the down arrow to the right of the **Identify From** selection box, you should see that we have several choices for the way in which the identify tool works. We can have it select on the topmost layer, the selectable layer, all visible layers, etc.

31. We could answer the chief fairly quickly by clicking on each point and then using the identify window results to count up the incidents that occurred in 2004. This may be a bit tedious but it could be done in a pinch.

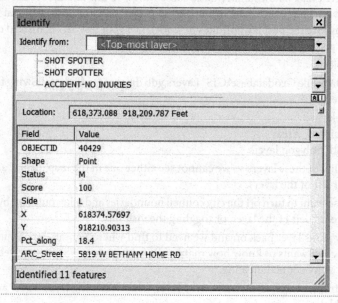

Figure E1–27

32. We want to explore the Tools toolbar a bit more. Again, you may refer back to Figure E1–3 for an image of the Tools toolbar.

33. The first two tools on the left of the toolbar are interactive zoom tools. If you were to select either of these tools and then click anywhere on your map display, the display would either zoom in (+ sign), or zoom out (– sign). The two tools that are fifth and sixth from the left also do the same thing, except you click the buttons and you zoom in from the current display or out from the current display. The interactive tools have the advantage of not only zooming in or out from where you click on the map display, but you can also click and hold the mouse button down and zoom in or out to an area within the box or rectangle you draw. Practice zooming in and out, using both the interactive and set zoom tools. Try zooming in to an area of town and turn on persons layers or calls for service to see what happens. You might also want to turn on the street layer we added so you have a spatial reference.

34. When you zoom in and out, you can see how **Scale** is important. Scale is the degree of accuracy with which we draw data to represent the Earth's surface. In our case, the streets might not always follow the center of the street exactly, or may look jagged when making a curve rather than be smooth.

35. In addition to the zoom tools, we have **Go back to Previous Extent**, and **Go to Next Extent**.

36. These are the blue arrows that are seventh and eighth from the left on the Tools toolbar.

37. As you practice zooming in and out, notice that ArcGIS keeps several of your zoom histories here so that you can go back and forth from where you zoomed during your analysis and map making.

38. If you find yourself in a situation where you see only white on your map display, it probably means that you have zoomed in too far (your nose is sticking in the grass in your backyard), or zoomed out too far (you are standing on Mars trying to make out someone in the pool).

39. This can be rectified by zooming to the full extents of the layers (extents are the outer boundaries of all layers in the TOC, or extents of a layer are the outer boundaries of that layer). Click on the small Earth symbol (fourth from left) for the full extent of all layers.

40. We might also want to slightly adjust where everything is in the map display area. When we zoom out to the full extents, the city is kind of small, so use the interactive zoom in tool (magnifying glass with plus sign) to zoom in to the city map. Draw a box around the street label boxes, so that all of them are just within the box you draw (click at one corner and hold the left mouse button down, then drag the rectangle around the rest of the city map and let go).

41. The **Pan** tool lets us make very small or large adjustments on where the map is displayed in the map display window. Click the white hand (third from left) in the Tools toolbar. Then click on the map, hold and move it left or right, up or down as needed.

42. You may have also learned that with the Tools toolbar, the tool functionality that you last chose remains chosen until you change it. When we do not remember this, we may often zoom in, pan, or identify when we did not want to, which can be annoying. A safe move is to always remember the **Select Elements** (11th tool from left—black arrow). After you have done something with a tool in the Tools toolbar, always go back and click the Select Elements tool as it is pretty harmless unless you have a lot of simple graphics in your map.

43. So, remember to default to the Select Elements Tool (black arrow) after every tool operation in ArcGIS to save yourself some grief and remember to SAVE your project.

44. Another thing we might want to do at times is to measure distances from one object to another.

45. The **Measure tool** (15th from left) is the tool we need.

46. Click on the Measure tool to activate it. A Measure tool dialog appears for us (see **Figure E1–28**). Our goal is to measure the approximate longest distance from north to south and west to east that Glendale represents on the Earth's surface.

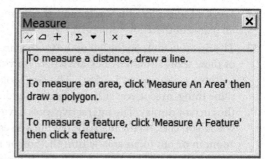

Figure E1–28

47. First, we need to set the measurement units with the fifth icon in the measurement dialog from the left that looks like a small down arrow. *Do not* choose the small down arrow all the way on the right. Click the Choose Units down arrow and choose **Distance**, then **Miles**.

48. Now click on the first tool in the dialog box, "Measure Line," and click once on the map at about Camelback Rd or as close as you can. Then stretch the measurement line up to the northern city boundary up by Pinnacle Peak Rd.

49. Double click at Pinnacle Peak Rd to get the measurement saved to the measurement dialog box. You should have received about a 12.99-mile segment.

50. Now do the same from about N 43rd Ave all the way west to Tuthill Rd. This reading should be about 17.89 miles.

51. The measure tool can be very useful to measure how far current crimes in a series are away from parks, freeways, major roads, etc.

52. Close the measure tool, click on the black arrow tool (Select Elements), and save the project.

53. The last item we will learn how to use is Bookmarks. Sometimes, we will be repeatedly drawing maps of the same geographic area, but may have more data outside that area than we want to keep in the project. We want to bookmark certain zoom scales we use often so we can quickly come back to them anytime we want.

54. At the moment you should be zoomed in on the city map where the street label boxes fill the screen so we can see all of them, and so we are zoomed in on the city as much as possible (see **Figure E1–29**).

55. We want to bookmark this view so that we can come back to it from any zoom scale we might have blundered into. On the menu bar, click on **Bookmarks**.

56. Click Create, call this view HOME, and click OK.

57. Now Zoom in to any area you wish (e.g., the area between N 43rd Ave and N 67th Ave and W Camelback Rd to W Northern Ave).

58. Click on Bookmarks again, then Create, and name this new area, "My Perfect Zoom," then click OK.

59. Now click on Bookmarks in the Menu bar and in the drop-down dialog you should see HOME and My Perfect Zoom. Click on HOME and you should zoom back to the full city boundaries. Pretty cool, right?

60. Save this project as EX_1e.mxd. Exit your project folder and close ArcGIS.

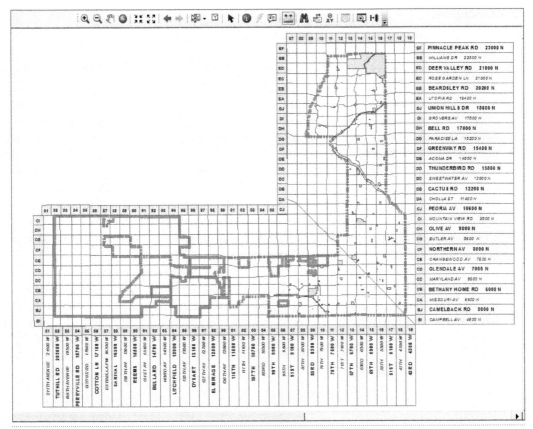

Figure E1–29

■ Exercise 1e: Graphics and the Draw Toolbar

Data Needed for This Exercise

- The project you saved as EX_1e.mxd (alternatively you can use the EX_1e.mxd located in the CIA\Exercises\EX_1 folder).

Lesson Objectives

- The student will discover how to use the draw tool.
- The student will learn how to select by graphics.
- The student will be introduced to combining select routines to get the data needed for analysis.
- The student will learn how to use the summarize function to make information out of data.
- The student will be given the necessary basic knowledge of how to classify data by categories, quantities, and charts.
- The student will learn about nominal, ordinal, interval, and ratio data and how they are used in classifications.

Task Description

1. Open EX_1e.mxd that you saved in the previous exercise (alternatively you can open the saved copy in CIA\Exercises\EX_1\EX_1e.mxd).

2. Once the project is open, you should have a map and TOC that looks similar to **Figure E1–30**.

3. We will start with a simple lesson in using the draw tool. The draw tool can be used to draw polygons, lines, or points on the map. This would equate to the old habit of placing a plastic colored "pin" into a paper map to record the location of a burglary. There is very little information that you can place on the head of that pin; the same goes for the graphics we draw with the draw toolbar (see **Figure E1–31**).

4. If you do not see the drawing toolbar at the bottom of the map display window, you can turn the toolbar on by going into the menu bar. Find the **Customize** menu item and left click it. In the drop-down dialog box, choose **Toolbars**. Now find the **Draw** toolbar and click it. Now that it is visible, we can drag it to the bottom of the map display window and dock it.

5. The most frequently used tools from the Draw toolbar are points, lines, or polygons drawing tools, and the tool that allows you to add graphic text to a map.

6. Our assignment is to find the total number of calls for service that were reported to police between N 43rd Ave to N 51st Ave, and W Glendale Ave to W Bethany Home Rd. We only need data for 2004. We need to do this quickly because the chief is waiting in your office for the data so he can take it to a city council meeting.

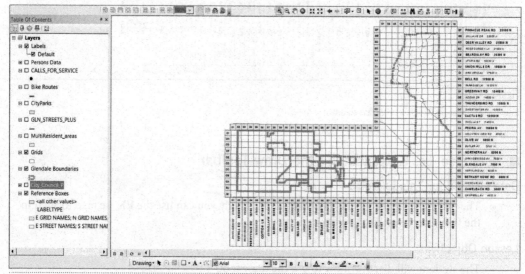

Figure E1–30

Figure E1–31

7. First, we need to look to see if we have data in our TOC that would allow us to answer this question.

8. Do we have a calls for service layer?

9. Yes, it is a point layer called CALLS FOR SERVICE in the TOC.

10. Do we have a streets layer or something we can use to get close to where the requested streets are located?

11. Yes, this layer is called GLN_STREETS_PLUS in the TOC.

12. So, the easiest way to accomplish this and find where all these streets are located is to do an attribute query.

13. Click once on the GLN_STREETS_PLUS layer to select it.

14. In the menu bar, click on Selection and then Select by Attributes.

15. When the dialog box comes up, we need to enter the following in the "Select*From Gln_Streets_Plus Where" window (see **Figure E1–32**):

   • "STREET_NAM" = '51ST' OR "STREET_NAM" = '43RD' OR "STREET_NAM" = 'GLENDALE' OR "STREET_NAM" = 'BETHANY HOME'

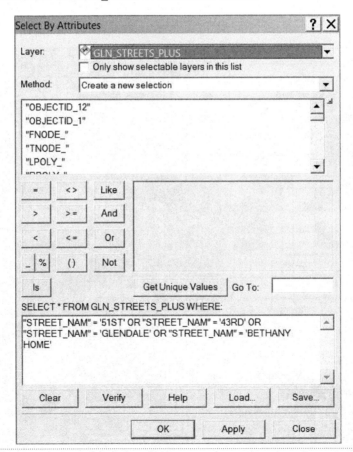

Figure E1–32

16. We need to make sure that the "Layer" section has GLN_STREETS_PLUS in it and that the "Method" section has Create a New Selection in it.

17. Click Apply to make the selection and then check the box next to the GLN_STREETS_PLUS layer to toggle the visibility to **ON**.

18. The area where all the streets with the names we selected is now light blue. Zoom into the small rectangle the selected streets make (**Figure E1–33**).

    Once zoomed in to this area, use the draw tool to draw a rectangle around the area between the selected streets. The Draw Rectangle tool looks like a small rectangle or square on the draw toolbar; it is the fifth item from the left on the draw toolbar (see Figure E1–31).

19. If you click on the small arrow to the right of the small rectangle, a popup dialog will appear showing that you can create several different kinds of polygon shapes with this tool. These include:

    a. Rectangle
    b. Free-form polygon
    c. Circle
    d. Ellipse
    e. Line
    f. Curve
    g. Freehand
    h. Marker (or point symbol)

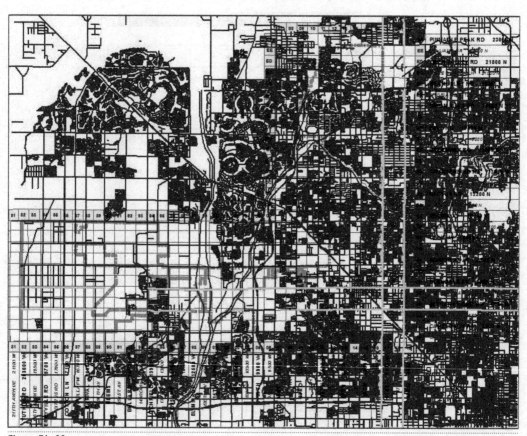

Figure E1–33

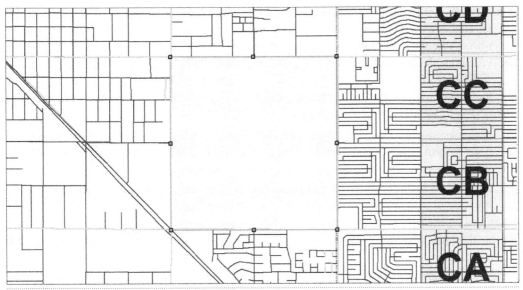

Figure E1–34

20. Make sure the Rectangle is selected and then draw your rectangle on the map. Your map should now look similar to **Figure E1–34**.

21. Save your project.

22. Right click on the rectangle you've drawn and choose **Properties**.

23. Click on the three tabs in the graphic item dialog box one at a time (Symbol, Area, Size, and Position) and get familiar with what is in each of these tabs. You can see in the area tab, for instance, what the total square miles are in this rectangle.

24. Under the Symbol tab, we can change the fill color (and can even make the fill color "no color," thus making the rectangle or polygon transparent, which allows us to "see through" the polygon).

25. Now that we have our rectangle encompassing the intersections of all our streets (N 43rd Ave, N 51st Ave, W Glendale Ave, and W Bethany Home Rd), we can select our calls for service.

26. Remember: The chief is waiting!

27. Close the graphics properties dialog box.

28. Make sure the rectangle is selected. If you need to resize it, grab the little boxes in the lines that make up the polygon and drag them by clicking them with your left mouse button and pulling them in the direction you want the box to go.

29. When done, make the calls for service layer visible, and then click on Selection in the menu bar.

30. Choose **Select by Graphics**.

31. After a few moments, the calls for service that intersect the rectangle you drew will be selected.

32. In order to find this number, we need to open the attribute table of the calls for service layer.

33. Right click the calls for service layer and choose **Open Attribute Table**.

34. Depending on the size of the polygon you drew and the one we did, you should have about 16,260 records selected, or that many calls for service.

35. Looking at the data in the attribute table we can see that calls in years other than 2004 are selected. We want to do a "down and dirty" yearly comparison for the chief. This can be done with a "summary" of a field from the attribute table.

36. We could calculate a new field and figure out the year of the reported date or something else, but we do have a field called "REPORTNOYR" in the attribute table, so we will use that.

37. Right click on the REPORTNOYR field name.

38. In the popup menu, choose **Summarize**.

39. In the Summarize dialog box (**Figure E1–35**), browse to where you want to save this new file (your student folder), name it, and choose to save as a .DBF(dBASE) table (**Figure E1–36**).

40. You also need to make sure the **Summarize on the selected records only** checkbox is checked.

41. It will take a few minutes for the summary table to be produced. Once done, a dialog will ask if you want to add the summary table to the map. Answer YES.

42. Close the attribute table.

43. At the very bottom of the TOC, look for the summary table you created, right click it, then **OPEN**.

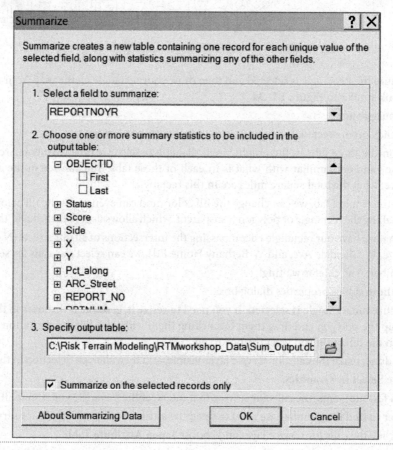

Figure E1–35

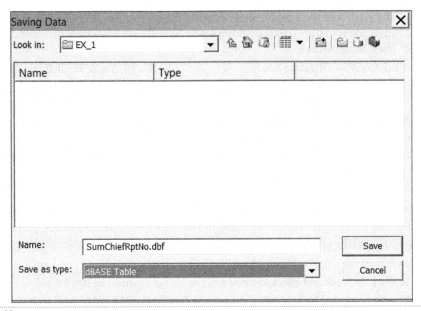

Figure E1-36

44. You should see **Table E1-1**, which you can provide to the chief.
45. The total then for 2004 within our graphically selected area of Glendale is 3775 calls for service to date.
46. Save your project again. It is never wrong to save the project and keep anything you have been working on.
47. Go up to Selection in the menu bar and choose **Clear Selected Features** in the dialog box.
48. Make sure to click on the Black Arrow (Select Elements) tool in either the Draw toolbar or the Tools toolbar and then click on the rectangle you drew to select it. Then hit the Delete key to delete it.
49. Turn off (make nonvisible) all layers except the GLN_STREETS_PLUS layer.
50. The Special Services Division has gotten word of a protest march for Occupy Glendale that is going to occur tomorrow. The marchers plan to walk from the intersection of N 43rd Ave and W Glendale Ave to the Rose Lane Community Park (near N 51st Ave and W Marlette Ave). The

TABLE E1-1

OID	REPORTNOYR	Count_REPORTNOYR
0	1	3890
1	2	4229
2	3	4366
3	4	3775

Commander has asked for a simple map showing the area, with a line showing the path of the march, and he wants to have points marking where he will have Solo-Motor officers doing traffic control. These locations are:

a. N 43rd Ave & W Glendale Ave

b. N 45th Ave & W Glendale Ave

c. N 47th Ave & W Glendale Ave

d. N 51st Ave & W Glendale Ave

e. N 51st Ave & W Maryland Ave

f. N 51st Ave & W Marlette Ave

51. We will draw the path and the points with our Draw toolbar functionality.

52. We can use the same zoom level that we are at from our last project, around N 43rd Ave to N 51st Ave, W Glendale Ave to W Bethany Home Rd. Use the Identify tool to check the street names if needed.

53. Let's set a bookmark for this view level.

54. Click on **Bookmark → Create** in the menu bar. Name this view Commander Jones View.

55. Make the City Parks layer visible, and, using the Identify tool, find Rose Lane Community Park.

56. We can also label the parks layer to find Rose Lane Park.

57. Double click on the City Parks layer to open the properties dialog.

58. Click on the Labels tab and check the box next to "Label Features in this Layer."

59. In the Text String Label Field section, choose the field called NAME.

60. Click OK to see the names labeling the parks now.

61. Now that you know where Rose Lane Park is, we can use the Identify tool to find the street names, or we can label the streets. Label the streets the same way you did the city parks, but use the ANNAME field for the labels.

62. Now you should be able to draw your map.

63. Using the Draw toolbar, find the tool we used to draw the rectangle earlier. Click on the down arrow to the right of the tool, and choose LINE from the choices.

64. Draw the line by clicking once at the intersection of N 43rd Ave & W Glendale Ave and then clicking once again at N 51st Ave & W Glendale Ave, then clicking once again at N 51st Ave & W Marlette Ave, and then moving right on W Marlette to about the middle of the park area, clicking once and then moving down to about the center of the park and then double clicking to end the line.

65. Now right click on the selected line you drew, and in the properties for the line, choose a Width of 5 and a color of red. Click OK.

66. **Figure E1–37** shows what your map should generally look like at this point.

67. Use the **ZOOM** tool to zoom in the extents of the march path you have drawn. Remember that you can zoom interactively with the zoom tool that appears to be a magnifying glass with a plus sign in it. Left click at one corner of the box you wish to zoom to, then hold the left mouse button down to complete the box and you will zoom in to the extents of the box you draw. Let go of the left mouse button to complete the zoom.

68. Now let's make this a bit prettier. Choose the Select Elements tool (black arrow) and double click on your path. In the popup dialog, click the **Change Symbol** button.

69. Find the symbol style that reads Dashed 6:1, then change the width back to 5 and the color back to red.

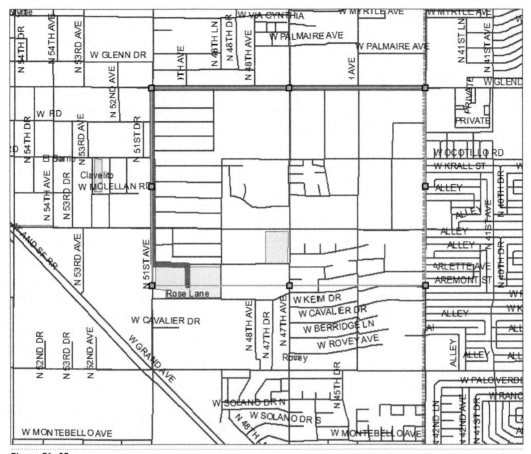

Figure E1–37

70. Click OK, then OK again to apply the changes.
71. Now, using the same tool we drew the rectangle and line with, click on the down arrow to the right and choose **Marker** as the element we will add now.
72. Click at each intersection indicated by the Commander in Step 51 of this exercise, clicking the Marker tool for insertion of each point.
73. When you have finished adding all the points or markers for the locations of Solo-Motor traffic control, we want to select all of these markers to change the type of symbol at one time.
74. Use the Select Elements tool (black arrow) and click on the first marker symbol. Hold the Shift key down and left click on all the other marker symbols, one at a time until all are selected.
75. Right click on any one of the markers.
76. Click on **Properties** and then **Change Symbol**.

77. Choose the **Star 4** symbol and make it 22 in size and a medium blue (for the police).
78. Click OK, then OK to make the changes.
79. Now let's use another Draw toolbar tool called "**New Text**."
80. This tool usually looks like the letter A and can be found to the right of the rectangle or marker tool we have been using.
81. Click on the down arrow to the right of this tool and choose "Callout" as the type of text.
82. You usually click on the point you wish to be the end of the callout (what is being labeled), and then drag the callout toward the direction you want it to be from the item being labeled.
83. Click on the first Star at N 43rd Ave & W Glendale Ave and label this position, "Officer Position 1."
84. Name each of the other positions along the path, Officer Position 2, 3, 4, etc.
85. Your map should now look about like **Figure E1–38**.
86. Save this project as EX_2.mxd and close ArcMap.

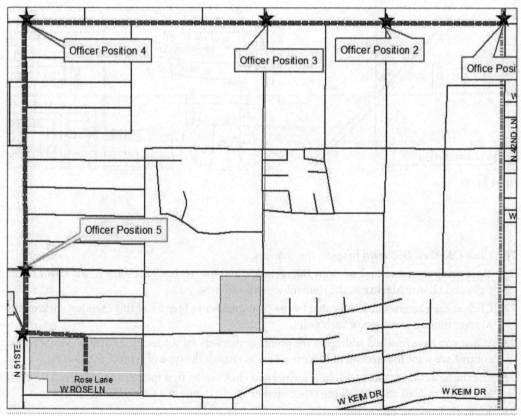

Figure E1–38

■ Exercise 2: Classification Types and Data Needs

Data Needed for This Exercise

- The project you saved as EX_2.mxd (alternatively you can use the EX_2.mxd located in the CIA\Exercises\EX_2\ folder).

Lesson Objectives

- The student will be given the necessary basic knowledge of how to classify data by categories, quantities, and charts.
- The student will learn about nominal, ordinal, interval, and ratio data and how they are used in classifications.

Task Description

1. Open EX_2.mxd that you saved in the previous exercise (alternatively the student can open the saved copy in CIA\Exercises|EX_2\EX_2.mxd).
2. There are four basic categories of data we can use in ArcMap to classify or display data in relation to data that are stored in the attribute table. We need to know what kind of data we are working with so that we can properly display the data in our map.
3. The lowest form of data we collect is *nominal* data.
4. Nominal simply means "name," and data we store in this category are usually text or string fields. Examples include "male or female," "blonde, brunette, or redhead." The order of the data does not have any significance and one value is not considered greater or lesser than another. We frequently see nominal data in law enforcement as descriptors of persons, or crimes.
5. An example can also be found in the City Parks layer. If you right click this layer and open the attribute table, there is a field called, "**PARK_TYPE**."
6. This field has names of park types in Glendale, but there is no order to the names.
7. Close the attribute table, and then double click the City Parks layer.
8. Go to the Symbology tab, and choose **Categories → Unique Values** (as in **Figure E2–1**; this step was already done in the saved copy of CIA\Exercises\EX_2\EX_2.mxd).
9. Choose the PARK_TYPE as your Value Field and choose the GREENS Color Ramp. You can find this color ramp by simply scanning the ramps available, or you can right click on the Color Ramp, and uncheck Graphic View to see the names of the Color Ramps.
10. Click on Add All Values and then OK to apply your changes. Turn on the City Parks layer on your map by clicking the checkbox in the table of contents (TOC).
11. As you zoom in and out on the map to the various parks, you can see what type of park they are by the color they are classified by.
12. The next type of data we encounter is *ordinal* data. Ordinal data are simply nominal data that have some order. Examples might be: "Chief, Asst Chief, Commander, Lieutenant, and Sergeant." Other examples could include specified ranges such as 0–10, 11–15, 16–20, 21–30, etc.
13. We might also think of temporal data as ordinal data where the day of week and time of day are important to stay in order. An example would be found in the calls for service data.
14. Turn off the City Parks layer and any other layer you do not think we need (like streets) at this time.
15. Turn on the calls for service layer.

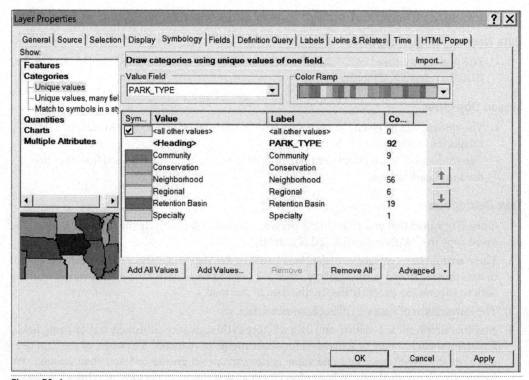

Figure E2–1

16. Right click the calls for service layer and choose **Zoom to Layer** from the dialog box.

17. Open the attribute table of the calls for service layer.

18. Browse the different fields in this layer. At the farthest right is a field called TOD. It contains a nominal (name) value which should be considered in an ordinal fashion or in order by time of day.

19. Close the attribute table and double click the layer to open the Symbology properties.

20. Use TOD as your value field, use a green to red color ramp, and click Add All Values. Once ArcMap is done calculating and finding the unique values in the TOD field, click OK to apply your changes.

21. Notice that in this case the data are also in ascending order based on time of day ranges, or are ordinal data. Be careful with text fields as they do not always sort as intended and you may need to manually move them around in the classification window using the up and down arrow buttons to the right of the classifications window.

22. Now that we have discovered the common uses and legend types for nominal and ordinal data, and that nominal and ordinal data can typically only be Single Symbol and Categories, we can move on to *interval* data.

23. Interval data are numbers instead of text. They are also usually integers such as "54 burglaries" or "24 robberies."

24. There are numerous ways these data can be classified. We can use Single Symbol, Categories, or Quantities to classify interval data in ArcMap.

25. Double click on the **Grids** layer in the Boundaries group in the TOC and when the Properties dialog opens, click the Symbology tab.

26. Click on Quantities classification type and choose Graduated Colors under it.

27. In the Value field section, choose "TotPop_All" as the field name, which is an interval value in this table. Interval also means you do not have any decimal data or ratio data. Interval data can also be from – infinity to + infinity in size but exist only as whole numbers.

28. Use a blue to red color ramp for the data and click OK to apply it.

29. **Figure E2–2** shows the results.

30. Another form and the final of the four we will use is *ratio* data. It is much like interval data in use, but can have decimal numbers. We can have 4 burglaries, but we cannot have 4.5 burglaries. We can have 4.5 burglaries average per household, or a ratio.

31. Another field in the Grids layer is called SQMILES. Open the attribute table and view the data entered in this field. We can create a ratio type of representation by choosing a normalization field in our classification.

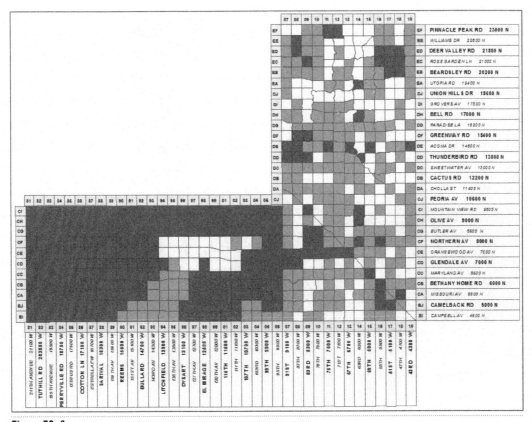

Figure E2–2

32. Double click on the Grids layer again to open the Properties. Go to the Symbology tab.

33. Under the Value Field is another section called Normalization.

34. Put in the field called SqMiles. This will give you a ratio of TotPop_All (or total population per the Census Bureau) divided by the SqMiles of each grid (see **Figure E2–3**). Click OK to apply these changes.

35. In addition to these classification methods, with interval or ordinal data we can use different class types to show our data in the best way depending on the data. There are several styles or methods of classification in ArcMap for quantities-type data (interval or ratio). These are:

   - Standard deviation
   - Natural breaks
   - Quantile
   - Equal interval
   - Defined interval
   - Geometrical interval
   - Manual

36. As a crime analyst you will probably use the natural breaks, standard deviation, and quantile classification methods the most often.

37. Open the Symbology properties of the Grids layer again.

38. Remove the field that is Normalizing this data and switch it back to **None**.

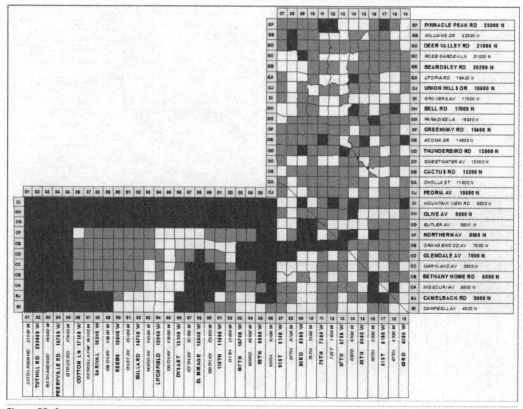

Figure E2–3

39. At the far right of the Symbology tab, it reads, "Classification" and under it probably Natural Breaks and a number in a small box. Click the Classify button to get the Classification Dialog box (see **Figure E2–4**).

40. This dialog box allows you to see if the data in your field are skewed (graph), and allows you to change what type of classification style or method you want to use.

41. Try the different methods of classification with the TotPop_All field in the Grids layer. Try different color ramps with the different classification types. See how they affect the data and your perception of it. You should notice how the Natural breaks, Equal interval, Quantile, and Standard deviation styles or methods change the overall distribution of the red or hottest grids for population. This is just why many cartographers cringe when they know that laypersons such as crime analysts are allowed to make these kinds of maps. If you do not really understand your data and the various statistical methods for displaying nominal, ordinal, interval, and ratio data, you can mislead your audience. You should spend some time looking at the help documents on the topics of natural breaks, standard deviation, and quantile classification methods in ArcMap. Look these items up in the help section and read about at least these three methods. Save your project if desired and close ArcMap.

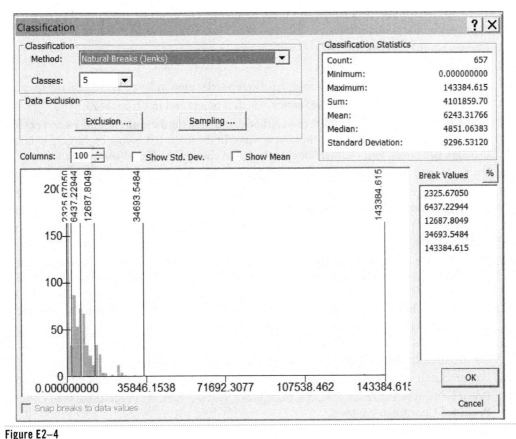

Figure E2–4

■ Exercise 3: Layouts

Data Needed for This Exercise
- CIA\Exercises\EX_3\EX_3.mxd
- Internet access is required for first part of exercise

Lesson Objectives
- The student will learn how to create a new map from a template.
- The student will learn how to work with a layout using several layout tools from the layout toolbar.
- The student will discover the common things found on maps.
- The student will use the group and ungroup of graphic elements function.

Task Description
1. Go to the Windows Start Menu and find Programs.
2. Find and open ArcMap 10.
3. Once opened, choose **New Maps** and then **Templates**. Go down to **Traditional layouts**, and then click on the **USA** section.
4. Choose **SouthWesternUSA**.
5. Click **OK**.
6. If a dialog asks you if you want to apply hardware acceleration indicate **Yes** to load the map.
7. All of these data come from an ArcService, which is online and free from ESRI.
8. Notice you have an almost complete map, although it is showing the entire Southwest and not just Glendale, and that the map opens in Layout View. In the lower left corner of the map window, there are two boxes. Run your cursor over them and click on the Data View option.
9. Try to zoom in to the general area of Glendale using the interactive zoom tool.
10. Add the City_Boundary_Player, which can be found in the CIA\Data\File Geodatabase\GIS_Layers.gdb Boundaries feature dataset section.
11. Right click on the City_Boundary_P polygon in the table of contents (TOC) and then choose Zoom to Layer.
12. Notice that the city boundaries layer is tilted slightly more than what we have been used to seeing. This is caused by the projection of the data we brought in first by using the template. It is not the NAD 1983 State Plane, AZ Central, Fips 0202, International Feet that all of our data are currently in. The actual projection can be found by double clicking on the data frame name at the very top of the TOC, which reads, "Southwestern United States."
13. If we then click on the Coordinate System tab we see that the maps projection right now is North_America_Albers_Equal_Area_Conic.
14. We can change the projection for the entire map by changing the projection in this dialog box.
15. Down below where it reads, "Select a Coordinate System," click on **Predefined**; then click on **Projected Coordinate Systems**.
16. Now click on **State Plane**.

17. Now click on **NAD 1983 (Intl feet)**.

18. Choose the **NAD 1983 State Plane Arizona Central Fips 0202 (Intl Feet)** projection, then click **Apply** and **OK** to exit the Map Frame Properties.

19. Right click on the **City_Boundary_P** layer again and choose **Zoom to Layer** if necessary.

20. If you zoom out you can see that the other data now also align with the Glendale boundaries and look like we might expect it to look, and not tilted.

21. Close this map but do not save it.

22. Now we are going to create a choropleth map for a CompStat meeting. Open CIA\Exercises\ EX_3\EX_3.mxd.

23. In this case, the hotspot analysis to determine how many gang members there are per grid has already been done. The various layers needed have also already been added and classified for the map.

24. In the lower left corner and at the bottom of the map display, there are four buttons. The first, as we already know, reads "Data View" when you hold your cursor over it. Think of this button as the "world as we see it" button. This is the view of the part of the Earth's surface we are trying to portray in our map. To the right of this button is the **Layout View** button.

25. Click this button. Think of this button as the "if I drew the Earth on a piece of paper" button. In other words, this is where we design the map that will be sent electronically or printed for our audience.

26. We can apply a template to get us started with this layout.

27. In the Layout toolbar (**Figure E3–1**), click on the Change Layout button (second item from the right).

Figure E3–1

28. Scroll to the right and choose the USA tab, and then the SouthwesternUSA template we used before. Click Finish.

29. After a few seconds our map is transformed from a drab layout to a nice one, although we still want to make some changes.

30. First of all we need to zoom a little tighter to the map data being displayed. So use the Zoom tools to zoom in until Glendale fills the layout.

31. We can also use the PAN tool (white hand) in the Standard Toolbar to move the map around in the Data Frame.

32. The blue background color is annoying, so click on the data frame with the Select Elements tool (black arrow), until you get the little handles, then right click on the data frame and go to Properties.

33. Go to the **Frame** tab.

34. Change the **Background** to none (see **Figure E3–2**).

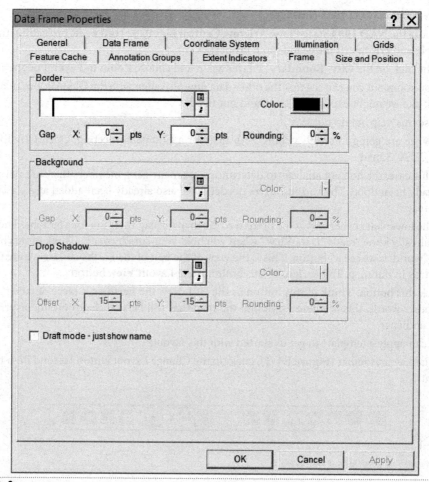

Figure E3–2

Screenshot used by permission. Copyright © Esri. All rights reserved.

35. Click OK to apply your changes.

36. Now, click on the legend and drag it up and left so that it is in the blank space on the Layout.

37. It is probably still being covered by a part of the city, so resize the legend a little by grabbing the bottom right handle and moving it up and left to shrink the legend slightly.

38. Delete the text at the bottom right side that describes the projection. Click on it with the black arrow tool, then hit delete on your keyboard.

39. You can also delete the ESRI graphic at the bottom right.

40. Delete the dividing line in the bottom section on the far left as well.

41. Resize the text that reads, "Southwestern United States" to size 18 and center it. If you click on the text and then right click, you can go to its properties.

42. Click on Change Symbol to change the text size.

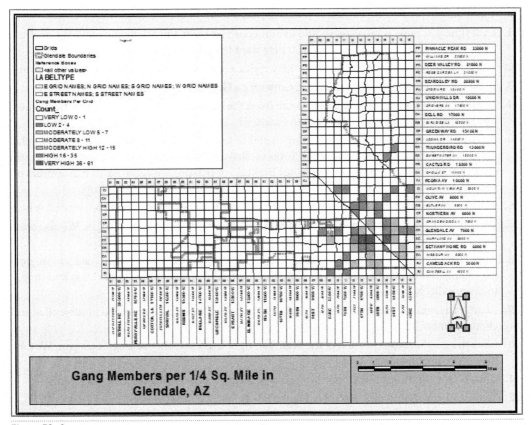

Figure E3–3

43. In the Properties dialog box, change the text to read, "Gang Members per ¼ Sq Mile in Glendale, AZ."
44. Position the text nicely in the left hand side of the bottom brown box.
45. Click on **Insert** on the menu bar.
46. Choose **North Arrow** and pick one from the list to add to the Layout.
47. Once added, move it into the open area on the map at the bottom right side of the city boundaries. Your Layout should now resemble **Figure E3–3**.
48. Save your project as "My First Layout" in your student folder.
49. Typically, every map you make should have the following items in the Layout:

- Map which shows one point of interest
- Supporting data in pastel colors which highlight the point of interest, or which give context to the area
- North arrow
- Legend

- Disclaimers
- Title
- Scale bar
- Other graphics needed to make the Layout more professional looking, or to add interest

50. You should avoid bright colors unless they are used to highlight the point of interest.

51. Each time you make a map you should let someone else see it and ask them to tell you what the map is showing. If they get it wrong, you may want to revise your Layout.

52. The last thing to learn about working with graphic elements is the group and ungroup actions.

53. Right click on the Scale bar and choose **Convert to Graphics** from the popup dialog box.

54. Use the Layout toolbar's Zoom tool to zoom in on the scale bar in the Layout. This is the leftmost tool on the Layout toolbar (refer back to Figure E3–1).

55. You can think of this toolbar as zooming in and out on the piece of paper you are making this map on. Use these tools instead of the Tools toolbar when working with Layouts. You can still use the Tools toolbar if you want to change the scale or perspective of the Earth that appears on your map, but generally always use the Layout toolbar tools when in Layout View.

56. After zooming in on the Scale bar, right click it and choose **Ungroup** from the popup dialog box.

57. We want to have the text "Miles" under the Scale bar, and we want it to be larger. We also want the black square on the right to be red instead of black.

58. After clicking Ungroup, we can see that instead of handles around the entire Scale bar, we now have handles around different parts of the Scale bar. Click once on the "Miles" text and drag it to the middle, below the Scale bar.

59. Change the symbol size of the "Miles" text to 14 and then reposition as needed (double click and choose Symbol button).

60. Click the graphic boxes portion of the Scale bar, right click, and choose Ungroup again. We now have even more handles.

61. Click on the rightmost black boxes and change their fill and outline colors to dark red.

62. Your Scale bar should now resemble **Figure E3–4**.

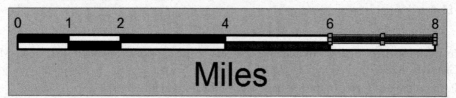

Figure E3–4

63. There are many times when you will need to Group and Ungroup different graphics in the map display. These could include creating a legend using graphics instead of the automatic and linked legend ArcMap provides. If you convert things such as the Scale bar to graphics, however, it no longer keeps automatic scale with the map data.

64. This means that your scale may not be accurate if you change the map view and not the Scale bar as well. Use the Zoom Whole Page tool in the Layout toolbar (fourth from left) to zoom to the full extent of your map. Your Layout should now look like **Figure E3–5**.

65. Save and close your project.

Take a brain rest now and eat lots of protein to replace all those brain cells lost up to this point.

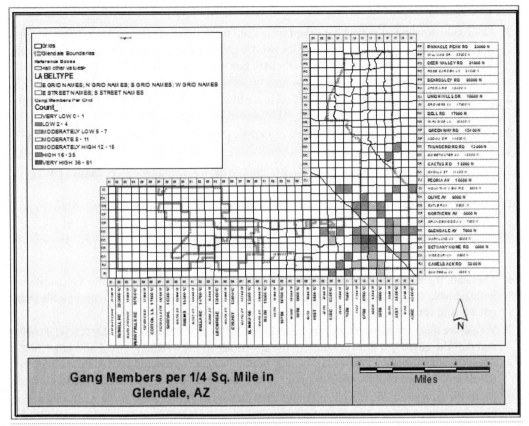

Figure E3–5

■ Exercise 4: Geocoding to Street Centerline

Data Needed for This Exercise
- CIA\Exercises\EX_4\EX_4.mxd

Lesson Objectives
- The student will learn about street centerlines and their attributes and create an address locator.
- The student will learn how to work with data tables and address quality.
- The student will learn about map projections.
- The student will geocode addresses in a table to a street centerline file address locator.
- The student will learn how to use lookup tables.
- The student will learn how to create attribute joins and how that will help add data to a map analysis.
- The student will learn how to use MS Excel and MS Access tables in ArcMap.

Task Description

1. This lesson provides a long but important set of skills for the analyst to know. Many times during a week or even a day the analyst may find the need to geocode address data to a street centerline file or address point. These are the typical methods of geocoding which are found within a law enforcement agency and street centerline geocoding, or "address matching," are the most predominant.

2. For this exercise we are going to match data in a DBF table to the City_Streets_L street centerline file. (Open the map CIA\Exercises\EX_4\EX_4.mxd.)

3. Let's take a look at the fields in the street centerline shapefile we will be using to geocode to.

4. Right click on the City_Streets_L layer and open the Attribute Table.

5. Browse through the fields and pay close attention to the following fields (see **Figure E4–1**):

   - STREET_PRE
   - STREET_NAM
   - STREET_TYP
   - STREET_SUF
   - L_FROM_ADD

   - L_TO_ADD
   - R_FROM_ADD
   - R_TO_ADD
   - L_CITY
   - R_CITY

6. These are the fields we need to set up our address locator. The address locator is basically an indexed table to help the geocoding process find an address on the street centerline file more quickly and convert a static set of addresses to points on the map.

7. We can see that the address ranges are in the L_FROM/TO_ADD and R_FROM/TO_ADD fields and that the name and directionality of the streets are in the STREET_NAM and other fields. Close the attribute table. We need to know how our data are created and edited in our street centerline and the names of these fields in our data. Our second step is to create an address locator.

8. Go to the far right of the map display and click on the tab ArcToolbox or the ArcToolbox icon near the right end of the Standard toolbar.

9. When it opens, find the **Geocoding** tools and then find **Create Address Locator** and double click on it.

STREET_PRE	STREET_NAM	STREET_TYP	STREET_SUF	CLASS	L_FROM_ADD	L_TO_ADD	R_FROM_ADD	R_TO_ADD	ANNAME	
W	SILVER SAGE	LN		D	6401	6421	6400	6420	W SILVER SAGE LN	
W	SILVER SAGE	LN		D	6423	6499	6422	6498	W SILVER SAGE LN	
W	VIA DONA	RD		D	6401	6435	6400	6436	W VIA DONA RD	
W	CORDIA	LN		D	6601	6699	6600	6698	W CORDIA LN	
N	65TH	LN		D	28200	28334	28201	26335	N 65TH LN	
N	PYRAMID PEAK	PKWY		B2	27600	28198	27601	28199	N PYRAMID PEAK PKWY	N
W	LUCIA	DR		D	6401	6499	6400	6498	W LUCIA DR	
N	65TH	LN		D	28412	28498	28413	28499	N 65TH LN	
N	66TH	LN		D	28400	28508	28401	28509	N 66TH LN	
W	CORDIA	LN		D	6401	6427	6400	6428	W CORDIA LN	
N	64TH	LN		D	28424	28598	28425	28599	N 64TH LN	
W	ROBERTA	LN		D	0	0	0	0	W ROBERTA LN	
W	DYNAMITE	BLVD		D	0	0	0	0	W DYNAMITE BLVD	
N	PYRAMID PEAK	PKWY		C	0	0	0	0	N PYRAMID PEAK PKWY	
N	64TH	LN		D	28200	28298	28201	28299	N 64TH LN	
W	VIA DONA	RD		D	6443	6699	6444	6698	W VIA DONA RD	
W	VIA DONA	RD		D	6437	6439	6438	6440	W VIA DONA RD	
W	PINNACLE VISTA	DR		D	0	0	0	0	W PINNACLE VISTA DR	
W	GAMBIT	TRL		D	6015	6099	6014	6098	W GAMBIT TRL	
N	60TH	AVE		D	0	0	0	0	N 60TH AVE	

1 ▶ ▶I (0 out of 23940 Selected)

CITY_STREET_L

Figure E4–1

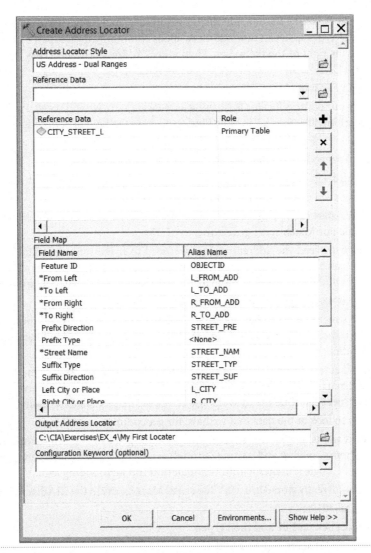

Figure E4–2

10. Complete the address locator **Toolbox Wizard** as follows (see **Figure E4–2** for reference as well):

a. Address locator Style = US Address – Dual Ranges

b. Reference Data = City_Streets_L

c. Feature ID = ObjectID

d. From Left = L_FROM_ADD

e. To Left = L_TO_ADD

f. From Right = R_FROM_ADD

g. To Right = R_TO_ADD

h. Prefix Direction = STREET_PRE

i. Street Name = STREET_NAM

j. Suffix Direction = STREET_SUF

k. Left City or Place = L_City

l. Right City or Place = R_City

m. Left ZIP Code = None

n. Right ZIP Code = None

o. Output Address Locator = Your student folder and name it "My First locator."

11. It will take a bit of getting used to, but the US Address – Dual Range is the most common of the address locator types. You can find out more about commonly used types, by clicking the Help button at the far right of the menu bar. Then enter "Address Locator Types" in the search bar. Then click on Commonly Used Address Locator styles in the help dialog.

12. Click OK to create our address locator.

13. To make sure our address locator is working as we want it to, we will try to use the **Find** tool on the Tools bar (binocular icon). Click the Find tool and in the Find dialog, click the **Locations** tab.

14. You should see My First Locator in the **Choose a Locator** selection box.

15. We will try to geocode the following address: 6201 W OLIVE AVE.

16. Enter this address in the **Full Address** selection box and click the FIND button.

17. Notice that we get a match, and the match score is 100%.

18. Delete the AVE part in the Full Address selection box and click Find again. Notice that without the Street Type our Match score goes down to 87.35%.

19. Whatever data we feed the address locator we need to make sure we include as much of the address as we can to make sure we get a good match. It could be that there is a 6201 W Olive Ave and a 6201 W Olive Circle, so we want to make sure that the point geocodes to the right location.

20. To see how this works, type in "7502 N 46th" and click Find.

21. We have two street segments that match at 87.35% and we need to avoid these issues, because typically when there is a match ArcMap matches to the first record found and that may be the incorrect location.

22. Obtaining and entering complete addresses for all address data we want to match is very important, and we need to make sure that the format of the address matches whatever format for each field in our street centerline file to avoid any errors or misgeocoded locations.

23. Now we need to look at the data that we have for geocoding.

24. The Vice Unit wants to start investigating illegal massage businesses in Glendale. You've spent the past few hours copying and pasting (special) several massage business addresses you found via Yahoo and Google searches within Glendale and the surrounding area.

25. These data are currently stored in a .CSV file called Massage.csv in the CIA\Exercises\EX_4 folder.

26. Open MS Excel 2010.

27. When opened, click on **File** and then **Open**.

28. Browse to the CIA\Exercises\EX_4 folder.

29. Change the Files of Type at the bottom right to **Text Files (*prn, *txt, *.csv)**.

30. We need to change the file types Excel is looking for so it will "see" them in the browse window. Choose our Massage.csv file and click Open.

31. Autofit column widths so you can see all the data. Browse through the data file and notice that you have some intersections in the data. Also, all of the city names are "GLN." These all need to be changed to "Glendale" to match the format of the L_City and R_City fields.

32. Change all appearances of GLN to Glendale in the City field. You can do this with find and replace (CTRL+F) or by changing the first one and dragging it down to the last record.

33. After making your changes, **Save As** "MassageBiz.xlsx" in your student folder.

34. Close Excel.

35. In ArcMap 10, click the Add Data button.

36. Find your Excel sheet and add it to the project.

37. You will probably get a second dialog box showing MassageBiz$ as a sheet in the Excel workbook. This is the one you want to click on and add.

38. Once added, right click this data and open the table.

39. Make sure nothing got messed up in translation to ArcMap, that all 34 records are in the table, no addresses were truncated, etc.

40. Once you are satisfied, take a mental note on which field contains your address and which contains the city and close the table.

41. Now right click on the MassageBiz$ data and choose **Geocode Addresses** from the popup dialog.

42. In the **Choose an Address Locator** popup dialog box, make sure **My First Locator** is chosen and click OK (see **Figure E4–3**).

43. We will then be brought to the geocoding setup dialog box (see **Figure E4–4**).

44. Make sure that **Address** is in the Street or Intersection Selection box and that **City** is in the City or Placename selection box.

45. Remember that Address and City are field names in the data we imported from Excel.

46. In the Output shapefile or feature class selection box, choose a location in your student folder and name it Massage Businesses.shp.

47. You do not have to follow a naming convention restriction such as no spaces, only 10 characters, etc., however, it is a good idea to get into the habit of following a naming convention so that you can find your files easily and quickly. For dated material you might start with the name of the data type (e.g., massage) and then the current date, for example, Massage20120302.shp. When you do this, you know what the data represents, and when it was created or geocoded.

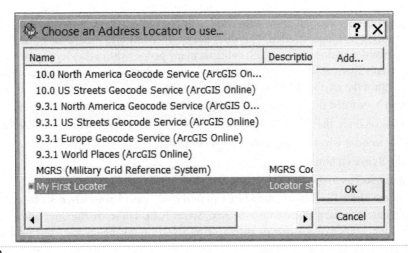

Figure E4–3

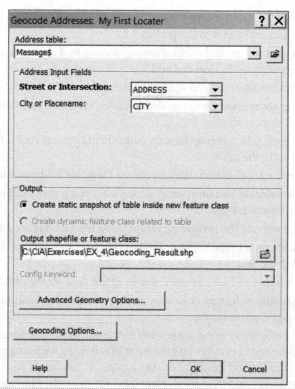

Figure E4–4

48. It is also a good idea to put all data from a project into the same folder. This way when you need to archive the data you can do so all at once with one folder, likewise you can delete the data in one step when no longer needed. This does not apply to any GIS Enterprise or centrally located geographic information system (GIS) data that many people within the city or police department use on a daily basis. A GIS Enterprise usually contains data that are updated regularly by many people within the city but used by others.

49. Once you have filled in the Geocoding dialog, click OK to geocode our addresses.

50. After a few seconds, the geocoding process should end with the dialog box shown in **Figure E4–5**.

51. Hmm . . . wonder why three records did not geocode?

52. Click the **Rematch** button.

53. This then takes us to the rematch dialog box shown in **Figure E4–6**.

54. Click on the **Show Results** selection box and find then select **Unmatched Addresses**. Scroll the results window to the right and find the **Arc_Street** field. These are the three addresses that did not geocode. Look to the **Street or Intersection** selection box below the word **Address**.

55. Notice that Glendale does not have a 5100 N 99th Ave. Change the City or Placename selection box to Phoenix and hit enter. Now we have a 100% match in Phoenix, so choose it in the match window and click the Match button twice.

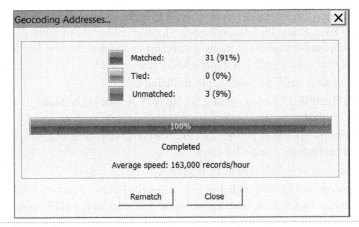

Figure E4–5

56. Use the Select Record arrows or select the next record manually by clicking on the small box next to the record in the upper match window.

57. The next address is 55th & Acoma, which is an incomplete address. It should be shown as N 55th Ave & W Acoma Ave.

58. Click on the button at the bottom left named **Geocoding Options**.

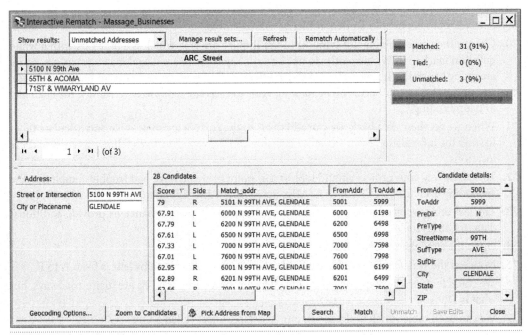

Figure E4–6

59. The match score on this intersection was only 78.19%, the Minimum Match Score in the Options dialog is set to 85%. This is the main reason this location did not automatically geocode. It found the right match, but because of the missing street types and directions it did not geocode higher than 85% and thus is here in the unmatched addresses results.

60. Click Cancel to close the Geocoding Options dialog box.

61. Let's go about fixing this first by entering N 55th & W Acoma in the Street or Intersection selection box and hit Enter.

62. Notice that we now get a match at 87.28% and we could stop here, but we want 100% as much as possible so we have no margin for error.

63. Change the address to N 55th Ave & W Acoma *Ave* and hit Enter.

64. You should now get a 93.64% match, but notice that the intersection match is to Acoma DR and not Ave, so change that and hit enter again. We should now have a 100% match. You should see from this exercise that the format of the street names, street types, direction, and address ranges as well as city name are important together to get 100% matches and have quality data.

65. Click **Match** to match this address.

66. Go to the next record.

67. We have no possible matches at all, but if we look at the address we can see that there is no space between the "W" and the "Maryland." Put a space in there and hit enter. We get an 89.1% match. Manipulate the intersection address (*hint:* street direction, street name, street type for both parts of the intersection) until you get a 100% match and then click the Match button to geocode it.

68. When "matched records" equals 34, click the **Close** button.

69. Save your project in your student folder as massage.mxd.

70. Change the current single dot symbols to the Inquiry symbol, which is a blue box with a white question mark in it. We currently do not know if any of these are illegal massage parlors, so we are going to ask the Tax and License Department if all of these have a current business license, and our undercover officers will be making visits to each site to try to determine if they can buy a "happy ending."

71. When we get these data back, we can add fields to the current attribute table and calculate them to store the information from Tax and Licensing and the vice detective's follow-up visits to these locations.

72. To see the way your project should look at this point or if you have had trouble completing the geocoding exercise, you can open CIA\Exercises\EX_4\EX_4Final.mxd.

73. The last thing we need to learn is how to use look-up tables to enhance or provide additional data in GIS layers.

74. Open the attribute table for the City_Streets_L layer.

75. Notice at the very far right we have a field called StType. This contains letters from A to F.

76. We could look on the map and get an idea that As are freeways and Bs are major roadways, but what is D?

77. We can use a table which is already in our ArcMap project called NONSTCO_LU.

78. Click on the List by Source button at the top of the TOC to see the NONSTCO_LU table. This is a DBF table that was loaded into the project using the Add Data button.

79. Right click on this table to open its attributes.

80. It has a field called CODE which is the same as the StType in the City_Streets_L table. There is also a field called TYPE that contains full-text description of those codes.

81. We can do what is called a "Join" and relate or link the code fields to get additional data into the City_Streets_L attributes.

82. Right click on the City_Streets_L layer and choose Joins and Relates and then choose Join to get the Join dialog box shown in **Figure E4–7**. *You may need to go back to the List by Drawing Order view in the TOC to see and select the City_Streets_L from the TOC.*

83. There are two types of joins available. One is the "Join data from another based on spatial location," which we will not discuss at this time. This other is "Join Attributes from a Table," which is what we will use.

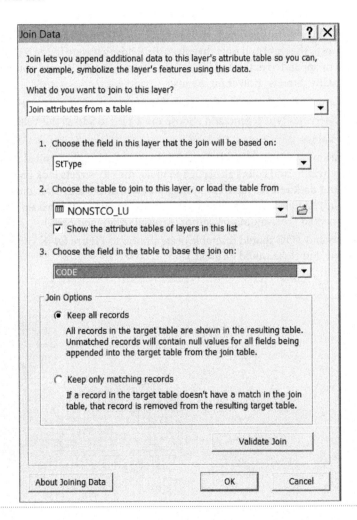

Figure E4–7

84. The field in the City_Streets_L that we want to use to match to is the StType field name. Browse in step number 1, find that field and select it. In Step 2, we need to identify the table we are going to join to the City_Streets_L attributes, and this is NONSTCO_LU.DBF.

85. In Step 3, we want to identify the field in NONSTCO_LU (Code), which we want to link to StType in the City_Streets_L table.

86. Now click the button, **Validate Join**.

87. This will advise us if there are any issues with the join.

88. After running it we can see that [Time] and [Type] might be reserved words for other database tools and that: *"The number of matching records for the join: 22834 of 23940 records matched by joining [StType] from <CITY_STREET_L> with [CODE] from <NONSTCO_LU>. Matching records may not appear in table view due to join validation errors."*

89. Close the Validate Join dialog box and click OK to run the join anyway.

90. Now right click on the City_Streets_L layer in the TOC and choose Open Attribute Table.

91. Scroll all the way to the right and note that all of the fields that were in the NONSTCO_LU table are now added or appended to the end of the City_Streets_L data. We can now use this to change the look of the City_Streets_L layer on the map.

92. Double click City_Streets_L to open the Symbology tab of the Layer Properties.

93. Click on the Categories type legend and choose the TYPE to add as the Value Field.

94. Click Add All Values.

95. Change the various symbols for each Type, by double clicking the symbol and changing each one to different widths and colors as needed to make the city streets look good. I might suggest 3 for a width and dark red for the freeways, light brown and width 3 for the major roads, very light grey for the residential streets, blue for the canals, purple for the private streets, etc. (Streets in this file are named Freeway, Major, Minor, Arterial, Alley, and Null.)

96. Your city streets and TOC should resemble or be similar to **Figure E4–8**. (It does not have to be exactly the same, but close would be great.)

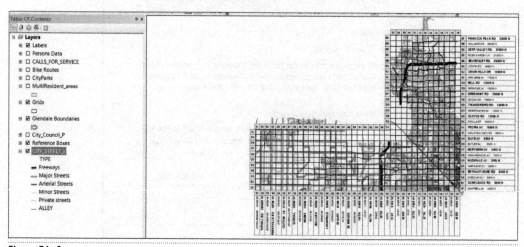

Figure E4–8

97. Remember to use your bookmarks to get back to the view shown in Figure E4–8 or the zoom in and out tools on the Tools toolbar.

98. Remember what you learned about classifying data as well. There are many levels and types of symbols we can use to represent these street types, so experiment with several and then choose the ones that are the most pleasing to the eye.

99. Save your project if desired and close ArcMap.

■ Exercise 5: Selection by Attributes

Data Needed for This Exercise

- We will create a brand new project to start this exercise and the data we will need come from the CIA\Data\File Geodatabase\GIS_Layers.gdb Geodatabase:
  - Boundaries: City_Boundary_P
  - Boundaries: Grids_P
  - Transportation: City_Street_L
  - Street_Labels
  - Basic_Street_Label_An
  - Persons: Probationers
  - Persons: Persons_Cited
  - CIA\Data\Shapefiles\Lookup_Tbls\ Nonstco_lu.dbf

Lesson Objectives

- The student will learn how to do various forms of Select by Attribute queries.
- The student will learn how to combine different Select by Attributes queries to get the right data.
- The student will learn how to create saved queries and load them.

Task Description

1. Open ArcMap and add the layers indicated in the *Data needed for this exercise* section.

2. Change symbology for each layer as needed to make a decent looking map.

3. You will need to create the join again between the City_Street_L layer and the Nonstco_Lu table and then change the symbology based on the Type field. (*Note:* A completed beginning project is available in the CIA\Exercise\EX_5 folder called EX_5.mxd if needed.)

4. Since we began a new project, all of the bookmarks we created in earlier exercises are gone. If you want, you can recreate the HOME bookmark and any other views you think might be needed.

5. This exercise covers finding data on the map using attribute queries. Attribute queries are just what they sound like—we are going to be searching fields and records within the data behind the graphic display on the map.

6. Right click on the **Probationers** layer and open the attribute table. (In the premade EX_5.mxd, the Probationer attributes appear to be empty. "Show selected records" was clicked, although no records were selected. Click "show all records.")

7. A detective has come to you to see if you can find any potential suspects who have a lightning bolt tattoo on their left arm. The suspect is further described as between 45 and 55 years old, has blue eyes and blonde hair, is about 5'7" to 5'9", and weighs between 165 and 185 lbs. The suspect committed a very violent armed robbery and threatened the victim not to call police because, "I am not going back to prison and will come and kill you first before that happens!"

8. Our goal is to see if we can find possible suspects from the adult probation data that are available to us.

9. You should have noticed that the HeightFt, HeightIn, and weight are all number fields in the Probationers layer. (Right click the field name and choose Properties, or just notice they are all right justified, strongly indicating they are number fields.)

10. With the Probationers Attribute Table still open, click on the **Table Options** button at the top left of the attribute table. In the drop-down dialog, choose **Select by Attributes**.

11. In the Select by Attributes dialog (see **Figure E5–1**) in the field list, find the HeightFt field and double click it to bring it down into the SQL query section. "SQL" stands for structured query language and it *"is a special-purpose programming language designed for managing data in relational database management systems (RDBMS)"* (see http://en.wikipedia.org/wiki/SQL). This means that there are special functions that we can use to edit, select, add, or manage fields, tables and data within a relational database. The general design of a standard SQL query involves the use of Select from (the fields of a dataset, or ∗ for all fields), Where (a certain value exists) to return a table of data for creating reports and other uses. ArcView allows us to create simple to complex SQL code using an easy to use interface, through the Select by dialog boxes.

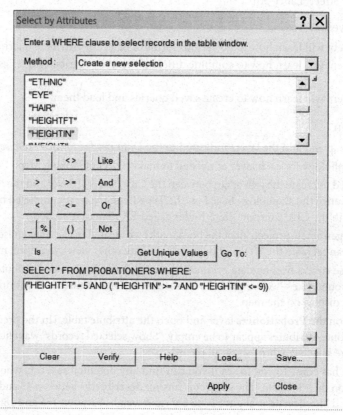

Figure E5–1

12. Click the = button to bring HeightFt down into the SQL Query section.

13. Then enter a value of 5 and click the AND button.

14. The SQL formula should now read:
    - "HEIGHTFT" = 5 AND

15. Enter an open parenthesis symbol, "(", then double click on the HEIGHTIN field to bring it down, and then click on the >= button (greater than or equal to). We want anyone who is between 5'7" and 5'9" so we enter 7, then click the AND button, and double click on the HEIGHTIN field again. Then click on the <= button (less than or equal to), enter 9, and a close parenthesis symbol, ")".

16. Highlight the entire formula and then click the "()" button.

17. Your formula should now be looking like:
    - ("HEIGHTFT" = 5 AND ("HEIGHTIN" >= 7 AND "HEIGHTIN" <= 9))

18. Make sure the Method of Selection box reads, "Create a new selection" (as shown in Figure E5–1).

19. Click Apply to run the selection.

20. The table should come to the front and show that 785 records were selected. We can't really give the detective a list of 785 people. Chances are he would not be happy and might stop asking you for help. Let's see if we can reduce this number a little more.

21. Click on the Selection Dialog box behind the Attribute table to bring it forward.

22. In the Method of Selection box, choose **Select from Current Selection**, and click the Clear button at the bottom.

23. Enter a new SQL formula in the SQL script section as follows:
    - "WEIGHT" >= 165 AND "WEIGHT" <= 185

24. Click Apply and see that we have reduced the number to 212.

25. This is still a lot of people to provide in a list. We know that the suspect was reported to have blue eyes and blonde hair. We can use the Select from current selection again to further reduce our number of potential suspects.

26. Click on the Select by Attributes dialog again to bring it forward. Click Clear and change the formula to:
    - "GENDER" = 'M' AND "EYE" = 'BLU' AND "HAIR" = 'BLN'

27. Click Apply and observe that you now have only 5 persons listed in the table as selected.

28. Five is a good number to provide to the detective, but we still had a lightning tattoo on his left arm left to search for. If we look in the Scar 1 and Scar 2 fields for these five candidates we might be able to see if one of them had a lightning tattoo on his left arm.

29. At the bottom of the attribute table, click the button that reads, "Show selected records."

30. Now we see only the selected records and it will be easier to browse this data.

31. If we scroll to the right to the Scar 1 and Scar 2 fields, we find that the only one listing a "Lightning" tattoo is Larry L. Chavez who has a date of birth (DOB) of 04/28/54. His DOB makes him to be about 58 years old, and that is very close to the suspect's reported age of between 45 and 55.

32. This Larry is likely our man based on the data available in the Probationer dataset. Also notice that Larry is on probation for a dangerous drugs possession charge.

33. We suggest that you learn how to combine different simple queries using the "Select from current selection," "Add to current selection," and "Remove from current selection" methods instead of one huge SQL statement. *It is possible to spend many hours creating very complicated queries only*

to have them fail to work and provide endless error messages. It is much easier to create several simple queries, save these queries, and load them as needed.

34. Close the attribute table of probationers, and in the main menu bar click **Selection** and then **Clear Selected Features**. As a side note, whenever you save a project you should Clear Selected Features because ArcMap remembers where the data is stored or the path to the data, the shape and views of windows, and where toolbars are docked, as well as any selections made. If it were a very large dataset, then when the project opened it would redo all those selections and slow down your ability to work with the project.

35. Let's see how to work with saved queries. This time, click on Selection in the main menu bar, then choose Select by Attributes. The **Layer** should be the **Probationers** layer and in the **Method** selection box choose: **Create a new selection**.

36. At the bottom of the dialog box click on the LOAD button and navigate to the CIA\Data\Saved_ Queries folder and click on the ProbRaceSex.exp file name. When you hit Open, it loads this into the SQL formula section. Click Apply.

37. Notice on the map that many records are now blue or selected.

38. Now hit the load button again to load ProbHeight.exp.

39. Change the method to "Select from current selection" and hit Apply.

40. We can see from the map that fewer records are now selected. Remember that if the offender was actually 5'5" to 5'7" we could change those values in our formula once it was loaded and Apply it without losing the saved query.

41. Now continue loading ProbEyeHair.exp and ProbWeight.exp and Apply each one with the Method of selection remaining: **Select from current selection**.

42. With each run the number of offenders that met the criteria went down from 619, 308, 98, and finally 24.

43. We could reduce it more if we had more descriptive factors for this query project like tattoo type being the word "Manda" on his chest or a ½" scar on his lip. (*The number of features selected can be found at the bottom left side of the screen under the TOC.*)

44. Each of these stored queries can be loaded, modified, and applied for the probationer dataset. If we wanted to create saved queries for the persons-cited dataset, we could and will as this exercise continues.

45. Take a break, step out of the room, inhale deeply, and get back into your Zen state of mind, then let's continue.

46. Choose Selection from the menu bar.

47. Choose Select by Attributes.

48. Change the **Layer** type to the **Persons Cited** dataset.

49. Choose *Create a new selection* in the **Method** section.

50. Enter the following formula in the SQL section:
    - "RACE" = 'H' AND "SEX" = 'M'
    - *Note:* If you are unsure of the data values, you can click on Get Unique Values and double click on the value to enter it in the SQL section.

51. Click **Save**.

52. Name the saved query, CitedRaceSex.exp, and put it in your student folder.

53. Turn off the Probationers layer (nonvisible) and turn on the Persons Cited layer (visible).

54. Apply the SQL formula and see if any records are selected.

55. You should see a lot of light blue on the map display.

56. Okay, let's create another formula and save it.

57. Clear out the SQL formula area so nothing remains (CLEAR button at bottom).

58. Double click on the "AGE" field and then click on the >= and then 20, then the AND button and then double click the AGE field again, then <= button, then 29. So our formula should look like:
    - "AGE" >= 20 AND "AGE" <= 29

59. Save as CiteAge.exp in your student folder.

60. Change the method type to **Select from Current Selection** and click **Apply**.

61. You should have seen a minor reduction in the number of records on the map display. You might have also noticed that on the bottom left side, under the TOC, it tells you how many records were selected.

62. Practice creating formulas for:
    - "CITY" = 'GLENDALE'
    - "VEHMAKE" = 'CHVY' OR "VEHMAKE" = 'FORD' OR "VEHMAKE" = 'HOND'

63. Save these queries as previously instructed and Apply them to see what happens. Practice with the **Add to current selection** and **Remove from current selection** methods to see what happens to the table (you may have to open the table, of course).

64. This concludes Exercise 5.

65. Save your project if desired and close ArcMap.

■ Exercise 6: Selects by Spatial Location

Data Needed for This Exercise
- CIA\Data\Basic Map Layers

Lesson Objectives
- The student will learn how to Select by spatial location in ArcMap.
- The student will learn how to select events which are completely within a source layer.

Task Description
1. Open a blank ArcMap 10 project.
2. At the right of the map display, click on the ArcCatalog tab. (If a tab is not present, click on the small yellow file cabinet icon in the menu bar to open.)
3. Navigate to the Folder Connections and find the CIA\Data folder.
4. Click on the Basic Map Layers folder and drag and drop each layer within this folder to the table of contents (TOC).
5. When dragging and dropping these "layer files" onto the TOC, you should observe that they are automatically symbolized. "Layer" files are special geographic information system (GIS) layers that remember the path to the data they are symbolizing and any symbolization you've placed on the data.

6. List the TOC by drawing order. Place each layer in the TOC in an order where the polygons are on the bottom and the point layers on top. Turn off the point layers (make nonvisible) and leave the patrol zones, grids, and city boundaries on.

7. Open the ArcCatalog tab again and navigate to the File Geodatabase folder and the GIS_Layers.gdb database. Load the Street_Labels and Basic_Street_Labels_An.

8. Street_Labels should be on the bottom of the TOC and Basic_Street_Labels_An would be on top.

9. Remember that in the TOC, everything draws in the display from the bottom up. So anything that is on top of something else will draw last and will cover or conceal what drew below it on the TOC.

10. We can work with the layers and make them semi-transparent, or make them hollow or have no-fill (polygons) to make sure the data we want to see are seen. (Your TOC should look like **Figure E6–1** at this time.)

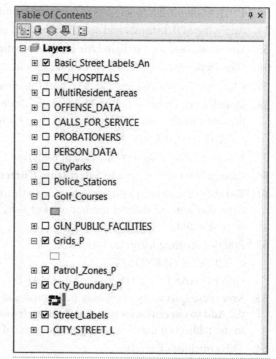

Figure E6–1

11. Now that we have a basic map, let's save it as EX_6.mxd.

12. Okay, now let's experiment with **Select by Location** queries.

13. A Select by Location query is just what it sounds like. A good example of how useful this query is, is to relate it to a database query using SQL, MS Access, or some other program. For example, if we wanted to query all traffic crashes within one-tenth of a mile along W Bell Rd, in a database query, I would have to enter all intersections where W Bell Rd was in Glendale and where another street had an intersection with W Bell Rd. This would involve entering at least 55–60 different intersections. With a GIS system you can easily query all intersections within one-tenth of a mile from W Bell Rd, and thus traffic crashes, which occurred near or at intersections along Bell Rd.

14. Let's give it a try, shall we?

15. First, we need to add the Traffic Crash shapefile from CIA\Data\Shapefiles\Traffic Crashes\Traffic_Crash.shp.

16. These are crashes that occurred between Jan 1, 2001, and Dec 31, 2004.

17. You can verify this by right clicking on the field called CV_DATE and sorting in Ascending then Descending order to see that these dates match.

18. First do an attribute query to find W Bell Rd. Make the City_Street_L layer visible.

19. Go to Selection in the menu bar, and choose Select by Attributes.

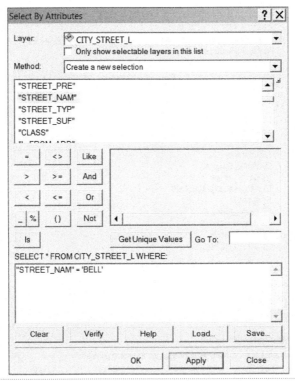

Figure E6–2

20. In the Select by Attributes dialog box, complete as follows:
    a. Layer to be selected = City_Street_L
    b. Method = Create a new selection
    c. SQL Query = "STREET_NAM" = 'BELL'
21. Click OK to select 34 street segments or records (see **Figure E6–2**).
22. Your map should now have Bell Rd selected (light blue), but notice that it is not just in Glendale. So we need to run a **Select by Location** query that selects from this selection to get only those within the city boundaries (see **Figure E6–3**).
23. Click on Selection in the menu bar, and this time use Select by Location. In the Select by Location dialog box, enter the following:
    a. Selection method = Select from the currently selected features in

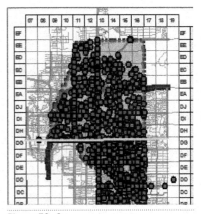

Figure E6–3

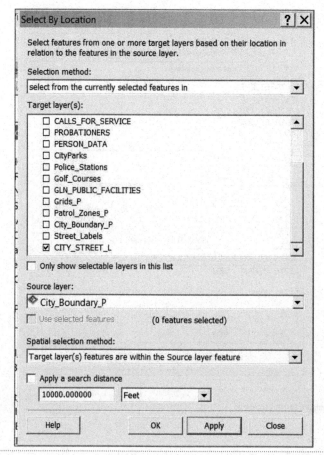

Figure E6–4

  b. City_Street_L
  c. Source Layer = City_Boundary_P
  d. Spatial Selection Method = Target layer(s) features
      are within the Source layer feature (see **Figure E6–4**)
24. Click OK to limit Bell to just those street segments totally
    within the city boundaries (see **Figure E6–5**).
25. Hey that works well, right? Now, for our final Select by
    Location query to find the number of crashes within one-
    tenth of a mile of W Bell Rd in Glendale.
26. Click Selection in the menu bar and Select by Location
    again.

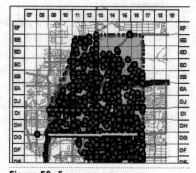

Figure E6–5

27. This time the setup in the dialog box is as follows:
    a. Selection method = Select features from
    b. Traffic_Crashes (*make sure this is the only layer selected*)
    c. Source Layer = City_Street_L (*also make sure the Use Selected Features checkbox is checked*)
    d. Spatial Selection Method = Target layer(s) features are within a distance of the Source layer feature
    e. Apply a Search Distance should be checked
    f. Enter 0.10 and Miles as the selected search distance

28. Click OK/Apply to make the selection.

29. Voila! 2061 traffic crash records should now be selected.

30. These are the traffic crashes that were within one-tenth of a mile of W Bell Rd within Glendale (see **Figure E6–6**).

31. We hope that you can now see the power that spatial or by-location queries can provide to the analyst. When these queries are combined with each other or combined with attribute queries, we can quickly zero in on the data we need.

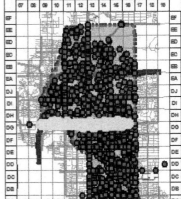

Figure E6–6

■ Exercise 6b: More Selects by Spatial Location

Data Needed for This Exercise
- CIA\Exercises\EX_6.mxd

Lesson Objectives
- The student will learn how to select items that intersect others on the map.
- The student will discover the concept of adjacency and distance queries.

Task Description
1. Open CIA\Exercises\EX_6.mxd.
2. We have the assignment from our commander to provide the total number of calls for service which occurred in Patrol Zone 20 in 2003.
3. He would also like to know which calls for service type were in the top 10 in total call count.
4. You should already be thinking about the fact that you will need a Select by Location and some sort of summary table that can sort the data in descending order by count of call type.
5. Let's start with the Select by Location. Click Selection in the menu bar and then choose Select by Location.
6. In the Select by Location dialog box, enter the following:
    a. Selection method = Select features from
    b. Calls_For_Service (*should be the only layer checked*)
    c. Source Layer = Patrol_Zones_P
    d. Spatial Selection Method = Target layer(s) features intersect the Source layer feature
    e. No *Search Distance* should be used

7. Click Apply to run the request.

8. OOPS! What happened? If we turn on the calls for service layer, we can see that we have data selected all over the city and not just in Zone 20, which is in the far south and east of the city. What we need to do is select Zone 20 first and then use that selection to Select by Location all those calls for service that intersect the Zone 20 boundaries.

9. Open the attribute table for the patrol zones layer (*right click, choose Open Attribute Table*).

10. Right click on the **PatrolDist** field and sort the field in ascending order.

11. At the far left of the PatrolDist record, which has "20" in this field, click the small box to select the Zone 20 record. Close the attribute table.

12. Now repeat the Select by Location process (steps 5–7), but this time make sure the **Use Selected Features** checkbox is checked.

13. Click OK/Apply to make your selection.

14. Now view the calls for service and you should have only those calls for service that were either entirely within the Patrol Zone 20, or they *intersected or touched* the boundary line of the patrol zone.

15. When using ArcMap 10 or any GIS software, if you can write out the things that you want to do, and the data you need beforehand, you can usually write down the steps in the order they need to be made so that you get the right answer in the end.

16. Okay, rest those brain muscles, relax, take a deep breath, and go Zen for a few minutes.

17. Now click on Selection in the menu bar, and then Clear Selected Features to clear out every selection in this project.

18. Let's try a slightly more complicated query that we might actually see in a journey-to-crime analysis to find an offender.

19. Add the BURGLARY_SERIES_CASES shapefile from the CIA\Data\Shapefiles\Offenses folder (if not already in the project). Turn on the burglary series cases and the journey-to-crime layer (JTC Burglary).

20. Turn off the calls for service layer and patrol zones.

21. Right click on the Burglary Series layer and then **Zoom to Layer**.

22. Turn on the **JTC Burglary** layer and turn on the **Burglary Weighted Mean Center** as well.

23. In this exercise, we will try and find potential suspects in a burglary series that our agency is investigating. We have a set of 20 burglaries we are tracking as a series.

24. The offender(s) is breaking the glass or front door of businesses in strip malls late at night. In two of the burglaries, witnesses have provided descriptions of white males between the ages of 14 and 22 who are 5'4" to 5'9" and weigh 130 to 170 lbs. In one burglary, witnesses grabbed one of the suspects as he was trying to exit out a back door and he then fought with the witness. The witness observed a tattoo on the offender's right forearm that resembled a flower or rose. The suspects have committed a great deal of criminal damage in each business that they have been successful in entering.

25. You have made a tactical prediction of when and where the offender will strike next, so undercover units are staking out the highest risk locations.

26. A detective working on the series has asked if there is anything you could do to narrow down the most likely location where the offender lived: You could look through your records to see if you could find anyone who matched the description given.

27. You advise that you could do a journey-to-crime estimate with CrimeStat III, which is what the JTC Burglary layer is. (It was created using the negative exponential mathematical method.)

28. You also know that other research has shown that the offender is most likely to live within 1 mile of the mean center of the crime series. The Burglary Weighted Mean Center is the result of that analysis using the spatial statistics toolbox.

29. Where do we begin? Think about this and think through the steps you want to take. What data do you have that has tattoo information? (*Adult Probationers, but does not include juveniles.*)

30. Since the highest peak area for the JTC analysis (red on map) is a good way to reduce the number of offenders, from citywide, we want to start there.

31. Right click on the JTC burglary layer and then choose properties. Go to the Symbology tab, and look to see what the bottom range is for the red category.

32. We can see that it is 35.187000.

33. So we want to query this layer for anything greater than that number to isolate just the red area in the JTC layer.

34. Click on Selection in the menu bar and Select by Attributes.

35. Enter the following in the appropriate fields:
    a. Selection layer = JTC Burglary
    b. SQL Formula = "Z" >= 35.187

36. Click the **Verify** button to make sure that you entered the formula correctly. If you did it correctly you will get back, "The Expression Was Successfully Verified!"

37. Click OK or Apply and then OK to make the selection. The reddest area should now be selected.

38. So we now have the peak profile area for our journey-to-crime analysis selected. This represents the highest likelihood of the offender's home address or anchor point for this series of crimes.

39. The concept is that this offender is a marauder or that he lives somewhere near the center of the crime series.

40. The fact that this offender is not taking large items like big screen TVs, but instead is taking cash and other smaller items, also supports that this may be a juvenile offender.

41. These two suspects have also been described as being between 14 and 18 years old. They also do a lot of damage within the building once they enter, which goes with many juvenile offenders' common modus operandi (MO).

42. Now let's select the person data using a spatial location query and the peak profile area of our JTC estimate (selected red area) as the "cookie cutter."

43. The point data are the "chocolate chips" or data we want to select, and the peak profile area of the JTC estimate is the cookie cutter.

44. Click on Selection in the menu bar, then Select by Location.

45. Complete the Select by Location dialog as follows:
    a. Selection Method = Select features from
    b. Check the boxes next to Persons_Data and Probationers. (*Make sure these are the only layers selected.*)
    c. Source Layer = JTC burglary
    d. Use Selected Features needs to be checked
    e. Spatial Selection Method = Target layer(s) features intersect the Source Layer Feature.
    f. Click Apply and OK.

46. 2755 records in the Persons_data layer should have been selected.

47. Forty-two Probationers should have been selected.

48. You can verify you have the same number by right clicking each layer, opening the attribute table, and looking at the bottom left side for the 42 out of 2534 records selected text (Probationers).

49. Now that we have several records selected we want to limit our choices by the physical description and tattoos if possible.

50. Let's start with the adult probationers as there are fewer records to sort through.

51. If we open the attribute table of the Probationers layer and sort it by the ETHNIC field in ascending order and then browse down the list to the W/M (white males), we see one suspect that should stand out quickly if we browse the Scar 1 field.

52. We find a W/M 5'9" 166 lbs named James Sepulveda who has a rose tattoo on his right forearm

53. We need to make a decision at this time if this person is a potential candidate, or if we need to search all offenders based on age, height, weight, etc. in this dataset. Close the Probationers attribute table.

54. For now we will move on to the Persons_Data dataset. Right click this layer and open the attribute table.

55. Click on the Table Options button (upper leftmost button).

56. Then click on Select by Attributes.

57. Change the method to: **Select from Current Selection**.

58. Enter in the SQL formula window:
    - "RACE" = 'W' AND "SEX" = 'M'

59. Click the Verify button to make sure your query is valid.

60. Click Apply, and now the number of selected records should be 565.

61. Click the Table Options button and then the Select by Attributes once more.

62. Leave everything the same as the last query, except in the SQL formula enter:
    - ("HEIGHT" >= 504 AND "HEIGHT" <= 509) and ("WEIGHT" >= 130 AND "WEIGHT" <= 170)

63. Make sure your formula is exactly as the one above with the parentheses correctly placed around each >= and <= statement.

64. Click the Verify button, and, if it runs correctly, click Apply. You should now have only 145 records.

65. Since several pieces of literature indicate that the offender typical lives close to the mean center of the crime series and we know where that is, we will examine the remaining 145 selected persons to see if they are within 0.5 mile from the mean center.

66. Close any and all attribute tables you may have open.

67. Click on Selection in the main menu bar, and then choose Select by Location.

68. In the Select by Location dialog box enter:
    a. Selection method = Select from the currently selected features in
    b. Target Layer = Persons_data is the only target checked now
    c. Source Layer = Burglary Series Mean Center
    d. Spatial Selection Method = Target layer(s) features are within a distance of Source layer features
    e. Check Apply a search distance and enter 0.5 and Miles in the two boxes.

69. Click Apply.

70. Click OK and your count should now be 110 persons.

71. Open the attribute table again for the Persons_Data table and find the last name field and sort it in ascending order.

72. You should find a Patrick Sepulveda in the list, whose description is close to that of James although he is a bit younger at 16 years old.

73. They do not live at the same address, but let's say for grins and giggles that you then ran those names in your records-management system (RMS) and found that they were cousins and had recently been arrested together on a shoplifting case.

74. This would be good information to bring to your property detectives and might just end in clearing 20 burglaries.

75. These are the sorts of queries you can apply to a practical situation in the law enforcement field. It is vital for the crime analyst to know how to perform all these queries.

76. Spatial queries are powerful for giving us information about where something is, how many calls occurred within a beat or city council district, or how many traffic crashes occurred along Bell Rd.

77. The analyst should be able to use spatial and attribute queries with ease in any situation. They provide a great deal of opportunities for analysts to view and use their data and get to know it better than any other person within their agency.

78. Please make all layers invisible except:
    - Grids_P
    - Street_Labels
    - Basic_Street_Label_An
    - City_Boundary_P

79. Save your project in your student folder as EX_7.mxd.

■ Exercise 7: Select by Graphics

Data Needed for This Exercise
- CIA\Exercises\EX_7\EX_7.mxd

Lesson Objectives
- The student will learn how to select by graphics.
- The student will learn when to use select by graphics instead of a buffer, or other select routines in ArcMap.
- The student will continue to learn how to combine queries to get the best result.

Task Description
1. Please open ArcMap 10, browse to the CIA\Exercises\EX_7\EX_7.mxd, and open it.

2. You may also use the EX_7.mxd that you saved to your student folder in Exercise 6.

3. A patrol zone lieutenant came to you recently and asked for all calls for service (CFS) "around the Bonsall parks," but was not much more detailed than that. He said that he felt that CFS were going up between 2002 and 2003 around the parks (imagine you are back in 2004 so this is recent).

4. Your analysis task is to find out how many calls occurred "around" Bonsall park during 2002 and 2003.

5. We could find the Bonsall park point, or the polygon representing the park and use the Select by Location queries we used in Exercise 6. Another way to query data is to use a graphic you draw on the map's surface to select points.

6. We can be much more accurate on how "around" is measured.

7. Click on the **Bookmarks** menu in the main menu bar and choose the **Analysis Area** view.

8. Turn on the CityParks layer.

9. We now see two square parks; one is called Bonsall North and the other is Bonsall South (yes, we do name things creatively here in Glendale).

10. We can also see a couple of grids near the park, and if we turn on the City_Streets_L we can see several small streets and two main streets that are near these parks.

11. Move your mouse over the streets and you should see the names of the streets. This popup is called Map Tips and is controlled in the Properties of the City_Streets_L layer. If you cannot see the map tips, this function has not been selected. To turn this function on, right click the City_Streets_L layer, go to Properties, and then to the **Display** tab.

12. There is a checkbox there that simply reads, "Show Map tips using the display expression."

13. We see that currently the ANNAME field is listed as the display field and this is the full name of the street and what we want.

14. Close the properties of this layer.

15. Using the Map tips function and your mouse, what are the two main streets that are near the parks?

16. You should have gotten N 59th Ave and W Bethany Home Rd.

17. Turn on the calls for service layer and by viewing the data, determine what you think "around" should consist of?

18. Perhaps we could use the measure tool (small ruler tool on the Standard tool bar) and see that within about 100 feet are all the calls for service that look like they are "around" the park. At this time we need to draw a graphic that encompasses this area we have decided to use.

19. Find the draw toolbar and the fifth tool from the left, and click on the down arrow to the right of the tool to get the type of draw item we want. In the pick list, choose the **POLYGON**.

20. Now we are going to draw several vertices, or nodes, or points on the map that will be the anchor points for the edges and corners of the polygon. Click once on the intersection where N 59th Ave and W Berridge Ln meet just north of N Bonsall Park.

21. Now click where Berridge Ln and N 58th Ave meet, then click again just south of Rancho Dr, about 100ft south of South Bonsall Park and in alignment with N 58th Ave. Finally, double click at the intersection of N 59th Ave and parallel with the point you clicked previously to complete your rectangle (see **Figure E7–1**).

22. To avoid drawing more polygons on the map display, click the Select Elements tool (black arrow) on the tool bar. Right click the rectangle you drew and choose Properties to get to the properties dialog for the polygon.

23. The yellow highlighted areas in Figure E7–1 show the points that anchor this polygon and result in the final polygon we see in this figure. The top left point should have been your first click,

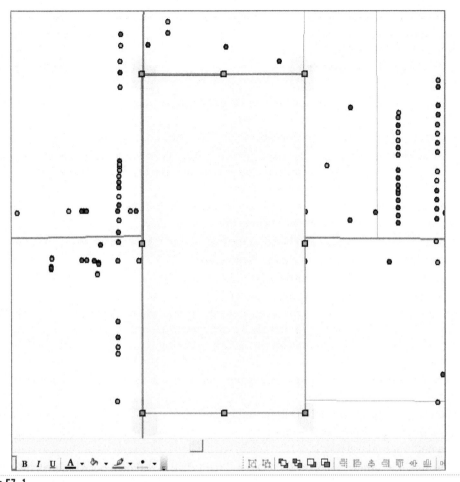

Figure E7–1

then you should have drawn in a clockwise direction to the bottom left point to end the polygon with a double click.

24. Make sure the Select Elements tool in the Tools toolbar (black arrow) is chosen.

25. There should be handles around your polygon, but if not select it now with the Select Elements tool. (Usually clicking on one of the lines of the polygon, rather than the center of the polygon, works the best.)

26. Click on the List By Selection button, which is the second from the right at the top of the TOC.

27. Make every layer nonselectable, except for the calls for service layer.

28. Make a layer nonselectable by clicking on the small button that looks like an envelope and is the first from the left after the name of the layer. A popup reads, "Click to toggle selectable," when you move over it with your mouse.

29. Now that every layer except the calls for service layer is nonselectable, we can click in the menu bar on the Selection item.

30. Next click on Select by graphics. Because our graphic was already selected, all of the CFS points intersecting the graphic have been selected.

31. Open the calls for service attribute table (right click, choose Open Attribute Table).

32. We can see that 1689 records are selected. If you click the small button to the left of 1689 that reads, "Show selected records," when you move your mouse over it, it will show only those selected records that intersect the polygon you drew.

33. Now we need to determine how many calls were received in 2003 and 2004. We can accomplish this with a summarize request on a field in the attribute table.

34. Find the field named, "YRMNTH" (near the right end of the attributes table).

35. Right click this field name and choose **Summarize...**

36. The following should be the entries in the dialog box:
   a. Select a field to summarize = YRMNTH
   b. Specify an output table = yrmonthcfssum.dbf in your student folder (this file is also saved in CIA\Exercises\EX_7\yrmonthcfssum.dbf if you need it)
   c. Make sure to check **Summarize** *on selected records only.*

37. Click OK to run our summary.

38. When the calculations are done, a popup box will ask if you want to add the summary table to the map. Click **Yes.**

39. Close the attribute table of the calls for service layer.

40. Click on the second button from the left at the top of the TOC that reads, "List by Source" when you hold your mouse over it.

41. Now find the summary table in the TOC and right click it, and then open the attribute table.

42. We could add all of these data and find the yearly totals for 2002 and 2003 using the calculator that comes with Windows 7, or we could open the data in Excel to do our calculations.

43. Open Excel; once open, click on File then Open.

44. Browse to where you saved your yrmonthcfssum.dbf table (alternatively you can use the file in the CIA\Exercises\EX_7\ folder).

45. Make sure you change the file type (use the drop-down field at the bottom right of the Excel browse dialog box) to dbase files (*.dbf).

46. You should then be able to see your file, click it, and click open.

47. Click on the box at the top left of grid in Excel to select the entire sheet. Then under the **Home** tab, click **Format** and then **AutoFit Column Width**.

48. Drag the individual years so they are side by side rather than in sequence as shown in **Figure E7–2.**

49. Now delete the columns that have the YRMONTH value in them for 2002, 2003, and 2004 (columns C, E, and G in Figure E7–2).

	A	B	C	D	E	F	G	H
1	YRMNTH	Cnt_YRMNTH						
2	200101	24	200201	26	200301	29	200401	39
3	200102	66	200202	50	200302	50	200402	36
4	200103	39	200203	24	200303	32	200403	38
5	200104	30	200204	21	200304	37	200404	40
6	200105	28	200205	43	200305	36	200405	56
7	200106	40	200206	44	200306	22	200406	49
8	200107	31	200207	35	200307	21	200407	52
9	200108	45	200208	29	200308	24	200408	36
10	200109	24	200209	50	200309	35	200409	33
11	200110	23	200210	22	200310	42	200410	55
12	200111	35	200211	22	200311	36	200411	23
13	200112	23	200212	34	200312	34	200412	26

Figure E7–2

50. Replace 200101 with JAN, 200102 with FEB, and so on. At the top of the data for 2002, 2003, and 2004, enter '2002, '2003, and '2004. Replace Count_YrMonth over the 2001 data with '2001. The prime symbol (') in front of the numbers will let Excel know these are actually text that represent a number and will make it easier to make charts without Excel trying to add the years in as a variable.

51. In addition, change YRMONTH in the A1 cell to read "YEAR."

52. Your worksheet should now look like **Figure E7–3**.

53. Now we can easily use the =Sum() function to add up each year. At the bottom of each year's data, click in the blank field below the last number and enter "=Sum(". Then click in the last number in that column (row 13) and hold your mouse down while you select the entire column of data to row 2. Press Enter on your keyboard to complete the calculation in each column.

	A	B	C	D	E
1	YEAR	2001	2002	2003	2004
2	JAN	24	26	29	39
3	FEB	66	50	50	36
4	MAR	39	24	32	38
5	APR	30	21	37	40
6	MAY	28	43	36	56
7	JUN	40	44	22	49
8	JUL	31	35	21	52
9	AUG	45	29	24	36
10	SEP	24	50	35	33
11	OCT	23	22	42	55
12	NOV	35	22	36	23
13	DEC	23	34	34	26
14					

Figure E7–3

54. You might also bold and center row 1 data cells and create borders that box in all of the cells. Add "Totals" to cell A14, and the formula in cell B14 should be =SUM(B2:B13). You might also highlight the Totals row.

55. As an alternative method to step 54 to copy the formulas across, drag the B14 values across to cell E14 to pull the formula and calculations for each column. **Figure E7–4** shows what your spreadsheet should now look like.

56. We can see that calls for service around Bonsall parks did not change much from 2002 to 2003 with only 2 less in 2003. We do, however, show an increase of 85 from 2003 to 2004. The percent change from 2002 to 2003 is calculated by the formula: (new-old)/old. So if we replace the values of 2002 and 2003 in the formula we get:

    a. (398–400)/400 or

    b. –2/400 = –0.005*100 = –0.05%

57. If we got a –0.5% from 2002 to 2003, what was the percent change from 2003 to 2004?

    a. (483–398)/398*100

    b. 95/398 = 0.23869*100 = 23.9% increase

58. This concludes the training. Save your project in your student folder and close ArcMap 10. Close Excel as well and save your Excel sheet in your student folder as Ex7. xlsx.

	A	B	C	D	E
1	**YEAR**	**2001**	**2002**	**2003**	**2004**
2	JAN	24	26	29	39
3	FEB	66	50	50	36
4	MAR	39	24	32	38
5	APR	30	21	37	40
6	MAY	28	43	36	56
7	JUN	40	44	22	49
8	JUL	31	35	21	52
9	AUG	45	29	24	36
10	SEP	24	50	35	33
11	OCT	23	22	42	55
12	NOV	35	22	36	23
13	DEC	23	34	34	26
14	**Totals**	313)	400	398	483

Figure E7–4

■ Exercise 8: SQL Queries of Attributes

Data Needed for This Exercise

- CIA\Exercises\EX_8\EX_8.mxd

Lesson Objectives

- The student will learn how to use SQL queries and know the right format for them.
- The student will learn how to use the create a new selection method.
- The student will learn how to use the select from current selection method.
- The student will learn how to use a .DBF table from a shapefile in Excel 2010.
- The student will learn how to create a pivot table in Excel 2010.
- The student will discover the add from current selection and remove from current selection functions.

Task Description

1. We have a lot of versatility with spatial and attribute queries, but they require a lot of knowledge about the data being used and within each field and record.

2. A proper attribute SQL query in ArcMap depends on the analyst entering the data correctly. The first thing we learn is that the format or syntax of the SQL query should be at least [FieldName], followed by an operator of like =, >=, <=, <, or >, and then a value such as 1, 'radar', or 20041231.

3. There can be any kind of data in a field within an attribute table. These data can be a string or text, a number, or a date. Common sense dictates that a string or text value must have quote marks around it and in ArcMap this is normally a single quote ('). A string or text query will often use an operator of "Like."

4. Numbers are entered as 1, 345, 356788, 35.872, etc., and will often use arithmetic operators: =, >, <, or a combination.

5. Open EX_8.mxd in CIA\Exercises\EX_8\EX_8.mxd.

6. A citizen watch group in Glendale has been pestering the chief of police at every public meeting, indicating that crime is horrible around apartment complexes. The local apartment association is yelling in his other ear about how false the other group's statements are.

7. We are going to create a complex SQL query to look for all the UCR offenses that occurred around any multiresident area in 2003 and 2004. We are also going to create a subquery of these selected data to find all Part 1 Uniform Crime Report (UCR) offenses.

8. So you should be thinking about what data we have in the table of contents (TOC) that we need to query and in what order?

9. First, we need to identify all the multiresident areas that are actually within the city of Glendale. The current multiresident area layer has data from all over Maricopa County if you make it visible and look at the polygons.

10. So what query do we do first? Yes, that's right, we need to do a Select by Location to find all the multiresident areas that at least intersect the city boundaries.

11. Can you think of the queries needed and in what order they should be performed? Maybe we can help a little with that, as follows:
    a. Select by location: City boundaries as cookie cutter to "clip" the data to within the city boundaries; multiresident polygons as data being clipped
    b. Selection by Location: Select all UCR Offenses that were within 500 feet of an apartment or multiresident polygon
    c. Select by Atttributes: Select all UCR offenses that occurred in 2003 or 2004 and those that were Part 1 offenses

12. Let's begin by going to the main menu bar and choosing Selection, then choose Select by location.

13. Fill the dialog box as follows:
    a. Selection method = Select features from
    b. Target Layer(s) = MultiResident_areas
    c. Source Layer = City_Boundary_P
    d. Spatial selection method = Target layer(s) features *intersect* Source Layer features

14. Click Apply or OK to make the selection.

15. Now that we have all the multiresident polygons selected, we need to select the UCR offenses that are within 500 feet.

16. Go to Selection → Select by Location again and this time complete the dialog box as follows:
    a. Selection method = Select features from
    b. Target Layer(s) = OFFENSE_DATA
    c. Source Layer = MultiResident_areas (The box to Use selected features should be checked.)
    d. Spatial selection method = Target layer(s) features *are within a distance of* Source Layer features
    e. In the Search distance boxes, enter "500" and "Feet."

17. Click Apply or OK to make our selection.

18. Now right click the MultiResident_areas and open the attribute table.

19. There are 302 out of 2661 records selected in the MultiResident_areas layer.

20. Now right click the Offense_Data layer to open the attribute table. There are 57,754 out of 104,597 records selected in the Offense_Data layer.

21. Click on the Table Options button at the top of the Offense_data layer's attribute table (leftmost button), and choose Select by attributes.

22. In the Select by attributes dialog box, complete the following:
    a. Method = Select from current selection
    b. Select* from Offense_data where:
       • "MIDPOINT" >= date '2003-01-01 00:00:00' AND "MIDPOINT" <= date '2004-12-31 00:00:00' (*Note:* You may only require the 2003-01-01 part of the value depending on the default date field your system is set to. Some systems require that 00:00:00 be added and others do not.)
23. Click Apply to run the query.
24. The number of records should have been reduced to 27,317.
25. Close the attribute table and we are now going off the lesson plan a little bit, because we also want to discover which apartment complexes are actually contributing the most to our crime problem around multiresident areas.
26. In the TOC, right click on the Offense_Data layer.
27. Choose Data → Export data from the popup menu.
28. The popup dialog menu should be completed as follows (see **Figure E8-1**):
    a. Export: = Selected features
    b. Use the same coordinate system as: = This layer's source data
    c. Output feature class to: = YourStudentFolder\Offense-DataSelected.shp
29. When asked, add the new layer to the ArcMapproject.
30. Now we want to use a little process called a "Join."
31. Joins are very powerful and allow us to join data as a lookup table to add information to a GIS layer, or to do a "spatial join" which lets us join data from one layer to another based on where they are located.
32. Our motivation is simple, get the name of the multiresident_area polygon which is closest to the points we selected so that we can

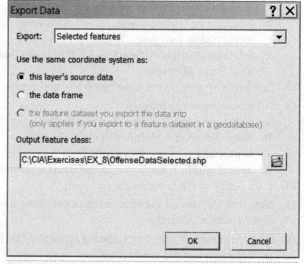

Figure E8-1

Screenshot used by permission. Copyright © Esri. All rights reserved.

use a pivot table in Excel to find out what crimes and which complexes are our biggest problems.
33. We want the multiresident name to be a part of the offense data file we exported in step 28. We always right click on the layer we want to add spatially joined data to in order to start the process.
34. So right click on OffenseDataSelected in the TOC.
35. Choose **Joins and Relates** from the popup menu and then choose **Join**.
36. Complete the join dialog as follows (also see **Figure E8-2**):
    a. What do you want to join to this layer? = Join data from another layer based on spatial location
    b. Choose the layer to join to this layer... = MultiResident_areas

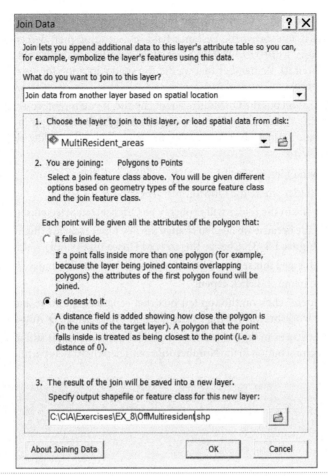

Figure E8–2

    c. Check = is closest to it

    d. Saves as OffMultiresident.shp in your student folder

37. Click OK to run our spatial join.

38. At your leisure, reopen the join dialog and review the Help for joins by clicking on the **About Joining Data** button on the join dialog.

39. Once your join is completed it should add the layer automatically, but if it does not it may again ask you if you want to add the new layer to current project. Indicate Yes, and then open the attribute table for this new layer.

40. At the right side of the offense data are new fields, which came from the multiresident_area attribute table. One of these new field names is DESC_, which is the name. At the far right is a field called "DISTANCE." This field records the distance this offense data record was from the multiresident area that was closest to it.

41. Notice we still have 27,317 records (if you did it correctly).

42. Notice also that if you sorted the Distance field in ascending then descending order, we have distances that range from 0 to 499.94062 feet (if your values are similar but not exactly the same do not worry about it). Remember that we did the spatial location for anything within 500 feet, so this makes sense.

43. Remember where you put the OffMultiresident.shp file. If you forgot, you can use the copy here: CIA\Exercises\EX_8\OffMultiresident.shp or you can right click the layer in the TOC, go to Properties, and then the Source tab and read what folder it is located in. Okay, close ArcMap for now.

44. Open MS Excel 2010.

45. Click on File, then Open in Excel.

46. Navigate to the folder where the OffMultiresident.shp file was saved.

47. The only visible file in the folder will probably be OffenseDataSelected.shp.xml.

48. We only see this file because we need to change the File types pick box (highlighted in the bottom right corner of **Figure E8–3**). Change this to read Dbase files (∗.dbf).

49. Once you have changed this selection box as indicated, you should now see OffMultiresident.dbf.

50. Click on this file name and click **Open**.

51. Once this file opens, click on the top left box that separates the rows and columns. This will select the entire worksheet. Click the Home tab, and then Format → Autofit Column Width.

52. To get rid of the extra 0s in the various fields, while the whole sheet is still selected, click once on the **Increase Decimal** button in the **Number** Ribbon. Then click on its partner **Decrease Decimal**.

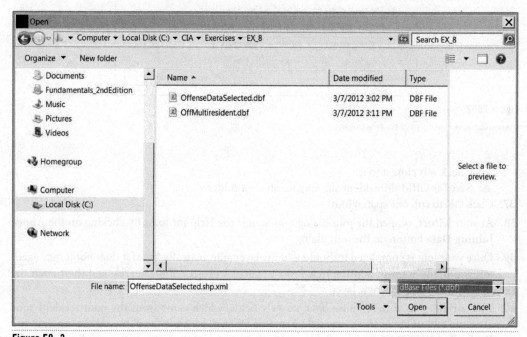

Figure E8–3

Screenshot used with permission from Microsoft.

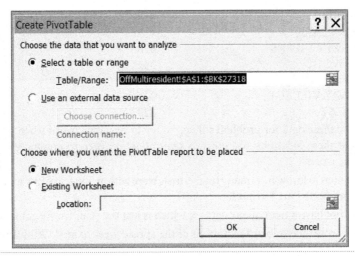

Figure E8–4

Screenshot used with permission from Microsoft.

53. Then click Format → Autofit Column Width again.

54. Now on your keyboard hit the CTRL+Home key to bring the cursor to the top left cell of the worksheet.

55. In the main menu bar, click on INSERT.

56. Then click on Pivot Table.

57. Click OK on the Pivot Table dialog as shown in **Figure E8–4** (*Note*: the range should have already been completed by Excel).

58. In the Pivot Table area created by this process, we need to tell Excel what we want to have as table values, column and row headings, and if we want to filter any of the data.

59. At the right side of the excel sheet, you should see the "Pivot Table Field List."

60. This is where we are going to make magic.

61. First find the field called **UCR Group** and drag it to the section called "Report Filter." (We will tell you what this is for later.)

62. In the section called "Values," drag and drop the field called "RPTNUM."

63. You should now see a count of 27,317 in the Pivot table but no column or row headers yet.

64. To see which apartment complexes were top both years in all UCR offenses within 500 feet, we can drag and drop the field called **DESC_** to the **Row Labels** section.

65. Now click in the first count in cell B4 and then choose **Sort largest to smallest** in the Pivot Table Options Ribbon. (*Note*: It looks like a red Z on top and a blue A on the bottom with an arrow pointing down to the right.)

66. You should see that these are the top 10 multiresident locations for UCR crimes in Glendale:

    a. COCHISE AT ARROWHEAD   703

    b. MONTEBELLO APARTMENTS   503

    c. OAKLAND VILLAS   471

d.	OLIVE TREE	459
e.	BETHANY PARK	451
f.	HALLCRAFT VILLAS	428
g.	RANCHWOOD	342
h.	SPRING MEADOW	338
i.	RIDGEWAY VILLAGE	331
j.	PARK WEST	329

67. We could use these data for problem solving to try to find which and when URC crimes were happening at these locations and create a tactical action plan to combat each multiresident area's specific issues.

68. Okay, we wanted to know how many total crimes were within 500 feet of an apartment complex, and how many were Part 1 crimes.

69. Since we do not have a field in our dataset, which is just the year, we are going to calculate one.

70. Click on the worksheet tab at the bottom of the spreadsheet named OffMultiresident. This is our original dataset. Find the Entry Date field.

71. Click on the column to the right of it, then right click and choose Insert from the popup menu.

72. At the top, and to the right of Entry Date, enter YEAR in the new blank column.

73. Below that enter this formula:

   • = YEAR(M2)

74. 2003 should appear. If it does not, first try to format the field to a General number. You click CTRL+1 to get to the format cells menu, and choose General under the number tab.

75. At the bottom right of the newly calculated year, there is a small black box. When you move your mouse over it, the cursor turns to a black plus sign.

76. Double click this black plus sign or black box.

77. This will calculate all the other fields below this one with the same formula relative to the date in that row.

78. We now have the year we can use in our pivot table.

79. Return to the pivot table by clicking the Sheet1 tab at the bottom of the spreadsheet.

80. Right click anywhere in the pivot table and choose **Refresh** to bring in the new data column.

81. In the Field List at the right, the field YEAR should now be visible.

82. Drag this into the Column Labels Section.

83. If it asks if you want to overwrite data, choose **Yes** to proceed.

84. Now we have the 2003 and the 2004 totals for each complex in order by the sum of both years.

85. We wanted to see UCR Class and year for all complexes.

86. Remove the DESC_ field from the Row Labels section by dragging it out of the section, and drag and drop the UCRType field to this location.

87. If you again sort the Grand totals column in descending order, Theft, Other, and Vandalism are the top three crimes.

88. We could create a chart or table from this point and provide it to the chief. We could also create multiple pivot tables of varying pieces of data to get as full a picture as we could of these data.

89. Now, our last question was what Part 1 crimes occurred within 500 feet of an apartment complex.

90. To solve this puzzle, at the top of the Pivot table where we see UCR Group, click on the drop-down arrow to the right of "(All)".

91. Check the box next to Select Multiple Items, and then click on ALL to uncheck everything. Place a checkbox in the Part 1 Violent and Part 1 Property items only and click OK.

92. See how this affects the pivot table?

93. Now we are only seeing the Part 1 crimes within 500 feet of an apartment complex.

94. Theft, Auto theft, Burglary, Agg. Assault, Robbery, Rape, Arson, and Murder are listed in that order.

95. We could also compare the number of units within the complexes to get a rate of burglary or theft, and then compare that to the rate of other single-family dwellings in the city (which we could obtain from census data).

96. Using this sort of data, we could potentially determine if these high numbers are due to an overwhelming crime problem as one of the chief's hecklers has indicated, or that crime in apartment complexes is no different residence to residence as surrounding single-family homes.

97. Save your Excel sheet as OffMultiresident.xlsx (*Note:* A sample version has been saved in CIA\Exercises\EX_8\OffMultiResident.xlsx for review as needed).

98. Within the Select by Attributes functions we have several different methods of selection:
    a. Create a new selection
    b. Add to current selection
    c. Remove from current selection
    d. Select from current selection

99. Each of these methods has its uses when trying to get just the data you need for a project.

100. **Create a new selection** allows us to create a new selection from scratch, and **Add to current selection** allows us to add variables and records based on other criteria.

101. **Remove from current selection** allows us to weed out records we do not want from a current selection set, and **Select from current selection** allows us to whittle down data we have selected through adding more criteria to the selection.

102. Each of these tools can be used singularly or together to get the exact data from a set of attributes we need for a project.

103. You should think of these tools as ones that help you make complex queries easier to handle. For example, let's say that we wanted to find all the Black Male suspects who are between the ages of 35 and 45 years, height of between 5'11" and 6'2", grey hair, weighing in between 134 and 195 lbs, and who live within 1500 feet of Glendale Ave. The steps you would take to query these data could be cumbersome in one Select by Attributes query. So, what we want to do is find the elements that can be done in the order in which we know we will not accidently remove items that should be included. In the example above we would:
    a. Select Glendale Ave using a Select by Attributes query
    b. Do a Select by Location query of all persons (probationers, etc.) who live within, say, 2000 feet of Glendale Ave
    c. Then Select from the Current Selection (Select by Attributes), all those [race] = 'B' and [sex] = 'M' subjects
    d. Then another Select by current selection of all those subjects who are [Age] >= 35 and [Age] <= 45

e. Another Select by current selection of [height]>= 511 and [height]<= 602

f. Then another select by current selection where [weight] >= 134 and [weight]<= 195

g. We could then remove from current selection all those subjects where [hair]= 'bld' or [hair] = 'bro' or [hair]='blk' for instance

h. If we then got additional information that the subject had a tattoo of a rose on his forearm, we could add to current selection where [race] = 'B' and [Sex]= 'M' and [Tat1] like '%Rose%' or something similar.

104. The concept is to do several short and simple queries instead of trying to write one huge query to accomplish the goal.

105. Hope you are enjoying the exercises—hang on for some more exciting knowledge!

106. Close and save your project as needed.

■ Exercise 9: Combining Query Methods

Data Needed for This Exercise

- Create a new map project with all the following basemap layers:
  - City boundaries
  - Grids
  - Streets
  - Street labels and annotation
  - Patrol zones
  - Offense data
  - Probationers

Lesson Objectives

- The student will learn about different types of map data and geodatabases.
- The student will learn how to use spatial and attribute queries together for a better result.
- The student will learn how use different attribute queries and methods to get a better result.
- The student will learn the right order in which to apply queries.

Task Description

1. Open ArcMap 10 and add the layers indicated under "Data Needed for This Exercise."

2. The data can be found in three different locations.

3. In ArcMap, we can have data stored in a variety of ways, and it does not take away from the quality of the data. There are, however, a few things you might consider:

   a. An ArcSDE (spatial database engine) is expensive software that sits in front of an SQL or Oracle database and is usually found in a city's GIS Enterprise system. These SDE layers can then be accessed by multiple persons and can have different versions of the data being worked on at the same time. These different versions can then be "reconciled" together with all updates from the versions added to the SDE Enterprise data for all to see and use. Since this requires servers and an SDE license, these data are not available for these exercises.

   b. File Geodatabases are the next best thing to an SDE geodatabase in that multiple users can be using the same data at the same time with little or no effect depending on the speed of your network. This is good for smaller units that need to share and use the same data at the same time; however, it does not like two people editing the same layer at the same time. To this point we have mostly used the file geodatabase data format.

c. Personal geodatabases are MS Access databases that store geographic information system (GIS) data. This database type is also good for small units; the advantage is that you can also link the GIS attribute table to other Access databases, which allows other units to query traffic crashes, adult probationers, and other data. The problem here again is that MS Access puts a lock on the data when someone is using it, so multiple users accessing the data can cause problems. This is especially true when editing. However, the data are very mobile, which can have its uses for small datasets.

d. The last GIS file structure we will discuss is the shapefile. Shapefiles are made up of several files. If you had a shapefile named MyData.shp that you looked at with Windows Explorer, you would actually see several files like:

- MyData.shp (*stores the graphic types*)
- MyData.shx (*stores the spatial location*)
- MyData.dbf (*stores the attributes or data*)
- MyData.prj (*stores the projection information*)
- MyData.sbn & .sbx (*spatial indexing and sorting info*)
- MyData.shp.xml (*this is the metadata—or data about the data that is stored in XML format*)

4. If we click on the Add Data button (in the menu bar), or open the ArcCatalog tab (right of the map display), we can see that the file structure of the data makes use of the File and Personal geodatabases as well as shapefiles. In each folder, the same data can be found in the other (see **Figure E9–1**).

5. In this way, you can begin to start using different data types, and in most ways it is seamless.

6. There are some differences when it comes to doing attribute queries.

7. After loading the basemap layers from any of the data sources, click on the Add Data or ArcCatalog options and add or drag and drop the File CIA\Data\File GeoDatabase\GIS_Layers.gdb\ UCR Crimes\Offense_data into the TOC.

8. After adding this layer, right click on it, go to Properties, and then to the **General** tab. Change the displayed name to Offense_Data – FileGDB and click OK. Now, Add Data again and find the Personal Geodatabase folder.

9. Add the CIA\Data\Personal Geodatabase\GIS_Data. mdb\UCR Crimes\Offense_Data layer.

10. Change the name of this layer to Offense_Data-PGDB.

11. Finally, find the CIA\Shapefiles\Offenses\Offense_Data.shp and add it to the project.

12. Change the name of this layer to Offense_Data-Shp.

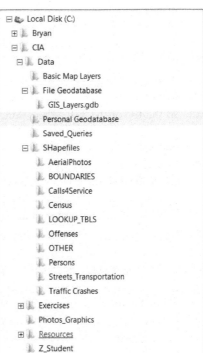

Figure E9–1

13. We are going to do the same query on all three datasets. These data are exactly the same, except for the different type of GIS storage or file format.

14. We want to find all the Uniform Crime Report (UCR) crimes in 2004 that were within 1000 feet from the main police station downtown. This address is 6835 N 57th Dr.

15. Click on the Binoculars icon in the Tools toolbar. Then choose the Locations tab.

16. 10.0 North America Geocode Service (ArcGIS Online) should be in the Choose a Locator window. (*Note*: You will need Internet access to use this geocoding service. If it is not available, the instructor will have to make other arrangements for a local geocoding locator to be available.)

17. In the Single Line Input box type, "6835 N 57th Dr., Glendale, AZ 85301" [without the quotation marks].

18. Click Find.

19. The first record in the match window at the bottom shows 100%. Right click on this match and choose **Add point**.

20. ArcMap puts a graphic point where the main station is located.

21. Close the find/search dialog window.

22. Turn off any other point layers that may be on.

23. Click on the Select Elements tool (black arrow) in the Tools toolbar and click on the point where the map station is located to select it and get the little handles around it.

24. Zoom in to the general area of the point. Use the draw tool to draw a circle that has an approximately 1000-foot radius from the center of the main station. The distance you are drawing is shown in feet at the bottom of the TOC and to the left side of the project window.

25. To create the circle, click as close to the middle of the point where the main station is located, and hold your left mouse button down while you drag it outward from the center.

26. It may be a bit difficult to get it right at 1000 feet. For this exercise +/−200 feet is acceptable.

27. Make sure the new circle you drew is selected.

28. At the top of the TOC, the second button from the right reads, "List by selection" when you hover your mouse over it. Click this button, and then make the three Offense_Data layers the only selectable layers in the project.

29. Note that the layers that are not visible are light grey in color, but they need to be visible to be selected. Click the small, diamond-shaped box (toggle visibility) to the left of each of the three Offense_Data layers to make them visible on the map display.

30. Click Selection in the menu bar again, and choose Select by Graphic.

31. Notice that a lot of blue dots start to show up as they draw.

32. To the right of each layer in the TOC is the number of records this process selected—approximately 1175 for each layer (or something similar depending on the radius of the circle).

33. If we wanted to be more exact, we might create a feature point for the main station, or use the public building polygons instead of a point and then use a buffer, or a Select by Location query to get as close to exactly 1000 feet as our data allow.

34. Remember that scale and accuracy play a part here. If the GIS data are not totally accurate, we might not be able to use them reliably to do such things as Megan's Law analysis where a sex offender cannot live within 1000 feet of a school, or Probation restrictions that indicate a probationer cannot live within 500 to 1500 feet of a bank, school, or another violent felon.

35. We will now query data from the Offense data from the File Geodatabase, Personal Geodatabase, and Shapefile sources of the Offense Data.

36. We will need to use slightly different SQL formulas based on the kind of data we are querying. Let's start with the File Geodatabase.

37. Right click on the **Offense_Data – FGDB** layer.

38. Open its attribute table.

39. Click on the Table Options button (leftmost button at the top left of the table).

40. Click on **Select by Attributes**.

41. Change the method to **Select from current selection**.

42. Enter the following formula into the SQL formula window:
    - "ARC_Street" LIKE '%5798%GLENDALE%' OR "UCRGROUP" LIKE 'PART 1%'

43. Make sure to make everything exactly the same text case as shown, as these formulas are typically case sensitive.

44. Notice that with a File Geodatabase, the field name is surrounded by double quotation marks.

45. Also notice that the wild card character (or a character we are putting in place of unknown characters) is a % sign for File Geodatabases.

46. We also use single quotes surrounding the value field to denote it as text.

47. Click Apply. This query will select from the current selection and return all Part 1 crimes and crimes that occurred at 5798 W Glendale Ave or any variations of that address.

48. Browse through the selected records by clicking the View Selected Records button at the bottom of the attribute table.

49. We have around 303 records now, depending on the radius of your circle, but there are different addresses than 5798 W Glendale Ave in the dataset.

50. All of the crimes are either Part 1 violent or Part 1 property crimes. The "OR" statement between the "ARC_Street" LIKE '%5798%GLENDALE%' **OR** "UCRGROUP" LIKE 'PART 1%' is the culprit. If we sort the address field in ascending order (right click the field name, then choose sort in ascending order) we can see that at the 5798 W Glendale Ave address our search has also returned several Part 2 crimes. So we got anything like "5798 W Glendale" OR any "Part 1 crime" (see **Figure E9–2**).

51. Close the Attribute table for the File Geodatabase layer. Right click on the Offense_Data – PGDB layer and open its attribute table.

52. Click on the Table Options button at the top left of the attribute table, and choose Select by Attributes. Change the method to Select from current selection as we did with the File Geodatabase layer.

53. Notice that the field names are surrounded by brackets [name] instead of with quotation marks—"name".

54. A Personal Geodatabase's fields are always seen and entered in the SQL formula window with brackets around them.

55. Enter the following formula into the SQL formula window:
    - [ARC_Street] LIKE '*5798*GLENDALE*' AND [UCRGROUP] LIKE '*PART 1*'

56. The wild-card character is now an asterisk (*) and the field names are surrounded by brackets—[].

57. We also only got back 2 records instead of 303. This time, because we used the AND operator, we got back only those part 1 crimes which occurred at 5798 W Glendale Ave.

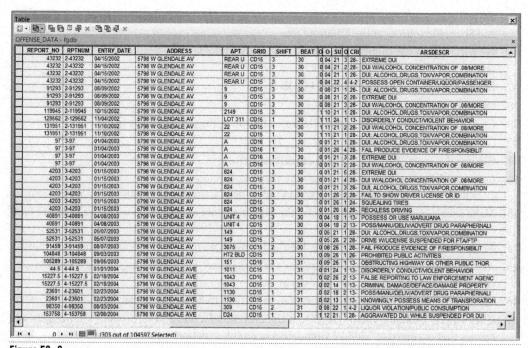

Figure E9–2

58. It is very important for an analyst to understand these operators and what order of operations we use in more complex formulas. Often we will use parentheses around different operations in a formula to designate that that happens before what is outside the parentheses. Let's give this a whirl with the Shapefile version of the Offense_Data.

59. Close the attribute table of the Offense_data – PGDB.

60. Open the attribute table of the Offense_Data-SHP layer (right click the layer in the TOC and choose Open Attribute table).

61. Click on the Table Options button again, and choose Select by Attributes.

62. Change the Method to **Select from current selection**.

63. We want to see all the offenses that occurred between Apr 15, 2002, and Oct 3, 2004, and between 0800 and 1630 hours, and that have the ARS Description or UCR Description fields contain the word "SEX" anywhere in the description.

64. This is going to be a bit more complicated than previous queries. Do you think you can do this on your own and figure it out? We are sure you could, but just in case we will give you a little bit of help.

65. We want to create each of these queries one at a time. As we are thinking, we need to figure out what should go first, second, third, etc., and decide if we are going to use ANDs or ORs in the SQL formula.

66. I am thinking that the first should be the date range, followed by the time range, and then the "SEX" variable.

67. So enter the formula as shown here:
    - (("RECVDATE" >= 20030415 AND "RECVDATE" <= 20041003) AND ("RECVTIME" >= '0800' AND "RECVTIME" <= '1630')) AND ("ARSDESCR" LIKE '%SEX%' OR "UCRDESCR" LIKE '%SEX%')

68. First we see that shapefiles use the double quotes around the field names. They also use the % sign as a wild-card character.

69. We use AND statements between the date ranges as well as the time ranges. Then we use an OR statement for the last piece in parentheses. We want ARSDESCR like "Sex" **OR** UCRDESCR like "Sex" to search both fields. We had to use an OR statement here because there may not be rows or records that have SEX in both fields at the same time.

70. Click Verify to make sure that your version of the query works properly and returns some records (we get 14 records returned). If it does, then click Apply to run it.

71. The verify button can save your bacon many times to allow you to correct errors in a query before actually running it. Another good thing to do is to highlight your entire formula and click CTRL+C to copy the formula to the clipboard. You can then save it off to a Word document or text document for use later. You can also click the SAVE button and save it as an expression.

72. Keep in mind that if you save it as an expression, when using it again, you need to make sure that the double quotes or brackets are correct for the data you are querying, as well as the wild-card character. This is easy to fix, but knowing what kind of data you are working with helps make these modifications easier.

73. Try the query in step 69 again, but this time choose **create a new selection** as the method. You should get back approximately 205 records citywide that meet the criteria.

74. This concludes Exercise 9. Please close ArcMap and save your project as EX_9.mxd to your student folder.

■ Exercise 10: Buffers

Data Needed for This Exercise
- Add all layer files from CIA\Data\Basic Map Layers
- CIA\Data\File Geodatabase\GIS_Layers.gdb\Street_Labels
- CIA\Data\File Geodatabase\GIS_Layers.gdb\Basic_Street_Label_An

Lesson Objectives
- The student will learn how to create buffers using the ArcToolbox.
- The student will learn how to add the buffer wizard to a toolbar.
- The student will learn how to use the buffer wizard to create buffers.

Task Description
1. Open ArcMap and add all the layers listed above and create a new map. Move the layers up or down in the TOC as needed to make the map easy to view and turn off any layers (make nonvisible) that are not needed or clutter the map display. Your map should resemble **Figure E10-1** at this stage.

2. Oftentimes we want to find how far something is from something else, or we want to do similar queries to the Select by Location query, however, we want to create a shapefile at the end of the distance query.

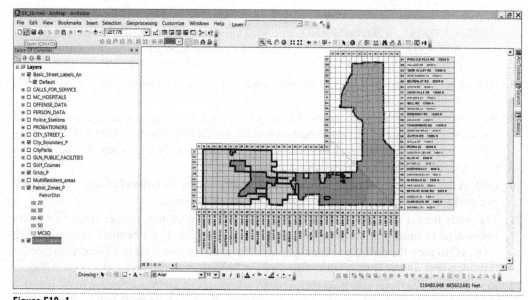

Figure E10–1

3. One example of needing this would be to check whether or not any probationer charged with a sex offense lives within 1000 feet of a school.

4. Click the Add Data button and find ..\CIA\Data\Shapefiles\Other\Area_Schools.lyr.

5. Add these data to our project. You should see several black stars on the map.

6. This .LYR file is a set of instructions on how to symbolize the Area_Schools.shp file. If you look in the same folder as the Area_Schools.lyr, you will find the GLN_SCHOOLS.SHP file which is the source for the *.LYR file.

7. Our task is to draw 1000-ft buffers around every school, then use the Select by Location query to find any Adult Probationers who are currently within 1000 feet of a school. We use a buffer, rather than just a Select by Location, mostly because we are going to be doing this query over and over again, and we want to make sure that each time it is done the same.

8. At the far right side of the map display, click the ArcToolbox tab and open it. (Alternatively, you can click the red toolbox icon in the main menu bar. There can be several seconds of delay while the toolbox opens so be patient.)

9. Go down to **Analysis Tools**, and then choose the **Proximity** toolbox.

10. Double click on the **Buffer** tool to open its dialog box.

11. Complete the dialog box as follows (see **Figure E10–2**):

    a. Input Features = GLN_SCHOOLS

    b. Output feature class – YourStudentFolder\Schools1000ftbuffer.shp

    c. Linear Unit selected

    d. Value = 1000

    e. Units = Feet

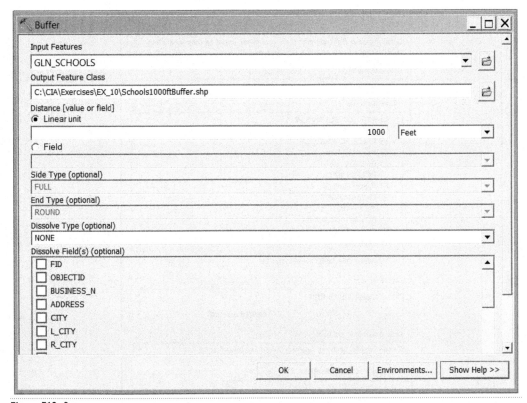

Figure E10–2

    f. Dissolve type = None (*Note:* "None" as dissolve type means that every buffer will be a record in the shapefile's table. If we chose one of the other options, wherever the buffers overlapped would dissolve or fuse together and create only one record.)

    g. Click OK and wait a moment for the tool to work.

12. Looking at the data from a citywide view, it does not look like much happened. However, using the interactive zoom tool, zoom in closer to several of the schools. (Remember that the interactive zoom tool is on the Tools toolbar, and resembles a magnifying glass with a plus sign in it.)

13. What is also cool, is that if you right click on the Schools1000ftBuffer layer in the TOC, and Open the Attribute table, we can see that all of the data from the schools layer was added to the buffer polygon shapefile so that we know which buffer involves which school.

14. Let's find out how many probationers may be in violation.

15. Click Selection in the Menu bar, and then click Select by Location.

16. Complete the Select by Location dialog box as shown in **Figure E10–3**.

17. We want to select any probationers who intersect the 1000-ft buffer around the schools.

18. Click OK to apply the selection.

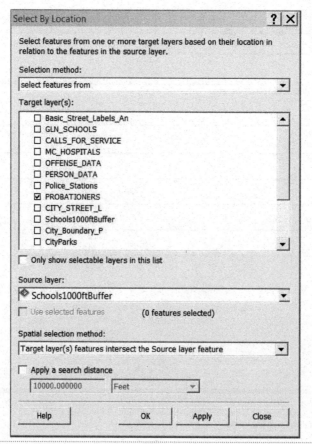

Figure E10–3

19. Open the attribute table of the adult probationers (right click the layer and choose Open Attribute Table).

20. We find 139 Probationers who live within 1000 feet of a school. We can then package up this list for Excel or create a report for our crime prevention or neighborhood response teams to make contact with these 139 probationers and find out if any are violating state laws. Brain Break!

21. You can also do multiple buffers with the ArcToolbox. Click on the ArcToolbox again, go to **Analysis Tools → Proximity → Multiple Ring Buffer**. View the dialog box and think about what data you would enter and then close it.

22. Let's say we have used Dr. Jerry Ratcliffe's Near Repeat calculator (www.temple.edu/cj/misc/nr/) and have discovered that we have a high chance that neighbors of burglary victims at 6201 W Olive Ave will be burglarized within 3 days at 1000 feet, 6–9 days within 2000 feet, and up to 30 days between 2000 feet and 3000 feet.

23. To use this for analysis and deployment we need to create a point or use a polygon of the 6201 W Olive Ave address.

24. Change the Schools1000ftBuffer and GLN_SCHOOLS layers to nonvisible. (One option is to check the List by Drawing Order button at the top left of the TOC, and then uncheck the boxes to the left of the layer name.)

25. Click on Selection in the menu bar, and then Clear Selected Features to clear any selections in all layers in the project.

26. Find the MultiResident_areas in the TOC (if this is not present locate it with the ArcCatalog window and add it to the TOC). Because of the type of symbol (a polygon shaped as a box) we know this is a polygon layer. If this symbol were a *marker* or point, that would tell us it was a point layer. Also if the symbol were a line style, the GIS layer type would be a line layer.

27. Click on Selection in the menu bar, and then Select by Attributes.

28. Enter the following as criteria in the dialog:
    a. Layer: = MultiResident_areas
    b. Method: = create a new selection
    c. SQL Formula = "ADDRESS" LIKE '%6201%OLIVE%'

29. Click Verify to make sure you have entered the formula correctly, and if you did, click OK to run it.

30. Right click the **MultiResident_areas** layer in the TOC.

31. Click on **Selection** in the popup dialog, and then choose **Zoom to Selected Features** in the second popup.

32. We are now zoomed in to the 6201 W Olive Ave apartment complex called the "Olive Tree" apartments. With the MultiResident_areas layer visible, your map should look like **Figure E10-4**.

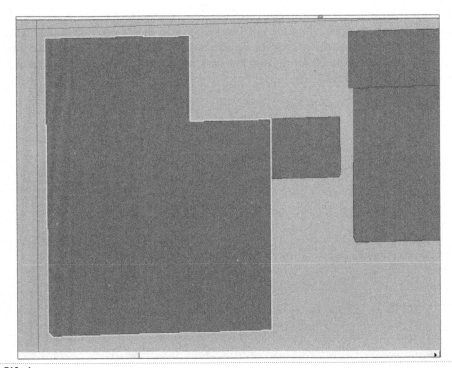

Figure E10-4

33. The polygon with the light gray line around it is our target location and we now want to create three buffers around it that are 1000 feet apart. We can use the Multiple ring buffer tool to set this up very quickly. Click on the ArcToolbox at the far right of the map display again. (*Note*: When first opening this toolbox, there can be a several second delay so be patient.)

34. Click on **Analysis Tools**, **Proximity**, and then double click on **Multiple Ring Buffer**.

35. When the multiple ring buffer tool dialog launches, enter the following:

   a. Input Features: = MultiResident_areas
   b. Output Feature Class: = YourStudentFolder\6201WOliveBuffers
   c. Where it reads "Distances" type in 1000 and click the button with the plus (+) sign. It will then bring 1000 down to the window below. Type in 2000 and hit the plus sign and then 3000 and hit the plus sign.
      • All three values should now be in the window below the field where you entered the values.
   d. Change the Buffer Unit (Optional) to Feet.
   e. Dissolve Option: = ALL
      • Click on the Dissolve Option field and then click Show Help. Read the help documentation about this selection box. Note that ALL means that each buffer will be a separate "donut" and contain only the areas within each buffer (see **Figure E10–5**).

36. Click on OK to run the buffer routine.

37. It may take a while for the new buffer layer to appear so be patient (ArcMap sometimes acts as if you had not hit the OK button and then all of a sudden the buffer layers appear). Zoom out to see the new buffer layer.

38. Now we have three buffers that are in increments of 1000 feet from the boundaries of 6201 W Olive Ave.

39. Assuming that the burglaries at 6201 W Olive Ave were the most recent, we would highlight the first 1000-ft buffer for patrol to look for burglaries that occur within the next 3 days, and move outward to the second buffer for the next 6–9 days, and finally the following 30 days in the next 3000 ft buffer. Brain Break!

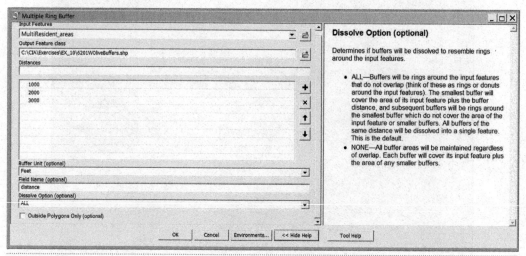

Figure E10–5

40. Save your project to your student folder again. Save often whenever you have done something you want to keep and at least after every selection, edit, or rearranging of items in the TOC.

41. The last item will be to find and add the Buffer Wizard to the Standard toolbar and use it to create buffers.

42. The buffer wizard is a great tool that has hung around for a while. It works well, is easy to use, and provides a lot of versatility with creating buffers in ArcMap.

43. This tool allows us to create single buffers around items like we did with the schools, and we have the option to also merge overlapping buffers when needed. We can make multipiece buffers, and we can use a field in the attribute table of the layer we are buffering as the length of the buffer.

44. In order to use these tools, we will need to customize our Tools toolbar. At the far right side of the tools toolbar (the one with the zoom tools and "hand" for panning), there is a down arrow.

45. The popup text will read "Toolbar Options."

46. When you click on this down arrow, Customize should be the only item in the popup dialog. Click this.

47. In the customize dialog, we want to click on the Commands tab (see **Figure E10–6**).

48. In the **Show commands containing** entry section, enter **Buffer Wizard**.

49. When you enter this text, the **Categories** window only shows one option, **Tools**, and the **Commands** window only shows **Buffer Wizard**.

Figure E10–6

Figure E10–7

50. Click on Buffer Wizard with your left mouse button, hold the button down and drag the buffer wizard to the far right side of the Tools toolbar then release it. Close the Customize dialog. Your toolbar should now resemble **Figure E10–7**.

51. Close the customize window and click on CityParks in the TOC to highlight this layer.

52. Click on the buffer wizard button you placed on the standard toolbar.

53. In the buffer wizard dialog, make sure the CityParks layer is in the Features of this layer section (see **Figure E10–8**).

54. Click Next.

55. We are going to create 1500-ft buffers around every park in this layer for an enforcement program geared at reducing street robberies.

56. In the top section, enter **1500** and make sure the **Distance Units** at the bottom reads **Feet** (see **Figure E10–9**).

57. Click Next.

58. Answer **No** to the question, "Dissolve barriers between buffers." We are answering No because we want each park to have its own 1500-ft buffer and not be joined or dissolved with others they may overlap (see **Figure E10–10**).

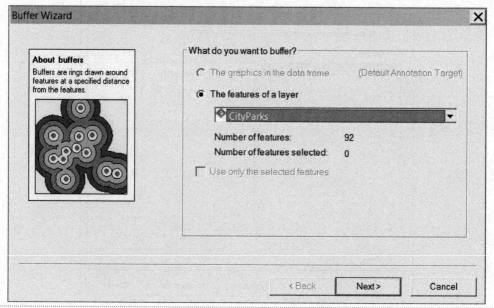

Figure E10–8

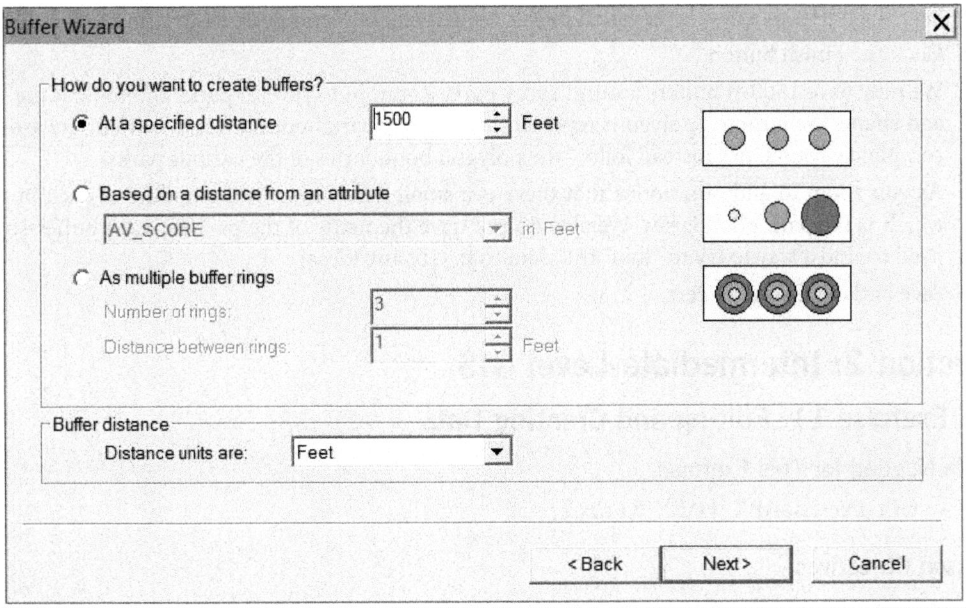

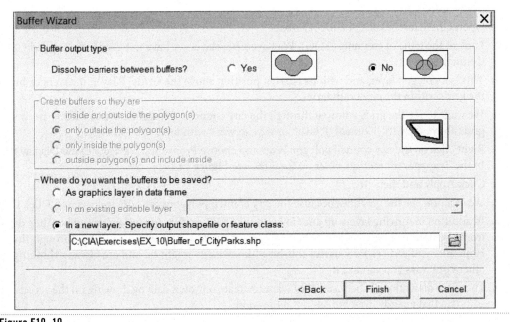

Figure E10-9

Figure E10-10

59. Save the buffer as a new layer called Buffer_of_CityParks.shp and save it to your student folder.

60. Click the Finish button.

61. We now have 1500-ft buffers around every park. Zoom in to several parks and look at the size and shape. We buffered polygons representing the city park boundaries, so our buffers are not completely round, but instead follow the polygon boundaries of the various parks.

62. As you zoom in and out, notice that there is a small donut hole in the middle of each buffer, which is the park boundaries. We also do not have the name of the park for each buffer so we need to find a way to try to "join" this data to it. Got any ideas?

63. Save and close your project.

Section 2: Intermediate-Level GIS

■ Exercise 11: Editing and Creating Data

Data Needed for This Exercise

- CIA\Exercises\EX_11\EX_11.mxd

Lesson Objectives

- The student will learn about layer transparency.
- The editor toolbar will be discussed and used.
- The student will learn how to edit a polygon layer.
- The student will learn how to use the auto complete polygon tool.

Task Description

1. Open CIA\Exercises\EX_11\EX_11.mxd.

2. Look at the table of contents (TOC). We have a new layer we have not used before called City_Council_P.

3. This is a polygon layer, and with its current position above the Grids_P layer, it covers or hides the grids within the city boundaries.

4. We want to see the grids running through the city council boundaries. We can either move the grids above the City_Council_P layer, or we can work with layer *transparency*.

5. Right click on the city council polygon layer and choose Properties. Navigate to the Display tab. In the **Transparent** section, enter 50 for 50% (see **Figure E11–1**).

6. Click Apply and then OK.

7. We can now see the gridlines because the city council polygons are 50% transparent. Click OK.

8. In addition to moving layers up and down in the TOC for drawing order (remember they draw from the bottom up), we can set the transparency of layers so that we can see through them. Hopefully you can see how useful this bit of knowledge might be and are already thinking of other cool ways you can use it?

9. There are many times when we might want to create our own data by drawing on the screen, or edit data that already exist but are not quite right.

10. We can use the buffer wizard and other tools to create new layers, but what if we want to edit existing data?

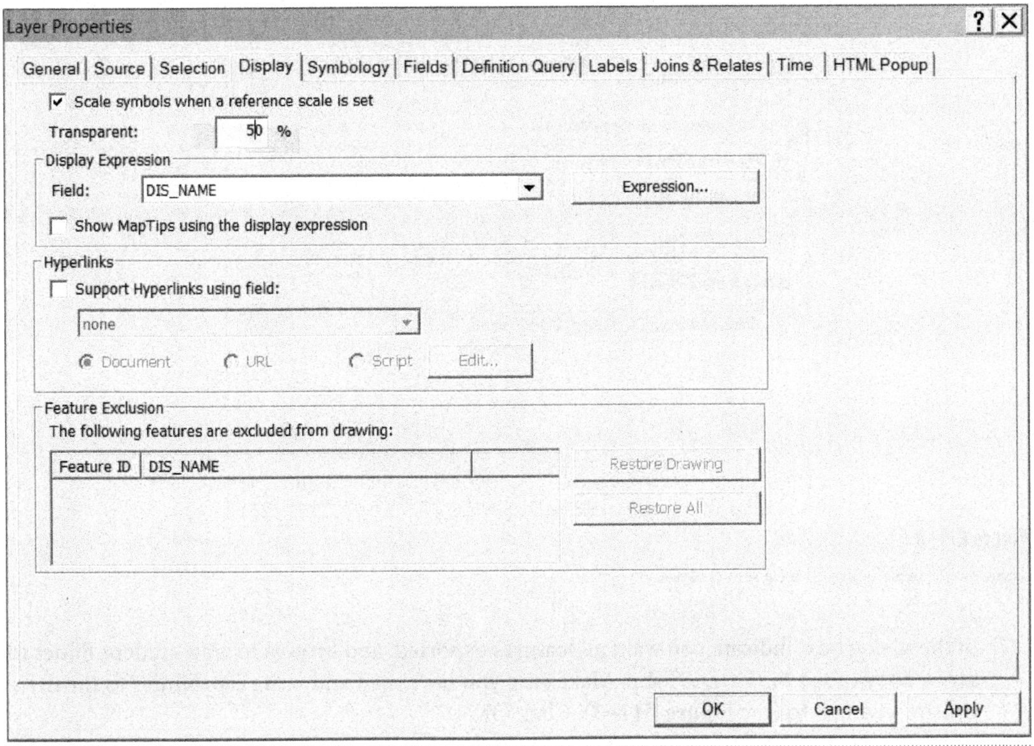

Layer Properties

General | Source | Selection | Display | Symbology | Fields | Definition Query | Labels | Joins & Relates | Time | HTML Popup

☑ Scale symbols when a reference scale is set

Transparent: 50 %

Display Expression
Field: DIS_NAME   ▼   Expression...
☐ Show MapTips using the display expression

Hyperlinks
☐ Support Hyperlinks using field:
none   ▼
⦿ Document   ○ URL   ○ Script   Edit...

Feature Exclusion
The following features are excluded from drawing:

Feature ID	DIS_NAME		Restore Drawing
			Restore All

OK   Cancel   Apply

Figure E11–1

11. Let's suppose that the city council districts changed last week and the engineering department said they would not be getting to the edits until 2 months from now. (Yes, not likely, I know.)

12. We can't let our officers be ignorant about this information and we need to make sure we create a new map of the council districts to inform them in a timely manner. So we will need to edit the city council polygons to add a new district.

13. We accomplish this feat of amazement by using the **Editor** toolbar (see **Figure E11–2**).

14. In the menu bar, click on Customize, Toolbars, and then click on Editor.

15. The Editor toolbar should now be floating on the map display.

16. Before we begin to edit the source data, let's make a copy to work from. Right click on the City_Council_P layer and choose **Data → Export Data**.

Figure E11–2

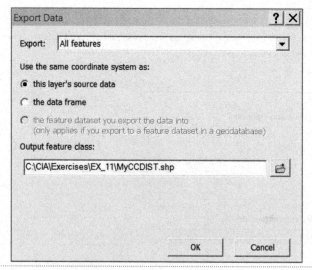

Figure E11–3

17. In the dialog box, indicate you want all features exported, and browse to your student folder to save a copy called MYCCDIST.shp. Make sure you have read and write capabilities to the drive you are saving it to (see **Figure E11–3**). Click OK.

18. Once you have exported your data, answer **Yes**, if asked, to adding it to this map project.

19. We want these data to be displayed like the other City_Council_P layer, and ArcMap comes with a tool to copy symbology from one layer to another.

20. Double click on the MyCCDIST.shp layer to open the Properties menu dialog. Click on the Symbology tab. At the top right of the symbology tab is a button named "**Import**". Click this button.

21. Complete the Import Symbology dialog as shown in **Figure E11–4**.

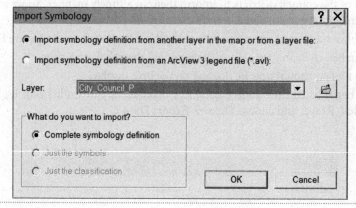

Figure E11–4

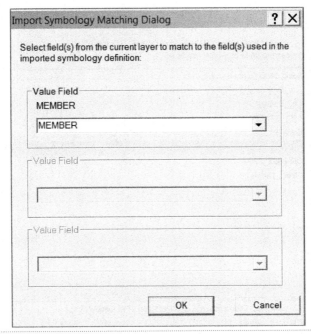

Figure E11–5

22. Click OK and OK again.
23. Another dialog box comes up that is basically asking what fields in this layer need to be symbolized the same as this new layer. Since they are basically the same data, the Member field is what we want, so click OK (see **Figure E11–5**).
24. Click Apply and then OK to make the symbology changes. This will not automatically add our transparency settings, so right click our new layer, choose properties, and the display tab. Change the Transparent setting to 50%. Click Apply and OK.
25. Now we want to edit our new layer and split a current city council district to create two where once there was only one.
26. We need to split the Cactus district (lower right corner of the city) along Glendale Ave to make two new districts from the current Cactus district.
27. Select the Cactus district from the MYCCDIST layer by opening the attribute table and clicking on that record. Zoom in to the area where Glendale Ave splits this council district.
28. In the Editor toolbar, click Editor.
29. Then click **Start Editing**.
30. Double click on the MYCCDIST layer in the dialog list (see **Figure E11–6**).
31. If you get an error message about the Basic_Street_Label_An layer, ignore this error and click Continue.
32. You are now in editing mode so anything you change in a layer will be saved.

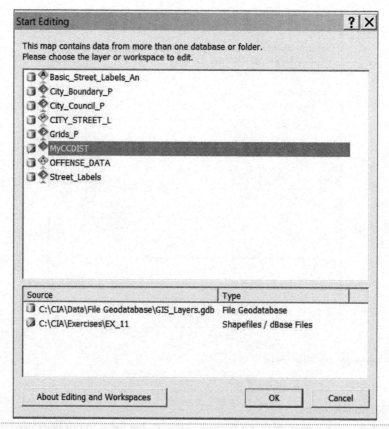

Figure E11–6

33. On the editor toolbar several buttons and tools became active when we started editing. The button that looks like the head of a black arrow to the right of the Editor text on the Editor toolbar is the **Edit** tool. Click this tool and then click anywhere ON the Cactus City Council District.

34. With the Cactus district selected we can now edit it. Make sure you do not click and drag your mouse on top of the Cactus district or you will move it. You can use the undo tool in main menu bar located under Edit to undo things you did in error.

35. On the Editor toolbar the sixth tool from the right resembles a rectangle with a line through it. When you hover your cursor over it, it reads, "Cut Polygons."

36. Click on this tool then move it over the line along Glendale Ave (the street sits *below* the label for Glendale Ave) that splits Cactus District.

37. Click outside or to the left of Cactus District once, release the mouse button, then drag the tool across Glendale Ave to the right of Cactus District and double click to split the polygon in half.

38. Right click on the MyCCDist layer to bring up the Open Attribute Table selection. Click this.

39. The software automatically prefilled all of the fields for both polygons with the same data from the original source polygon.

40. We want the polygon to the south to be called Turquoise district.

41. The polygon to the north will remain Cactus.

42. Click the left edge of the Attribute table to select the record on the top, FID = 6; if this is not the Southern polygon, select the other, FID = 2. Light blue lines will appear on the map display around the polygon selected.

43. In the table, Click on the DIS_Name, Member, and Hansen_Dis fields one at a time and enter:

   a. DIS_Name   =   Turquoise
   b. Member   =   Mitt Romney
   c. Hansen_DIS   =   Turq

44. Click **Editor** in the Editor toolbar and choose **Stop Editing** from the popup dialog.

45. Say YES to saving your edits.

46. Change the symbology and labeling of this layer from single symbol to Categories → Unique Values, to include the new Mitt Romney District.

47. Save your project.

■ Exercise 11b: Creating Data

Data Needed for This Exercise

- CIA\Exercises\EX_11\EX_11b.mxd

Lesson Objectives

- The student will learn how to create a new feature class (polygon).
- The concept of "snapping" will be discussed.
- The student will learn how to add a new polygon.
- The student will learn how to use the auto complete polygon function.
- The student will learn how to edit the attributes of a polygon layer.

Task Description

1. Open CIA\Exercises\EX_11\EX_11b.mxd.

2. In this exercise we will learn the concept of digitizing our own data. One of the patrol division lieutenants has asked that we divide up patrol zone 20 into 4 balanced workload areas. We have done the analysis and placed the data in the field called "BalWork" in the GridBal polygon in this exercise.

3. The data here show a weighted value based on total work time on calls and average response times on calls for patrol zone 20. First, let's change the symbology for the GridBal polygon so that the different values in the grids are a different color based on our weighted value.

4. Right click the layer, choose Properties (alternatively, double click the layer), and then the symbology tab.

5. Choose a quantities legend method (left side of symbology tab where it reads "Show"). Select "BalWork" for the Value field.

6. Choose the BalWork value field and a graduated colors scheme and then click Apply.

7. Click OK.

8. Now we can see the new report areas in the southeast end of the city the lieutenant asked for and we can begin.

9. We need to create a feature class to store the data we are going to draw. We can create a point, line, or polygon feature class, but for this project we need a polygon.

10. Open the ArcToolbox by clicking on the tab at the far right of the map display.

11. In the ArcToolbox, find the **Data Management** tools, then click on the **Feature Class** toolset, then double click on **Create Feature Class** (see **Figure E11–7**).

12. The directory where you save your version should be the path to your student folder. (Figure E11–7 shows the CIA\Exercises\EX_11 folder—replace this with your student folder.) In the Feature Class name field, call this layer **Sector20ReportingAreas.shp**.

13. **Geometry Type** should be set to **Polygon**.

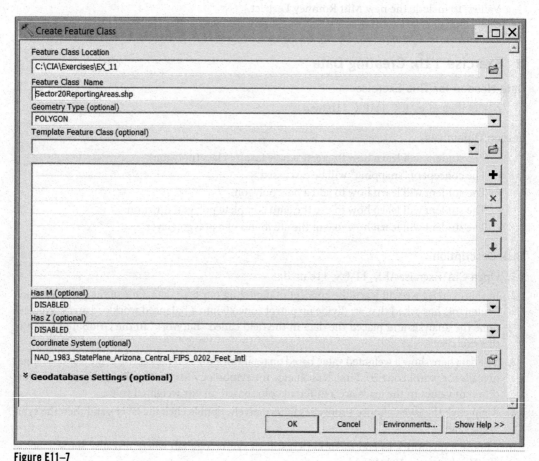

Figure E11–7

14. Coordinate System should be set to **Nad_1983_StatePlane_Arizone_Central_FIPS0202_Feet_ Intl**. To get to this, click the browse button to the right of this field, then click on the **XY Coordinate System** tab. In the dialog box, click on the **Select** button. In that dialog choose **Projected Coordinate Systems** → **State Plane** → **Nad 1983 (Intl Feet)** → **NAD 1983 StatePlane Arizona Central FIPS 0202 (Intl Feet).prj**. Click Add (see **Figure E11–8**).

15. Click **Apply** → **OK** to add the correct projection.

16. Your Create Feature dialog box should now look like Figure E11–7.

17. Click **OK** to add the new polygon feature class.

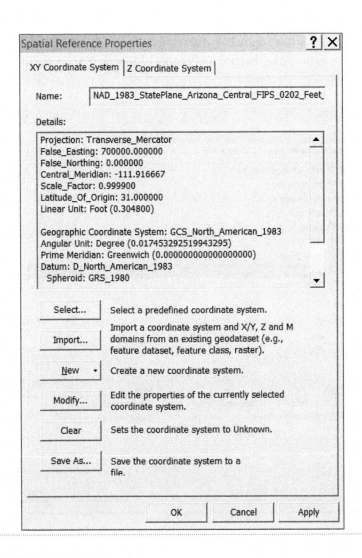

Figure E11–8

18. It may take several seconds, but be patient and soon the new layer will be added to the table of contents. Once you see the new layer in the TOC, right click our new layer and open the attribute table. Notice that we have no records in the table and no graphic representations on the map display. This makes sense as we have not actually drawn anything yet. We have to go into **Edit** mode in order to add polygons to this polygon feature class. Close the attribute table.

19. Click on **Customize** → **Toolbars** → **Editor**. (*Note:* If the editor toolbar is already turned on, you can skip this step.)

20. Once the Editor toolbar is open, click on Editor → Start editing.

21. Double click our Sector20ReportingAreas layer in the Start editing dialog box (see **Figure E11–9**).

22. Click Continue and ignore the warning about the Basic_Street_Labels_An layer.

23. Zoom in tightly to Zone 20 and our visualization of the report areas the lieutenant wants. Your map should look like **Figure E11–10**.

24. Click on Editor in the Editor toolbox and choose Snapping → Snapping toolbar in the popup dialog.

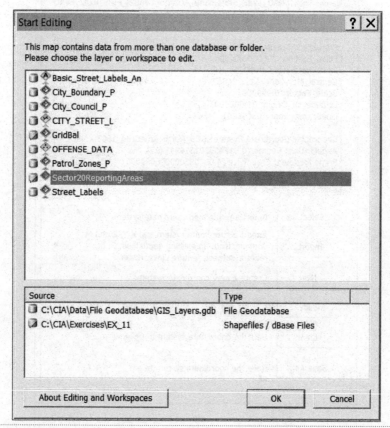

Figure E11–9

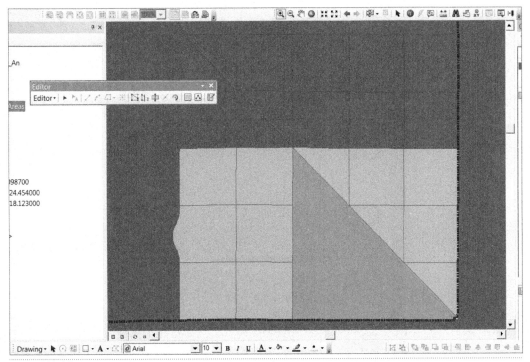

Figure E11–10

25. Select all of the buttons in the snapping toolbar. They will appear shaded slightly when selected.

26. In the drop-down dialog, click on Snap to Sketch. When we draw each polygon we want the edges, vertices, and end points to snap to one another. This will avoid holes or slivers where the lines and end points do not join exactly. These slivers or even overlaps can sometimes distort our data and any aggregation we may do at some point with crime data. The lieutenant will want updates monthly on how well each squad is combating the crime problems in Zone 20, and within each reporting area for his sergeants.

27. In the Editor toolbar, click on the Edit tool, which is a small black arrow. At the far right of the Editor toolbar click the **Create Features** button.

28. At the far right of the map display a new **Create Features dialog** should be showing; click on the Sector20ReortingAreas layer in this Create Features window.

29. Now at the bottom of the Create Features window, choose Polygon (see **Figure E11–11**).

30. In the Map display area, click on any corner in one of the four areas of the GridBal layer to start our first digitization of the polygon.

31. Now click on the next vertex, or every half mile, which is every intersecting gridline in the Grid-Bal layer within our study area. (We want to snap our new polygon to this grid layer and at each

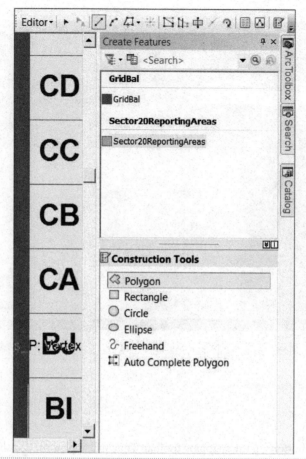

Figure E11–11

point in the underlying layer at every point where one grid intersects, or shares an intersection with another grid.)

32. Double click once you are done going all around one of the new reporting areas. We chose the northern most reporting area and our progress is shown in **Figure E11–12**.

33. We will now use a tool called Auto Complete Polygon to create the rest of the reporting areas.

34. Under **Construction tools** in the **Create Feature** window, choose **Auto complete polygon**.

35. Click anywhere in the first polygon we created, and then click on one corner point where a polygon area adjacent to the one we have drawn shares that corner point.

36. Click at each corner of the grids you see and then click on the final corner where the first polygon intersects the one you are drawing. Move the cursor into the first polygon and then double click to end the drawing and create our second polygon.

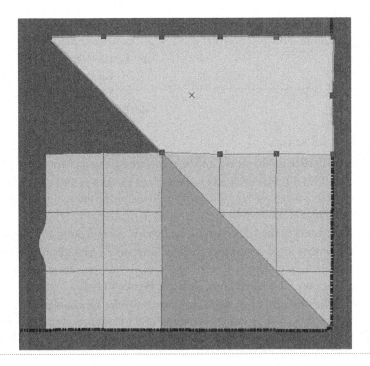

Figure E11–12

37. Do this same process for the other two polygons. When done, click Editor in the Editor Toolbar and choose **Stop Editing** and make sure you **Save edits.** You may find that you have to place more vertices along the bottom left polygon to get it to fit around the curve nicely.

38. Now we want to edit the attribute table of each polygon to add some information. We want to add two new fields:
    a. RA as text 4 characters in length
    b. SgtName as text, 35 characters long

39. Right click the Sector20ReportingAreas layer in the TOC and choose Open Attribute Table.

40. Click on the **Table Options** button (leftmost button) and choose **Add Field**.

41. In this add field dialog complete the following:
    a. Name = RA
    b. Type = Text
    c. Field Properties/Length = 4

42. Then create another field as follows:
    a. Name = SgtName
    b. Type = Text
    c. Field Properties/Length = 35

43. Once both fields are added, go back to the Editor toolbar and start editing again, selecting Sector20ReportingAreas.

44. In the attribute table, click on the small box at the left of the record to select it. You will see light blue lines appear around the polygon that is selected. The fields should be completed as follows:

    a. Northmost
- RA = 4J24
- SgtName = S Walker

    b. RightBottom
- RA = 4J25
- SgtName = K Kulaga

    c. LeftBottom
- RA = 4J26
- SgtName = R Jones

    d. BottomCenter
- RA = 4J23
- SgtName = B Hill

45. To edit, you need to click on the record and field you are editing and enter directly into the field.

46. Make sure to hit ENTER after each edit, especially in the last record edited and then click in another record before stopping edits. This will avoid losing the edits you made to the last record when you stop editing and save your edits.

47. Click on the Editor text in the Editor toolbar and choose Stop Editing and save your edits.

48. Change the symbology for this new polygon to a Categories legend using the RA values as the Value field.

49. Your map and attribute table should now look like **Figure E11–13**.

50. If you had any difficulty with this exercise, don't worry. There are not many times that an analyst has to create their own GIS data, but this depends on the resources your police department and local jurisdiction has available. We would strongly urge you to find a best friend in the engineering, planning, and GIS department of your jurisdiction as you may find they have a lot of data you need.

51. This concludes EX_11b; save your project and close ArcMap.

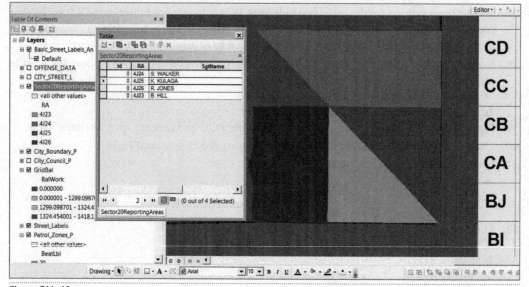

Figure E11–13

■ Exercise 11c: Creating Data

Data Needed for This Exercise

- CIA\Exercises\EX_11\EX_11c.mxd

Lesson Objectives

- The student will learn how to add and edit a point layer.
- The student will learn how to use merge, intersect, union, and find and replace functions in edit mode.

Task Description

1. Open ArcMap and the CIA\Exercises\EX_11\EX_11c.mxd project.
2. For this project we have a need to digitize a point for each apartment complex located in the Sonorita area of Glendale. Sonorita was an area where the local landowners and farmers lived. East of Grand Ave is where the migrant farm workers lived, the majority of whom were from Sonora Mexico. They would come on the train from the Yuma area and be dropped off in Little Sonora, or Sonorita, so that they could work in the fields.
3. Our assignment is to draw a point for every building in each apartment or multiresident area. The high-resolution aerial photo and a 50% transparent polygon layer of the MultiResident_areas layer are already listed in the TOC. Turn on these layers so that they are visible. Zoom in to the extents of the Sonorita aerial photo. Zoom in and out of the data over each multiresident area so you can see the different buildings. We want to draw a point in the approximate middle of each building.
4. To begin we need the ArcToolbox again.
5. Click on Data Management Tools → Feature Class → Create Feature Class.
6. Complete the Creature Feature Class dialog as shown in **Figure E11–14**.
7. Make sure the Geometry Type is Point and set the Coordinate System as we did in CIA\Exercises\ EX_11\EX_11b.
8. Click OK.
9. Wait until the new point shapefile is added to the project.
10. Turn on the MultiResident_areas layer in the TOC if not already on. Zoom in to the small yellow box on the far right side of the aerial image.
11. There are two buildings at this location so we need to draw two points, one for each building, in the center of the building.
12. Click Editor in the Editor toolbar and choose Start Editing.
13. Click Create Feature button at the far right of the editor toolbar.
14. In the create feature window, click on SonoritaPoints, and in the Construction Tools section, click on Point (see **Figure E11–15**).
15. Click once in the approximate middle of both buildings to add a point for each building. Click Editor in the Editor toolbar and then save edits. Zoom out and then in to another one of the multiresident polygons.
16. Add the other points to the center of each building.

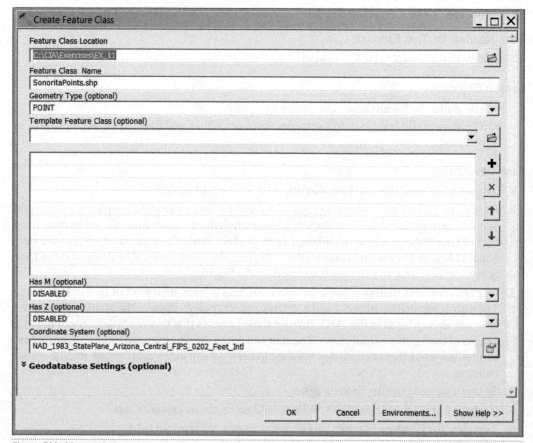

Figure E11–14

17. After you are done with one apartment complex, zoom out and then in to another, and continue the process until all points are drawn.

18. There are seven multiresident polygons that intersect the aerial image and have buildings in them (or eight areas if you include the far right lower corner with about seven buildings).

19. There were approximately 123 buildings or points in these areas.

20. Now we want to populate what complex each of these points are in. We can use a join to accomplish this.

21. Click on Editor → Stop Editing, and Save your edits. Save this ArcMap project to your student folder as EX_11c.mxd.

22. Right Click on SonoritaPoints and choose Joins and Relates → Join to get the join dialog.

23. Complete the Join dialog as follows:

    a. What do you want to join to this layer? = **Join data from another based on spatial location**

    b. Choose the layer to join to this layer or load spatial data from disk = **MultiResident_areas**

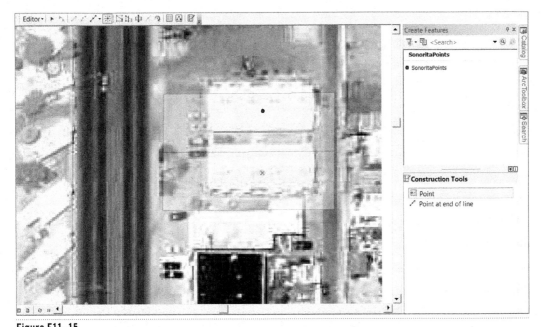

Figure E11–15

24. "It falls inside" should be checked (see **Figure E11–16**).

25. Save the new joined layer to your student folder as 11CJoin.shp.

26. Click OK.

27. Now if we open the attribute table for the 11CJoin layer we can see that all of the multiresident data from that polygon are now in this table. So we were able to use the multiresident polygon layer to populate the point layer's attributes, making them now more useful (see **Figure E11–17**).

28. There are several fields we probably do not need so let's get rid of them. With the 11CJoin attribute table open, right click on FRMR_NAME and click on Delete Field. Answer Yes to deleting the field.

29. Delete the following other fields in the same way:

    a. ID_1   g. STARTEXTEN
    b. MAPID   h. CATEGORY
    c. PLANREF   i. IMANAGEFIL
    d. FILE_   j. FILETYPE
    e. POLYID   k. FILEAUTHOR
    f. ROTATION

30. Now we need to change some data: We can use the find and replace function to make those changes.

31. Leave the attribute of 11CJoin open and click Editor in the Editor toolbar and Start Editing 11CJoin. Click OK and Continue.

32. Click on the Table Options button, which is the leftmost button at the top of the attribute table.

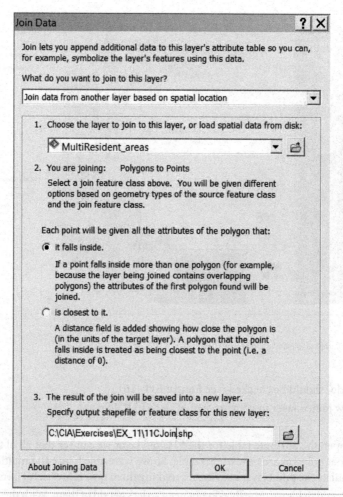

Figure E11–16

33. Choose Find and Replace.
34. Click the Replace tab.
35. Enter PARADISE GROVE in the find section.
36. Enter PARADISE GROVE APARTMENTS in the replace section.
37. Click the Replace All Button.
38. The data should now be changed in the data table.
39. Find "APARTMENT COMPLEX" and replace it with "BRITTLE GLASS APARTMENTS" as we did with the Paradise Grove example.
40. Stop editing and save the edits.
41. Save the project to your student folder.

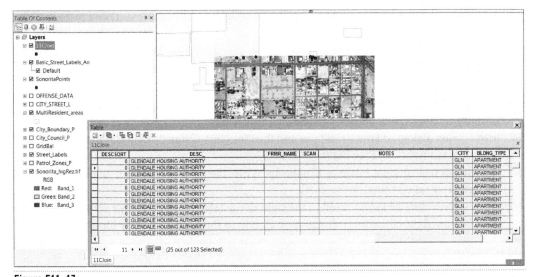

Figure E11–17

42. Now we will discover the power of the Intersect function.

43. Our objective is to create a street centerline file that is only within the Patrol Zone 20.

44. First, we need to select Zone 20 from the Patrol_Zones_P layer using the map graphics and the Select Features by Rectangle tool or Open the attribute table and then clicking on the row that contains 20 in the BeatLbl field.

45. Make your selection using one of those methods and then click **Geoprocessing** in the main menu bar.

46. Choose Intersect and in the dialog box enter the following:

    a. Input Features = City_Street_L and then Patrol_Zones_P

      • *The order is very important: You first choose the layer you want an intersection of (streets) and then the layer you want them clipped or intersected by (selected patrol zones).*

    b. Save this to your student folder as Intersect.shp

    c. JoinAttributes = ALL

    d. XY Tolerance = <blank>

    e. Output Type = INPUT

47. Click OK and wait a moment to create this new file.

48. Make sure the new layer is visible and notice how we have a perfect selection of streets that are within (intersected by) Patrol Zone 20, which we initially selected from the Patrol_Zone_P layer.

49. There are three other tools in the Geoprocessing part of the main menu bar.

50. These functions are Union, Merge, and Dissolve.

51. Union is used when we want to mesh two layers together that overlap the same geography.

52. Merge is often used when we want to add new data to an existing layer. This is often used by analysts when they have a set of data like a year's worth of offense data. They geocode new data and then merge the new geocoded layer to the year-long set.

53. A Dissolve is used when we want to create a new geographically aggregated layer from an existing one.

54. Union can be used to add data to an existing layer that it overlaps. For instance, if we look at the attribute table of the Grids layer, we see that we do not have the City Council district information in the attributes.

55. We can add these data by using a Union function.

56. Click on Geoprocessing in the menu bar, and then Union.

57. In the Union dialog, add the Grids layer and then the City_Council_P layer in that order. Again, order is very important. (See **Figure E11–18**.)

58. Save this to your student folder as Union.shp. When the process is done, it will eventually add the new layer called Union to the TOC.

59. Open the attribute table and scroll to the right of the table. We can see that several fields were added to the right of the table. If you look closely to the edge of the city limits, you will also

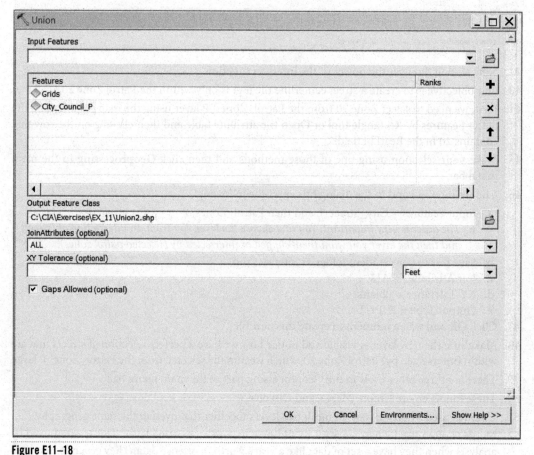

Figure E11–18

notice that the city limits were split where the city council boundaries did not go all the way to the grids boundary.

60. Another of the functions we can use to massage our data into compliance is the dissolve function. With the dissolve function, we are trying to make new data from old data by combining all the current geography into bigger components based on one field in the attribute table. So, we will take our new Union layer, and we want to create a layer that has the characteristics of the Union but aggregated up into the city council–sized areas. Everything outside the city council areas will be aggregated into one area.

61. Click on the Union.shp layer and right click to open the attribute table.

62. First let's select all the records where the DIS_NAME field is blank.

63. Click on the Table Options button at the top left of the attribute table. Click on Select by Attributes.

64. In the Select dialog box, enter the following:
    a. Method: = Create a new selection
    b. Sql Query = "DIS_NAME" = ''

65. Click Verify to make sure your query will run (see **Figure E11–19**).

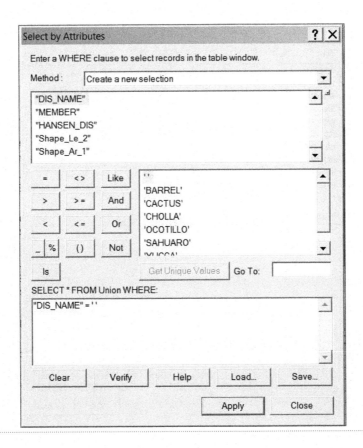

Figure E11–19

66. Click Apply.

67. Browse through the attribute table and observe that all the DIS_NAME blank records are selected. This amounts to 488 out of 938 records.

68. Right click the DIS_NAME field and then click Field Calculator.

69. In the Field Calculator dialog, enter "Outside Glendale" in the window at the bottom of the dialog (see **Figure E11–20**).

70. Click OK.

71. After it is done calculating, click on the Table Options buttons and choose Clear Selection. We need to clear any selections so when we run the dissolve function it performs it on all records and not just the selected ones.

72. Close the attribute table.

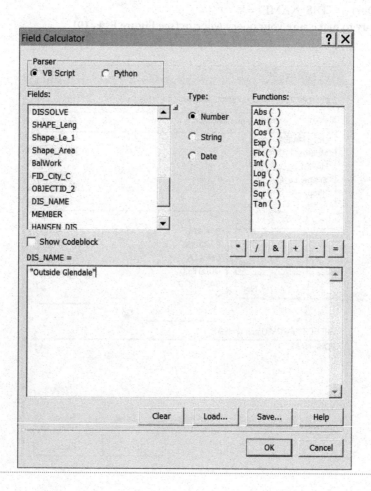

Figure E11–20

73. Now click on Geoprocessing in the menu bar and then choose Dissolve.
74. Complete the Dissolve Dialog box as follows.
    a. Input Features = Union
    b. Save this to your student folder as Dissolve.shp
    c. Dissolve Field (s) (Optional) = DIS_NAME
    d. Statistics Field(s) (optional) = Shape_Area
    e. Statistic Type = Sum
75. Click OK once all the settings are made (see **Figure 11–21**).

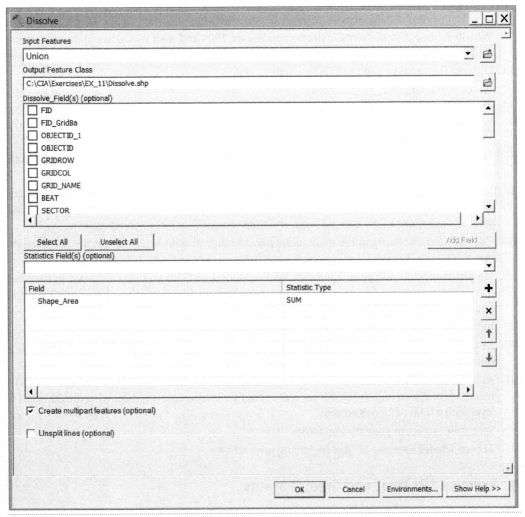

76. Zoom out to the extents of the Dissolve layer by right clicking it in the TOC and choosing Zoom to Layer from the popup dialog.

77. The gridlines have all disappeared and the boundaries of the grids have been dissolved into just the city council boundaries and the Outside Glendale boundaries. Change the symbology as a categories legend using the DIS_NAME field.

78. Also open the attribute table and see that there are only a few fields in this new layer: DIS_NAME, Sum_Shape_, FID, and Shape.

79. So, only those fields we created in the dialog (the dissolve field and our Statistics on the Shape_Area field) were preserved in the new layer.

80. The last function we will cover in this exercise is the Merge function.

81. Although merges can be performed both spatially and attribute wise, we most often do merges based on new layer data we want to add to a repository.

82. We will assume that we have a collection of data for 2004 and wish to add new data in the same format to an already established layer.

83. Observe the two layers in the TOC named:
    a. OffData20040101_to_20040930
    b. OffData20041031_to_20041231

84. We want to merge the 10-31 to 12-31 data to the 01-01 to 09-30 data for 2004. We need to make sure that the fields are as close to the same as possible and share the same field names.

85. Browse the attribute tables of both layers and verify that the field names are the same in both attribute tables.

86. In most cases, we would be pulling the same data from the same fields of our records-management system (RMS), then geocoding the data each week or month, and merging it to our main geocoded data. We will make a new merged layer, and then rename it to our main repository.

87. Click on Geoprocessing in the main menu bar, and then choose Merge. Select the two datasets that begin with "OffData" as described in step 83, and choose them to be input datasets.

88. We can change the merge rule for each field name, delete fields you may not want in the final merged layer, and in a few minor cases you can add fields to merge when they might have different names like UCRGroup and UCR_Group.

89. In this case, we do not need to change anything.

90. Save this to your student folder called OffData.shp (see **Figure E11–22**). Click OK and wait a moment for the merge.

91. As we can see if we now open the attribute table of OFFDATA.shp, we can see that the 5647 records of one layer and the 18,001 records of another layer are now combined in the OFFDATA layer with a total of 23,648 records.

92. Save your project in your student folder.

93. This concludes Exercise 11. Are we having fun yet?

■ Exercise 12: Meet and Greet: Layouts

Data Needed for This Exercise

- CIA\Exercises\EX_12\EX_12.mxd

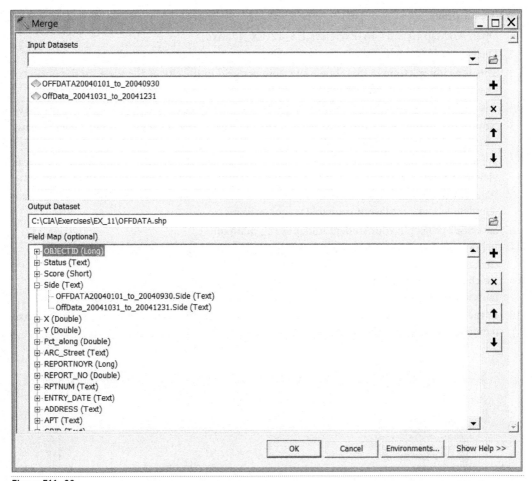

Figure E11–22

Lesson Objectives

- The objective of this lesson is to create an informative and pleasing layout that depicts the total offense data from October 1, 2004, to December 31, 2004.
- The student will learn about using map templates to quickly design a layout.
- The student will learn about working with graphics—resizing, drawing handles, and adding other graphics items.
- The student will learn about working with text on a layout for titles and other disclaimer items.
- The student will learn about white space, how to create one point of interest, and the five vital elements of a map.

Task Description

1. Open ArcMap 10 and CIA\Exercises\EX_12\EX_12.mxd.

2. Once open, view each of the layers and see how they are currently symbolized.

3. This is a choropleth map that shows all crime per grid in the city of Glendale for the period of October 1, 2004, through December 31, 2004.

4. Take several minutes to make sure all the symbolization looks good and depicts what we need it to.

5. Now, at the bottom left of the map display window, click on the button that reads, "Layout View," when you hover your cursor over it.

6. We are now viewing the Layout or map we would send to the printer. It is probably a portrait view with only an outline around the map, the visible layers in the map display, and nothing else.

7. We are in a hurry as we need this for a meeting in just a few minutes so we want to use a current template to make the layout printable for the meeting.

8. Save your project in your student folder as EX_12.mxd.

9. In the Layout Toolbar (see **Figure E12–1**), click on the second button from the right which reads, "Change Layout," if we hover our cursor over it.

Figure E12–1

10. In the Change Layout dialog, choose the "USA" tab, then click on the SouthwesternUSA.mxd template (see **Figure E12–2**).

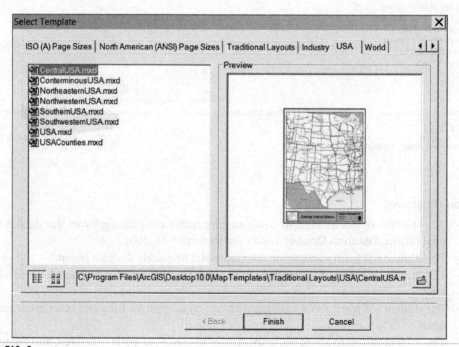

Figure E12–2

11. Our map is transformed and almost all necessary formatting is done in a few minutes.

12. There are a few things that do need to be changed, however.

13. First, let's change the background color of the map display window to white.

14. Click anywhere on the light blue area surrounding our map. Handles should appear around the map display window. Right click, then click on Properties to open the Frame Properties dialog.

15. Click on the Frame tab.

16. In the Background area, click the small down arrow to the right of the selection window and choose White for the background color (see **Figure E12–3**).

17. Click Apply and then OK.

18. Use the Zoom tool on the **Tools** toolbar to **Zoom In** (magnifying glass with plus sign) tighter to the map.

19. Then use the Pan tool (white hand) to move the entire map as far right as it goes while still leaving a little white space surrounding the entire map.

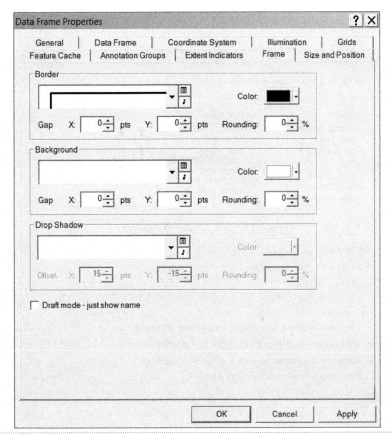

Figure E12–3

20. Change the tool to the Select Elements (black arrow).
21. Click on the visible portion of the legend, then right click and in the dialog choose Order → Bring to Front.
22. This will move the legend in front of the other objects on the map. Now position it in the top left of the open space in the map.
23. While the legend is still selected, right click on it and choose Properties.
24. Click on the **Items** tab.
25. Click on Grids in the right window and check Place in New Column.
26. Click Apply (see **Figure E12–4**).
27. The City Boundary stays in one column and the other legend items are moved to a new column.
28. Using the < arrows in the middle of the two windows, move every layer except for Grids and City_Boundary_P to the left window.
29. Click Apply. This eliminates all but the two layers from our legend.
30. Click OK to close the legend properties dialog. Drag or resize the legend box to fit in the space.

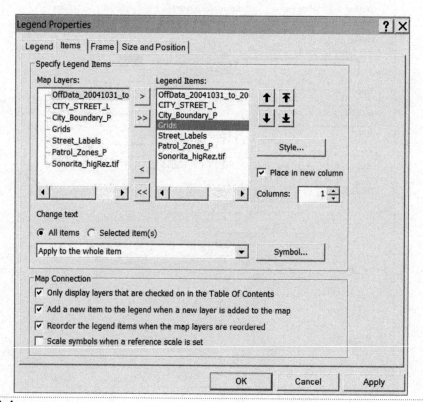

Figure E12–4

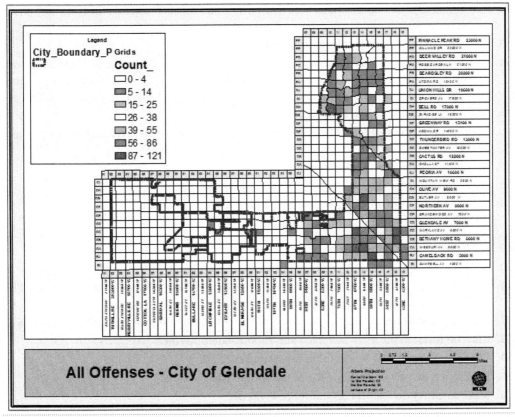

Figure E12–5

31. At the bottom in the information bar, click on the small vertical line on the left until handles appear, then click the delete key.
32. Our Title needs to be edited, so click on the "Southwestern United States" text to select it, then right click on it and choose Properties.
33. Change the text to read, "All offenses – City of Glendale." Click Apply and OK.
34. While it is still selected, click on it and hold the left mouse button down to move the text to the approximate center of the leftmost box.
35. Your map should now resemble **Figure E12–5**.
36. We need to add another bit of text under this to hold the time period of the data.
37. Click on Insert in the main menu bar, then Text.
38. Enter, "Date Range: Oct 1 – Dec 31, 2004".
39. Resize this text to size 18 font and position it centered beneath the "All offenses – City of Glendale" text.
40. Click on the ESRI symbol at the bottom left until you get handles around it, then select Delete.
41. Click on the small text to the left of the ESRI graphic, then right click and choose Ungroup.

42. You should now see two selection boxes. The top one has "Albers Projection" in it and the bottom has the other details of this projection.

43. Click once on the top text (Albers Projection).

44. As you should have noticed with text only a small thin blue line denotes it is selected, but with other graphics we get the line and small boxes or handles in the corners. Make sure you have selected just the text and nothing else.

45. Now right click and choose Properties.

46. In the textbox, change the text to read, "Created by: My Name" (please replace your name where My Name is). Click OK.

47. Now click on the other part of the text, and choose Properties after right clicking it.

48. In the text box here enter:
    a. Glendale CAU
    b. Jan 2, 2004
    c. Source: GPD GIS Data

49. Click Apply then OK to change the text.

50. Select both sets of small text and right click and choose Group.

51. Move both sets of small text together (draw a box around both sets of text with the Select Elements tool [black arrow]) to the bottom left of the leftmost brown textbox.

52. Click on the scale bar to select it and move it to the bottom right side of the rightmost brown box.

53. Click on Insert in the main menu bar and choose **North Arrow**.

54. Choose a North Arrow to add to the layout and click OK.

55. Fit it so it is just left of the Scale Bar in the bottom right textbox.

56. Make sure they do not overlap and resize as needed.

57. Click on Insert again and this time choose Picture.

58. Navigate to the CIA\Photos_Graphics folder.

59. Find the image named GPDBADGE_CLRCHECK.JPG.

60. Click on this image and then click **Open**.

61. Resize the badge so it fits in the small white box next the bottom right of the map display. The white box is created by the street label boxes at the bottom right of the map display.

62. We can resize the badge by clicking and dragging one of the small handles at each corner of the badge.

63. Your map should now look like **Figure E12–6**.

64. Save your project as EX_12.mxd to your student folder.

65. There are many things we have learned in this lesson:
    • How to group or ungroup items to preserve items in the right order as we move things around the map
    • How to add or insert new items to the map
    • How to resize graphics
    • How to work with text
    • How to make a map look nice without being too colorful

66. In this map, we see only one real center of attention—the darkest red areas on the map.

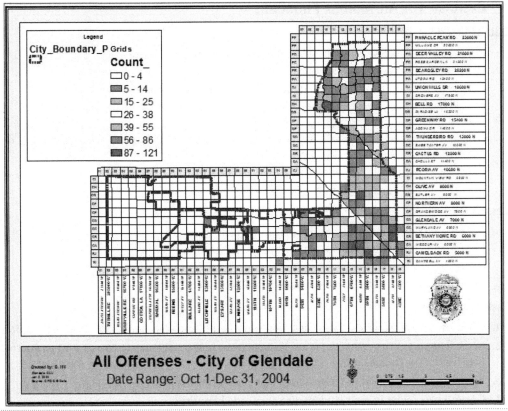

Figure E12–6

67. We have tried to leave white space between items to make the map readable.

68. We have made the map so it reads left to right and top to bottom.

69. We have included the five most critical elements of a map:

   a. The map itself, with one center of attention

   b. North arrow

   c. Scale bar

   d. Legend

   e. Title and other disclaimer text

70. Are you an expert cartographer now? Not even close, but we are crime analysts not cartographers, so if we get our point across easily to officers, we are probably doing something right even if it is not at the high standards of a cartographer.

71. A good idea is to show your maps to others and ask them, "What is this map telling you?"

72. If they say, "Shows me the locations of the McDonald's restaurants," you might want to try again. If they say, "Well, it looks like the red boxes are where all UCR crimes were the highest between Oct 1 and Dec 31, 2004," then you have done a tremendous job.

73. Save and close your project.

■ Exercise 13: ArcToolbox Functions

Data Needed for This Exercise

- Add all the data layers in the CIA\Data\Basic Map Layers folder to a new map project.
- Make all unnecessary layers nonvisible.
- Change the symbology as needed for all layers so that they look good for the map.
- Add the Street_Labels and Basic_Street_Label_An layers from the CIA\Data\File Geodatabase\GIS_Layers.gdb geodatabase.
- Change the symbology on the above two layers so they resemble other maps we've made in previous exercises.
- Add the CIA\Data\File Geodatabse\GIS_Latyers.gdb\UCR Crimes\VideoSeries data and symbolize each point in the series as a blue triangle.

Lesson Objectives

- The student will learn how to clip map elements.
- The student will discover how to use the Spatial Statistics toolbox.
- The student will learn how to create the mean center of a crime series.
- The student will learn how to create StDev ellipses for a crime series.

Task Description

1. Open ArcMap and create the project as described in the "Data Needed for this Exercise" section.
2. In the first part of this exercise, we are going to learn how to clip map features based on another map feature (or cookie cutter).
3. In this exercise, we want to create a map with just Foothills data.
4. Create a new folder in your student directory called **Foothills**.
5. Our first step is to clip the grids based on the Foothills patrol division boundaries.
6. First we need to select all the Patrol Zones that make up the Foothills Division. Right click **Patrol_Zones_P** and choose **Open Attribute Table**.
7. Sort the PatrolDist field in ascending order. Find the 3 rows that have either 40 or 50 in them and select them by clicking the leftmost box of each row.
8. Once highlighted, close the attribute table.
9. In the main menu bar, click Geoprocessing.
10. Click **Clip** to open the clip dialog.
11. Complete the clip dialog as shown in **Figure E13–1**.
12. The Input Features section is always set to the feature class you want to clip, and the Clip Features section is always the feature class that will be the *cookie cutter* or feature that is used to clip the feature dataset or Input Features. Name this new layer FHGrids.shp and save it to the Foothills folder you made in your student folder.
13. Click OK.
14. When the new layer is done being created by ArcMap, turn off the Grids_P layer and observe that the FHGrids layer stops at the Foothills boundaries.
15. Now right click on the Patrol_Zones_P layer and choose Data → Export Data from the popup dialog box.

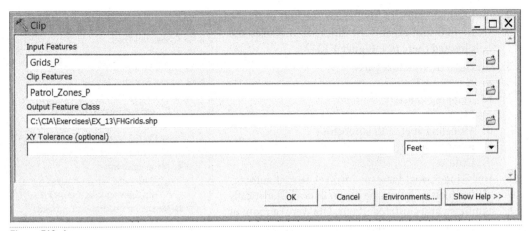

Figure E13–1

16. Name the new feature class FHPatrolZones.shp and save it to your Foothills folder.

17. Zoom in to the Foothills Division as close as possible.

18. Make every layer nonvisible except for the Foothills layers we've just created (left click the List by Visibility button at the top of the TOC, then click the small box to the left of the layer to make nonvisible).

19. Make the FHGrids layer hollow with a light grey outline.

20. Make the patrol zones a different color based on the PatrolDist field. Your map should now resemble **Figure E13–2**.

21. If our goal was to make a Foothills-only map, we could clip the streets layer, create new annotation boxes around it by drawing them, and create a new annotation for a Foothills-only map. We will not do that right now, but keep it in mind as something you may want to do with your own data sometime.

22. We will now begin exploration of the Spatial Statistics toolbox. This toolbox is located in the ArcToolbox.

23. Click the ArcToolbox to open it.

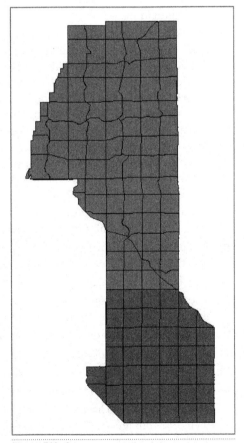

Figure E13–2

24. Find Spatial Statistics Tools near the bottom of the ArcToolbox and expand the different toolboxes and tools located there (see **Figure E13–3**).

25. The different toolboxes are:
    a. Analyzing Patterns
    b. Mapping Clusters
    c. Measuring Geographic Distributions
    d. Modeling Spatial Relationships
    e. Rendering
    f. Utilities

26. Analyzing Spatial Patterns involves spatial autocorrelation tools to determine if your data are statistically significant and clustered. If our data were random or evenly distributed, none of the crime analysis methods we typically use would be useful.

27. The Mapping Clusters section covers creating hotspots using a specific statistical method called Getis Ord GI and a local Moran's *I*.

28. We'll skip over the Measuring Geographic Distributions set of tools for now and move to the Modeling Spatial Relationships tools. This set of tools allows us to calculate *geographically weighted regression* on a set of variables aggregated to a polygon layer and *ordinary least squares* spatial regression to develop a model to determine what affects crime. Although the typical crime analyst may not use these tools daily, they do provide a new set of functions inside ArcMap for determining cause-and-effect relationships for crime.

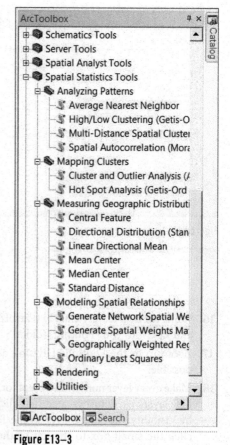

Figure E13–3

29. The Rendering toolbox allows you to create symbology for a variety of functions we can run in the clustering and hotspot areas. This set of tools also allows us to create a repeat address or graduated point map of data.

30. Last but not least is the Utilities toolbox. These tools allow us to collect events (graduated points again), calculate the square area of polygons, and export features to an ASCII format.

31. Now back to the Measuring Geographic Distributions Toolbox.

32. The first thing we want to calculate will be the mean center, or average of the *X* and *Y* Coordinates, of a set of locations in a crime series.

33. Turn on the visibility of the VideoSeries layer in the table of contents (TOC).

34. Zoom to the extents of this layer.

35. Turn back on the citywide grids and the city boundary layers if not already on.

36. Change the series symbology to blue triangles.

37. These five robberies have all occurred at video stores and have involved two Hispanic males in their 20s; both are about 5'6" and 145 lbs with dark hair and eyes. Only one suspect carried a silver semiautomatic; he has a tattoo of a snake.

38. Open the Properties of the Video Series and go to the labels tab. Check the **Label features in this layer** checkbox. Change the Method to **Label all the features the same way**. Change the Label Field to Sequence and click Apply.

39. Now each of the robberies is listed in the order the crimes have occurred, and they are numbered on the map display.

40. In the ArcToolbox → Spatial Statistics Tools → Measuring Geographic Distributions toolbox double click on the Mean Center tool. Complete the mean center dialog as follows (see **Figure E13–4**):

   a. Input Feature Class = VideoSeries
   b. Output Feature Class = YourStudentFolder\VideoMeanCtr
   c. Weight Field = Sequence

41. Click OK to calculate. The weight field will "pull" the mean center toward whatever the weight value is. In this case, we used the sequence in which the robberies occurred, so the newest records have a higher weight than older records.

42. When the new layer is added to the TOC, change the symbology to the "Circle 17" symbol in the symbol list (green circle with cross within it).

43. Your map should now resemble **Figure E13–5**.

44. The orange square shown on Figure E13–5 shows where the mean center would be located if we had not used the weighting.

45. In much of the journey-to-crime literature, we can discover that many criminals will live within a mile of the mean center. So, armed with this knowledge, we can create a rudimentary journey-to-crime analysis with this mean center. We could use the buffer tool to create a buffer at 1 mile around our mean center.

46. Within this 1-mile buffer, we could select by location many of our person's layers and data and then do a Select by Attributes of these selected person records to try to find potential candidates who might be our robbery offenders.

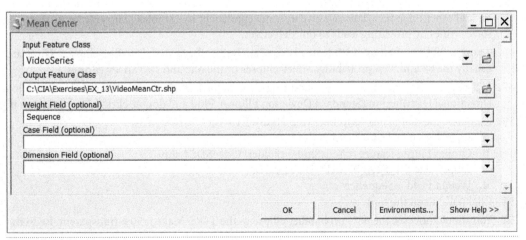

Figure E13–4

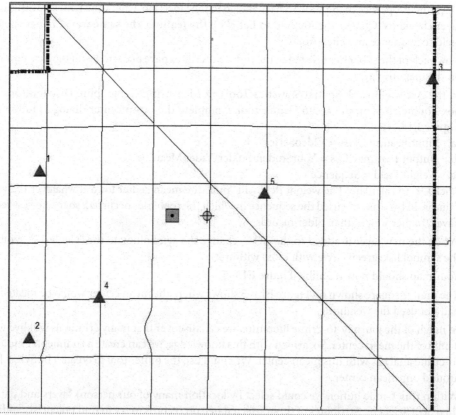

Figure E13–5

47. Everything we have been learning to this point could be used to help us identify robbery offenders and other offenders. This can give us some enjoyment in our jobs—knowing we are helping solve crimes by providing leads to our detectives.

48. Another tool we often use with tactical crime analysis is the spatial deviation ellipses. These are usually the 68 and 95% probability StDev ellipses or the one and two StDev ellipses.

49. In the Spatial Statistics Toolbox → Measuring Geographic Distributions toolbox, this tool is called Directional Distribution (Standard Deviation Ellipse). Find and double click this tool to open it.

50. Complete the dialog box as follows (see **Figure E13–6**):
    a. Input Feature Class = VideoSeries
    b. Output Ellipse feature = YourStudentFolder\VideoSDE1.shp
    c. Ellipse Size = 1_STANDARD_DEVIATION
    d. Weight Field = Sequence

51. Click OK to run the tool.

52. You should now see the 68% probability ellipse in the TOC. Make it 50% transparent. Redo the same Directional Distribution (Standard Deviation Ellipse) tool, but this time in the Ellipse Size field choose 2_STANDARD_DEVIATIONS. Name this new layer as VideoSDE2.shp and save it in your student folder. Click OK to calculate.

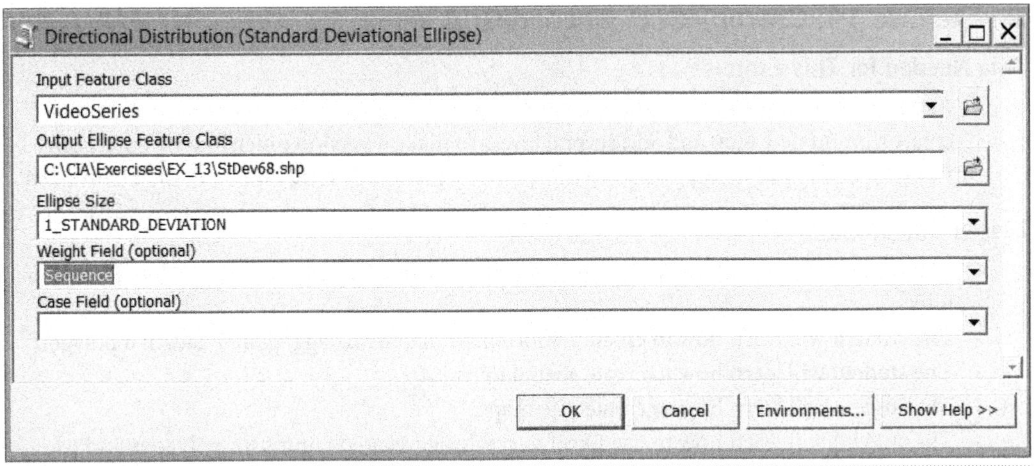

Directional Distribution (Standard Deviational Ellipse)   _ □ X

Input Feature Class

VideoSeries

Output Ellipse Feature Class

C:\CIA\Exercises\EX_13\StDev68.shp

Ellipse Size

1_STANDARD_DEVIATION

Weight Field (optional)

Sequence

Case Field (optional)

OK   Cancel   Environments...   Show Help >>

Figure E13–6

53. Make it 50% transparent as well and move it under the VideoSDE1 layer in the TOC.
54. If we look at the two standard deviation ellipses, we can see that they follow the directionality of the crime series, and that we could use these layers to predict where the next crime would occur in this series.
55. It is not an exact science and we cannot always predict human behavior, but the standard deviation ellipses do sometimes get us into the right area.
56. Your map should now look like **Figure E13–7**.
57. Please save your map in your student folder as EX_13.mxd and close your map to end this lesson.

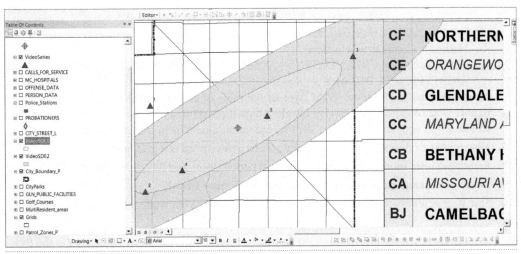

Figure E13–7

■ Exercise 14: Choropleth or Shaded Grid Maps

Data Needed for This Exercise

- By now you should be like the little bird in its nest. You are ready to fly on your own, so create a brand new map and add several layers to make a version much like we have been using up to this point. You will need the quarter square mile Grid layer, and the offense data.

Lesson Objectives

- The student will learn how to aggregate data from a point layer to a polygon using a spatial join.
- The student will learn how to create a choropleth map using aggregated data in a polygon.
- The student will learn how to create spatial joins.
- The student will learn how to create rate maps.
- The student will learn how to use Excel to create aggregated counts for polygons and use these data as a look-up table within ArcMap.

Task Description

1. One of the first types of hotspot maps an analyst learns how to create is a choropleth, or shaded grid map. This is a map based on polygons that uses an aggregate count per each polygon of calls for service, robberies, burglaries, or all Uniform Crime Report (UCR) crimes, as we need.

2. The first thing we need to learn is how to aggregate data to a polygon layer. For this we need to use the smallest polygon we can and still have useful data. For this map we will aggregate data to the Grids_P layer, in which each square is about ¼ of a square mile.

3. Make a copy of the grid layer first. Right click on the Grids_P layer and choose Data → Export Data from the popup dialogs. Save this to your student folder as GridCounts.shp.

4. Now we need to create another layer of all the burglaries that occurred in Glendale in 2003. Click on Selection in the menu bar and choose Select by Attributes.

5. Enter the following in the Select by Attributes dialog box and then click OK:
   a. Layer = CIA\Data\File Geodatabase\GIS_Layers\Offense_Data
   b. Method = Create new selection
   c. SQL Formula = ("RECVDATE" >=20030101 AND "RECVDATE" <=20031231) AND "UCRTYPE" = 'BURGLARY'

6. Now right click the Offense_Data layer in the table of contents (TOC) and choose Data → Export Data to export the selected burglary data for 2003 to a new layer called **Burg2003.shp** and save it in your student folder; 1819 records should now be in the new layer.

7. Now we have a new set of burglary points and a new copy of our grid layer.

8. Right click once on the GridCounts layer and choose Joins and Relates → Joins.

9. In the Join dialog, enter information as shown in **Figure E14–1**.

10. Save your new polygon layer with aggregated count data to your student folder as GridBurgs.shp.

11. Click OK.

12. Now double click the GridBurgs layer in the TOC and in the properties dialog go to the Symbology tab.

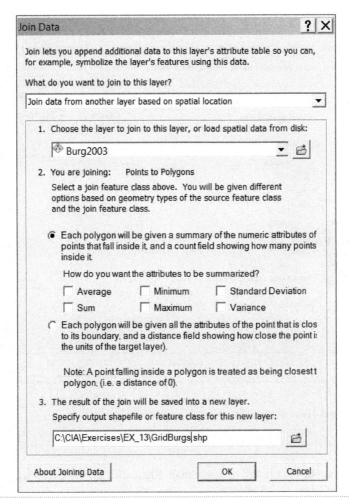

13. Click on the Quantities type legend and make the Value field = Count_.

14. Make it classified by Natural Breaks with seven classifications.

15. Double click on the First or least number class range in the classification window and make the color white. The symbology window should appear similar to **Figure E14–2**.

16. Click Apply and then OK.

17. Your map should now appear as shown in **Figure E14–3** with the darkest areas indicating the highest counts of burglaries per grid.

18. Now we are going to introduce you to rate maps. Rate maps are ratio data, or basically data we use to do comparisons between two different data. We often see this in the number of burglaries per population where burglaries are the numerator and population is the denominator.

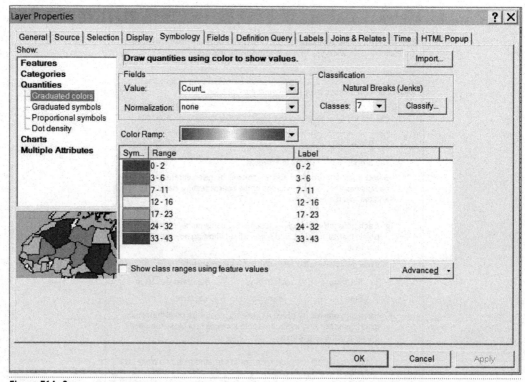

19. So let's see what our data reveal in a rate map. Right click on the GridBurgs layer and choose Open Attribute Table.
20. Browse through the table until you find a field called TotPop_All. This field has data on the 2010 total population aggregated to each grid.
21. Close the attribute table, then **right click** the layer again and choose the **Properties** dialog. Click on the **Symbology** tab, which should still be displaying Quantities → Graduated colors.
22. Under the Value field is a field called **Normalization**.
23. Click on the down arrow to the right of this field and choose the **TotPop_All** field.
24. Change the lowest or top field to white again and click Apply and OK (see **Figure E14–4**).
25. Save your map as EX_14.mxd.
26. Notice that only a certain small number of grids are now red. These grids that are red are now # of Burglaries/Total Population and are a fraction in the legend as they represent a ratio or percentage.
27. The red grids have between 0.4 and 0.6 burglaries per person.
28. Close and save your project as EX_14.mxd.

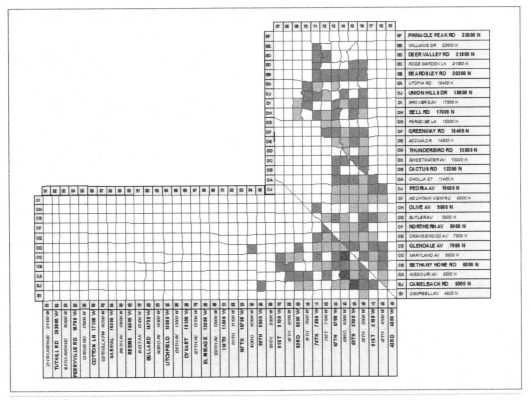

Figure E14–3

■ Exercise 14b: Introduction to Hotspots with CrimeStat III

Data Needed for This Exercise

- CIA\Exercises\EX_14\EX_14.mxd

Lesson Objectives

- The student will learn how to download a copy of CrimeStat III software.
- The student will learn how to set up data for preparation to use it in CrimeStat III.

Task Description

1. Open EX_14.mxd that you saved from the previous exercise. (Alternatively, you can open EX_14 .mxd from the CIA\Exercises\EX_14 folder.)

2. In this exercise, we will explore the single "interpolation" routine in CrimeStat III. An interpolation is similar to a choropleth or shaded grid hotspot analysis in that it creates a map that shows where more crime occurs. These hotspots can then be used to direct police services in the right areas.

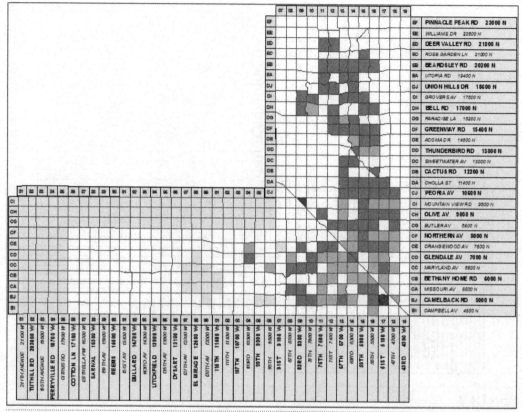

Figure E14–4

3. Hotspots by themselves do not often give us enough information to deploy resources, and they are only the first analysis effort we want to attempt in our problem-solving path. *There could be other steps we want to take prior to hotspot mapping, however, for spatial analysis this is often the first step and answers the question, "Do I have clusters of crime, or high-density locations of crime?"*

4. We may need to create a **kernel density** or **interpolation** of point data to analyze how many crimes within a square mile occurred within an area (hotspots or density maps; see **Figure E14–5**). We should then look at a graduated point layer (where different points are larger or smaller based on count of offenses) to exclude or point a finger at a business/residence within the hotspot that is actually where the majority of criminal activity occurs (hot location; see **Figure E14–6**).

5. We may then want to zoom in to the hotspot and perhaps create another hotspot map that is specific to the geography of the initial citywide hotspot (see **Figure E14–7**).

6. Or we could look at a "pin" or point location map, which shows every crime (also shown in Figure E14–7) along with the hotspot map.

7. We need to be sure we advise our audience that each point could actually have more than one event at that same location. Point maps are only useful at these scales when we are looking at one neighborhood, but consider the caveats to the data and how it is shown on the map.

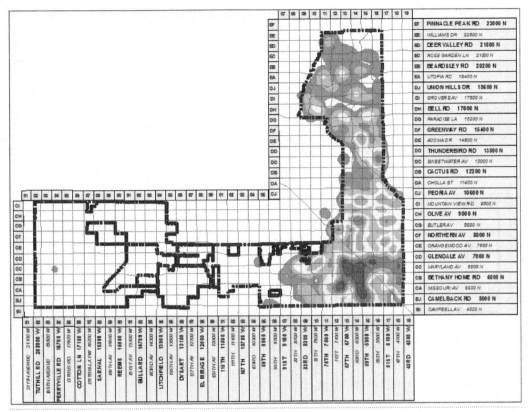

Figure E14–5

8. When we create hotspot maps we will need to make sure that whatever cell size and search radius we use will not distort the true hotspots.

9. The cell size really only controls how smooth the final hotspot map is. In Figures E14–5 and E14–7, the cell sizes were different because one showed the entire city (150 cell size) and the other only a small portion of it (cell size of 25).

10. As we analyze areas that are neighborhoods, we want to use a smaller number for the cell size, and when we are looking at analysis for the entire city we use a larger cell size. In Glendale, for citywide analysis, a cell size of about 100–300 works fine.

11. The search radius determines how far out the program looks from inside each cell for nearest neighbors. In a simplistic description, each cell is created as a 25 × 25 foot cell and then each cell in turn goes out to the search distance we set to find points and counts them.

12. So if the search radius is 100 feet, then each cell searches that far out for points in the point data. In kernel density estimation, points are given values according to their distance, with those farthest receiving slightly lower values, and points inside the cell receiving highest values.

13. We could decide in some cases that a simple choropleth map is most useful, and in other cases, we may want a density map made with CrimeStat III or perhaps the Spatial Analyst Extension to

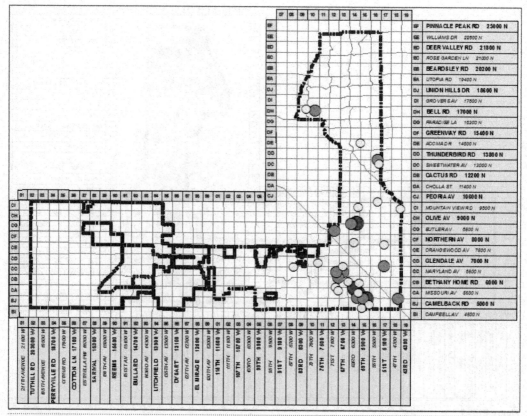

Figure E14–6

ArcMap 10. At other times, a graduated point map is the most useful to tell the story that needs to be told after our analysis. We might also resort to a pin map depending on our audience and need. A good analyst will also look at graphs, charts, and executive summaries of the analysis as a medium instead of a map, when the map does not provide any additional information.

14. Remember that your audience is most often police officers and police executives and they like to see everything they need to know in one to two pages. In addition, do not get too fond of your maps and analyses; you will do hundreds of them in your career and they could be obsolete in a week.

15. CrimeStat III is free from the National Institute of Justice and can be downloaded from www .icpsr.umich.edu/CrimeStat/.

16. Open your web browser and download the CrimeStat III software from www.icpsr.umich.edu/ CrimeStat/download.html.

17. You will only need to download the first item: *CrimeStat* **Program (version 3.3) (ZIP 1MB) (Updated 2010-07-31)** by clicking on it once.

18. At some point, you may want to download the manuals and tutorial data, but for now just the program will do.

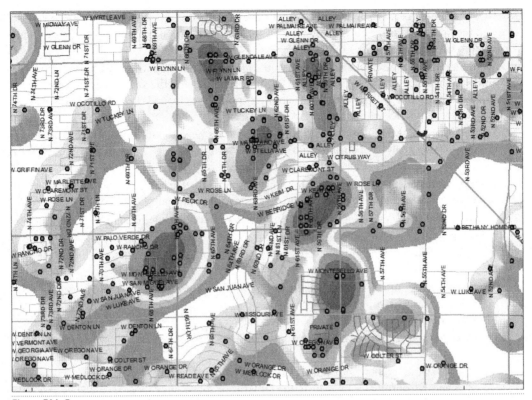

Figure E14–7

19. In the popup menu, choose **Save**.

20. Save it to your student folder.

21. Once the program finishes downloading to your student folder, find the CrimeStat-3.3.zip file in Windows Explorer and double click it to open it.

22. Highlight all four files and then click on the Extract All button in the top left section of Windows Explorer (in Windows 7 this feature is located by right clicking the .ZIP file and choosing **Extract to…** from the popup menu).

23. You can also extract the data using WinZip or a variety of other software that works with zipped files.

24. After the files have been extracted, you will notice we have four files:

    a. **Crimestat.exe** (the program itself)

    b. **CRIMESTAT.HLP** (the help dialog)

    c. **License.txt** (the license information and text that should be on any analysis product that you've used CrimeStat III with as a courtesy to the creator, Ned Levine. This disclaimer text is as follows: Ned Levine, *CrimeStat III: A Spatial Statistics Program for the Analysis of Crime Incident Locations* [update version 3.3]. Ned Levine & Associates, Houston, TX, and the National Institute of Justice, Washington, DC, July 2010.)

    d. **Readme.Txt** (contains known bugs and other disclaimers)

25. Our assignment is to create a hotspot map using a kernel density function in CrimeStat III to find the hottest spots for burglary in 2003 (using our Burg2003.shp from the previous exercise or from CIA\Exercises\EX_14).

26. We want to advise the chief and the staff in the CompStat meeting where the hottest spots are, and what locations have had more than five burglaries during the year. The chief would also like a summary of *all* UCR crimes in the hottest spot of the city and the hottest times and days of week for burglaries within the hottest hotspot.

27. So, we have several things to think about here. First, we need to know how to create a density or interpolation analysis of our Burg2003.shp data. Second, we need to create a graduated point map of every location that has had five or more burglaries during the year.

28. Then we need to identify the hottest of the hotspots, and from that hotspot, determine the number of all UCR Crimes that have occurred during the year (not just burglaries).

29. Our final step is to determine *when* the burglaries were occurring during the year within the hottest hotspot.

30. While seemingly overwhelming, this is a pretty commonplace request and so we'll walk through the steps together.

31. There are several things we need to prepare when using CrimeStat III:
    a. A minimum bounding rectangle (MBR)
       - Lower left X and Y coordinates of the MBR
       - Upper right X and Y coordinates of the MBR
       - Square mileage of the MBR
    b. A set of crime "points" with at least five cases
       - X and Y Coordinates must be in the DBF file or shapefile of those incidents
    c. You must know the projection of the data and know if the map units are decimal degrees, feet, meters, etc.
       - We would re-project to state plane (feet) if we had decimal degree data
    d. Feet or miles of each street segment in the MBR

32. First, we need to make sure we have all the data we need and that we have the right information in the attribute table we will need.

33. Right click the Burgs2003.shp in the TOC and click on **Open Attribute Table**.

34. Browse the attribute table and look for a field that contain the X and Y coordinates of these data.

35. Did you find it? Hopefully, it was not too hard!

36. The fields are called "X" and "Y". We need to make sure we have no missing data in either of these fields, and the easiest way to do this is simply to sort each field in ascending then descending order.

37. Right click on the X field name and choose **Sort Ascending** from the drop-down menu.

38. Uh oh, looks like we have at least 27 records that do not have an X coordinate and 0 is in that field instead. If we sort the Y coordinate field in ascending order, we see that the 0s in that field line up with the 0s in the X coordinate field. This is good. Sorting the data in descending order does not show any issues, so we are good to go there. We don't see any huge numbers that are atypical from the other coordinates in these two fields when sorting in descending order.

39. We can now exclude these records in CrimeStat III later because we know that 0 means null or missing values in these fields. Remember this little tidbit of information when we get ready to set up CrimeStat III.

40. While we are browsing fields, let's look and see if we have time of day (TOD) and day of week (DOW) fields in our data already.

41. If you scroll to the far right, we do have MPTOD and MPDOW fields.

42. The "MP" stands for midpoint of occurrence. In other words, in some cases we would have a date range during which a crime occurred. For example, a victim left to go camping on Friday night and came home Monday morning to find his house was burglarized. The midpoint would be calculated as the average, or halfway, between the start and end dates and time reported to police.

43. So for our final step in this exercise, we will be able to use these fields to summarize when burglaries in the hottest spot occurred.

44. We also meet the criteria of five cases or more so we are good there.

45. We also know the projection of these data because it is the same for all of the data in these exercises:
    • AZ NAD 1983 Fips 0202, AZ Central, Int'l Feet. (This can be found in the Properties for a dataset under the Source tab.)

46. Okay, now what is a minimum bounding rectangle (MBR) anyway? In simplest terms, it is a rectangle that, when drawn around the points you are analyzing, bounds all points within the rectangle.

47. We can use the Draw toolbar to draw our rectangle. We need to be mindful of the fact that all points are completely within it, and that the MBR is shaped so that it makes sense for the analysis we are doing. In this case, we are doing a citywide analysis, so our MBR should reflect that as well. Good and bad examples are shown in **Figures E14-8** and **E14-9**. (Actually, it is more like bad and better, as good is dependent on the extent area we want to analyze and not always where the points are now.)

48. In Figure E14-8 all points are within the rectangle, but in Figure E14-9 several points in District 30 are outside of the rectangle.

49. It could be that those points outside the rectangle in Figure E14-9 are not necessary, however, without doing the analysis we won't know and including them makes the most sense for this citywide analysis.

50. Using the Draw Rectangle tool from the Draw toolbar, draw a rectangle around the city limits so that all the points are completely within the rectangle.

51. Right click on the graphic and choose Properties.

52. Make the fill transparent and the outline dark red and size 3 in thickness.

53. With the Properties still open, check the tab that reads, "Size and Position."

54. In the bottom left side of the tab menu, there are nine small blue boxes. The bottom left represents the X and Y coordinates of the corner of the rectangle. Select the bottom, leftmost box and copy down the X and Y coordinate values to Excel (or a piece of scratch paper).

55. Now click on the box in the upper right corner and record these X and Y coordinates as well.

56. We will need these data when we setup CrimeStat III to create a density map for us.

57. We also need the total Area of this rectangle.

58. Click on the Area tab and record the total square miles on your Excel sheet or scratch pad.

59. Now we need to find the total street miles within this rectangle. Do you remember what function we use to do this and where it is located?

60. Do not worry; I will not leave you hanging. We will use the Select by Graphics functions in the Selection menu bar.

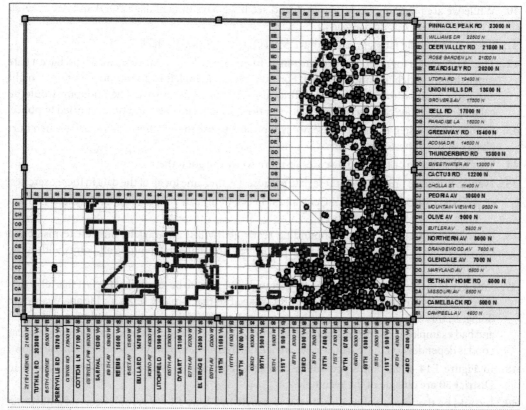

Figure E14–8

61. Close the Graphics Properties dialog.

62. Make sure the handles are around the rectangle to show it is selected. If not, choose the Select Elements tool from the tools toolbar and click it anywhere in the box until the handles appear.

63. Click to select the GLN_STREETS_PLUS layer in the TOC, then click on the Selection menu item in the main menu bar, and choose Select by Graphics.

64. After a few seconds, the streets that intersect the rectangle will be selected. Now we need to know the total street footage that has been selected.

65. Right click on the GLN_STREETS_PLUS layer and choose Open Attribute Table from the popup menu.

66. Find the field called **Length** or alternatively **Shape_Length**. Right click on either field name and choose **Statistics** from the drop-down menu.

67. The number in the Sum row (it will be a doozy) is what you want to save where you are recording the lower left *XY* coordinates, the upper right *XY* coordinates, and the total square mileage of the rectangle. You should have something that looks like:

- Lower Left XY: 531,057.0115/910,076.8481
- Upper Right XY: 631,230.5833/984,095.8866

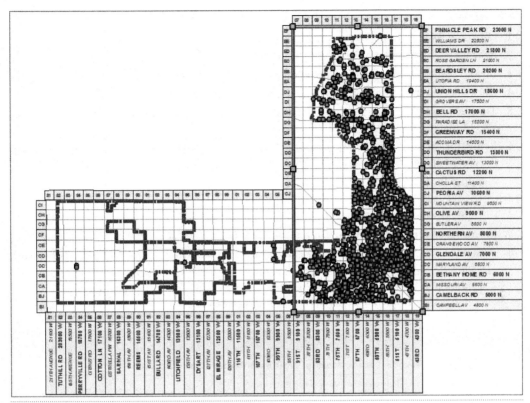

Figure E14—9

- Total Square Miles: 265.9676 square miles
- Total Street Footage: 15912820.500304

68. This ends this part of the hotspot analysis using CrimeStat III.

69. Save your project as EX_14.mxd. Then close your project (if you are continuing on to EX_14c you do not need to close the project to proceed).

■ Exercise 14c: Continued Introduction to Hotspots with CrimeStat III

Data Needed for This Exercise

- CIA\Exercises\EX_14\EX_14.mxd

Lesson Objectives

- The student will learn how to set up their data for preparation to use in CrimeStat III.
- Directions on loading data into CrimeStat III will be provided.
- The student will learn how to create a single kernel density map.

Task Description

1. Open EX_14.mxd from the previous exercise.
2. Now we need to open the CrimeStat III program.
3. In your student folder, double click on the CrimeStat.exe file to open the program.
4. Click once on the opening screen to go to the data setup and CrimeStat menu.
5. The file we are going to analyze with CrimeStat is the Burgs2003.shp located in the CIA\Exercises\EX_14 folder.
6. Remember that we have the data for our MBR already saved so we can use it to set up CrimeStat:
   - Lower Left XY: 531,057.0115/910,076.8481
   - Upper Right XY: 631,230.5833/984,095.8866
   - Total Square Miles: 265.9676 square miles
   - Total Street Footage: 15912820.500304
7. In CrimeStat menu, click on the **Data Setup** tab if not already selected.
8. Within the Data Setup tab, click on the **Primary File** tab and enter the following (see **Figure E14–10**):
   a. Click the **Select Files** button and then navigate out to the CIA\Exercises\EX_14 folder. Find and double click the Burgs2003.dbf table (the attribute table part of the shapefile) and then click OK in the primary file dialog (see **Figure E14–11**).

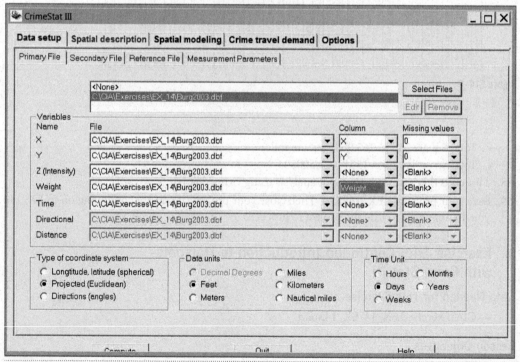

Figure E14–10

Ned Levine (2010). *CrimeStat III: A Spatial Statistics Program for the Analysis of Crime Incident Locations* (v 3.3). Ned Levine & Associates, Houston, TX, and the National Institute of Justice, Washington, DC. July. http://www.icpsr.umich.edu/CrimeStat.

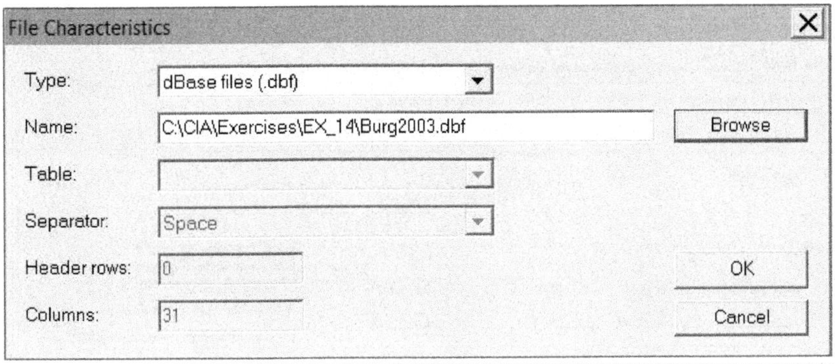

Figure E14–11

Ned Levine (2010). *CrimeStat III: A Spatial Statistics Program for the Analysis of Crime Incident Locations* (v 3.3). Ned Levine & Associates, Houston, TX, and the National Institute of Justice, Washington, DC. July. http://www.icpsr.umich.edu/CrimeStat.

b. Now we need to set the variables (fields) needed to fill the requirements of CrimeStat III. Under the column field sections, select the following:
- X Coordinate = X; missing values set to 0 (see, we told you that we would need that sometime)
- Y Coordinate = Y; missing values set to 0
- Weight = Weight

c. Type of Coordinate System = Projected (Euclidean)

d. Data Units = Feet

e. Time Units = days (but we will use this some other time)

9. Now we need to click on the **Reference File** tab.

10. Complete the Reference File tab (MBR) using the coordinate values for the lower left and upper right *XY* coordinates from our MBR (see **Figure E14–12**).

11. In some cases, CrimeStat is "buggy" when you try to cut and paste numbers instead of just entering them manually.

12. For the time being in the Cell Specification section, we are going to leave this as checked—By Number of Columns = 100. This field is where we basically control the size of the cells. In this case within the extents of our MBR, we will have 100 columns and 100 rows creating our cell size. We can also create cells using the cell spacing, or the specific size of the cell we want to see. We can make it smaller or larger by changing how smooth the resulting kernel density is.

13. Click on the **Measurement Parameters** tab now.

14. Enter the values from the MBR calculations we did in EX_14b (see **Figure E14–13**).

15. Click on **Indirect (Manhattan)** under the **Type of distance measurement** section.

16. We will use indirect, or based on Manhattan street walking, distances. We could also use the Direct (as the crow flies) or Network (actual street network) options. The Euclidean or Direct method is another option, but most research indicates that the Manhattan option more closely resembles how an offender walks to a crime. Network analysis requires other data to setup the network and we have found that the Indirect or Manhattan distance provides the best results in our analyses.

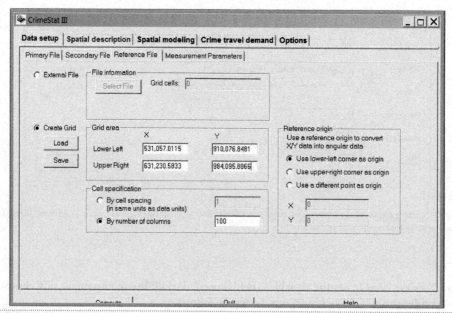

Figure E14–12

Ned Levine (2010). *CrimeStat III: A Spatial Statistics Program for the Analysis of Crime Incident Locations* (v 3.3). Ned Levine & Associates, Houston, TX, and the National Institute of Justice, Washington, DC. July. http://www.icpsr.umich.edu/CrimeStat.

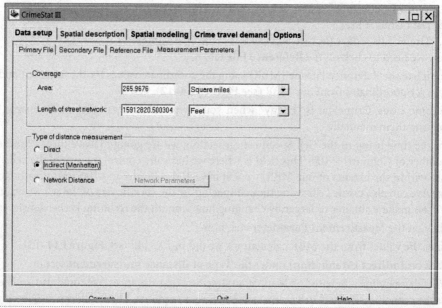

Figure E14–13

Ned Levine (2010). *CrimeStat III: A Spatial Statistics Program for the Analysis of Crime Incident Locations* (v 3.3). Ned Levine & Associates, Houston, TX, and the National Institute of Justice, Washington, DC. July. http://www.icpsr.umich.edu/CrimeStat.

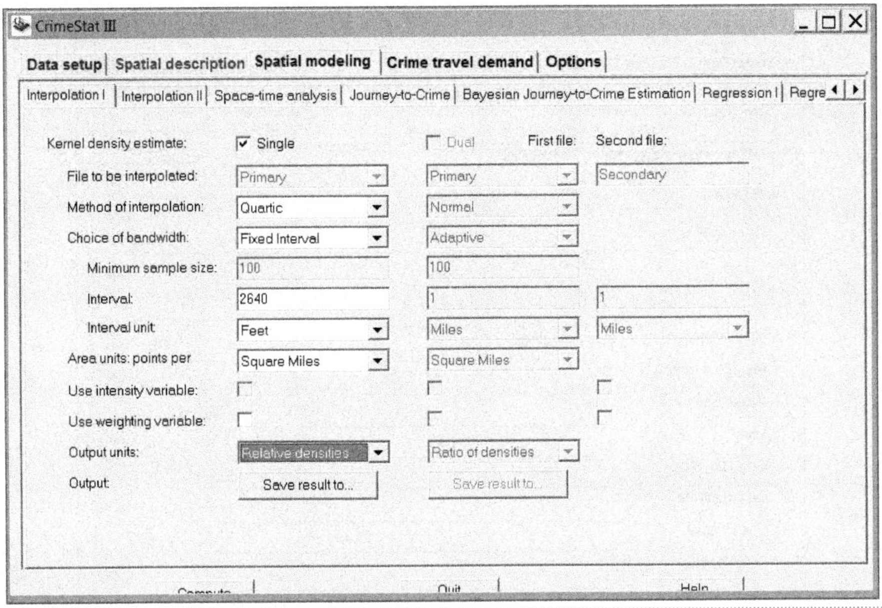

Figure E14–14

Ned Levine (2010). *CrimeStat III: A Spatial Statistics Program for the Analysis of Crime Incident Locations* (v 3.3). Ned Levine & Associates, Houston, TX, and the National Institute of Justice, Washington, DC. July. http://www.icpsr.umich.edu/CrimeStat.

17. We have setup CrimeStat to do Interpolation or kernel density estimation of our burglaries, so now all we need to do is tell CrimeStat what routines we want to run.

18. Click on the **Spatial Modeling** tab.

19. Click on the **Interpolation I** tab and complete the tab as shown in **Figure E14–14**.

20. Click on the **Save result to** button.

21. In the popup dialog, Enter the following:
    a. Save Output to: = ArcView 'SHP'
    b. Save to your student folder as Burg2003HS.shp
    c. Click OK (see **Figure E14–15**)

22. We will create several of these hotspots and rename them before each run so we can see the results of our changes in the software. The output of this will be small polygons the size of our cell specification in the data setup stages.

23. Click the **Compute** button at the bottom left of the CrimeStat window to run this hotspot analysis. The results window will appear after a few seconds (see **Figure E14–16**). You could print these results or save these results to a text file, although for the typical crime analyst you will simply close this window after it runs—we are just looking for error messages.

24. Click the **Close** button once, but do not close the main CrimeStat window.

25. Go to ArcMap and click the Add Data button.

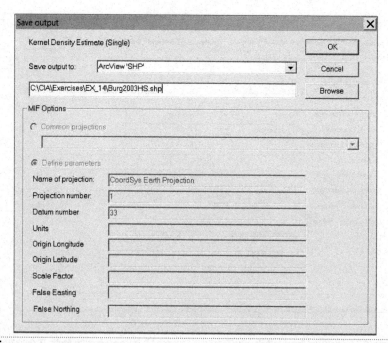

Figure E14–15

Ned Levine (2010). *CrimeStat III: A Spatial Statistics Program for the Analysis of Crime Incident Locations* (v 3.3). Ned Levine & Associates, Houston, TX, and the National Institute of Justice, Washington, DC. July. http://www.icpsr.umich.edu/CrimeStat.

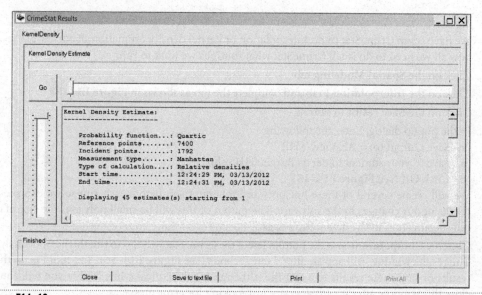

Figure E14–16

Ned Levine (2010). *CrimeStat III: A Spatial Statistics Program for the Analysis of Crime Incident Locations* (v 3.3). Ned Levine & Associates, Houston, TX, and the National Institute of Justice, Washington, DC. July. http://www.icpsr.umich.edu/CrimeStat.

26. Find the KBurg2003HS.shp file you saved to your student folder—CrimeStat III always adds a K in front of any kernel densities you create, so when you look for the file you entered, make sure you also look for those with a K in front of what you entered.

27. Answer OK to the warning about Spatial Reference if prompted.

28. Right click this layer in the TOC and choose Properties → Symbology.

29. Click on the Quantities, graduated colors type of classification, and in the value field use the Z (score). Use natural breaks classification type and seven classes. Use a blue to red color ramp. Change the first, or lowest value, color to white or "No Color."

30. Click Apply and OK.

31. Your map should now resemble **Figure E14–17**.

32. Okay, we have lines around every polygon and we want to eliminate them: Open the Properties → Symbology tab again, and click on the top symbol *(where the color boxes are located)*, then hold the shift key down and click on the bottom symbol. Right click the selected symbols and choose Properties for Selected Symbols. Change the outline color to No Color, Click OK, and OK again to see the new hotspot map.

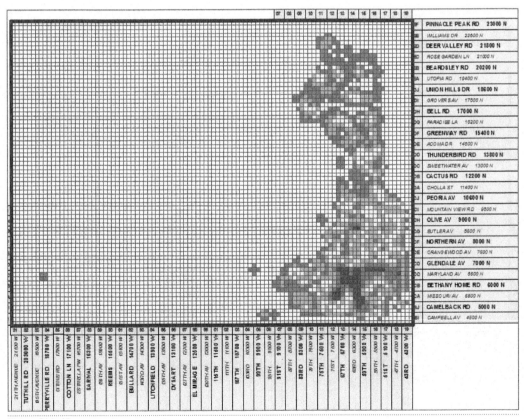

Figure E14–17

33. Notice how our map looks a little pixelated? This is because of our 100 × 100 row and column size in the cell specification area.

34. Click on the CrimeStat window to make it active.

35. Go back to the Data Setup tab, and select the Reference File section.

36. In the Cell Specification box, check the box that reads, "By Cell Spacing (in Same Units as Data Units)."

37. In the box to the right of this, enter 250.

38. Click on the Spatial Modeling tab, and then click on the Interpolation I tab.

39. Click on the Save result to button again.

40. Make the output a Shapefile again (ArcView 'SHP') and save it to your student folder as Burg2003250cellSize.shp.

41. Click OK and then Compute again.

42. When this is completed (notice that it took longer because we increased the size of the cells), close only the results window of CrimeStat III, then open ArcMap and add the KBurg2003250 cellSize.shp file from your student folder. Symbolize it like the first hotspot layer.

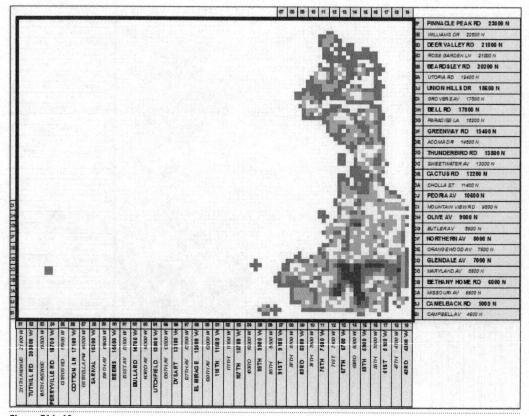

Figure E14–18

43. *Note*: If you get a popup message indicating that the sample size has been exceeded, do the following:

   a. Click OK to this message.

   b. Click on the Classify button.

   c. Click the Sampling button.

   d. In the popup, add two or three zeros at the end of the Maximum Sample Size window.

   e. Click OK, and OK again to finish symbolizing your map. When finished, click Apply and OK to get back to the map.

   f. Change the lowest classification range to a fill of white or "no color."

44. Do you notice the difference in how much smoother the hotspots are, but that they are in the same places and are almost the same size and shape?

45. **Figure E14–18** shows the first hotspot map and **Figure E14–19** shows the second or more improved hotspot map based on how smooth (or prettier) it looks. (You may not see the differences in the graphics in the workbook, but you should see obvious differences in the hotspot layers in ArcMap.)

46. Save your project.

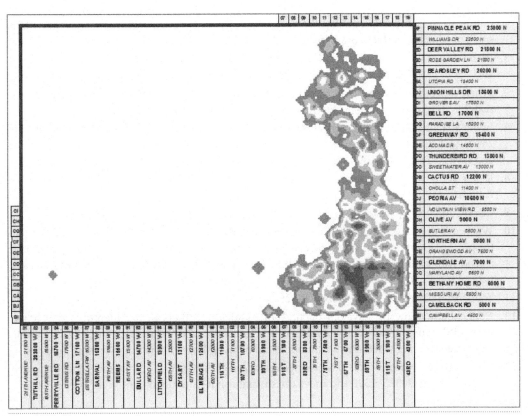

Figure E14–19

■ Exercise 14d: More Hotspots with CrimeStat III

Data Needed for This Exercise

- CIA\Exercises\EX_14\EX_14.mxd

Lesson Objectives

- The student will learn how to set up their data for preparation to use it in CrimeStat III.
- Directions on loading data into CrimeStat III will be provided.
- The student will learn about the mode function in CrimeStat III to create graduated point data.
- The student will learn how to create a single kernel density map.

Task Description

1. Open EX_14.mxd from the previous exercise.
2. If you are continuing from EX_14c and CrimeStat is still open, we can continue. If not, please open CrimeStat III and do the data setup as we did in steps 4–22 in EX_14c.
3. We will now see how the search radius affects the final result. Basically, the larger your search radius the bigger the blobs are, and the smaller your search radius the smaller they are.
4. We need to work with our agency data to make sure that we do not choose so large a search radius that we have only one large hotspot in the city, and not so small that we have too many small hotspots as problem areas for police.
5. In the City of Glendale, which is about 57 Square miles, we have found that 2640 feet as a radius and a 100- to 250-foot cell size gives reliable results for a citywide analysis.
6. When we zoom into a neighborhood or other smaller part of geography, we will reduce this search radius to 1000–1320 feet to identify smaller hotspots in a neighborhood.
7. In the Spatial Modeling → Interpolation I tab, change the search radius to 5280 feet (instead of 2640), and click the Save result to button. Save this new hotspot layer as an ArcView .SHP file and save it to your student folder as Burg2003250_5280HS.shp.
8. *If you are setting up CrimeStat III again, make sure you set the cell size to 250 as we did in Exercise 14c.*
9. Click Compute.
10. When it is done running, switch to ArcMap 2010 and load the KBurg2003250_5280HS.shp to the project. Right click the layer and choose the Properties → Symbology tab. Make a quantities legend with a blue to red color ramp, white for the lowest value, no color for the outline, and natural breaks with seven classes using the Z field as the Value Field.
11. Your map should look like **Figure E14–20**.
12. Notice that we now just have one big hotspot and that the others we had identified at 2640 feet were a little more spread out. We could call this "generalization." As we use a larger search radius, we are generalizing where the hotspots are and often end up with just one "hottest" hotspot.
13. Now go back to CrimeStat III and change the search radius to 1320. Make sure to save this new output as Burg200325_1320.shp so we can distinguish it from the others.
14. Click Compute.

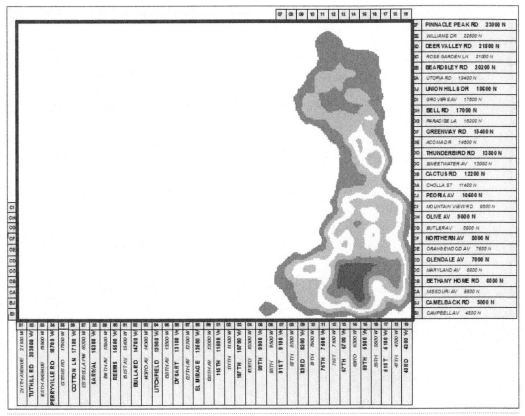

Figure E14–20

15. When it is done running, add the new layer to the ArcMap project and make the legend the same as our previous hotspot layers (see **Figure E14–21**).

16. We now have several more, smaller hotspots (which can be difficult to prioritize for enforcement).

17. For the next part of the exercise, we will use the KBurg2003250cellSize.shp file. Make sure this is loaded in your TOC.

18. It is a good idea to clean up your TOC by deleting data you are not using and give yourself some space.

19. Click on any other hotspot layer you have in the TOC except for the one above and remove them (right click and choose Remove).

20. Also, collapse (+ or – sign to the left of the layer in List by Drawing Order view for the TOC) any layers we are not currently using.

21. Move the KBurg2003250cellSize.shp layer to the bottom of the TOC, and right click to go to Properties.

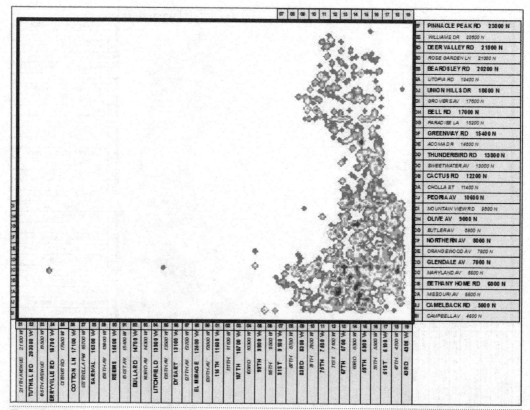

Figure E14–21

22. Click in the Label section in the Symbology tab and change the values in each label section as shown in **Figure E14–22**.

23. We do not want to show these numbers because they really do not mean anything that most officers and command staff will understand. It is the total number of **crimes *per square mile*** based on any place where you would touch on the map surface.

24. Converting them to Very Low through Very High when using a Natural breaks classification schema with seven classes seems to work out well.

25. We need to select all UCR crimes that occurred in the hottest hotspot. So we need to choose the hottest hotspot from this layer's data. As we can see, Very High values on the map are greater than or equal to 124.4. (Your value may vary slightly depending on differences in the size of the original MBR we created.)

26. We can now do a Select by Attributes to select these areas.

27. Close the Properties dialog after you have applied your changes to the labels.

28. Go to Selection in the menu bar and choose Select by Attributes.

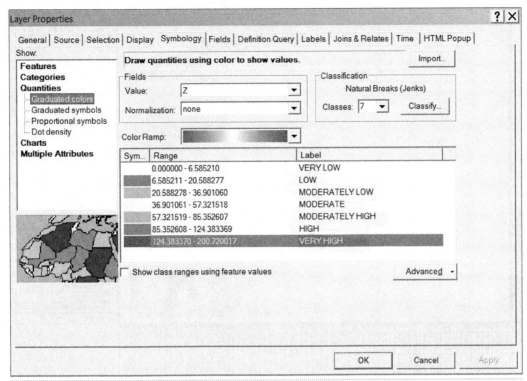

Figure E14–22

29. In the Select by Attributes dialog, we need to choose the KBurg2003250cellSize layer and then our SQL formula will be: "Z" >= 124.4.

30. Click Verify to make sure it runs and then click OK.

31. We should now see several "blobs" on the map selected in light blue, as shown (in black) in **Figure E14–23**.

32. We can now use a Select by Location query using this as the cookie cutter part of the selection process.

33. Click on Selection in the menu bar and choose Select by Location from the popup dialog.

34. We need to select the features from OFFENSE_DATA that intersect the selected features of KBurg2003250cellSize layer (see **Figure E14–24**).

35. To get a summary of the UCR crimes by type that have occurred in 2003 within the "hottest spots for burglary," you can open the attribute table for the Offense_Data layer.

36. Click the button at the bottom that reads, "Show Selected Records" when you hover your cursor over it.

37. Now we see only the selected records and can see that 16,077 were selected. (*Note*: This may be slightly different depending on how you drew your MBR.)

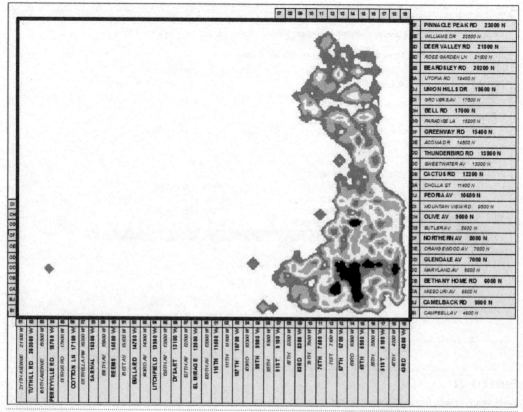

Figure E14–23

38. Find the field called UCRType and right click it.

39. Choose Summarize from the drop-down menu.

40. Save the summary table as UCRSUM.dbf and make sure to change the Save As Type section to dBbase Table.

41. Click OK.

42. When it asks if you want to load the data to the current map project, say YES so we can see the summarized data.

43. We could then bring this table into Excel 2010 and massage it and get something like **Figure E14–25**.

44. Okay, what are we missing? Well, we need to see a map of graduated points for locations that had five or more burglaries during the year. We also need to show the top time of day and day of week for burglaries within the hotspot areas.

45. Since we still have CrimeStat open, let's create the Mode of the points in the burglary layer.

46. Click on CrimeStat to bring it to the front of your computer screen.

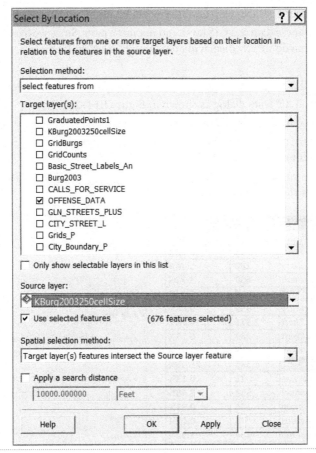

Figure E14–24

47. Click on the Spatial Description → Hotspot Analysis I tab, then check the checkbox next to Mode.

48. At the right of Mode, click the Save result to button.

49. Save this to your student folder as a dBase Table "Dbf" and name it GP.dbf. CrimeStat will add a prefix to the name as well.

50. Go to the Spatial Modeling → Interpolation I tab and uncheck the Single checkbox so we do not rerun our density analysis.

51. Click Compute.

52. This will save a .DBF table out to your student folder named ModeGP.dbf.

53. Close the Compute screen, and leave CrimeStat open.

54. Click the Add Data button in ArcMap and add the ModeGP.dbf table to the project.

55. Right click on this file and choose Open.

56. This table is a frequency table with a rank, frequency, and *X* and *Y* coordinates fields.

57. We need to show these data as a GIS layer and not just a table. Since we have *X* and *Y* coordinates in the table, we can do this by displaying the table as an event theme.

58. Close the table.

59. Right click the table in the TOC again and choose **Display XY Data…** from the popup dialog.

60. Complete the Add XY Data dialog as shown in **Figure E14–26**.

61. Click OK to add the data as an XY event theme.

62. Make sure to turn off the kernel density layer (make nonvisible) so we can avoid waiting for it to draw all the time.

63. ModeGP data is currently displaying as single feature symbols and we need to change this to a graduated point classification type.

UCR TYPE	COUNT	% OF TOTAL
Murder	7	0.04%
Rape	36	0.22%
Robbery	280	1.74%
Aggravated Assault	600	3.73%
Total Part 1 Violent Crimes	923	5.74%
Burglary	955	5.94%
Theft	2,371	14.75%
Auto Theft	989	6.15%
Arson	18	0.11%
Total Part 1 Property Crimes	4,333	26.95%
Curfew	21	0.13%
Disorderly Conduct	559	3.48%
Drug-Cocaine/Opium	134	0.83%
Drug-Dangerous	3	0.02%
Drug-Marijuana	244	1.52%
Drug-Synthetic	700	4.35%
Dui	643	4.00%
Embezzlement	18	0.11%
Family Offense	1,353	8.42%
Forgery	277	1.72%
Fraud	45	0.28%
Indecent Exposure	132	0.82%
Liquor Laws	190	1.18%
Misconduct w-Weapons	141	0.88%
Other	2,265	14.09%
Prostitution	7	0.04%
Runaway	285	1.77%
Simple Assault	1,292	8.04%
Stolen Property	102	0.63%
Traffic Only	539	3.35%
Vagrancy	12	0.07%
Vandalism	1,859	11.56%
Part 2 Crime Totals	10,821	67.31%
Overall Totals	16,077	100.00%

Figure E14–25

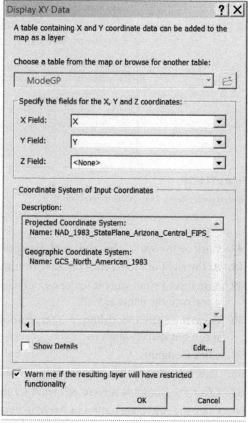

Figure E14–26

64. Right click on the New Events layer → Choose Properties → Symbology tab. Click on a Quantities classification type → Graduated symbols.

65. The value field will be the FREQ field.

66. Change the point size to 3 to 18.

67. Click OK.

68. Now we have points that are larger or smaller depending on the number of burglaries that occurred there.

69. But we want only those where the FREQ was greater than five, right? Any ideas how to do this?

70. Okay, I'll bail you out again. Click on Selection in the menu bar, then Select by Attributes.

71. Query the ModeGP Events layer attributes where FREQ >= 5.

72. When done, right click on the events layers and choose Data → Export Data.

73. Make sure you export only the selected records and save it to your student folder as Graduated Points.shp.

74. Click OK.

75. Add the new layer to the current map (yes).

76. Turn off the ModeGP Events layer and then change the symbology on the Graduated Points layer to a graduated symbol classification type.

77. Change the range from 4 to 18 to 2 to 18 and Apply.

78. We can make this even better by changing the display transparency to about 30%, and changing the color of the highest frequency of events to red size 18, the next smallest orange, then yellow, light blue, and blue as shown (in grayscale) **Figure E14–27**.

79. Now we have a map that shows us the hottest locations within Glendale for Burglary. We could then do a spatial join to find out what addresses these are, or simply turn on the burglaries and click near the center of the graduated points until you find the addresses that match the counts. This does seem crude, but it works.

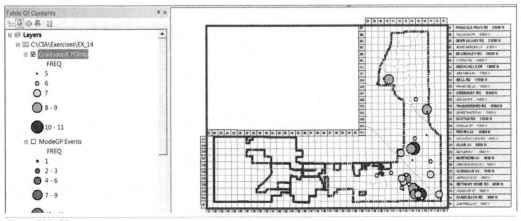

Figure E14–27

80. Our last assignment was to find out when burglaries were occurring in the hottest spots.
81. Close CrimeStat III at this time.
82. If you have the hottest spots still selected, we are ready to go; if not, Select by Attributes from KBurg2003250cellSize where Z >= 124.4.
83. Then do a Select by Location where Burg2003 intersected the selected polygons in the KBurg-2003250cellSize layer (see **Figure E14–28**). Click OK.
84. Now you should have all the burglaries in 2003 in the selected hottest hotspot area.
85. Open the attribute table to the Burg2003 layer.
86. Click on the Show Selected Records button.
87. Right click on the MPDOW field and choose Summarize. Choose your student folder and call this MPDOWSUM.dbf.

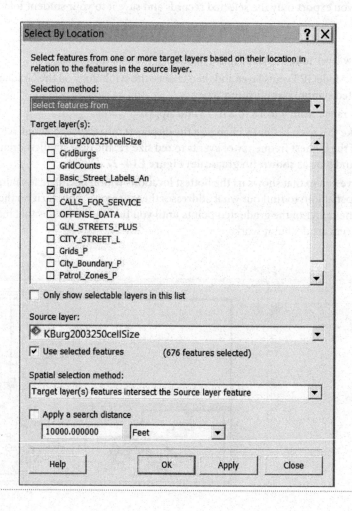

Figure E14–28

88. Add the summary table to the project.
89. Right click on the MPTOD field and choose Summarize. Choose your student folder and call this MPTODSUM.dbf.
90. Add the summary table to the project.
91. Close the Burg2003 table.
92. Right click and open both dbf tables to see the contents. Work with the MPDOWSUM table first.
93. Click the Table Options button and then choose **Create Graph** from the popup dialog.
94. In the graph type, choose **Vertical Area**.
95. Fill the remainder of the graph dialog box as shown in **Figures E14–29** and **E14–30**.
96. Click Finish.
97. We now have a chart we can add to our layout if desired. Unfortunately, since the day of week was in text and the days do not sort in proper order, our chart is a little out of sync, but we can easily see that Thursday and Sunday have the highest counts.
98. Now graph the MPTODSUM table as we did with the day of week.

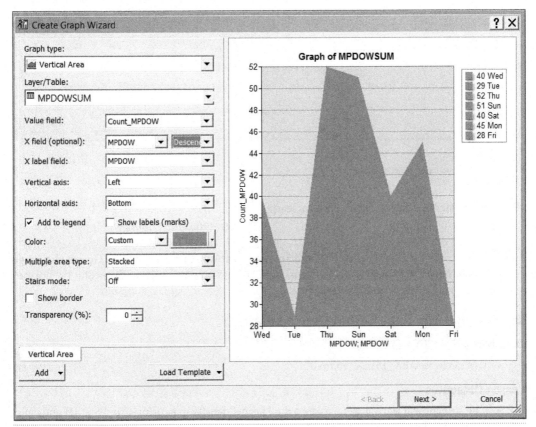

Figure E14–29

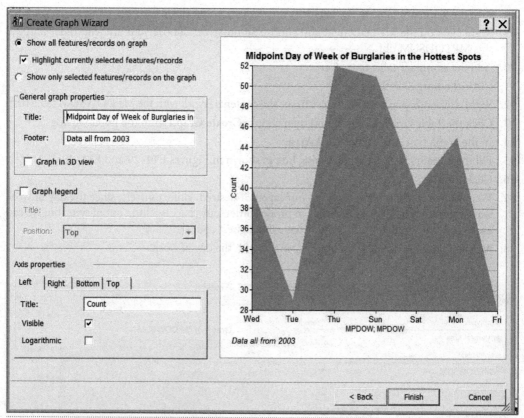

Figure E14–30

99. Your highest time periods should be at least:

    a. 0300–0359 hours
    b. 0200–0259 hours
    c. 1200–1259 hours
    d. 1300–1359 hours

100. Save your project and close ArcMap and any other software that may be open. Go get a beverage of your choice, sit back in your chair, and sigh. You are now an expert at CrimeStat III, hotspot maps, and all their related masterfulness.

■ Exercise 15: Dual Kernel Density Maps

Data Needed for This Exercise

- CIA\Exercises\EX_15\EX_15.mxd

Lesson Objectives

- The student will learn how to create a dual kernel density map using CrimeStat III and calls for service data.

Task Description

1. Open EX_15.mxd from the CIA\Exercises\EX_15 folder.

2. The chief has asked if some interventions we instituted are potentially having the desired effect, which was to reduce calls for service during Apr–Jun 2003 from the number that occurred during Jan–Mar 2003. The police department has been putting resources into a few areas and he wants to know if the goal of reducing calls for service has occurred.

3. Our steps are to:
   a. Create two new shapefiles:
      - Jan–Mar 2003
      - Apr–Jun 2003
   b. Make sure both shapefiles have *X* and *Y* coordinates and no nulls.
   c. Create MBR:
      - Get lower left *XY*
      - Get upper right *XY*
      - Get area in square miles
      - Get total street length (in feet) for the minimum bounding rectangle (MBR)
   d. Open CrimeStat III and:
      - Set up primary file (Apr–Jun 2003)
      - Set up reference file
      - Set up measurement parameters
      - Set up secondary file (Jan–Mar 2003)
      - Create dual kernel estimate
   e. Add data to ArcMap from CrimeStat and symbolize properly.
   f. Make a "pretty" map for the chief and an executive summary about what we have accomplished.

4. In this case, the Jan–Mar 2003 and Apr–Jun 2003 data have already been created for you and are in the table of contents (TOC). If you had wanted to do this yourself, you would begin by selecting by attributes on the calls for service layer where the RECVDATE >= 20030101 and RECVDATE <= 20030331 for one layer, then you can figure out the rest.

5. Take a peek at the attribute tables of each layer (right click and open attribute table), to make sure we have an *X* and *Y* coordinate in each table and that we have no 0s or missing data.

6. Wow, we have 252 records in the Jan–Mar data that have 0 for the *X* and *Y* coordinates. We will throw these out for now. In real life we might try to geocode all these incidents again, but in this case we will just place a disclaimer on the map.

7. The Apr–Jun has 292 missing *X* and *Y* coordinates, but remember that 0 is the null value in these data.

8. More disclaimers!

9. Now we need to create our MBR. Turn on both point layers to see where they are and draw your MBR.

10. At this point, we usually create a new Excel spreadsheet with cells to capture the values for use later in CrimeStat (refer ahead to Figure E15–4).

11. Your map should look something like **Figure E15–1**.

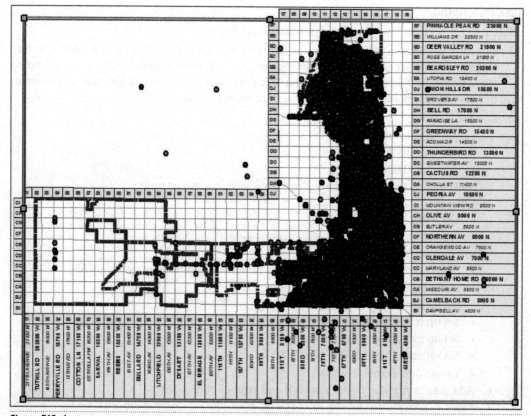

Figure E15–1

12. Now right click on the MBR, choose Properties, then choose the Area tab. Record the value (approximately 434 square miles).

13. Click on the Size and Position tab and record the lower left *XY* coordinates and the upper right *XY* coordinates of the MBR (see **Figure E15–2**).
    a. Lower Left: 527,467 / 888,879 (approximate)
    b. Upper Right: 658,239 / 987,343 (approximate)

14. Close the MBR properties.

15. Make the City_Streets_Plus layer visible and use a Select by Graphics function to select all the street segments intersecting the MBR.

16. Open the attribute table of the City_Streets_Plus layer, find the length field, right click this field, and choose **Statistics**.

17. Copy the sum of the street length (about 30842325.671376 feet) to a safe place for later.

18. Right click each of the calls for service layers and open the properties for each one. View the source tab and see where these data are stored. You will need to find these when looking from inside CrimeStat. You can see that both are stored in the CIA\Exercises\EX_15 folder (see **Figure E15–3**; alternatively, you could click on the List by Source button at the top of the TOC).

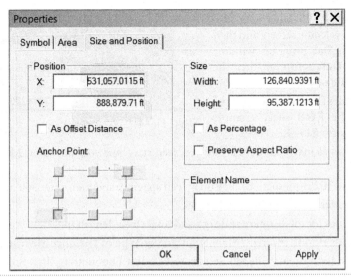

Figure E15–2

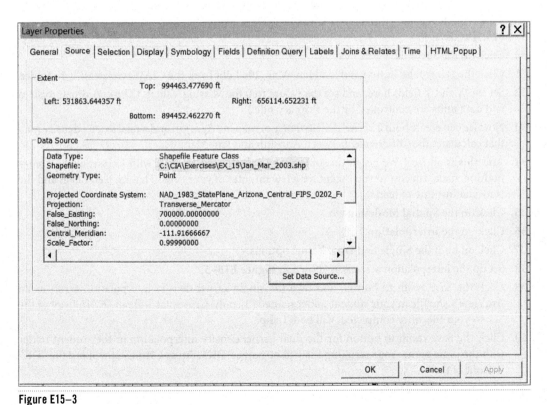

Figure E15–3

19. Now open CrimeStat.
20. Click on the welcome screen, and then in the CrimeStat program window click on the **Data setup** tab, then the **Reference File** tab.
21. Enter the values from where you stored them like the Excel sheet example shown in **Figure E15–4**.

	A	B	C
1	Statistic	Value or "X"	Value or "Y"
2	Lower Left MBR	527,467	888,879
3	Upper Right MBR	658,239	987,343
4	Sq Miles	434	N/A
5	Total Street (Feet)	30842325.7	Feet

Figure E15–4

22. *Note*: Your values may be different due to screen size, how you drew your MBR, and how you rounded up.
23. In the **cell specification** section, click on **by cell spacing**, and then enter **300** in the cell size box.
24. Click on the **Measurement Parameters** tab.
25. Enter the values for total **square mileage** and total **street length** in feet.
26. Check that box next to Indirect (Manhattan) in the **Type of Distance Measurement** section.
27. Now click on the Primary File tab and browse (Select Files button, then Browse) to the CIA\Exercises\EX_15 area and find the Apr–Jun_2003.dbf file and load it into CrimeStat.
28. Once added to the Primary file tab, set the *X* and *Y* coordinate fields and do not forget to set the missing values to 0 for both the *X* and *Y* coordinates.
29. Check the **Projected (Euclidean) Units** box, **Data Units** should be feet, and **Time Units** can be left at days.
30. Click on the **Secondary File** tab.
31. Click the Select Files button and load Jan–Mar_2003.dbf from the CIA\Exercises\EX_15 folder.
32. Set the *X* and *Y* fields here, and set the values to 0 for Missing Values. (The coordinate system and data units are controlled by the Primary File.)
33. Now we can create both a kernel density hotspot map for Apr–Jun and a dual kernel density map that calculates the "difference" between Apr–Jun and Jan–Mar 2003.
34. And this is all free! We get to do some very sophisticated analysis with CrimeStat for free—nothing, nada, zip cost to you except for a few minutes of your time. Thanks, Ned Levin and the National Institute of Justice.
35. Click on the **Spatial Modeling** tab.
36. Click on the **Interpolation I** tab.
37. Click on both the **Single** and **Dual** kernel options.
38. Set up the interpolation screens as shown in **Figure E15–5**.
39. Click the Save result to button, and save the single kernel density interpolation result as an ArcView *.shp file in your student folder named "1" only. CrimeStat will put "K" In front of the "1," so your file, once completed, will be **K1.shp**.
40. Click the Save result to button for the dual kernel density interpolation in the student folder with the same name. Your resulting file will be named **DK1.shp** as CrimeStat will put the "DK" in front of the "1."
41. Click the **Compute** button.

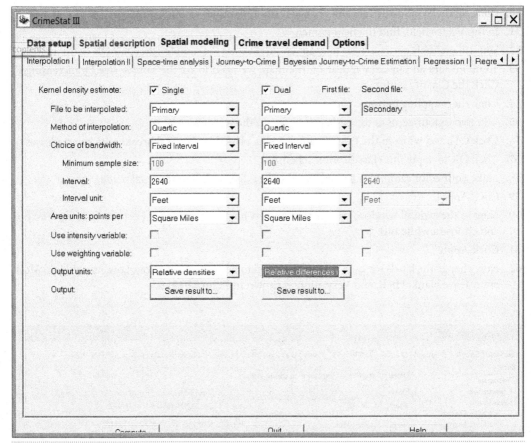

Figure E15–5

Ned Levine (2010). *CrimeStat III: A Spatial Statistics Program for the Analysis of Crime Incident Locations* (v 3.3). Ned Levine & Associates, Houston, TX, and the National Institute of Justice, Washington, DC. July. http://www.icpsr.umich.edu/CrimeStat.

42. After a few moments the functions will be done running. Click the Close button of the **CrimeStat Results** screen *only*, but DO NOT CLOSE CrimeStat at this time.
43. Minimize CrimeStat.
44. Go back to ArcMap and click the Add Data button.
45. Add the K1.shp and DK1.shp layers into the ArcMap project.
46. If prompted, answer OK to the warning about Spatial References for the two layers.
47. Save your project in your student folder as EX_15.mxd.
48. Uncheck the DK1 layer in the TOC for the time being and move both the K1 and DK1 layers to the bottom of the TOC.
49. Double click K1, and in the General tab of the Properties dialog, change the Layer Name to Apr–Jun 2003 CFS Hot Spots.

50. Click on the Symbology tab, and change it to a Quantities classification type.

51. In the Values field, find the field named "Z."

52. You will probably get a warning message about meeting the sample size. Click OK to this message.

53. To make sure all our data appear on the map, we need to fix the sample size by increasing it. Click the Classify button.

54. Click the Sampling button.

55. Add two to four zeros at the end of the value in the window.

56. Click OK, and while in the Classification menu, classify as Natural breaks with seven classes.

57. Click OK to apply this classification schema.

58. Make your color ramp Blue to Red ("cold to hot diverging" is the actual name).

59. Click Apply.

60. Now in the symbol window, change the "coldest blue" to a white fill (double click the blue box and choose a white fill).

61. Click Apply.

62. Now change the labels for each symbol from top to bottom as Very Low, Low, leave blank, Moderate, leave blank, High, and Very High as shown in **Figure E15–6**.

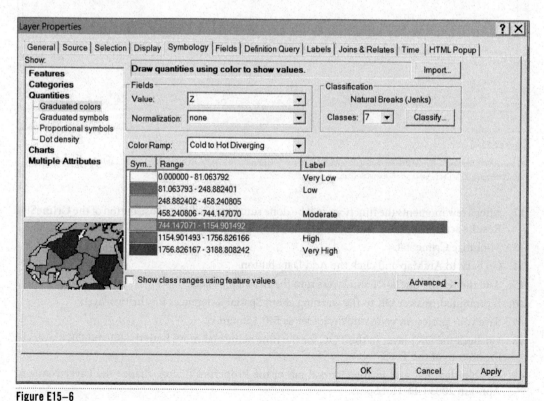

Figure E15–6

63. Click Apply and then OK.

64. Observe on the map that we have color, but we have outlines around every polygon that has an interpolated Z value (zoom in to see this). We need to get rid of the outlines. Double click the Apr–Jun 2003 CFS Hot Spots layer to open the properties and go to the Symbology tab.

65. Click on the top Symbol box (white), hold the shift key down, and click on the bottommost box (red) to select all the symbols.

66. Right click on the selected symbols, and choose Properties for Selected Symbols.

67. Change the outline color to No Color and click OK.

68. Click Apply and OK.

69. Your map should now resemble **Figure E15–7** (with the CFS point layers turned off).

70. We have at least five very distinct hotspots that we could point out to the chief as he requested. If we turn on the Focus Area layer in the TOC, we can also see that several of the focus areas overlap these hot areas.

71. Now we need to see if our interventions have had any effect between the two time periods.

72. Make the Apr–Jun 2003 hotspot layer nonvisible, and make the DK1 layer visible. Rename the DK1 layer as "Spatial Trend of CFS" in the TOC.

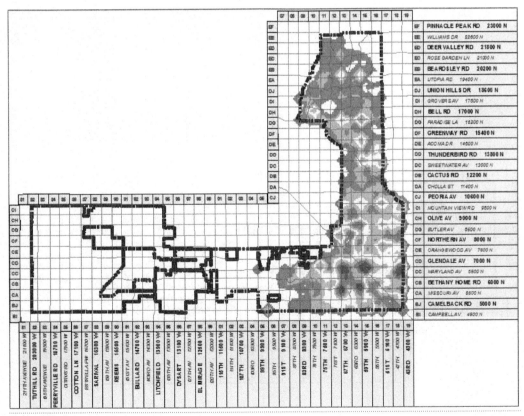

Figure E15–7

73. Change the Symbology to be about the same as the Apr–Jun hotspots except:
    a. Make it a green to red color ramp and do not make the lowest value white—leave it dark green. Remove the outline from all colors.
    b. Make the value that covers most of the map (probably yellow or orange) have a white fill.
    c. Change the labels to read:
        i. Relative decrease
        ii. Decrease
        iii. Slight decrease
        iv. Blank
        v. Blank
        vi. Stable
        vii. Relative increase
    d. This usually works, but you have to look closely at the values. If all values are negative, then all we saw were decreases.
    e. If all were positive, then we saw all increases.
74. Your map should now look like **Figure E15–8**.
75. Your legend will likely look similar to **Figure E15–9**.
76. Observe that five of the seven classifications are showing negative values or a decrease in calls for service to some degree.

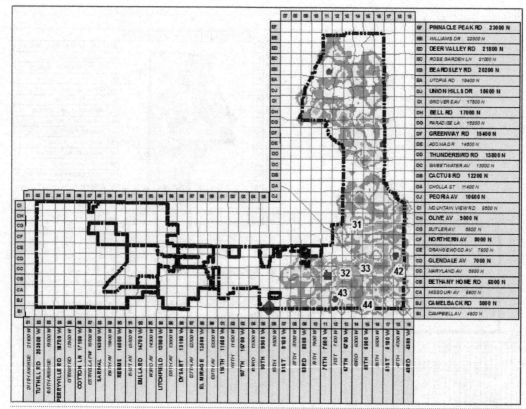

Figure E15–8

77. The sixth value goes from a negative value to a positive value, which basically means that calls for service are fairly stable in these areas.

78. All the positive values in the seventh classification show increases in calls for service between the two time periods.

79. Because these values are somewhat speculative, we will not usually show the values in the legend and only show the wording of relative decrease, increase, etc. The values are shown in Figure E15–9 for demonstration purposes.

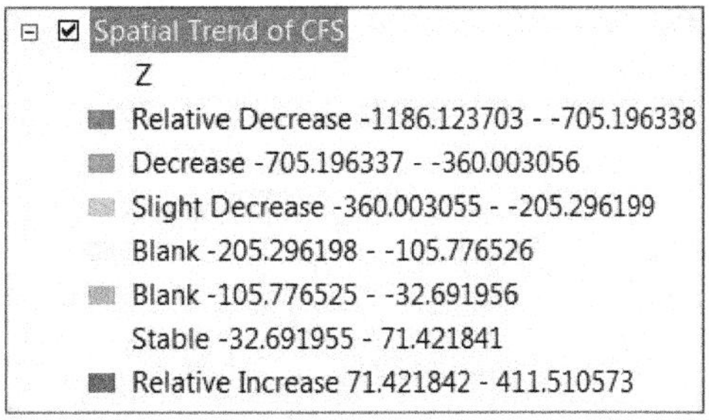

☐ ☑ Spatial Trend of CFS
      Z
   ▨ Relative Decrease -1186.123703 - -705.196338
   ▨ Decrease -705.196337 - -360.003056
   ▨ Slight Decrease -360.003055 - -205.296199
      Blank -205.296198 - -105.776526
   ▨ Blank -105.776525 - -32.691956
      Stable -32.691955 - 71.421841
   ▨ Relative Increase 71.421842 - 411.510573

Figure E15–9

80. Now check out the Focus Areas, right click, and uncheck the Label Features item so you can see what effect the interventions have had on the various areas.

81. We can see that Focus Areas 33 and 44 saw the highest decreases, but all of them saw some level of decreases.

82. Using a Select by Location, we could create a table that showed the actual numbers for each Focus Area.

83. Click on Selection in the main menu bar, and then Select by Location.

84. Select from both the calls for service time period layers that intersect the Focus Areas layer. Click Apply and OK.

85. Right click on both selected layers (one at a time), then Data → Export data to make the selected records two new shapefiles.

86. Call them Jan–Mar.shp and Apr–Jun.shp and save them to your student folder.

87. Add the new layers to the current project.

88. One at a time, do a spatial join from the Focus Areas layer to the CFS point layer. You do not need to add these to the current project, but save them to your student folder as Jan–MarJoin .shp and Apr–JunJoin.shp.

89. Open Excel and open both of the DBF tables for these two shapefiles.

90. Create a pivot table to include all data in each spreadsheet. (Focus Area is in the ID column and count values on REPORT_NO.)

91. Create a final table that looks like **Figure E15–10**.

92. We can see that the spatial trends shown in the dual kernel density map represent the actual data for each focus area through this combination. We can show the change both spatially, and through a table analyzing the data from a spatial join.

FOCUS AREA	JAN-MAR	APR-JUN	% CHANGE
31	351	314	-10.5%
32	1,017	939	-7.7%
33	983	737	-25.0%
42	735	671	-8.7%
43	595	511	-14.1%
44	606	439	-27.6%
Grand Total	4,287	3,611	-15.8%

93. Thank you for joining us in the exploration of the powerful density tools within CrimeStat. Did we mention that it was FREE?!

94. Close CrimeStat and Save and close your project.

Figure E15–10

■ Exercise 15b: Creating Repeat Address Maps

Data Needed for This Exercise

- Create a new map from scratch and load the following data at a minimum:
  - CIA\Data\File Geodatabase\GIS_Layers.gdb
    - Street_Labels
    - Basic_Street_Label_An
    - Boundaries → Grids_P
    - Boundaries → City_Boundaries_P
  - CIA\Exercises\EX_15
    - Apr_Jun_2003.shp
- Symbolize the data as needed to make it look good visually and ready yourself for the rest of this lesson.

Lesson Objectives

- The student will learn how to create a repeat address analysis using the Spatial Statistics toolbox.
- A comparison of this to the mode and fuzzy mode and the Spatial Statistics Tools option will be demonstrated.

Task Description

1. After completing the creation of your new map, save it to your student folder as EX_15b.mxd (alternatively, you can open CIA\Exercises\EX_15\EX_15b.mxd).
2. No hotspot map ever ends with the actual map. As we found in the dual kernel density exercise, we will often analyze the data within our focus areas, or other parts of the map along with the map. We not only want to tell officers *where*, but also whenever possible: *who, what, when,* and *why*. We also want to advise them *how many* for most of our analyses.
3. One of the additional *where* items is to find those addresses within focus areas or generally citywide that have more than 1, 5, or 10 criminal events or calls for service occurring over time. These are called repeat addresses analysis, or for a map, a graduated point map.
4. We can create these with CrimeStat or with the Spatial Statistics tools in the ArcToolbox.
5. We will start with CrimeStat.
6. To demonstrate, open the attribute table of the Apr–Jun cfs data. Right click the Address field and sort in Ascending order.
7. Click on the Table Options button, and choose Find and Replace.
8. In the Find and Replace dialog, type: 6199 W OLIVE AV.
9. Now click the Find Next button.
10. This will take you to the first occurrence of this address. Notice that there are several.
11. Highlight this record, then at the far left box in the same row, right click and choose Zoom to Selected.
12. Observe on the map that there appears to be only one dot.
13. Choose the Identify tool from the tools toolbar.
14. Click on this point.

15. There are actually 99 calls for service at exactly this point (see bottom of the Identify window).

16. These points are at exactly the same place but we could not tell that visually. A hotspot map would possibly show this area as a hotspot, but would not show this address as responsible for 99 of the events within the hotspot.

17. This is where graduated point maps come in.

18. Open CrimeStat 3.3.

19. It is very easy to use CrimeStat to calculate the mode and fuzzy mode.

20. *Mode* might be defined as finding all those locations that are the same, and creating a summary table of all the values at an *X* and *Y* coordinate. *Fuzzy mode* creates a similar table, but uses distances between *X* and *Y* coordinates and comes up with a summary table counting the totals events that occurred at and around a point.

21. The output for both of these is a .DBF table.

22. In CrimeStat, set up the primary file to be the Apr–Jun calls for service data (Apr_Jun_2003.dbf) found in CIA\Exercises\EX_15 folder as with EX_15.

23. For this hotspot routine, we do not need a Reference File or Measurement Parameters.

24. Click on Spatial Description → 'Hotspot' Analysis 1.

25. Click the checkboxes near Mode and Fuzzy mode.

26. Under the Fuzzy mode section, enter 1000 and Feet in the Radius section. This determines how far away the routine searches for events.

27. Save result to your student folder for both layers as MyStudentFolder\1 (as a .DBF).

28. Click Compute.

29. When done, close the Results window, but do not close CrimeStat (the reason we do not close CrimeStat here is so that if something did go wrong, we could recheck our settings, find any errors, make changes, and then run it again).

30. Make ArcMap the active window, and click the Add Data button. Add the Mode1.dbf and the Fmode1.dbf files to the project.

31. Right click Mode1.dbf, and choose Display XY Data from the popup dialog.

32. Choose whatever defaults come up for projection and click OK.

33. Double click on the Mode1 event theme and go to the Symbology tab.

34. Make this a quantities classification type.

35. Choose Graduated Symbols as the classification type under Quantities.

36. The Value Field = FREQ.

37. Change the Symbol Size from 1 to 18.

38. Click Apply and OK.

39. Check this out! It shows all the locations where a call was received based on how many calls were received at the identical *X* and *Y* coordinates. There are 7833 records or 7833 unique *X* and *Y* coordinates.

40. Make this layer nonvisible.

41. Recreate steps 31–39 for the FMode1.dbf.

42. Notice how we still have 7833 records in the table, but the values for the FREQ are much higher. It is showing the results of the locations plus counts of a 1000-ft radius around each point.

43. We can sometimes use this to show which bars, for instance, are problematic, both because of calls that occurred there, and also of calls occurring within 500 feet, 1000 feet, etc. We might think of these as the highest risk locations. In our case, we are just feeding CrimeStat total calls for service, but we could use the example for bars by all violent crimes, or even metal thefts.

44. If you zoom in and out of both layers (one at a time, of course), you will see different clusters of graduated points based on the number of crimes at or around the points the program found.

45. We can also perform the "mode" analysis from within ArcMap and the ArcToolbox → Spatial Statistics Tools.

46. Make both of our CrimeStat layers nonvisible.

47. Open ArcToolbox at the right of the map display.

48. When it opens, double click on the **Spatial Statistics Tools** item.

49. Double click on **Rendering** then double click on **Collect Events with Rendering**.

50. In the dialog window enter the following:
    a. Input Incident Features: = CIA\Exercises\EX_15\Apr_Jun_2003.shp
    b. Output Layer File: = YourStudentFolder\Apr_Jun_2003_CollectEvents_C.lyr
    c. Output Weighted Point Feature Class: = YourStudentFolder\Apr_Jun_2003_CollectEvents

51. Click OK to run it.

52. It will take a minute or so to run. You can tell if a routine is running by looking at the bottom right of the map display. If a routine is running, a light blue scrolling banner will be visible.

53. Once added to the project, change the Symbology to 1 to 18 as we did with the other event layers from CrimeStat.

54. Open the Properties → Symbology tab for the new layer and observe that the Value field is ICOUNT and the classification type is equal interval. (If yours is something else, that is okay, it is just that someone has set the default display to the default.mxd on the computer.) This is usually acceptable for these types of frequency tables and we see that we get more of a difference between the graduated points than with natural breaks that we used for the Mode and Fuzzy mode layers.

55. Play around with the different classification types for the mode (CrimeStat) and the spatial statistics "mode" result (from the Spatial Statistics tools in ArcMap) and see how they appear the same depending on the classification type you use.

56. In addition, if we add a hotspot layer of the same data to the project (CIA\Exercises\EX_15\ K1.shp), we can identify what locations are high by zooming in and out of our hotspots on the map and clicking on the largest of the graduated points to determine which addresses contribute most to a hotspot.

57. Give this a try.

58. When finished observing how these two types of hotspot indicators could help you provide better information to your staff and officers, save and close your project.

■ Exercise 15c: Hotspot Clustering Methods

Data Needed for This Exercise
- YourStudentFolder\EX_15b.mxd

Lesson Objectives

- The student will learn how the clustering method of Nearest Neighbor Hierarchical clustering (NNHC) works in CrimeStat.
- The student will learn how the K-Means hotspot method works.
- The student will learn how the clustering hotspot routine called Stac works in CrimeStat.

Task Description

1. Open your saved file from the exercise (alternatively, you can open CIA\Exercises\EX_15\EX_15b .mxd).
2. We are going to explore some less commonly used methods of determining hotspots. These methods are often discussed as distance measures or clustering methods for determining hotspots. Here we are using statistical methods that measure how many points are within a certain distance of each other. This is a density calculation, however instead of using cells, it bases everything on how clustered the data are.
3. Go up to Selection → Select by Attributes in the main menu bar.
4. Enter the following:
   - Layer: = Apr_Jun_2003 [checked?]
   - Method: Create a new Selection
   - SQL Query: = "X" <> 0
5. Click OK to run the query.
6. This query gets the events that did not geocode out of the analysis, because distance and clustering are going to be analyzed and those events are not in their correct places so we have to throw them out. Once points are selected, right click on Apr_Jun_2003, go to Data and click on Export Data to create a new shapefile of the selected features (those with *X* and *Y* coordinates only). Name it Apr_Jun_2003XY and save it to your student folder. Now, in the Spatial Statistics Toolbox, double click on the Analyzing Patterns toolbox.
7. Double click on the Average Nearest Neighbors tool to open it.
8. In the Average Nearest Neighbor dialog box, enter (see **Figure E15–11**):
   - Input Feature Class = Apr_Jun_2003XY
   - Distance Method: = MANHATTAN_DISTANCE
   - Check: Generate Report (optional)
9. Click OK to run the function. This analysis checks to see if the data are clustered, random, or dispersed and thus is checking for spatial autocorrelation.
10. It will take several minutes for this to run and when it is done a popup notice will appear at the bottom right of the project area (see **Figure E15–12**).
11. Click on this notice to open it. (If the notice closes before you can click on it, you can bring the results window up by clicking on **Geoprocessing** in the menu bar and then **Results** in the popup dialog. See **Figure E15–13**.)
12. Find the HTML Report part that will look like:
    - HTML Report File: NearestNeighbor_Result1.html
13. Double click this report file to open it in Windows Internet Explorer.

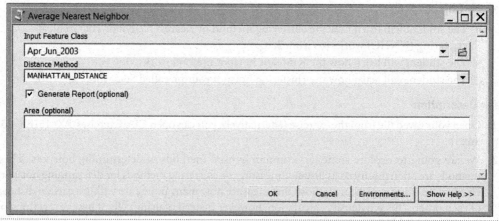

Figure E15–11

Figure E15–12

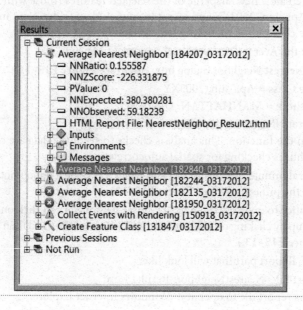

Figure E15–13

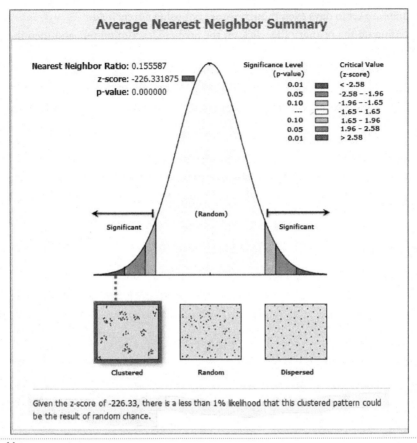

Figure E15–14

14. The report will advise you that the data appear to be clustered (see **Figure E15–14**). Considering this, we can now use the Nearest Neighbor Hierarchical Clustering hotspot routine along with the K-Means and STAC clustering routines.

15. As a sidebar, in the Analyzing Patterns toolbox, we can check to see if aggregated data to polygons are clustered, random, or dispersed, or do other point analyses like the Ripley's K analysis.

16. Although we will not go into these other options, you should explore them and see how they could be used to determine if your data are patterned such that analysis would actually show something.

17. So now that we know our data is clustered, we can apply the other tools in the CrimeStat toolbox.

18. Close the Results window.

19. Save your project as EX_15c.mxd in your student folder.

20. Now open CrimeStat and set up the primary file as Apr_Jun_2003XY.dbf as the source file. Set the *X* and *Y* fields accordingly (if you still have records without an *X* or *Y* coordinate value set the missing values to 0).

21. The data are Projected (Euclidean), the Data Units are set to feet.

22. Time units are set to days even though we are not using a time field.

23. After setting up the primary file, click on the Spatial Description tab, and then the 'Hot Spot' Analysis1 tab.

24. Check the box next to Nearest Neighbor Hierarchical Clustering.

25. Complete the NNH dialog as shown in **Figure E15–15**.

26. Save Ellipses and Save Convex Hulls to… should both be set to ArcView 'SHP' (shapefiles), and they should be saved to your student folder with the file name of 15c.

27. Now click the Compute button.

28. This will take a while to run and will go through many different phases while you watch. When done, close the Compute dialog window, but leave CrimeStat open for now.

29. Add the NNH files and the CNNH files to the map project from your student folder.

30. NNH115c is the first order of ellipses, which are the smallest, or most distinctly clustered, data.

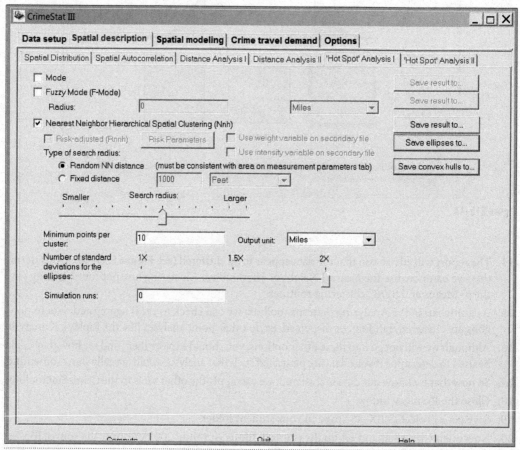

Figure E15–15

Ned Levine (2010). *CrimeStat III: A Spatial Statistics Program for the Analysis of Crime Incident Locations* (v 3.3). Ned Levine & Associates, Houston, TX, and the National Institute of Justice, Washington, DC. July. http://www.icpsr.umich.edu/CrimeStat.

31. NNH215c are a little bigger, and NNH415c ellipses are the largest and highlight most of the city.
32. In crime analysis, we most often use the first or second order ellipses.
33. The CNNH115c convex hulls are the smallest and include all the clustered points in that order.
34. The other convex hull polygons get larger as those clusters get larger.
35. Make each layer visible and nonvisible and see how they change with each layer.
36. Now let's run the K-Means and STAC clustering methods in CrimeStat.
37. Make CrimeStat the active program and uncheck the Nearest Neighbor Hierarchical clustering checkbox in the 'Hot Spot' Analysis 1 dialog. Click on the 'Hot Spot' Analysis 2 tab.
38. Check the box next to the Spatial and Temporal Analysis of Crime (STAC) and K-Means functions.
39. Click the STAC Parameters button and complete the dialog window as shown in **Figure E15–16**.
40. Make sure the Boundary section is checked as **From data set**.
41. Click OK.
42. Now change the number of clusters for the K-Means section to 20, and the separation to 6.0.
43. Save the ellipses and the convex hulls for both functions (4 total) as 15c in your student folder (i.e., YourStudentFolder\15c).
44. Save them all as ArcView SHP (shapefiles).
45. Click the Compute button.
46. It will take a few seconds to run and then we can add the data to the project.
47. Close the Compute window and leave CrimeStat open.
48. Make ArcMap active and then add the following layers from your student folder:
    - CKM15c (K-Means order 1 convex hulls)
    - KM15c (K-Means level 1 ellipses)
    - CST15c (STAC order 1 convex hulls)
    - ST15c (STAC order 1 ellipses)

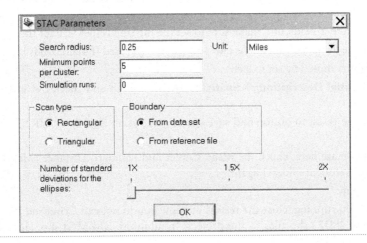

Figure E15–16

Ned Levine (2010). *CrimeStat III: A Spatial Statistics Program for the Analysis of Crime Incident Locations* (v 3.3). Ned Levine & Associates, Houston, TX, and the National Institute of Justice, Washington, DC. July. http://www.icpsr.umich.edu/CrimeStat.

49. In my crime analysis career, I've never found much usefulness in K-Means results. If you view them one at a time, you will see that the K-Means results are all over the city and include every point.

50. The STAC results are more precise and useful, and better mimic a density map. They typically show the same areas that are "hot."

51. Save your project and close ArcMap and CrimeStat.

■ Exercise 16: The Spatial Statistics Toolbox

Data Needed for This Exercise

- CIA\Exercises\EX_16\EX_16.mxd

Lesson Objectives

- The student will learn how to create Stdev ellipses in CrimeStat III and ArcToolbox.
- The student will learn how to create StDev rectangles in CrimeStat III.
- The student will learn how to create a Mean Center in CrimeStat III.

Task Description

1. There are a few reasons why we might want to create standard deviation ellipses. One is for tactical analysis, and another is to see how data might be distributed in different zones. Open CIA\Exercises\EX_16\EX_16.mxd.

2. Our first view of the map is zoomed in to several burglaries that we feel are part of the same offender's modus operandi (MO).

3. We are going to use CrimeStat to create the mean center and standard deviation ellipses (68 and 95% probabilities).

4. Open CrimeStat III and set up the primary file to be CIA\Data\Shapefiles\Offenses\BURGLARY_CASES_ALL.dbf.

5. Set up the X and Y fields, and make sure to set the missing values to 0 for these two fields.

6. Make sure the Projection section is checked where Projected (Euclidean) is located.

7. The Data units should be set to feet.

8. Click the **Spatial Description** → **Spatial Distribution** tab and check the Standard Deviation Ellipses item.

9. Click the Save result to button and save your results as an ArcView .SHP file to your student folder\1.

10. Now while we are here, check the Mean Center and Standard Distance (Mcssd) option. Save result to your student folder\1 again.

11. Click Compute.

12. When finished running, close the results window but do not exit CrimeStat III. Add the SDE1 .shp and the 2SDE1.shp files to the project. In addition, add MC1.shp, HM1.shp, Gm1.shp, XYD1.shp, and SDD1.shp.

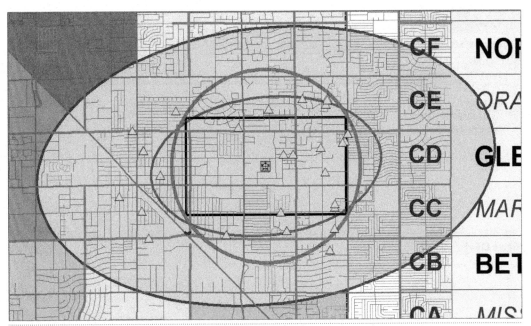

Figure E16–1

13. Change the symbology so that you can see SDE1 above the 2SDE1 layer. In addition, change the mean center (MC1) to a large blue box, and symbolize the other point and polygon data so we can see all of them.

14. The map should look like **Figure E16–1**.

15. The offender will most likely hit within one of these standard deviation ellipses (SDE1 and 2SDE1) about 80% of the time, based on research by one of the authors. We also have the 68% probability rectangle (XYD1) and the 68% probability circle (SDD1), and if we overlap all of these, we have a smaller area where the next crime would occur. We can easily geoprocess this using the draw tool to highlight the areas where the various spatial statistics overlap.

16. The Mean Center (MC1) can also be used to identify the area where the offender is most likely to live. Research by Ned Levine (CompStat III's creator) has shown that in many cases the offender may live or have his or her anchor point within 1 mile of this mean center.

17. In addition, the GM1, or geometric mean, and the HM1, or harmonic mean, are different ways to calculate the mean. Author Bryan Hill has seen in his experience that the more often that these three methods of determining the mean appear in the same place, it is more likely that the offender lives near the mean center or within a mile of it and is a marauder instead of a commuter.

18. Turn off the SDE layers for the next part of the exercise.

19. We want to find out how our data is distributed in our patrol beats for calls for service between April and June of 2003.

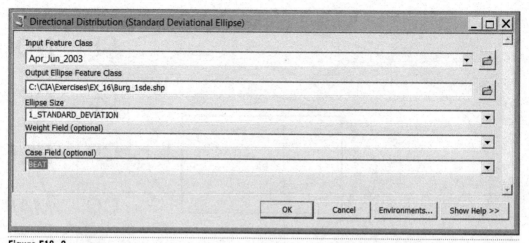

Figure E16–2

20. Observe that we have Apr_Jun_2003 data in our TOC. Zoom to this layer. Right click this layer and open the attribute table.

21. Go all the way to the right and see that we have added a field called BEAT, which is a text field that is a two-character defined field.

22. Close the attribute table.

23. Click on the ArcToolbox and the Spatial Statistics toolbox.

24. Double click on the **Measuring Geographic Distributions** toolbox, and then double click on the **Directional Distribution (Standard Deviation Ellipses)** tool.

25. Complete the SDE ellipse dialog as shown in **Figure E16–2**.

26. Save the Output Feature class to your student folder as Burg_1SDE.shp. Click OK.

27. After this is done, repeat steps 23–26, however, change the Ellipse Size to 2_Standard_Deviations.

28. Also, change the name to Burg_2SDE.shp.

29. If we look at the Burg_1SDE layer, we can see that we have a Stdev ellipse for each beat and one representing citywide.

30. The individual beat Stdev ellipses show the general directionality of calls for service for this time period within each beat.

31. After some symbolizing, your map should look like **Figure E16–3**.

32. This is most often used in research to detect change in the directionality of data. It may also lead to discovery of what directional pattern is evident in the data for each area we create ellipses for.

33. These different spatial techniques can be created in either CrimeStat III or the Spatial Statistics toolbox. I will admit that the Spatial Statistics toolbox has a few more options, but you need to decide for yourself which one you are most comfortable with and use it enough to be competent with it.

34. This concludes Exercise 16. Save your project and close ArcMap and CrimeStat III.

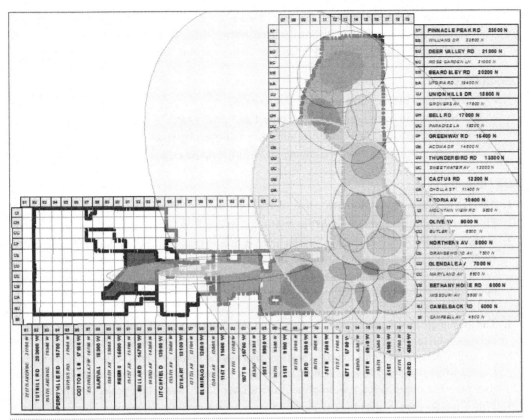

Figure E16–3

Section 3: Advanced-Level GIS

■ Exercise 17: Problem Solving Using Hotspots

Data Needed for This Exercise

- In this exercise you will need to add data to a map. The list below shows the layers we need to make our map and do the analysis. You will need to use your knowledge to decide what layers are actually needed:
  - A street layer
  - Grids
  - Political boundary
  - Robberies
  - Street label annotation
  - Street label boxes
- The layers above are suggestions, but you decide what layers to use and where to obtain them. (The CIA\Data folder is always a good place to start looking.)
- Your objective is to analyze robberies in 2004, and determine where the hottest areas are. We also want to see if there are any repeat addresses for robbery in the top 3 hottest areas.

- You will need to create charts of the days of week and times of day when these robberies are occurring citywide and possibly for the three hottest areas as desired.
- You will then need to complete a bulletin or analysis report showing all of this information.

Lesson Objectives

- The student will learn how to create a hotpot map.
- The student will learn how to create a repeat addresses map.
- The student will learn how to create summary tables and graphs.
- The student will learn how to combine into a bulletin and report.

Task Description

1. This is a regular analysis effort in a crime analysis unit and is problem-solving policing at its finest.
2. First, create your map and symbolize everything so that it looks good and presents the data well.
3. In many Crime Analysis Units, a master map is often created and then the map is Saved As another name, usually named after the analysis project being undertaken at the time. In this case you could start from scratch and practice creating a brand new map project, or you could open CIA\Exercises\EX_1\EX_1d.mxd and then Save As Robbery2004.mxd in your student folder as an example.
4. The idea of creating a master map project is to save time creating all of the layers and classifications we want to use all the time. Another option would be to create a folder with several *.LYR, or layer, files. A layer file holds the classification information and points to the data wherever it was located when the layer file was created. In the layer file method, when you want to create a new standard-style map project, you simply add all the layer files to a new map project and get to work.
5. With a master map project file (master.mxd), you want to add the layers you want to use in the majority of the maps you will create or analyses you will work on. Then you do not do any actual analysis with this project, but only copy it or save the map project as another name when you want to do analysis. If you start doing analysis, or change the master file in any way, then you run the risk of it being corrupted and you may find yourself having to create a new master project file.
6. Depending on the work you do in crime mapping, you may find the master project is the way to go, you may find that creating layer files works the best for you, or you might even find that creating a new map from scratch each time is most appealing to you. Practicing creating and developing many new maps from scratch will give you the skills needed to make the decision on a master map at a later time.
7. If you copy EX_1d.mxd, you will then need to add the Offense_Data layer from the File or Personal Geodatabases area, or the shapefile to continue (alternatively, you could open EX_17. mxd and use it).
8. Complete an attribute query to find the robberies in 2004.
   a. In the menu bar, click Select → Select by Attributes
      - Enter: "UCRTYPE" = 'ROBBERY' AND ("MIDPOINT" >= date '2004-01-01 00:00:00' AND "MIDPOINT" <= date '2004-12-31 00:00:00')
9. Create a new shapefile of the results of your query:
   a. Data → Export Data → Selected records only
10. Add the new layer to the current project.

11. Use the draw rectangle tool to create a minimum bounding rectangle (MBR) and right click the rectangle and choose Properties from the dialog box. In the Size and Position tab, collect the:

    a. Lower *X* and *Y* coordinate
    b. Upper *X* and *Y* coordinate
    c. Total Square Mileage of MBR

12. Now, make the City_Streets_L layer the only selectable layer by clicking the **List by Selection** button at the top of the TOC (fourth from left) and then gather the following data after choosing Selection → Select by Graphics:

    a. Total street length in feet inside MBR

13. You will need to open the City_Streets_L layer's attribute table and get *statistics* on the length field.

14. Use CrimeStat to create a hotspot map (single interpolation; refer to Exercise 14 for assistance).

15. Decide on a MS Word bulletin template you might want to use (suggestion: templates are saved in CIA\Resources\Sample_Bulletins). After the hotspot analysis is done, your map should resemble **Figure E17–1**.

16. Now we need to identify the top three hotspot areas.

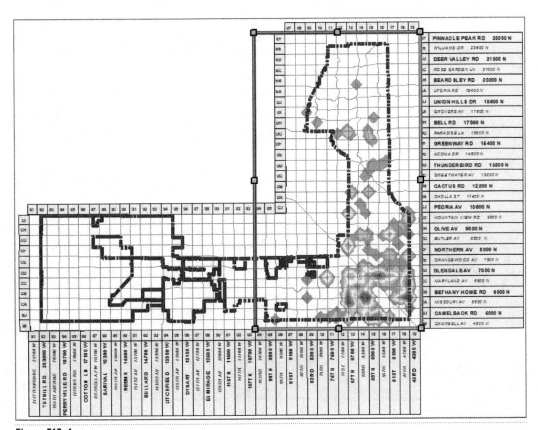

Figure E17–1

17. In the Properties → Symbology tab for the interpolation (K1.shp) layer, look at the highest Z score range; it should be between 0.000186 and 0.000295 approximately (your scores may be different due to the size of your MBR, and the settings you used in CrimeStat). The settings used in CrimeStat for these results were:

   a. Cell Specification = 150 ft
   b. Fixed Interval = 2640 feet
   c. Probabilities Output

18. To start, let's select our interpolation layer (K1 if you named the output 1) where the Z value is >= 0.000186.

19. We could also classify our data by standard deviation and use the top three classification ranges to make up our top three hottest spots. While this would likely give us larger areas than we want to deal with for this project, it is an option.

20. You may need to experiment with step 17 to get only the top three areas. (For my interpolation layer "Z" >= 0.000215 worked to give me just the top three areas.) Your map and selection should appear just like or similar to the map in **Figure E17–2**.

21. Now that we have these areas selected, we want to highlight a little more around them to make sure we do not miss any points that make up these hottest spots, so we will do a Select by Location for those additional areas within one-tenth of a mile around these selected areas. (Go up to Selection → Select by Location and choose the K1 hotspot layer as the target layer, and choose The Source layer to be the same layer. Then choose Target layer(s) features that are within a distance of the Source layer features as the spatial selection method and add 0.10 mile as a search distance.)

22. Once you've identified these three hottest spots, export them to a new shapefile (3HottestSpots.shp).

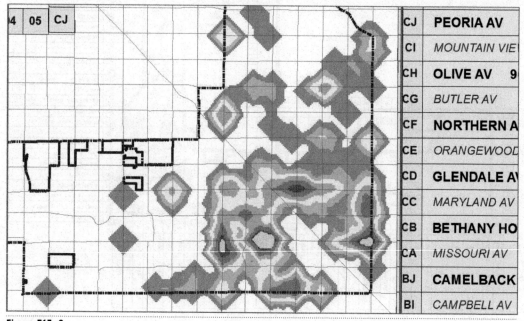

Figure E17–2

23. Add a new field to the three hottest spots called Dissolve as a short integer. In order to calculate a field, we need to right click on the field name (dissolve), then choose Field Calculator. In the box below the field listing, enter the value and click OK. Since these are numbers, we can enter them directly as 1, 2, and 3. If this was a text field, we would need to enter them as "1," "2," and "3."

24. We can use the same values we used to determine the ranges we will call our top three hottest spots. Select the first hotspot by drawing a box around it with the Select Features tool in the standard toolbar. Now field calculate the dissolve field to be 1. Repeat this operation for the second hottest area and calculate the dissolve field to be 2. Repeat this for the third hottest spot, and calculate the dissolve field to be 3.

25. Unselect any records in the 3HottestSpots layer so that the dissolve process will run on all of the data and not just the last selected records.

26. Now click on **Geoprocessing** in the main menu bar, and choose **Dissolve** from the popup dialog.

27. Complete the dissolve dialog as shown in **Figure E17-3**.

28. Name this layer 3Hot.shp and save it to your student folder. You could also add the Z field as a statistics field and ask for the sum as the type of statistic you wanted.

29. Once completed, you should have three polygons that outline the three hottest spots for robberies in 2004 year to date (which in this case is only 6 months of data). Now we need to do some analysis of the robberies that are within these three areas, and possibly for all robberies during this time period.

30. You might want to turn off the (original) 3Hottestspots layer at this time to avoid confusion. (Removing it from the project might be even better.)

31. Use the Select by Location function to select all of the robberies that are within the 3hot.shp layer.

32. The first thing we might note for our bulletin is that there are 242 robberies in 2004, and 41 of them intersected the 3 hottest spots. (Again, your results may be slightly different depending on

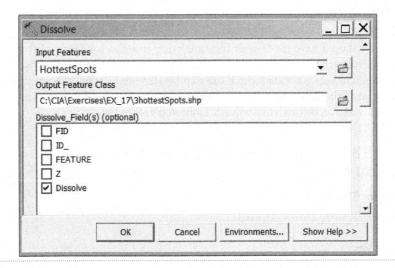

Figure E17-3

the size of your MBR, your Interpolation settings, and your search criteria when defining the sizes of the three hottest spots.) This represents 16.9% of the total robberies.

33. Now open Excel and create a spreadsheet and pivot table to do a repeat address analysis, time of day and day of week, and other similar analyses found in CIA\Exercises\EX_17\Rob2004.xlsx.

   To get the data ready, you may want to do a spatial join between the 2004 robberies and the 3Hottestspots layer. First, make sure there are no selections on any data in the map project. To do this you would need to select the 2004 robberies layer, then right click on this layer and choose Joins and Relates → Join from the popup dialog. Then choose **Join data from** another layer based on spatial location. Now choose the 3hot.shp layer as the layer to join to robberies. Then check "it falls inside." We only want the robberies that are within the three hottest spots polygons. If we wanted all of the robberies, then we might choose the "is closest to it" option. In this case we would get all the robberies, and a distance to the closest three hotspot polygons. Experiment with both and see what data you get in the end, and which would better suit your analysis. (I chose "closest" to get all the robberies. Thus, any robberies where the hotspot number was 1 and the distance was 0 were entirely within that hotspot. This way I can do analysis on all robberies and those within the three hottest spots as well.)

34. Review the Rob2004.xlsx worksheet at this time and consider what analysis you would have left out. Also review the Robbery2004HotSpots.docx MS Word document, which is our final analysis on robberies in 2004 and consider what you may have added, or left out.

35. In order to do the join between the robbery points and the 3hot.shp layer, you will first need to find an ArcToolbox tool that allows you to define the projection of the 3Hot layer to AZ State Plane, Nad 1983 AZ Central Intl Feet (try the Data Management Toolbox).

36. After doing analysis in Excel, we can pull together a bulletin in Word that shows the most important information we need (see Robbery2004HotSpots.docx in CIA\Exercises\EX_17).

37. Create a graduated point map of the robbery data to see where we have repeat locations for the crime (alternatively, and my first choice, do the analysis in Excel).

38. Complete your version of the bulletin, and then save it and the project into your student folder.

39. Close ArcMap and all other applications.

40. This exercise should have made your own analytical muscles ache as we left you alone to do most of this from memory, or your own experience. In the next few exercises, we'll be a bit more hands on again to help you along with more step-by-step instruction. This exercise is a good one though for you to begin thinking of what you need to do more, and to be less dependent on the exercises to walk you through the process. Hope you enjoyed it!

■ Exercise 18: More of the Spatial Statistic Toolbox: Ready for Tactical Analysis?

Data Needed for This Exercise

- CIA\Exercises\EX_18\EX_18.mxd

Lesson Objectives

- The student will learn how to create standard deviation ellipses and use them to predict a new hit in a series.

- The student will learn to manually create a distance between hits buffer analysis to use for predicting where a serial offender will go next.
- The student will learn to manually derive a directionality analysis polygon to use for predicting where a serial offender will go next.
- The student will learn to use the mean center to find offenders in a database that may meet a serial suspect's description.

Task Description

1. In this exercise, we are trying to do a forecast of when and where a new crime might occur in a series of indecent exposures.
2. We need to do some time calculations as well as some geoprocessing to predict when (with Excel) and where (with ArcMap) the offender will strike again and forecast where the offender may live or identify the highest peak profile area where the offender's anchor point may be.
3. Several of the tools we have already used might be applied, and CrimeStat will again come into play to create a weighted kernel density probability forecast.
4. Open EX_18.mxd and see that we are zoomed in to a map of the 13 indecent exposures already in this series. See **Figure E18–1**.
5. Open the attribute table for this series and get familiar with the fields and the data within the table. First, let's label each crime in the series in the order that they occurred. If you look at the attribute table, the only field that is numbered in order of occurrence is the FID field. It begins with 0 and ends with 12. We want it to read 1–13 instead.

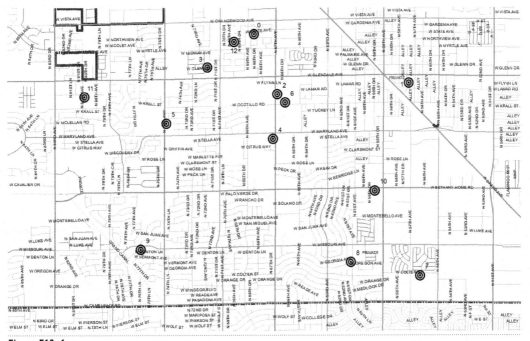

Figure E18–1

6. Right click on the layer, and go to the **Properties → Labels** tab.

7. Check the Label features in this layer.

8. The Method should be **Label all the features the same way**.

9. Change the Label Field to FID.

10. Now click the Expression button.

11. Change the Expression to [FID]+1 as shown in **Figure E18–2**.

12. Click OK, change the label font if needed for readability, and then Apply and OK.

13. Look at the incidents and observe the path between hits (visually follow the crimes in order of occurrence).

14. We will work with this later, but think about which direction you think the offender will go next and if there is a pattern.

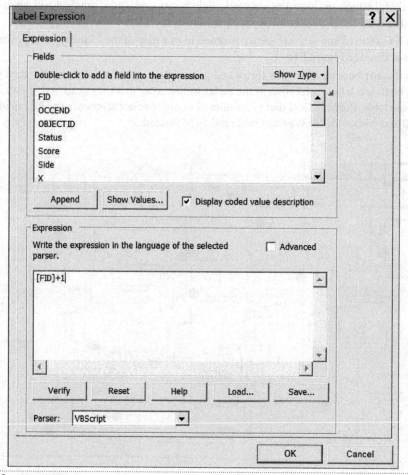

Figure E18–2

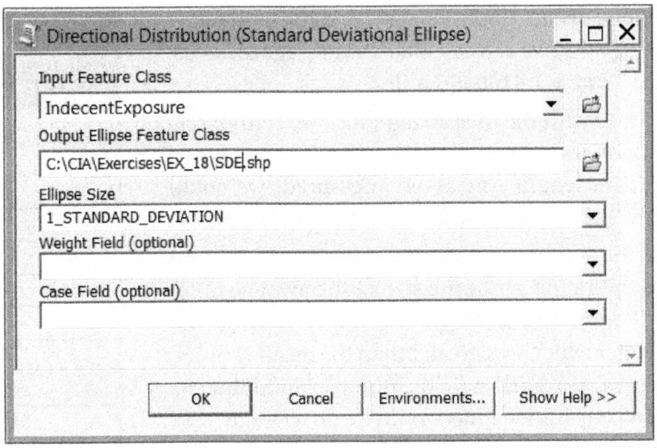

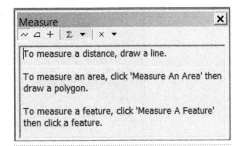

Figure E18–3

15. Now, open the Arc Toolbox and the Spatial Statistics toolbox. Double click on the Measuring Geographic Distributions. Double click on the Directional Distribution (Standard Deviation Ellipses).

16. Complete the tool's dialog box as shown in **Figure E18–3**. Save the file to your student folder as SDE.shp. You could add 18 to the end of SDE, to remember these ellipses are for Exercise 18.

17. This will have created a 1 Stdev Ellipse. Do steps 17 and 18 again, however, this time the Ellipse Size will be 2_Standard_Deviations. Save this file as 2SDE.shp.

18. Now we are going to draw a distance between hits buffer to determine what the average distance between hits has been, and we can then assume that the next travel distance will be at least the Mean1 StDev of that distance.

19. We can use the measuring distance tool to accomplish this easily and manually.

20. On the tools toolbar, click on the measuring tool which looks like a small ruler with double arrows on top.

21. Then make sure to change the distance units to miles (see **Figure E18–4**).

22. After selecting miles, click on the first crime in the series. You do not have to be exactly in the middle, but close when you click.

23. Now the measuring tool is like stretching a rubber band between points. We need to create anchors at each crime location to measure the total distance between the hits. We could also write down or otherwise collect the individual segment lengths if desired.

24. Click on each point once in turn and in sequence of the crimes occurring. When you get to the last crime (13, and be careful because it is near #1 so do not forget it), double click and record the total segment length. It should be around 17 miles.

Figure E18–4

25. If we know the total distance between hits, and the total number of trips (13 − 1 = 12) we can calculate the average distance. This would be 17 / 12 = 1.4166666 miles.

26. Using this method (with the measuring tool), we cannot calculate the standard deviation of the distances. If we recorded what each segment length was as we measured, we could calculate that the StDev was 0.65252 (see **Figure E18–5**).

27. If we used just the average, we would draw a buffer around the most recent hit in the series the size of the average miles between hits. If we used the Mean and StDev method, we would draw a buffer which was greater than the mean−1 Stdev, but less than the mean+2 StDev. This "donut" would then be where the most likely hit location would be on average.

28. In our case, we are just going to draw the average distance as a buffer around the last hit in the series.

29. Open the Indecent Exposure layer's attribute table and sort the data in order of occurrence. Then select the last or most recent crime in the series (remember to imagine this is 2004).

30. Close the table.

31. Now click on ArcToolbox → Analysis Tools → Proximity.

32. Double click on the Buffer tool to open its dialog.

33. Complete the buffer dialog as shown in **Figure E18–6**.

CRIME TRIP NUMBER	CRIME TO	MILES
1	1-2	1.46
2	2-3	1.19
3	3-4	0.68
4	4-5	0.87
5	5-6	0.98
6	6-7	1.09
7	7-8	1.96
8	8-9	0.64
9	9-10	1.90
10	10-11	2.18
11	11-12	2.75
12	12-13	1.44
	Mean	1.43
	StDev	0.65
	Median	1.32
	Mode	#N/A

Figure E18–5

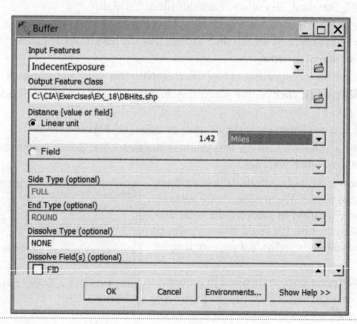

Figure E18–6

34. Save this as DBHits.shp in your student folder and enter the average distance in linear unit (in miles).

35. Click OK.

36. Make the Distance Between Hits Buffer hollow with a bright green outline.

37. Another piece we can use to help us figure out where the next hit will be located is a guess on the direction the offender is going to next. If we rehearse the distance between hits process, we may have observed that the offender would be going back south and west slightly. So we want to create a new polygon shapefile and draw it in that direction like a pie piece.

38. Double click on ArcToolbox → Data Management Tools → Feature Class → Create Feature Class tool.

39. Complete this dialog as shown in **Figure E18–7**.

40. Make sure to go all the way to the bottom and set the Projection to be NAD_1983_StatePlane_Arizona_Central_FIPS_0202_Feet_Intl.

41. Save it to your student folder as Directionality.

42. The new shapefile will be blank and have no attributes.

43. Click on Customize on the main menu bar, and then choose Toolbars. Check the Editor toolbar.

44. With the Editor toolbar open, click Editor and Start Editing. Choose the Directionality layer.

45. If an error message about the spatial relationship comes up, click OK to proceed. If you do not see Directionality in the editing window at the right side of the map display, click on the Organize Templates button at the top, second from left of the editing window. Once open, click on the Directionality layer, and choose New Template.

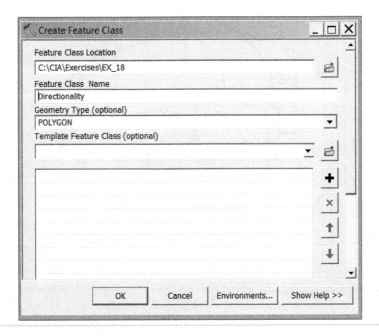

Figure E18–7

46. Check the Directionality layer and click Finish. It should now appear in the editing window. Click on it in the editing window.

47. At the bottom in the second window, you should now see polygon. Click on it to make this your editing tool. Click on Incident 13, and then stretch the polygon out at least as far as the distance between hits buffer just south and west of Point 13. Then click along the 2 Stdev Ellipse or the Distance between hits layer boundaries, and click several times moving left to right (west to east). Double click to finish the polygon.

48. You should end up with a map that looks similar to **Figure E18–8**.

49. Click Editor and Stop Editing when done, and save your edits.

50. We could then use these data as is to give risk areas for a new hit in the series. The area where the SDE ellipses, the Distance between hits buffer, and directionality layers overlap would be the highest risk areas.

51. Our jobs as analysts do not stop with the easiest way to do things each time. Our goal is to use whatever we can to better assist the investigation and give the best possible prediction we can. The pin map of the crimes should really never be done. Yes, it shows where the crimes have occurred, but there is no "analysis" in that.

52. The investigator might like it, but in reality you were hired for your predictive capabilities—so give it a try. With these three layers, we can actually get down to some pretty small areas in some crime series.

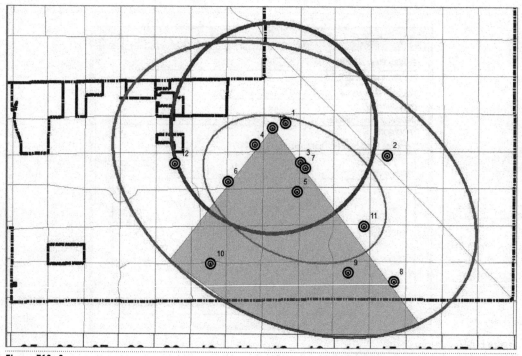

Figure E18–8

53. The smaller the area predicted, the less surveillance is needed and it can be focused into a few areas instead of where the entire series occurred.

54. The more we know about the victims and other geographic features of the past crimes, the better we can determine other "risk factors" we operationalize on the map to further reduce the area that is at highest risk.

55. Examples might be such things as using the locations of all existing apartment complexes (the offender in our series flashed people within 500 feet of our victims' apartment complexes). It might also be distance from a freeway (showing they may be using the freeways to travel to crimes).

56. Other possible operationalization of risk factors might be census blocks with higher volumes of persons over 60 years of age (targeted by Travelers), or census or land-use areas where the median house value is the same as high value homes being burglarized in a series, etc.

57. So now we have made a map, which could be given to investigators with our date and time analysis. We also need to do some day of week and time of day analysis and predict when the next crime will likely occur for our product to be the most useful.

58. Open EX_18.xlsx found in the CIA\Exercises\EX_18 folder.

59. Look over the spreadsheet and see how simple and easy analysis can be performed with graphs and a few summary tables for temporal aspects of your prediction. (*See more in the Excel appendix to the textbook and the exercises with Excel.*)

60. It is important for you to advise what specific hours per day are best for surveillance and nothing more. You do not need to predict the next hit to the minute, and an hour or date range is sufficient depending on the accuracy the series allows you to have.

61. After reviewing the Excel sheet thoroughly, close Excel.

62. Now let's go back to the map and create a simple journey-to-crime analysis using the mean center.

63. Open ArcMap and turn off the ellipses and other items we added to create the forecast for the next hit in this series.

64. Now double click on the Spatial Statistics toolbox, and then the Measuring Geographic Distributions.

65. We are going to run the Mean Center, Median Center, and the Central feature tools.

66. Start by double clicking the Mean Center tool to open its dialog. Complete the dialog as shown in **Figure E18-9**.

67. Save this to your student folder as MeanCtr.shp.

68. Click OK.

69. While you are waiting, make sure that all of the records are either selected, or none of them are selected. ArcMap will perform the majority of these functions on the selected records only, so if your mean center does not appear where it is shown in **Figure E18-10** that could be the cause.

70. The location of your mean center should be just west and slightly south of crimes 3 and 7 as shown in Figure E18-10. Now, let's run the median center function. Double click Median Center in the Spatial Statistics toolbox.

71. The input feature class will be the Indecent Exposure incidents again, and the output will be to your student folder named MedianCtr.shp.

72. Click OK to run this.

73. In this case, the median center wound up exactly on top of the mean center.

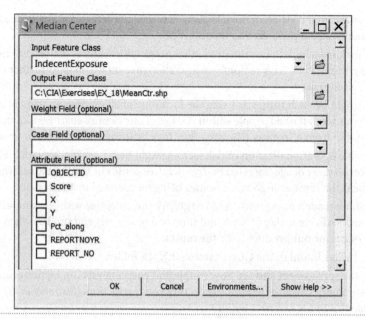

Figure E18-9

74. Now double click the Central Feature tool in the Spatial Statistics toolbox.

75. This is set up like the others, as the indecent exposure layer is the input feature class. Save it to your student folder as CentFeature.shp. In the Distance Method field, choose Manhattan Distance.

76. Click OK to run this tool.

77. This result indicates that hit number 3 in the series is the central feature since it is in the same place.

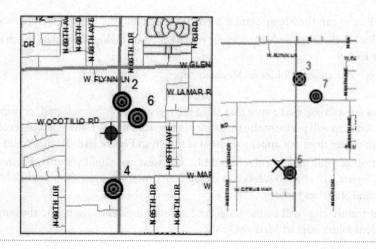

Figure E18-10

78. Several analytical reports and studies suggest that an offender who commits crimes like these typically lives very near the center of the crime series. There are some dissenting studies that argue the areas around the mean center, median center, or central feature are where we want to begin to search for the offender.

79. Distances such as 1 mile and others have been thrown out as search distances around one of these points to begin, or prioritize the search.

80. Coauthor Hill has done research in Glendale with 50 different serial offender cases. The results of that study showed that in 20% of the cases, the offender was reported to live within a peak profile area of a journey-to-crime analysis using CrimeStat and a calibrated model.

81. In addition, it was also found that in 20% of those cases, the offender lived within 1 mile of the mean center.

82. About 40% of the offenders lived just outside the peak profile area of a journey-to-crime analysis, and an analysis of 8328 series revealed that the average distance between the home of the offender and the mean center was 0.98 miles, well within the 1-mile tolerance.

83. The other 40% of cases analyzed during the serial offender research showed those offenders lived completely outside of Glendale in many cases or at least 3 miles away.

84. Create a buffer of 1 mile around the mean center, or alternatively, select all probationers and persons listed as "S" in a police report who live within that 1-mile area (using a select by location query).

85. If using the buffer option, after creation of the buffer, select by location those persons and probationers within the buffer.

86. You should get about 16,552 persons from the Persons_Data layer and 390 Probationers.

87. We need to whittle this list down a bit before we can even think about giving the results to an investigator.

88. In a thorough review of the police reports, all victims reported that the offender was between 5'11" and 6'2", 45–55 years, 180–220 lbs, with grey hair, and blue eyes.

89. One victim also thought that the offender had tattoos on both arms, although she could not tell what the tattoos were.

90. To perform an age query in the Probationers data, you will first need to figure out what years you are looking for. So 2004 − 45 = 1959 and 2004 − 55 = 1949, so we want to Select from Current Selection all those records that fit this:
   - "DOB1" >= '19490101' AND "DOB1" <= '19591231'

91. Unfortunately there are no 45–55 year olds that live within the 1-mile buffer in the Probation data.

92. So let's check the persons data.

93. Here we have MINAGE and MAXAGE fields and we also have everyone from police reports, not just suspects.

94. Our first query against the attributes (Select from Current Selection) might be:
   - "INVCODE" = 'S' OR "INVCODE" = 'FI' OR "INVCODE" = 'IL'

95. This will give us all the Suspects, Investigative Leads, and Field Interrogations persons who live within the 1-mile buffer.

96. What did you get? I got 5465 left from the initial 16,000.

97. So let's refine this some more and Select from Current Selection:
    - ("MINAGE" >= 45 AND "MINAGE" <= 55) OR ("MAXAGE" >= 45 AND "MAXAGE" <= 55)

98. Now we have all the 45–55-year-old offenders, and we are down to 861. Continuing, we want to check for the height of 5'11" to 6'2" which looks like:
    - "HEIGHT" >= 511 AND "HEIGHT" <= 602

99. We are now down to 133 records and need to query for the weight range of 180–220 lbs. (*Note:* In many cases, we might add an inch or so to each end of the height range, and 20–30 lbs on either end of the weight range because witnesses are not always very good at guessing about these.)
    - "WEIGHT" >= 180 AND "WEIGHT" <= 220

100. We now have only 59 records.

101. We could do another query for grey hair and blues eyes, but it is just as easy to sort the hair color field in descending order to see we only have two persons with grey hair. One has hazel eyes and the other blue eyes:
    - Kevin Shake
    - Robin Hisel

102. Now you could obtain driver license photos for these two offenders and check their history.

103. It turns out that Hisel has been arrested in the past for exposing himself to his female neighbor. You could then put together a photo-lineup for the detective with Hisel and another one with Shake and give them to him with a brief explanation of their histories, etc.

104. Close ArcMap and any other programs you have open.

105. Save any files to your student folder as needed.

■ Exercise 19: Tactical Analysis 1—PGM: Step 1 Building the Data

Data Needed for This Exercise
- CIA\Exercises\EX_19\EX_19.mxd

Lesson Objectives
- The student will learn the probability grid method (PGM) for tactical analysis.
- The student will learn about combining layers and performing geoprocessing.

Task Description
1. This exercise is a little more involved than others we have provided. To begin with, you will have reading assignments before working on this exercise. The reading assignments can be found in the CIA\Exercises\EX_19 folder. They are:
    a. Catalano_Hill_Long_SecurityJournal_article53668.pdf
    b. PGM_Final.pdf
    c. PGM_AppendixA.pdf
    d. StepsPGMAnalysis.docx

2. These are not very long, so you should not have to spend more than 30–45 minutes reviewing these publications, and it will help you better understand this process of analysis.

3. First we need to open the EX_19.mxd located in the CIA\Exercises\EX_19 folder.

4. After this project is open, view the occurrence of five armed robberies of video stores. The offender is described as a black male, 17–25 years old, 5'6"–5'9", 133–145 lbs. He is usually wearing a black "hoodie" and armed with a chrome or silver large-caliber semiautomatic handgun. In the last two robberies, witnesses saw him leave in a grey or silver two-door Honda Civic.

5. The offender enters the video store, picks up a few movies, waits until the store empties out some, and then approaches the cashier and brandishes the chrome, large-caliber weapon over his head and yells at anyone else in the store to get down on the floor.

6. He then points the weapon directly at the clerk and says, "Listen up scumbag, place all the money in my blue bag and don't hit any alarms, or you are dead," or words to that effect in each robbery.

7. The blue bag was described as the kind you get at Safeway stores to save from using the plastic bags.

8. He then flees out the back door and apparently always runs behind the store, possibly to the waiting Honda.

9. For this analysis, we have the crime series point layer, and a point layer of other video stores in Glendale, along with all the supporting layers we need to make a nice looking map.

10. Now that we have read all the cases and have all the data we need for the time being, let's start doing some analysis.

11. We are going to create the following spatial statistics layers for this crime series:
    a. Drawing Toolbar
        i. Create the minimum bounding rectangle (MBR)
    b. CrimeStat
        i. Probability interpolation
        ii. Convex hull
        iii. 1 StDev rectangle
        iv. Mean center
    c. ArcMap's ArcToolbox
        i. Spatial deviation ellipses: 1 Stdev and 2 Stdev
        ii. Mean center
    d. Manually
        i. Distance between hits buffer
        ii. Directionality pie polygon (if able)
        iii. Find the MBR square area
        iv. Find the MBR lower left X and Y
        v. Find the MBR upper right X and Y
        vi. Find the total street footage within the MBR

12. We are going to use the interpolation results from CrimeStat as our base polygon. All others will be selected by location to score the interpolation polygon layer, so we will need to add some fields to it as well.

13. Look to see that the VideoSeries data are located here: CIA\Data\SHapefiles\Offenses\VideoSeries.shp

14. We will need to remember this path for when we need to find it and pull it into CrimeStat.

15. Okay, we can begin now that you have all been forewarned that this will use all of the ArcMap skills you have developed up to this point.

16. Zoom out once from the video robbery crime series (we are going to call him the "Film Noir Bandit").

17. We want to zoom out to give a small buffer around the points when we draw the MBR.

18. Use the Drawing toolbar → Draw rectangle feature to draw an MBR around the crimes in this series (see **Figure E19–1**). Make the fill hollow, with a red outline about 4 in size. (At this point, you might want to turn off the streets to keep from having to wait for them to draw.)

19. Now right click on the rectangle and choose Properties and collect the Total Square Area in Miles and the Lower Left *XY* and Upper Right *XY* coordinates:
    a. 15.574587 square miles
    b. 604,637.8807/914,396.1034 Lower Left
    c. 631,221.2141/930,729.4367 Upper Right
    (*Note:* Your results may be different due to the size of your screen, and the size and shape of your MBR.)

20. Now we need to select the City_Streets_L by where they intersect the MBR graphic. Make the City_Streets_L layer visible, and click on it to make it active. Now, in the menu bar, click on Selection → Select by Graphics.

21. After several moments, the city streets that intersect the MBR should be selected. If none are selected, make sure the layer is selectable under List by Selection in the table of contents (TOC) and run the selection again.

22. Right click the streets layers in the TOC, then choose Open Attribute Table from the popup menu. Find the Length field, right click this field, and choose Statistics for a value of about 1739561.570505 feet.

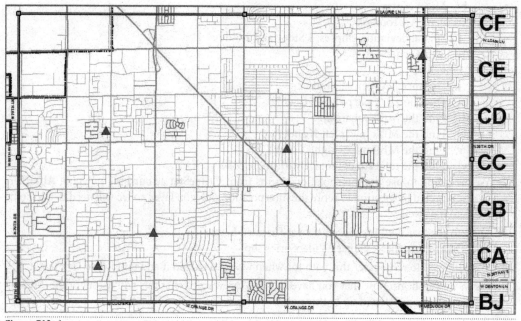

Figure E19–1

23. Open the attribute table of the VideoSeries layer and make sure that there are X and Y Coordinates in this attribute table. Yup, they are there!

24. Choose Selection → Clear Selected Features from the main menu bar.

25. Now close any open tables you may have open.

26. Open CrimeStat 3.3.

27. Complete the Primary file screen as shown in **Figure E19–2**.

28. The Reference File tab should be completed as shown in **Figure E19–3**.

29. The Measurement Parameters tab should be completed as shown in **Figure E19–4**.

30. Notice we have added a Weight variable called "Sequence," which is nothing more than a count of the crimes, so that crime 5 will have a higher weight than crime 1.

31. We are going to use a 500 foot by 500 foot cell size (Cell Specification). We will be using indirect or Manhattan distance measurements for this analysis.

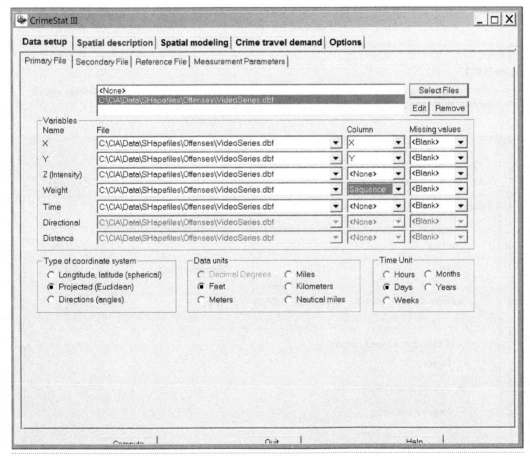

Figure E19–2

Ned Levine (2010). *CrimeStat III: A Spatial Statistics Program for the Analysis of Crime Incident Locations* (v 3.3). Ned Levine & Associates, Houston, TX, and the National Institute of Justice, Washington, DC. July. http://www.icpsr.umich.edu/CrimeStat.

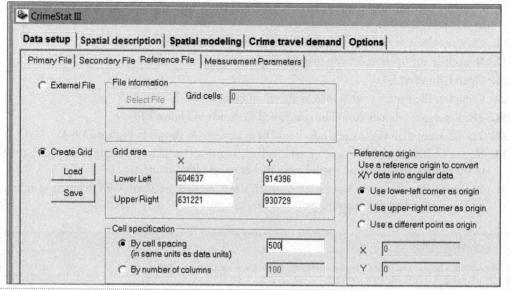

Figure E19–3

Ned Levine (2010). *CrimeStat III: A Spatial Statistics Program for the Analysis of Crime Incident Locations* (v 3.3). Ned Levine & Associates, Houston, TX, and the National Institute of Justice, Washington, DC. July. http://www.icpsr.umich.edu/CrimeStat.

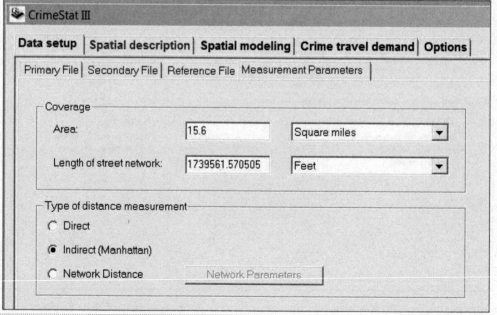

Figure E19–4

Ned Levine (2010). *CrimeStat III: A Spatial Statistics Program for the Analysis of Crime Incident Locations* (v 3.3). Ned Levine & Associates, Houston, TX, and the National Institute of Justice, Washington, DC. July. http://www.icpsr.umich.edu/CrimeStat.

32. Direct distance is also called Euclidean, or "as the crow flies," distance and connects two points.

33. Manhattan distance is also called street distance, or the distance one would have to walk if they were using city streets to get to one point from another point. When you have completed all three primary file setup tabs, click on the Spatial description tab.

34. Check the box next to **Mean Center and Standard Distance (Mcsd)** and the **Convex Hull** at the bottom, and Save result to your student folder as "1" as an ArcView *.SHP file; CrimeStat will add text in front of whatever you enter (CHULL for the convex hull, MC for the mean center, and XYD for the standard deviation rectangle).

35. It is often a requirement to redo these analyses every time the offender strikes again. So naming them 1, 2, 3, etc. allows you to know which bulletin each version of the analysis was for and keeps them in order. Over time you can amass a large quantity of good data that you can then use for forecasting research.

36. Now click on the Spatial modeling tab.

37. On the Interpolation I tab, click on the **Single** checkbox for Interpolation.

38. Now complete the Interpolation form as shown in **Figure E19–5**.

39. Save result to your student folder named "1."

40. Click the Compute button.

41. When CrimeStat is done running all three functions, close the Compute window, but leave CrimeStat open until we've verified that we got what we wanted.

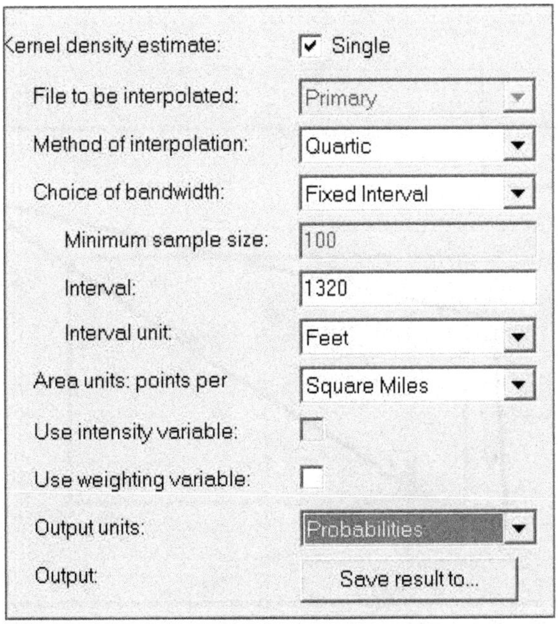

Figure E19–5

Ned Levine (2010). *CrimeStat III: A Spatial Statistics Program for the Analysis of Crime Incident Locations* (v 3.3). Ned Levine & Associates, Houston, TX, and the National Institute of Justice, Washington, DC. July. http://www.icpsr.umich.edu/CrimeStat.

42. Reopen ArcMap and use the Add Data button, or Arc Catalog to add the four files to the current project.

    a. XYD1.shp   **c.** CHULL1.shp

    b. MC1.shp   **d.** K1.shp

43. Answer Yes to the Projection Missing message and then look at the resulting data.

44. Add the K1 to the map and move the K1 layer below the other layers in the TOC.

45. Change the symbology of the K1.shp file to a quantities type of legend, with seven classes, Natural Breaks classification Schema, blue to red color ramp based on the Value Field of "Z."

46. Make the Chull1 layer hollow with a thick black outline.

47. Change the MC1 layer to "Mean Center" and change this to a bull's eye–type symbol.

48. The XYD1 layer is the 1 StDev rectangle; make it hollow with a dark green outline.

49. You should now have a map that looks similar to **Figure E19–6**.

50. Notice how the density, or probability interpolation, pretty much said the next crime would occur at the places where they have already occurred. We could increase the search radius from 1320 to 3960 (3/4ths of a mile) and we would get larger hotspots around the points. If we kept increasing the distance, it would resemble one large hotspot in the middle of all of the crimes.

51. But we forgot to include our weight field in the calculation. Go back to CrimeStat and the Interpolations screen. Check the box next to **Use Weighting Variable**.

52. Hit the Compute button again to rerun this function. CrimeStat will rerun each of the checked functions and save them over the previous shapefiles, essentially updating the map automatically.

53. In ArcMap, right click the K1 layer in the TOC and choose Properties.

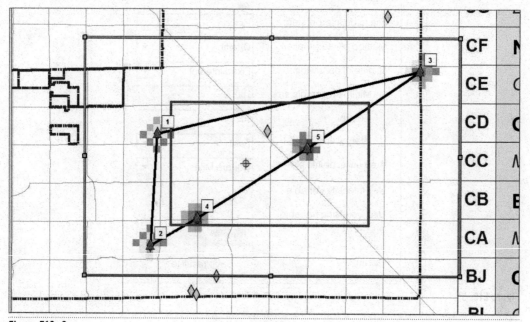

Figure E19–6

54. Click on the Symbology tab and click the value field and choose Z again. (I know it is already checked, but we want ArcMap to change the legend and refresh the data from this field because we changed it when we reran CrimeStat.)

55. Now hits 4 and 5 are the hottest, with the other crimes being less hot.

56. Open the attribute table for the K1 layer.

57. Notice how we have five fields? The Z field is the values of the interpolation for each polygon. Select one row and look for the selected feature on the map display. These are all 500 ft × 500 ft polygons and mimic what a city block might be.

58. Now, let's create the distance between hits buffer.

59. First we need to measure the distance between trips, or between the hits in the series in sequential order.

60. Using the measure tool, measure the distance from hit 1 to hit 2 and record the data in an Excel worksheet.

61. Measure from hit 2 to hit 3, record it, and then 3 to 4 and 4 to 5.

62. When you have all four measurements, you should then calculate the mean and standard deviation:

    a. Hit 1 to Hit 2 = 1.45 miles
    b. Hit 2 to Hit 3 = 4.25 miles
    c. Hit 3 to Hit 4 = 3.53 miles
    d. Hit 4 to Hit 5 = 1.73 miles
    e. Average = 2.74

    f. Standard Deviation = 1.36484
    g. Median = 2.63
    h. Mean + 1 Stdev = 4.1 miles
    i. Mean + 2 Stdev = 5.46 miles

63. Using the ArcToolbox → Analysis Tools → Proximity → Multiple Ring Buffer tool, create a three-ring buffer where there are three values: (1) mean, (2) mean +1 StDev, and (3) mean + 2 StDevs.

64. Select hit number 5 from the VideoSeries layer. Use whichever method you prefer (open table—select record, select on map display, or select by attributes).

65. Our buffer needs to be drawn around this last hit in the series, so we need to select this last hit first.

66. Once selected, open the Multiple ring buffer tool by double clicking it.

67. We are going create buffers of 2.74, 4.1, and 5.46 miles around the most recent hit in the series.

68. Enter each distance in the distance field, and then click the plus sign to move it down. *Do not hit enter or the window will close.* Complete the buffer dialog box as shown in **Figure E19–7**. Click OK.

69. When the buffer analysis is done and added to the TOC, change all of the rings to hollow and right click the layer name and choose Zoom to Layer.

70. Notice how far away the offender could go? Turn on the Video_Stores layer and see if there are any stores within these rings.

71. It looks like many are outside our MBR, and we may have to change the interpolation result to be larger, but for now we will stick with what we have so we do not have to recreate the fields we added.

72. Now on your own, create the two standard deviation ellipses (1 and 2 Stdev) from the Spatial Statistics toolbox.

73. Make sure that you Clear All Selected Features before running any of the other tools.

74. Your map, when finished, should look like **Figure E19–8**. (*Note:* If you get lost, all of these layers are already created in the CIA\Exercises\EX_19 folder for your use.)

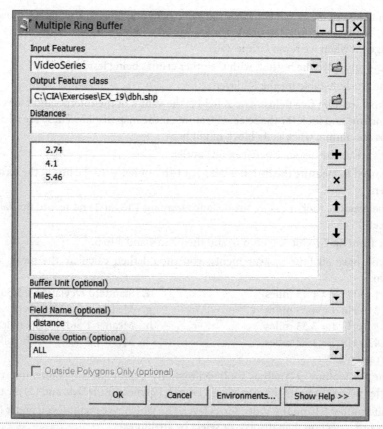

Figure E19–7

75. Save your project and work to this point to your student folder.

76. You can then close this exercise and continue to Part 2 later, or continue to Part 2 to Scoring the PGM.

■ Exercise 19b: Tactical Analysis 2—PGM: Step 2 Scoring the PGM

Data Needed for This Exercise

- CIA\Exercises\EX_19\EX_19.mxd

Lesson Objectives

- The student will learn to score the probability grid method.

Task Description

1. Open EX_19 in the CIA\Exercises\EX_19 folder.
2. Add the K1 layer from the EX_19 folder and open its attribute table.

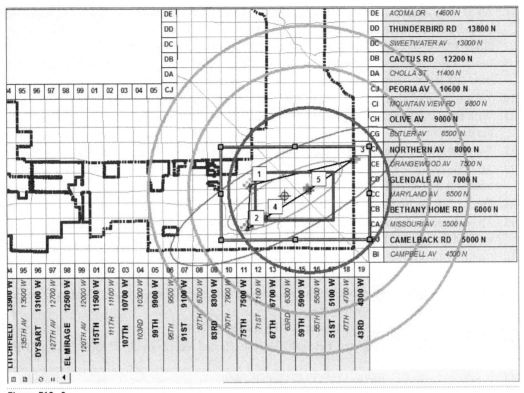

Figure E19–8

3. We are going to add eight new fields to this attribute table in total to score various "risk factors" for a next hit in the series.

4. Since our offender has only been robbing video stores up to this point, scoring the polygons in the K1 layer, which contains a video store, is also a good risk factor.

5. We also need a TOTAL field. The total field will eventually contain our overall score or risk level for each polygon in the K1 layer.

6. Click on the Table Options button at the top left of the table and add the following fields. Make the **type** for all of them DOUBLE:

   a. CHULL (convex hull polygon)
   b. SDE1 (1 Stdev ellipse)
   c. SDE2 (2 Stdev ellipse)
   d. DBH (days between hits buffer)
   e. DIR (directionality pie)
   f. XYD (1 Stdev rectangle)
   g. TARGET (other video stores on the map)
   h. TOTAL (sum of all scores)

7. Now determine what the score should be for every one of the fields we've added. The scores can be anywhere between 0 and 3. Generally, here is how these variables are typically scored:

   a. CHULL = 1.75 to 2.25
   b. SDE1 = 1 to 1.5
   c. SDE2 = 1.5 to 2.25
   d. DBH = 1.5 to 2
   e. DIR = 0.25 to 2.25
   f. XYD = 0.25 to 1
   g. TARGET = 2 to 3

8. All of these numbers are subjective, and the more you know about the victimology and travel behavior of your offender, the more you will adjust these. It is important, however, that the values given are between 0 and 3 only, so that one value does not "overpower" another in the final result.

9. In this case, we have an offender who is hitting only video stores to our knowledge, so this is a large risk factor, whereas the others are general spatial statistics and not as high in the scoring.

10. We want to give all of them value, but the polygons with stores in them will get the highest score.

11. With the K1 table open and all of our fields added, click on Selection → Select by Location in the menu bar.

12. We want to select features from the K1 layer that intersect the CHULL1 layer to begin with.

13. After the Select by Location query is finished, right click on the CHULL field in the K1 attribute table and choose **Field Calculator**.

14. Enter 1.5 in the bottom window and then click OK.

15. All of the K1 polygons that intersected the convex hull polygon were selected and now have a value in that field of 1.5.

16. Continue to do a Select by Location for each layer, one at a time, where they intersect the K1 layer. Keep the attribute table of the K1 layer so we can do the calculations.

17. Let's start with the easiest layers—the standard deviation ellipses. Click on Selection → Select by Location in the main menu bar.

18. Select the features from K1 that intersect the features of SDE1.

19. Once the polygons are selected, field calculate the selected records in the K1 layer and the SDE1 field to be equal to 0.65.

20. Repeat this process with the SDE2 layer and give it a score of 1.25.

21. Select the features of the K1 layer that intersect the XYD1 layer and then calculate the XYD1 field in the K1 layer to be a value of 0.5.

22. Now calculate the Distance between hits buffer, which is a bit more complicated. One of the author's research has shown that the Mean+ 1 StDev distance has 65% of the next hits. The Mean distance has only 25%, and the Mean+ 2 StDev has the remaining 10%. So we want to score them accordingly. We will assign the Mean distance buffer a value of 0.5, and the middle ring, or the Mean+ 1 StDev distance a value of 1, while the farthest out ring will get a value of 0.25.

23. Open the attribute table of the DBH layer.

24. Click on the 2.74 distance ring to select it.

25. Now do a Select by Location of the features of K1 where they intersect the features of the DBH layer.

26. Field calculate the selected rows of the DBH field in the K1 attribute table to be 0.5.

27. Repeat this process with the 4.1-mile and 5.46-mile buffer rings.

28. Because we chose ALL in the Dissolve Option when we did the buffer rings, they do not overlap (see Figure E19–7) and we can do the select by locations in this manner for each individual geographic location or buffer. (Although in this case the entire grid is within the first buffer, so the other buffers will have no value.)

29. The only thing we do not have is a guess on what direction the suspect will go next. In this series that would be very difficult to determine, so we will ignore this analysis.

30. Okay, now we need to add all the data together in the various columns into the Total field.

31. In the K1 attribute table, click the Table Options button and choose Clear Selected Features (if anything is selected).

32. Now turn off all the spatial layers we've created except for the K1 layer. Open the attribute table for the K1 layer if it is not already open.

33. Right click on the TOTAL field, and choose Field Calculator.

34. In the field calculator window, calculate the value of TOTAL to be:

   • [Z] + [CHULL] + [SDE1] + [SDE2] + [DBH] + [DIR] + [XYD] + [TARGET]

35. Yes, I know we have no values in the DIR and the TARGET columns yet, but we will get to the TARGET one in a few minutes. Click OK.

36. Now classify the K1 layer by the Total field instead of the Z field.

37. Your map should now resemble **Figure E19–9**.

38. We can see that the highest risk areas are where hits 4 and 5 were located based on just these spatial statistics layers that overlapped. If we stopped here, we would indicate to detectives that these stores were at highest risk for a new hit. So now let's add the other video stores into the mix. Click on Selection → Select by Location in the main menu bar.

39. Select the features of K1 that Intersect the Video_Stores layer.

40. Open the K1 layer's attribute table and Field Calculate the TARGET field with a value of 3.

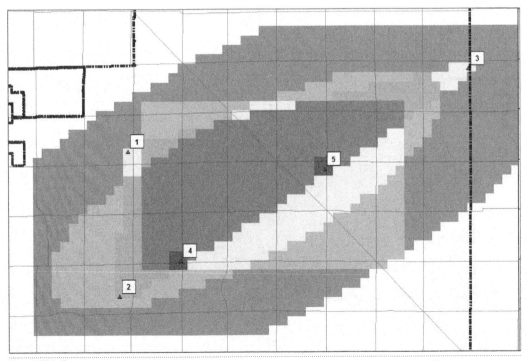

Figure E19–9

41. While we are here, we want the interpolation analysis to have equal footing with the other layers. Clear the selection, then Right click on the Z field and sort in descending order.

42. Right click the field and choose field calculator, and enter the formula, [Z] * 50, and click OK.

43. Now our Z values of 0.64 are full numbers (3.2, etc.), so we can use them with equal weight as the other layers which are at least 0–3. We do not want to exceed the value of 3 if we can, but we want to give the interpolation results some influence on the final result.

44. Now recalculate the Total with our previous formula from step 35.

45. Reclassify the K1 layer by the TOTAL field to renew it and apply. Make the top color (dark blue) white, and click Apply and OK.

46. So if we look at this map with an analyst's eye, we can see that the 15.6 square miles of highest risk area (where the crimes have already happened) have been reduced considerably.

47. We now have only three highest risk areas around hits 3, 4, and 5, with secondary areas at higher risk where there were video stores.

48. Your final map should look like **Figure E19–10**.

49. We could then tell the investigators and other units that the following four stores were at highest risk for a new crime in this series and let them decide which ones to sit on:

    a. Condaca Video Center at 6830 N 55th Ave
    b. Hollywood Video at 7910 N 43rd Ave
    c. Blockbuster Video at 6702 W Bethany Home Rd
    d. Netflix at 5952 W Palmaire Ave

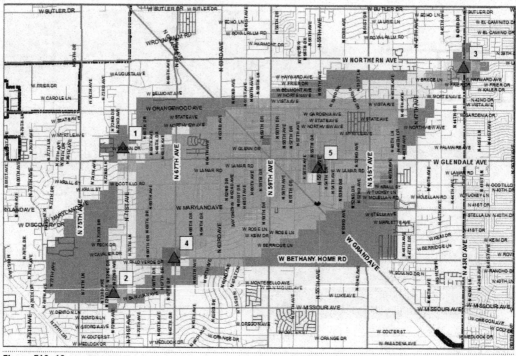

Figure E19–10

50. This concludes this lesson on how to create a probability grid method analysis for tactical predictions.

51. There are many other layers we could consider, such as a weighted density by how much money the offender got, distance from main roads, and distance from mean center buffer (much like the distance between hits buffer, but from the mean center, sometimes called spider diagram analysis).

52. There is an infinite number of risk factors you could use, depending on how specific the offender is to targets or other factors you can see on the map. You want to use the ones you are at least 50% sure apply to the current crime series.

53. Finding good business data can be a struggle, but it will be one of your best friends over time. Try your local tax and licensing department, or you can buy the data from ESRI and many other sources.

54. We hope you will use the PGM tactical prediction method. If each of these individual prediction methods works in certain circumstances, then why not combine them into one good prediction?

55. There is also an exciting method from Rutgers University and Dr. Joel Caplan and Dr. Leslie Kennedy called Risk Terrain Modeling (RTM; see www.rutgerscps.org/rtm/).

56. It is more for strategic predictive value where you are trying to predict robberies that will be in the next 3 months compared to a previous time period.

57. Instead of using past crimes to predict future locations, the RTM process uses "risk factors" of crime such as analytically derived distance around parks or apartment complexes for street robberies, and density of drug-related crimes as a risk factor for shootings.

58. In theory, we could combine an RTM model with the spatial statistics we have created for the PGM method to get an even more accurate prediction of a new hit in a crime series.

59. One further note, Hill (coauthor of this text) has found that when the PGM predicts a very small area for a new hit, it has been correct every time he has done the analysis. When the highest risk area is very large, the prediction has been correct in a large number of cases, however, the larger the area of the prediction is, the less useful it is to surveillance units.

60. Close everything that is open, and save your project in your student folder as EX_19.

■ Exercise 19c: Tactical Analysis—Vandalism

Data Needed for This Exercise

- CIA\Exercises\EX_19\EX_19.mxd

Lesson Objectives

- The student will learn how to create a tactical analysis product independently, using skills learned in the previous exercises.

Task Description

1. Using the knowledge you have gained on how to create the various layers that could be used in a tactical analysis project, and using EX_19.mxd as the basemap, create a tactical analysis using the Vandalism layer (Vandalism.shp) already located in the EX_19 project.

2. Create the various tactical analysis layers you feel would best suit this crime series and develop a bulletin complete with next hit prediction for this series.

3. An example can be found in the CIA\Exericses\EX_19 folder called Vandalism.docx.

■ Exercise 19d: Tactical Analysis—Indecent Exposure

Data Needed for This Exercise

- CIA\Exercises\EX_19\EX_19.mxd

Lesson Objectives

- The student will learn how to create a tactical analysis product independently, using skills learned in the previous exercises.

Task Description

1. Using the knowledge you have gained on how to create the various layers that could be used in a tactical analysis project, and using EX_19.mxd as the basemap, create a tactical analysis using the Indecent Exposure layer (IndecentExp.shp) already located in the EX_19 project.
2. Create the various tactical analysis layers you feel would best suit this crime series and develop a bulletin complete with next hit prediction for this series.
3. An example can be found in the CIA\Exericses\EX_19 folder called IndecentExp.docx.

■ Exercise 20: Basic Journey to Crime with CrimeStat III

Data Needed for This Exercise

- CIA\Exercises\EX_20\EX_20.mxd

Lesson Objectives

- The student will learn how to set up data to do a journey-to-crime analysis.
- The student will learn the main objectives of a journey-to-crime analysis and perform some research concerning this process.

Task Description

1. Open EX_20.mxd in the CIA\Exercises\EX_20 folder.
2. In this exercise, we will learn about a method of geographic profiling called journey-to-crime (JTC) analysis.
3. JTC analysis is used in a tactical environment to:
   a. Help prioritize suspects
      i. Investigators may already know about other suspect's names from tips or other leads, but the JTC estimate will give them the most likely offenders to start with.
   b. Identify the peak profile area, or highest probability area where the offender may have an anchor point (home, business, girlfriend, etc.), to organize responses and canvasses for the offender.
      i. The typical anchor point is offender home address, but this is not always the case.
   c. Provide crime analysts with the opportunity to search police databases for the offender.
      i. Analysts can use the description of the suspect and the peak profile area to limit the possible candidates.
      ii. This will take a fairly long time and may involve a list of 100 or more likely offenders, depending on the size of the peak profile area and the number of persons in the databases living there.

      iii. An analyst will want to create a weighting for the individuals found to help get only the top contenders at the top of the list.

4. Now that we know we can find an offender not already known, prioritize suspects investigators may already know about and find a peak profile area to organize canvasses and other searches we need to create a JTC analysis.

5. We will start out the same as a hotspot analysis in that we need to create the minimum bounding rectangle (MBR):
   a. Lower Left X and Y **c.** Total Square Mileage
   b. Upper Right X and Y **d.** Street Length

6. First, Observe that we are working with a set of burglaries that are all part of a series. We can visually inspect the data available to us and see that there is a big hole in the middle of the crime series where no burglaries have occurred (see **Figure E20–1**).

7. Common logic says that the offender may live close to the mean center of the crime series. Use the Spatial Statistics Toolbox → Measuring Geographic Distributions → Mean Center tool to create the mean center of the BURGLARY_SERIES_CASE layer.

8. Double click the mean center tool, and complete the dialog as shown in **Figure E20–2**.

9. Save your BurgMeanCtr.shp to your student folder and click OK. When the mean center has been created, change the symbol to the Circle 17 symbol in the symbol selector dialog. (Right click BurgMeanCtr, choose Properties → Symbology tab. Click on the Symbol, find Circle 17 in the list to the left and click OK to get back to the map display.)

Figure E20–1

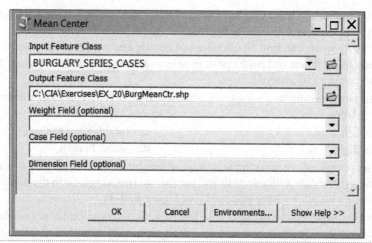

Figure E20–2

10. The mean center is in the middle area where no burglaries have been occurring.

11. We need to look over this area and make sure that the reason that no residential burglaries are occurring in this middle area, is that there are no residences. (Consult layers that show residential zoning, parcel layers, or satellite images.) Since this is not the case, we have our first hint that the burglar may be following Brantingham and Brantingham's (1981, 1984, 1993) concept of a "buffer area" around him where he will not commit a crime.

12. The reasons might be that the burglar fears his neighbors who know them and will see him committing a burglary, or that the targets around his home have less property to steal.

13. Okay, let's create an MBR around these burglaries.

14. Zoom out at least once using the Zoom Out button on the Tools toolbar (see **Figure E20–3**).

Figure E20–3

15. Use the Draw Rectangle tool in the Drawing toolbar to draw an MBR around all the burglaries so that all of them are well within the MBR.

16. After the MBR is drawn, right click it and choose Properties. Click the Symbol tab, and choose No Color for the fill and a size 3, medium blue outline.

17. With the graphic Properties open, click on the Area tab and record the square mileage of the MBR: 6.445976 square miles.

18. Now click on the Size and Position tab and click the light blue box in the bottom left corner. Record the X and Y coordinates of the lower left X and Y:
    a. X = 614,224.8561
    b. Y = 918,623.5631

19. Now click the light blue box in the upper right corner. Record the X and Y coordinates:
    a. X = 631,124.8561
    b. Y = 929,256.8965

20. Close the properties dialog.
21. Now turn on the City_Streets_L layer if it is not already turned on (visible).
22. Highlight the City_Streets_L layer in the TOC, and make sure the MBR is selected (handles at the corners and sides).
23. Click on Selection → Select by Graphics to select all the city streets within the MBR.
24. Right click the City_Streets_L layer, and choose Open Attribute Table.
25. Find the Shape_Length field. Once found, right click this field name and choose Statistics.
26. Save the SUM value from the Statistics function: 866880.476926 feet.
27. Close the streets table and click on Selection → Clear Selected Features to clear everything in the project.
28. Save your project as EX_20.mxd in your student folder.
29. The only thing we need to do now is to verify that the burglary series cases have X and Y coordinates in the attribute table.
30. Right click the BURGLARY_SERIES_CASES in the TOC and choose Open Attribute Table. We see that we do not have X and Y coordinates in this table. To add them we need to go back to the ArcToolbox.
31. Click on ArcToolbox to open it and then go to Data Management Tools. Click on the **Features** toolbox, and double click on the Add XY Coordinates tool.
32. The Input Features will be the Burglary_Series_Cases. Click OK to run the tool.
33. Now open the attribute table. At the far end of the Burglary_Series_Cases, we now find the fields POINT_X and POINT_Y. These are the fields we will use when setting up the primary file in CrimeStat.
34. We have everything we need now, so open CrimeStat.
35. Click on the Primary file tab and complete it as shown in **Figure E20–4**. (Note the location of the Burglary_Series_Cases shapefile in the CIA\Data\Shapefiles\Offenses folder.)
36. Click on the Reference File tab and complete it as shown in **Figure E20–5**.
37. Click on the Measurement Parameters tab and complete it as shown in **Figure E20–6**.
38. Be sure to enter all of the data exactly as shown—do not add any extra spaces or characters in the fields.
39. When you are done entering data into Data setup tabs, click on the Spatial Modeling tab.
40. Click on the Journey-to-Crime tab.
41. There are two different ways we can calculate JTC: with mathematical functions or with a calibrated function. For our analysis, we are going to run both.
42. We will start with the mathematical functions. Check the box next to "Journey-to-crime estimation (jtc)."
43. Check the box next to "use mathematical formula" and then click the down arrow to the right of the field called Distribution. We have five different mathematical formulas we can use:
    a. Negative exponential
    b. Normal distribution
    c. Lognormal distribution
    d. Linear distribution
    e. Truncated negative exponential

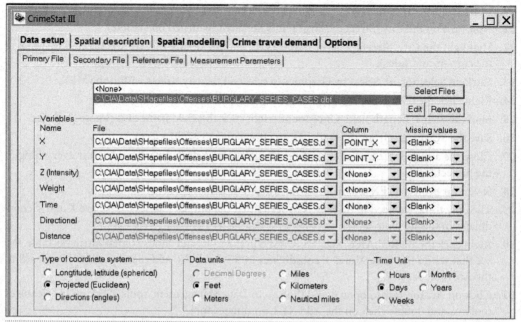

Figure E20—4

Ned Levine (2010). *CrimeStat III: A Spatial Statistics Program for the Analysis of Crime Incident Locations* (v 3.3). Ned Levine & Associates, Houston, TX, and the National Institute of Justice, Washington, DC. July. http://www.icpsr.umich.edu/CrimeStat.

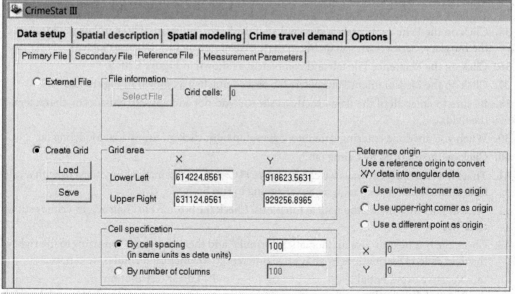

Figure E20—5

Ned Levine (2010). *CrimeStat III: A Spatial Statistics Program for the Analysis of Crime Incident Locations* (v 3.3). Ned Levine & Associates, Houston, TX, and the National Institute of Justice, Washington, DC. July. http://www.icpsr.umich.edu/CrimeStat.

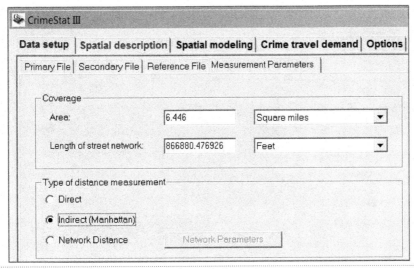

Figure E20–6

Ned Levine (2010). *CrimeStat III: A Spatial Statistics Program for the Analysis of Crime Incident Locations* (v 3.3). Ned Levine & Associates, Houston, TX, and the National Institute of Justice, Washington, DC. July. http://www.icpsr.umich.edu/CrimeStat.

44. Each of these can be used for different types of crime and some research into this is contained in the CrimeStat manual.
45. We will run each one of these formulas so we can see the result in ArcMap. Choose the Negative exponential to start with.
46. Click the **Save Output to** button, save this as an ArcView *.SHP file type.
47. Save it to your student folder as BurgNegExp.shp.
48. Click Compute.
49. CrimeStat will add JTC to the front of BurgNegExp.
50. Now close the results window, and change the formula to normal distribution. Click the Save Output to button and change the file name to BurgNormDist.shp.
51. Click compute.
52. Do these steps for the remaining three mathematical formulas. Name your files without "JTC."
53. When completed, reopen ArcMap and add these five layers:
    a. JTCBurgLinearDist
    b. JTCBurgLogNormDist
    c. JTCBurgNegExp
    d. JTCBurgNormDist
    e. JTCBurgTruncNegExp
54. After adding these layers, change the symbology for each layer to be Quantities, Natural breaks, seven classes, blue to red color ramp, with the Z field in each layer as the Value field. Change the outline to No Color for all symbols.
55. Move them all below all other layers in the TOC.
56. Turn off all the JTC layers except the negative exponential analysis (see **Figure E20–7**).

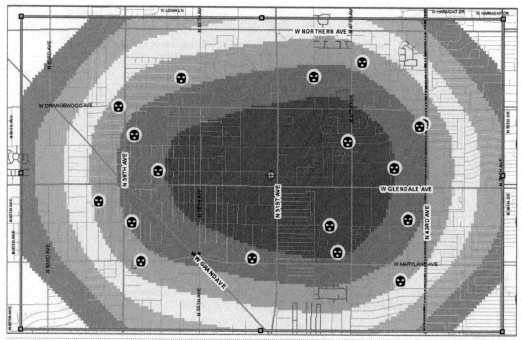

Figure E20–7

57. Turn on and off each layer one at time to see that the shapes of the peak profile areas are similar in that most highlight the center of the crime series as the likely area where the offender's residence would be located.

58. The result of the Normal Distribution is opposite of what we might think, which is indicating the offender residence is outside the crime series (see **Figure E20–8**).

59. The Lognormal distribution formula gives us a result that identifies the peak profile area to be very close around the crimes in the series (see **Figure E20–9**).

60. The Linear Distribution formula appears very similar to the normal distribution (see **Figure E20–10**).

61. The Truncated Negative Exponential formula gives us a result that seems to be the best for this crime series. It clearly identifies the mean center area, and areas closer to the crimes in the series (see **Figure E20–11**).

62. Another way we can do a JTC estimate is to use a calibrated model. We collect data from known offenders in our jurisdiction and we geocode their home address and the address of where they committed a crime. We create a table that has their information and both the origin (home) X and Y coordinates and the destination (crime) X and Y coordinates.

63. To see how this looks, use Windows Explorer to navigate to CIA\Data\JTC\SerialCrime.dbf and open this file. Open this file with Excel. (Excel does not usually automatically open DBF tables anymore, but you can open it after changing the file type in the open file dialog to dBase *.DBF. In some cases, depending on how your system is set up, it may only take double clicking the .dbf file name to open it in Excel.)

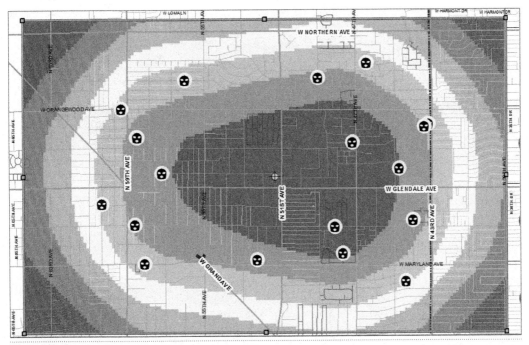

Figure E20—8

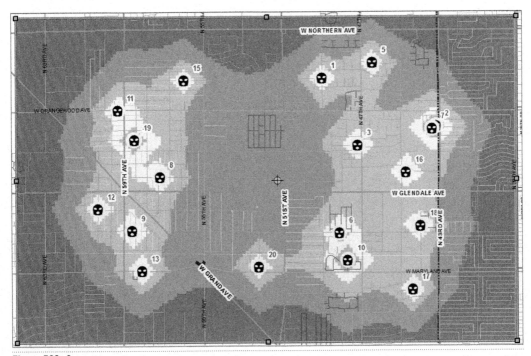

Figure E20—9

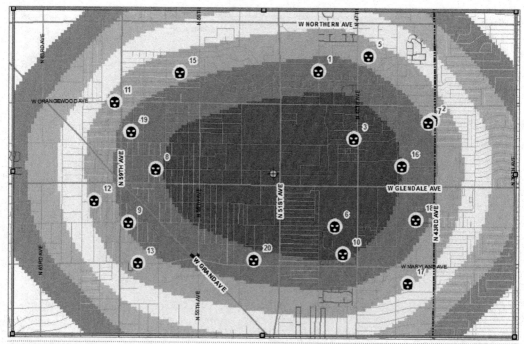

Figure E20–10

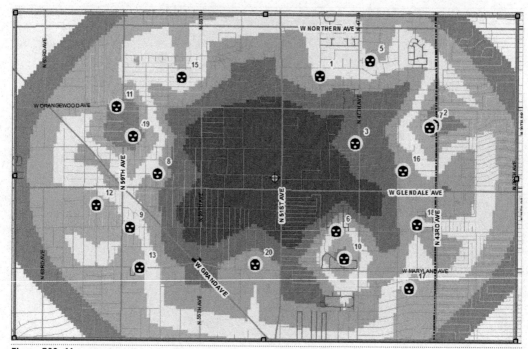

Figure E20–11

64. This file contains all of the serial crime trips for about 10 years' worth of serial crimes in Glendale.

65. The table contains the *XY* coordinates of the origins (home address of offender), and the destinations (location where crime occurred).

66. We will use this table in CrimeStat to create a calibration file.

67. Reopen CrimeStat to the journey-to-crime tab and click the Save Output to button.

68. Change the name to Calibrated1.shp in your student folder.

69. Click on the **Select Data File for Calibration** button.

70. In this dialog, click on the Select Files button, navigate to CIA\Data\JTC\SerialCrime.dbf, and click OK to load the file.

71. Complete the rest of the calibration dialog as shown in **Figure E20–12**.

72. Click OK.

73. Click the **Select Output File** button.

74. Choose Plain Text from the first box and save the file to your student folder as EX_20.txt (be sure to enter the .txt at the end).

75. Click OK.

76. Click on the Select Kernel Parameters button.

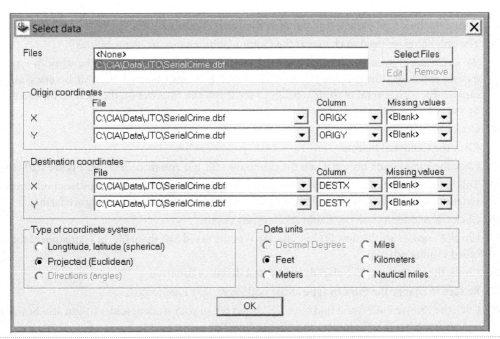

Figure E20–12

Ned Levine (2010). *CrimeStat III: A Spatial Statistics Program for the Analysis of Crime Incident Locations* (v 3.3). Ned Levine & Associates, Houston, TX, and the National Institute of Justice, Washington, DC. July. http://www.icpsr.umich.edu/CrimeStat.

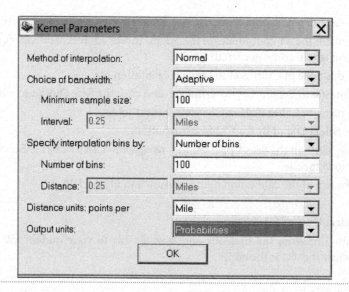

Figure E20–13

Ned Levine (2010). *CrimeStat III: A Spatial Statistics Program for the Analysis of Crime Incident Locations* (v 3.3). Ned Levine & Associates, Houston, TX, and the National Institute of Justice, Washington, DC. July. http://www.icpsr.umich.edu/CrimeStat.

77. Complete the kernel parameters dialog as shown in **Figure E20–13**.
78. The only thing we need to change is the Output Units; change to "Probabilities."
79. We could make these similar to what we do with hotspots and change the bandwidth type to quartic and adjust the cell size (interval) and search radius (distance bins). It is very good to experiment with several of these settings to see if you can improve on the final result and get a tighter, smaller peak profile area.
80. Click OK.
81. Click the Calibrate! button.
82. Click the View Graph button when the calibration file has run its course (see **Figure E20–14**).
83. This is the "distance decay" curve. This graph shows that the majority of trips from our known serial offenders were relatively short, and that more trips are closer than they are farther.
84. Click OK and then close the Calibration results popup.
85. Check to make sure the new JTC estimation is being saved as a shapefile, in your student folder, called Calibrated1.shp.
86. Check the box next to **Use already calibrated distance function**.
87. Be sure to change the **Files of type** at the bottom to Text Files (*.txt).
88. Click the Browse button and find your EX_20.txt file in your student folder (it can also be found in CIA\Exercises\EX_20 folder) and choose this file.
89. Click Compute.

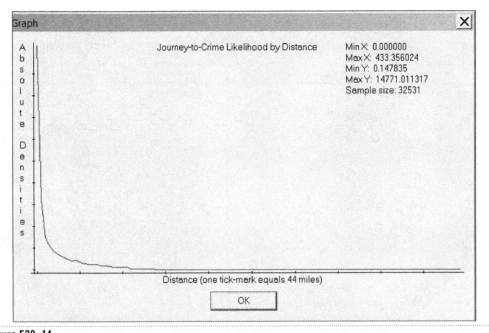

Figure E20–14

Ned Levine (2010). *CrimeStat III: A Spatial Statistics Program for the Analysis of Crime Incident Locations* (v 3.3). Ned Levine & Associates, Houston, TX, and the National Institute of Justice, Washington, DC. July. http://www.icpsr.umich.edu/CrimeStat.

90. When it is finished running, close the results window but not CrimeStat, return to ArcMap, and add the JTCCalibrated1.shp from your student folder to the ArcMap project.

91. Symbolize the new layer as you did with the five mathematical formula versions.

92. Your calibrated version of journey-to-crime should appear as shown in **Figure E20–15**.

93. Our calibrated version shows more emphasis on locations around the clusters of burglaries in the series. The red areas are the peak profile area and this demonstrates the graph we viewed on paper.

94. In one of the author's experience, the offender's home residence would probably be somewhere along a line you drew between the mean center, and the centers of each of the red "high" areas.

95. In some occasions, we might want to run every model and then take only the peak profile areas from each model and combine them into one analysis estimate of JTC as shown in **Figure E20–16**.

96. By combining all of the JCT estimates, we get an estimate that shows that the area near hits 6 and 10 in the series is the highest peak profile.

97. The area around hit 19 is also in the peak profile (red) classification on the map. This was an imaginary crime series, based on a real crime series and the real offender lived between hit 6 and 10.

98. Save and close your project.

99. Close CrimeStat.

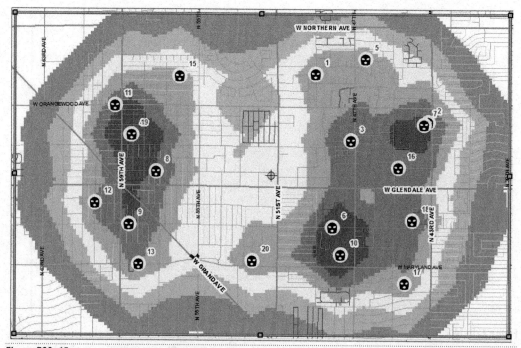

Figure E20–15

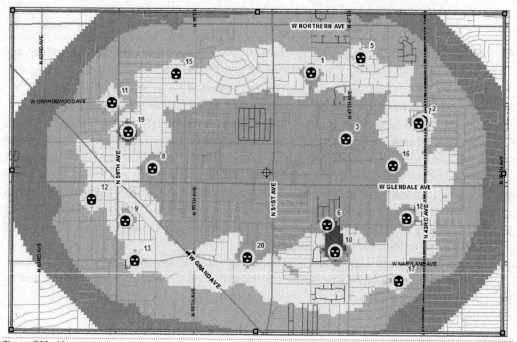

Figure E20–16

■ References

Brantingham, P. J., & Brantingham, P. L. (Eds.). (1981). *Environmental criminology*. Beverly Hills, CA: Sage.

Brantingham, P. J., & Brantingham, P. L. (1984). *Patterns in crime*. New York, NY: Macmillan.

Brantingham, P. L., & Brantigham, P. J. (1993). Environment, routine and situation: Toward a pattern theory of crime. In R. V. Clarke & M. Felson (Eds.), *Routine activity and rational choice* (pp. 259–294). New Brunswick, NJ: Transaction.

■ Exercise 21: Correlated Walk Analysis in CrimeStat

Data Needed for This Exercise

- CIA\Exercises\EX_21\EX_21.mxd

Lesson Objectives

- The student will learn to set up data.
- The student will learn to set up CrimeStat III for correlated walk analysis (CWA).
- The student will learn to use directionality, distance to next hit, and time variables in a tactical analysis.

Task Description

1. The correlated walk analysis attempts to predict the actual point where a new crime in a crime series might occur. Open CIA\Exercises\EX_21\CorrelatedWalkAnalysisHill.pdf and read it prior to doing this exercise so you have an idea of what you will be doing and further support your learning.

2. For a very ordered direction and distance crime series, the CWA works quite well and very nearly puts the point directly on top of the next crime location based on prior hits.

3. We will work with one of these very predictable and ordered series as well as a typical one we might find while working in a crime analysis unit. Unfortunately, most crime series are not as easily predictable and ordered.

4. The CWA is very good for predicting the next date in a crime series, as well as the distance a new hit will be from the last hit in the series.

5. Directionality does not work that well, and the simple manual observation of directionality from hit to hit serves the analyst better (in the authors' opinion). (Research on this routine by practicing analysts could make it better and is very much needed, however.)

6. Open EX_21.mxd in the CIA\Exercises\EX_21 folder.

7. As with the Interpolation hotspot routine, and the journey-to-crime routine, we will need to make sure that the series data we wish to analyze have the X and Y coordinates in the attribute table.

8. You will find three different crime series: the very predictable made-up series, a robbery series, and a burglary series.

9. Open the attribute table for the very Predictable_Pattern series (see **Figure E21-1**).

10. You should find that this table contains Point_X and Point_Y, as well as two other fields: DBH and CDBH. These stand for days between hits and cumulative days between hits.

Table

Predictable_Pattern

FID	Shape *	Id	POINT_X	POINT_Y	OCCDATETIM	DBH	CDBH
0	Point	1	607596	959883	1/23/2012	0	1
1	Point	2	612882	959879	2/6/2012	14	15
2	Point	3	619527	960930	2/21/2012	15	30
3	Point	4	623215	963110	3/6/2012	14	44
4	Point	5	620611	965746	3/13/2012	7	51
5	Point	6	617896	968270	3/21/2012	8	59
6	Point	7	614752	968208	3/29/2012	8	67
7	Point	8	610354	968220	4/4/2012	6	73
8	Point	9	607772	967807	4/14/2012	10	83
9	Point	10	604945	965166	4/20/2012	6	89
10	Point	11	604462	962161	5/3/2012	13	102
11	Point	12	604960	959877	5/18/2012	15	117

Figure E21–1

11. The data are sorted in order of occurrence, and then the number of days between each hit was calculated. We don't have anything in the first row except 0 because of course there were no hits before this one. The CDBH field is what we will give to CrimeStat as the "Time" variable. Now that we have verified the fields that we need are in this table, close the table and open CrimeStat. In the primary file tab, complete it as shown in **Figure E21–2**.
12. The Predictable_Pattern.dbf file is located in the CIA\Exercises\EX_21 folder.
    - **a.** X = Point_X
    - **b.** Y = Point_Y
    - **c.** Time = CDBH
    - **d.** Type of Coordinate System = Projected (Euclidean)
    - **e.** Data Units = Feet
    - **f.** Time Unit = Days
13. After completing the Primary File tab correctly, click on the **Spatial Modeling** tab.
14. Click on the **Space-time analysis** tab.
15. Check the box next to Correlogram.
16. Check the box next to Regression Diagnostics.
17. Check the box next to Prediction.
18. Leave the Time, Distance, and Bearing methods as Mean, Lag 1.
19. Click the **Save Output to** button to the right of the Prediction item, and save this to your student folder as PMean.shp.
20. We do not need to save the output of the Correlogram as it is just there to inform us if the CWA routine will work well.
21. Click Compute.
22. We will get three tabs of functions that have run CWA-C, CWA-D, CWA-P.
23. Click on the CWA-C tab to view the results (see **Figure E21–3**).
24. Scroll down until you see Adjusted Lag.

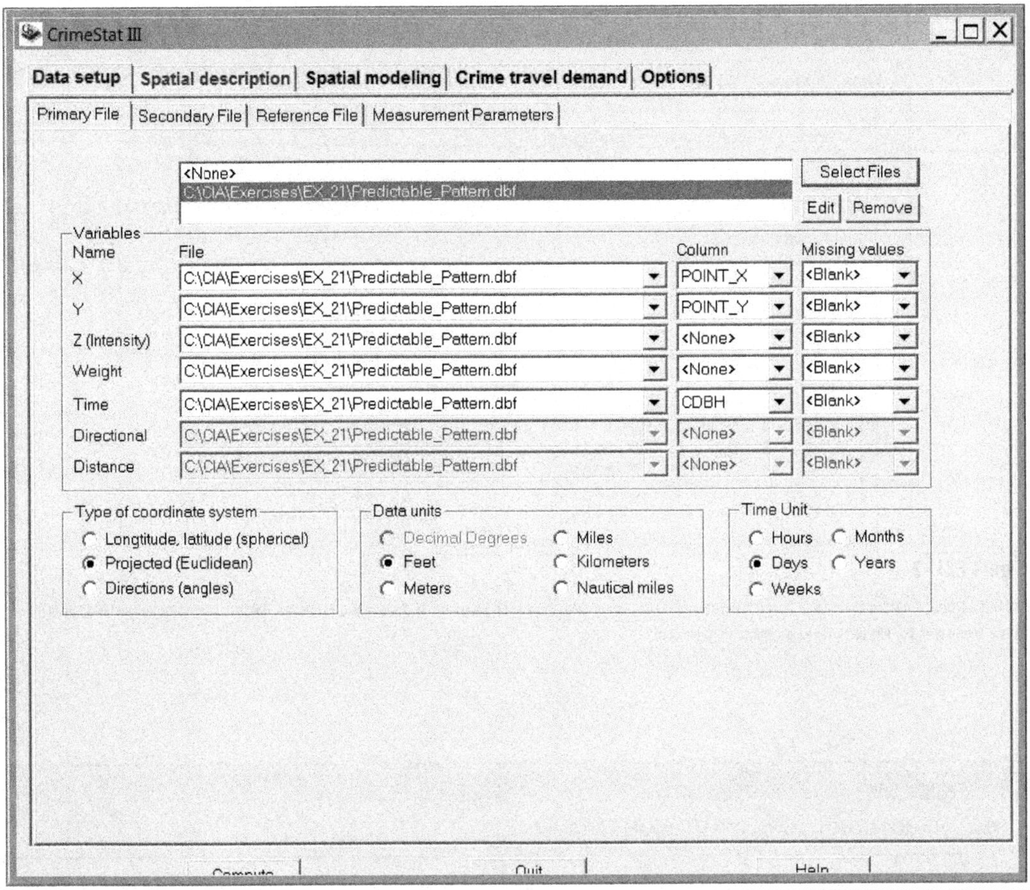

Figure E21-2

Ned Levine (2010). *CrimeStat III: A Spatial Statistics Program for the Analysis of Crime Incident Locations* (v 3.3). Ned Levine & Associates, Houston, TX, and the National Institute of Justice, Washington, DC. July. http://www.icpsr.umich.edu/CrimeStat.

25. This is a lag calculation for the time, distance, and bearing factors from the X and Y coordinates and time variables we set in the primary file section.

26. We need to find the lags for each variable that are the largest; it looks for the time variable we get −0.40413 at Lag 4.

27. For the distance variable, it is Lag 1 with 0.38822. (Do not worry if your values are slightly different from mine—the lags should be the same.)

28. And finally, for the bearing variable (or direction) we get Lag 7 with 0.30255.

29. Record the lags for each of the variables—time, distance, and bearing.

30. Now click on the CWA-D tab.

31. This tab is really to let you know how predictable CrimeStat thinks each variable is. We are looking for the Multiple R value for each variable (see **Figure E21-4**).

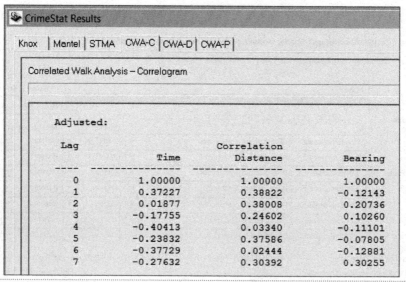

Figure E21–3

Ned Levine (2010). *CrimeStat III: A Spatial Statistics Program for the Analysis of Crime Incident Locations* (v 3.3). Ned Levine & Associates, Houston, TX, and the National Institute of Justice, Washington, DC. July. http://www.icpsr.umich.edu/CrimeStat.

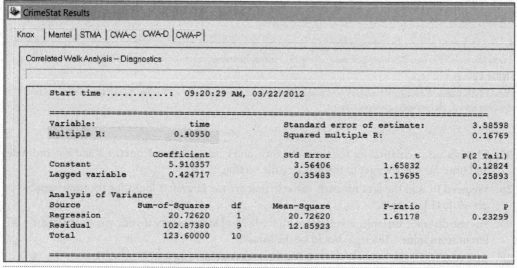

Figure E21–4

Ned Levine (2010). *CrimeStat III: A Spatial Statistics Program for the Analysis of Crime Incident Locations* (v 3.3). Ned Levine & Associates, Houston, TX, and the National Institute of Justice, Washington, DC. July. http://www.icpsr.umich.edu/CrimeStat.

32. We have observed that when these Multiple R values for the variables of time, distance, and bearing are over +/–0.25 they seem to be reliable predictors of future behavior. This is only subjective, but we look at these values just to see if we can rely on the data being produced. You can see that the bearing Multiple R value is –0.13357, which really does not seem too good.

33. Okay, now click on the CWA-P tab.

34. This is our first prediction of where the next crime would occur in this series and is based on the mean of the variables. Scroll down until you find the Predicted Time wording (see **Figure E21–5**).

35. The value of our predicted time is 127.54545. Record this value someplace and once we get the data back into ArcMap, we will see what we do with it.

36. The *X* and *Y* coordinates of the predicted point are also shown here.

37. Now close the CrimeStat Results window and go back to the Spatial Modeling Tab → Space-time analysis section.

38. Uncheck the boxes next to Correlogram and Regression Diagnostics.

39. Change the Mean in each of the boxes for time, distance, and bearing to Median.

40. Leave the Lag at 1, but click on the Save Output to button and save it as PMedian in your student folder.

41. Click Compute.

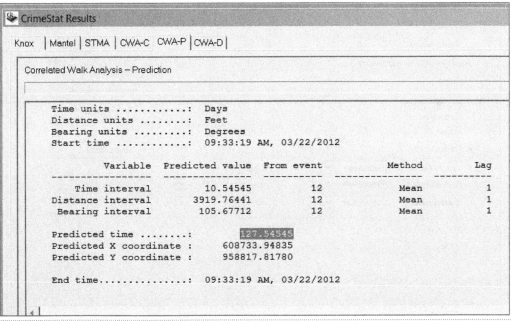

Figure E21–5

42. When the results window is done calculating, go down to the predicted time section again and record this value. We have found that this is the most accurate prediction of time from the three versions we will be running. Our value is 127.0000.

43. Close the CrimeStat Results window, and now change the boxes that have Median in them to Regression.

44. Do you remember what those lags were for time, distance, and bearing? (See steps 25–30.)

45. Enter Lag 4 for Time, Lag 1 for distance, and Lag 7 for bearing and click the Save Output to button.

46. Change the saved file name to PReg in your student folder (see **Figure E21–6**).

47. Click Compute.

48. In the results window, collect and write down the time prediction again; it is 126.59105.

49. Close the results window but leave CrimeStat open.

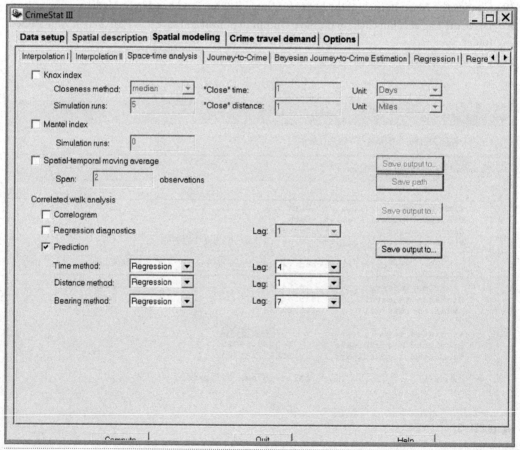

Figure E21–6

Ned Levine (2010). *CrimeStat III: A Spatial Statistics Program for the Analysis of Crime Incident Locations* (v 3.3). Ned Levine & Associates, Houston, TX, and the National Institute of Justice, Washington, DC. July. http://www.icpsr.umich.edu/CrimeStat.

50. Open your ArcMap project and add data from your student folder.

51. You will be looking for a "PredDestL" prefix to find the predicted points in this pretend series. There are three of these files:

    a. PredDestLPMean.shp
    b. PredDestLPMedian.shp
    c. PredDestLPReg.shp

52. Load these three points. At your leisure, review the other files the function provided along with these three points. We will not go over these files in this lesson as they are not pertinent to the final predictions.

53. Now view the crime series and your new points on the map. Notice how the crime series starts about 7500 W Bell Rd and circles counterclockwise back to about 7900 W Bell Rd. Simple deductive reasoning would have you place the next point in this series between 6700 and 7500 W Bell Rd (between points 1 and 2).

54. Change the symbology of each point layer so that you can distinguish between them on the map. We have two of the points, PredDestLPMean.shp and PredDestLPMedian.shp, which are very close to where we would logically think the next hit might be.

55. The PredDestLPReg.shp layer is also very close and either one of these points might predict the next hit very accurately.

56. If only other crime series were as predictable. I have had crime series that were as predictable, but there have been very few in my 17-year career as a crime analyst (see **Figure E21–7**).

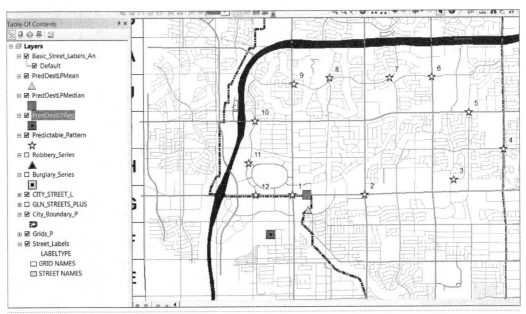

Figure E21–7

57. Now back to the time variables and how to use them: Right click the Predictable_Pattern layer in the TOC and choose Open Attribute Table.

58. The last cumulative value in the CDBH field is 117. Our values from the three analyses we did were:
    a. Mean = 127.54545
    b. Median = 127.0000
    c. Regression = 126.59105

59. So we have 3 different days since the last hit, during which the new hit could occur. 10.5 days (mean), 10 (median), and 9.6 (regression) days from the last hit in the series. If you look at the number of days between hits, 9.6–10.5 does not seem unreasonable at all.

60. We could say that, "if the offender continues to behave in the manner that they have in the past, the next crime in this series should occur on May 27 or May 28, 2012."

61. Recreate this analysis with the Robbery and the Burglary series data. Your final maps should look like **Figures E21-8** and **E21-9**.

62. Be observant and make sure you check each attribute table first to be sure the X and Y fields are there and populated. Also make sure the CDBH field is there and that the name is not different for that field.

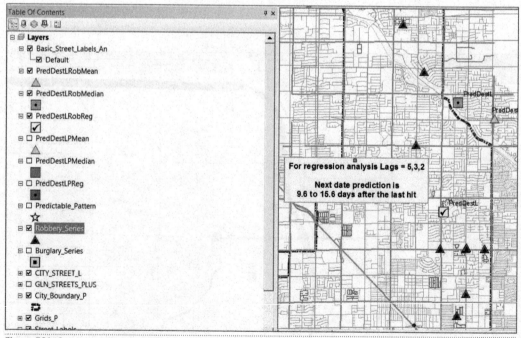

Figure E21-8

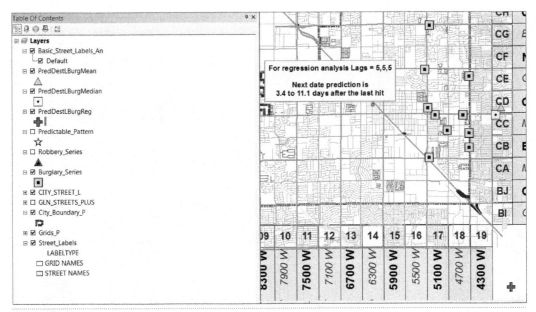

Figure E21–9

■ Exercise 22: Administrative Analysis Example

Data Needed for This Exercise

- Figure E22–1

Lesson Objectives

- The student will learn how to create a reference map for patrol beats.
- The student will learn basic skills on creating layouts through practice.

Task Description

1. This exercise is geared toward creating a map that is used by all units within the police department; the beat map. The goal is to recreate the map shown in **Figure E22–1** using the skills you have been practicing to this point.

2. Make sure to use white space effectively and do not have too much on the map that distracts from what it is meant to tell the reader.

3. The primary purpose is to make a beat map, so do not lose sight of this goal. Be professional and remember to include:

   - North arrow
   - Scale bar
   - Title
   - Map with one center of attention

   - Disclaimer text
   - Legend
   - Other text or graphics, as needed
   - Keep colors pastel except for the center of attention

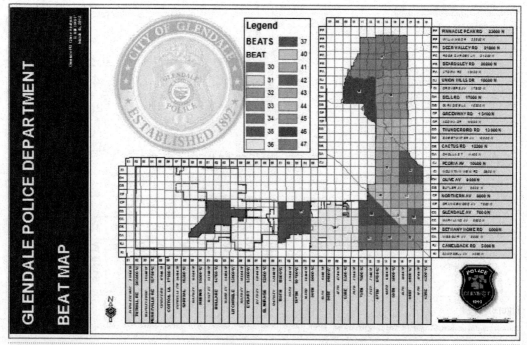

Figure E22–1

■ Exercise 23: Strategic Analysis Problem Solving Example

Data Needed for This Exercise

- Add reference layers (streets, boundaries, etc.).
- Add event data layers that you feel are needed to answer the question.
- Add additional data you feel enhance the analysis.

Lesson Objectives

- The student will learn how to analyze data for a strategic, problem-solving perspective.
- The student will learn how to work with different data layers to come to a conclusion and identify problem areas.
- The student will get more practice with hotspot and hot address analyses.
- The student will achieve further discovery of graphs and charts.
- The student will learn the use of reports in ArcMap 10.
- The student will discover how to find and identify problems and do the analysis a police agency would require of an analyst as well as discover how to use these same tools to answer a common question.

The commander of the Gateway Patrol Division has asked that you do a long-term (January 2001–December 2004) study to determine where robberies have occurred the most within her division. She would also like to know if there are any businesses or other addresses that have repeat offenses of robbery. She has also asked for day of week, time of day, and any other information you think the patrol units working this area should know about the crime of robbery. You have already given her a breakdown of the offender types—race, sex, ages etc.—responsible for the robberies in the Gateway division. You have even provided a general study of the vehicle types used in robberies in this division. Your goal then is to create a hotspot map and a graduated point map showing the top 10 locations where the robberies have occurred between January 1, 2001 and December 31, 2004. Once you have these data, you need to compile statistics on the hottest days of week and times of day robberies occur.

Task Description

1. Create your base map as shown in **Figure E23–1**.
2. First, we need to do a select by attributes on the Offense_Data layer for all robberies that occurred between January 1, 2001 and December 31, 2004:
   - "UCRTYPE" = 'ROBBERY' AND ("RECVDATE" >= 20010101 and "RECVDATE" <= 20041231)
3. Complete the Select by Attributes query.
4. Once you have all the robberies during this time period, **Data → Export data** this file to your student folder as AllRobberies.shp and add it to your map.
5. You should end up with 1035 records.
6. Do the following steps:
   a. Verify the attribute table has XY coordinates.
   b. Verify the robbery data have no missing XY values (15 records have 0 for the X and Y).
   c. Create your minimum bounding rectangle (MBR) around the robberies.
   d. Find the Lower Left X and Y.
   e. Find the Upper Right X and Y.

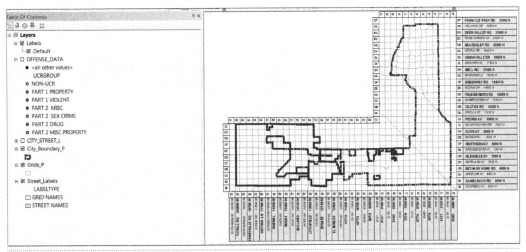

Figure E23–1

   f. Find the total square area in miles.

   g. Find the total street footage within the MBR.

   h. Set up the primary file in CrimeStat to point at your AllRobberies.dbf in your student folder.

   i. Set to Projected (Euclidean).

   j. Set the distance units to Feet.

   k. Enter the Reference File data (lower left *XY* and upper right *XY*).

   l. Set cell specification, cell spacing size to 150.

   m. Enter measurement parameters data (square mile area and total street feet, Indirect [Manhattan] distance measurement).

   n. Click Spatial modeling, Single Interpolation:

       i. Quartic

       ii. Fixed interval: 2640 feet

       iii. Probabilities

       iv. Save results to your student folder as an ArcView .SHP file.

7. Click Compute.

8. Close the CrimeStat Results window but do not close CrimeStat until you have verified the routine settings were correct.

9. Add the shapefile to your project (say yes to projection missing).

10. Symbolize with blue–red color ramp, quantities legend type, Value field = Z, Natural breaks classification schema with seven classes, change the sampling size if needed. Make the darkest blue symbol have a white fill. Make all symbols have no outline. Change values in Symbol labels to Very Low, Low, <blank>, Moderate, <blank>, High, and Very High.

11. Apply the legend and close the properties dialog. Move the kernel density lower on the table of contents (TOC) to draw behind the other layers.

12. Change to the layout view and change the layout to resemble **Figure E23-2**.

13. Work hard and remember everything we do should look as professional as possible.

14. When done with this map, click File → Export Map and save as a *.PDF; we can now move on to the next step.

15. Use either the CrimeStat Mode function or the Spatial Statistics tools Collect events with rendering tool, and create a graduated point map.

16. You will have to then edit this file and provide only the top 10 locations for the map. (Note that the top frequency is 15, which would be the locations with an *XY* of "0" and should be excluded from the top 10.)

17. Normally, we would save the original and then export just the top 10 as its own layer.

18. When done with this map, it should resemble **Figure E23-3**.

19. Export this map as a PDF and we are halfway through.

20. Now close ArcMap and open Excel 2010.

21. Open the AllRobberies.dbf table with Excel. Create a pivot table based on the MPDOW and MPTOD fields.

22. Your pivot table can look like **Figure E23-4** by simply applying Home Ribbon → Conditional Format → Color Scales.

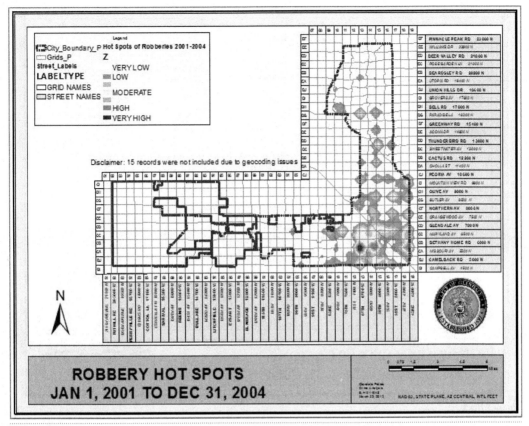

Figure E23–2

23. Or you can create day of week and time of day charts separately (see **Figure E23–5**).

24. Another option in Excel is the Surface chart as shown in **Figure E23–6**.

25. These are all good ways to demonstrate the day of week and time of day peaks, and which one you use will be dependent on how well you train those persons who are viewing them.

26. Be careful not to assume the audience always knows how to read a complex chart like the surface chart shown in Figure E23–6, and you may want to use the conditionally formatted table or the separate graphs for day of week and time of day. You must know your audience.

27. At this point, you would likely put together a bulletin or a report concerning everything you know about the robberies.

28. To create a report from ArcMap, right click the AllRobberies layer and choose Open Attribute Table.

29. Click on the Table Options button, and near the bottom of the popup dialog click Reports.

30. Then click Create a report.

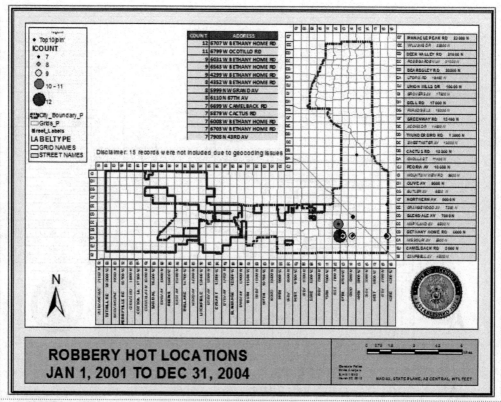

Figure E23–3

TIME OF DAY	Sun	Mon	Tue	Wed	Thu	Fri	Sat	TOTALS
0000-0059 hr	9	14	7	5	6	9	14	64
0100-0159 hr	7	12	7	5	3	6	7	47
0200-0259 hr	5	7	5	9	7	8	9	50
0300-0359 hr	8	3	1	8	1	4	8	33
0400-0459 hr	2	4	4	3	3	2	1	19
0500-0559 hr	2	2	2	7	2	3	3	21
0600-0659 hr	1	5	5	1	2	3	1	18
0700-0759 hr	0	4	5	3	3	6	1	22
0800-0859 hr	2	3	2	2	3	1	1	14
0900-0959 hr	5	6	6	3	3	3	1	27
1000-1059 hr	4	3	9	5	4	8	2	35
1100-1159 hr	2	0	7	6	4	1	2	22
1200-1259 hr	2	7	2	6	5	14	3	39
1300-1359 hr	4	4	9	5	5	6	4	37
1400-1459 hr	7	7	12	8	3	3	1	41
1500-1559 hr	5	9	7	7	10	9	7	54
1600-1659 hr	8	7	11	9	4	11	4	54
1700-1759 hr	4	6	7	7	6	2	4	36
1800-1859 hr	7	10	7	9	13	9	9	64
1900-1959 hr	5	10	8	11	11	15	7	67
2000-2059 hr	9	8	11	10	13	7	9	67
2100-2159 hr	12	11	12	9	10	11	6	71
2200-2259 hr	16	9	13	8	7	11	7	71
2300-2359 hr	15	4	9	6	4	12	12	62
TOTALS	141	155	168	152	132	164	123	1035

Figure E23–4

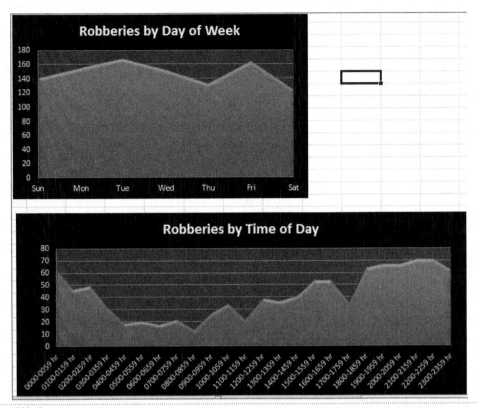

Figure E23–5

31. There are several option screens that you will need to go through and from which you want fields in the final report, and you will be able to decide if you want to group by field name and which fields the data will be sorted by. Then we can decide what look we want for the report and what to title it (see **Figures E23–7** to **E23–13**).

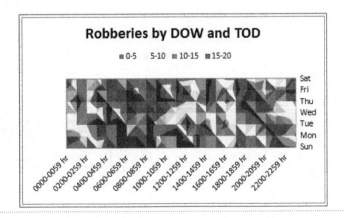

Figure E23–6

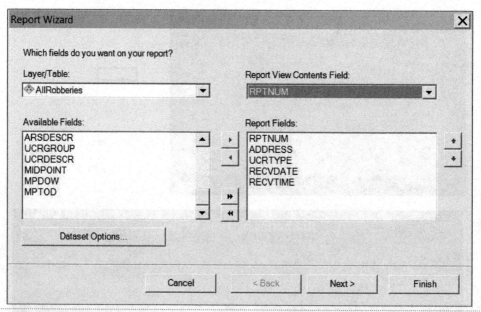

Figure E23–7

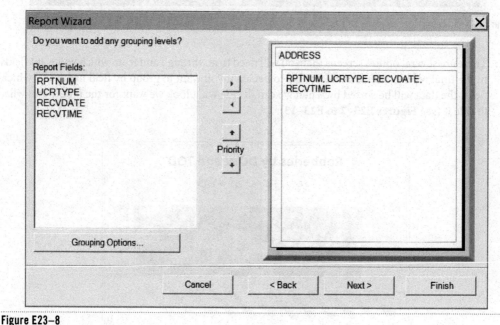

Figure E23–8

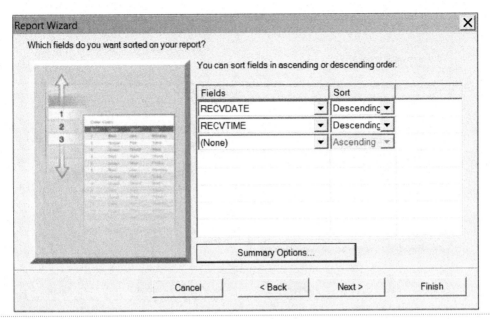

Figure E23–9

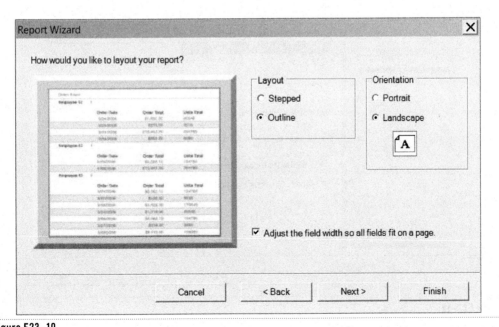

Figure E23–10

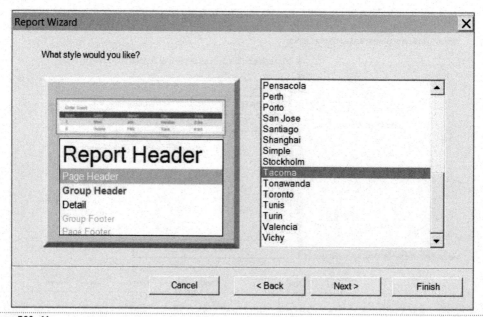

Figure E23–11

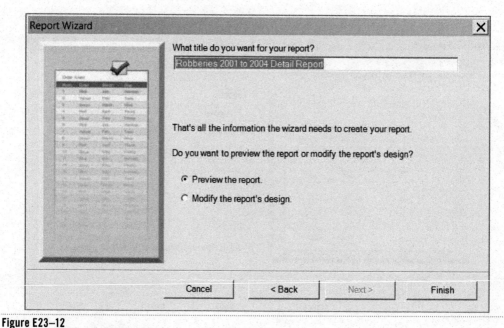

Figure E23–12

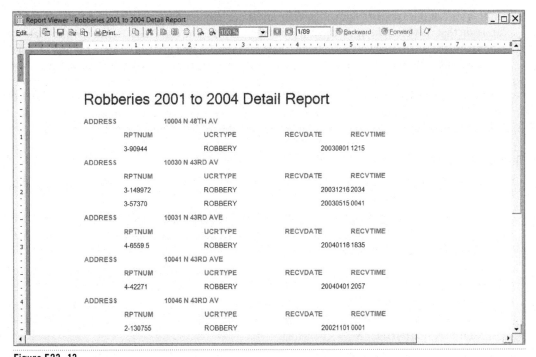

Figure E23–13

32. Once we click Finish, we get a standard-looking report that could be useful for sorting and looking at details of events.

33. You can also save reports and use them again later. Save your project because you can use it for the next part of this assignment.

■ Exercise 23b: Strategic Analysis Information Example

Data Needed for This Exercise

- Add reference layers (streets, boundaries, etc.).
- Add event data layers that you feel are needed to answer the question.
- Add additional data you feel enhance the analysis.

Lesson Objectives

- The student will learn how to analyze data from a strategic, problem-solving perspective.
- The student will learn how to work with different data layers to come to a conclusion and identify problem areas.
- The student will get more practice with hotspot and hot address analyses.
- The student will discover uses for graphs and charts.

In this part of the exercise, you will answer an ad hoc request from the city council concerning an issue that was brought up to them from a constituent. The complaint is that a white male—approximately 45–55 years of age, with grey hair, between 5'7" and 5'9" tall, weighing approximately 145 lbs, with a "beer belly" and large glasses—has been exposing himself to several women jogging up and down the Thunderbird Paseo linear park. Apparently the offender is getting more and more aggressive with the women and the chief has directed you to create a bulletin for patrol with the dates and times of this offender's crimes (provided you can find any cases). If possible, a prediction of when and where he may be again in the future could be useful.

Task Description

1. You will need to start by opening the project from EX_23, or creating a new project with the layers you need for this analysis.
2. First select the Thunderbird Paseo park using a Select by Attributes query.
3. Then use a Select by Location query to find all the UCR offenses from the Offense_Data that are within 1000 feet of the park.
4. You will then want to right click the Offense_Data layer and choose open attributes. You have more than just indecent exposures within 1000 feet of the park. You need to click on the Table Options button and choose Select by Attributes.
5. Choose **Select from Current Selection** of the Offense_Data, which matches "UCRDESCR" = 'SEX OFFENSES/INDECENT EXPOSURE'.
6. Once you have the 18 indecent exposures within 1000 feet of the park, export these indecent exposures to a new shapefile and add to the map.
7. Since we don't have access to the police reports, we are going to "pretend" we read all of them and found that they all fit the same basic modus operandi (MO) and physical description of this offender.
8. So, gang, we have a crime series going on here, what do we do?
9. First, we would likely talk to the investigator assigned to these cases and make sure they are not already doing something, and then join the game of finding this offender. Be sure to advise your detective that the chief has made a request for a report for city council so he can ensure the integrity of his investigation if necessary.
10. Then we would likely advise the chief and create a city council report indicating that these 18 crimes are all part of the same offender's crime series and what we are doing as a department to find and arrest this offender.
11. Then we would create a tactical analysis, using whatever method you wish, to predict where the offender would strike again.
12. We have now moved into a more tactical response and project than a strategic analysis but this is how these things go sometimes. The strategic analysis we did identified the crime series.
13. Create a tactical analysis prediction of where and when the next hit will occur using the many tools and skills taught thus far in these exercises.
14. We hope you would try to replicate a probability grid method prediction, but in any case your analysis should end up looking like **Figure E23–14**.
15. Our date and time analysis would look like the charts in **Figures E23–15** and **E23–16**.

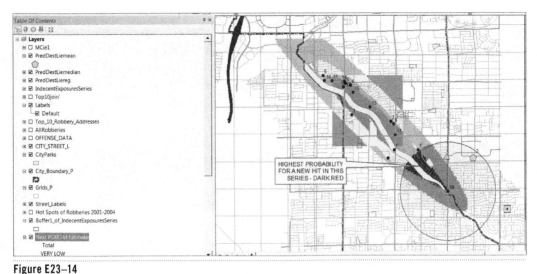

Figure E23–14

16. Using the correlated walk time estimate, the offender is expected to hit again between October 11, 2004 and November 7, 2004.

17. Create your layout, and, if needed, a bulletin analyzing this crime series (see **Figure E23–17**).

18. When finished, save this project as EX_23.mxd in your student folder and close all open programs.

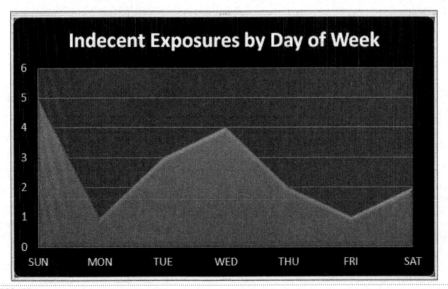

Figure E23–15

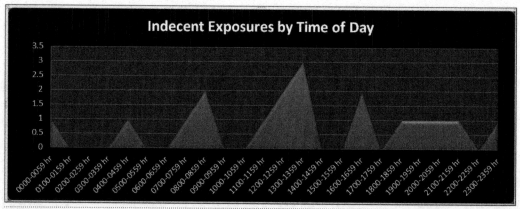

Figure E23–16

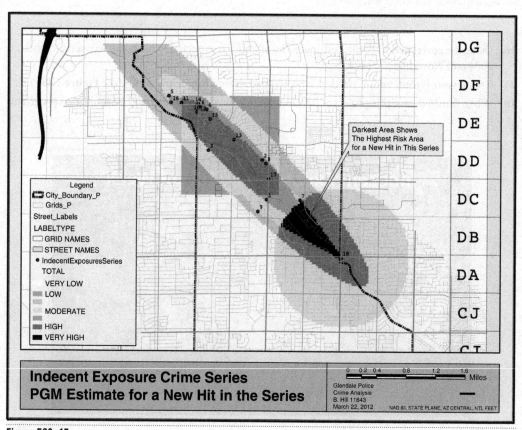

Figure E23–17

■ Exercise 24: Tactical Analysis Example

Data Needed for This Exercise

- You will need to start a new project or use an existing one you can save as EX_24.mxd.
- The crime series you will be analyzing is at
  CIA\Data\Shapefiles\Offenses\XSTASY_METH_CASES.shp

Lesson Objectives

- Create an ArcMap project from scratch.
- Do a tactical analysis and predict where the meth suspects will hit next.
- Create a bulletin with the information above plus the day of week and time of day the next hit is likely to occur.
- Use good technique when creating the map and the layout for the audience of investigators this map and bulletin are for.

Task Description

1. Create a new ArcMap Project.
2. Analyze the XSTASY_METH_CASES.shp data for the next hit to determine *where* it will be.
3. Analyze the XSTASY_METH_CASES.shp data to determine *when* the next hit will be (date range).
4. Analyze the XSTASY_METH_CASES.shp to determine what *day of week* is the most likely.
5. Analyze the XSTASY_METH_CASES.shp to determine what the most significant *time of day* the next hit will be.
6. Your final analysis should resemble the bulletin found here: CIA\Exercises\EX_24 folder named XstasyBulletin.pdf.

■ Exercise 24b: Tactical Analysis: More Practice on Your Own

Data Needed for This Exercise

- You will need to start a new project or use an existing one you can save as EX_24.mxd.
- CIA\Data\Other\TacticalAnalysisPractice.xlsx.
- This exercise gives you a chance to do more tactical analyses using actual crime series from the city of Glendale.

Lesson Objectives

- Practice creating tactical analyses, journey-to-crime (JTC) analyses, and developing bulletins on these crime series.
- The data the student will show should contain the multiple crimes in a series and the X and Y coordinates for the offender's home address.
- Practice developing a PGM analysis using whatever layers you feel are most appropriate. You can also use weighting to create the Interpolation density from CrimeStat as you feel best fits the series.
- Practice developing JTC analyses on the series in the Excel sheet. See if you can successfully predict the offender's home address.

Task Description

1. Open any one of the series in the TacticalAnalysisPractice.xlsx workbook. Bring them into your map project and perform the PGM tactical analysis, or *another analysis you feel confident doing.*

2. Consider completing a JTC analysis for each series and predict the peak profile area.
   a. Think of how a detective or a surveillance unit would use this information.

3. The crime series data are located here: CIA\Data\Other\TacticalAnalysisPractice.xlsx.

4. Remember who your audience is, and try to think of what information they would need the most when doing these analyses.

5. Consider the type of maps you are going to create and any ancillary documents, graphs, or charts you should create to give your audience the best information.

6. Think about and plan out your analysis before you begin:
   a. Determine what GIS data files you need.
   b. Create a new project with these data.

7. Since the series data are in an Excel 2010 spreadsheet format, you should go into the spreadsheet and create a unique name for the offenses in each tab (this works the best when bringing into ArcMap 10).
   a. Bring these in as event themes and then convert them to shapefiles (so we have the *.dbf file for CrimeStat).

8. Run the different spatial statistics (CrimeStat or ArcMap) you feel apply to these series based on what you see on the map, how close they are to other cases in the series, and how close they are to other things on the map.
   a. What is the directionality of the offender between hits?
   b. Apply other knowledge you may know about the victims if any.

9. Create one analysis result from all the layers you have created to determine the most likely hit location.

10. Do any temporal analyses you feel are important to give to investigators so they can set up surveillance on those places.

11. Create your map and bulletin and be proud of what you have done, but not so proud that you cannot take constructive criticism from your peers as needed. (Use that criticism to make a better analysis the next time around.)

12. Do not be afraid to ask detectives what they know about the crime series and learn what they are doing in the investigation. If you do not agree, you can speak up, but beware the consequences (good or bad, depending on how you came across).

13. When first starting, it is a good idea to sketch on a piece of paper what you think your map or bulletin should look like. Once done, figure out what data are needed to draw that map in ArcMap, and then work toward getting it done one step at a time.

14. Good luck and have fun with these series. They are actual crime series from the city of Glendale.

15. See if you can predict where they are going next, and see if your JTC analysis shows where their home address is.

16. When finished, try one of the other series in the Excel workbook. The more you practice performing these functions, the more proficient you will become, and the less time it will take you to run the analyses.

■ Exercise 25: Using Data from ArcServices/Internet

Data Needed for This Exercise

- In this exercise, we will create a new ArcMap 10 project using data from the ESRI Arc Services basemap data.

Lesson Objectives

- The student will learn how to create a new map from an ESRI template which uses data from an Internet connection.

Task Description

1. For this exercise, you must have Internet access on the computer you are using.
2. Click on the ArcMap icon in **Start → All Programs → ArcGIS → ArcMap 10**.
3. When the program opens, it will provide you several opportunities to select from several templates.
4. Click on the **Traditional Layouts → USA → USA** (see **Figure E25–1**).
5. This will allow us to go online and download these basemap data, then it will create the map for us.
6. Click OK to create the map.
7. You should now have a map that looks like **Figure E25–2**.

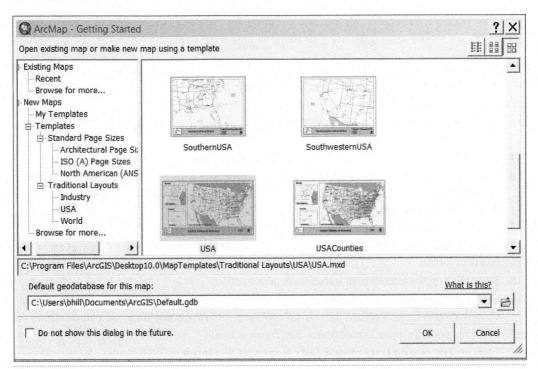

Figure E25–1

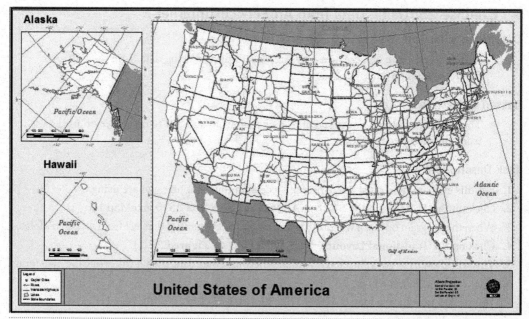

Figure E25–2

8. Zoom in to Arizona using the Tools toolbar's interactive zoom tool. Draw a rectangle around Arizona and zoom in to it on the main map to the right.

9. Make sure you use the Tools toolbar and not the layout toolbar.

10. Click the button at the bottom left of the map display that reads, "Data View" when you hover your cursor over it.

11. This exercise will also introduce you to multiple **Data Frames**.

12. Look in the table of contents (TOC). There are three data frames: (1) Alaska, (2) Hawaii, and (3) conterminous United States. Also observe that the conterminous United States data frame is **bold** because this is the active frame.

13. Right click on the Alaska data frame and choose **Activate**.

14. Now the data within this data frame are active and all we see are the Alaska data layers within this data frame.

15. Right click on the Hawaii data frame and make it active.

16. In this manner, you can create much more complex maps that show graphs, charts, close-ups of certain areas in question, a citywide hotspot map, and nearly anything else you can think of.

17. Make the conterminous United States data frame active.

18. Click on **File → Add Data → Add Data from ArcGIS Online**.

19. In the Search field, type "Arizona" and hit the Enter key.

20. Click the Add button under the USA Topo maps.

21. After a few seconds, you will now see the topographic (topo) maps for the United States.

22. Drag and drop the new layer to the bottom of the conterminous United States data frame (if it did not go there automatically).

23. Turn off the States layer so we can see the new Topo layer.

24. Zoom in to the area around where Phoenix should be (the intersection where most freeways area located).

25. Zoom in and notice how the data refreshes after each zoom, allowing us to see more detail in the data.

26. Right click this layer and choose Properties. Read about these data in the General tab: "This map presents land cover imagery for the world and detailed topographic maps for the United States..."

27. Close the Properties dialog.

28. There are many more datasets available from ESRI online. Add data from ArcGIS online again and search for Phoenix, or Glendale.

29. If we search for Glendale, we find a map layer that is coming directly from the Spatial Database Engine (SDE) servers at Glendale. Add the data.

30. The majority of these datasets are free and some are for a fee, but you can see how if you do not already have some of these data, this could be a great source to find some.

31. Zoom in to the approximate extents of the City of Glendale (using the Glendale SDE_ NeighborhoodMapServerObject data from a search of Glendale, and then zooming to the extents of this layer).

32. Now right click any of the basemaps within the conterminous United States data frame, and choose Save As → Layer File.

33. Save the *.lyr file as EX25Layer.lyr, and save it to your student folder.

34. Now close the ArcMap project (you can save it as EX_25.mxd if you choose).

35. Open ArcMap 10 again, and then find your EX25Layer.lyr file and load it into the new map.

36. After several seconds, all of our data is back. (*Note:* Often the data does not preserve the view we had, but it is all there and we can zoom back in.)

37. Close ArcMap; this concludes this exercise.

■ Exercise 26: Creating a Simple Model

Data Needed for This Exercise

- CIA\Exercises\EX_26\EX_26.mxd

Lesson Objectives

- The student will learn how to create a simple geographic information system (GIS) model to separate different Uniform Crime Report (UCR) offenses for a specific time period from a main dataset.

Task Description

1. Many times we find ourselves doing repetitive tasks over and over again. One of those tasks would be to select subsets of UCR crime data, by crime type, and a date range.

2. In this exercise, we are going to create a simple model that will do this for us, so we do not have to do it manually.

3. Open EX_26.mxd from the CIA\Exercises\EX_26 folder.

4. Our objective is to run multiple Select by Attributes queries on the Offense_Data layer:
   a. By UCR type
   b. By date range

5. We want to begin by creating a new toolbox to store our new model when we are done with it.

6. Create a new folder called "MyTools" in your student folder.

7. Now open ArcCatalog and navigate to where you saved your MyTools folder. Once found, right click the MyTools folder and choose New → Toolbox. Change the Toolbox.tbx to read My Crime Analysis Tool Box.tbx.

8. Now, go back to ArcMap and open ArcToolbox.

9. Right click anywhere in the blank space around the tools, and choose Add Toolbox from the popup dialog choices.

10. Navigate to the MyTools folder and add the My Crime Analysis Tool Box.tbx.

11. Examine ArcToolbox and see your toolbox as it appears alphabetically in the lineup.

12. Right click on your new toolbox, and choose **New → Model**. The model builder window will appear.

13. Our first objective is to create three variables:
   a. StartDate
   b. EndDate
   c. UCRCrimes

14. From the model builder window, click on **Insert → Create Variable** (see **Figure E26–1**).

15. In the list, find Double and click OK.

16. Repeat steps 15 and 16 to create a second Double variable (it may show up directly on top of the first double ellipse, so you should move them as they are created so you can see both variables. We are going to be querying the RECVDATE field in the Offense_Data and need to make sure our format matches that of the data we are going to query—see Figure E26–1).

17. Now create another variable that is of the **String** type.

18. Right click on the first Date variable, and choose Model Parameter. A small "P" will show up above and right of the Date variable. Click Save!

19. Repeat this for the other two variables, and click Save after each change (see **Figure E26–2**).

20. Now right click on the first date variable and choose **Rename**. (*Note*: At times when you change the variable names in Display Properties and then when you save and reopen the model later, the variables may all have returned to unnamed String or Double, this is an issue with model builder.)

21. Where it currently reads "Double," change this to StartDate and click Save.

22. Close the window and change Double2 to EndDate and click Save.

23. Close the window and change the name of the String variable to UCRCrime and click Save.

24. Save the model by clicking on the save icon (*computer disk*) in the menu bar. We will not worry about naming it for a few more steps.

25. Okay now we have the variables created and have set them as a parameter in the model we are going to create. A parameter simply means that these three items will be the inputs to our Select by Attributes function we are going to develop with this model. A parameter is the data in your SQL statement, or the fields and values that must be in the SQL statements to get the data we want.

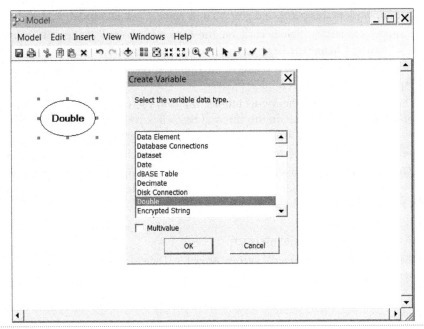

Figure E26–1

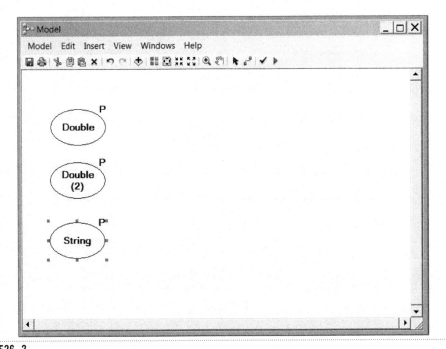

Figure E26–2

26. Let's save our work to this point, and give it a new name. Click on **Model → Model Properties**.

27. In the model properties dialog, click on the General tab, and change the Name field to SelectUCRCrime. Change the Label to read "Select UCR Crime."

28. Make sure you do not get this switched, as the *Name* cannot have any spaces, but the label can. Click Apply and OK. Click on Model → Save.

29. If you have not maximized the Model builder window, you can see the ArcToolbox tab at the right of the map display. Click on this tab, and then click your toolbox (if needed) to see your new tool called Select UCR Crime. You are entering the programming world!

30. Now we need to find the model function we want to run, which is a Select by Attributes function.

31. Click Geoprocessing in the main ArcMap menu bar (you may have to move the model aside while you do this, and if you have maximized the model builder window, you will need to reduce its size to see ArcMap in the background).

32. Choose **Search for Tools**.

33. Type in Select by Attributes and hit enter.

34. Drag the first item returned (Select Layer By Attribute [Data Management]) to the model window (see **Figure E26–3**).

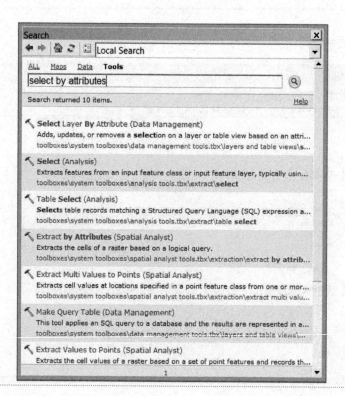

Figure E26–3

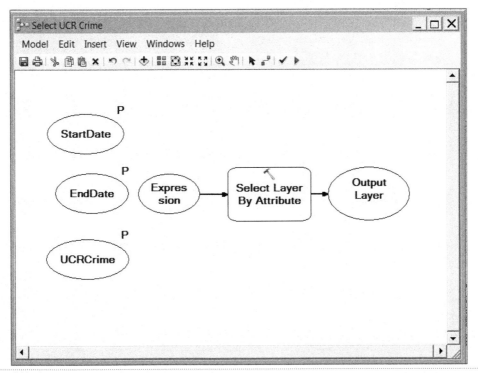

Figure E26–4

35. Now right click the Select Layer By Attributes function and choose Make Variable → From Parameter → Expression. This new variable field will hold our SQL expression to query the main dataset. Your model should now look like **Figure E26–4**.

36. Right click the Output oval to the right of the Selection function, and choose Display Properties from the popup dialog box. Change the Name to UCRChoice, the Tooltip to UCR Choice, and click Save to save the model to this point (see **Figure E26–5**).

37. Your model should now resemble **Figure E26–6** (your colors and names may not be exactly the same six, but the number of ovals should equal five with one rectangle).

38. To see what we need to feed the Select function to get it to run, double click on the Select Layer by Attribute rectangle (see **Figure E26–7**). This is the dialog that will appear when the model runs from ArcToolbox and shows what variables will be needed.

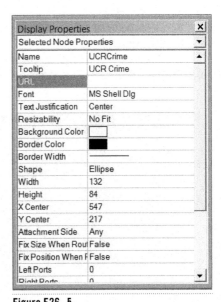

Figure E26–5

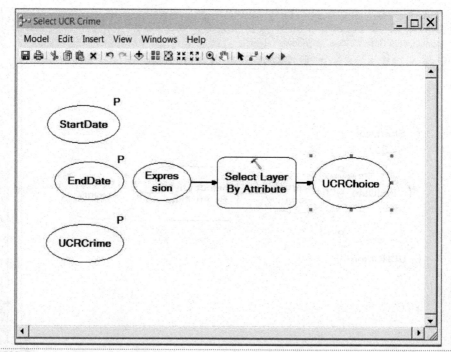

39. We see we need:
   a. Layer name or table view
   b. Selection type
   c. The Expression (or SQL Formula)
40. Close the Select Layer by Attributes dialog box.

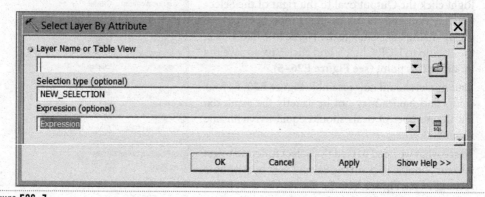

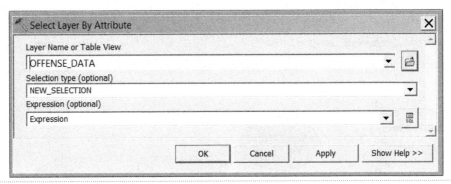

41. In order to have the actual expression show up in the model dialog when we run it, right click on the Expression oval and choose Model Parameter. A "P" will appear to the upper right of the Expression.

42. In step 36, we created a parameter to hold the SQL expression and we can enter something here or create a more advanced query. (Well, of course, we are going to create a more advanced query! You are all experts by now!)

43. Double click on the Select Layer By Attributes rectangle again and in the Layer Name box, click the drop-down arrow to the far right and choose the Offense_Data layer in the ArcMap project (see **Figure E26–8**).

44. Notice how the word "expression" is already in the expression section or field in this dialog (Figure E26–7). We will enter this expression in our string and double variables we created at the beginning of this exercise, so that we can rerun this as much as we want to by just changing the variable values.

45. Click Apply and then OK to close the dialog. Your model should now resemble **Figure E26–9**. (You may need to move the parts around to see the entire model, or click View in the menu bar, and then Auto Layout and then reorganize as needed.)

46. Now double click the StartDate parameter field and enter 20040101 (represents January 1, 2004, as a number value—this will now be our default value).

47. Close this parameter by clicking Apply and then OK.

48. Right click the EndDate field and enter 20041231 as the second default value for the date range. Click Apply and OK.

49. Double click on the String field and enter 'ROBBERY' including the single quotes.

50. Click Apply and then OK. Save the Model again! (See **Figure E26–10**.)

51. Double click on the Expression parameter and enter the following SQL expression exactly as shown:
    a. ("RECVDATE" >= %StartDate% AND "RECVDATE" <= %EndDate%) AND "UCRTYPE" = %UCRCrime%

52. There are two buttons in the main menu bar at the right of the toolbar in the model builder.

53. One is a black checkmark. This allows us to validate the model to see if we have everything in proper order. It does not actually tell us where the errors are.

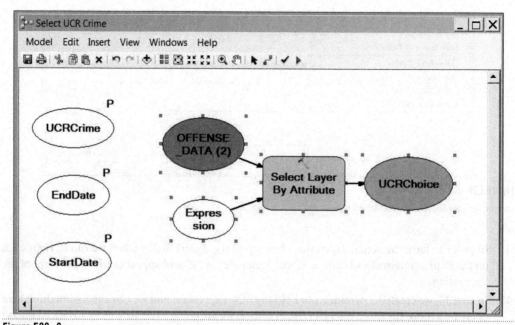

Figure E26–9

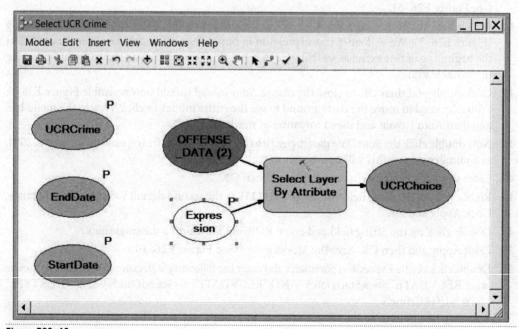

Figure E26–10

54. Click the checkmark. If everything is in order, nothing happens. If there are errors, a popup message will appear indicating there are errors.

55. Now click the blue arrow at the right of the checkmark to run the model.

56. A window should come up showing that your model is running and will disappear after the model is completed (or, if you have unchecked the "Close dialog when completed successfully" checkbox, it may remain open showing any errors). If it did not run correctly, go back and check each box individually to see if there are any typos or missing data.

57. In ArcMap, open the attribute table for the Offense_Data layer and observe that 242 records are selected—all robberies. Save the model one more time.

58. Close the model editor and then open ArcToolbox.

59. Find your My Crime Analysis Tool Box and then the new model we've created, called Select UCR Crime.

60. Double click Select UCR Crime to open the tool.

61. The tool dialog pops up and allows you to change the parameters in the three fields (StartDate, EndDate, and UCRCrimes) and shows you what is in the expression section for the model. All of these were Model Parameters, or had a "P" to the upper right of the graphic.

62. Try entering different date ranges and UCR Crimes as follows:
    a. 20030213 and 20030418 and 'BURGLARY' (total records = 283)
    b. 20010301 and 20010630 and 'AGGRAVATED ASSAULT' (total records = 206)
    c. 20020601 and 20021231 and 'DUI' (total records = 523)

63. Be aware that the UCR crime field is case sensitive and you MUST include the single quote marks at the beginning and end. Whatever you enter must also match the UCRType field values, and of course the RECVDATE field values.

64. Okay, what if we wanted to have the output of this query exported to a new layer?

65. Right click the Select UCR Crime model and choose Edit.

66. Right click on the Expression oval and uncheck the Model Parameter item (click on it). We no longer need this as a parameter value since the SQL statement is working correctly.

67. We want to recreate the Data → Export Data functionality we can do manually from any layer. In the model builder, for this exercise, we are going to use the copy features function.

68. Navigate in the ArcToolbox → Data Management Tools → Features → Copy Features and drag it to the edit window.

69. Double click the Copy features rectangle.

70. Review the inputs this function typically needs.

71. Change the default output feature class field to be your student folder and named UCR (i.e., C:\MyFolder\UCR.shp).

72. Click Apply and OK.

73. In the main menu bar of the model builder, there is a tool that looks like a line with boxes on the end. When you hover your mouse over this tool it reads, "Connect."

74. Choose this tool and then draw a line between the Output of the Select by Attributes function (UCRChoice) and the Copy Features rectangle.

75. A link line between the selected records and the Copy Features box is created, and the rest of the copy features function boxes are colored in. Choose Input Features from the popup box.

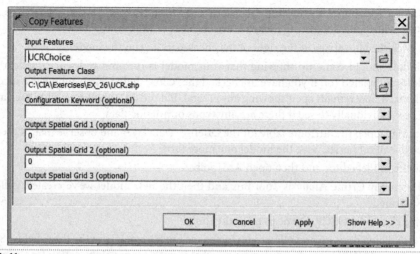

Figure E26-11

76. Double click on the Copy Features rectangle again and make sure the top two sections are completed as shown in **Figure E26-11**.

77. Save your model! Right click on the Output Feature box to the right of Copy Features, and choose Model Parameter. A "P" will appear next to this output box. We want this to be a parameter so that we can choose a different location and name for our files we create with this tool (see **Figure E26-12**).

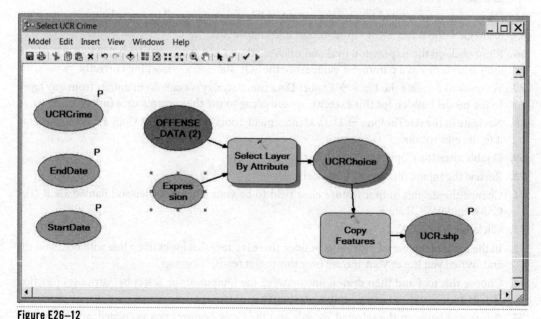

Figure E26-12

78. Save the model and close the model builder.

79. In ArcMap, open ArcToolbox, find and run your model with one of the original date ranges and a UCR crime type as shown in step 65.

80. If it works, you are a straight A student. If not, we still like you, but you are not getting anything for Christmas this year. Ha ha ha.

81. This ends the "simple" model building exercise.

82. Think of ways on how you could modify this tool, by making changes to the SQL expression and copying what we have already done for one UCR crime type and a single date range to run multiple UCR crime types and date ranges.

83. Models can be frustrating to get working as you want them to at times, but when you do work them out they can save you a lot of time with repetitive tasks and data queries that you do all the time.

84. Save and close your project.

■ Exercise 27: Downloading and Using Data from the U.S. Census Bureau

Data Needed for This Exercise

- www.census.gov/geo/www/tiger/shp.html

Lesson Objectives

- The student will learn how to download data from the U.S. Census Bureau website.
- The student will learn how to add sociodemographic data to the GIS Tiger data.

Note: The Census Bureau website went through numerous changes in 2011 and 2012, and will likely continue to, so what is there one day, may not be there on another day. *Because of this potential change, this exercise may need reworking by the instructor for the processes to work correctly.* The U.S. Census Bureau site may have changed again since this was written, but generally the data are still in about the same locations, but may be referred to in some other fashion, or located in a slightly different spot. Please try to work through the exercise, but be ready to make changes on the fly as the Census site changes.

Task Description

1. Open a web browser and navigate to www.census.gov/geo/www/tiger/shp.html.

2. We want to create a choropleth map of thefts by census block.

3. So we need to download the blocks shapefile from the Census website. Click on "**2011 TIGER/ Line® Shapefiles Main Page—Released December 12, 2011**".

4. Read the notice under **What are the TIGER/Line Shapefiles?**

5. Then click **Web interface** under **Download**.

6. In the drop-down box named Select a Layer Type, choose Block Groups.

7. Click Submit.

8. Change the selection box for states to Arizona, and then click Download.

9. If you have popup blockers turned on, you may need to answer yes to a popup indicating the web browser has blocked content, so you will need to click on this popup and indicate you wish to allow the download.

10. Save the file to your student folder (we suggest creating a new folder called EX_27 to save these files in).

11. It will take quite a while to download all the census blocks for Arizona. (This could take 20 minutes or more to download. While waiting, proceed to step 22 and set up a basemap in the meantime! When the download is complete, return here and get the downloaded data ready to be used in a GIS.)

12. When completed, open Windows Explorer and navigate to where you saved this file.

13. Double click on the *.ZIP file to open it, and then in Windows 7, click on Extract All Files in the menu bar of Windows Explorer. (If you are using Windows XP, you can also extract files by right clicking the *.ZIP file and choosing **Extract to** from the drop-down menu.)

14. You will get five files that are all part of the shapefile.

15. Double click on the .PRJ file to see what the projection is for this data.

16. If a dialog comes up asking you to specify what program to open this with, choose Word Pad.

17. You will then see the projection for this data is:
    GEOGCS["GCS_North_American_1983",DATUM["D_North_American_1983",
    SPHEROID["GRS_1980",6378137,298.257222101]],PRIMEM["Greenwich",0],UNIT
    ["Degree",0.017453292519943295]].

18. Close Word Pad and the *.PRJ file.

19. These data are in decimal degree format.

20. Create a new project and add the following layers:
    a. Street_Labels.lyr
    b. Basic_Street_Labels_An
    c. Grids_P.Lyr
    d. City_Street_L.lyr
    e. City_Boundary.Lyr
    f. Offense_Data.Lyr (see **Figure E27–1**)

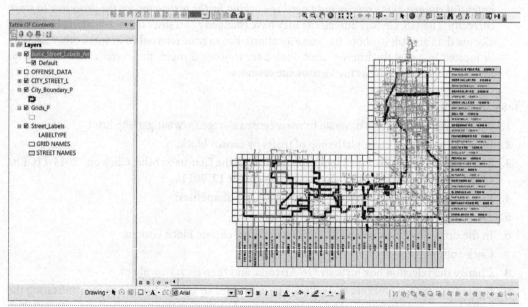

Figure E27–1

21. We need to add all *our* data first so that the decimal degree data will be displayed in our state plane projection automatically in ArcMap.

22. Now add the Census Block data.

23. These are for the entire state but since we only want Glendale, we can use the Clip tool to clip the Glendale data to the Grid_P polygon layer.

24. Open ArcToolbox.

25. Double click on Analysis tools → Extract → Clip.

26. In the clip tool dialog, enter the data as shown in **Figure E27–2**.

27. Save this to your student folder and call it 2011Blocks.shp.

28. Once this is done running, we will have a census block layer which is clipped to the grid boundaries (see Figures E27–2 and **E27–3**).

29. Now we need to aggregate our theft data to the census blocks, which takes two steps:

    a. Create a layer of only thefts.

    b. Do a spatial join to the 2011Blocks from the thefts layer.

30. Click on the ArcToolbox and find your toolbox we made in Exercise 26. Not there? Right click and choose Add Toolbox.

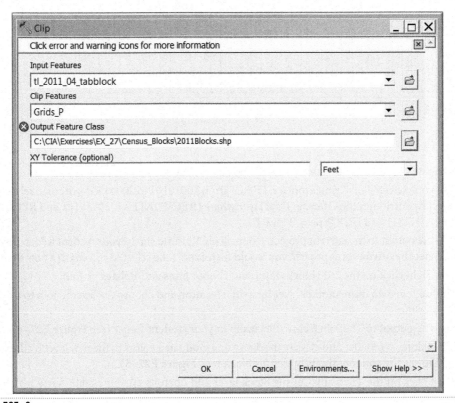

Figure E27–2

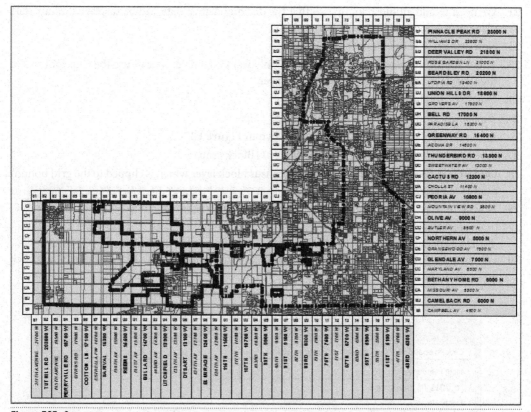

Figure E27–3

31. Navigate out to where you saved this toolbox and add it to the ArcToolbox.

32. Run your Select UCR Crimes tool for THEFT from 20010101 to 20041231. Alternatively, you can Select by Attributes the Offense_Data layer where (RECVDATE >= 20010101 and RECVDATE <= 20041231) and UCRType = 'THEFT'.

33. Add the output to the current project. (Name it UCRCrime.shp in your student folder. If you did the Select by Attributes approach, you would then export the selected records to a new shapefile.)

34. Now right click on the 2011Blocks layer and choose Joins and Relates → Join.

35. Choose Join data from another layer by spatial location and choose the layer to join to this layer: UCRCrime.

36. Save the output to TheftsbyCensusBlock.shp in your student folder (see **Figure E27–4**).

37. When done, symbolize and classify the data using graduated colors in the new layer by the Counts field to see the count of thefts by census block (see **Figure E27–5**).

38. Right click on the Thefts by Census Block layer and open its attribute table. View which fields are present.

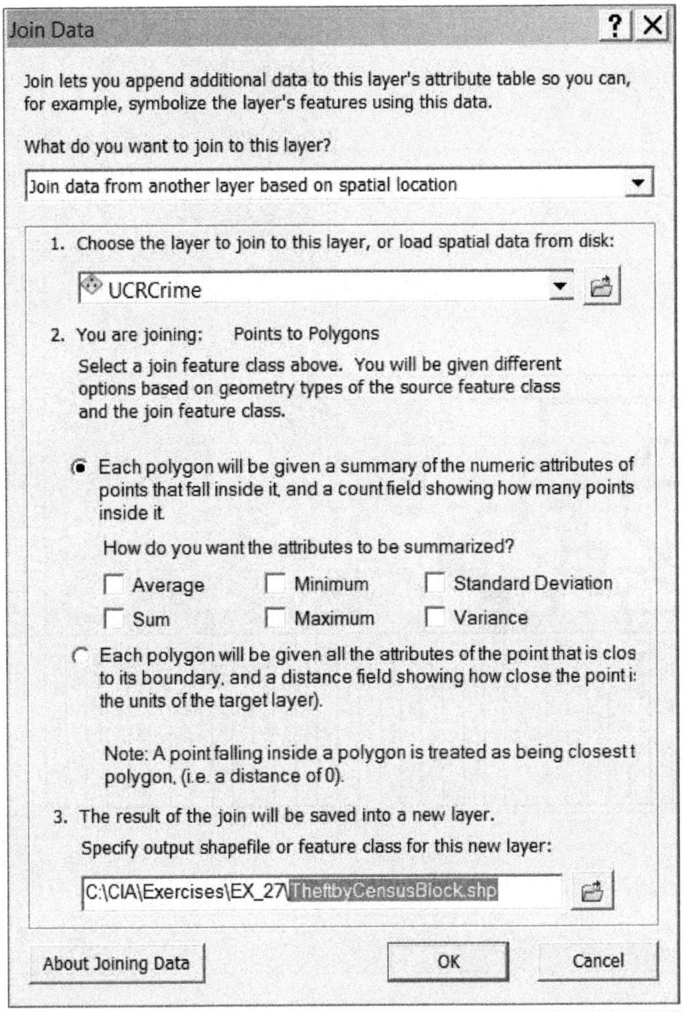

Figure E27–4

39. We have a field called GEOID, which we will use for the next part of this exercise.
40. Now let's create a Z score–weighted hotspot analysis of these census blocks and the Count_ field.
41. Double click on the Spatial Statistics Toolbox → Rendering → Hot Spot Analysis with Rendering (see **Figure E27–6**).
42. Complete the Hotspots with Rendering dialog as shown in Figure E27–6 and then click OK.
43. Add the layer to the map as needed and change the outline for all symbols to "no color" and view the results. We have hotspots everywhere and for the entire city (**Figure E27–7**).
44. Close all census block layers, save the project in your student folder, and close all programs.

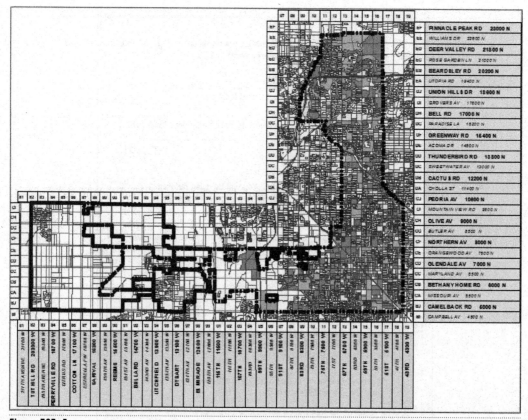

Figure E27–5

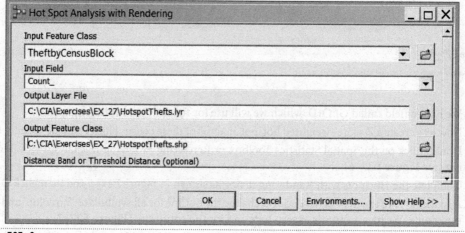

Figure E27–6

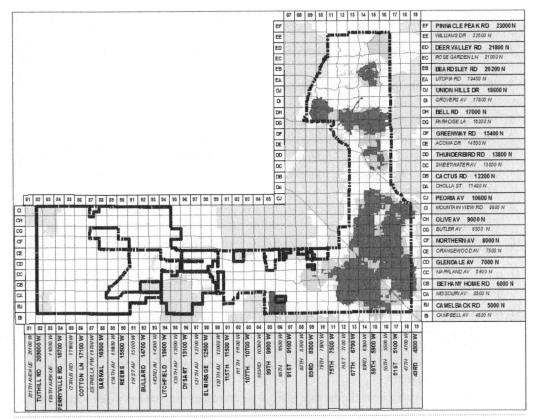

Figure E27–7

■ Exercise 28: Finding Other Data on the Internet to Use in Your GIS Project

Data Needed for This Exercise

- http://data.geocomm.com/catalog/US/61081/index.html

Lesson Objectives

- The student will learn how to find data on the Internet and use it for his or her projects.
- The student will learn how to find data within their own agency, or other local sources.

Task Description

1. To start off, we recommend calling your own or nearest City Engineering Department, City Clerk's Office, or Planning Department.
2. These departments within a municipality are treasure troves of good quality geographic information system (GIS) data covering a variety of data types.

3. You can find good street centerline files, and address points for doing address matching (geocoding).

4. The planning and engineering departments offer layers such as good census data already pulled for your own municipality.

5. They also have things such as land-use layers, population updates by city, city council district, and possibly by police department zones.

6. You can find data on business locations and parcel data.

7. You will also probably find a great source for aerial imaging for your municipality.

8. There are so many layers these different departments could have, you would be remiss if you did not call them and start up a conversation with them to see what they have and what they would be willing to share.

9. If your city already has a GIS department, you will probably find that they know who has what data, and can potentially be a great ally in getting new data and resources for your projects.

10. The Land Resource Department within your state may also be a great resource for free data (see, for example, www.land.state.az.us/alris/layers.html).

11. Many of these sites require you to fill out a form to obtain the data, and others allow data downloads right from the site.

12. Two things you need to ask yourself are:
    a. What projection are these data in?
    b. What units are these data in?

13. Without knowing what projection the data are in, you may not be able to get them to overlap existing data correctly.

14. We need to know what units the data are in so we get correct measures when we do statistics on the length or area fields, or use the data with our own, and to make the layers line up properly as well.

15. So always look for information on the website about what the projection and units are when downloading data from a website.

16. Another awesome thing to know is when it was last updated. This is important to know how accurate it may be.

17. Along with state and county websites where you can order various free datasets, universities and colleges can also be a great source for some GIS data (see http://lib.asu.edu/gis/data or www .library.arizona.edu/help/how/find/maps/gis/datasets.html).

18. Now you give it a try and see how many different data sources you can find online. Open a web browser (if it is not already open) and enter "Free GIS Data for Arizona" in the search field and then press Enter.

19. There are pages and pages of websites offering some free data. Many vendor sites lure you in with the promise of free data, so you will look at the fee-based data they also have available.

20. In Exercise 25, we showed you how to find free data from ArcGIS Online right from within ArcMap, but you should have seen that these data are usually very general, and not to the detail and completeness that we often need when doing crime mapping.

21. In the browser window, enter the following URL: http://sco.az.gov/website/geoserver/ (or pick it from the list you got back when searching on "Free GIS Data for Arizona").

22. Zoom in on the map so you are approximately zoomed in to Glendale.

23. Use the Select button to draw a box around Glendale and the surrounding area.

24. At the bottom left is yellow text that reads, "Download Data."

25. Click the Download Data text.

26. In the popup dialog, click on Maricopa (shapefile).

27. Save the file as Maricopa.zip to your student folder.

28. Back on the webpage, Click on the yellow Site Info button at the top left and look for the text, "The data are displayed in Latitude/Longitude - Decimal Degrees."

29. Close the web browser.

30. The data we downloaded are in decimal degrees and we need them to work with our data, so we need to find a *.PRJ file within our downloaded data.

31. Extract all the files within the Maricopa.zip download.

32. When we look at the extracted data, we see a maricopa_ngs.prj file, which shows (in WordPad) the data to be NAD 83 HARN decimal degrees, but since there is a *.PRJ file we should be good.

33. Open ArcMap and add your traditional files. We need to add our own data so that the projection of the data frame is in our known units, which are International feet and in our projection of AZ Central Fips 0202, NAD 83 State Plane.

34. ArcMap always assumes the first layer loaded as the default projection. You loaded our data first, so now the data we downloaded will be forced to display as our projection. The actual projection of these data will not have been changed, however—just how it is displayed.

35. Now load the data we downloaded from the website.

36. A warning will come up indicating we are loading data that is different from the current data frame (see **Figure E28–1**).

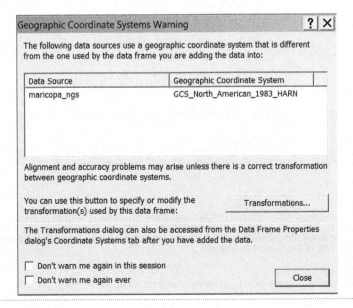

Figure E28–1

37. Click Close.

38. Our data are now loaded and we have a bunch of points. To see what these data are, we will look at the metadata behind it.

39. Open ArcCatalog at the right of the map display. Under File Connections, find your student folder and navigate to where this file is located.

40. Right click on the Maricopa_ng.shp file and choose Item Description.

41. Well, shucks, we should be seeing metadata about this file, but apparently there is none.

42. Close the item description dialog window.

43. To see what this should look like, navigate to the CIA\Data\File Geodatabase\GIS_Layers.gdb\Boundaries\City_Boundary_P layer and right click on it.

44. Choose Item Description and view the metadata for this layer (see **Figure E28-2**).

45. When done browsing the metadata, close the item description window.

46. Save your new project as EX_28.mxd in your student folder and close ArcMap.

47. Close any other programs or windows that are still open. This concludes this exercise.

For more exercises, please visit our companion website.

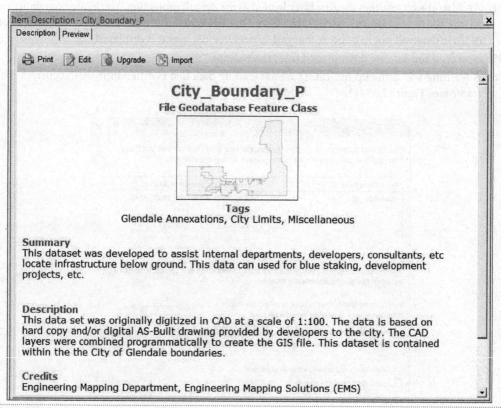

Figure E28-2

Index